951
.2505
Dim

Dimbleby, Jonathan.
    The last governor : Chris Patten & the handover of
Hong Kong / Jonathan Dimbleby. --Toronto :
Doubleday Canada, c1997.
    xvi, 461 p., [24] p. of plates : ill.

    Includes bibliographical references (p. [447]-448) and
index.
    813380   ISBN:038525637X

(SEE NEXT CARD)

316   97SEP08   3688/kc   1-482207

THE LAST
GOVERNOR

THE LAST GOVERNOR

Chris Patten
& the Handover
of Hong Kong

JONATHAN DIMBLEBY

DOUBLEDAY CANADA LIMITED

Canadian Cataloguing in Publication Data
Dimbleby, Jonathan
The last governor
Includes index.
ISBN 0-385-25637-X
1. Patten, Chris, 1994 –   2. Hong Kong — History
Transfer of Sovereignty to China, 1997   3. Great Britain
Foreign relations — China   4. China — Foreign relations
Great Britain   I. Title.
DS796.H757D55   1997   951.2505   C97-930548-9

Typeset in Bembo by M Rules
Jacket photo by Topham Picture Point
Printed and bound in the USA

Lines from 'The Ship' by W.H. Auden reproduced
by kind permission of Faber and Faber

Published in Canada by
Doubleday Canada Limited
105 Bond Street
Toronto, Ontario
M5B 1Y3

For Bel

CONTENTS

ACKNOWLEDGEMENTS

Over the five years of this project, I have received kindness and hospitality in abundance from many people in Hong Kong and London. For that and more I owe them a huge debt of gratitude. All of those listed below have not only been generous with their time but have helped me to a better understanding of the issues that form the subject matter of this book. Many of them have spent long hours exploring with me their differing and frequently rivalrous viewpoints on Hong Kong. Some of them will disagree bitterly with my interpretation and judgement. None of them should be blamed for my opinions. One or two of those who have offered particularly helpful insights have asked not to be identified. I am in their debt no less than I am to the following.

David Akers-Jones, Martin Barrow, Sir Jack Cater, Anson Chan, Professor Edward Chen, George and Rowena Chen, Cheung Man Yee, David Chu, Francis Cornish, William Courtauld, Sir Percy Cradock, Hugh Davies, Dr Michael Degoylyer, Martin Dinham, Jamie Dundas, Baroness Lydia Dunn, Major-General Bryan Dutton, William Ehrman, Sir David Ford, Sir Alastair Goodlad, Leo Goodstadt, Han Dongfang, Mike Hanson, Hari Harilela and his family, Richard Hoare, Michael Howard, Lord Howe of Aberavon, Christopher Hum, Douglas Hurd, Jimmy Lai, Albert Lam, Norris Lam, Emily Lau, Allen Lee, Commander Dick Lee, Martin Lee, Dr C. H. Leong, Bowen Leung, Edward Llewellyn, Vincent Lo, Christine Loh, Ma Yuzhen, Kerry McGlynn, Sir Robin McLaren, the Lord MacLehose of Beoch, Richard Margolis, Simon Murray, Ng Koon Leung, Margaret Ng, Bob Peirce, Sir Charles Powell, Peter Ricketts, Malcolm Rifkind,

William Shawcross, Michael Sze, David Tang, Baroness Thatcher, Nancy Thompson, Peter Thompson, Hank Townsend, Tsang Yok Sing, Simon Vickers, Wong Oi Ying, Lord Wilson of Tillyorn, Peter Woo, Minky Worden, Grace Wu, Gordon Wu and Lord Young of Graffham.

Chris and Lavender Patten have had many burdens to bear in Hong Kong. I added to these by consuming many hours of their precious time. Like many others over the last five years, I have been a beneficiary of their goodwill, their kindness, the warmth of their hospitality, and – wondrously – their sense of perspective.

Caroline Courtauld has been a consummate guide and mentor. Her diaries, which have been a delight to read, were also an invaluable source of illumination. Sister Helen Kenny's religious duties command many hours of commitment and yet for the love of the subject, she managed to find time, throughout the last five years, to create and maintain a beautifully ordered cuttings library without which I would frequently have been lost. Both Sister Helen and Caroline Courtauld were assisted by Fanny Wong, who also helped to organise my life on most of my whistle-stop visits. Gary Pollard provided me with his extensive research notes into the Hong Kong media and related issues. Jonathan Mirsky, a distinguished foreign correspondent, was generous with his knowledge, his opinions and his Italian home cooking. He took the trouble to make available to me the original drafts of many of his articles for *The Times*, and for this, and more, I am in his debt. Stella Ma was a skilful and sensitive interpreter. I am grateful, too, to Robin Allison Smith for the care and speed with which he took many of the photographs in this book.

As a longstanding colleague and friend, Francis Gerard was in at the start of this project. His judgement, his enthusiasm and his company have made a sometimes daunting task far easier to accomplish than it would otherwise have been. These qualities are shared by my PA, Georgie Grindlay, who not only transcribed hundreds of hours of taped interviews (forming her own fierce views about Hong Kong in the process), but made sense of incoherent notes and half-formed ideas written on the backs of envelopes. I have benefited greatly from her opinions and her commitment.

Philippa Harrison, the chief executive of Little, Brown, had the original faith to commission the book and has been astute and wise throughout. Caroline North, my editor, has not only been meticulous but contrived to restructure key parts of my original manuscript with skill and tact and at great speed. Cheung Man Yee, Francis Gerard, Mike Hanson and Caroline Courtauld read all or parts of my text and made many helpful criticisms and suggestions. All of them should share the credit for any virtues that may be detected in *The Last Governor*; they bear no responsibility for any of its vices.

Bel, my wife, has been stoical, wise and my unfailing support in times of stress. But then, she always is.

Somewhere a strange and shrewd To-morrow goes to bed,
Planning a test for men from Europe; no one guesses
Who will be most ashamed, who richer, and who dead.

from *The Ship*
by W.H. Auden

FOREWORD

Hong Kong brags shamelessly. In all Asia it lays claim to the boldest tycoons, the best-educated and most industrious workers, the most important financial centre, the most innovative trading houses, the highest living standards, the most billionaires, the most spendthrift gamblers, the largest gold market, the largest diamond market, the busiest port, the most crowded skies, the most exciting skyscrapers, the widest range of luxury shops, the most expensive apartments, the lowest taxes, the most efficient civil service and the least corrupt police force. Hong Kong spews out statistics about itself which show that – on one level – it is indeed a jewel in Asia; at another, deeper, level it reveals the fragility of the identity about which its apologists boast with such abandon. If this city state has any culture, it is that of the marketplace – a free-for-all world where the pursuit of profit is unashamed and the possession of wealth is admired, not envied. If Hong Kong has a commitment, it is to today and tomorrow. The day after tomorrow will take care of itself – or so many of its denizens have wished to believe.

On 1 July 1997, Hong Kong was to be released from British colonial status to be incorporated as a special administrative region (SAR) of the last major communist power in the world, the People's Republic of China. With a population of 1.3 billion people, which accounts for almost a third of the world's population, China is still in the throes of a social and economic upheaval caused by an attempt to graft the practice of capitalism on to the precepts of totalitarianism. It is an awesome venture fraught with uncertainty.

This book is about the last five years of British rule in Hong Kong and its principal focus is the remarkable political drama which began to unfold once it became clear, within a few months of his arrival, that the new governor, Chris Patten, and the rulers of China were on a collision course. From July 1992 to the end of June 1997, Patten had to make judgements of a nature and on a scale unimaginable to most men and women. Uniquely in the history of British colonialism, he had the responsibility of accomplishing the peaceful transfer of sovereign power from one state to another, rather than into independence.

The book's main vantage point is the perch I was allowed to occupy inside Government House, where I had easy access to the governor and his team. With the proviso that what he said would be embargoed until after the handover, Patten agreed in advance to discuss – for the future record – his strategy and his tactics at every stage of what was to become a serious and sustained diplomatic crisis, the consequences of which are still uncertain. He not only did so with extraordinary candour but, self-evidently, without benefit of hindsight. As a result, his own testimony will surely be of unusual historical interest.

Patten's task was to meet three overlapping but not necessarily compatible challenges. First, he was to negotiate the final stages of the transfer of sovereignty over Hong Kong from Britain to China. Secondly, he had to prepare the people of the colony to face the uncertainties enshrined in that prospect. Thirdly, he had to convince public opinion in the United Kingdom and internationally that Britain's withdrawal from Hong Kong had been accomplished with at least a modicum of dignity and honour. Patten did not himself enumerate his objectives in precisely these terms, but, from the standpoint of history, they serve as useful yardsticks by which to evaluate his governorship in the sunset years of British colonialism.

Inheriting a basket of unfinished business which affected the basic rights and freedoms of more than 6 million people, Patten was charged with assessing how best to prepare Hong Kong to face the unpredictable imperatives of the gerontocracy which formed the ruling politburo in Beijing. Sino–British relations had long been marked by suspicion, which, in the case of China, verged on paranoia. Disposed to regard the outgoing colonial power as an agent of 'Western imperialism', the old men in Beijing were swift to conclude that any failure by Britain to yield to the 'principles' of sovereignty to which they adhered was evidence of a Western plot to subvert the People's Republic.

The prospects for a smooth transfer had been dramatically and immeasurably undermined by the gathering storm of protest in China during the early months of 1989 which culminated in the killings in

Tiananmen Square – and in other major cities beyond Beijing – on 4
June 1989. This atrocity shattered the illusions harboured about the
nature of the regime by those who had chosen to interpret the economic reforms introduced by Deng Xiaoping, China's 'paramount
leader', a decade earlier as an irreversible process leading inevitably to
fundamental social and political reform. Hong Kong's horror at the
shedding of so much innocent blood was matched by China's fear that
Hong Kong would become a base for internal subversion against their
regime. The fact that the constitution of the People's Republic pledges
to uphold democracy and to protect human rights throughout China,
including the SAR of Tibet, did little to reassure the people of Hong
Kong that the principle of 'one country, two systems' – the term used
by Deng Xiaoping to express the ideal relationship between the mainland and the new SAR of Hong Kong – would survive for long.

Even under conditions of mutual amity, negotiations between Britain
and China were bound to be fraught with difficulty and misunderstandings. As it was, the distrust which had bedevilled their relationship
before Patten's arrival was compounded by the intense suspicions harboured by the people of Hong Kong about both present and future
sovereign powers.

Although I have sought to preserve an observer's detachment
throughout, my proximity to Government House is bound to have
shaped, if not distorted, my authorial perspective. In an attempt to
remedy this, my narrative is also driven by the experiences and opinions
of many other individuals in Hong Kong and, to a lesser extent, in
Britain, whose competing aspirations formed part of the backdrop
against which Patten defined his own priorities. On the understanding
that nothing they said would be published until 1 July 1997, several of
these people freely confided their thoughts and feelings about the
drama in which they were all central characters. I have variously attributed motives, opinions, and beliefs to all these individuals, and
especially to Chris Patten. Although my judgements are based on close
observation, they remain mine alone unless they are duly attributed.
This book may have the authority of first-hand experience, but it is my
own account of events and not 'authorised' by anyone.

As an outsider, I cannot claim to 'understand' Hong Kong, and this
book makes little attempt therefore to penetrate what remain to me
the cultural and social opacities of its 6 million inhabitants. However,
in charting the crucial milestones along the 150-year history of
Britain's last significant colony, I have drawn extensively on the scholarship of others to chronicle the most pertinent episodes in the long
march from the Opium Wars to Patten's appointment as Hong Kong's

last governor. Since it is impossible to understand the predicament inherited by Patten without some appreciation of the colony's recent political history, I have explored in some detail, with the help of those most closely involved (including the former prime minister, Baroness Thatcher, her former political adviser Sir Percy Cradock and two former foreign secretaries, Lord Howe and Douglas Hurd), Britain's diplomatic objectives in the years between 1979 and 1992.

It was originally my hope to balance this portrait of Hong Kong's last years by including the 'Beijing perspective'. At first, in the person of the Chinese ambassador to London, the authorities of the People's Republic showed keen interest in this idea. However, they soon retreated into vague promises about what they might be able to deliver once the 'misunderstandings between our two countries' had been resolved. I gave up. As the text shows, I have been obliged as a result to rely on the authority of press conferences, official statements and other much-quoted 'sources'. However, I suspect that these have yielded as much of the truth as I would have discovered for myself if I had been able to penetrate the carapace of secrecy in China to forge a more productive relationship with one or more of its luminaries.

Inevitably, *The Last Governor* has been written on the run. For that reason alone, it is essentially a work of extended journalism of the sort that its proponents like to describe as 'contemporary history'. That it contains material which has historical significance I have no doubt, but even though I have been privileged to witness at close quarters 'history in the making', my perspective lacks the enchantment of distance. At the time of writing, the future of Hong Kong is uncertain and precarious. I have to declare a twofold bias: first in favour of the last governor of Hong Kong, and secondly in favour of democracy. As a friend, I am disposed to judge Chris Patten sympathetically; more pertinently, as a democrat, I am inclined to look askance at those who use their own freedom to argue that others can do very well, thank you, without democracy.

Of great matters in contention, it is sometimes said that 'history will judge'. History, of course, does no such thing. People judge and, as of now, we can only guess at what, in the case of Chris Patten, that judgement will be. I like to believe that he will be shown to have been on the 'right' side of history; that his faith in individual freedom is well founded, and that, for this reason, future generations in Hong Kong, and even in China, will look back on his struggle on their behalf with gratitude.

Jonathan Dimbleby, June 1997

'A Terrible Feeling
of Falling'

*The New Governor
Arrives in Hong Kong*

W estern writers have been by turns entranced and appalled by their experience of Hong Kong. Ian Fleming, writing in the early sixties, described the city as 'the last stronghold of feudal luxury in the world . . . a gay and splendid colony humming with vitality and progress, and pure joy to the senses and spirits'. A decade later, John le Carré set a memorable episode of *The Honourable Schoolboy* in Hong Kong. Describing a taxi ride in bad weather up the winding road from the city centre to the top of the Peak, he wrote that the car 'sobbed slowly up the concrete cliffs', which were engulfed by 'a fog thick enough to choke on'. Outside the taxi, 'it was even worse. A hot, unbudgeable curtain had spread itself across the summit, reeking of petrol and crammed with the din of the valley. The moisture floated in hot, fine swarms.' On a clear day it would have been possible to see far out over the harbour across Kowloon towards the New Territories, and beyond a vagueness of mountains that marked the border with the People's Republic of China.

The Peak has long been de rigueur for tourists, who usually prefer to travel to the top in the Peak Tram which clanks up the sheer side of the mountain. Jan Morris, Hong Kong's finest apologist, took this route in the seventies, accompanied by a 'foreign devil' who showed her the 'kingdoms of the world' which lay below them: 'The skyscrapers of Victoria, jam-packed at the foot of the hill, seemed to vibrate with pride, greed, energy and success, and all among them the traffic swirled, and the crowds milled, and the shops glittered, and the money rang.' By no means starry-eyed, however, she also saw this throbbing megalopolis as a 'permanent parasite' upon the skin of China, wherein the British

and the Chinese, springing from 'two utterly alien cultures, from opposite ends of the world' are 'fused in the furnace of Hong Kong, and
made colleagues by the hope of profit'.

The last governor of Britain's last colony landed at Kai Tak Airport on
9 July 1992, on schedule at two o'clock in the afternoon. Accompanied
by his wife, Lavender, and two of his three daughters, Laura and Alice,
Chris Patten stepped off the aircraft to face a battery of television cameras and journalists corralled on the tarmac by officials of the
Government Information Services. The weather was routinely swel-
tering and the humidity nudged towards 100 per cent. Hong Kong's
new first family, the source of much excited chatter in the local media
since the announcement of Patten's appointment, smiled self-consciously and disappeared into the merciful cool of the VIP lounge.
    After a pause for refreshments, the Patten motorcade left the airport
to drive through the heart of Kowloon to the public pier, where the
family boarded the *Lady Maurine*, the elderly and elegant motor yacht
provided by the Hong Kong government for the personal use of the
governor and which, along with an equally ancient Rolls–Royce, was
one of the gubernatorial perks to provoke in some a titter of envy. Led
by a Royal Navy warship and surrounded by a flotilla of naval and
police launches and a convoy of pleasure craft, the Patten family made
stately progress across the harbour to disembark at Queen's Pier. A
couple of fireboats sprayed a welcoming spume of water as she passed.
RAF jets and army helicopters flew low overhead. Foghorns blasted
and the sound of a seventeen-gun salute from the naval landbase *HMS
Tamar* ricocheted around the waiting crowd. There was a guard of
honour and a Gurkha band played the national anthem. Patten took the
salute with his wife and children beside him, their dresses swishing
slowly in a sultry breeze. For aficionados it was colonialism encapsulated
in a single image – even if their new overlord, surrounded by so much
gold braid, did cut an underwhelming figure in a plain grey suit and
without the gubernatorial plumed hat favoured by his predecessors.
    In the dog days of colonialism it had become customary for the
media in London to caricature the motley selection of superannuated
politicians dispatched to govern Britain's dwindling possessions as
faintly ridiculous refugees from a Gilbert and Sullivan opera strutting
their way into the imperial sunset. Patten had no intention of either
joining that twilight galaxy or dressing the part, which was one of the
reasons why he had decided to forgo both the plumed hat and the ceremonial uniform. There was also an aesthetic consideration: 'If you are
built like one of those sketches for a Daks suit from Simpson's, you can

get away·with wearing a hat – as someone said to me rather indelicately – with a chicken on top and that wonderful white tropical kit. If you are built like me, medium-sized and lumpy, you do look extremely foolish.' His friends had been disappointed. 'The prime minister said that I had been a frightful spoilsport. Lots of people who were looking forward to a rather more cheerful breakfast when they looked at photographs of me in the paper were to be denied that pleasure.' A more pertinent, if no less self-conscious reason for his abstinence lay in his determination to impress upon popular opinion in Hong Kong that in style and character he was cast in a quite different mould from his predecessors; that his governorship would be 'more open and accessible and without some of the flummery' which had been traditionally associated with the post.

The power vested in the governor of Hong Kong under the Letters Patent, which gave him absolute executive authority over the colony as the head of government and commander-in-chief of the armed forces, was a sharp reminder to Patten that he lacked the popular legitimacy of an elected leader, and it made him vaguely queasy. With this in mind, he not only resisted the 'flummery' of his new office but also turned down the knighthood that traditionally went with it. 'There were negotiations and the Palace was receptive and helpful,' he confided. 'I've got my house colours as a privy councillor, which, for a politician, is the most important honour you can have . . . I think the time for an additional honour, if there does come a time, should be when I've actually done something for Hong Kong, not just because I've taken a job.'

The welcome he was given was friendly but not effusive. Foreign tourists and expatriates, as intrigued by the Patten daughters as by the new governor himself, all but outnumbered the local population. The people of Hong Kong had seen too many British officials alight on their soil to be anything other than sceptical about the latest arrival. However, even the sceptics acknowledged that Patten was a little different. For weeks the local media had regaled their public with every recycled titbit about the new governor and his family: how Lavender had been a barrister in London; that their eldest daughter Kate was in South America before starting a degree course at Newcastle University; that Laura, a photogenic seventeen and given to stylishly short dresses, would stay for a while but might return to work in London; and that thirteen-year-old Alice would be living at Government House and would become a pupil at the Island School in the Midlevels. Patten himself was a good deal younger than any of his recent predecessors, who had been rewarded with the governorship towards the close of their careers. And unlike his predecessors, he was already a public figure, even – in Britain at least – something of a star. As written up by the assiduous Hong Kong press, the Pattens had all the makings of a genuine first family: politically glamorous and pleasingly enthusiastic about the adventure ahead of them.

It was not merely that Patten exuded bonhomie; nor that he waved from the Rolls and searched for hands to shake with the manic energy of a campaigning politician; nor that his face easily creased in what seemed to be a genuinely eager smile, even if, on the first humid day, his complexion assumed an ever-deepening shade of puce. All that helped, but there was something else: from the start, he exuded a self-confidence and certainty which implied, even via the unyieldingly attentive television cameras recording his arrival, that he had a purpose and he knew what it was. Even the cynical – which included most of those of whatever viewpoint who had taken more than a spasmodic interest in the unfolding drama of the previous decade, and who knew Albion to be perfidious – could not help feeling a frisson of anticipatory excitement. For better, for worse, life with the new governor – Peng Dingkang in the official Cantonese translation, or Fat Pang, as he soon came to be called – at least promised to be far from boring.

Chris Patten had been preceded to Hong Kong by a formidable repu-tation as one of the Conservative government's heavyweights. The prime minister's close friend and most trusted confidant, he was deemed to have snatched electoral victory for his party from what the polls had predicted to be certain defeat. In the process, he became, in his own characteristic phrase, 'the only Cabinet minister careless enough to lose his seat' in his own west-country constituency of Bath.

In Britain, Patten had been a skilled political communicator. His way with the English language had earned him a reputation as a thoughtful and fastidious politician who avoided the coarse public dialogue in which so many of his colleagues indulged. His was by no means a high Tory background: his father worked in what was then called Tin Pan Alley (Patten would recall proudly that he published the hit song 'She Wears Red Feathers and a Hooly-Hooly Skirt'). A scholarship boy, he was educated at Catholic schools and read history at Balliol College, Oxford, where he edited a humorous magazine called *Mesopotamia*, which had been started by the founders of *Private Eye*, in which he updated fragments of Aristophanic comedy. Patten evinced no interest in politics until, having won a Coolidge Travelling Scholarship to the United States, he was given a job as a researcher with the team running John Lindsay's 1965 campaign to become mayor of New York. Enthused by this experience of politics in the raw, he returned to

London and eschewed a BBC traineeship to join the Conservative Research Department. After four years he went to the Cabinet Office, and two years later, in 1972, he became private secretary to the party chairman, Peter Carrington. On his return to the research department as director in 1974, he soon fell foul of the new party leader, Margaret Thatcher, who regarded him as deplorably hostile to her radical vision. Although he remained at the research department he was effectively ostracised by Thatcher. As one of his friends told the writer John Newhouse, 'Chris protested and then went into outer darkness.'

In the 1979 election Patten won the marginal seat of Bath, going on to serve his ministerial apprenticeship as a PPS at Social Services and a parliamentary under-secretary at the Northern Ireland Office before rising to become minister of state, first at the Department of Education and Science and then, between 1986 and 1989, in the Foreign Office, where he was in charge of overseas development. Despite his relatively slow progress, he had already been cast by his peers in all parties in the role of 'future leader'. Although he was averse to the style of Thatcherism, and semi-detached from much of its content, he had managed to overcome his distaste to the point of toiling annually in the arid vineyard of the prime minister's speeches to the Conservative Party Conference, attempting to bring eloquence to her thought and life to her prose. His reward, in 1989, was a place in the Cabinet as secretary of state for the environment, charged with steering Thatcher's community charge – the hated poll tax – on to the statute book. Though Patten regarded the poll tax as a catastrophe, the last gasp of a leader who had lost touch with political reality, he did not hesitate to bludgeon the bill through the House of Commons – to the amazement of his political opponents and the dismay of his admirers beyond Westminster, who could not understand how such a decent politician could impose so manifest an injustice upon the nation. In failing to appreciate the iron laws of collective responsibility, they also underestimated the careful ambition of a politician which was obscured by a beguiling persona in which high seriousness and dry humour were, in that grey age, refreshingly entwined.

Patten had comforted himself by letting it be known at Westminster that he found the 'old girl' faintly ridiculous. In private he was also scathing about the vainglory of lesser colleagues. Contemptuous of romantic argument, whether it emanated from the right or the left, his response to it had been to acquire the disconcerting habit of slowly rolling his eyes in exaggerated bewilderment, as if to indicate that its proponent had to be off his – or, in the case of Thatcher, her – trolley.

Patten's 'success' in imposing the community charge on a resentful populace helped precipitate Thatcher's downfall. Forced to defend her leadership in a party election, she failed to win outright in the first ballot. Believing her to be mortally wounded, Patten joined the home secretary, Kenneth Clarke, in telling her that it was time to retire gracefully. He warned that if she did not follow their advice, they, like many of their colleagues, would be unable to support her in the second round. She departed for the House of Lords, blessing John Major as her successor in the Commons. Major duly defeated the foreign secretary, Douglas Hurd, and the former defence secretary, Michael Heseltine, to emerge as leader and prime minister.

Patten was appointed chairman of the party to mastermind John Major's victory over a resurgent Labour party. The 1992 campaign was not an elevated affair. Bending himself to the task of achieving victory, Patten started to deploy terms like 'double whammy', 'gobsmacked' and 'porkies', as if to demonstrate to genuine street-brawlers like Lord Tebbit (a predecessor in the post) that he, too, was an upper-echelon bruiser. Many commentators were genuinely taken aback by his vulgarity, while his opponents affected dismay that such an eminently reasonable politician should stoop to such abuse. Yet those who knew him well were already accustomed to his private, if quaintly anachronistic earthiness, and were surprised only that this trait had not emerged earlier in his career. The Patten they knew was a complex individual, a man of pragmatic conviction, blessed with religious faith, who lived for politics but also had what Denis Healey had memorably called 'a hinterland'. He had one of the best political brains of his generation among the Tory high-flyers. An ideologue who wore his commitment lightly, he was a Conservative in the mould of 'Rab' Butler and Sir Edward Boyle, formal photographs of whom had become part of his office furniture. Yet unlike those icons of 'one-nation' Toryism, he was also, in the political sense, more of a thug than his genial demeanour suggested.

Armed with a swift wit and a gift for the apposite phrase, he had long been the leading figure in a group of sympathetic contemporaries which included such luminaries as William Waldegrave, Tristan Garel-Jones, his namesake, John Patten, and John Major, before the latter's meteoric rise at the behest of Margaret Thatcher. Perhaps not as clever as Waldegrave, nor so artful as Garel-Jones, and less volatile than John Patten, he nonetheless dominated the group with effortless aplomb. To the chagrin of political journalists, even the most ambitious of his colleagues, who were usually swift to deprecate each other in private, stayed their hands. He was the one to whom others turned for advice and reassurance, and whose judgement was trusted, even by his fiercest rivals. Some likened him to Lord Whitelaw, whose benign countenance disguised a shrewd political wisdom on which Margaret Thatcher had learned to rely. But the comparison was inapt: Whitelaw lacked ambition and the 'killer' instinct to go with it. Patten wanted to be prime minister, and he was not nearly so squeamish about it as his self-deprecatory manner might have implied. His asperity in argument left none of his friends in any doubt that the master of the emollient soundbite was very much tougher than his image might suggest.

In his final weeks as the Conservative MP for Bath, that political armour was tested to the limit. Patten had been resigned to the prospect of defeat from the start of the election campaign. Damaged by his association with the poll tax, he was also held responsible for the injustices of the uniform business rate – not least in his own constituency, where some traders faced consequential ruin. As party chairman he was obliged to be in London under the daily scrutiny of the media, and although he was ferried to Bath by helicopter, his campaign in what had long been a marginal seat was inevitably spasmodic. In his constituency he became a scapegoat for the government's unpopularity and, as the canvass returns seemed to confirm, enough of his sophisticated electorate had resolved to vote 'tactically' against him to ensure that at least one member of the Cabinet would be driven from office.

The rejection was more painful than he had anticipated. Afterwards he tried to draw comfort from Adlai Stevenson's reaction after his defeat in the 1952 US presidential elections. Like a small boy who had stubbed his toe, 'It hurt too much to laugh but I was too grown up to cry.' Patten resisted the temptation to blame the burghers of Bath, but he was to harbour lasting resentment about the raucous delight with which some of his opponents at the count greeted his defeat. His farewell speech was dignified, decent and generous, but his successor, the Liberal Democrat Don Foster, failed to offer the customary condolences, an omission or oversight which rankled. Reports that some right-wingers at an election gathering in London hosted by the party's treasurer, Lord McAlpine, had toasted his demise even as they celebrated the victory of which he had been the principal architect did little to soothe his wounded spirits. Exhausted by an election campaign which had been more than usually demeaned by personal abuse and vilification, Patten left Central Office in the early hours of Friday morning, sustained by the gratitude of a jubilant prime minister but conscious that, for the moment, his own career in British politics was at an end.

Knowing that Patten was unlikely to hold his seat in Bath, the prime minister had held out the promise of the Hong Kong governorship to his friend some weeks earlier. On the day after the election, Major renewed the offer, but at the same time intimated that he would dearly like Patten to reject the Hong Kong option in favour of remaining in his Cabinet. It was common knowledge that the prime minister had come to rely heavily on Patten's acute political intelligence as well as on his skills as a communicator. Patten exuded that air of relaxed assurance that Major could never master; it would be invaluable to have such a 'safe pair of hands' close by to help navigate the government through the turbulent waters of domestic politics that lay ahead. As Patten recalled their conversation a few days later, Major made it clear that 'he'd have liked me to stay around, but he recognised that Hong Kong was a big job . . . [and that] without being too vain, I sort of fitted the bill . . . I guess quite a lot of my friends, while recognising the importance of the job and flattering me into thinking I could do it, also flatteringly, hoped that I'd stay in London.'

Indeed, within hours of the election some of his closest friends were counselling him to find a 'safe' seat (in Chelsea, for instance, former minister and fellow 'wet' Sir Nicholas Scott had indicated that he would be ready to stand down in favour of such a formidable successor), or to accept John Major's offer of a peerage and a place in the Cabinet with the prospect of succeeding Douglas Hurd as foreign secretary. Patten demurred. 'I did have a very strong feeling,' he said privately a few weeks later, 'that I didn't want to hang around on the margins of contemporary domestic politics, collecting directorships, doing a bit of writing, with the terrible danger of starting to be afflicted with a sense of what might have been. I think it's important, since we're only here once, to look forward, not backward.'

Patten had long stated his private aversion to political carpet-bagging, or joining the 'chicken run', as the demeaning search for a safe seat was later disparagingly described. Moreover, he was too astute to presume that any Conservative seat would be safe in a high-profile by-election following the return of an unloved government. If he accepted a peerage, his future in public life would depend exclusively on the prime minister's patronage: for an ambitious individual who was not yet fifty years old, the Lords seemed a remarkably precarious pinnacle from which to establish a position of sustained influence. He had no wish to become a supplicant at the court of Westminster.

Yet party politics had been his life, and he felt bereaved. On the Saturday following the election he helped the prime minister to select the new Cabinet and, he said, felt 'a certain wry detachment' when three of the new appointees rang him for advice about what to do and how to do it. Yet he had no sense that he should have been in their shoes: the 'stabs and twists of anguish' that did assail him sprang from the inevitable loss of companionship, the feeling that he was no longer a member of an intimate club and the recognition that half a dozen of his closest friends now inhabited a world from which he was excluded. He resolved to resist the temptation to resort to envy or bitterness. 'Some people might find this barking mad, but the first time I had dinner with them, and practically all of them had to go off at ten to ten, I did feel slightly gutted,' he confessed later. 'What really came nearest to emotional disembowelling, though, was not just missing them, but realising they were going to miss you.'

By this time, Patten had virtually decided to accept John Major's offer to become the last governor of Britain's last significant colony, Hong Kong. Despite the passionate entreaties of Tristan Garel-Jones, one of the wiliest insiders at Westminster, who organised an informal lobby of sympathetic Tories to ring Patten urging him to stay, he was not to be persuaded. On the Sunday he told Douglas Hurd on the phone that he was 'very attracted' to the job. Lavender, his wife, was also enthusiastic. From the outset, she had said, 'If you don't take it, you'll spend the rest of your life regretting it.' Only his loyalty to the prime minister still made him hesitate. That evening the Pattens and the Hurds dined together. Although other names had been canvassed for the governorship (including that of the former foreign secretary David Owen), Hurd made it clear that Patten was, in his judgement, the best available choice. The two men and their wives rehearsed the pros and cons, but the foreign secretary was gently adamant: 'Without pushing me into doing it, Douglas made the point that it would be much more interesting than most of the jobs I might have been doing in domestic politics,' Patten recalled. 'It is unique in public service. Dangerous – not in a physical sense – but difficult enough to be fascinating . . . Almost the second the prime minister knocked the ball over the net, I wanted to knock it back again.' As Hurd put it, 'I was very sad for Chris when he lost his seat, but when the thought was sown that he might go to Hong Kong, I jumped at it, because I could see there were going to be problems.'

It was later reported that Patten was so agonised by the decision facing him that he and Lavender had to remove themselves to France for a heart-searching weekend. 'Pretty average bilge,' Patten commented. The die had already been cast.

The decision to replace a diplomat, Sir David Wilson, with a politician for the final years of British rule had first been mooted by Douglas Hurd some months before the election. Hurd explained later that this 'had nothing to do with Chris Patten', although, as he saw it, the argument in favour of a 'political' governor was compelling: 'The last five years were going to be very difficult, and we needed someone in Hong Kong who was in tune with the world of Westminster and the British media; someone who could operate in Hong Kong in a more political way than had been traditional, finding allies and supporters in a way which a traditional governor had no need to do.' It was, he insisted, no criticism of David Wilson, just 'a clear view on my part that we needed a different kind of governor for the last five years of British rule'.

When the decision to replace Wilson became known, it was rumoured that the prime minister and the foreign secretary (both of whom had been recently bruised by failed missions to Beijing) regarded the outgoing governor as one of the principal advocates of the 'appeasement' of China, an approach which they believed could no longer be sustained after the atrocity of Tiananmen Square in June 1989. Hurd has conceded that his visit to Beijing in 1991 – to follow up a 'memorandum of understanding' about the construction of a new airport for Hong Kong signed by Major during an official visit to China earlier that year, on which Beijing was soon to renege – had been 'extremely frustrating'. The groundwork for this doomed effort had been prepared by Wilson in co-operation with Major's foreign affairs adviser, Sir Percy Cradock. As a result, both sinologists fell foul of the media, which – led notably by *The Times* and the *Spectator* – were scathing about the 'kowtowing' diplomats in the Foreign Office who had masterminded Britain's relations with the 'butchers of Beijing'. Hurd has dismissed as 'a journalistic cliché' the suggestion that his and the prime minister's experiences in Beijing turned them against the Foreign Office 'kowtowers', but he has acknowledged that the decision to replace a diplomat with a politician did involve a shift of emphasis by the government: while 'co-operation and consultation', he explained, remained 'highly desirable and necessary', they 'don't mean waiting to establish what the government of the People's Republic wants and then doing it'. The implied rebuke was self-evident.

For his part, Lord Wilson has been reticent about his departure, confirming only that he was 'very sorry to leave', and that had he been asked to remain, 'I'd certainly have regarded it as my duty to do so.' It was 'very crude indeed' to suggest that he had been sacked for failing to stand up to the Chinese and to make way for someone who would. However, Wilson shared the view held by many of his peers in the Foreign Office that the restoration of good relations with China following the shootings in Tiananmen Square was of paramount importance. 'I was trying to build a house that had decent foundations,' he has since explained. 'Now that meant . . . Chinese support is perhaps putting it too strongly; Chinese acquiescence, yes, for sure.'

To this end, he confided to at least one senior colleague in Government House that he was quite ready to be pilloried by the media in Britain and Hong Kong as one of the 'arch-appeasers' of China. Appointed in 1988, Wilson had been expected to retire before the handover, but he was bitterly disappointed by the prime minister's decision to remove him at a moment when, he claimed, 'We had recovered in a quite remarkable way from all the problems of 1989.' According to his friends, he felt especially betrayed by the failure of government ministers to quash publicly the rumours that he had been sacked to make way for a figure of greater resolution and substance.

The prospective governor had been to Hong Kong as overseas development minister and before that, in 1979, as one of a group of backbench MPs who took it upon themselves, in the words of one official who was present, to 'harangue' the governor of the time, Sir Murray MacLehose, about democracy. Why, Patten and his colleagues wanted to know, had the colonial authorities been so dilatory about the introduction of democracy? Were not the Hong Kong people mature enough to accept a parliamentary system? And would not democratic reform reinforce Hong Kong's precious 'way of life'? By the prevailing standards in Government House, such questions must have seemed irredeemably jejune. Nevertheless, this encounter between the Tory young Turks and the colonial old guard did, in fact, help to nudge the colonial administration towards the establishment, in embryonic form, of the hydra-headed quasi-democracy which the new governor was to inherit over a decade later.

Aside from these brief encounters, Patten's knowledge of Hong Kong was rudimentary, while his acquaintance with the delicate latticework of diplomacy between Britain and China in the intervening years was negligible. He was tangentially familiar with the Joint Declaration (the 1984 treaty, lodged at the United Nations, defining the terms under which the sovereignty of Hong Kong would revert from Britain to China in 1997), and the Basic Law (China's codification of the Joint Declaration into a constitutional and legal framework for the governance of Hong Kong as a special administrative region of the People's Republic of China). However, he had had no cause to pay close attention to the recent history of Hong Kong and he was thus not au fait with the carefully contrived ambiguities of either document, or with the tortuous diplomacy through which, under relentless pressure from China, Britain had negotiated its retreat from sovereignty.

Throughout May and June of 1992, therefore, Patten immersed

himself in the detail of Hong Kong's recent history. Briefed by Foreign
Office officials and former diplomats, he was also lobbied by industrialists, financiers and several of Hong Kong's most prominent public
figures, who flew to London to deliver their competing recipes for triumph and disaster. He worked his way through a daunting collection of
files – memoranda, briefing notes, telegrams and correspondence –
reading between the lines to piece together not only the order of events
but the aspirations and assumptions which underlay the process of
diplomacy. As he noted at the end of those two months, 'It's dragged
me up the learning curve and in the process I've acquired some prejudices. But I'm absolutely convinced that when I actually get to Hong
Kong and see things for myself, and allow my nostrils to twitch in the
breeze – if there is any in July – it'll feel different.'

Sir Percy Cradock – who had been the principal architect of
Sino–British relations in the 1980s and who, as foreign affairs adviser to
Margaret Thatcher and, latterly, to John Major, was still the most influential sinologist in Whitehall – had opposed the appointment of a
'political' governor. His aversion, which predated Patten's availability for
the post, sprang from his fierce belief that the accommodations he had
engineered with Beijing would be jeopardised by the more aggressive
approach that a politician, driven by other imperatives, would almost
certainly adopt. In particular he was convinced that a politician as governor would be overly swayed by the media in Hong Kong and
London, a large sector of which, to Cradock's chagrin, had already
decided that his own approach had been pusillanimous. Cradock
thought that 'there were great springs of emotion bubbling away below
the surface about this' in the hothouse of Westminster, and that these
threatened to undermine the prospect of a smooth transition which, he
believed, his 'realism' had managed to secure. He feared that a politician
would too easily yield to unrealistic but vociferous demands to extend
the bounds of democracy in Hong Kong before 1997, and that any project of this kind would be doomed to fail amid acrimony and conflict
with China. By his own account, Cradock told Major, as he had previously told Thatcher, 'It's no good shuffling the cards; you are not
going to change the situation.'

He made no headway with the prime minister; Douglas Hurd,
meanwhile, privately believed that Cradock and his fellow sinologists
had 'missed the change in Hong Kong' following the killings in
Tiananmen Square and the new strength of the demand in Hong Kong
for political advance. This internal conflict was concealed until some
months after Patten's appointment, but it went to the heart of the
bitter divisions, within Whitehall and between the Foreign Office and

Government House, which were soon to provoke an undeclared war of attrition between them. This was only resolved in Patten's favour precisely because he was the kind of heavyweight politician to which Cradock had taken such exception.

Patten had foreseen that there would be tensions. 'I'm sure that, from time to time, there will be differences of view. I'm sure there will be people who say, "It just shows what happens when you appoint a politician,"' he commented on the eve of his departure for Hong Kong. 'I guess there'll be people who'd say, "It just shows that with a job like that at the crossroads of Asia, you really needed to have an old Asia hand stroking their nose. Needed a sinologist. Good lad – but didn't speak Mandarin."' However, he had no premonition of how prolonged, how vituperative and – in the case of Cradock and a motley array of superannuated diplomats and politicians – how public this fundamental dispute would become.

The new governor's insouciance was underpinned by his confidence that Major and Hurd would, in his own phrase, give him 'a great deal of authority and a great deal of elbow room to manufacture policy with them'. Indeed, according to Patten, the three of them never even discussed the issue because: 'They both know I'm not a turf warrior . . . it didn't need to be said that I would have the authority I needed.' The mutual trust that existed between Major, Hurd and Patten would, they all three recognised, be critical in sustaining that authority as Patten sought to navigate Hong Kong through the political and diplomatic rapids ahead. At the Rio Summit soon after the announcement of Patten's appointment, John Major duly described the elevated status of the new governor to the Chinese premier, Li Peng. As reported to Patten, the prime minister in effect said, 'This is one of my closest personal and political friends in Britain. He's one of the leading politicians in my party and the country, and there is no point in thinking you can slip bits of tissue paper between him and Number Ten. If you are talking to him, you are talking to me.' This blunt statement served only to intensify Beijing's growing suspicion – paranoia is perhaps a better term – about Britain's purpose in Hong Kong in the run-up to the handover. It also confirmed Cradock and his allies in the Foreign Office in their belief that Britain was about to embark on a hazardous course of confrontation rather than conciliation.

Patten was clear about the competing pressures that would be placed on him by China, Britain and a volatile community in Hong Kong. He also knew that if he was to impose himself on the drift of events – not to turn the tide but to direct the flow – he would have to act swiftly, and to be seen to do so. As he focused more precisely on his objectives, he was sharply conscious that the eyes of the world would be on Hong Kong, and on him. 'This is the last big job in our colonial history. I don't mean to give the impression that I want a place in history – I think politicians who talk like that are pretty dangerous – but it is a literal description . . . Britain's colonial history is going to be judged, to a considerable extent, through the prism of the next five years in Hong Kong.' He was also aware that the decolonisation of Hong Kong was quite different from any other. Hong Kong was not to acquire independence, but to be transferred from one sovereign power to another; from a liberal democracy to a communist dictatorship. In 1980 the Chinese leader, Deng Xiaoping, had used the phrase 'one country, two systems' to characterise the prospective relationship between the 1.3 billion people on the mainland and the 6 million of Hong Kong. This slogan had acquired an almost mystical significance, becoming a mantra for optimists and pessimists alike, to be chanted with ritual fervour in the knowledge that, like all phrases devoid of intrinsic meaning, it was reassuring precisely because it was opaque.

To define his own objective as governor, Patten had taken to using – or, by his account, abusing – an intergalactic metaphor. The traditional process of decolonisation, he noted, involved 'designing' a constitution, complete with an independent judiciary, an honest civil service and the Westminster model of democracy. The next step was to 'put this on the launchpad, light the blue touchpaper and hope the satellite will go into orbit. Sometimes it is successful and sometimes it isn't – which is when you fetch up with judges being murdered, the public service corrupt and Sandhurst having rather more influence on government than Westminster.' In the case of Hong Kong, however, there had to be 'a docking of shuttles in outer space'. If this intricate manoeuvre were to succeed, the applause would be muted and, in the case of 'a lot of Americans and others who take sometimes a rather dangerously moralistic view of global issues', absent altogether. However, failure to dock would be calamitous. One of his mentors commented: 'Of course, if it goes smoothly it'll be frightfully boring. If it doesn't, you'll have people rioting on the streets and you'll have civil disorder. You'll have a collapsing Hang Seng Index. You'll have half the people wanting to run you out of town for causing instability and the other half for not standing up to China with sufficient vigour.'

The prospect of severing his ties with the intimacies of the political club to which he had belonged for most of his adult life for the uncertainties of Hong Kong was bittersweet. By the time of Patten's departure, the shock of his election defeat had given way to a lingering sense that this new appointment had brought his career in domestic politics to an end. 'It is difficult,' he noted wistfully, 'to think of any-body who has taken off for a flight round the airfield and has managed to touch down again. Christopher Soames [the last governor of Rhodesia] didn't manage. I don't know whether Sir Leon Brittan [a European commissioner] will manage . . . Our system slightly distrusts those who show from time to time that Westminster isn't the only place in the world.

'I have woken up once or twice early in the morning with a terri-ble feeling of falling. It's an adventure.'

2

'RECKLESS AND UNSCRUPULOUS ADVENTURES'

Britain Acquires a Colony

The new governor lacked the reverential approach to China's past with which so many British sinologists were afflicted. A few days after his arrival at Government House, he stood in his study examining a map of China as he reflected breezily on Beijing's attitude to the handover of sovereignty in 1997. 'I think for most Chinese, but certainly for the immortals, the Long March generation – pretty fatal, literally, once you start calling yourself an immortal – for that generation, it is about the national humiliation of the Opium Wars. It is about reasserting Chinese sovereignty and, in the process, closing a humiliating episode in Chinese history.' His own knowledge of that history was, as he readily acknowledged, decidedly sparse.

The British flag was planted on Hong Kong for the first time in January 1841. The foreign secretary, Lord Palmerston, was dismayed when he heard the news, and reprimanded Captain Elliot, who had taken this 'barren island', pronouncing that Hong Kong would never be 'a mart of trade'. The Chinese emperor, Daoguang, was no less baffled, but concluded of the invaders: 'These barbarians always look on trade as their chief occupation . . . It is plain they are not worth attending to.'

The seizure of Hong Kong was a classic if accidental triumph of gun-boat diplomacy. The island was one of a hundred or more scattered around the estuary of the Pearl River, seventy miles downstream from the capital of southern China, Canton. By the early eighteenth century, Canton was already an elegant city whose grandest quarters, graced by fine squares and magnificent triumphal arches, reminded one contemporary correspondent of St Germain in Paris. By the end of the century it had become an established entrepôt where the great trading nations of the world had taken up residence to exploit the huge but virtually untapped market of an ancient but ramshackle empire which already had a population of 300 million subjects. In Britain, liberal ideology was in the ascendant, most aggressively in the form of a commitment to free trade, which had acquired the status of a quasi-moral imperative. It was underpinned by a genuine belief that international peace and prosperity could not otherwise be secured: the alternative to free trade, it was argued, was war. British merchant venturers, with the Royal Navy in support, criss-crossed the trading routes of the globe in pursuit of the rapidly growing opportunities for trade and investment. In Canton, these buccaneers operated under the protective authority of the East India Company, which was formally entrusted with quasi-governmental responsibilities on behalf of the British empire. Like their European rivals, the scions of the great trading houses, such as Messrs Jardine and Matheson, regarded themselves, in the words of the latter, as the 'princes of the earth', the advance guard of a new world order.

Unhappily for these self-appointed 'princes', this obeisance before the altar of commerce clashed fundamentally with some of the basic tenets of Confucianism. In the celestial empire, the deference owed to traditional hierarchies was rigidly enforced. The merchant class was to be found almost at the bottom of the social scale, above beggars and prostitutes but beneath peasants and craftsmen. In Canton, the self-esteem of the 'princes of the earth' was thus put severely to the test. As *fan-kwais,* or 'barbarians', foreign merchants were required to segregate themselves from contact with the indigenous population, which regarded them with suspicion and even hostility. Forbidden to live inside the city walls, they were restricted to their own compounds while their womenfolk were banned altogether from landing on Cantonese soil. Even more frustratingly, their terms of trade were severely restricted and they were only permitted to do business with China during the summer months, after which they decamped, reluctantly, to the island of Macau at the mouth of the Pearl River delta.

These constraints were not only irksome but, far more importantly, they violated the new Western orthodoxy according to which all nations not only had the right but the obligation to open their borders in the cause of free trade. This imperative, it was widely agreed, was a cause which could legitimately be pressed to the point of war. In 1793, following pressure from the East India Company, the British government sent Lord Macartney on the first 'embassy' to Peking to urge His Celestial Majesty to liberalise Chinese trading regulations and, more broadly, to put Britain's diplomatic relations with China on a more substantial footing by allowing His Britannic Majesty's government to establish a presence at the Imperial Court. He failed. In a courteous but firm rebuff, the old emperor, Qianlong, sent Macartney back with a missive for George III informing the British monarch that the changes he sought were 'not in harmony with the state system of our dynasty and will definitely not be tolerated'.

By the end of the eighteenth century, opium, cultivated in India and shipped to Canton, had become the most valuable commodity traded with China. An imperial edict banning the import of this addictive substance had been widely ignored by local merchants, who smuggled the contraband ashore under the eyes of well-bribed officials. Everyone – with the possible exception of opium addicts – benefited. As Frank Welsh has observed in his masterly *History of Hong Kong*, 'It was in everyone's interest that the Canton trade continued uninterrupted: the prosperity of Canton, the comforts of Peking, the livelihood of thousands of officials, and, through the duties levied on tea [the celestial empire's principal export], a substantial part of the revenue of the British government, all depended on it.' As a result, efforts by the Chinese authorities to stamp out the illegal trade were at best desultory. On one occasion, after a ritual engagement with a departing convoy of opium traders, the Chinese naval authorities issued a proclamation stating: 'His Celestial Majesty's Imperial fleet, after a desperate conflict, has made the Fan-kwais run before it.' This sound and fury concealed the fact that, as always, the Chinese gunboats had followed the British merchant ships, as Welsh puts it, 'at a respectful distance and at a deliberate pace, but with the minimum discharge of ordnance'. Great care was taken to ensure that no one was hurt and no ships suffered more than superficial damage.

In Britain opium was still highly regarded as both a painkiller and a soporific. Its addictive properties were well known, but caused concern only to a minority. In China, the use of the narcotic was as commonplace as that of tobacco in Britain. So opium itself was not a casus belli between the two countries. As Welsh has argued persuasively, the underlying cause of the Opium Wars between Britain and China was principally the dispute over free trade which sprang from mutually incompatible attitudes. It is conceivable that if the emperor had been willing to open negotiations with the first British envoy to visit Peking, the 'embassy' led by Lord Macartney in 1793, armed conflict between Britain and China, and more than two centuries of resentment and distrust, might have been avoided. It is clear from the available evidence that the British authorities would have been quite willing to suppress the opium trade in return for the liberalisation of legitimate trade, which had far greater potential. That happy outcome, however, would have required the statesmen of both sides to bridge the cultural chasm that separated their two empires – an improbable vision to contemplate, even with the benefit of hindsight.

Throughout this period, the British government came under growing domestic pressure from the merchant classes, who demanded the right to trade as directly and freely with China as with the other parts of the world over which Britannia held sway. Towards the end of the nineteenth century British exporters were facing intense competition from rival European nations and from the United States of America. They were anxious for new outlets in which to market the products of the industrial revolution. For them, China was an untapped source of unimaginable wealth: if only they could trade freely through Canton and move unhindered about China, then, as Welsh has noted, 'the Chinese masses would rejoice at being able to buy Staffordshire mugs, Birmingham trays and Lancashire frocks, all brought to them cheaply by British-built railways'. A petition to Parliament in 1820 demanded action; the government of Lord Liverpool, its collective mind elsewhere, for the moment demurred.

In Canton, the British merchants became ever more fretful. In 1831, they petitioned London again, complaining that the Cantonese authorities were 'a venal and corrupt class of persons, who, having purchased their appointments, study only the means of amassing wealth by extortion and injustice'. Worse, they subjected the foreign community to 'privations and treatment to which it would be difficult to find parallel in any part of the world'. The petitioners proposed that if the Cantonese authorities could not be persuaded to mend their ways, the British government should 'by the acquisition of an insular possession near the coast of China place British Commerce in this remote quarter of the globe beyond the reach of further despotism and oppression'.

The imperial arrogance of this demand did not find immediate favour in London, where the government faced conflict rather closer to home: an agrarian uprising, riots in major cities, a financial crisis, and, in the form of the Great Reform Bill, a constitutional drama of the first magnitude. Indeed, in 1833, even with the bellicose Lord Palmerston as foreign secretary, a British government mission to Canton was enjoined to 'cautiously abstain from all unnecessary use of menacing language . . . to ensure that all British subjects understood their duty to obey the laws and usages of the Chinese empire . . . to avoid any conduct, language, or demeanour, which should excite jealousy or distrust among the Chinese people or government . . .' Evidently the British empire's policy towards China had yet to live up to the bloodcurdling reputation that later mythology was to bestow on that period. However, this injunction failed to impress the man chosen by Palmerston to lead the mission, Lord Napier, a former naval officer without experience of diplomacy or trade, who, in the words of the Tory *Morning Post*, knew as much about Canton as an orang-utan.

The reaction of the Chinese to the British envoy at the start of what was intended to be a confidence-building exercise was instructive. Reporting the 'arrival of a ship's boat at Canton, about midnight, bringing four English devils', one of the local viceroy's officials warned: 'We think that such coming as this is manifestly stealing into Canton.' And as a representative of the British government, Napier had indeed violated Chinese protocol. Instead of announcing his arrival to the local viceroy by letter, he should first have presented himself at the court in Peking. As it was, he lacked the requisite permits even to land at Canton. The viceroy, however, stayed his hand, choosing to give an impudent but ignorant 'barbarian' the benefit of the doubt.

At a meeting with the viceroy's representatives, Napier displayed all those attributes of British imperialism that the Chinese most deplored. Upbraiding his hosts for keeping him waiting, his Lordship declared that the delay was an 'insult to His Britannic Majesty'. Moreover, he made it clear that he was quite ready to deploy armed force to secure Britain's diplomatic and mercantile objectives in China.

The relationship between two mutually uncomprehending cultures rapidly deteriorated. In a wholly unprovoked gesture, the British envoy engineered a skirmish between two British warships, which happened to be in the vicinity, and a couple of lightly armed Chinese patrol boats, near the Chinese fortress at Whampoa, downriver from Canton. The Chinese response was immediate and, for once, unequivocal. They announced a boycott of all British goods and the death sentence for any local merchant caught trading with the barbarians. The British envoy's foray into diplomacy had been a disaster. He departed soon afterwards for Macau in disgrace. His enduring, if only, legacy was a dispatch to London in which he urged the occupation of 'the island of Hong Kong, in the entrance of the Canton River, which is admirably adapted for every purpose'.

The tensions did not abate. There were misunderstandings, disputes and skirmishes. If the Chinese were stubborn and disdainful, the British merchants in Canton were arrogant and uncouth. The quality of their collective character was embodied in the person of James Matheson, who wrote in 1836, 'It has pleased Providence to assign to the Chinese – a people characterised by a marvellous degree of imbecility, avarice, conceit and obstinacy – the possession of a vast portion of the most desirable parts of the earth, and a population estimated as amounting to nearly one third of the human race.' There was, Matheson avowed, only one course of action open to the thwarted British empire: 'We must resolve upon vindicating our insulted honour as a nation, and protecting the injured innocence of our commerce.' The alternative was to humble ourselves in 'ignominious submission, at the feet of the most insolent, the most ungrateful, the most pusillanimous people on earth'. Matheson's grandiloquence was patently absurd, but in his vulgar way he voiced the opinion of many leading figures of the British merchant class.

As free trade faltered, the smugglers continued to flourish, and by 1838, the drug-runners were landing no fewer than 40,000 chests of opium a year at various points along the south China coast. Increasingly frustrated by this impertinence, the authorities in Peking faced two options. Either they could concede defeat and legalise the opium trade, or they could opt to stamp it out altogether. There seemed to be no middle path. After intense debate with his advisers at court, the emperor decided on the latter course of action.

It was not the barbarians but the local Chinese who were the first to experience the full sting of the imperial lash. James Matheson's business partner, William Jardine, recounted: 'The Governor-General has been seizing, trying, and strangling poor devils without mercy . . . We have never seen so serious a persecution.' Napier's successor in Canton, Lord Admiral Sir Charles Elliot – a man of greater sensitivity and judgement who genuinely supported the imperial edict against opium – warned his recalcitrant compatriots that owners of craft 'engaged in the said illicit opium trade' would receive no support from Her Majesty's Government 'if the Chinese Government shall think fit to seize [them]'. He also warned them that any smuggler causing the death of a Chinese in the course of his illicit trade should expect the death sentence.

On 18 March 1839, the imperial commissioner, Lin Zexu, who had been dispatched from the celestial court in Peking to oversee the clampdown, had sixty of the most notorious Chinese smugglers detained. Four of them were later executed. However, he was swift to reassure the expatriate community that it would come to no harm unless the imperial diktat was defied. To this end he ordered that all stocks of opium were to be surrendered and that all foreigners should pledge themselves never again to deal in the contraband. Otherwise, he warned, they would face the full rigour of the Chinese law: imprisonment, expropriation, and perhaps decapitation. Lin, who was both famously incorruptible and notably sophisticated, laced these warnings with an eloquent reminder that the opium smugglers were undermining the growth of the legal trade in properly bartered goods, which alone was the proper basis on which to conduct economic relations between nations. In a note to the emperor he advised that 'the said barbarians are from a far-off country . . . our policy is to be rigorous without resorting to any offensive action'. Nevertheless he ordered a military cordon to be thrown round the compound of foreign-owned factories outside the walls of the city, incarcerating its European inhabitants until every last ounce of opium had been surrendered. After six weeks, Lin and Elliot (who had himself been immured in the compound) contrived to secure the surrender of more than 1,000 tons of opium, valued at more than £2 million, which was ceremoniously burned on the banks of the Pearl River by the Chinese authorities.

In Britain, the London East India and China Association, which represented the merchants trading in the Far East, tendered their advice to Palmerston. 'We have no desire that it should for one instance be supposed that we are advocating the continuance of a trade against which the Chinese government formally protest,' they insisted. 'British merchants trading in China must obey the laws of that country.' The association urged the government to press the case with China for free trade and for the opening of specified ports to make that possible. These recommendations were adopted, yet soon afterwards a delegation from the association, led by William Jardine, managed to convince Palmerston that the Chinese should nonetheless be persuaded to compensate the British traders for the destruction of the opium which they had quite legally purchased from India. The foreign secretary was further assured that the dispatch of a naval task force to the South China Seas would help expedite this outcome. One member of the British Cabinet recalled in a dry aside, 'We had resolved . . . on a war with the master of one third of the human race.'

In Canton, the imperial commissioner pressed his advantage. Explaining to the emperor that 'the barbarians never break an agreement', he demanded that every British trader put his signature to a formal document promising that if 'one little bit of opium was found out in any part of my ship by examination, I am willingly deliver up the transgressor and he shall be punish to death according to the correctness law of the Government of the Heavenly Dynasty'. Lin's translators may not have served him well, but the import of the document was self-evident and, to Admiral Sir Charles Elliot, unacceptable. Recognising the scope for abuse it offered the Chinese authorities, and mindful of the vagaries of celestial justice, he instead ordered the British community in Canton to cease trading with China and to withdraw to the Portuguese colony of Macau.

A drunken brawl between some British sailors and local Chinese in Tsim Sha Tsui on the southernmost point of China was enough to cause a deteriorating relationship to plummet. One of the Chinese involved in the fracas died of his injuries. Elliot at once ordered an official inquiry into the 'grave offences' which had been committed. Although it proved impossible to identify a single culprit, five sailors were arraigned to stand trial before a special court convened by the British envoy and conducted according to British domestic law. Although the jury threw out the charge of murder, all five of the accused were convicted of riotous assault, fined and sentenced to short terms of imprisonment. This did not satisfy the imperial commissioner, who demanded that a culprit – any culprit – be handed over to the Chinese authorities. When Elliot refused, Lin Zexu's response was to pressurise the governor of Macau to expel the British community. On 15 August 1839, the several hundred men, women and children were, as described by Elliot's wife, Clara, 'turned out of our houses' to be transferred into British ships moored in the natural harbour formed between the protective land mass of Kowloon on the southern coastal tip of mainland China and the island of Hong Kong.

In an attempt to maintain the pressure, Lin decreed that the British ships should be denied fresh food and water by the Chinese traders on Kowloon. Elliot went ashore to persuade the local traders to ignore the edict. He had some success: on 4 September, a convoy of small craft set off to supply the British fleet, only to be intercepted by Chinese naval junks. Exasperated by this obduracy, Elliot ordered three of his vessels to fire on the Chinese. In what was the first of the several skirmishes which were to enter Chinese mythology as the 'Opium Wars', no casualties were reported by either side.

On 3 November, despite frantic efforts by Elliot to broker a truce, an assemblage of Chinese naval junks challenged the local might of the British navy: four junks were destroyed and one British sailor was wounded. Thereafter hostilities were suspended until, early in 1840, with some reluctance, Palmerston dispatched a small task force to the South China Seas. Its mission was to demonstrate the potential of the British navy rather than to pursue a still undeclared war, but this 'diplomacy' could hardly have been more provocative, even if in military terms it was largely free of risk. The task force first blockaded the Pearl River, then the Yangtze, and later the Yellow River. After this show of force, it proceeded to the approaches to Peking and awaited orders.

In the late autumn the British fleet sailed south again to regroup in the Pearl River. On 7 January 1841, the *Nemesis*, a prototype for the British gunboat, led an attack against the Chinese fortifications which

guarded the approaches to Canton. Lin's successor as imperial commissioner was swift to negotiate with Elliot. On 28 January, knowing
that his own demands had fallen far short of Palmerston's orders to
secure a commercial treaty opening up every major Chinese port to the
benefits of free trade, Elliot secured 'the cession of the island and harbour of Hong Kong to the British Crown'. Under the Convention of
Ch'uen-pi, he also secured payment of a $6 million indemnity and the
right both to trade again in Canton and in future to conduct official
negotiations 'upon equal footing'. At 8.15am on 26 January, Captain
Edward Belcher RN of the *Sulphur* raised the Union Jack on Hong
Kong and Admiral Sir Charles Elliot, aboard *HMS Wellesley*, declared
himself governor of Britain's first colonial acquisition in the Far East.

The shame and grievance at the seizure of Hong Kong was deeply
felt in Peking. In London, Lord Palmerston was no less aggrieved by
Elliot's decision to settle for the 'barren island'. In consequence the
governments of both empires declined to accept the terms of the convention which their respective emissaries had agreed on their behalf.
The imperial commissioner was escorted back to Peking in chains;
Charles Elliot, rebuked by the foreign secretary for treating his instructions 'as if they were waste paper', was summoned back to London to
be replaced by Sir Henry Pottinger, an altogether cruder exponent of
gunboat diplomacy.

The Opium Wars were in military terms more a splutter of skirmishes than a struggle of Titans. The Treaty of Nanking (1842) ended
the First Anglo–Chinese War by securing in perpetuity British sovereignty over the thirty square miles of the island of Hong Kong and the
opening of five Chinese ports (including Canton) to foreign trade.
Officially, and only with the reluctant consent of a sceptical British government, Hong Kong became a crown colony on 26 June 1843. But
this did not settle matters: in the struggle for free trade, one skirmish led
to another. After the Second Anglo–Chinese War (1856–8), the
emperor gave his approval to the Treaty of Tientsin, which granted
Britain the right to permanent diplomatic representation in Peking.
However, the military sparring resumed the following year, and as a
result, in 1860 the Convention of Peking formally ceded the southern
tip of Kowloon (fifteen square miles) to Britain as a base for a garrison.
The physical framework for the early development of Hong Kong as a
British trading station, a minor entrepôt in the Far East, was now in
place. The cost in military terms had been negligible; in diplomatic
terms, however, though it was not yet apparent, the price would prove
far higher.

The 'unequal treaties' (as, more than a century later, the People's

Republic of China would refer to the cession 'in perpetuity' of both the island of Hong Kong and the southern tip of Kowloon) did not complete the process of British acquisition. Following the Japanese invasion of China in 1895, the European powers scrambled for advantage against each other. Britain, anxious to ward off the marauding interest of France and the United States, extracted a further concession from the Celestial Empire. Under the second Convention of Peking in 1898, the British secured a ninety-nine-year lease on the so-called New Territories, which comprised 287 square miles of the Chinese mainland to the north of Kowloon and 235 small and largely uninhabited islands around Hong Kong. It was agreed that the lease would expire on 1 July 1997.

In the years following the establishment of the People's Republic, the Chinese politburo constructed a version of the nineteenth-century conflict with Britain from which no deviation was permitted. According to this mantra-like revision, the 'motherland' had been ruled by a succession of weak and corrupt Manchu emperors. Among their subjects, however, were a number of patriotic soldiers who fought heroically against the opium trade and its British sponsors. The obstinacy shown by the British imperialists forced China to take up arms, but despite great resistance, the imperialists were able to impose their will on a dynasty that was physically and psychologically on the point of collapse. Thereafter, the struggle in China took place on two fronts: emancipation from feudalism and liberation from Western imperialism. In the words of the usually urbane Chinese ambassador to St James's, Ma Yuzhen, speaking in 1992, the loss of Hong Kong was 'a national humiliation' that was followed by a number of 'unequal treaties' which were unacceptable to the Chinese people. This outrage was compounded by the attempted 'carve-up' of China by the European powers at the end of the nineteenth century which left Britain in occupation of the New Territories. Thus, as judged from Beijing, 1997 offered a restoration of 'national dignity, national independence and national sovereignty' by erasing for ever an historic mortification at the hands of Britain.

The sincerity of this communist revisionism was not doubted by the sinologists at the Foreign Office, and it had a powerful impact on British diplomacy in the years leading up to Patten's arrival in Hong Kong. According to Percy Cradock, for instance, 'When it comes to the crunch, memories of 1840 are at the top of the bill. China's determination to expunge those humiliations and to recover their national territory on their own terms comes absolutely top . . . I can't emphasise the importance of this too much.'

Under Britain's colonial administration, the fruits of China's defeat slowly began to blossom in Hong Kong. The population of the island at the time of the seizure was no more than 2,000; within a year it had grown to 15,000. In large measure this was due to the foresight of Charles Elliot. Before his recall in August 1841, the disgraced plenipotentiary had not only authorised the sale of commercial land along the harbour's edge but had witnessed the auction of the first tranche of potentially valuable real estate on 14 June 1841, before the British government had even acknowledged the acquisition of Hong Kong to be anything more than a tactical manoeuvre. By the spring of the following year, the Royal Engineers had built a four-mile road along the foreshore. Storage sheds had started to sprout from building plots; merchants oversaw the construction of grand mansions. Soon there were police stations, post offices and a jail, as well as the inevitable sprinkling of gambling dens and whorehouses. By the following year the first of many theatrical touring companies performed in the Opera House and the first newspaper (the *Friend of China*, later named the *China Mail*) went on sale in the streets. Within four years, the waterfront had taken shape: naval and military installations of a permanent nature rose elegantly alongside the two- and three-storey warehouses and offices.

Elliot's swift move to authorise the sale or lease of development land which had not been sanctioned by London was reinforced by the decision of his successor, Sir Henry Pottinger, to allow the publication of official statements implying a British commitment to Hong Kong which had not yet been made. As a result the establishment of Hong Kong as a British colony had become a fait accompli before the Cabinet had resolved the matter one way or the other.

In the official summary of the colony's history, compiled by the Hong Kong Information Services, it is recorded, in an otherwise somewhat Panglossian account, that 'the new settlement did not go well at first. It attracted unruly elements, while fever and typhoons threatened life and property. Crime was rife.' In fact Hong Kong rapidly acquired the nastiest characteristics of the worst kind of frontier town. Piracy on and around the coastline was matched in the centre by a violence and lawlessness which made the streets quite unsafe for all but those accompanied by bodyguards. In the absence of an effective police force, the Europeans armed themselves with handguns against marauding bands of murderous thieves.

This anarchy was attributed to a rapid influx of Chinese from the mainland in search of easy pickings. Within the first ten years of the seizure, the Chinese community multiplied sixteenfold to over 32,000. According to the Rev. Charles Gutzlaff, one of the colony's most

influential figures of that time, 'Many of them are of the worst characters, and ready to commit any atrocity . . . It is very natural that
depraved, idle and bad characters . . . should flock to the colony
where money can be made . . . The moral standard of the people . . .
is of the lowest description.' Fugitives from mainland justice mingled
easily with the local population. As one observer noted, 'The shelter
and protection afforded by the presence of our fleet soon made our
shores the resort of outlaws, opium-smugglers, and, indeed, of all persons who had made themselves obnoxious to the Chinese laws . . .
Hong Kong has been invested by numbers of the Triad Society, the
members of which . . . perpetrate the grossest enormities.' The triads
had emerged in the eighteenth century as a quasi-liberation movement
with a mission to rid China of its Manchu – 'foreign' – rulers.
However they had soon degenerated into a Mafia-like alliance of criminals and their activities had already begun to pollute both China and
Hong Kong.

By 1845, the situation had become so bad that the governor of the
time, Sir John Bowring, introduced a range of emergency measures to
combat the lawlessness. These included pass laws providing that 'any
Chinaman found at large . . . elsewhere than in his own Habitation not
having a pass . . . shall be summarily punished by any Justice of the
Peace . . .' The available chastisements ranged from fines and imprisonment to 'Public Whipping and Personal Exposure in the Stocks'.
Vigilante groups, defined as 'every person lawfully acting as Sentry or
Patrol', were authorised 'to fire upon with intent or effect to kill'.
They were doubtless stiffened in their resolve by the knowledge that
'no Act done or attempted in pursuance of this Ordinance shall be
questioned in any court'. In the early years exemplary punishment in
the form of public hangings and floggings had little impact. Public
hangings were later abandoned, but that Victorian favourite, corporal
punishment (administered with the cat-o'-nine-tails), persisted.

In their own way, the expatriate community behaved no less
deplorably than those over whom they held sway. As if to compensate
for their own treatment in Canton, the British lost no time in reminding the Chinese who were now the masters. Some of them behaved
with such arrogance, braggadocio and brutality that one Anglican cleric
was driven to comment that the merchant venturers of Hong Kong
treated the Chinese as though they were 'a degraded race of people'. A
later traveller, Miss Isabella Bird, noted: 'You cannot be two minutes in
Hong Kong without seeing Europeans striking coolies with their canes
or umbrellas.'

The social niceties of colonial life, while less formally applied than in other outposts of the empire, were nonetheless carefully observed. The Chinese were effectively barred from the Midlevels and the Peak, the high ground with a view on which the Europeans set about creating an outpost of Western civilisation. The segregation on the Peak was later extended to a 20,000-acre site on Kowloon, ostensibly in the name of (European) public health. The Chinese were also forbidden to enter the 'whites-only' clubs and sports grounds, those semblances of British culture without which colonial settlers of that era would have been bereft. Miss Bird was not altogether impressed by expatriate Hong Kong, with 'its cliques, its boundless hospitalities, its extravagances in living, its quarrels, its gaieties, its picnics, balls, regattas, races, dinner parties, lawn tennis parties, amateur theatricals, afternoon teas, and all its other modes of creating a whirl which passes for pleasure', from all of which, of course, the Chinese were wholly excluded, except in the role of servant.

The Victorian settlers not only found the Chinese culture hard to fathom but were evidently reluctant to make the effort. Prejudice was much simpler – and there was ample opportunity for its indulgence. Although the authorities in Hong Kong outlawed infanticide, they were unable to make much impression on the traditions of foot-binding, child marriage and concubinage, despite much hand-wringing outrage on the subject from social reformers in London. The living conditions in the Chinese community served to reinforce European prejudices. As the population of the indigenous Chinese expanded (by the turn of the century, with a population of 240,000, they outnumbered the Europeans by twenty-five to one), their quarters became synonymous in the minds of the uptown settlers with disease and squalor. Governor Sir John Pope-Hennessy, who took up office in 1877, noted: 'The dwellings of the Chinese working classes are inconvenient, filthy and unwholesome. Accumulations of filth occur in and around them . . . Above all, the water supply is miserable.' But he added, as if to reproach his fellow countrymen, 'It is unjust to condemn them as a hopelessly filthy race 'til they have been provided with reasonable means for cleanliness. I conceive that it is the duty of the Government to see that these means are provided and applied . . .' Unfortunately, the resources to achieve this were not readily forthcoming in a colony of free-traders which was already prone to regard all taxation as a form of administrative theft, and where subsequent overlords were not always so enlightened. Sir William Robinson, for example, writing in the last decade of the nineteenth century, detected that the Chinese were 'educated to insanitary habits, and accustomed from infancy to herd together, they were quite unable to grasp the necessity of segregation; they were quite content to die like sheep, spreading disease around them so long as they were left undisturbed'.

Although the Chinese were gradually to emerge from the degrading status imposed on them by the settlers, the process took a very long time. In 1896, a leading businessman by the name of Granville Sharp deplored the beginnings of change. 'When first I came to Hong Kong every Chinese coolie doffed his cap and stood to one side to allow you to pass. When do you see a coolie do that now? We do not exercise our undoubted superiority. We must rule by power.' His attitude was widely shared, and remained institutionalised until well into the twentieth century. It was defined in 1935 by an incoming governor as a form of 'mental arrogance', the basis for which, he wrote, was 'the assumption that the European is inherently superior to the Asian'. At least until 1940, one of Hong Kong's leading hospitals, the Matilda, which Granville Sharp had endowed, still reserved admission for Europeans only. Chinese subjects of the crown were not allowed to serve in the police force until the Second World War, and it was not until 1942 that the Colonial Office dropped its requirement that all candidates should be 'of pure European descent'. It was only in 1946 that the ordinance imposing residential segregation was finally repealed.

The two communities did have some occasion for closer intercourse. As befitted the 'new frontier' atmosphere of Hong Kong's market economy, the red-light zone, with its illegal gambling dens and brothels, grew to accommodate an apparently insatiable need. The Chinese, in particular, were addicted to gambling, and for them games of chance carried no whiff of moral opprobrium. In Victorian England a range of complex (and, from a late twentieth-century perspective, arcane) set of laws sought to control the popular taste for what was regarded as a degrading appetite. However, it soon became evident to the administration in Hong Kong that gambling was impossible to suppress. Ignoring the cries of anguish from social reformers and Christian missionaries, Sir Richard MacDonnell (who became governor in 1867) therefore sanctioned the opening of eleven gaming houses. However, Victorian humbug was not to be thwarted. The MacDonnell reform was soon reversed and a veil of discretion was once again draped over a 'vice' which prospered to the great benefit of the triads, whose 'protection' soon became an ineradicable feature of the colony's subculture.

Like gambling, prostitution proved impossible to abolish by administrative fiat. The official statistics for venereal disease revealed that by 1880, a quarter of the soldiers and sailors stationed in Hong Kong were so adversely affected by syphilis – known locally as Havana flu – that they were unfit for duty. In an attempt to control the disease, which not only incapacitated its victims but caused them terrible suffering, the colonial authorities had instituted a system of licences for 'approved' brothels and inspections for those which were not registered (except for those used exclusively by the Chinese, which were exempt from scrutiny). Unhappily, this pragmatic approach appeared to condone in Hong Kong a 'vice' which was outlawed in Britain. Upon the repeal of the Contagious Diseases Act (which permitted the forcible medical examination of those at risk) by the Westminster Parliament, Hong Kong was driven to abandon licences and inspections. By the turn of the century, no less than half the Hong Kong garrison was infected by venereal disease, a problem which was only solved with the discovery of penicillin some years later.

The expatriate community protected themselves from these disagreeable aspects of Hong Kong by a veneer of gentility which over the years ossified into a set of small-town snobberies that were cruelly observed by the novelist Stella Benson, writing in the 1930s. 'There is nobody here who reads, nobody who is interested in European politics,' she noted. 'Really nobody likes even the mildest honesty here . . . Faces shut like doors unless we talk about games or the weather.'

The stifling mores that ruled social intercourse in the European ghetto contrasted sharply with the economic rapacity of its occupants, whose character found little favour with the British civil servants dispatched to impose administrative order on their buccaneering fellow countrymen. In the words of a senior official from the Board of Trade, writing in 1863, 'The class of Britons who press into this new and untrodden field of enterprise is mainly composed of reckless and unscrupulous adventurers who seek nothing but enormous profits on particular transactions and care little for the permanent interests of commerce – still less for the principles of truth and justice. These men always cloak their injustices under the guise of patriotism and civilisation.'

Even so, Hong Kong did not at first prosper; indeed, it remained a colonial backwater until the second half of the twentieth century. Widely regarded, in the words of one contemporary, as a 'remote and completely unimportant settlement', the colony bore no comparison to Canton and Shanghai as a trading port. In 1845, a deputation of merchants complained to the colonial secretary that 'Hong Kong has no trade at all and is a mere place of residence of the government and its officers with a few British merchants and a very scanty, poor population'. Yet, as Frank Welsh has noted, the overblown expectations of the merchants themselves were almost certainly the root cause of their disappointment. Even as Hong Kong built its basic infrastructure, utilities and services, the throughput of goods in the port grew sluggishly and the economy remained virtually stagnant. The merchants' investment in Hong Kong, in the form of seventy-five-year leases for their waterfront warehouses, seemed, for a time, distinctly insecure.

The most fundamental change in Hong Kong's prospects did not occur until after the Second World War, during which the colony was occupied by the Japanese and its inhabitants subjected to the harsh treatment characteristic of the Japanese Imperial Army. The governor, Sir Mark Young, who had been held in captivity by the Japanese and suffered terrible privations at their hands, was reinstated at Government House in 1946. In 1949 hundreds of thousands of refugees began to pour across the border from southern China and to arrive by boat from Shanghai. The former were peasants fleeing from hunger; the latter were principally merchants fleeing from expropriation and repression after the fall of Beijing, Shanghai and Canton to the Communists. Mao Zedong's Long March had reached its revolutionary destination, and those who feared that the People's Republic would not be to their taste saw in Hong Kong an alternative route to individual and communal salvation.

As a result the population of Hong Kong virtually doubled within a single year, and by the end of 1950, altogether upwards of 2 million people had crossed the border. The authorities in the British colony, mindful of the need to preserve diplomatic relations with the new regime in Beijing, referred to these hapless people as squatters to avoid the implication that they had fled from persecution. This linguistic obfuscation sprang in part from the fear that Mao might use the excuse of nationalist subversion in Hong Kong to launch a pre-emptive strike against the colony to restore Chinese sovereignty by force. Tens of thousands of the opponents of the Nationalists, led by Chiang Kai Shek, had fled to Hong Kong before the Nationalist army collapsed, and it would have been a simple matter for Beijing to stimulate an internal uprising of communist sympathisers against the latest wave of refugees which would almost certainly have been beyond the powers of the war-weary colonial authorities to contain. Similarly, Chiang could easily have roused the no less fervent nationalist supporters of his 'exiled' regime in Taiwan. Hong Kong faced a social, economic and political problem on an alarming scale.

In the literal sense, the refugees were indeed squatters. Camped on the hills around Hong Kong and Kowloon, filling every available piece of land, they lacked any basic amenities. Gradually the authorities imposed a semblance of administrative order: they screened the squatters for resettlement, marked out plots of land on which they could build, provided standpipes and paved the paths through each settlement as it was established. Nothing was done to indicate that these migrants had any right to settle in the colony, or that the authorities had any responsibility for them. Then, on Christmas Day 1953, a fire in the squatter camp at Shek Kip Mei made 50,000 people homeless. Overnight, the governor, Sir Alexander Grantham, was forced into taking a fateful decision: the government would have to build houses for the squatters. By 1956, 200,000 former refugees had been accommodated in tenement rooms, each individual allocated a living area somewhat smaller than the square footage of a double bed. It was a modest but, given the resources of the Hong Kong government, gallant effort to rehouse the dispossessed. More significantly, Grantham's initiative established a principle from which the British government could not possibly retreat. As a result, within a generation the phrase 'refugee community' had come to denote not a physical environment, but the psyche of most of the territory's inhabitants.

To the relief of the authorities, the new settlers were, in general, peaceable, law-abiding and hard-working. Sir Jack Cater, then a junior official, later to become chief secretary, was astonished by the degree to which the immigrants accommodated the privations of this period: 'It was extraordinary for me to visit one of these areas where many thousands of people were living, with one standpipe for two hundred people, and then to see the girls going off to work in the factories in the morning looking pretty, smooth and clean. It was absolutely fantastic.'

The fears of internal upheaval gradually faded until, in 1956, on the anniversary of the 1911 October Revolution (which had led to the downfall of the Ch'ing dynasty), a British resettlement officer took it upon himself to order the removal of some nationalist flags. This crass decision provoked a riot: shops were looted and factories owned by communists came under attack; known communists were rounded up, taken to Nationalist headquarters and brutally assaulted. They were forced to chant nationalist slogans and some of them were killed in cold blood. It took two days for the police and army to restore order, by which time fifty-nine people were dead, forty-four shot by the police, who had been ordered to fire 'without hesitation', and fifteen murdered by the rioters. The adjournment debate in the Commons on this grave breakdown of order in a British colony did not take place for almost a month after the riots, and then it lasted a mere thirty minutes – an accurate measure, as Frank Welsh has pointed out, of the 'very low priority accorded Hong Kong'. After guttering for a moment, the candle of curiosity about Hong Kong was soon snuffed out by more pressing matters closer to home.

In the sixties Hong Kong's economy took off. Under the direction of financial secretary Sir John Cowperthwaite, a laissez-faire economist, the British colony acquired all the characteristics of a free-trade port. Long before Milton Friedman or Margaret Thatcher summoned up the gods of the free market, Cowperthwaite imposed a regime of minimum public spending and minimal restraint on the maximisation of profits. Between 1960 and 1970, wages rose on average by 50 per cent and the number of people living in acute poverty fell from over 50 per cent of the population to under 16 per cent. The annual report for 1971 was able to boast that Hong Kong had become a 'stable and increasingly affluent society comparable with the developed world in nearly every respect'. This was an exaggeration: an ideological hostility towards the concept of the welfare state, combined with the financial secretary's refusal to countenance public borrowing, left Hong Kong's basic services woefully underfunded. Health and education in particular languished far behind what the developed world would regard as appropriate for a thriving modern society. Yet, in the latter half of the sixties, the departments of education, health and social welfare managed to record large budget surpluses apparently without provoking criticism.

Across the border, the People's Republic of China lurched from one slogan to another. The 'Let a Hundred Flowers Bloom' years of the early fifties gave way to the 'Great Leap Forward' in 1958 – and upwards of 20 million people starved to death in the process. Mao's authority soared. In 1966, he initiated the Cultural Revolution, a regime of persecution and terror under which the intelligentsia were purged and the Red Guards held terrifying sway. It was not difficult to visualise how the same generation in Hong Kong, appropriately subverted from the mainland, might erupt with similar revolutionary fervour. In April of that year, a protest against a rise in fares on the Star Ferry which plied its trade between Hong Kong and Kowloon was the pretext for an outbreak of unrest in Kowloon, in which one demonstrator was killed. In comparison with neighbouring Macau, where rioting Red Guards were fired on by Portuguese troops, the Hong Kong disturbances were easily contained. However, any complacency was misplaced. The frustration of the young and the poor, the badly housed and ill educated, was tinder waiting to be ignited. And in May 1967, a rash of demonstrations did escalate quickly into full-scale rioting. Day after day thousands of people, old as well as young, took to the streets in the name of the Cultural Revolution. There was arson and looting. Urged on from the mainland by Red Guards, who had seized control of Canton, saboteurs in Hong Kong planted bombs which killed fifteen people.

Meanwhile, the lives of ordinary citizens were frighteningly disrupted. Loudspeakers from the Bank of China directed an incessant bombardment of anti-British propaganda into the centre of the city. Even schoolchildren were urged to rise up against the British colonialists. The police, stretched to capacity, reacted severely, using batons and tear gas. On one occasion they chased a group of rioters to a power station, where five young revolutionaries leaped into an empty bucket on a conveyor-belt which scooped coal to the furnaces. They were drawn down into the coalstack, and buried alive. This incident, along with one or two others, was later used to support claims that the police had acted with great brutality.

Bearing in mind, however, that ten police officers had been killed and scores more seriously wounded, it might be fairer to say that in general the police acted with remarkable restraint. Nonetheless hundreds of people were arrested, charged and imprisoned, some of whom would never forgive the British for what they complained was the summary justice handed down by the courts. Although the Hong Kong authorities affected an air of insouciance, they were close to despair. According to Sir David Ford, a civil servant with military and media expertise who was drafted in to liaise between the government and the army, the insurrection put the administration under extreme pressure.

> People were very apprehensive. A lot of people were saying that Hong Kong was finished . . . the fear was that China would simply take over . . . There were bodies floating down the Pearl River in their hundreds every day. In Hong Kong, there were major marches up to Government House, with everybody chanting Maoist slogans. And underneath that, there was the ferment of labour strikes, transport strikes, food strikes. There is no doubt that if it had continued, and if the Chinese government had sanctioned the cutting off of water or food supplies, that would have been the end of Hong Kong.

In August, a crowd laid siege to the British embassy in Beijing and, on the night of 22 August, a mob invaded the compound and broke into the embassy building. Soon the embassy was on fire, and the British officials who had barricaded themselves inside were forced to surrender. They were paraded through the crowd by the police, who did little to prevent frenzied onlookers from beating and kicking these emissaries of 'stern imperialism'. Eventually they were taken into what passed for protective custody before the authorities finally sanctioned their release. This episode had a lasting effect on the victims, who included Percy

Cradock, then chargé d'affaires, who has vividly described the incident in his memoirs, *Experiences of China*.

In Hong Kong this episode fuelled the authorities' fears of a similar fate. As it turned out, Beijing was not so incautious as to attempt such a démarche. According to Ford: 'The Chinese government clearly made the decision to tell the compatriots in Hong Kong who were causing the trouble to stop.' Even in this period of acute turmoil, the leaders in Beijing had evidently not entirely lost their reason.

Despite the setbacks of 1967, Hong Kong's economy continued to grow. By the early seventies, the Chinese entrepreneurs who had fled to Hong Kong twenty years earlier had not only restored their fortunes but added to them. Men like Sir Y.K. Pao, who began with one small cargo boat, and K.S. Li, a manufacturer of plastic flowers, who had started businesses in the early fifties with almost no assets, had become international tycoons, rivalling (in influence and acumen, if not yet in scale) the long-established British companies like Swires and Jardine Matheson. The stock exchange flourished; banks multiplied. Takeovers and reverse takeovers accelerated as 'old' money merged with 'new' to generate fabulous wealth for speculators and investors alike in a market that was artificially sustained by the soaring value of land and property.

Under the governorship of Sir Murray MacLehose, the authorities reinforced Hong Kong's burgeoning international reputation by instigating an all-out drive against the corruption endemic in Hong Kong from the early years. The problem was personified by Joseph Godber, an expatriate chief superintendent in the Royal Hong Kong Police who had distinguished himself in the 1967 riots. Godber was also at the heart of a web of corruption which had made him a Hong Kong-dollar millionaire several times over. His exposure as a criminal led to the creation of the Independent Commission Against Corruption (ICAC). Under the unrelenting leadership of Sir Jack Cater, the ICAC set about its task with a vengeance. Hundreds of police officers were arrested in a drive against bribery and back-handers that penetrated deep into the world of organised crime and came perilously close to exposing some of the colony's most prominent entrepreneurs. The realisation that the ICAC was in earnest appeared to have a transforming effect on behaviour, if not on attitudes, in both the public and private sectors. The consequent dawning awareness that Hong Kong, unlike almost every other entrepôt in Asia except for Singapore, was now relatively free of corruption enhanced the colony's standing as the most attractive financial-services centre in the region. Following Deng Xiaoping's economic 'reforms', which began in 1978, mainland China began to invest in Hong Kong with growing self-assurance, helping to propel the colony to the very centre of the Far Eastern stage. By the end of the seventies, Hong Kong thus found itself at both the trading and the financial hub of a region that was developing with spectacular speed.

So in the twenty years before Chris Patten's arrival, the face of what had once been a colonial backwater had been transformed as Hong Kong grew upwards and outwards at an astonishing rate. A network of new bridges, roads, tunnels, railways and a metro system gave the colony the appearance of a great American metropolis, a cross between New York and Los Angeles. This hugely ambitious transport pro-gramme, financed by the vast government surpluses that flowed from the city's runaway economic expansion, included the development of a clutch of satellite cities linked umbilically to Hong Kong and Kowloon by every means of modern communication. Taipo, Shatin, Sheungshui and Fanling were designed to accommodate upwards of 2 million people between them. They would have schools, hospitals, universities, sports stadia and, in one case, even a racecourse. The New Territories, which had been a quiet, rural area dotted with traditional villages, now sprouted great clusters of high-rise apartment blocks, sports grounds, shopping malls, stations and car parks. It was a bold vision, planned unequivocally to embrace a refugee community as permanent residents of what had become one of the most dynamic societies in the world. Of course, you could still find poverty, squalor and homelessness, but in this, as in other respects, Hong Kong was much like any Western soci-ety.

There was one glaring omission: the failure of the colonial authori-ties to make any significant concession to a cardinal principle of twentieth-century governance – that no society could claim to be civilised until the will of the people, as expressed freely through the ballot box, was held to be inviolable. This shameful, if explicable, fail-ure of foresight, imagination and courage by the British government would soon return to haunt Hong Kong.

3

'WE HAD NO OPTION'

Deciding Hong Kong's Fate

In 1949, flushed with victory though they were, the Communists had stopped short of crossing the border and overrunning Hong Kong. Of course, they made it clear that they rejected the 'unequal treaties' by which Hong Kong had been prised away from the motherland and asserted that Hong Kong had always been part of China, but stated that the issue could be resolved by negotiation at an appropriate date in the future. During the extreme privations wrought by the Great Leap Forward in the late fifties, China was preoccupied with the internal crisis generated by Mao's programme of economic 'reform', but even during the heady days of the Cultural Revolution, Beijing (Peking) took no action. However, the Chinese premier, Zhou Enlai, warned that the future of Hong Kong would be settled by 'patriots' and not 'imperialists'. In 1971, during the hangover induced by the excesses of the Cultural Revolution, he was more specific, indicating that the Chinese would indeed seek to recover Hong Kong, but not until the expiry of the leases on the New Territories – the area north of Kowloon and the 235 small islands surrounding Hong Kong – which was then still more than a quarter of a century away.

The issue lay dormant until 1979. According to Sir Percy Cradock, 'Up to this point Hong Kong had been only one refrain of the sometimes dissonant music of Sino–British relations. Never absent, and, on occasion, as in the Cultural Revolution, harsh and threatening. But still a secondary theme. From 1979 onwards, however, it gathered strength and from 1982 became the main motif, drowning virtually all others.' As Britain's chargé d'affaires in Beijing at the height of the Cultural Revolution, Cradock's experience of that 'collective madness' as a de facto hostage in the embassy scarred him permanently. 'It was like having the French Revolution at the bottom of the garden and being asked every now and then to join in. It is participatory theatre of a very violent and brutal kind. It was a great hardship,' he acknowledged after his retirement in 1992. Although he was later to be labelled by critics in Britain and Hong Kong one of China's arch-appeasers, a charge he bitterly repudiates, his analysis of the Chinese leadership was caustic if not lacking in awe. Even before the Cultural Revolution, he had found Maoism, 'that unholy marriage of Chinese culture and Western communism', an almost overpowering force. The leaders who orchestrated the cruelties of the revolution seemed isolated, arrogant, inflexible and secretive. Appearing to believe themselves predestined to be at the centre of the world, they were acutely suspicious of the West, and in particular of Britain, and – although they no longer used the term in public – it seemed to Cradock that they considered the description 'barbarian' to be as apt in the twentieth century as they had in the nineteenth. They were 'a very emotional, violent people who feel they have to assert themselves'.

Cradock was never in any doubt, therefore, that for the old guard in Beijing, the issue of Hong Kong was both real and symbolic, a struggle against Britain, an adversary which would use every wile capitalism could devise to frustrate the recovery of their territory. Cradock also believed that the Chinese held virtually all the cards and that 'the ground was slipping away under the British feet every day'. To him, therefore, the question had always been not whether, but when, they would assert their claim on Hong Kong. For Cradock, the 'bottom line' was that China was the preponderant political and military power: the People's Liberation Army could overrun Hong Kong at any time and Britain could do nothing about it. This bleak assessment thoroughly infected the handful of Foreign Office officials who, under Cradock's intellectual leadership, were responsible for defining Britain's stance throughout the tortuous negotiations which led to the 1984 Joint Declaration and beyond. If this entailed what his critics were to describe as a policy of appeasement, Cradock was irritated but not ashamed to be so castigated: in his mind, it was 'a policy of co-operation. The only sensible policy. The policy of realism.'

Nevertheless, until 1979, in London:

There was no clear view of the likely terms of any such settlement. It was acknowledged that the long-term trend was probably unfavourable to Hong Kong's existence as a colony. But there was always the chance that the status quo might quietly be maintained, particularly if there was a bow in the direction of Chinese sovereignty.

In Hong Kong, the matter was regarded with rather less insouciance. China's assertion of sovereign rights over the colony hovered perpetually in the background, menacingly to some, beguilingly to others. The economic reform programme initiated by Deng Xiaoping, however, gave confidence that the post-Mao generation of Chinese elders would at least not deliberately undermine Hong Kong's crucial role as a rapidly expanding entrepôt. In a community which lived for the short term and where entrepreneurs took high risks and expected quick returns, 1997 was a faraway precipice which almost no one greatly cared to contemplate and which was, therefore, only discussed sotto voce.

It was against this background that in 1979 Hong Kong's governor, Lord MacLehose, flew to Beijing as the guest of the Chinese government. Unlike Sir Percy Cradock, MacLehose was an unabashed enthusiast for China. Recalling his postwar experiences there, he remembered: 'The thrill of that different world . . . It has a strong effect on people. Either they love it or they hate it. I love it . . . You know what they say about the Foreign Office "always loving our enemies"? I think they are a fascinating people, and provided you take them on their own terms, very rewarding.'

As the governor of Hong Kong, MacLehose had been preoccupied with social and economic matters: driving through a vast housing programme; reforming a police service which, in the aftermath of the Cultural Revolution, had become exhausted and excessively prone, for a consideration, to turn a blind eye to the protection rackets operated by the triads; and enhancing Hong Kong's identity as the region's economic miracle. Although the 'bamboo curtain' between Hong Kong and China was still firmly in place, MacLehose did what he could to filter his own goodwill across the border, becoming the first governor to celebrate China Day and signing the book of condolence at the New China News Agency on the death of Mao.

In a sense, the invitation to Beijing was a reward for his assiduous efforts to cultivate better relations with the mainland. His would be the first official visit to China by a Hong Kong governor since 1949, and he made it clear to his Chinese counterparts that he would only go if he could meet 'leading personalities' and if the visit were to 'have some substance'. With this confirmed, it was MacLehose who advised the Foreign Office, that, inter alia, the future of Hong Kong should form part of Britain's agenda for the talks.

The Foreign Office assented at once. Although Hong Kong was flourishing, the Foreign Office took the view, in Cradock's recollection, that there would shortly come a point when fears about the future would begin to overshadow that prosperity. He and his officials concurred with MacLehose's opinion that, with land mortgages in Hong Kong lasting usually for fifteen years, prospective purchasers were likely to shy away, and that business confidence might rapidly evaporate. It was imperative to give investors at least some security about their holdings after 1997. This, combined with the apparently reformist character of the Deng leadership, made the moment seem propitious. The question, therefore, was not whether but how to raise what was recognised to be a matter of the very greatest delicacy.

Instead of tackling the issue head on, MacLehose suggested that they should take what Cradock described as a 'sidelong' approach, treating the matter as if the issue at stake were merely a technical one. The British side would seek Chinese authority for the sale of individual leases in the New Territories that would straddle 1997, in the hope that the constitutional deadline might thereby be blurred. Were the Chinese to assent to this in principle, it might then be possible to amend the Order in Council under which Britain administered the New Territories until 1997 by simply removing the terminal date. In retrospect, given the well-known suspicions of the Chinese, this ruse seems almost comically transparent and diplomatically inept, but Cradock, at this time British ambassador in Beijing, has explained that he thought it worth a try. The game plan was endorsed by the Labour foreign secretary, Dr David Owen – although, according to his own account, he gave instructions that MacLehose should not go so far as to mention the Order in Council.

The decision to raise the issue at all was taken in the teeth of opposition from one or two of MacLehose's most senior colleagues, including his chief secretary, Sir Jack Cater, who argued, 'Don't go and see the Chinese; they are reactive, not proactive. Don't raise the question at all.' Cater relates:

I was being told by Murray that there was grave concern about the leases in the New Territories; that the subleases were getting shorter and shorter; that people and the bankers were getting worried about the mortgages. This was nonsense. We did not even have mortgages at that time – or at least in no great number. And I'd certainly not heard about it and obviously I would have done.

There was concern [in the Foreign Office] about the leases. No doubt. But basically it seemed to me that they wanted to get shot of Hong Kong but in the nicest possible way . . . It was simply the East of Suez policy of 1964. Hong Kong was indefensible. It was the government's policy for Hong Kong to be handed back.

It is true that MacLehose presumed that China would reclaim Hong Kong. It is also true that David Owen had put the future of Hong Kong high on his own agenda for discussion during a forthcoming visit scheduled for April, and that he was intending to propose a 'pre-emptive' transfer of sovereignty in return for a guarantee of continued British administration after 1997. As it was, to Cradock's great relief, the Owen visit was torpedoed by the fall of the Callaghan government in the wake of the 'winter of discontent'. Yet even if Cater's analysis of the Labour government's intention to 'surrender' Hong Kong contained an element of truth, it is, with the benefit of hindsight, naive to suppose that his alternative strategy – studiously to ignore the problem – might have prevailed. In MacLehose's view it was 'bunkum' to think that 'the Chinese might have drifted past 1997 . . . [or] that we could drift by without any arrangements being made for four million people who had no legal title to Hong Kong under international law and no domestic title as landowners . . . The mind boggles.'

The British team was ushered into the Great Hall of the People in a state of some trepidation. In Hong Kong the visit was the subject of much press excitement and speculation, but only a handful of people were aware of MacLehose's real purpose: any rumour to the effect that Hong Kong's future was 'up for grabs' would have been certain to trigger precisely those fears which they hoped this meeting could be used to allay. But what if Deng Xiaoping were to rebuff them? Or if he simply refused to discuss the matter? They felt themselves to be on a high wire without a safety net.

As it was – and as if to confirm the British contention that the issue could not have been allowed to drift – Deng at once wrong-footed MacLehose by seizing the initiative himself. Like other British envoys, the Hong Kong governor was magnetised by Deng's presence. He was relieved when the Chinese leader spoke in mollifying terms, conveying in a somewhat rambling way (as summarised by Cradock): 'Of course Hong Kong will return to China. Sovereignty belongs to China. But 1997 is quite a long way off. Don't worry down there, you'll be all right.'

According to Beijing's official version of the chairman's statement,

Deng reasserted China's sovereignty over Hong Kong and insisted that a negotiated settlement should be based on that premise. At the same time he conceded that Hong Kong would be a 'special region' where capitalism would be allowed to flourish 'for a considerable length of time'.

MacLehose took the cue from Deng to raise the issue of the leases in the New Territories. Deng either failed to grasp the point or affected to misunderstand what the governor had said. When MacLehose tried again, Deng cautioned him that, in any mention of land leases, there should be no reference to British administration. He also advised that China had not yet decided on a political structure for Hong Kong after 1997. However, he repeated, in what Cradock has described as 'an all-weather quote' upon which the British seized to use later for public consumption, that investors should 'set their hearts at ease'. And that, for the next three years, was that.

The British had not been entirely rebuffed, but they had failed to make any headway. The future for Hong Kong after 1997 was essentially no clearer after the visit than it had been before. Cradock was frustrated: 'We were not satisfied because we had dropped a rock into the Chinese pool and seen some ripples but we weren't quite sure even yet that the full meaning of what we said had been taken aboard.' In a further attempt to broach the issue, Cradock had a meeting with the vice-foreign minister. The response was unequivocal: 'We advise you not to go ahead with any proposal to extend British sovereignty beyond 1997.'

Cradock was anxious to maintain the dialogue but MacLehose was nervous. London sided with the governor, and Cradock was refused the go-ahead. In the following months the subject of Hong Kong was raised in 'bilateral' meetings between British and Chinese officials, but in a desultory fashion. It was clear that Beijing had temporarily redirected its diplomatic attention to the even more formidable problem of Taiwan, which for a moment seemed to offer China a promise of peaceful reincorporation. This hope proved forlorn following the election of President Reagan, who was all but ready to offer Taiwan a place in the United Nations as an independent state. However, it was not until 1982 that Chinese officials began to indicate that Hong Kong was again on their minds. Just before the outbreak of the Falklands War, the former British prime minister Sir Edward Heath, known as a 'friend of China', returned from Beijing to report that Deng Xiaoping had told him bluntly that China intended to reassert its sovereignty over the entire territory of Hong Kong. The 'unequal treaties' would be abrogated accordingly, and while Hong Kong would continue to enjoy economic and social autonomy, there would be no role for Britain after 1997. Deng coined his 'one country, two systems' slogan to embrace the concept to which China was now wedded. His message to the British elder statesman was clearly intended for 10 Downing Street, but the new prime minister was preoccupied by the conflict with Argentina and, as Heath no longer had government status, Whitehall decided that his message did not require an official response. It did, however, provoke serious discussion among the sinologists at the Foreign Office, whose own prejudices were confirmed by Deng's words.

The trigger for the next stage was the official visit the British prime minister, Margaret Thatcher, was due to make to Beijing in September 1982. Rather late in the day, the Foreign Office briefed her for the first time on the unappetising options facing her government. Three years into her premiership, Thatcher was not only viscerally opposed to communism but, fresh from leading Britain to victory against the Argentinian junta, she had also become the most charismatic leader of the 'free world'. In the view of one of her closest advisers on China, 'This had left her with a great disposition to military solutions, tough solutions and a certain degree of suspicion of the Foreign Office.' According to Sir Percy Cradock, Thatcher's attitude towards the policy of the Foreign Office on Hong Kong was essentially: 'Here is another colonial outpost they want to sell off.'

By this time, the Foreign Office – where the views of Sir Percy Cradock held sway, although he himself was still in Beijing – had decided to ditch the 'sidelong' approach essayed by Lord MacLehose. In its place Cradock now favoured what was in effect a pre-emptive retreat on sovereignty, arguing that the best Britain could now expect was to persuade Beijing to agree to leave the administration of Hong Kong after 1997 in British hands in return for 'making a bow' in the direction of the Chinese claim to the island. Since it was clear to him that the Chinese intended to take over the territory in 1997, when the lease on the New Territories expired, there was little practical point in counter-asserting the legality of the 'unequal treaties' by which Hong Kong and the southern tip of Kowloon had been ceded to Britain in perpetuity.

Margaret Thatcher was not at all impressed. 'Look, I would have loved to have kept it,' she recalled fourteen years later.

Sovereignty means something to us. We recognised sovereignty. I believe it would have been recognised in international law . . . Being brought up on the rule of law, it hadn't occurred to me that the sovereignty of Hong Kong would not be respected. I thought they would respect it because it's a treaty . . . I would have liked to have kept the sovereignty of Hong Kong island for Britain . . . [Or, alternatively] I would have loved for them to have their independence and to be a small member of the United Nations . . . It would have been marvellous.

The hapless officials at the Foreign Office were the victims of the whirlwind whipped up by that assumption. Evidently contemptuous of what she regarded as their timid approach, Thatcher was at her most relentless and abrasive – or as Cradock has put it, 'combative and unco-operative'. Her approach, he recalled, was 'one of free, not to say hostile, inquiry, with a predisposition to solutions based on legal, or even military strength'. In the words of one official, 'She looked quite hard at the idea that we should simply stand pat, hold our own, and tell the Chinese to take a running jump.'

Margaret Thatcher only succumbed when she was persuaded, as she later described it, that Britain had no option.

Hong Kong island is less than 8 per cent of the territory. All the rest is China mainland. There is no way we could say, 'We're going to keep the sovereignty of Hong Kong.' There was no way in which we could defend it. More than that: they didn't need to march in. The Chinese could have just turned off the supply of water and food which came from the mainland. So I had very few cards in my hand.

Nonetheless, the prime minister remained a reluctant convert. On more than one occasion in the months ahead, she sought to recant. Cradock described her stubbornness. 'There was resolution in plenty at those meetings, but it tended to resolution of a one-dimensional kind, with little or no sense of the other side of the struggle, their prejudices, strengths and likely reactions; and in such an embattled setting it was not always easy to supply the missing elements in the equation – in other words, to give a realistic assessment of the prospects – without sounding negative or even faint-hearted.' On more than one occasion, according to Cradock, the defence secretary, Michael Heseltine, was summoned to the prime minister's presence to confirm the Foreign Office line that Hong Kong could indeed not be held by force of arms against a regime which, Cradock says, she regarded as 'bad, tough and cruel'.

Eventually even the prime minister was driven to concede Cradock's case for beating the retreat: since Hong Kong was indefensible by military means, there had to be a negotiated settlement. Whether Britain liked it or not, there would be a reversion of the whole territory in 1997, and what would matter would be the terms of that reversion. Strategically, Cradock's view was straightforward, if somewhat lacking in heroism: 'If there was to be a retreat, it had to be an orderly retreat from one carefully defended point to another . . . and this was the first position: sovereignty to China, administration staying with Britain.'

It was in this spirit that in September 1982 the prime minister followed the well-trodden path into the Great Hall of the People. Cradock's strategy, accepted by Thatcher, was to negotiate for continued British administration of Hong Kong after 1997 in return for which Britain would be willing to 'consider' the question of sovereignty. The proposition was, as Cradock intended, highly qualified, but it also dangled the carrot of concession.

The prime minister's first meeting was with her opposite number, the Chinese premier Zhao Ziyang. Although in Thatcher's view he was 'the kindest, the most understanding of the lot', he was also unyielding. He insisted that in 1997 China would recover sovereignty over both the New Territories and Hong Kong itself, and it was, he indicated, nonsense to suppose that any other state would be permitted to administer any of the territory on China's behalf.

The following day, 24 September, Thatcher was ushered into the presence of Deng Xiaoping. Like Lord MacLehose, she was impressed:

> The volume of personality compared with the physical volume – he is small, not very tall – makes the personality even more obvious. Very much in charge. Oh, very much . . . Now, this man had known what it was like to be put in prison by the communist system. His son had been grievously injured during the Cultural Revolution – thrown from the top of a building and left to lie there for twenty-four hours. Now we think, 'That must have been a terrible experience for Deng; it must have made him more human and sympathetic.' Do you know, I don't believe it did . . . He is a really tough guy.

The meeting did not go well. Thatcher rehearsed the British position with what Cradock called 'great charm and clarity'. Deng, chain-smoking and gesticulating dismissively, was unmoved. He would allow up to two years for consultations, and then China would announce its decision. The British prime minister retorted that, while of course Britain accepted the termination of the lease on the New Territories, the treaties ceding Hong Kong to Britain were valid in international law and therefore could not be abrogated unilaterally. Deng became tetchy. Thatcher responded forcefully, on the grounds that: 'If you are going to argue with someone, you might as well be frank; there is no point to me in putting it all in diplomatic language. They don't understand that.' As she recalled the meeting in 1996, the two leaders then had the following exchange:

> Deng: 'Look, I could walk in and take the whole lot this afternoon.'
> Thatcher: 'Yes. There is nothing I could do to stop you. But the eyes of the world would now know what China is like. Everything would leave Hong Kong. You'd have its prosperity and you would suddenly have lost the lot.'

This was the heart of the matter: would China really risk the destruction of Hong Kong and international obloquy to reclaim sovereignty? Or would it have been possible to call Deng's bluff and to have counterproposed a diplomatic and economic modus vivendi between the British island and the Chinese mainland? Although the British side had already half ceded the case, Deng's response to Thatcher's riposte was instructive: 'The whole atmosphere changed. I think he and the people watching him were absolutely amazed . . . He had never been brought face to face with what he could do to China in the eyes of the world.' Allowing for any histrionic quality in the former prime minister's recollection of the moment, Deng's reaction does raise the question of whether Cradock's eagerness to concede the reversion of Hong Kong essentially on the terms demanded by Beijing was not infected by defeatism.

As it was, the die was cast. The two sides tussled over a communiqué – which was sufficiently ambiguous to cause months of mutual recrimination afterwards – to the effect that negotiations over the future of Hong Kong would begin in earnest. Whether or not these were to be conducted on the premise that Hong Kong would revert to China, as Beijing demanded, or whether the issue of reversion was one of several yet to be decided, as the British claimed, remained unresolved, but, on the British side at least, the matter had already been settled in favour of further retreat. Not only would the sovereignty of Hong Kong revert to China in 1997, but Britain would no longer genuinely contest the case for continued administration after that date. So far as the Foreign Office was concerned, the latter issue would be no more than a negotiating ploy, as much for domestic consumption as to salvage concessions.

The prime minister left Beijing for Hong Kong with a sense of some foreboding. She has recalled:

I realised that the people of Hong Kong somehow thought that we could pull something out of the hat. And I realised we weren't going to be able to. Just as they didn't understand our system, I didn't realise that the Chinese would overturn a treaty which gave us sovereignty over Hong Kong; that they would take this view of law. Because if you do that, you've no international law and no treaty is ever worth anything.

If the British prime minister was touched by a degree of self-delusion, the pro-Chinese media responded with characteristic bombast: Thatcher's 'fallacy imbued with colonialism', Hong Kong's leading pro-Beijing paper, *Wen Wei Po*, thundered, 'has aroused the indignation of Hong Kong patriots and has once again recalled to the 1 billion Chinese people the history of aggression against China by the British Empire . . . Is it not that she wishes to enjoy once again the aggressions of the past?' There was much more in the same vein. In the view of Sir Percy Cradock, who would have preferred reticence on Thatcher's part, the impact of her words in Beijing 'provoked an angry reaction which had the effect of complicating the already arduous task of getting negotiations started'. In what now became a gruesome war of diplomatic attrition, Britain began to retreat inch by inch towards China's bottom line. On the question of sovereignty Cradock has insisted, 'They were prepared to go to the brink of breakdown and virtually ruin Hong Kong financially.'

The evidence for this claim is persuasive, though whether this prospective démarche would have been a deliberate act of economic sabotage or simply a byproduct of incompetence is debatable. During Margaret Thatcher's visit, Hong Kong investors had one of their periodic bouts of anxiety and the Hang Seng Index began to plummet. According to the former prime minister, at one point Deng turned to her and rasped, 'Money is going out. You must stop it.' Thatcher replied, 'I can't. I have no powers to stop it.'

'Of course you can!'

Thatcher repeated, 'I can't. I have no power suddenly to step in and stop the market operating. I have no powers under the law.' She was bewildered: 'He didn't understand. He just had no comprehension at all.'

The negotiations stalled. In the spring of 1983, to Cradock's horror, the prime minister fell to canvassing a host of ideas, including a UN-sponsored referendum on the future of Hong Kong, or even independence. Instead she was persuaded to write to the Chinese premier shifting Britain's stance. If the two sides could reach agreement over the administration of what China had designated the 'special administrative region' of Hong Kong, then she would not only 'consider' the sovereignty issue, but she would be prepared to recommend to Parliament the reversion of sovereignty to China. Cradock called this the 'first finesse'. It was not enough; by the autumn of 1983 the negotiations had reached the point of collapse.

Although key officials at the Foreign Office, where Sir Geoffrey Howe had become foreign secretary a few months earlier, had acknowledged among themselves that the Chinese would never accept the prospect of a British administration of Hong Kong after 1997, even one operating under Chinese sovereignty, they had continued to press the case. This tactic was designed in part to extract better terms from the Chinese in the process of retreat. It was also thought to be important, in the words of Sir Robin McLaren, political adviser in Hong Kong from 1981 to 1985, to 'convince British ministers, and above all the prime minister, that we had done everything possible'. Thatcher remained sceptical. 'Margaret's heart kept on cherishing the alternative,' Lord Howe recalled in 1995, 'dreaming of a way in which we could have something more permanent and more durable. And heart and mind were constantly in conflict. And we had to keep on restoring the sovereignty of mind over heart.'

The Foreign Office also had to cope with fierce resistance from within the colony itself, led by Lord MacLehose's replacement as governor, Sir Teddy Youde, and his principal officials, and leading members of the community.

Much against the will of the British diplomats involved, the prime minister had insisted that the leading members of the Executive Council, the governor's appointed advisers, should be kept abreast of the negotiations and allowed to comment on their progress. 'Diplomats are a coterie who rather prefer the idea of negotiating with their fellows in secret,' noted McLaren. 'I think it was their instinct that it is better, and easier and tidier, to deal with these things in private rather than negotiating in public.' In this hall of mirrors, the British negotiators were under no less pressure from London and Hong Kong than they were from Beijing. It is at least arguable that Britain would have been free to retreat more rapidly to China's bottom line, as defined by Cradock, if there had not been a countervailing imperative to persuade the most influential figures in Hong Kong that the territory had only been surrendered after fierce and prolonged resistance. As it was, the Chinese proved as obdurate as the British team had always presumed they would be, insisting that their Twelve-Point Plan, which appeared to confirm Hong Kong's future status as an independent economic entity, should allay any residual doubts, and that to suggest otherwise was mere colonial arrogance on Britain's part.

On paper at least, the Twelve-Point Plan appeared to offer the reassurances that the people of Hong Kong would need. Stipulating the basic principles which would govern Hong Kong's future under Chinese sovereignty, the twelve points confirmed, inter alia, that Hong Kong would become a special administrative region with 'a high degree of autonomy, except in foreign and defence affairs', which would become the 'responsibilities of the Central People's Government'. The SAR would be vested with 'executive, legislative and independent judicial power, including that of final adjudication', while the laws currently in force in Hong Kong would remain 'basically' unchanged. The current social and economic systems and 'lifestyle' would also remain unchanged: 'Rights and freedoms, including those of the person, of speech, of the press, of assembly, of association, of travel, of movement, of correspondence, of strike, of choice of occupation, of academic research and of religious belief' would be protected by law. Hong Kong would retain its status as an international financial centre.

Although they were encouraged by the tenor of the twelve points, the British negotiators were unwilling to accept these commitments at their face value. They sought clarification, precision and exegesis. The diplomatic impasse between the two sides provoked an atmosphere of crisis in Hong Kong. In September, the Hang Seng Index again fell precipitously and, more alarmingly, the value of the Hong Kong dollar dropped by 8 per cent in one day. Huge queues formed at Hong Kong supermarkets as the population panicked itself into stocking up on essential goods. In London, treasury officials worried that the sterling reserves would have to be called upon to support the local dollar, a prospect which was averted when, in October, officials rushed through a decision to peg the Hong Kong currency to the US dollar. In a mood of suspicion and recrimination, there were strong rumours that the Bank of China had been used by Beijing to precipitate the collapse of the currency, while Beijing accused the British of manipulating the Hong Kong dollar for the same duplicitous purpose. The financial crisis served only to confirm Cradock's pessimism about Beijing's determination to regain sovereignty over Hong Kong regardless of the economic consequences. The foreign secretary was easily persuaded to Cradock's view, explaining that he soon realised: 'There was no stopping that, whatever we tried to do. We couldn't stop them by force or by appeal to world opinion or anything of the sort.'

In the summer Cradock had drafted what he liked to describe as a 'second finesse', the next staging post on the long retreat 'in good order' to which he sought to commit the government. He urged that Britain should now be willing to 'explore' whether the foundations of lasting prosperity in Hong Kong could be established in the absence of continued administration by Britain. If they could, Her Majesty's government would no longer resist the transfer of sovereignty required by the Chinese. But even after the autumn financial crisis, a majority of Hong Kong officials and advisers still opposed further concessions, declaring that the Chinese were still bluffing and that there was no need for further retreat. Although Thatcher and Howe both accepted the Foreign Office view that the Chinese were deadly serious, it was only when the Hong Kong establishment had been assured that the proposal was 'conditional' that they assented to Cradock's 'second finesse'.

In truth, the 'conditionality' of the talks which now began in earnest was of an entirely theoretical kind. The British had already concluded that Beijing's claim on Hong Kong could not be resisted and that this should not be permitted to precipitate a breakdown in negotiations. Although the prime minister still yearned – romantically, in the view of her advisers – either to retain British sovereignty or to achieve independence for Hong Kong and Kowloon, the Foreign Office had implicitly accepted both the premises and the preconditions set by China. As a result, the deadlock was at last broken, and the negotiations, even if they were intense and sometimes combative, now took place in an altered and more cordial atmosphere. Howe and Cradock still had trouble with both what Cradock described later as the 'unyielding' British officials of the Hong Kong government and Hong Kong's appointed politicians, who, he later recalled acidly, were 'poised uneasily on the windowledge, threatening to jump, with myself desperately clutching their coat-tails'.

In April 1984 the foreign secretary finally acknowledged in public that British administration over Hong Kong would terminate in July 1997. Sir Geoffrey Howe had flown to Hong Kong from Beijing, where he had endured a two-hour audience with Deng Xiaoping. It had been, he said, a 'daunting' experience. In an earlier meeting with the Chinese foreign secretary, Wu Xueqian, Howe had devised a metaphor to express the common interest of each side. Hong Kong, he told his interlocutors, was like 'a Ming vase, an object of priceless value', which was to be handed over like the baton in a relay race. It would be disastrous to drop it. His emollience paved the way for agreement on a timetable for negotiations leading to the restoration of Chinese sovereignty which did not yet formally exclude a continued but unspecified 'British role' in Hong Kong after 1997.

The Sino–British negotiations had been conducted in secret. Although there had been much speculation about them, it still came as a shock to hear the British foreign secretary inform Hong Kong's Legislative Council in his 'unveiling statement' that 'it would not be realistic to think in terms of an agreement that provides for British administration in Hong Kong after 1997'. There were gasps in the assembly and many people broke down in tears at the recognition of a finality which, in the interests of diplomacy, had been kept from them for so long.

By the autumn of 1984, the final deal was almost in place. It was agreed that the twelve points should, as the Chinese had insisted from the beginning, form the basis of a Joint Declaration which would define the terms under which sovereignty over Hong Kong would revert to China. However, the Chinese conceded that these principles would be elaborated in an annex of substantially more detail than they had originally been willing to accept. The two sides also agreed that the twelve points and the elaboration of them in the annex would be stipulated 'in a Basic Law of the Hong Kong Administrative Region of the People's Republic of China, by the National People's Congress', and that these policies would remain unchanged for fifty years.

The only outstanding Chinese demand – that they should be free to establish a commission in Hong Kong to oversee the final phase of transition – was also agreed, although, at Britain's request, this body was to be renamed the Joint Liaison Group (JLG). After prolonged haggling, it was determined that the JLG would begin work in July 1988, a small concession by the Chinese, who had wanted it to be set up in January of that year. This modest triumph of diplomacy seems to have given the British team an inordinate amount of satisfaction.

After another marathon set of negotiations in Beijing, the two sides finally reached agreement on the key clauses of the Joint Declaration. Deng Xiaoping emerged from the last round of talks in ebullient mood, smiling and joshing with an equally relaxed Sir Geoffrey Howe, who was delighted when Deng declared: 'We have decided that we can trust the British people and the British government. Please convey to your prime minister our hope that she will come to sign the agreement. And to Her Majesty, your Queen, our hope that she too will be able to visit our country.'

The Joint Declaration was initialled in September 1984, thus meeting the deadline set by Deng two years earlier. In December the prime minister flew to Beijing to join Deng for the official signing ceremony, at which point the Joint Declaration became the basis for all future discussions about Hong Kong's future with China. Before long, the agreement was acknowledged across the political spectrum in Hong Kong and in Britain to have been a consummate achievement, and one for which Sir Percy Cradock's sinuous intellect and strategic perspective were very largely responsible. The media in Hong Kong, reflecting widespread relief, commented with jubilation on China's apparent commitment to preserving Hong Kong's social and economic freedoms in the name of lasting prosperity and stability. In London, *The Times* was more cautious, asserting: 'Just as it would be wrong to celebrate the agreement as a victory, so too it would be wrong to criticise it too severely. It has managed to secure some unusually specific assurances from Peking, and as such holds out the prospect of order, stability and business confidence in Hong Kong at least for the next few years.'

In 1990, six years after Margaret Thatcher and Deng Xiaoping put their signatures to the Joint Declaration, the National Congress of the People's Republic rubber-stamped the Basic Law, which codified the principles outlined in the Joint Declaration in the form of a detailed mini-constitution for Hong Kong.

And what of democracy? Not a mention of that issue seems to have passed the lips of any negotiator until, as if it were an afterthought, a mere seven days before the Joint Declaration was submitted to both governments for approval, Sir Geoffrey Howe raised the question of Hong Kong's internal governance. 'My important proposal', as he would later describe it, was that the post-1997 Legislative Council should be constituted by elections and that the executive should be accountable to the legislature. This cryptic commitment, inserted into the agreement at the very last moment, is the only reference to the concept of democracy in the entire 8,000-word document. Given Sir Percy Cradock's assertion twelve years later that the phrase 'constituted by elections' was approved by the British in the full knowledge that the Chinese had therein made no commitment to democracy whatsoever, it is hard to understand Howe's later self-satisfaction. Nonetheless, this fragile clause was Chris Patten's most vital inheritance – a conceptual chalice filled in equal measure with the elixir of ambiguity and the poison of self-deception.

4

'NO ONE IS SAFE'

Alarm Bells Across the Border

A few months before Chris Patten's arrival in Hong Kong, Professor Gong Xiang Rui of Beijing University concluded the draft of a lecture which he intended to deliver at the Hong Kong Human Rights Conference in 1992. The words he wrote eloquently expressed Patten's own conviction.

> There are some rights which are inherent in a system of democracy, whether it is capitalist or socialist. So long as there are free elections based on public opinion, it is always possible to compel the government not to overstep the boundaries of its powers, for there is a minority who would give attention to any abuses, and persuade the electorate to oppose those abuses. And if the government is not responsive, it may be turned out. There will be no democracy if minority opinions cannot be expressed, or if people cannot meet together to discuss their opinions and their actions, or if those who think alike on any subject cannot associate for mutual support and for the propagation of their common ideas. Yet these rights are vulnerable and they are most likely to be subject to attack. Therefore the fundamental liberty is not only of free election but also of the limitation of government powers.

The lecture was never delivered. Just before the Human Rights Conference, Professor Gong Xiang Rui was informed by the authorities in Beijing that he was forbidden to leave China for Hong Kong.

In China the gerontocracy was still in control. Deng Xiaoping, lingering for an apparent eternity on his deathbed, held a dead hand over the regime he had created. The old guard and the new guard were both imprisoned by his immobile authority. China's conversion to capitalism was irrepressible but wayward. Impoverished peasants drifting from the countryside to the towns and cities in search of work formed a migratory army of perhaps 20 million people competing for jobs with a similar number of unemployed urban workers. Higher up the economic scale the pickings were rich. Businessmen, lawyers, soldiers, party cadres – any individuals with a place to protect in the anarchic web of negotiation and transaction by which an arthritic socialist economy stumbled into the new age of global capitalism – survived and prospered by demonstrating their commitment to the new order which involved, inter alia, endemic corruption on a massive, if unquantifiable, scale.

The price of rampant growth was not only inflation but social insecurity and, in so vast a country, a perpetual sense of incipient disorder. The political freedoms and civil liberties elaborately enshrined in the constitution of the People's Republic were conspicuous only by the severity of the punishment imposed on those seeking to exercise these rights. The cynicism with which the regime espoused the cause of freedom while crushing any perceived threat to the arbitrary exercise of its 'revolutionary' authority made even the most insouciant observer recoil. In Hong Kong, the idea of 1997 was inseparable from an anticipatory shiver of anxiety.

On 19 May 1989, the Chinese premier, Li Peng, introduced martial law in China to combat the students and workers who, exercising their rights under Article 35 of the constitution, had taken to the boulevards of Beijing to campaign for democracy. Two days later in Hong Kong, 50,000 people braved a typhoon to stage the first of several huge demonstrations in the colony supporting the democracy movement on the mainland. They marched through torrential rain and high winds to the headquarters of China's de facto embassy, the headquarters of the New China News Agency (NCNA) in Happy Valley, where they staged a protest. At a request from the platform they all sat on the sodden ground and, to enable everyone to see the proceedings, they obediently folded their umbrellas as the leaders of the demonstration spoke in support of the Chinese students who, in defiance of Li Peng, had occupied Tiananmen Square in Beijing.

The organiser of the Hong Kong protest was Martin Lee, a leading barrister and a member of the colony's Legislative Council, who had recently emerged to prominence after conducting a well-orchestrated media campaign for fully democratic elections and a Bill of Rights. In a second demonstration a week later, a million people – one sixth of the entire population of Hong Kong – took to the streets.

On Saturday 4 June 1989, in Beijing, the People's Liberation Army was ordered to cleanse Tiananmen Square of the 'subversive elements' occupying it. At 8pm the tanks rolled in and the first of several hundred unarmed civilians were mown to the ground. The massacre horrified the world. The following day, a million people of all races and creeds again took to the streets of Hong Kong. Once more they walked in silence through the city to Happy Valley, in mourning and dread. In a gesture of despair and defiance, Martin Lee, who was a member of the Drafting Committee responsible for formulating the Basic Law, symbolically burned his copy of the draft. In Beijing the Queen's counsel was accused of violating Article 1 of the Chinese constitution, branded a subversive and formally expelled from the committee.

In Britain, the public feeling of disgust and impotent rage found powerful expression in the British media, notably in newspapers like *The Times*, the *Telegraph* and the *Spectator*, which, with varying degrees of vehemence, warned that the diplomatic triumphalism over the Joint Declaration five years before now seemed horribly misplaced. The *Spectator*, indeed, urged that the document be torn up altogether. Margaret Thatcher later admitted to feeling such revulsion that she, too, wondered whether she had been right to put her signature to what was by now a binding international treaty. She was one of the first world leaders to denounce the perpetrators of Tiananmen Square and the very first to endorse a range of (albeit modest) sanctions against the regime.

Martin Lee was born in southern China in 1938, the son of a Chinese army officer. His father had been a student activist in France, where he was a contemporary of Zhou Enlai, but despite the entreaties of the latter, he supported the Kuomintang nationalists rather than Mao Zedong's revolutionaries. When the Long March reached the Yangtze, the Lee family fled to Hong Kong, where Martin's father spent much time resisting Zhou Enlai's efforts to enlist him in the revolutionary cause.

Martin himself did not become involved in politics until he was in his forties. He was chairman of the Hong Kong Bar Association from 1980 to 1983, and it was in that capacity that in 1982, shortly before Margaret Thatcher's visit, he had been invited to Beijing. It was there that, for the first time, he had become aware of China's determination to resume sovereignty over Hong Kong in 1997. The prospect made his heart sink. Though he soon discovered that many local tycoons, who had likewise become aware of China's intentions, had chosen to sell their assets in Hong Kong to buy US dollars and thus to secure American passports for themselves, he decided that he would stay in the colony to oppose a takeover by the communists.

Lee had been selected by China to join the Basic Law Drafting Committee in 1985. As a supporter of the Joint Declaration, he had soon become disillusioned by the way in which that hard-won treaty was gradually being eroded. 'I felt China was really trying to control Hong Kong,' he said later. He and his colleague Szeto Wah had found themselves at odds with other members of the committee, who seemed far too ready to yield on points of substance that, once surrendered, would drain Deng's original concept of 'one country, two systems' of its unique potential. The two of them were keenly aware that the Basic Law was itself subordinate to the Chinese constitution, Article 1 of which stated: 'The People's Republic of China is a socialist state . . . Disruption of the socialist system by any organisation or individual is prohibited.' Martin Lee argued not only that more 'democracy' should be written into the Basic Law itself, but that interpretation of it should be exclusively a matter for the Hong Kong courts to settle rather than for the Standing Committee of the National People's Congress in Beijing, which he knew to be a 'paper tiger' mouthpiece of the polit-buro. It was to no avail. It was pointed out to him that he should not be alarmed: after all, Article 35 of the Chinese constitution also stated that 'citizens of the People's Republic of China enjoy freedom of speech, of the press, of assembly, of association, of procession and of demonstration'.

In 1987, Deng Xiaoping had addressed the members of the Basic Law Drafting Committee in Beijing, warning them that the Chinese leadership would not permit any activities which, in the guise of 'democracy', would turn Hong Kong into a base for subversion against China. The next day, in response, Martin Lee departed from his pre-pared speech to declare that those who 'genuinely loved Hong Kong' had an inalienable right to criticise the Chinese government when mistakes were made. From then on, so far as Beijing was concerned, he had been a marked man.

During the pro-democracy demonstrations in Hong Kong which immediately preceded Tiananmen Square, members of both the Legislative Council and the Executive Council, swept along by the wave of public feeling, had agreed unanimously that the pace of demo-cratic change in Hong Kong had to be accelerated. They called then for 50 per cent of the sixty-seat Legislative Council to be elected directly, on the basis of universal adult suffrage, in 1991, rising to 100 per cent in 1995.

On his first secret mission to Beijing at the end of 1989, Sir Percy Cradock raised the question of increasing the number of directly elected seats to the Legislative Council. He was given a dusty answer. Tiananmen Square, he said later, had exacerbated the 'profound suspicion on the Chinese side of Western-style democracy as a force for political change and instability, even chaos'. Nevertheless, after two further months of negotiation involving a formal exchange of letters between the British and Chinese, the two governments agreed, in principle, to the creation of eighteen directly elected seats in 1991, rising to twenty by the handover, and to thirty by 2003. For good measure, however, the Chinese made it clear that any unilateral departure from those figures would lead to what was described to Cradock as 'big trouble'.

To the dismay of Martin Lee and others, and despite strenuous argument from the British, Article 23 of the Basic Law contained a general prohibition of 'subversion against the Central People's Government', while Articles 158 and 159 respectively vested the power of interpretation of, and amendment to, the Basic Law in the National People's Congress. In the same month Martin Lee and like-minded liberals formed the United Democrats to campaign for greater freedom and democracy than the Basic Law appeared to envisage.

In the 1991 elections the United Democrats took seventeen of the eighteen seats elected on the basis of universal adult suffrage. Martin Lee's landslide was a fierce rebuke not only to China, but to the colonial administration as well. Lee had become an outspoken critic of the British government and contemptuous of the outgoing governor, Sir David Wilson, whom he regarded as one of the archetypal Foreign Office diplomats 'who only believe in kowtowing to Beijing' and whose philosophy was 'to push a little for Hong Kong', but only to the point that 'they consider to be China's bottom line'. In China the United Democrats were regarded as a threat to the state, and Martin Lee himself was routinely excoriated in the Beijing press as a 'subversive'.

The killings in Tiananmen Square had alerted the world to the fact that, in one vital respect, Deng Xiaoping's regime was no different from its predecessors. According to a detailed report by Amnesty International, 'Death in Beijing', published a few months later, 'at least 1,000 civilians – most of them unarmed – were killed and several thousands injured by troops firing indiscriminately into crowds in Beijing

between 3 and 9 June 1989 . . . Since early June, at least 4,000 people
are officially reported to have been arrested throughout China in con-
nection with pro-democracy protests, but the total number of those
detained is believed to be much higher . . .' Reports reaching Amnesty
suggested that many of those who had been detained were subjected to
severe beatings and torture; others, it was said, had been sent for show
trials followed by summary execution.

The introduction to Amnesty's report was written by Jonathan Mirsky,
who was in Tiananmen Square as the correspondent for the *Observer*. He
had witnessed PLA troops firing indiscriminately into the huddled mass
of demonstrators, and seen the dead and wounded lying in pools of
blood. He put the atrocity in illuminating context. 'Any Tibetan could
have foretold the violence to come, after years of experience of the PLA,
most recently in March, when Chinese soldiers mowed down monks and
nuns.' He recalled China's long record of brutality. In April 1956,
Chairman Mao had informed the politburo that 2 to 3 million counter-
revolutionaries had been executed, imprisoned, or placed under control
in the past. The term 'counter-revolutionaries' has long been used by the
Chinese Communist party as a justification for abusing its adversaries – a
'catch-all for rapists, thieves, murderers and "troublemakers"'. Although
Beijing had occasionally expressed regret for some excess or other, the
use of 'extra-judicial execution' was regarded as routine punishment for
what the party referred to as 'evil members of the herd'. During what
Chinese commentators have since described as the 'terrible decade' of the
Cultural Revolution, from 1966 to 1976, nearly 1 million people were
killed by mobs urged on by Chairman Mao. A further 100 million were
officially acknowledged to have been treated illegally. Between 1986 and
1989, it was estimated that as many as 10,000 'counter-revolutionaries'
were shot, usually on the day of sentence and without right of appeal.
Mirsky wrote: 'During this horrendous period, which equalled anything
in Stalin's Russia, few voices arose from the international community and
none from any government, except in the case of the UK, when its own
nationals were badly treated. On the whole China is treated as a grand
exception. Its assertion that human rights is an internal matter is barely
challenged.' He was scathing about those in the West who chose to claim
that 'the Chinese have different concepts of human rights and democracy
from our own, and therefore the routine use by the Chinese of the
familiar tools of repression – execution, torture, labour camps, and internal exile – that Amnesty has detailed, is somehow acceptable'.

Three years on, little had changed, except that there was no longer
any reason for the world to be ignorant of the repression of their own
citizens and in their name by the rulers of the People's Republic of

China. Thanks to individuals like Jonathan Mirsky and human-rights organisations like Asia Watch and Amnesty International, it was virtually impossible in the early nineties to be unaware of China's continuing brutality. From 1989 onwards, Amnesty accumulated a body of convincing evidence which demonstrated that, despite the economic reforms in China, the authorities still used the law, the administrative system and the prison service to persecute those who dared to oppose their will. Citing well-documented individual cases, Amnesty identified the victims as political dissidents, human-rights activists, workers' representatives, peasants, Tibetan nationalists, ethnic minorities and religious groups. 'No one,' Amnesty judged, 'is safe in China . . . political repression and abuse of power mean that everyone is at risk.'

The authorities have invariably denied that the People's Republic holds any political prisoners. China has acknowledged, however, that thousands of 'counter-revolutionaries' have been jailed or executed. The provisions of the criminal law most widely used to jail 'prisoners of conscience' have been Articles 98 and 102, which outlaw respectively 'organising, leading or taking part in a counter-revolutionary group' and promoting 'counter-revolutionary propaganda'. Dissidents have also been detained as common criminals for 'disturbing public order' or 'hooliganism'.

Two years after the events in Tiananmen Square, Chen Yanbin and Zhang Yafei were arrested and charged with carrying out 'counter-revolutionary propaganda and incitement' by writing articles in a political journal called *Iron Currents*, wherein they allegedly 'slandered' the rule of the Chinese Communist party. They were further charged with forming an organisation, the Chinese Revolutionary Democratic Front, 'with the purpose of overthrowing the leadership of the CCP and the political power of the people's democratic dictatorship'. The two men were found guilty and sentenced to terms of imprisonment of fifteen and eleven years respectively.

In July 1992, in one of the most infamous of many examples of political persecution, a senior Communist party apparatchik, Bao Tong, was given a seven-year sentence for 'leaking' state secrets. A former assistant to Zhao Ziyang, who was forced to resign in disgrace as the CCP general secretary just before the imposition of martial law in Beijing on 20 May 1989, Bao Tong was arrested the following week. He was held for a year in solitary confinement and then put under house arrest until his detention and trial in January 1992. His conviction was based solely on a conversation he was alleged to have had with another senior official of the party, the content of which, of course, had to remain a state secret.

A formal trial, however arbitrary in character, was not the only means available to the state for persecuting dissidents. The use of 'administrative detention' was also widespread. According to official Chinese statistics, hundreds of thousands of citizens are detained each year either for 'shelter and investigation' or for 're-education through labour'. Under the former provision, the police are given the authority to hold anyone suspected of committing a crime for up to three months without charge, even for 'minor acts of law infringement'. In 1990, the Ministry of Public Security reported that 902,000 individuals were held for 'shelter and investigation', up to 40 per cent of whom, according to Chinese legal scholars who examined the official figures, were detained for longer than the prescribed three-month period. Despite Article 48 of the 1979 Criminal Procedure Law, which imposed a ten-day limit on detention without charge, some held for 'shelter and investigation' were subsequently 'sentenced' by local government committees to a term of 're-education through labour' lasting up to three years.

A handful of cases have reached international attention, but they constitute only a minute proportion of the several thousand unearthed by Amnesty International over the years. The leaders of the democracy movement have been targeted with particular venom. Since 1989, according to Amnesty, 'large-scale arbitrary arrests have been carried out around the anniversary of the 4 June massacre'. In 1991, fifteen such 'dissidents' held in Beijing were indicted the following year on a range of 'counter-revolutionary' charges. Having spent two and a half years in detention they were eventually to be convicted in December 1994, after a trial lasting five months, of forming dissident groups and writing and printing political pamphlets for publication. Five of these 'counter-revolutionaries' were 'exempted' from further punishment, one was given two 'supervision orders' and nine were jailed for terms ranging from three to twenty years.

Throughout this period, the use of torture, explicitly banned by Chinese law, remained endemic. The most common forms of torture identified by Amnesty include 'severe beatings with fists or a variety of instruments, whipping, kicking, the use of electric batons which give powerful electric shocks, the use of handcuffs or leg-irons in ways that cause intense pain, and suspension by the arms, often combined with beatings'. Amnesty documented further forms of torture or 'cruel, inhuman or degrading treatment' such as incarceration in unlit cells without heat, ventilation or sanitation; exposure to intense cold or heat; and deprivation of food and sleep.

A group of political prisoners held at the Lingyan Number 2 Labour Reform Detachment in Liaoning province claimed that they were repeatedly tortured between 1991 and 1992. The abuse apparently started when a group of eleven newly arrived dissidents refused to acknowledge that they were 'criminals'. All were severely beaten and four were sent to the 'correction unit'. Here, they said, they were stripped naked, held down on the floor and repeatedly given shocks with high-voltage electric batons to their heads, necks, shoulders, armpits, stomachs and the insides of the legs. One of their number, Leng Wanhao, who remained silent during this ordeal, had an electric baton forced into his mouth.

In a number of the reported cases, the victims did not survive such ordeals. According to the *Henan Legal Daily* of 7 October 1993, forty-one prisoners and 'innocent suspects' died from torture under interrogation between 1990 and 1992 in Henan province alone. Among the forms of torture listed by the newspaper were instances of victims being hung up, having boiling water poured over them, being hit with bottles, burned with cigarettes, whipped with leather or plastic belts or having electric prods placed on their genitals. Citing this and other reports in the Chinese press, Amnesty International has noted starkly that 'deaths as a result of torture are not rare'.

According to a former police officer in Shanghai, for every case investigated by the authorities and reported in the press, there were hundreds of unacknowledged cases. A few of the allegations have apparently been investigated by the judiciary but, Amnesty says, the Chinese authorities have 'erected a wall of silence around torture and ill-treatment' from which the only conclusion to be drawn is that the Communist party acquiesces in this massive violation of human rights.

Throughout this period the authorities in Beijing forbade any reputable international organisation or group to investigate the grave allegations against China. Refusing to accept the terms on which the International Committee of the Red Cross conducts its inquiries, the foreign minister, Qian Qichen, was to offer the view that these standard requirements were 'hardly feasible for China'. Amnesty's own efforts to gain access to China have yielded no response. This refusal to permit outside scrutiny led Amnesty to the view that China has much to hide; that the scale of human-rights violations may be far worse than can be documented, and that the Chinese authorities still believe that they can do what they like to people and are not accountable for their actions, either internally or externally.

Across the border in Britain's last significant colony, the persecution and punishment of dissidents and the repression of political freedom was observed with growing alarm. In 1976, Britain had ratified the two UN covenants (the International Covenant on Civil and Political Rights and the International Covenant on Economic, Social and Cultural Rights) which codified in treaty form the Universal Declaration of Human Rights adopted by the UN General Assembly in 1948. The ratification of both covenants applied simultaneously to all British dependent territories, including Hong Kong. In 1984, the two signatories of the Joint Declaration agreed that the provisions of both treaties should remain in force in Hong Kong after 1997, an agreement confirmed in Article 39 of the Basic Law of 1990. In the meantime, pressure grew in the community for a single piece of legislation, a Bill of Rights, to bring together under domestic law all relevant rights included in the covenants. During 1989, in the diplomatic phrase of an official British booklet on the issue, 'public support for such a bill increased'. Backed by an overwhelming majority of the Legislative Council, the bill came into force on 8 June 1991. With characteristic bluntness, Chris Patten was later to volunteer that the Bill of Rights was a 'measure introduced in the wake of the killings in Tiananmen Square in 1989 to meet understandable anxieties at the time'.

Except in the case of six ordinances, any previous legislation that was held to be 'plainly' in conflict with the Bill of Rights was automatically repealed, and any future legislation that failed to conform to the twenty-three articles in the new bill would be invalid. The overarching authority of the Bill of Rights meant that a number of key laws relating to the rights and freedoms of the individual would have to be withdrawn or amended. Patten's inheritance, therefore, was the obligation to oversee draft legislation to amend the Societies Ordinance, the Public Order Ordinance, the Emergency Regulations Ordinance and the Crimes Ordinance – all of which gave draconian powers to the Hong Kong authorities in clear violation of the new Bill of Rights. The Emergency Regulations, for example, enabled the police to ban demonstrations and assemblies, to detain suspects without trial and to suspend habeus corpus.

Although the Joint Declaration and the Basic Law did contain a commitment to protect the individual rights and freedoms enshrined in the UN Declaration of Human Rights, the relevant articles did not identify how, after the handover, China proposed to implement this laudable objective within a framework that placed 'affairs of state' outside Hong Kong's jurisdiction and in the hands of the National People's Congress. Indeed, neither the Joint Declaration nor the Basic Law provided a final blueprint for the principles they both appeared to embody. The ambiguities and opacities in both documents reflected a set of conceptual imprecisions that left open a range of possibilities which still had to be negotiated. The new governor was thus trapped between his obligation – and his desire – to reform these anachronistic laws and the likelihood that to do so would provoke the wrath of China.

Indeed, Chris Patten had taken on a whole basket of unresolved and contentious issues dating back to the colonial mists of time. One matter which went to the heart of Hong Kong's survival as a free and prosperous society was the judicial system, and, in particular, the status and composition of the Court of Final Appeal, which was due to replace the Privy Council after 1 July 1997 as Hong Kong's court of last resort. Under Clause 3 of the Joint Declaration it had been agreed that the Hong Kong SAR would be vested with 'independent judicial power, including that of final adjudication'. In the Basic Law, China elaborated this point, indicating that the judicial system in Hong Kong after 1997 would remain as it had been under British rule, 'except for those changes consequent upon the establishment of the Court of Final Appeal'. Following the publication of the Basic Law in April 1990, a number of legal matters remained in negotiation between China and Britain, at the conclusion of which it was hoped that the powers of the Privy Council could be transferred smoothly to those of the Court of Final Appeal.

The prevailing ethos before Patten's arrival dictated that these negotiations were conducted in absolute secrecy. However, in a society like Hong Kong, where the rule of law was universally regarded as a vital element in preserving the community's unique way of life, the core issues were not hard to identify.

As a member of the Basic Law Drafting Committee in the late eighties, Martin Lee had challenged Beijing to insert a clause guaranteeing the autonomy of the Court of Final Appeal against interference by China, pointing out that, in the absence of such a guarantee, the court's independence would be undermined by the powers given elsewhere in the Basic Law to the National People's Congress. He lost the argument. As promulgated, Article 17 of the Basic Law gave the Standing Committee of the National People's Congress the power to invalidate any law enacted by the legislature of the SAR of Hong Kong which the committee considered to be not in conformity with the provisions of the Basic Law 'regarding affairs within the responsibility of the Central Authorities, or regarding the relationship between the Central Authorities and the region'. These 'responsibilities' were not precisely defined, but were held to include, inter alia, foreign affairs and security. In addition, under Article 18, the National People's Congress reserved the power to issue an order applying the relevant national laws to Hong Kong if, 'by reason of turmoil . . . which endangers national unity or security', it were to decide that the region was in a state of emergency. Article 19 explicitly underlined this, stating that Hong Kong courts would have no jurisdiction over 'acts of state, such as defence and foreign affairs'. The question of what activities, if any, apart from foreign affairs and defence, would constitute 'acts of state' hung in the air, unanswered. However, it was already clear that 'internal security' – a term dreaded by human-rights activists in China – was unlikely to be excluded by Beijing from the list of 'acts of state' over which, at best, Hong Kong would have limited jurisdiction.

The ambiguities of the Joint Declaration and Basic Law were not confined to the fundamental questions of human rights and democracy. The fact that Britain and China were unable to resolve the complex issues of nationality in the Joint Declaration was a further cause of concern in Hong Kong. In 1962, following large-scale immigration from the 'new' (i.e., non-white) commonwealth countries, the Commonwealth Immigration Act had for the first time imposed tight controls over the number of immigrants allowed into Britain from these newly independent states. Under the 1981 Nationality Act, the concept of British citizenship was redefined to exclude the 'right of abode' from these British passport-holders. Among them, more than 3 million Hong Kong subjects of the crown suddenly found themselves reincarnated as 'second-class' British citizens free to travel on their new 'dependent territory' BDTC passports, free to enter the United Kingdom without a visa, but, for the first time in 150 years, denied the right to settle in Britain.

But the predicament of Hong Kong's British subjects was unique: unlike every other major community affected by the 1981 act, they were not citizens of a new independent state but colonial subjects due to be transferred from the sovereignty of Britain to that of the People's Republic of China. For this reason, Britain's 'betrayal' of its citizens in Hong Kong caused not only deep offence but a great fear. In Hong Kong, 'right of abode in Britain' had become virtually synonymous with 'means of escape from China'. Britain itself had long ceased to be the chosen destination for more than a handful of the 20,000 to 30,000 people who emigrated from Hong Kong each year; the United States, Australia and Canada were far more enticing destinations to those anxious to establish a base outside the British colony. Moreover, the overwhelming majority of Hong Kong's citizens had no desire whatsoever to leave their homes or their jobs in one of the most prosperous communities on earth for the uncertain prospects of a Britain in relative decline. For those people, the right of abode in Britain had represented not a licence to swamp Britain with their presence but a safety net against persecution, a reassurance that in case of catastrophe they would not be left entirely at the mercy of the People's Liberation Army. From the perspective of almost everyone in Hong Kong, the removal of that precious shield by the 1981 act was an abdication by the British government of a moral duty to protect its own citizens, and it was greatly resented.

In the Joint Declaration, Britain and China exchanged memoranda on the status of BDTC passport-holders. As Hong Kong would cease to be a dependent territory on the handover, Britain undertook to replace the BDTC passport (which would be invalid after 1 July 1997) with a document of similar status, except that it could not be passed on to the next generation and would only provide consular protection outside China. It was later decided to call this document the BNO (British National Overseas) passport. The Chinese memorandum confirmed that former holders of BDTC passports could use travel documents issued by the British government 'for purposes of travelling to other states and regions', and that, as Chinese nationals, they would not be entitled to British consular protection on Chinese soil.

Year after year, throughout the remainder of the 1980s, campaigners from Hong Kong took their case to Westminster, lobbying politicians of all parties in the forlorn hope of amending the 1981 act to take account of the colony's unique situation. When the People's Liberation Army's tanks rolled into Tiananmen Square in 1989, and a million people in Hong Kong responded by taking to the streets, the governor, Sir David Wilson, hurried to London for a meeting with the prime minister, Margaret Thatcher. At 10 Downing Street, in the presence of Sir Geoffrey Howe, the foreign secretary, he proposed that full British passports should be granted to all BDTC passport-holders to help restore confidence to a community in despair about the future. His case was, as he recalled five years later, that such a move 'would give a sense of security to those people; they would feel that if things went really badly wrong, there was a door out – and it would have rooted in Hong Kong those people most necessary for its success'. Margaret Thatcher, whose own fear of a Britain swamped by immigrants had paved the way for the 1981 Nationalities Act, gave Wilson short shrift. Howe was no more sympathetic, arguing then, as he related later:

> The risk of three and a half million Hong Kong people actually claiming their right to come here would have created the most impossible social problems in this country, however brilliant and

marvellous they are . . . Even the most generous society in the world
could not have accommodated what could have happened . . . A
government cannot give an undertaking that it will receive those
people as British citizens unless it is prepared to mean what it says.
We couldn't deliver, and it would have been quite wrong to suggest
that we could.

In the House of Commons, the underlying consensus was so firm that
even when the foreign secretary saw fit to point out that the arrival of
over 3 million people from Hong Kong would sharply increase Britain's
'ethnic-minority population', no senior politician, with the exception of
the leader of the Liberal Democrats, Paddy Ashdown, murmured in
protest, or even squirmed with embarrassment. None felt it relevant to
mention that 30 million or more white commonwealth citizens living in
Australia, Canada and New Zealand – not to mention the 260 million
citizens of the European Community – all had the right to 'swamp'
Britain at will; or indeed that many of the 100,000 ethnic Chinese inhabitants of Hong Kong's neighbouring colony, Macau, also enjoyed right of
abode in Britain as holders of full Portuguese passports with the same
freedom of movement as any other citizen of the European Community.

Nonetheless, the Cabinet realised that Britain could not ignore the
risk that the brightest and best in the civil service and the professions
might lead an exodus from Hong Kong, draining the colony of precisely the talent it most needed to weather the transition into 1997. So,
ten months after Tiananmen Square, the government introduced the
British Nationalities (Hong Kong) Bill, under which 50,000 heads of
household would be offered full British citizenship, giving them, their
spouses and their offspring under the age of eighteen the right of abode
in the United Kingdom. This elite would acquire a BNS (British
Nationality Scheme) passport, carrying identical rights to those enjoyed
by any other UK citizen. The selection of the 50,000 heads of household was to be made on a points system designed to favour those
whose skills and services were thought most vital to Hong Kong, or
who had the education, training and resources to make a 'positive contribution' to life in Britain.

The debate on the bill was a shabby and ill-tempered affair in which
the House of Commons showed itself in its worst light. The home secretary, David Waddington, plodded through his set-piece speech
without conviction; Sir Norman Tebbit reinforced his reputation as the
leader of the 'little England' tendency of the Commons by warning in
sub-Powellite rhetoric of 'social upheaval'. The shadow home secretary,
Roy Hattersley, was splenetic but inconsequential, scoring cheap points

off the government without offering a serious alternative of his own (the Labour party being as fearful of appearing 'soft' on immigration as the Conservatives). Once again, only the Liberal Democrats found the measure of the moment, but as they would not have to take the responsibility for their principles, their opinions were widely discounted. Aside from Paddy Ashdown, no significant politician ventured the opinion that the government's bill was mean-spirited, nor hinted that it was riddled with racism. It was duly passed.

Sir Percy Cradock, who had become Margaret Thatcher's foreign policy adviser, regarded her horrified reaction to the events in Tiananmen Square as an understandable but regrettable emotional spasm which threatened to cloud the underlying realities of the relationship with China and thereby to make it even more difficult to resolve the vital issues which had not been settled in the Joint Declaration. By December 1989, Cradock had again prevailed. Encouraged by the intervention of Dame Lydia Dunn, Hong Kong's most senior politician, the prime minister agreed that Cradock, accompanied by Robin McLaren, the assistant under-secretary at the Foreign Office, should fly to Beijing in an attempt to break the diplomatic impasse.

The visit was undertaken in great secrecy to avoid further accusations about Britain's readiness to 'kowtow' to Beijing, which was, even now, putting its 'subversives' on 'trial' before their summary execution. Cradock took with him a mollifying message from the prime minister, which he had drafted himself, and which said, in effect, 'We are two great powers, fellow members of the Security Council. We have worked together very well. It is very sad to have these rifts. We have important issues to discuss.'

The two diplomats were welcomed by every senior member of the regime, including the prime minister, Li Peng (widely credited as the principal agent of the killings), the secretary general, Jiang Zemin, and the foreign minister, Qian Qichen. Ostracised by the world community for its complicity in mass murder, the Chinese leadership was delighted by the timing of Cradock's arrival and by the prime minister's readiness, as Cradock put it, to 'pick up the threads again' so soon. They warmly consented to his proposal that they should look forward rather than dwell on the past, and agreed that it was in both countries' interests to abide by the Joint Declaration.

According to Cradock, the Chinese were 'touchy' about Tiananmen Square, and reminded the British envoy that they had been dealing with 'rebellion, a counter-revolutionary act; that they were entitled to act as they had done; that they had done no harm to Britain, and yet [the

British] had been one of the first in the cabal to produce sanctions against us'. They went on to inform the British duo that Hong Kong was a base for subversion against China, producing evidence which Cradock claims he was unable to refute: money had indeed been sent from Hong Kong to provide tents used by the demonstrators in Tiananmen Square, while political activists in the territory had indeed taken it upon themselves to denounce the leadership of the People's Republic. Cradock did not respond to this complaint with the contempt which others might have thought it deserved. Instead he reiterated on Britain's behalf that

> we had no intention of allowing Hong Kong to be used as a base for subversion against the mainland; that while of course each country applied its own laws – and those of the British were different from those operating in China – it remained the policy of the British government that if any individuals arrived in Hong Kong seeking deliberately to make trouble with China, they would be expelled.

From the standpoint of a Western liberal, this was an unedifying exchange, but it served its immediate purpose: to restore some of the trust without which it would be impossible to explore further three vital and interrelated issues – the Chinese commitment to 'elections' in Hong Kong, the status of British passports held by residents of Hong Kong after 1997, and the airport at Chek Lap Kok, which, since the project spanned 1997, could not be realised without Chinese consent. The airport was the last item on that agenda to be raised, but from the perspective of the business community and even some of the diplomats involved, it was the most critical of the three.

The development of the new airport was a precondition for sustaining the phenomenal growth rates to which it had become accustomed. The old airport at Kai Tak was reaching saturation point; it was antiquated and dangerous. Although the runway was constructed on reclaimed land jutting into the harbour, the final approach involved a sharp bank to the right only a few hundred feet over the surrounding densely populated high-rise apartments, a flight path regarded by pilots as one of the most hazardous in the world. The prospect of a catastrophe in the heart of Kowloon was too terrible to contemplate.

By 1990, Beijing's traditional paranoia about Britain had resurfaced to be focused, inter alia, on the new airport. Prone in any case to believe that the outgoing colonialists intended to empty the public coffers before their departure, they were by now suspicious that the British would use the Chek Lap Kok project to enrich British companies in the process. As Cradock was swift to detect, they were also mindful that such a major undertaking gave them a very powerful lever with which to extend their efforts to control Hong Kong in advance of the handover. 'One of the bad effects of Tiananmen was their view that the relationship with the British was much more struggle than co-operation: the hostile elements took control.'

Throughout 1990 the airport project remained in limbo as the Chinese made more and more extreme and strident demands for a central role in Hong Kong affairs generally. Clearly dismayed by the increasingly vocal calls for greater democracy emanating from Hong Kong, they were also, it seemed to Cradock, extremely worried by the speed with which communism in Europe had collapsed. With the fall of the Romanian dictator Nicolae Ceausescu, they were friendless and ideologically exposed. Although they claimed that they wanted to reach a 'consensus', it was plain that they really sought a veto over Hong Kong's development. From the British standpoint, this implicit insistence flew in the face of the Joint Declaration.

In the spring of 1991, in an attempt to break the deadlock, the new foreign secretary, Douglas Hurd, flew out to Beijing. After what he would later describe, with characteristic understatement, as a 'frustrating' encounter with the leadership, he returned empty-handed. Two months later, in June, the Chinese threatened to leak details of Cradock's secret negotiations which, the diplomat foresaw, would lead to 'a slanging match in which everything would get out of hand'. To avoid that, Hong Kong's governor, David Wilson, proposed that the new prime minister, John Major, should write to Li Peng warning, in the mildest terms, that if 'clarity and certainty' were not forthcoming, then the airport project should simply be cancelled.

A few days later, David Tang, a ubiquitous and colourful Hong Kong businessman, accompanied by another prominent, if precariously successful entrepreneur, T.T. Tsui (who had intimate links with the Beijing leadership), asked to see the prime minister. These unlikely envoys, ushered into 10 Downing Street on the advice of Sir Percy Cradock, suggested that the time had arrived for some 'personal diplomacy'. Towards the end of the meeting, Major slipped his foreign-policy adviser a note asking for his opinion. Cradock scribbled, 'Worth a try.' Within a fortnight, Cradock was once more on his way to Beijing, where his old ally, Robin McLaren, had recently been appointed British ambassador. Cradock, who relished such cloak-and-dagger diplomacy, called this 'secret visit number two'. He thought the position was 'fairly desperate' and that the chances of a breakthrough were at best 50 per cent.

As it turned out, the talks went far better than either British diplomat had dared to hope. The two sides agreed on the size of the reserves to be left in the Hong Kong treasury on Britain's departure, and instead of a bruising battle of 'principle' over Beijing's right to have a veto over the airport project, they devised a form of words that merely conceded China's right to be consulted – and then only within the terms of the Joint Declaration. At first the two British diplomats were bemused that the Chinese were suddenly so amenable. Then, in their meeting with the Chinese premier, 'the scales fell from our eyes', as one of them put it. Li Peng was clearly interested in only one thing: that John Major should be prevailed upon to fly out to Beijing to sign a 'memorandum of understanding' on the airport which had eluded them for eighteen months. The trade-off was obvious: a visit from the British prime minister would do much to rehabilitate the discredited regime in the eyes of the outside world. From Cradock's perspective it had the makings of a very good deal indeed.

The agreement was announced on 4 July 1991 and Major duly arranged to fly to Beijing for the official signing, where he would be obliged to become the first Western leader to shake hands with the 'butcher of Beijing' under the glare of the media's sceptical spotlight. Cradock was delighted with the breakthrough he had helped to negotiate. It was 'big stuff', he claimed later, convincing evidence that relations between the two nations were about to enter what he then saw as a 'new golden age'. Some officials in the Foreign Office were reluctant for the prime minister to be seen saluting the Chinese flag or inspecting a guard of honour in Tiananmen Square itself, but Cradock, who had no sympathy with such squeamishness, knew that the Chinese would demand no less. Yet again he prevailed over not only his colleagues in the Foreign Office but ministers as well. For the one or two ministers who were 'mooning around, viewing the visit as a shameful episode', his contempt was boundless: 'You cannot help Hong Kong unless you talk to China. It is self-defeating, indeed, it is self-indulgent, to say we are not going to talk to these people.'

The prime minister arrived in Beijing in September 1991. As a sop to the liberal sentiment which Cradock so despised, he was careful to raise the issue of 'human rights' and to make sure that it was known that he had done so. However, the television coverage showing a British prime minister exchanging pleasantries with Li Peng left some commentators aghast. It was widely judged that Major had allowed himself to be manipulated by the Chinese into endorsing their campaign for international rehabilitation.

It was rumoured that the prime minister, who had looked decidedly ill at ease as he inspected the guard of honour provided by the People's Liberation Army, soon came to regret the visit Cradock had orchestrated. Although Cradock had been the decisive figure throughout, Sir David Wilson had to shoulder much of the subsequent opprobrium. Wilson's friends blamed Cradock for offloading on to Wilson his responsibility for the prime minister's damaging international foray. However, Cradock maintained that Major 'was very pleased with the outcome – as well he might have been . . . As regards Sino–British relations, they were back to a peak.'

Not for long, however. Within weeks the Chinese were once again jibbing over the airport, arguing over issues which the British assumed had been settled with the prime minister's visit and insisting on guarantees over the financial arrangements. In short, despite the negotiations, despite the memorandum of understanding, and despite the prime minister's trip, the airport project was once more in limbo, a hostage to China's paranoia about the British.

5

'NO MORE GAMES'

The Governor Assesses his Options

The Hong Kong people are often spoken of as if they formed an undifferentiated mass with uniform aspirations and values and a shared belief in the means required to attain their common goals. In reality, Hong Kong was a disparate and divided community with competing objectives, though the political conflicts thereby generated had been skilfully muzzled by the informal alliance of senior civil servants and business leaders who between them had charted the colony's meteoric rise to prosperity.

Even before setting foot in Hong Kong, Chris Patten had convinced himself that he could not navigate honourably towards 1997 without widespread public support within the colony itself. Since as governor he had no formal mandate from the electorate, he had already resolved to take to the streets to secure the popular endorsement for his leadership without which, he feared, he would soon become a 'lame duck'.

> I've got to earn people's trust and understanding by trying to appeal directly to them. To try through my presence on the streets to establish that I'm working in the interests of the six million people who live out there . . . And the more they think I'm a decent bloke and think that at least I'm trying to understand them, the more likely it is that I'll be able to penetrate the carapace of the newspapers and the media.

To this end, on his second day in Hong Kong, more in the manner of an American president than of a British politician, Patten strode through the heart of Kowloon with Lavender at his side, flanked by police and bodyguards, to 'press the flesh'. Given that this personal approach was beyond the experience of the security services, the media and the public among whom he had so miraculously descended, the resulting 'Australian rugby league scrum' was inevitable. 'I want to meet the people of Hong Kong as well as the photographers,' he complained to an aide, but he was hemmed in by both. In the narrow streets of Mong Kok, he surrendered to the enthusiasm of a bewildered populace which clearly welcomed the governor's démarche as a novel form of street theatre. The camera teams duly recorded the scene for the next day's news. For their benefit as well as his own, he grasped outstretched hands, kissed at least two toddlers (only one of which cried), lifted another into his arms, and accepted petitions from two groups of protesters who immediately joined in the applause for what was, everyone agreed, a bravura performance. He seemed genuinely touched by the reception he was given. Here, said the reporters to one another, was a real political star: 'Who could imagine any of his predecessors behaving like this?'

It was indeed a break with tradition, and those of more conservative opinion in Hong Kong were not overly impressed. Muttering to each other about the dignity of the governor's office, they also worried that the Chinese would not approve. It began to dawn on them that Patten's 'charm offensive' could only too easily be deployed against Beijing. The prospect that Patten might use public opinion as a diplomatic weapon, an informal court of appeal, was almost as distasteful to Hong Kong's elite as it was alien to the gerontocracy in Beijing. This, the first of many walkabouts, was indeed a pre-emptive strike – part of a strategy which Patten had already planned before his departure from London, from which the Hong Kong establishment had been deliberately excluded. As he confided two days after his arrival, his ploy was to 'get the benefit of the doubt' on the home front before advancing on Beijing with a set of proposals that was bound to produce tremors in the Chinese capital, if not an earthquake.

The new governor found the resources of his private office quite inadequate for his needs. Accustomed to running a government department with a well-oiled bureaucratic machine at his disposal, he had inherited a ramshackle arrangement in which the responsibilities of the officials closest to him were at best ill defined. At his very first meeting with them he asked, 'Who keeps my diary?' To his amusement, three people put up their hands.

His inclination was to create within Government House a replica in miniature of the structure at 10 Downing Street.

Without, I hope, folie de grandeur, I want to establish an office a bit like the one the prime minister has, which can provide a transmission mechanism between me and the government machine – one hundred and eighty thousand civil servants responsible for the eleventh-largest trading territory in the world. It has a vast housing programme, educational programme. There is law and order and security. All that as well as politics. One of the bits of jargon which Beijing is keen on is 'executive-led government', and I don't think we've got the machinery to have that . . . Maybe all that is the most appalling vainglory, but that's the way I feel about it.

A priority was the establishment of a secure telephone link between Government House and Whitehall. The absence of such a line was a telling illustration of the status in the diplomatic hierarchy enjoyed by his predecessors. 'I've been used to phoning the prime minister once or twice over the weekend and maybe a couple of times in the week,' he explained. 'I've nattered at Douglas [Hurd] on the phone, and other colleagues – I'm not suddenly going to stop doing that . . . I don't want to spend all my time writing telegrams. I want to go on dealing directly with people.' The scrambler was installed at once.

The governor's principal advisers were drawn partly from the Hong Kong civil service and partly from Foreign Office diplomats seconded to the colony. They were highly trained, well informed and capable, but they were not his own appointees. Feeling the need to have about him one or two people whom he could trust absolutely, he had circumvented the official structure by bringing with him two personal advisers, neither of whom had significant experience of either China or Hong Kong: Martin Dinham as his private secretary, and Edward Llewellyn as his political adviser. Dinham, 'the best private secretary I ever had', had worked for Patten when he was the minister for overseas aid. The governor respected his strategic judgement, his insider's knowledge of Whitehall, his skill as a draughtsman (if not as a speech-writer) and his toughness as an infighter. Llewellyn had been fresh from university when he became a private secretary to Margaret Thatcher in the last years of her premiership. He joined John Major's team at Number 10 for the 1992 election campaign, where he worked closely with Patten, then party chairman, who learned to respect his political acumen and to admire his 'networking' skills within the Conservative party and the British media. Both men were blessed with personal charm; Patten enjoyed their company and knew that they would be unswervingly loyal. With Dinham and Llewellyn, more than the others, he could freely share doubts and anxieties in the knowledge that neither adviser would leak them into the wider community of the civil service or the media.

Unlike other senior aides, Dinham and Llewellyn worked in Patten's private office, a few yards away from his study and only a short walk down the stairs from his private apartment. Initially, their privileged position caused some resentment among less favoured colleagues, who feared – correctly, as it turned out – that the two outsiders would enjoy an influence greater than their own. Foreign Office diplomats, especially those in Beijing, who were in any case dubious about Patten's appointment, discerned in his choice of lieutenants a deplorable tendency to buck the Whitehall system which had hitherto largely left China and Hong Kong in the hands of the sinologists.

The inadequacies of Patten's press team proved another cause for concern. The cultivation of local and international media was a crucial plank in his efforts to secure popular goodwill, and Patten devoted much thought to the subject.

> I hope I'll get my message through and my argument through by being as open and accessible as is reasonable to the media. I think if I take the initiative with the press in a fairly deliberate and calm way, it might help me to reduce some of the frenzy with which political events are covered. I don't want to find myself constantly driven by the rather frantic preoccupation of the media with each nuance of somebody's remark or speech . . . It doesn't make delivering a sensible policy terribly easy if one allows oneself to be buffeted by all that.

Patten's goal, commonplace in Western democracies, but hitherto untested in Hong Kong, was to charm the media into unwitting complicity with his efforts to woo public opinion, and thereby to protect his flank from potential critics within the foreign-policy establishment in Britain and the business community in Hong Kong.

On that second day in office, the governor broke with precedent to call a press conference in the grounds of Government House. The media were corralled on the lawn by the director of information services, Mrs Irene Yau, with a brusqueness to which local correspondents had long been inured. Patten came down the steps from his office to deliver what he intended to be a genial but authoritative statement at the start of what, in his mind, was to be an extremely important relationship. One reporter described the moment to his readers: 'Facing the media behind a yellow and black nylon cord ten paces away, the great man spoke. "Good morning," he probably said. A bank of incredulous faces opposite said something was seriously wrong. "Is the microphone working?" It wasn't. He tapped it. Nothing doing. And again. Eventually he decided to shout. "Speak up!" yelled the assembled press.' It went from bad to worse, and, finally conceding defeat, a clearly exasperated governor concluded his first press conference by saying, 'I dare say we'll meet in these circumstances again in the future.'

'I hope not,' one intrepid reporter yelled back. 'Not without a microphone.'

Patten did not need to be told that the press conference had been, in his words, 'a pretty spectacular shambles'. From his point of view, it merely served to highlight some of the problems which were waiting to be sorted out. The GIS, on which his predecessors had relied to impart their occasional public utterances to the populace, was, in Patten's view, 'very good at producing glossy brochures on Hong Kong economic policy', but hopeless at conveying any political message. 'The whole thing needs pulling together and to be given a sense of direction – not least in relation to getting across what the government is trying to do and handling the media. I think the operation tends to be firefighting and damage-limitation rather than getting out and selling what we are up to.'

To remedy this shortcoming, Patten decided to import another idea from the prime minister's office. 'I'm going to have a spokesman for me, here in Government House, just as Bernard Ingham was at Number Ten. Someone who can speak for me but can also make sure that the operation of the information service right across the departments is pulled together.' The man he chose was an energetic and approachable government official on the GIS staff, Mike Hanson. Hanson had served as refugee co-ordinator during the critical period of 1989–91, when tension over the Vietnamese refugees in Hong Kong was at its peak, and his experience had honed his natural flair for public relations. At first the chief secretary, Sir David Ford, looked askance at Patten's decision to appoint someone else to the task which had hitherto been his responsibility, but he soon came to appreciate Hanson's ability to promote the governor's cause. Patten himself was to judge that Hanson hardly put a foot wrong. As information co-ordinator, Hanson joined Dinham and Llewellyn in the inner circle surrounding Patten. They became a devoted triumvirate which helped to refine his ideas, protect his flank and articulate his case both privately and publicly. Other key players included Ford, whose bland and jovial manner concealed a shrewd and edgy intelligence; Leo Goodstadt, who combined an air of semi-detached all-knowingness with a sceptical intellect and a deep understanding of Hong Kong; Michael Sze, one of the first 'local' civil servants to be entrusted, as constitutional secretary, with a role worthy of his ability; Hamish McLeod, the reliable and diligent financial secretary, and William Ehrman, a shy and languid official on secondment from the Foreign Office, who was far more loyal to Patten than some of his peers.

With the help of others in the Foreign Office, the embassy in Beijing and the local community, Patten and his advisers had a little over two months in which to draft his first policy address to the Legislative Council, in which he had committed himself to define the parameters of the historic task ahead.

Government House was built in a neoclassical style reminiscent of the American deep south. Completed in 1855, it had once enjoyed a fine view over the nineteenth-century harbour. Surrounded by a well-manicured garden which ran down steeply towards the waterfront, and which, in March, displayed the best show of azaleas in the colony, Government House was a very splendid little mansion. Viewed from any one of the towerblocks by which it was now entirely surrounded, it had the air of a colonial amphitheatre, an appropriate setting for Scarlett O'Hara and Rhett Butler to stroll down the front steps and pause awhile in the soft evening breeze. From the opposite perspective, it was disconcerting for the mansion's inhabitants to be so obviously exposed, hemmed in and dwarfed by the brilliant, brassy and assertive monuments to modern capitalism which reared up from the stalls to the gods with intimidating disinterest. The Hong Kong and Shanghai Bank, designed by the British architect Sir Norman Foster, presented its backside – likened by traditionalists to the rear of a giant fridge – to the main verandah of the house, entirely obliterating the view towards Kowloon. A little way away to the east, the Bank of China rose effortlessly above its myriad rivals, by common consent the most elegant high-rise in the colony – all silvery steel and reflecting glass, austerely delicate, but, according to local superstition, directing its shards of bad *feng shui* towards the Pattens' drawing room. During the day, the sounds of the city ricocheted around this colonial oasis; by night, when all else was still, the throb of air-conditioning units gave no peace.

The Pattens' new home provided a private flat in the east wing, a range of reception rooms for official entertaining, and a substantial private office. Several commentators in Britain had adopted a reproachful if not envious tone about the tax-free £150,000 salary and expense allowance which went with his new job, which greatly exceeded his earnings as a government minister. Slightly needled by this media focus, he commented before leaving Britain: 'They write as though it were a matter of hitting the jackpot. I think it fair to say that I could have been pretty comfortably looked after doing all sorts of other things I was asked to do. This job is well paid. The facilities, the houses [Government House itself, and the 'country' residence in the New Territories on the edge of a golf course at Fanling] are all very comfortable. But there is an awful lot of responsibility that goes with them.'

Once in Hong Kong, he and Lavender did not allow themselves to dwell on the tabloid murmurings back home. Patten reflected with some contentment:

> For the first time in our lives as a family we're not going to be slightly concerned about the bank statement at the end of every month . . . I have never believed in much mortification of the flesh, Catholic though I am, and I certainly don't bear a metal-studded thong around my upper thigh. I therefore confess freely to looking forward with some enthusiasm to living in a bit of style. And I think that a lot of Lavender's friends would look forward to not having to do the ironing.

To take possession of Government House, was, he volunteered, 'terrific fun'. The Pattens thought that their new residence needed to be spruced up; that it had become somewhat faded and dated, and that the public areas, at least, needed a facelift. 'There are some nice pictures here,' the new proprietor remarked, wandering through the hall and into the drawing room. He cast a baleful glance at the anodyne designs for the armchairs and the sofas chosen by the previous incumbents. 'One has to do something about the covers, which are a bit tacky . . .'

Until a couple of months before, Hong Kong's new first family had commuted between a modest flat in Victoria and a small cottage in Patten's Bath constituency. As a government minister, he was used to 'doing' his red boxes on a dining room table spread with his daughters' homework. The last governor was determined, at the very least, to relish the experience of such unaccustomed space. 'I don't think it is impossible to be both quite grand and quite welcoming.' Certainly he was not to acquire the reputation locally for miserliness with which, perhaps unfairly, his predecessors had been burdened. The empty wine cellar left by the Wilsons was to be filled with the best that a substantial budget could afford – or at least, wine good enough to match the quality of the multicultured cuisine on offer from the Chinese chefs, which, in the opinion of the many connoisseurs who would pass through in the months ahead, rivalled all but the best restaurants in either China or the West. Every room would be employed to the full. 'At present there is an awful lot of kit which is simply unused,' Patten mused. 'There are rooms we've discovered that haven't been used for years.'

Unaware of the sensitivities involved, he later observed, in the presence of a journalist, that he and Lavender wanted to get rid of 'all that Laura Ashley' with which several of the official rooms had been decorated. Those who had helped the Wilsons to implement their taste in decor were greatly offended when this remark was duly published, and Patten was accused of denigrating a great fashion house. He responded that he and Lavender intended to redecorate the house to reflect the best of Chinese design and to capture the feel of Hong Kong. This aspiration was later formalised in a glossy booklet in which the theme of the restoration work was defined as 'East meets West'. The plan, according to the design team responsible, was 'to treat this renovation project as an opportunity to display to world leaders who come calling on the territory – as well as to local leaders and the general public – the impressive workmanship of Hong Kong's craftsmen and engineers in architectural, interior and industrial design and manufacturing.'

The idea of combining occidental taste with oriental colours, patterns and fabrics, led to a blueprint (produced by the Taoho Design Architects Ltd) which stressed 'a soft, warm, muted' look. There were lavish new rugs in pinks and greens, each woven around the motif of Hong Kong's 'official' flower, the pink bauhinia. Out went almost all the existing furniture, utilitarian but characterless, which was described tactfully by the design department of the Hong Kong Trade Development Council, under whose auspices the renovation was commissioned, as symbolising 'the legacy of the building's previous residents'; in came a collection of rosewood chairs, tables and sideboards reproduced in the light but elegant style of the seventeenth-century Ming dynasty. There was a nineteenth-century camphor-wood chest with an elm stand, two elm money chests, and two solid elm armchairs, all chosen by the Pattens and carefully restored to their original patina. They also selected a set of twenty-eight light green clay pots, each one individually knife-carved with Chinese designs created by local artists. Four of them were filled with plants and flowers to decorate the portico at the main entrance, the galleried lobby and the main corridor leading to the grand ballroom. The floors were to be relaid in polished limestone of the mildest pink hue; balustrades, latticework and bookshelves were stripped of tarnished paint to reveal the teak, cherry and oak wood beneath. The formal drawing room was decorated in soft shades of peach, rust and cream, colours echoed in the striped curtains into which a delicate oriental pattern of flowers was woven. The sofas, large, squashy and European, were upholstered in cream and rust

damask. The dining room, over which the Annigoni portrait of the
Queen reigned supreme, featured a mahogany dining table which could
seat up to thirty guests. Its formality was softened by walls sponged in
two shades of yellow and an oval carpet in a pattern of green leaves
edged in gold.

The royal portraits were to remain in place over the lofty entrance
hall, but they would be joined by a selection of the best of contemporary Chinese art and artifacts – a celebration of local culture in an
otherwise quintessentially British environment. It was a choice which
the governor was resolved to make himself, indulging a passion which,
perforce, as a mere minister of the crown, he had been obliged to
restrain. Sculpture and paintings by Chinese artists from Taiwan, Hong
Kong and the mainland adorned the main hall and all the principal
rooms; some works were donated, others borrowed from museums
and galleries and one or two were bought for what became a rotating
collection of the best of Asian modern art.

Then there was the ballroom – bare on the Pattens' arrival apart from
a stack of chairs and the faded aura of grand entertainments long since
forgotten. It had been used by his predecessors on formal occasions, but
Patten planned to exploit its grandeur far more frequently. 'I think we
should have a concert once every month on a Sunday evening. We
should have people in for drinks, have a buffet – you can fit a hundred
people in with no difficulty. I think we should get a bit of sponsorship
and have the Pavilion Opera here – it's a stunning room.'

The overall effect of the restoration was to create an atmosphere that
contrived to be elegant rather than sumptuous; imposing and yet informal. The dowdiness of earlier decades yielded to a last colonial hurrah
which looked to the future, not to the past – even if, as some wags
remarked, Government House was to be re-established as the Museum
of Colonial Atrocities after 1997.

Hong Kong does not encourage self-doubt. True, the city may be
cramped, noisy, overcrowded, polluted and often foul-smelling; its air
laden with fumes from belching trucks and commuter-crowded high-
ways. It may vibrate with the sound of a million air-conditioners
throbbing against the swirling humidity which engulfs the island for
nine months of the year. Its surrounding waters may be a cesspit of
toxic waste and its landscape may be pock-marked by sprawling junk-
yards. It may offer little other source of refreshment than the betting
windows at the racecourse in Happy Valley, a clutch of manicured golf
courses and a number of breathtaking views from the well-trodden
footpaths that criss-cross the tropical hillsides, too steep for even the

most rapacious developer to destroy. Hong Kong may lack a developed taste for literature and the arts, importing virtually all its music and theatre from elsewhere in Europe and Asia. In short, it may lack many of those ingredients which the affluent Westerner has come to regard as prerequisites for a civilised existence. But, as its elite are quick to point out, such disdain misses the point. Hong Kong, they explain, using a weary cliché, is 'a borrowed place living on borrowed time' – and its purpose is to make money.

John Krich, an American travel writer visiting the city in the early eighties, described it as 'a long shot . . . one bookie joint operating under the nose of the Maoist vice . . . a high volume, low overhead trading post', where the British offered 'one prize rock's worth of real estate on which cling the addicts of property'. If his tone was jaundiced, Krich nonetheless went to the heart of the matter. Hong Kong's raison d'être as an entrepôt was, and is, defined physically and psychologically in terms of property. Yes, the harbour is the most exciting in the world, the water churned permanently by aggressive flotillas competing for right of way: glossy liners, dilapidated coasters, container ships, tugs, lighters, barges, fishing smacks, hydrofoil ferries and a vulgar glitter of private motor yachts. Yes, Kai Tak Airport, which reaches out into the harbour on a spit of reclaimed land, does growl with Jumbo jets coming in from and going out to every continent, a layman's measure of Hong Kong's financial and commercial preeminence. Yes, the traffic between Hong Kong and China is ceaseless, the defining purpose of a parasitical community. But for the great majority of the people of Britain's last colony – whether they sit before computers, thirty, forty or fifty floors up a towerblock, insulated in artificially cool isolation from the throbbing streets below, or whether they toil on the new bridges, roads and subways, or in the factories, warehouses, shopping malls and street markets – property, or the promise of property, is all.

Simon Murray, one of the handful of expatriates with a genuine feel for Hong Kong's recent history, understood this cast of mind and approved of it.

> This is a refugee community. It is tough to say it, but they are on the run. People in Hong Kong are mesmerised by money. Not so much because of greed – it is to get security . . . Today China is getting closer, and they think, 'We've got to make some money, because with that money we can buy our security. We can buy our ticket out of here. We can buy some property overseas. We'll be OK.' Without money you are dead.

Murray had arrived in Hong Kong twenty years earlier, almost penniless, himself a refugee, from six years in the French Foreign Legion,
where he had survived to acquit himself with distinction. He applied
himself with verve, charm and talent to making money in Hong Kong.
'I was turned on by this place,' he explained. 'I like selling things, I like
people, I like the Chinese. Genuinely. People say they do, but they
don't. I think they are fabulous. And, yes, I saw a chance to make some
money.' By the late eighties he had risen to become the chief executive
of one of Hong Kong's largest conglomerates, Hutchison Whampoa,
and the trusted lieutenant of its tycoon owner, K. S. Li, one of the richest men in the colony. Murray had no illusions about the world in
which he now moved with such aplomb. 'It is absolutely as bloody as
you could possibly imagine. Lots of grins and shaking hands and banquets, but underneath that, it is lethal. There are huge jealousies. It is
very clannish: they really gang together and they have their loves and
hates. They are very tough.'

Murray, by now a millionaire, was a member of an influential elite,
many of whose most powerful figures – men like K. S. Li, Stanley Ho,
Peter Woo, Robert Kuok, Cheng Yu Tung, Sir Run Run Shaw, H. C.
Lee, Walter Kuok and Ronnie Chan – had prudently diverted a hefty
proportion of their assets into financial havens well away from the
uncertainties of 1997. The biggest players were not only traders, but
gamblers in real estate who had made most of their money out of land.
Given that over 6 million inhabitants had to be squashed into an area
only half the size of greater London, the better part of which was
composed of steep hills, the demand would have been intense even if
Hong Kong had not been the eighth-largest trading community in the
world. As it was, the supply was controlled by the government, which
released development land in annual tranches at a rate which did not
begin to meet the ever-growing need. As a result, property prices
inflated in value far faster even than the Hang Seng Index, the fastest-
growing stock market in the world. Simon Murray tells how he bought
a flat for HK$1.5 million. The following day he left for his summer
retreat in southern France. Two weeks later the telephone rang. 'There
was a man on the phone who said he wanted to buy my flat for ten million dollars. I thought it was a joke. Hysterical. But it was for real.
Imagine the guys who were doing this on a scale not of one flat, but of
ten thousand flats.'

The thought that such riches might not be entirely beyond the
realms of their reasonable aspirations was never far from the collective
consciousness of the restless millions who comprised the great majority of the population. The great disparities in wealth in the colony

appeared to provoke no significant discontent among those at the bottom of the pile: on the contrary, their vision seemed unclouded by envy and untrammelled by the odds against them. They laboured furiously to work their way up towards the edge of that financial future which for them was measured in square feet and bounded in bricks and mortar, a cornucopia that remained elusively just out of reach but always in sight.

In the street markets of Kowloon, you enter a world which is far removed from the ersatz elegance of Hong Kong's commercial centre. Trucks and vans and taxis, belching diesel fumes, thread their way through line upon line of hawkers and vendors. Everyone is in a hurry, buying and selling. A van stops outside a butcher's and the carcasses of five fat, freshly slaughtered pigs are thrown on to the road, slithering across the tarmac to be picked up and carried fireman-style to a long wooden slab of a table, where they are slapped down on the knife-scarred surface. Within minutes, each carcass has been hacked into neat pieces of instantly cookable flesh for the gathering crowd to purchase. At a nearby stall, there are large green frogs, eyes popping, sliding over one another in a wire colander. A few feet away, live snakes in a basket wait to killed and skinned. Sitting beside a small tank in which fish thrash helplessly in three inches of water, there is an old woman, her face leathery and lined, dressed like the Western image of a coolie. She is selling vegetables discarded by other vendors, piled higgledy-piggledy on a battered handcart. The awnings over the booths selling cheap and garish T-shirts, blouses, shorts, slacks and trainers have been faded by the sun and rotted by the humidity; tattered and frayed, they sway listlessly in a fetid breeze. The streets here are overshadowed by decrepit apartment blocks, paint blistered, plaster falling. Wires trail from one window to another; television aerials sprout haphazardly. Air-conditioners whirr and rattle, incompetent against the weight of humidity and heat. There are balconies crowded against each other, filled with fresh flowers and washing lines.

It is tempting for the liberal commentator to detect in such grime-laden localities a great social injustice, an unforgivable Dickensian squalor. This would be to miss the point. In Hong Kong, as the official statisticians are quick to remind the sceptic, malnutrition is almost unknown, education is universal and free, and unemployment is lower than in any country in Western Europe. Even the tenements which now cover virtually all the habitable terrain of the New Territories, transforming this rural oasis into a cityscape of identikit towerblocks, can mislead. Most of these apartments, so drearily monochrome in design and structure, were owned privately, family assets of rapidly growing value in a market where the scramble for real estate seemed never to be tempered by the fear that the property bubble might one day burst.

By 1992, Hong Kong's economic prosperity was already entwined with that of China, itself careering anarchically towards capitalism with a growth rate in excess of 9 per cent a year. For this reason, from the viewpoint of Peter Woo – chairman of the Wheelock Group, which had assets worth US$10 billion in property, telecommunications, hotels, retailing and distribution, financial services, public transport and a container terminal – it made no commercial sense to view Hong Kong in isolation. 'We are not just talking about the six million people of this city. We are talking about an economic region that is composed of Hong Kong and southern China. That's almost sixty million people – the size of the UK.'

Woo was one of Hong Kong's grandees, a member of one of the most powerful families in the colony. He had easy access to Government House and top civil servants would juggle their diaries to suit his. Appointed by China to the Basic Law Consultative Committee, he was also a vice-president of the Prince of Wales' Business Leaders Forum. His office was ritually adorned with photographs of himself with world leaders and members of the royal family, the Chinese gerontocracy competing for space with President Bush, Margaret Thatcher and the heir to the British throne. In such a competitive environment, rival members of the good and the great did not shy away from self-promotion, but Peter Woo was inclined to reticence and lacked that Hong Kong taste for vulgar ostentation which makes the colonial classes cringe. Tall and sleek, he was suave in style and calculating in conversation. He gave no indication that he was troubled by self-doubt or an overdeveloped social conscience. Although he liked it to be known that he was a public benefactor who gave away several million US dollars each year in charitable donations, he was coldly hostile to Western ideals of social welfare. He regarded the United States, from his own elevated perspective, as an exemplar of the 'socialist' model of development which had drained the West of its competitive potential.

Happily gliding through the harbour on his motor yacht, he pointed out his possessions on either side of the busiest waterway in the world. 'See this?' he said, indicating a long expanse of newly reclaimed land on the Kowloon waterfront, which was already sprouting embryo office blocks and apartments. 'As far as you can see in either direction, it belongs to the company.'

Peter Woo's manner was deceptively bland, his analysis of Hong

Kong's success embalmed in the smooth jargon of the Columbia Business School, of which he was among many of Hong Kong's alumnae. The raw certainties of Hong Kong's business ethic pepper his discourse. Hong Kong, he has explained, is 'the world's only merchant city', a conveyor-belt for goods between China and the rest of the world. 'Cargo is the essence of Hong Kong. The creation of cargo and the movement of cargo. That is our prosperity. You know that Felixstowe is the largest port in the UK? Our growth is one Felixstowe every year.'

The liberalisation of the Chinese economy authorised by Deng Xiaoping had further inflamed the entrepreneurial senses of the community. Peter Woo explained the enthusiasm this had generated:

> Someone will say, 'Look, I haven't got much money but I have a flat. I'll mortgage the flat to buy two hundred sewing machines . . . and suddenly I am in business.' And before long they say, 'I've got to move across the border into mainland China. Then I can start up an eight hundred-sewing-machine factory.' And before long he's got two hundred workers. Soon this guy's a multimillionaire through hard work and the opportunity to move very, very fast. Those guys are our champions.

For Peter Woo the vitality of the 'borrowed place, borrowed time' cliché sprang from the need to secure the economic growth of Hong Kong beyond the last five years of British rule. 'We knew the British lease was running out. So we shrink our timetables. We work faster. The returns are faster.' The sense of an ending is untouched by false sentiment. The merchant city could collapse almost overnight. 'You've got to have freedom of movement – freedom of goods, services and capital . . . If the entrepreneurs see the environment has changed, they'll vote very quietly with their feet and you won't even know they have left until you see that, rather than cargo throughput increasing by one Felixstowe a year, it is decreasing by one Felixstowe a year.'

In his analysis of Hong Kong's achievements, Peter Woo volunteered not a single mention of freedom of speech or assembly, of civil rights or democracy. Like the overwhelming majority of his peers, he had enjoyed the benefits of a liberal education under the British or (usually at graduate level) in the United States. Yet concepts of freedom and democracy, at least in the context of Hong Kong, had remained, for them, alien and problematic. Pressed about his apparent disregard for these Western values, Peter Woo's opinions, in comparison with those of some of his opposite numbers, sounded remarkably sophisticated. 'I don't think anybody in Hong Kong has anything against democracy, but people know that democracy has its own limitations. The issue is not whether we have democracy or not, the issue is how to maintain Hong Kong as a merchant city.' Though he held these views tenaciously, he refrained from expressing them in public, or even, although he had ample opportunity to do so, in private with the governor. Peter Woo disdained Patten's principles, but, for a while, liked to bask in the reflected glory of his company.

Apologists for this view in the Hong Kong civil service and the Foreign Office chose to focus world-wearily on the need to protect the future prosperity of the 'merchant city' by accommodating China's distaste for democracy. Their guru, Sir Percy Cradock, would freely acknowledge that, under Deng Xiaoping, the gerontocracy in Beijing was composed of an unreconstructed communist tyranny or, as he once noted, 'a bunch of thugs'. More than a decade earlier, Jiang Zemin, then the general secretary of the Chinese Communist party, had warned him: 'We want Hong Kong back. We want it back, of course, prosperous. Like everyone else we want to have our cake and eat it. But if it comes to the crunch, we'll have it back a wasteland.' Cradock did not for a moment doubt that the Chinese leader meant what he said – and his response, as a British negotiator, had been to make accommodations accordingly.

The international business community had fastened on Cradock's rationale with alacrity and relief. With one bound, he seemed to have liberated them from the charge of collaborating with the 'tyrants' in Beijing in a purblind scramble for a slice of the lucrative Chinese market. Yet they also knew that the widespread aversion to democracy among their Chinese counterparts in Hong Kong was not merely driven by 'realism' about the recidivists in Beijing. Though they rarely put it so baldly in public, the Hong Kong elite had persuaded themselves that democracy was intrinsically a threat to their 'merchant city'. In private, Peter Woo was delicately explicit: 'I think democracy arouses debate, and debates are healthy. But what is the ultimate objective? To ensure Hong Kong's prosperity and stability. Hong Kong is the only merchant city in the world, and that happens because of sovereign policy . . . Now, if you look at the Basic Law, it spells out very, very clearly that the Chinese want Hong Kong to be a merchant city.' Throughout the eighties he thought that Hong Kong had heard a great deal, indeed too much, from what he referred to as 'the so-called democratic lobby'. Now, he advised, the business people were venting their concerns about democracy, which they believed threatened to erode Hong Kong's pre-eminence: 'For me it would be a shame to destroy Hong Kong's role as a merchant city because it can never be created again.' The trouble with Western democracy, he averred, was that it too often produced 'one-party control'; in Asia, and especially in Hong Kong, people wanted a political system where different seg-ments of the community had an opportunity to express their views. 'So the whole debate is basically on the basis of "Let's have a system whereby the consensus of the community becomes the rule of the day rather than anyone who has more votes than anyone else."'

Did this mean, in essence, that Hong Kong's elite should make the decisions in collaboration with the elite in Beijing? 'We know what happens in Washington or Whitehall . . . things don't happen. I mean, it's a joke,' declared Peter Woo. 'In business, when you don't want something to happen, you put it through a committee . . . If you want Hong Kong to be a merchant city then there have to be certain para-meters. If you don't want that, then I think "one man, one vote" seems very plausible – to a Western eye.' Why, though, should 'one person, one vote' be inherently incompatible with the prosperity of a 'merchant city'?

> Very simply, it is this. If you look at the electorate in any society, they are a small minority. And therefore if you go to a one-man, one-vote situation, then the so-called bottom of the pyramid – where people are concerned for their own welfare – will dominate the way the government is run . . . Hong Kong has been successful and the entire population has benefited. We really should not tamper with it.

The self-satisfaction with which so many of the Chinese elite in Hong Kong displayed their 'robber-baron' status was a source of entertain-ment, laced with admiration, to the expatriates whom they had gradually usurped. By the 1990s, only a tiny proportion of the colony's population were offspring of the colonial power and the British had ceased to dominate the expatriate community. Although they still held the key posts at the top of the civil service, they were of dwindling sig-nificance in trade and commerce. The senior positions in Hong Kong's most important international conglomerates were still occupied by white expatriates, but the Indians, Eurasians and, latterly, the indigenous Chinese had begun to take an increasing share of senior management jobs.

The leading banks and legal firms proved the most reluctant to accommodate non-white talent in the boardroom. The latent rivalries between the expatriate minority and the Chinese majority sprang from a variety of cultural and social divisions, of which racial antagonism –

covert in public, overt in private – played no small part. In this respect, Hong Kong was stiflingly parochial, and from an outsider's perspective, embarrassingly trapped in its colonial past. The Hong Kong Club and the Captain's Bar at the Mandarin Hotel were both haunts which most Chinese preferred to avoid. The former preserved the traditions of a Pall Mall club in the environment of an upmarket American hotel. Secure in these cloisters, the prejudices of those who were nostalgic for the colony's *ancien régime* could still be heard above the tinkle of ice in a whisky glass.

The Captain's Bar was altogether less subtle. A bolt-hole for youngish men on the make – some of whom lacked the talent to make it elsewhere – it was occupied every evening by noisy advocates of Thatcherite brutalism. Stuffed into city uniforms, their faces flushed by expensive claret, they brayed about financial deals, sexual conquests and, when the spirit took them, about the deficiencies of the Chinese – 'chinks' or 'little yellow buggers' – among whom they were obliged to live and work. In the last outpost of British rule, they disported themselves with the arrogance of the worst of their forebears. Incurious and insensitive, they lived in self-delusion cushioned by self-regard, and protected by the ersatz authority which, even in its dying days, colonialism still bestowed upon the second rate. They lived for the moment: for quick money, flash apartments, glossy cars, motor yachts, weekend parties, the cheap supply of domestic servants and the pleasure of reinforcing each other's certainties.

Mercifully, these arrivistes were not in the majority among the expatriate community. Hong Kong was also peopled by academics, writers, journalists, civil servants, doctors, nurses, clerics and community workers who were ashamed of their raucous and racist compatriots. Many of the colony's established emigrés understood Hong Kong's past and cared greatly about its future – not for their own sake, but for that of an indigenous community which they did not necessarily understand but which they held in high regard and even affection. Although many of them looked towards the uncertainties of 1997 with trepidation, others were determined to remain in Hong Kong after the handover, apparently indifferent to the change of sovereign. For them, Hong Kong was not merely about money: it had become their home, and they felt themselves to be part of its peculiar culture and civilisation. Hong Kong was more comprehensible and more secure to them than the 'old world' to which they now felt themselves to be formally but elusively attached by the possession of what, after 1997, would become a foreign passport.

British expatriates were easily lost among other Europeans and

Americans who had come to Hong Kong for one purpose only: to maximise their own profits or those of the international conglomerates for which they worked. None of them cared much for democracy: safe in the knowledge that they were temporary exiles from a free society, they were, in general, dismissive about the virtues of democracy in the context of Asia and Hong Kong. The more established among them had developed a genuine regard for the Chinese entrepreneurs who had displaced them or their forebears. In private conversation they seemed anxious to demonstrate the baldness of their commitment to capitalism without the constraints of democracy. In their entrepreneurial dynamism, they could not fail to impress; within these limits, it was easy to appreciate why they were more at ease with the short-term certainties of autocracy than with the vagaries of twentieth-century liberal democracy.

Vincent Lo, a property developer, was like Peter Woo, an influential voice in both Hong Kong and Beijing. 'We are obviously not an idealistic people,' he volunteered. 'Hong Kong is not an idealistic place. To put it bluntly, we are very materialistic, very capitalistic – and that's how we survive. That's how we prosper. We make no apologies for that.' And democracy? 'I don't think we necessarily associate freedom with democracy, because we believe that economic prosperity is our protector, our guarantee for the future, the assurance of individual rights.'

In the judgement of the majority of people like Peter Woo and Vincent Lo, Hong Kong was fortunate to have been spared the draconian levels of taxation needed to finance state pensions, unemployment benefits and a national-health service, all of which they regarded as crippling burdens imposed by the West's commitment to the welfare state. 'Western observers say, "Boom, democracy! You like it, you're a good guy. You don't, you're a bad guy,"' said Peter Woo. 'I don't think it is as simple as that.'

If in 1992 it was thought to be impolitic to avow such sentiments in public, they were nonetheless the common currency of off-the-record and private conversations. It was clear to any close observer that long before the arrival of Chris Patten, the business community in Hong Kong found themselves in collusion with Beijing against democracy, a situation tacitly but powerfully endorsed by their international counterparts. This was not so much because they feared a Chinese démarche against the subversive threat allegedly posed by the democratic aspirations of their fellow citizens, but because they detected from the same source an equally insidious political threat to their established position as Hong Kong's ruling elite. Their overriding concern was that a new governor, driven by other imperatives, would upset the delicate balance of power in Hong Kong which, for several decades, had given them an effective veto on political and social progress and had preserved their financial and trading citadels intact. In this respect, Hong Kong's capitalists and Beijing's communists formed a potent coalition against the kind of freedom and democracy for which the majority of Hong Kong's citizens had already declared their enthusiasm.

This enthusiasm was embodied in the person of Martin Lee, who, in 1989, had spearheaded the mass demonstrations in Hong Kong in support of China's fledgling democracy movement and to protest against the atrocities of Tiananmen Square. Having led his party, the United Democrats, to a handsome − but, for the business community, spine-chilling − victory in Hong Kong's first quasi-national elections in 1991, he had become something of a popular hero in the colony, albeit an unlikely one. Mild-mannered, ascetic and studious in appearance, he possessed neither obvious charisma nor the politician's gift for sound-bite rhetoric. Yet his evident gentleness and integrity, combined with the courage of a prospective martyr, made him a potent symbol of Hong Kong's fate.

Although the 1991 elections were regarded as the first to be freely and openly contested, they were far from democratic in any conventional sense of the word. Forty-two of the sixty members of the Legislative Council were either appointed directly by the governor or selected by 'election committees' and from 'functional constituencies' representing the dominant professional and business groups in the colony. The intrinsic absurdities of this deformed and flagrantly gerrymandered franchise would have been ridiculed out of existence long ago in any genuinely open society. It was no surprise, therefore, that Lee's United Democrats won seventeen of the eighteen directly elected seats.

Insofar as the citizens of Hong Kong had been given a voice in the 1991 elections, they had spoken with remarkable unanimity in favour of precisely those principles and aspirations that so alarmed both the business community in Hong Kong and the gerontocracy in Beijing. Although only a minority of the electorate had been confident or assertive enough to enter the polling booths, there had been little doubt that those who did spoke for most of those who did not. Even before Patten's arrival, the potential for a political confrontation within Hong Kong, let alone between Hong Kong and China, could hardly have been more apparent.

This was certainly clear to the Hong Kong government and the Foreign Office. To those diplomats who were charged with the delicate task of negotiating the transfer of sovereignty from Britain to China, Martin Lee was neither villain nor hero. From their perspective, his principal offence was not that he argued for universal adult suffrage, nor that he was bitterly critical of the collective tyranny which ruled China, but that he seemed to attract overwhelming popular support for his heresies – support which was bound to make their project even more difficult to accomplish. Traditionally accustomed to exercising their benign and usually efficient authority over a generally compliant legislature, Hong Kong's civil servants – especially the 'local', that is Chinese, members of the service – tended to be ambivalent about the virtues of democracy. Their attitude towards Martin Lee was touched by disdain: yes, he was a brave man, but he was also foolhardy and naive. In challenging China so directly, he had been provocative to the point of irresponsibility. It irked them that this local hero was also fêted in Britain by the handful of politicians and journalists who made it their business to take an interest in Hong Kong, and who were likewise unhealthily addicted to democratic reform. They faced enough problems effecting a smooth transfer as it was without the agitation of well-meaning but ill-informed commentators 'back home'.

Patten had pledged himself to work in the interests of all 6 million people of Hong Kong, but what did this mean? Was it to deliver what they wanted, assuming this could be established, or was it to deliver an outcome which they could be persuaded was in their interests?

> I suppose, if I'm honest, both. I hope I'll be able to comprehend what they want, though what they want sounds more than a shade paradoxical. They say, 'You've got to stand up for Hong Kong, show you're firm.' At the same time they say, 'Don't have a fuss with China. We've got to have a nice smooth life with China.' Somehow one has to square that circle.

The governor used his swearing-in ceremony, which took place in the City Hall in the presence of local dignitaries, the representatives of foreign governments and a massive contingent of local and international journalists, to make his first speech on Hong Kong soil. Though it contained the usual genuflections towards the colony's 'formidable assets' and its status as 'one of the most spectacular examples of a free economy known to man . . . a capitalist heart beating at the centre of Asia, pumping prosperity even more widely', Patten identified some guiding principles, expressing them more bluntly than was usual in Hong Kong. His focus confirmed the impression that he was 'different'.

Stressing the importance of the rule of law, freedom of speech and democratic participation, he undertook to listen carefully but to lead

from the front. 'To govern is to choose, and choice is invariably difficult. Good political leadership involves facing up to hard decisions,
taking them, setting out clearly what has to be done when all the talking is over, and winning consent for the course that has to be
pursued . . . the ultimate responsibility of government rests with me.'
Promising to devote all his energies to representing the interests of the
people of Hong Kong as strongly and wisely as he could, he undertook
to stand up for the colony 'courteously and firmly'. Of all his tasks, the
most vital and challenging was to remove misunderstanding and to
build up trust between Britain and China which was, he avowed, his
sincere aim and his profound wish. But trust, he added, was a 'two-way
street'. Departing from his written text, he added, as if to reassure – or,
perhaps, to rebuke – Beijing, 'I have no secret agenda.' It was a confident performance in front of a sceptical audience – and it was his own
speech. 'I dictated what I wanted to say . . . It was circulated round the
world for comments by embassies, and we managed to avoid taking too
much notice of what people said . . .' Nonetheless he contrived to avoid
causing offence to anyone.

Hong Kong's most prominent figures, protecting themselves against
an uncertain future, publicly offered him a wary welcome. Tycoons
praised his 'balanced approach', and Peter Woo, in particular, com-
mended his 'refreshing' style. A deputy to the National People's
Congress in Beijing was reported to have said, 'I'm moved by the governor's pledge to remove misunderstandings', while Martin Lee
promised to co-operate with the new governor. Yet of those quoted,
only Simon Murray, the managing director of Hutchison Whampoa,
appeared to register the full import of Patten's speech. 'He is terrific,'
Murray declared. 'His message [to China] is very clear. No more
games.'

In private, Patten's critics had been swift to deride his walkabouts
as attempts to earn cheap applause from the Hong Kong gallery. The
new governor's instinctive populism confirmed their intuitive prejudice against Major's decision to appoint a politician – especially one
so skilled in the black arts of public relations – to such a sensitive
diplomatic post. Had they known that the cultivation of public opinion was at the very heart of Patten's strategy for seizing the diplomatic
initiative, they would have been even more disconcerted. In the
endgame to which he was now committed, the apparently trivial
decisions about the plumed hat and the knighthood were in fact the
first shots in a 'hearts-and-minds' campaign which he would pursue
with vigour.

Martin Lee confided:

Here you have the consummate politician kissing babies and always appealing to the people. I almost feel he's trying to run against me in the next elections . . . But I've got to be cautious because I don't know ultimately what the British government's intentions are: whether they just want to do a better PR job so that the free world will look at them trying to discharge obligations towards Hong Kong, and yet finally failing – or whether they really want to do something for Hong Kong even at the risk of offending China.

It was the latter prospect which most worried Martin Lee's namesake and political rival, Allen Lee. An appointed member of both the Legislative Council (LegCo), and the Executive Council (ExCo, the governor's official advisory body), Allen Lee had been in public life for longer than any other of Hong Kong's emerging political leaders. Always responsive to the wind blowing from Beijing, he was a toughened but compliant advocate of the business community and their allies in China. 'I fear that Mr Patten will do things by himself without consulting the Chinese,' he admitted. 'I don't believe he will, but he is a very powerful politician.' Immediately before Patten's arrival Lee had been in Beijing to see Lu Ping, the director of the Hong Kong and Macau Affairs Office, who had told him, 'We want to talk to Chris Patten as soon as possible.' Lee was swift to pass this message on to Government House and optimistic that Patten would act accordingly before settling on his priorities in the run-up to 1997.

Emily Lau, an elected member of LegCo and a searing critic of both Britain and China, was the only public figure to be openly sceptical of Patten's credentials:

We are like people swimming and drowning, and we will grasp at anything which is thrown at us. Now we are being thrown Chris Patten . . . He sounds tough, a skilful politician and so on. Doesn't cut any ice with me. I only believe in actions, and I wait to see what he's going to do. The next six months or even less is going to be decisive. If he's not going to do anything in the next six months I think we can kiss ourselves goodbye.

6

'A DEMOCRATIC TIME BOMB'

Patten Draws Up a Blueprint

The Pattens adjusted easily to the regular routine imposed on them by their responsibilities. At least twice a week, soon after daybreak, the governor began the day with a game of tennis on the Government House court a few yards from the front door. He usually played with a coach, but sometimes with Lavender or one of his guests. By 8.30am he was back in the flat at the top of Government House, showered and ready for the day. After breakfasting with his wife, he invariably went down to his study to face the first of the day's official papers and meetings. Every morning, at 'prayers', he met his personal aides to talk through the day ahead, to monitor the local media and to discuss the most pressing dilemmas facing the team. Then there would be routine meetings with departmental officials, business leaders, local politicians and other representatives of the community, as well as the steady stream of visiting dignitaries from Britain and elsewhere who invariably stopped off in Hong Kong en route to other destinations in the Far East. In the afternoon, there were more meetings, public and private consultations, and, frequently, visits to housing estates, schools, shopping centres or factories throughout the community.

Patten soon realised that local officials were prone to treat these visits as quasi-royal tours, and therefore took pains to escort him round the most modern and cleanest block of flats, the refurbished home for the elderly, or the school which had just acquired a new science laboratory. To avoid becoming the star character in a self-serving, if well-meaning, pantomime, he decided to make unannounced visits to outlying districts, giving local officials and the police only as much notice as they needed to arrange the itinerary he had chosen. As a result he began to discover more about the genuine worries and grievances of the public: the leaking roofs, broken lifts, toilets which flooded in rainstorms, officials who failed to respond to repeated requests for assistance. His 'subjects' treated him with a combination of deference and frankness that was reminiscent of petitioners in a feudal monarchy. He listened, took note, and, sometimes directly, but more frequently through his staff, agitated on their behalf with the appropriate branch of the civil service. In so small a community, his reputation as someone who genuinely cared about 'ordinary' people spread rapidly; to his great political advantage, this perception was played back in the opinion polls, which confirmed and entrenched his reputation as a sincere and honourable governor.

In the last week of August 1992, Patten put the finishing touches to his plan for the reform of Hong Kong's electoral system. At the core of his proposals was the creation of a constitutional framework for the 1995 elections, which, it was hoped, would be adopted by the Chinese for the first elections after the transfer of sovereignty, which were due to be held in 1998. In the jargon of their earlier negotiations, the British and Chinese had alighted on the metaphor of the 'through train' to describe the guiding principle that any electoral system put in place by the British before 1997 should remain after the handover. Although he knew that his reforms would raise eyebrows in Beijing, Patten had convinced himself that they would not derail the 'through train', not least because he was confident that they fell within the ground rules established by the Basic Law, which was itself designed to be consistent with the Joint Declaration.

Patten's proposals were the product of his determination to open up new ground. While they were still in preparation he said privately:

> What I feel very strongly is that we have to break out of the cul-de-sacs in which all the political arguments have been taking place; that I have to make it into open country . . . I think there is quite a lot I can do to broaden and deepen democracy in Hong Kong without necessarily taking on the Chinese on things which they have said they won't accept. They still might not much like the agenda I put forward, but I think we'll be in rather better country when it comes to manoeuvring.

It was a bold vision, even more fraught with hazard than Patten appreciated. In retrospect his insouciance would seem precariously optimistic. Hitherto, public debate about the framework for the 1995 elections had focused on the demand made by Martin Lee, and endorsed by Dame

Lydia Dunn, the doyenne of Hong Kong's politicians, that the number of directly elected seats in the sixty-seat Legislative Council should be increased from twenty to thirty by the handover date, 1 July 1997. Patten knew, because it had been made unequivocally clear to him by the Foreign Office, that any such increase would be unacceptable to the Chinese, and that for Beijing this was a fundamental issue. Consequently he had no intention of allowing himself to be side-tracked into a dead-end route by reopening the question. Instead he resolved to 'raise some of the issues which I think are actually more important and interesting'. The only room for manoeuvre available to him, therefore, lay in the arcane electoral system for the thirty seats representing the 'functional' constituencies, and the ten chosen by an Election Committee – both of which had been originally devised for the precise purpose of restricting democratic participation to those inside the charmed circle of Hong Kong's commercial barons and political powerbrokers.

In London Patten had pored over the Basic Law and discovered that nowhere did it proscribe either an extension of the voting base in the functional constituencies or a change in the composition of the Election Committee. In both cases, he realised, with a frisson of cautious delight, there was 'quite a lot of space, quite a lot of elbow room between the Joint Declaration and the Basic Law. What I propose to do is to find all those bits of elbow room for bedding down democracy or extending it.'

Notwithstanding his optimism, he was not indifferent to the pitfalls ahead. 'I could find myself with a very sensible, rational, carefully worked out policy that is politically adroit, guileful and wily, but which no one agrees with . . . I'm only too well aware of the fact that I could find myself in no-man's-land without a compass.' The Chinese in particular would be exceptionally dubious: 'I think some of them suspect that, having come to democracy rather late in Hong Kong, we're trying to construct some democratic time bomb to blow their system to smithereens.' This prospective reaction could only have been sharpened by his refusal to attend in person upon the leadership in Beijing before his arrival in Hong Kong. On the announcement of his appointment, Beijing had used the 'usual channels' to invite him to visit China to discuss the development of Hong Kong's new airport on Chek Lap Kok Island, the construction of which had been delayed by the disputes between the two sovereign powers. According to Patten, Beijing intimated that 'I could have the airport if I'd give them certain undertakings on political issues.' He had refused to accept this linkage, confiding, 'Even if we had – which I wouldn't have done – it would have leaked straight away, and I'd have been a completely lame duck for five years: somebody who'd kowtowed even before he'd arrived in Hong Kong.' Patten's first stand-off was not widely known about. Likewise, he shared his ideas on extending democracy only with his most trusted colleagues. By mid-September, however, he and his team had honed his ideas into a fully fledged – and wholly transparent – constitutional proposal ready to present to LegCo in early October.

Contrary to the myth long peddled by some of the Foreign Office's most influential sinologists, the debate about the future of democracy in Hong Kong long predated the 1989 massacre in Tiananmen Square. Indeed, it first surfaced almost 150 years ago. The charter establishing Hong Kong as a colony in 1843 included provision for both an Executive Council and a Legislative Council. The former was to consist exclusively of crown servants, who were to meet only when summoned by the governor, and then to discuss matters which he alone had tabled. The latter was to have no powers, except those of scrutiny, and its members could be dismissed by the governor at will.

Hong Kong's fourth governor, Sir John Bowring, who arrived to take up his duties in 1854, tried to put his reformist instincts to good effect by proposing that Hong Kong should be given at least an element of genuinely 'representative government', from which the Chinese should not be excluded. His suggestion was that LegCo should be expanded to accommodate three 'unofficial' members, elected directly by all residents of the colony in possession of land worth £10 per annum, and that they should hold office for three years. The response from the colonial secretary, Henry Labouchere, sharply illuminates subsequent policy:

> I believe that the present is the first proposal that has been made for introducing those institutions amongst an Asiatic population, containing but a very small proportion of British or even European residents: I have, therefore, thought it the more necessary to weigh carefully the reasons for and against it . . . The testimony of those best acquainted with them represent the Chinese race as endowed with much intelligence, but as very deficient in the most essential elements of morality. The Chinese population of Hong Kong is, with perhaps a few honourable exceptions, admitted to stand very low in this respect.

The British community, too, was disqualified by the colonial secretary, but for different, and arguably sounder, reasons:

Few if any of the British residents in Hong Kong are persons who go
to establish themselves and their descendants permanently in that
place; they merely sojourn there during a limited time, engaged in
commercial or professional pursuits, but intending to quit the colony
as soon as circumstances will permit.

To whatever extent the control of local affairs might be conferred
on this class by the partial introduction of representative government, the effect would be, to give power over the permanent
population to temporary settlers, differing from them in race, language, and religion, and not influenced by their opinions. However
respectable the character of the residents may be, I cannot believe that
such an arrangement could work satisfactorily.

Thus thwarted, Bowring abandoned his cause. The assumptions
underlying the colonial secretary's rebuff, being unchallenged,
remained intact. Notwithstanding his decision, Labouchere's colonial
instincts were liberal – far more so than those of the settlers for whom
he had ultimate responsibility. He advised Bowring that if the governor could find suitable candidates from within the Chinese community
'whom you may think fit' to hold administrative office, 'I should be
willing to assent to such appointments'. Encouraged at least to this
extent, Bowring began the process of incorporating the leaders of the
Chinese community into the public life of the colony by allowing
them access to the legal profession with a view to appointing the first
tranche of Chinese magistrates. For this, as for all progressive decisions,
he was bitterly vilified by the expatriate community, which was
delighted to see the back of him in 1859.

The slow process of Chinese emancipation was accelerated by the
arrival of refugees fleeing from the long and bloody Taiping rebellion
on the mainland. Unlike the rapacious 'coolies' of the early days, the
new immigrants were prosperous families. By the year of Bowring's
departure, sixty-five Chinese firms were registered as 'Hongs', a title
accorded to the larger, well-established merchants. Within the next
twenty years, several famous Hong Kong families entrenched themselves as major entrepreneurs, or in the middle ranks of the civil service,
and in 1880, one of their scions, Ng Choy, became the first Chinese
member of the Legislative Council. The influence of the Chinese
community soon grew to the point where their needs and aspirations
could no longer be ignored by the expatriate minority or by the colonial administration, whose response was to cede them greater
institutional authority.

The emerging concepts of Western democracy played no part in the complex structure of relationships within which the Chinese community organised its own affairs and began to play a more assertive, albeit still segregated, part in the life of Hong Kong. Guided by Confucian principles of family and hierarchy, and driven by the imperatives of Western commerce, its leadership was profoundly conservative in attitude. To this extent, and no further, it found common cause with the expatriate elite, which had no patience at all with the highfalutin notions of emancipation and universal suffrage which emanated from English radicals far away in London.

In the 1880s, under the governorship of Sir George Bowen, the composition of the Legislative Council was modestly adapted to take account of Hong Kong's growing sophistication. Five seats of the sixty-member council were to be taken by 'unofficial' appointees selected to represent specific interests. One of these went automatically to a representative from Jardine Matheson, which had graduated from the murky waters of the illicit opium trade to become the most powerful 'Hong' in the colony. Another seat was reserved for one or other of the lesser business houses. The third went to the justices of the peace, the fourth to the Chamber of Commerce, and the last was reserved for a Chinese subject of the crown, also selected by the governor. Except for one or two minor changes, the structure created by Bowen survived intact for very nearly a hundred years.

This constitutional inertia has been explained away by recent apologists with the breezy assertion that until very recently the issue had not arisen because there was no popular demand for democracy. This self-serving revision of history, which was to be blandly repeated by a succession of government ministers and Foreign Office officials, does not do justice to the available evidence, or to those who sought fundamental constitutional reform but were repeatedly outmanoeuvred by a powerful coalition of timid diplomats in Whitehall and over-mighty merchants in the colony itself.

The modern argument for democracy in Hong Kong had its birthplace in London towards the end of the Second World War and was enthusiastically backed by the wartime governor, Sir Mark Young – who had been held in captivity by the Japanese and subjected to appalling privations – when he was reinstated at Government House. Based on the widely accepted premise that the outcome of the war had been a triumph of democracy over dictatorship, the Young Plan, as it became known, advocated a fundamental restructuring of Hong Kong's antiquated political system to bring it more into line with the democratic precepts of the postwar world. The British civil servants who had been instrumental in preparing the ground for this plan assumed that the people of Hong Kong would expect and demand more than the restoration of the prewar status quo.

Young's original plan was to create a forty-eight-member Municipal Council representing the urban areas of the territory (the term 'colony' gradually faded from use in official communiqués), with thirty-two directly elected members, sixteen representing the Chinese and sixteen the non-Chinese communities. A further sixteen members would be 'nominated' by Chinese and non-Chinese bodies, again in equal numbers, to represent the two communities. Young envisaged that the Municipal Council would be given a high degree of financial autonomy and that it would have responsibility for public sanitation, education, social welfare, building, town planning, the supervision of public utilities, general licensing, the fire brigade and the management of parks and playgrounds. Although the franchise was to be restricted by age limits, literacy and property standards and residency qualifications, his proposals nonetheless represented a huge step along the road towards democracy. The council would have enjoyed complete control over its own affairs within the framework of an overall budget allocated by the administration and approved by the Legislative Council. Young also wanted to extend the principle of direct representation for a number of seats in the legislative assembly. It was his hope that Hong Kong would steadily develop the idea of representative government at central and local level, on the basis of a combination of directly and indirectly elected seats.

Young made it clear that his plan was open to debate. Indeed, he believed that the education in democracy which such public participation would entail was crucial to the success of self-government in Hong Kong, especially given the uncertainties which were bound to arise if and when China reasserted its claim on a territory it considered to have been snatched from the motherland. In such an uncertain climate, democracy could only take root with the understanding and commitment of public opinion. Young envisaged that the consultation period would last nine months. In fact, for a number of reasons which he had failed to foresee, the debate turned into a war of diplomatic and political attrition which took place largely over the heads of the people of Hong Kong and endured for almost six years.

The spectrum of opinion in 1946 ranged from the standpoint of the colonial secretary, Arthur Creech-Jones, who thought the Young Plan did not go far enough, and who favoured the immediate reform of the legislative assembly on the basis of direct elections, to the fears of the colony's merchant venturers that any democratic reforms would pose a threat to the economic hegemony they enjoyed, and which they identified as Hong Kong's raison d'être. That the latter view was to prevail is testimony not only to the enduring power of the business community in Hong Kong. For those who believed, even in the late forties, that Hong Kong's 'unique way of life' could be protected in the long term only by entrenching individual rights and freedoms within a democratic framework of law and administration, it also testified to the moral astigmatism which afflicts those whose vision is transfixed by the Hang Seng Index.

The Young Plan foundered in uncharted waters. Some civil servants feared that whatever the outcome of the civil war then ravaging China, any attempt at extending democracy in Hong Kong would fall foul of subversion either by the Kuomintang or by Mao Zedong's communist revolutionaries. Many British expatriates were viscerally prejudiced against Chinese emancipation. The Hong Kong General Chamber of Commerce argued against any extension of democracy which did not guarantee to leave a majority of the votes in the hands of the 'responsible' minority of the population (namely themselves), a view echoed by the China Association, which represented British Far East trading interests in London. This demand for a British veto was endorsed by a majority of the expatriate members of the Legislative Council, several of whom were also leading members of the Chamber of Commerce. The Chinese members of the Legislative Council chose, conspicuously, to refrain from making any public comment, on the astonishing grounds that they did not wish to exercise undue influence on the debate. Not unnaturally, this was widely interpreted as a statement of tacit opposition to reform.

Ranged against this weight of opinion, the response of the Chinese community at large was initially muted. Most of its members were too shell-shocked by their experiences, too uncertain as refugees and too desperate to claw a living for themselves and their families to pay any attention to the debate, let alone to follow its intricacies. Their leaders had no expertise in constitutional affairs, and it is likely, in any case, that they assumed the Young Plan was a blueprint for reform which would be imposed from above, regardless of their views. However, in the autumn of 1946, the grass roots began to stir. According to a survey of several thousand Chinese citizens, there was overwhelming support for the Young Plan, even though the electoral system would conceivably yield only a token majority for their community.

As the Chinese scholar Steve Tsang has pointed out in his monograph *Democracy Shelved*, any assessment of this response must take into account the 'traditional' Chinese character: 'Important policy ought to originate at the top . . . the local leaders would support it if it was

acceptable . . . The vast majority of the illiterate and semi-literate considered public affairs to be the domain of the government and of the
educated; their main concern was to make ends meet.'

Despite these inhibitions, Chinese opinion slowly coalesced around
the need for constitutional reform. By 1949, three years after the
prospect of extending democracy to their community had first been
mooted, no fewer than 142 representative bodies were, according to
Steve Tsang, 'clamouring' for reform. By this time, however, Young
had retired to be replaced as governor by Sir Alexander Grantham, who
came from a very different school of thought.

Grantham arrived in Hong Kong in July 1947. Having announced
his support for the Young Plan, he at once set about dismantling it.
With the active support of the business community, the majority of the
appointed members of LegCo and a growing number of Foreign Office
officials who, like him, feared communist subversion in Hong Kong,
Grantham contrived to delay, prevaricate and obstruct until, two years
later, he was ready to introduce what were in effect a set of elaborately
contrived counter-proposals. Stripped of its cosmetic modifications,
Grantham's blueprint tore the democratic heart out of his predecessor's
plan. Effectively abandoning the idea of a Municipal Council, he
argued instead that a proportion of seats on the Legislative Council
should be directly elected. It was claimed on his behalf that this constituted a more radical reform than that advanced by Young. However, by
insisting that only British subjects should be given the vote, he effectively excluded the overwhelming majority of the Hong Kong
community who would have been enfranchised by the Young Plan: in
1949 Hong Kong's population had risen to 1.8 million, of whom a
mere 14,000 were non-Chinese. Of the 16,000 British subjects entitled
to vote, only 4,000 would be Chinese.

Later Grantham explained confidentially to a newly receptive
Colonial Office that the great merit of his plan was that it safeguarded
Hong Kong from communist infiltration while the allocation of seats in
LegCo was so devised as to guarantee that potentially 'unreliable' members could never defeat the administration on any issue of political
substance. By this time, the Colonial Office, once so enthusiastic about
the Young Plan, had come to the view that the electoral system for
LegCo should be so gerrymandered to ensure that votes would always
stack up in favour of the government. When pressed by the Committee
of Inquiry into the Constitutional Development of the Smaller
Territories, which judged that his approach 'left the election of the legislature in the hands of the representatives of the richer classes' and was
'undemocratic', Grantham merely countered that any Chinese

government, communist or nationalist, would press for the return of Hong Kong, and that the advent of direct elections in the colony would 'result in the dominance in Hong Kong of Chinese politics'.

It had now become impossible to assert with any credibility that Hong Kong was 'apathetic' about democracy. A cursory glance at the press or at petitions from more than a hundred communal institutions showed conclusively that support for genuine constitutional reform had become widespread among both the Chinese majority and expatriate professionals in the media and the law. However, Grantham remained adamant that articulate opinion in the colony was not to be trusted, particularly when it was non-British.

By this time other forces were at work. While the debate about constitutional reform in Hong Kong stumbled irresolutely onward, the Long March in China had reached its destination. In October 1949, with the formal establishment of the People's Republic of China, the flow of refugees from the mainland into Hong Kong became a flood. The Colonial Office now joined the Foreign Office in fearing internal subversion or a guerrilla attack from across the border.

To make any announcement about constitutional reform in Hong Kong, they believed, would be to tempt fate. It could easily be criticised by the communists in Beijing as an 'instance of the hypocritical insincerity of the imperialist oppressors' aimed at 'brutally crushing the rightful interests of the Chinese in the colony'. To press ahead with the reforms was bound to provoke the Chinese communists into a propaganda attack on Britain at a time when the Far Eastern position was 'particularly serious'.

The outbreak of the Korean War further fuelled the case against any constitutional change in Hong Kong. Members of the British garrison there had been dispatched to face Chinese communists on that battlefield, and the Colonial Office had to prepare itself for the 'international police action' in Korea to spill over into Hong Kong. Sir Alexander Grantham, who had always regretted the 1946 commitment to democratic reform, willingly conceded that the issue should be temporarily put aside. Although it was briefly resurrected again late in 1951, by which time the Conservatives, led by Winston Churchill, had replaced Clement Attlee's Labour party in government, the new colonial secretary, Oliver Lyttelton, was swift to judge that 'responsible and professional' people had not demanded reform; only a 'vocal minority' at 'a lower level' who 'could not be regarded as responsible' were still agitating for the introduction of democracy.

On 20 October 1952, Lyttelton announced in the House of Commons that the time for significant constitutional change in Hong

Kong was 'inopportune'. In the colony, Grantham announced that he at least was 'at all times ready to consider further proposals for constitutional changes, provided they are not of a major character'. Thus the foremost agent of British 'betrayal' managed to leave the impression that, far from sabotaging the reform process, he was willing to resuscitate it. In any event, democratisation was dead. The repercussions on the future rights and freedoms of the people of Hong Kong, and on the international reputation of Britain, were to be incalculable.

Twenty-five years later, in a momentary spasm of resolve, an attempt was made to resurrect the corpse. In 1979, the colony's chief secretary, Sir Jack Cater (who had worked closely with the Chinese community as the first registrar of co-operative societies in Hong Kong), was one of the small handful of expatriate civil servants to decide that 'the time was right for us to have a good dose of democracy'. As chief secretary, Cater was aware that Britain, in the person of the governor, Sir Murray MacLehose, was about to approach China directly at the start of the process which led to the Joint Declaration five years later. For this reason he was anxious to move swiftly so that, in terms of democracy, 'we would have something on which to base our future'. MacLehose was unlikely to be sympathetic: in private, he had never disguised his opinion that the principal threat to Hong Kong's survival was any suspicion in Beijing that the British colony might become a base for subversion against the mainland. In MacLehose's view (which, by the late seventies, had congealed into the diplomatic consensus), a democratic election in Hong Kong would constitute just such a threat by turning the hustings into the battlefield for a civil war between nationalists and communists. As he explained much later, 'If the communists won, that would be the end of Hong Kong. If the nationalists won, that would bring in the communists. So it seemed a thoroughly unhelpful line to develop.'

Early in 1979, while MacLehose was away in London, Cater summoned a small group to his official residence, Victoria House, to work out 'possible plans for democracy – or more democracy – in Hong Kong'. Those present included two future chief secretaries: David Akers-Jones (who subsequently became a 'China adviser' and one of Patten's bitterest critics), and David Ford, who was in the post for the first two years of Patten's governorship. The 'Victoria House Group' conducted their discussions in secret because Cater knew how unpopular he would become with his colleagues for even convening such a gathering. After several meetings, according to Cater, 'we worked out a skeleton of what might have been . . . When Murray returned, I put our proposal to him. He was not very happy.'

Cater persisted, and as a result he was allowed to present a much watered-down proposal to the governor's advisory body, the Executive Council. At that meeting, MacLehose made it clear to Cater that he still disapproved of any constitutional change and that Cater was on his own. In the face of such resistance, Cater made very little ground. 'It was quite clear that the majority of ExCo, including the Chinese members, were certainly dead set against democracy in principle . . . To me it was a great disappointment. If we had had those ten, twelve years to experience democracy . . .'

Cater's efforts were not entirely in vain, however. In 1981, the Executive Council agreed to the introduction of direct elections for eighteen newly created District Boards. Although the powers of these quasi-parish councils were very limited and their elected members were again in a minority, at least a principle had been established. Campaigning occurred, votes were counted and the roof did not fall in. Perhaps more importantly, as the contemporary historian of these events, Robert Cottrell, has astutely observed, 'It enabled British politicians to talk a few years later . . . about the "continued development" of "representative government" in Hong Kong as though it were a longstanding process rather than merely an adjunct of 1997.'

Even this claim was far less valid than it might have been. More to the point, Hong Kong still lacked any significant degree of democratic accountability by the time negotiations with China on Hong Kong's future began, at which stage it was almost too late to make any significant progress.

In retrospect, MacLehose was to concede that the fear of provoking Beijing which led him to sidestep the pressure for democracy 'sounds remarkably feeble'. But he has explained: 'I felt my job was to make Hong Kong as contented and prosperous and cohesive as possible . . . Insofar as I don't sleep at nights, that is the sort of thing one looks back at and wonders whether one should have done it. I still think I was right.' According to John Walden, director of home affairs between 1975 and 1980, democracy was a 'dirty word' throughout his thirty years as an official in Hong Kong. Walden has written that the handful of expatriate civil servants who favoured democratic reform were regarded as disloyal, or even dangerous.

Pressure groups advocating political reform or grass-roots democracy were carefully monitored by the government and the Special Branch of the Hong Kong Police and, where possible, their activities were discreetly obstructed or frustrated, sometimes by the use of highly questionable tactics. This deliberate and active discouragement of the growth of the democratic process by the government continued right up to 1980, to my certain knowledge.

These allegations are dismissed by MacLehose as 'absolute moonshine', and it is fair to say that they have not been given great currency except by the most ardent conspiracy theorists in Hong Kong.

Whatever the truth, as Robert Cottrell has pointed out, the civil servants at the heart of this history lacked both foresight and imagination. Their defence has been that Hong Kong enjoyed the benefit of an admittedly authoritarian executive which was, nonetheless, itself bound to the precepts of Britain's democratic tradition. However, this rationalisation of their inertia founders on their failure to think coherently beyond 1997; their failure to accommodate the argument of those who believed, as Lord MacLehose dismissively phrased it, that 'somehow the democratic process would insulate Hong Kong against China', or to appreciate that, in Cottrell's words, 'should any rendition of Hong Kong eventually occur, the seeding of democracy there would encourage British public opinion to feel slightly nobler about the process, and probably also make rendition more acceptable to Hong Kong itself'.

It was perhaps with these considerations in mind, but almost as an afterthought, that the concept of a representative government for Hong Kong 'constituted by elections' was slipped into the final draft of the Joint Declaration at Britain's request. As we have seen, neither party interpreted this to mean that a future legislature would be elected by universal suffrage (except 'ultimately', whatever that term was supposed to mean in this context). The British were reconciled to the view that such elections might be 'indirect' and that the franchise might be severely limited. As Cottrell says, 'In the Chinese political lexicon "elections" could have meant almost anything.' It is difficult to resist his scathing conclusion that 'the British government was more concerned at this juncture with the political benefits which would derive from the *idea* of democracy for Hong Kong, than it was with the implementation of democracy as such.'

In November 1984, following agreement on the final draft of the Joint Declaration, the government published a White Paper advocating that the Legislative Council should be restructured to the extent that two fifths of its membership would be indirectly elected through the creation of the twelve 'functional' constituencies representing various professional and business interests, while twelve more seats would be allocated by an 'electoral college' formed by local government organisations. 'A very small number of directly elected members' was proposed for 1988, building up to what was carefully described as 'a significant number' by 1997.

In both Houses of Parliament, ministers expressed in the most sententious language that they all fully accepted that a firmly based democratic administration should be built up in Hong Kong before 1997. Backbenchers, among them the former prime minister Sir Edward Heath, who was later to become one of Patten's most strident critics, urged the government to move rapidly towards that goal. More than 140 years after the seizure of Hong Kong, this belated commitment carried little conviction among those on whose behalf the Mother of Parliaments had been so dilatory.

The sceptics were right. In perhaps the most blatant act of perfidy in this shabby little history, the British soon reneged on even the modest commitment made in the 1984 White Paper. Within a year the Chinese had made it clear that Britain's unilateral decision to promise a 'very small number' of directly elected seats in the 1988 elections constituted a violation of the commitment made in the Joint Declaration to securing 'a smooth transition'. According to the Chinese, this objective could only be achieved if Britain refrained from any change to the political structure of Hong Kong that might be construed as a contravention of the Basic Law – by which Hong Kong would be bound after 1997, but which, in a Kafkaesque tweak of diplomacy, had yet to be finalised, let alone promulgated. 'Convergence' was the buzzword used by the Beijing officials to characterise Britain's 'obligation' to honour this self-serving interpretation of the 1984 agreement. Nonetheless, Britain consented to what one government minister described as this 'important' principle with no apparent qualms. As a result, as Cottrell has noted, 'China could claim the right to co-determine pre-1997 policy decisions, and also, prior to the Basic Law's publication, to delay any major decisions which Britain might wish to take until China, too, was ready to pronounce on the matter.' To this extent, Britain had meekly submitted to a Chinese armlock over all major political developments relating to Hong Kong for the next decade and, in a shameless volte face, conceded that direct elections, after all, should not be essayed in 1988.

Given the strength of feeling on the issue, a Green Paper in 1987 did not entirely rule out the option of direct elections for the following year, but buried the prospect in the small print. This subterfuge backfired, however. Altogether 368,431 individuals exercised their right to register a formal response to the Green Paper. Of these, 361,398 expressed an opinion about direct elections: 265,078 were in favour, 94,565 against, and 1,755 had no definite view. The verdict in favour of direct elections could hardly have been more clear cut.

Yet, in a breathtaking sleight of hand, the Hong Kong Survey Office, which had the task of collating these responses, under instructions from Government House, and at the behest of the Foreign Office, contrived to suggest that the reverse was true. The campaign against direct elections was orchestrated by the 'united front' pro-China groups, led by the trades unions, working with the business elite. They distributed preprinted forms around offices and factories which respondents merely had to sign and return to the Survey Office. By contrast, most of the signatures in favour of direct elections were attached to petitions collected by liberal groups led by the United Democrats. Offering no explanation for its decision, the Survey Office decided to treat every signature on the preprinted form as an individual submission, but not to accord the same value to the signatures on the petitions. Thus, with an effrontery usually associated only with totalitarian states and banana republics, the Hong Kong government blithely announced that, on the basis of the submissions to the Survey Office, 'more were against than in favour of the introduction of direct elections in 1988'. Progress towards the ultimate goal was postponed yet again.

In fact it was not until 1991, by which time the principle of 'convergence' had been called into question by the atrocities in Tiananmen Square, that a system of direct elections was at last introduced for a minority (eighteen) of seats in a legislative assembly which (despite its honorific title) was still essentially a debating chamber without significant legislative authority. Following that year's elections, the constitutional structure of Hong Kong remained much as it had been for the previous 150 years. Absolute power still resided at Government House in the hands of the present sovereign power, very much as the future sovereign power might have wished. Yet although Martin Lee's victorious United Democrats were still outnumbered two to one in the sixty-seat assembly by those either indirectly elected or appointed by the governor, they had a legitimacy, conferred on them by the endorsement of a genuine electorate, which threatened to confound the Tammany Hall assumptions on which the legislative assembly had been constructed almost a century and a half earlier.

Against such a background Chris Patten's self-imposed goal of escaping from the 'cul-de-sacs' of the past would have been fraught even in normal circumstances. As it was, he was not yet fully acquainted with this convoluted history, and his predicament was massively aggravated by the fact that the handover was a mere five years away. China was bound to be even more dubious about any further tinkering with the electoral system, while the people of Hong Kong, who had learned to view any proposals for reform emanating from Britain with suspicion, were themselves divided about how far to appease or to challenge China. At the very least, the new governor had set himself a daunting task.

Patten's informal drafting committee included Sir David Ford, William Ehrman, Michael Sze, Martin Dinham and Edward Llewellyn. Other groups and individuals also played a part. In other circumstances, the product of their work during the summer of 1992, though novel, would hardly be described as controversial. The voting age, for example, was to be lowered from twenty-one to eighteen, which did no more than bring it into line with China's own constitution. The number of seats in the Legislative Council which were to be contested by direct elections was in any case due to rise from eighteen to twenty, again with Beijing's tacit consent: despite pressure from Martin Lee and others to increase the number to thirty, Patten did not deviate from his original intention to refrain from incurring the wrath of China by 'revisiting' that issue. Neither of these proposals was therefore expected to provoke an adverse reaction in Beijing.

Patten focused his search for the 'elbow room' exactly where he expected to find it: in the future structure of the functional constituencies and the Election Committee. So far as he understood it, neither of these anachronistic arrangements had been the subject of negotiation with China, and to that extent, he believed himself to have a free hand to democratise them. The structure of both, as Patten was well aware, was a coruscating indictment of a deeply flawed and often corrupt process for which the term gerrymandering was barely adequate.

As Patten well knew, the immediate 'victims' of his reforms would be Hong Kong's mercantile and financial elite, the corporate voters heavily overrepresented in LegCo. Patten's blueprint, as it became known, proposed that in the functional constituencies 'all forms of corporate voting should be replaced by individuals who own or control the management of the corporations concerned'. Thus, for example, 'all directors of companies that are members of the General Chamber of Commerce would be able to vote, instead of just the companies themselves, as was the case hitherto'.

The importance of this seemingly modest reform was far greater than it might at first appear. In 1992, Simon Murray, who, as group managing director of Hutchison Whampoa, was directly responsible for assets in excess of £11 billion and for 20,000 employees, was almost alone among his peers in acknowledging the failings of the existing structure. 'Take my group, which has thirty companies which are members of the Chamber of Commerce,' he explained. 'Theoretically, each of those companies has a vote. But of course, if I tell them to vote for Smith, they are likely to do that.' Under Patten's proposals, which Murray was to endorse with enthusiasm, the individual directors of the thirty companies in the Hutchison Whampoa group – some 150 people – would each cast a personal vote by secret ballot, making the outcome very much more difficult to gerrymander. The repercussions would not only echo through every boardroom in Hong Kong but ricochet all the way to Beijing.

Patten had quite deliberately not only challenged the entrenched power of Hong Kong's mercantile autarchies but also threatened their discreet but cosy relationship with Beijing. Once again, the General Chamber of Commerce was to supply a pertinent example. In 1992, a few months before five directors of its Executive Committee were due to retire, but expecting to stand again and to be voted in automatically, Beijing intervened. Simon Murray explained at the time: 'China let it be known that they had their own list, people who they wanted to stand against the five guys who were retiring. They passed that list round to many of the 3,000 companies in the Chamber of Commerce. They also got many Chinese companies, which weren't members, to join the chamber.' In eighteen months membership of the Chamber of Commerce increased by 900, the fastest-ever growth in its long history. As Murray was to observe later, 'When the votes came in, the five guys on China's list all got 900 votes. Of course, it was the Chinese companies voting them in. Over time, if that were to continue, the committee of the Chamber of Commerce – theoretically – will be run by people put in by China.' As a result, under the existing system, the selection of the chamber's representative in LegCo would, in effect, be determined by Beijing. And, Murray went on, 'they operate in the same way with the lawyers and with the banks'. So, in the absence of reform, he had no doubt that China would acquire 'a very menacing control over LegCo, which cannot be good for anybody, because they will just be puppets doing what they are told'.

Patten's proposed reforms of the existing twenty-one functional constituencies were designed to cut the ground from under this form of corruption. Extending the franchise in all of them would increase the potential number of eligible voters by a factor of five; moreover, by loosening the grip of a few powerful individuals over the votes of their subordinates, he would ensure that the democratic gain was likely to be greater than the bare arithmetic would suggest. It would not be surprising, therefore, if the thin skein of trust between Britain and China unravelled in this constitutional knot to the point where the architect of these reforms would be reviled in language not heard since the Cultural Revolution.

This was not all. As agreed with China, Patten was also obliged to create nine new functional constituencies to replace the seats hitherto taken by government appointees. It was here that he found the further 'elbow room' to advance the cause of democracy quite dramatically. Under the chief secretary's direction, a small team of civil servants constructed these new constituencies to meet Patten's requirement that, as far as possible, they should embrace 'the entire working population'. This was to be achieved by giving a vote to all those working in Hong Kong's existing industrial and commercial sectors: in agriculture and the fishing industry, power and construction, manufacturing, import and export, textiles and garments, wholesale and retail, hotels and catering, transport and communication, financing, insurance, real estate and business services, as well as in community, social and personal services. At a stroke, Patten had contrived to extend the franchise to 2.7 million people without, he believed, violating the terms of the Joint Declaration or the Basic Law.

In addition to the twenty directly elected seats and the thirty elected by the functional constituencies, the sixty-seat chamber was to be completed by ten seats selected by an Election Committee. Hitherto, the Election Committee had been composed principally of members who were themselves members of one of the District Boards. Here Patten had alighted on another aspect of Hong Kong's gerrymandered political system. Without condemning the prevailing structure, he advocated that the system of appointments to District Boards should be abolished in favour of direct elections. A group led by one of the colony's foremost legislators, Jimmy McGregor, came up with a proposal that the Election Committee for the 1995 elections should 'draw all or most of its members' from the District Boards which, for the first time, would themselves be overwhelmingly composed of individuals who had been directly elected into local government. This would not only have the effect of enhancing local democracy but would yet again serve to strengthen the democratic credentials of the Legislative Council. As McGregor would later explain to the legislative assembly: 'The ideal would be to ensure that the Election Committee became genuinely representative of the community.' If all members of LegCo were to be elected in 1995, it made sense that the electors on the committee should themselves have been elected. 'Anything less,' he observed dryly, 'might be taken as appointment by proxy.'

Taken together, Patten's proposals would seriously impair Beijing's ability to influence, directly or indirectly, the outcome of an election in

Hong Kong. Although the leadership of the People's Republic had subscribed in principle to the concept of elections for Hong Kong, this commitment, it was tacitly acknowledged – even by Beijing's most ardent advocates in the expatriate community – had been made on the assumption that the electoral system could be guaranteed to deliver a compliant majority in the Legislative Council. From Beijing's crabbed and fearful perspective, the governor was indeed proposing to place a 'democratic time bomb' in Hong Kong. Patten was in little doubt that Beijing would react badly, regardless of whether his proposals did or did not violate either the Joint Declaration or the Basic Law. His schemes to promote the democratisation of Hong Kong violated a cardinal principle of colonial governance, to which, from their differing viewpoints, both the outgoing and incoming masters of the colony had long tacitly subscribed: that the electoral process should be so structured and manipulated as to ensure that its people could not mount a significant challenge to either sovereign power in the name of democracy. This complicity, which was a source of growing resentment among Hong Kong's thwarted intelligentsia, was about to be blown asunder in the name of freedom and, albeit in a stunted form, democratic accountability.

Once completed, the Patten blueprint was sent to the Foreign Office and to a number of key embassies around the world, including those in Beijing and Washington. Not one official raised any objection of substance to what was proposed, although Sir Robin McLaren, the recently appointed British ambassador in Beijing, warned that the Chinese would react badly to it. On 25 September 1992, with the full support of the prime minister and the rest of the Cabinet, the foreign secretary, Douglas Hurd, handed a copy of Patten's proposals to his Chinese counterpart, Qian Qichen, in New York, where they were both attending the autumn session of the United Nations. Patten himself sent a written message to Lu Ping, who, as the director of the Hong Kong and Macau Affairs Office, was, strictly speaking, his opposite number.

To Hurd's surprise they heard nothing for a week. Then, on the first Saturday in October, the British ambassador in Beijing was summoned to receive what Patten described privately as 'a stern note from Lu Ping'. Two calls 'along private channels' confirmed that the Chinese were 'furious'. The message was clear and simple: Patten should shelve his proposals until he had discussed them with China. For once, the British government refused to allow itself to become trapped in this familiar diplomatic cul-de-sac. According to Hurd, the Chinese 'expected a long period of confidential discussions in which they would express their views and we would accede to them. Well, that was unrealistic.'

'We've been getting storm warnings, rather than signals, for the best part of a week,' Patten elucidated a few days later. 'Of course, it is the way Peking customarily does business, so it's a bit difficult to know whether it's any different from other times. But I expect Peking to be pretty savage and to try to frighten the community here . . . I imagine that the rhetorical thunderbolts will start raining down.' He was aware of the precariousness of his own position. 'Of course, it's true that if, after a couple of months of banging the dustbins and making a lot of noise, the community here has flooded away from supporting any notion of more democracy, then it will be difficult to get any package through the Legislative Council or to make it stand up. But I hope that doesn't happen. I hope the community has some self-confidence. We shall see.'

7

'YOU DESERVE BETTER'

An Agenda for Hong Kong

On 7 October 1992, the day of Patten's first policy address to the Legislative Council, Hong Kong was abuzz with rumour and speculation. Overworked phrases like 'moment of truth' and 'turning point' filled the newspapers; politicians, some of whom had been briefed by Patten on the broad thrust of his proposals, were quoted extensively on what they thought he might say. There were warnings of a 'backlash' from disgruntled legislators, while 'sources in Beijing' warned that if the governor's speech breached the Joint Declaration then the Foreign Ministry would register a formal protest. The columnist Margaret Ng, writing in the *South China Morning Post*, discerned that his speech would clarify two fundamental questions about the new governor: whether his style of government was to be 'co-operative' or 'confrontational', and whether he was in the colony 'to do the greater good for Hong Kong or for Chris Patten'. The mood of excited anticipation in the Legislative Council, and in the wider community, was almost palpable as Patten launched into what he described self-mockingly as a speech of Castro-length proportions, entitled 'Our Next Five Years: The Agenda for Hong Kong'.

His address was not, nor was it intended to be, entertainment: it was devoid of the jokes and rhetorical flourishes for which he was renowned, and delivered with a deliberation reminiscent of the sovereign's speech at the state opening of the British Parliament. 'My goal is simply this: to safeguard Hong Kong's way of life,' he declared emphatically at the start. He dealt with local issues first, unveiling a massive five-year programme of public spending on health, education, housing and law and order. There would be enough teachers to reduce average class sizes to twenty; the public housing authorities would build an average of a hundred new flats a day; an extra 800 police officers would be recruited in the forthcoming financial year; spending on health would rise by almost 5 per cent per annum. He also announced a public-works programme on infrastructural projects and community buildings worth $HK78 billion. As a result of these and other plans, annual public spending – the former Conservative Cabinet minister was proud to boast – would rise by 21 per cent in real terms over the five years to 1997, a figure that could comfortably be maintained by economic performance and without depleting Hong Kong's traditionally prudent level of reserves.

Then there was the proposal to construct the new airport at Chek Lap Kok which, he reminded his delighted audience, would confirm Hong Kong's position at the crossroads of Asia. Designed to be the largest and most modern airport in Asia, it promised to be one of the world's greatest engineering feats. It would require a small but mountainous island off the coast to be levelled; a supporting network of new motorways; a suspension bridge to rival the Golden Gate, and a new metro system. Although the project had fallen prey to the mutual antipathy and mistrust which had bedevilled Sino–British relations following Tiananmen Square, work was already underway, underwritten for the moment by the Hong Kong government. But it had become an issue of such financial, commercial and political magnitude that the word 'crisis' hovered around every mention of the subject. By 1992, the Chinese had once again decided to use the airport in a blatant attempt to exert leverage on the political process in Hong Kong. This time, however, they found themselves hoist by their own petard.

Instead of displaying the constructive ambiguity favoured by diplomats, Patten was unequivocal. 'I will not be judged on whether in 1997 I fly out for the last time from Chek Lap Kok,' he reminded his audience in the legislative chamber and beyond.

> I remain convinced that if we discuss the airport on its merits, then our very able negotiators could sort things out in a morning, perhaps even with a break for coffee. . . . If, in the event, we cannot achieve the breakthrough we need, and if, because the timetable slips, the costs rise and I have to fly out of Kai Tak or leave on the *Lady Maurine*, it will not be for want of effort or ingenuity in seeking out a timely solution. But the delay would be a great pity for Hong Kong; and it would be just as great a pity for China.

The message was clear: Patten was not going to allow anxiety over the new airport to derail his proposals for constitutional reform.

I owe it to the community to make my own position plain. I have spent my entire career engaged in a political system based on representative democracy. It would be surprising if that had not marked me. It has. I have always been moved by Isaiah Berlin's description of democracy as 'the view that the promotion of social justice and individual liberty does not necessarily mean the end of all efficient government; that power and order are not identical with a straitjacket of doctrine, whether economic or political; that it is possible to reconcile individual liberty – a loose texture of society – with the indispensable minimum of organising and authority'. I bring those opinions to the task of governing Hong Kong, where the ink of international agreements and the implacable realities of history, geography and economics shape and determine the way in which such views can be applied.

It was a powerful credo, plainly stated in terms which the citizens of Hong Kong had not heard before from any British official. The words were spoken slowly and with great emphasis, and with a touch of defiance. Yes, Patten acknowledged, the pace of democratisation was necessarily constrained, but, he stressed, 'It is *constrained*, not stopped dead in its tracks.' That established, he defined a crucial role for democracy in a way which was to cause great controversy within Hong Kong and, when he elaborated on his theme elsewhere, throughout the region. 'Democracy,' he declared, 'is more than just a philosophical ideal. It is, for instance, an essential element in pursuit of economic progress.'

This sentiment flew in the face of the received wisdom to which the business elite in Hong Kong had always clung. It challenged the premise on which the authoritarian leaders of several Asian 'tigers' had constructed their economic miracles; and, implicitly, at least, it was a rebuke to the Chinese leadership, which was struggling to establish capitalism within the political and bureaucratic constraints of its own deformed 'dictatorship of the proletariat'. Patten was unrepentant. In the absence of the rule of law buttressed by democratic institutions, and without an independent judiciary enforcing laws democratically enacted, he insisted, investors were vulnerable to 'arbitrary political decisions taken on a whim'. The new governor could hardly have described his outlook more bluntly or more precisely. Many of his listeners were visibly affected by what he said: some mesmerised by his vision, others aghast at his temerity. These contrasting responses reflected precisely the profound schism by which the community had long been divided.

Patten then revealed his blueprint for electoral reform, prefacing it with two crucial commitments. First, that most of the community, he was sure, wished any constitutional reform to be compatible 'as far as possible' with the Basic Law, and, accordingly, to transcend 1997, which meant that his proposals would require 'serious discussions with Peking'. Secondly, that while 'it would be very easy diplomatically and, perhaps, politically, to draw a line here and to declare that, in due course, this council will be informed of the outcome of the negotiations', he had not been so tempted. 'You deserve better,' he promised, 'and I believe my first duty is one of frankness to this council and to the community.'

In that brief statement of intent, Patten repudiated the stance which had been adopted by all his predecessors, and which had been enshrined in the Cradock doctrine of secret diplomacy endorsed by all previous British ministers. Two related factors were at the root of his approach: the fundamentally altered environment created by Tiananmen Square, and the growing demand for democracy in Hong Kong which that atrocity had accelerated. He had taken it upon himself to invest the Joint Declaration with a passion for democratisation that neither signatory had intended their complicit ambiguities to imply. More than that, he had pledged himself to a style of diplomacy which reflected that commitment. Any lingering doubts that the appointment of Patten might have been a cosmetic diversion had now been swept away. For better or for worse, the people of Hong Kong were to be put to the test in ways which had not been demanded of them before. Some shrank from the prospect; others rejoiced. Most resolved to wait and see.

The headlines in Hong Kong the following day reflected the excitement and concern Patten's speech had provoked. 'PATTEN "VOTES FOR ALL" PLAN', trumpeted the front page of the *South China Morning Post*. In an enthusiastic editorial which carefully refrained from judging the package itself, the leading English-language newspaper commented:

> Chris Patten has never been one to duck a fight . . . Yesterday he demonstrated to a new audience in Hong Kong that he is not short of political courage . . . Those who thought he would back away from confrontation ahead of his first visit to Beijing later this month were proved wrong. Fears of jeopardising an agreement on airport financing did not sway him from his purpose yesterday . . . He pressed on with his ambitious plan to extend the franchise to

include every eligible member of Hong Kong's working population through an extension of the functional constituency system. China will denounce the move as bringing in more democracy through the back door, in contravention of the Basic Law . . . After three months of shadow boxing, the first appearance in the ring of Hong Kong's new champion was no let-down . . . Let nobody say that the territory is short of leadership, however controversial it proves.

On the first page of an eight-page supplement, under the headline 'CHINA HITS OUT AT PLANS FOR POLITICAL SHAKE-OUT', the *Post* confirmed that the private 'storm warnings' from China a few weeks earlier were in earnest. A 'Hong Kong-based senior Chinese official, who declined to be named' was quoted as saying that the proposed reforms were 'incompatible with the Joint Declaration and the Basic Law' and 'a far cry from the provisions of the two documents'. Moreover, the source indicated:

What Mr Patten said was contrary to repeated assurances by the British side that Britain would consult China on major issues concerning Hong Kong . . . We are gravely disappointed that he did not have the intention of consulting us in the first place. Sincerity is absent from his speech. Against this background, it would be difficult to expect Mr Patten's policy outline, in its present form, would be accepted by the Chinese side.

The same criticism was echoed in almost identical terms by Beijing apologists like Edmond Lau Ting Chung, a Hong Kong affairs 'adviser' to Beijing, who warned, 'If China does not agree, all these changes will be dropped by 1997 when China will organise another round of elections according to the present arrangements . . .' For good measure, he added, 'He's just putting on a show for the British people and for his future career in Britain.'

Other members of the Legislative Council were more reticent. Even the most ardent advocate of 'standing up' to China, Martin Lee, who was prone to denounce almost any statement emanating from Government House as some form of 'sell-out', had been wrong-footed by the governor's speech and merely expressed the hope that the governor would 'do what was right' even if Beijing were to oppose him.

After the United Democrats' landslide victory in the 1991 elections, Martin Lee had been in no doubt about the message that result had conveyed to Beijing. As he said later, 'The battle lines were drawn thus: on the Chinese side they said, "Be careful in casting this sacred vote. Vote for those who can work with China. Don't vote for those who can't" — namely us. The verdict from the ballot box was crystal clear.' Buoyed up by their result, the United Democrats had persisted in their campaign for half the Legislative Council — thirty seats — to be directly elected in 1995, rather than 2003, as Beijing had insisted. Lee was to recall a conversation of that time with Sir David Wilson, in which the governor chided him for adopting a confrontational approach towards the mainland. 'You know that China is not going to let you have that sort of democracy,' Wilson told him. 'And is it really in the interests of Hong Kong to go on fighting for it in these circumstances?' Martin Lee was convinced that by this stage, the British government simply 'wanted us to go quietly and to accept our fate. They didn't want trouble from us, because if we were to shout it would make Britain look bad in the eyes of the world. After all, which other government in the world was handing over six million people to a repressive communist regime?'

On the basis of his first meeting with Patten, which took place before the new governor's arrival in Hong Kong, Martin Lee had immediately concluded that Patten was different. Nonetheless, when the governor invited him for a briefing a few hours before the announcement of his proposals, Lee remained sceptical. The outline of what Patten intended to say was, however, enough to send the leader of the Democratic party (as the United Democrats had by this time renamed themselves) hurrying back to his colleagues to prepare them for a remarkable turnabout in British policy. They were not convinced.

A few hours later, when they heard Patten lay out his proposals in full, they were incredulous. 'They were so thrilled,' said Martin Lee. 'They just couldn't believe it. Disbelief. The good ideas . . . I mean, it is almost like a fully democratic election . . . Last night, after a long session, some of our people actually went and had drinks to celebrate. We've never celebrated anything before.'

Yet Patten's 'modest proposals' posed a dilemma for the Democrats. Hitherto the essence of their stance as a political party had been fierce opposition to both China and Britain: to the former as a despotic regime bent on the destruction of freedom and human rights; to the latter for 'kowtowing' to the malign purposes of the former. Now Patten had rudely unbalanced the neat symmetry of this political platform. Martin Lee described his problem and his solution to it with candour.

> I think our official line will be that we still want ten more directly elected seats; that we expect the British government to talk to the

Chinese to give us those ten; and that even if they don't get Chinese approval, there is nothing to stop them going ahead. But we won't be able to go too hard on that or we'll lose the support of the people of Hong Kong. They will think, 'These people are idealists. They are just banging their heads against the wall. They are not realistic because the alternative [the Patten proposals] is perfectly acceptable already . . .' When they have an alternative which is almost as democratic as the American system of electing their president, and which is not inconsistent with the Basic Law, and we can go ahead without Chinese agreement, they will say, 'Of course, ten directly elected seats is more democratic, but China will go through the roof. Let's take the lesser option. It is not as good, but it has the advantage of not really offending China.' So if we continue our present policy, we will have real difficulty bringing the people behind us.

After prolonged internal discussion, the Democrats agreed to maintain their commitment to direct elections but to soften their rhetoric. Their objective now was to manoeuvre into a position where they could retain both their democratic credentials and their public support by endorsing the Patten proposals without appearing to compromise the principles on which they had been elected. For a group of individuals who were fresh to the realities of party politics, and who belonged to a community which was still widely regarded by the British and Hong Kong civil service as politically immature, they showed a remarkable understanding of the realities of the democratic process.

And how would Martin Lee carry off this triumph of compromise? Would he be able to conceal his delight? To celebrate in private while in public continuing to insist that Patten should have gone further? 'Oh, that's not difficult. I mean, I just pull a long face in public,' he explained disarmingly. The following day he duly wrote an article for the *Guardian* in Britain in which he accused Patten, who 'does not seem willing to stand up to pressure from Beijing', of appeasing China by failing to increase the number of democratically elected seats in the Legislative Council and thereby failing to fulfil Britain's responsibilities towards its major colony.

Martin Lee was astute, but it did not occur to him that this criticism from the Democrats could be used by Patten as a tactical weapon, a counter to those strident voices who decried his proposals as 'irresponsible' – or, in the words of Sir Percy Cradock, 'fatal, fatal, fatal'. To have Martin Lee, China's bête noir, pay tribute to him in the eye of that gathering storm would, as Patten was only too well aware, only have intensified its violence. As it was, the governor was able to assert that he had contrived to steer a careful course between the competing aspirations of the community he served. And if Martin Lee was to have a serious go at him, would that be a problem? 'No. And I don't think he will. It would be more of a problem if he was hagiographical about me.' Patten had been convinced from the start that:

> The alternative to an argument with China wasn't a quiet life, but four or five years of argument with pro-democracy politicians in Hong Kong, and with pretty well everyone one respects here and outside . . . I could have had hunger strikes and people chained to railings and people resigning from the Legislative Council and forcing by-elections and political turmoil of that sort without any great difficulty at all if I'd simply gone along with whatever China had wanted.

Later Martin Lee was to embroil himself in a bitter row with Patten over another unresolved 1997 issue – the powers and structure of the Court of Final Appeal – in which each would be wounded by the other. At this stage, however, his admiration for the governor was unclouded, while Patten, for his part, already viewed the Democrats' leader as 'the most formidable politician in Hong Kong', and felt a strong political affinity with him. The thought was never far from the governor's mind that individuals like Lee, of high, even self-destructive, principles, might one day find themselves behind the iron bars of a Chinese jail for asserting those principles and campaigning for objectives from which no one educated even minimally in the concepts of freedom and democracy could conceivably resile. 'I think one of my tasks,' Patten explained in these early days, 'is to ensure that people like Martin Lee, along with the whole notion of a more plural approach to government, are accepted by China by 1997. And I've got to ensure that people like Martin Lee don't push it too far with China. To help in some accommodation between Martin Lee and China would be a great success . . . It may well be beyond me.'

Other politicians in Hong Kong, who were inclined to believe that the mantle Chris Patten had privately thrown around Martin Lee should more properly be theirs, were distinctly less enthusiastic about the governor's proposals. Martin Lee's rival, Allen Lee, was now the leader of the recently formed and quaintly named Co-operative Resources Centre (CRC), a quasi-political party representing the interests of the business community, but anxious to be seen as independent of Chinese influence. When pressed, he tended to speak in favour of democracy, but he preferred to regard himself as a political realist: in the fragile hothouse of Hong Kong politics, he was regarded more as a weathervane than as a leader, and he had long been treasured by civil servants because he could be relied upon to take a 'sensible' if sometimes opaque position on matters of controversy.

Allen Lee had been, for many years, an uncomplaining colonial subject. Born in Shanghai in 1940, he was smuggled into Hong Kong fourteen years later aboard a cargo ship. His father, a merchant, had already fled to the United States, so as a teenager, Lee lived alone in Hong Kong until the family was reunited in 1957. When Allen Lee had finished his schooling, his father sent him to the United States, where he studied engineering and mathematics at the University of Michigan. He returned to Hong Kong in 1966 as an employee of Lockheed Electronics, but was soon headhunted to become managing director of what was then the colony's largest engineering company, employing 3,800 people. In 1977, he was introduced to the governor of the time, Sir Murray MacLehose, who was evidently impressed by the eager young executive. The following year, at the age of thirty-eight, he became the youngest person ever to be appointed to the Legislative Council. In 1986 he was also appointed to the Executive Council. In the 1980s Lee had been an assiduous champion of open government and democracy; by the time of Patten's arrival he had fallen under the influence of the tycoon Sir S. Y. Chung and, along with his mentor, had switched allegiance to the future sovereign.

On the day of Chris Patten's address, Allen Lee was one of several public figures summoned to Government House to be relieved of their duties as advisers to the government on the Executive Council. It is true that Patten had not been greatly impressed by Lee, but the ExCo member's dismissal was not a reflection on him personally: he was a casualty of the governor's decision to separate the function of the Executive from that of the Legislative Council, a distinction which had previously been blurred.

Patten's reform of these functions, which he had announced in his address, was straightforward: henceforth no member of LegCo could simultaneously serve on ExCo. As the former would be an exclusively elected body, the members of the latter would be appointed from the existing pool of senior civil servants and co-opted leaders of the wider community. ExCo's role, on a miniature scale, would be similar to that of the US Cabinet. 'My intention,' Patten said, 'is to ensure that we have vigorous and effective executive-led government that is properly accountable to this Legislative Council.' The 'confusion and muddle' which was endemic in the existing structure was a threat to the effective development of the legislature as an independent check on government. 'It is the legislature which is the main constitutional element, and which must be developed.'

By separating ExCo from LegCo, Patten hoped to streamline the process of government and to reinforce open political debate. As his chosen advisers, members of the Executive Council were bound by confidentiality and collective responsibility. 'What kind of democracy,' he asked rhetorically, 'seeks to take open political debate away from the legislature and shut it up in confidential discussion hidden from the eyes of the voters who elect the legislature?' This reform fell well within the terms of the Joint Declaration. Patten had carefully preserved the concept of 'executive-led government', a phrase which had become a mantra recited by both governments in the full knowledge that, if driven to assert their constitutional authority, the British governor or his Chinese successor could legitimately override the wishes of a troublesome majority in the Legislative Council by exercising their 'executive-led' veto. Patten did not add that his reform of the Executive Council extricated him from a grave dilemma: as the leader of the largest democratically elected party, Martin Lee would previously have had a powerful claim to a place on ExCo, which Patten would have found it hard to deny him. To have appointed China's 'subversive-in-chief' as one of his senior advisers would have angered Beijing and alarmed the Foreign Office. So Patten's reform not only had intrinsic merit but also the rare virtue of defusing a potential battle with both Chinese officials and British mandarins.

In public, Martin Lee again excoriated the governor for deciding to 'bar elected representatives from sitting on the Executive Council', a decision which, he asserted, 'constitutes a significant backward step in Hong Kong's democratic development. Put simply, he is thumbing his nose at the voters.' In private, he acknowledged, 'I can't push too hard . . . It would be very bad for the Chinese community in Hong Kong to get the message: "Martin is doing all this just to get himself a place on ExCo."' He was honest enough to add: 'Of course, I wouldn't, in any case, enjoy the prospect of going to ExCo, because that would mean giving up the best part of my legal practice.' As in the case of direct elections, the Democrats made their point but soft-pedalled the issue and soon dropped it altogether.

Patten also used his reform of the relationship between LegCo and ExCo to rid himself of another lurking problem. In their first meeting with him, several members of ExCo had informed him that they would not be willing to support a significant extension of democracy. Though he did not admit it in these terms, the 'constitutional' argument for the reform of ExCo provided a convenient cover for the expulsion from his inner council of potential adversaries whose loyalty was extremely uncertain.

Some of the Executive Council members who lost their positions through the reform were disgruntled. Patten confirmed, 'I'll be hearing more from one or two of them . . . There will be a certain lack of "house spirit". And in a sixty-member Legislative Council, one or two people can cause a lot of difficulty. They will feel that they did their best to support the administration. If the administration doesn't want their help, maybe they should kick over the traces.' But Allen Lee, the leading casualty, insisted that he felt no resentment: 'I don't feel bruised . . . His options are very limited. Either he has to separate LegCo from ExCo, or he has to appoint people like Martin Lee to the Executive Council and the Chinese will give him hell.' In his own time and his own style, however, Allen Lee was indeed to 'kick over the traces' in ways which irritated the governor and confirmed his instinct that Allen Lee was a distinctly less substantial figure than Martin Lee.

In public, Allen Lee confined himself to bromide statements about the desirability of a 'smooth transition' and 'convergence', but confidentially he was more forthcoming.

> Mr Patten is going to use his charm and his political wisdom to try to convince the Chinese, but I don't think they will be convinced. They're going to give him a very difficult time. So what's he going to do? That's the key question. When he comes back from his visit to China, he will have a choice: either negotiate with the Chinese again and come up with a package which leads to his being accused in Hong Kong of 'kowtowing', or take unilateral action. Now, if he takes unilateral action, we can throw convergence out of the door . . . Don't forget, after 1997, the consequences will be lived by the Hong Kong people, not Chris Patten. He will be leaving Hong Kong. How is China going to treat Hong Kong then? That is the important question.

While he stressed that he supported Patten's drive towards greater democracy, Allen Lee privately signalled his shift towards 'realism' by confessing that he had some sympathy with the complaint from Chinese sources that Patten's proposals had violated the spirit of the Basic Law. 'I mean, the Chinese expected to have dialogue with Chris Patten on this particular issue and the dialogue isn't really there,' he explained. 'Mr Patten wants to give Hong Kong as much democracy as he can, so he's looking at the loopholes in the Basic Law . . . and that, too, causes a problem with the spirit of the Basic Law.'

In October 1992, the message from Beijing was still not clear. The Foreign Ministry spokesman had been relatively restrained, but Patten's 'other channels' of intelligence, about which the governor was coy, were less encouraging. 'We've had some private messages from those who claim to be in the know, whose role in life I should perhaps not describe,' he confided, 'that the Chinese are furious and that Li Peng is furious.' The gist of the information was that the 'important people' in Beijing would refuse to meet him and that the airport project would be held hostage to his intransigence. In short, according to Patten, they were saying, 'We'll get you for this.'

As an accomplished public figure, Chris Patten was familiar with the round of official meetings, luncheons and dinners which consume so much of a politician's working life. He was blessed with an easy authority and a relaxed approach towards the public duties of high office. As the sovereign's representative in Hong Kong, he delighted in referring to himself mockingly in private as Hong Kong's 'Queen'. At the newly refurbished Government House, the Pattens were generous hosts. Dispensing with much of the formality favoured by some professional diplomats, they presided over luncheons and dinner parties with bonhomie, though they took care not to destroy that sense of occasion many of their guests craved. While her husband held court at one end of the table, affable, anecdotal, but dryly ferocious in argument, Lavender contrived to be solicitous, but never ingratiating, at the other. It was to become a testing role. Given to the expression of strong, independent opinions behind closed doors, she contrived to conceal her distaste for her husband's critics and adversaries, who were, according to protocol, only too often seated on her left and right. If it was disagreeable to entertain guests from Britain and Hong Kong whom Lavender knew were bent on frustrating his purpose, she never allowed her guard to slip. Invariably charming and discreet, she waited until they had departed before venting her loyal wrath against the 'rats' and 'traitors' whose company she had been obliged to endure on Patten's behalf.

Lavender had never been at ease with her husband's political ideology – 'I'm not one of your Tory wives,' she retorted defiantly when Patten teased her about failing to wear a hat for one official engagement – but she had been an assiduous campaigner in his Bath constituency. When Patten was in the Cabinet, she had pursued an independent career as a barrister specialising in family law. Now she had to play the part of first lady. Not all of her friends thought she would succeed. Her reserve, which disguised a gentle and affectionate nature, could be faintly intimidating. Lacking any streak of flamboyance, she

did not display that superficial panache which leads social commentators to describe a hostess as 'legendary'. Nor, at first, did it seem that she
would enjoy the round of duties that would inevitably envelop her:
how, her friends wondered, would she adapt to the tedious obligations
of a public spouse under constant, critical scrutiny? Would she dress the
part? Would she *play* the part? Or would she succumb to frustration and
irritation at what they imagined to be the suffocating proprieties
imposed upon her? They need not have worried. With no inherited
wealth, and with three daughters to educate, the Pattens had lived
modestly, if not with frugality, in Britain. Now, blessed for the first time
with a substantial income, Lavender blossomed. Elegant in dress,
modest in demeanour and sympathetic in manner, she swiftly reinvented herself as the very model of a modern first lady. Before long, it
was established in the community that Mrs Patten, unlike her husband, could do no wrong. She started to learn Cantonese (though she
never mastered more than a few phrases and soon gave up); she patro-
nised important charities with sustained conviction; she discovered
how to make effective speeches – short, simply expressed and genuinely
felt – and she became a familiar sight around town or walking on the
Peak, accompanied by her two terriers, Whisky and Soda, who became
local stars and the subject of affectionate cartoons. When Whisky disappeared one afternoon, Mrs Patten was correctly reported to be
distraught. A clumsy joke by an Australian diplomat, who speculated
that the dog had been spirited across the border to be consumed as a
delicacy by the Chinese leadership, offended the local community no
less than its first lady. When the dog was recovered, the rejoicing was
not confined to the Patten household.

In the days following his address, Chris Patten and his team sifted
through the mound of press cuttings culled from Hong Kong's
seventy-eight newspapers and the British press. In general they were
encouraged. The English-language dailies were supportive, one of
them describing Patten admiringly as a 'marathon man' for taking his
case to the people via phone-ins and a quartet of public meetings. The
latter innovation caused great excitement, and he was able to demonstrate his popular touch – though not without testing the mettle of his
translator with his characteristic irony and colloquialisms like 'sick as a
parrot'. One or two pro-Beijing papers referred to Patten 'playing the
public-opinion card' at these rallies. The gulf of incomprehension
between China's apologists and the former chairman of the British
Conservative party on the question of the status of 'public opinion' in
a free society was ominous. Patten detected in his critics an 'awful

contempt' for their fellow human beings and only just resisted saying so.

The public meetings bore little relation to their nearest equivalents in Britain. Patten was greeted more like a royal visitor than a politician. Many of those in the audience seemed to have come simply to be able to tell their grandchildren about it. The only questions which contained an element of confrontation were from pro-China activists, who had evidently been closely briefed. The form of words used was virtually identical, focusing either on Britain's colonial record or on Patten's apparent failure to understand the importance of 'convergence'. The governor was, in either case, brusquely dismissive. 'I could tell straight away who they were. They were close to the microphones and it was the standard line you get in polite conversation with Chinese negotiators – that we wrecked every country we ever left, and that we'll wreck Hong Kong. It's standard Chinese Marxist kit. Crap, of course.'

If the Hong Kong citizenry appreciated their governor's eagerness to press the flesh, the encounters also boosted his own resolve. Although his demeanour was unflappable, his style concealed an intellectual restlessness which led him to constantly re-examine every option facing him. By nature he was pragmatic: the grand gesture or the high risk was not greatly to his taste. Yet he had found himself, by political conviction and through his sense of history, driven to occupy the high ground. It frequently disconcerted him to be thus exposed, so perilously close to the territory favoured in 'gesture' politics, and, although he sought to hide his moods from even the closest of his advisers, the pressure of the great political gamble on which he had embarked sometimes told heavily. Direct contact with a supportive public, therefore, was not merely a matter of shoring up the polls but an experience from which to draw encouraging conclusions, however extravagant they might seem in the cold light of the morrow. After one of his public meetings, which was attended by 3,000 people, Patten said:

> You saw tonight – even though there were some loonies in the audience, and even though there was every opportunity for people to react in an excitable way – they actually behaved perfectly well. So I think we can make things work and, if they work, the Chinese are not going to change them. Because, boy, are they going to be worried about how to make this work as well as we've made it work.

Exactly who were these Hong Kong citizens whose support the governor was going to such lengths to retain? It is impossible, of course, to generalise, except by stating the obvious: that most were either refugees from mainland China or the offspring of refugees; that they worked, by

European standards, very long hours; that for them capitalism was not
a political question but the only economic answer; that the individual
and the family mattered more than the community or the state; that the
future mattered more than the past; and that, in their individual lives,
they were more usually given to optimism than to pessimism. Though
their differing attitudes were doubtless reflected in the opinion polls
which so assiduously charted the shifting hopes and fears of an insecure
and shallow-rooted society, their horizons were not bound by the vicissitudes of the 'through train'. To the outsider, they represented Hong
Kong only in the most imprecise fashion, as representatives of some of
the most significant sectors of the community and, unusually, in being
willing to talk about their lives openly to a stranger.

Ng Koon Leung, for example, ran a market stall when Chris Patten
first arrived in Hong Kong. He was not interested in politics and for
him, Patten was merely another British overlord. He was intrigued to
see the new governor in the streets among the people, but his life was
bounded by a set of basic imperatives which gave him no time to
follow in any detail the tortuous details of the diplomatic drama which
was to be played out not only over his head but without his participation. He worked hard, but he was unable to earn enough from selling
cigarettes and trinkets to support his two children, aged fourteen and
eight. His wife, Wong Oi Ying, a lively and practical woman, supple-
mented his income by working part-time as a seamstress. They lived in
a high-rise flat in a vast concrete block on one of the public housing
estates that had mushroomed all over the New Territories in the 1970s.
They had a small living room, which was dominated by a television set;
a bedroom just large enough to take a double bed, a bunk room, six
feet by six; a galley kitchen, six feet by four; a shower and toilet. It was
cramped but spotless, and it did not cross their minds that they were in
any way deprived.

Ng Koon Leung's father had arrived in Hong Kong in 1948, aged
eighteen, driven out of China by poverty and the depredations of the
Japanese. He found work as a labourer, and after a few months he
returned to his village across the border to meet the bride who had
been chosen for him and brought her back to Hong Kong. Like hundreds of thousands of similar immigrants, the couple worked with the
tenacity of desperation until they had secured for themselves the basic
means of subsistence. They had virtually no contact with the British,
except in the form of officialdom, and then only remotely. Their abid-
ing memory of their colonial masters was of their vast physical size: the
white man was tall and intimidating.

Soon after Patten's arrival Ng Koon Leung gave up his market stall to become a lorry-driver, collecting scrap. He was efficient and trust-worthy, and soon became a foreman. The work was dirty and tiring but he relished the responsibility: 'We collect anything and everything, and you have to try to assess how much the stock is worth. For machinery you have to decide if it can be reconditioned or whether it should be scrapped. You have to decide that for yourself . . . Yes, it is satisfying.' He worked eight hours a day, six days a week for HK$10,000 (£850) a month. His wages were soon put up to HK$13,000, and he considered himself fairly rewarded in what he knew to be a fiercely competitive sector of the economy. Each month he handed over HK$10,000 to his wife to keep the family. Their basic living expenses – food, rent, water and electricity – consumed half that amount, while extra tuition for the children and clothing cost another HK$2,000. The remainder, according to Wong Oi Ying, 'we put aside for a rainy day'. In the absence of a state insurance scheme to cover healthcare, unem-ployment benefit or a pension, HK$3,000 was scarcely enough to provide for their future security, let alone for the luxury of an occa-sional outing or holiday.

For this reason, Wong Oi Ying decided to boost their income by babysitting two small children, a boy aged three and a girl of eight months. Both children were brought to her on Monday mornings by their parents and collected again five days later, after work on Fridays. The elder child slept on a mattress in the living room, the baby in a cot in the Ngs' bedroom. Wong Oi Ying enjoyed looking after them, but it was 'quite hard work – twenty-four hours a day'. The extra HK$5,500 a month, however, made all the difference. She explained that the practice of 'boarding out' children in this way was becoming increasingly common: 'In Hong Kong both partners have to go out to work to keep their family. The working day is long: they must be at the office for a nine o'clock start, and with overtime, they are frequently not home until after eight in the evening.'

Despite their own economic insecurity, the Ngs did not resent the absence of a welfare state. Though they could appreciate the advantages of unemployment benefit, they thought that, on balance, it would mainly benefit the idle and incompetent. 'Of course it would be nice to have it, but in other countries people live on benefits rather than going out to work. Here, if you are disabled or off sick, the Welfare Council will help, but it is only a thousand dollars a month, which is not enough even for the basics. If they gave more it would be a burden on the econ-omy.' As for pensions and healthcare, they shared the view that, since there was no state scheme, it was incumbent on individuals to look after themselves, and not to take a 'shortsighted view of the future'.

The Ngs had recently started to follow the debate about the destiny of Hong Kong and had formed the impression that Patten was 'smart'. But they could not understand why Britain and China could not resolve their differences amicably. 'There is no need to shout at each other,' Wong Oi Ying said. 'They should just sit down together and discuss these things.' They felt there was little they could do to influence matters: 'We are just ordinary citizens. We just listen and let others speak.' Although the concept of democracy was still alien, they were not indifferent to its attractions. 'It is better to have the right to speak out. If you have the right to put forward your views, it doesn't matter if what you say is accepted. At least you have the chance to say it.' Wong Oi Ying was optimistic about the future, her husband less so. 'At the moment you can say anything and you can sign any petition, but after 1997, the Chinese can do what they like. There is nothing you can do. They might be more open than one expects but, in my opinion, it will be very much like China here in Hong Kong after 1997 . . . If there is restriction on freedom of speech it will not make much difference to us ordinary citizens.'

Hong Kong's freedoms, however, mattered greatly to Grace Wu, an antiques-dealer specialising in Ming furniture, on which she had become an authority with a rapidly growing international reputation. An elegant woman in her forties, she was as much at home in London and New York as in Hong Kong, where she now lived with her teenage daughter. Grace was born in China but her parents fled Shanghai soon after the Communist takeover for Singapore, where she spent her early childhood until her family decided to settle permanently in Hong Kong. She was sent to school in Canada and the United States, and later lived in England for a time. Despite her Western demeanour, she had always considered herself to be an exile from her homeland, a refugee, loyal to Hong Kong but, culturally at least, a 'Chinese patriot'.

Like others in the thriving antiques trade in Hong Kong, Grace Wu's business was expanding quickly. The delicate fifteenth- and seventeenth-century chairs, tables, bedsteads and wardrobes she imported from China were particularly in demand in the United States, where the best-quality items in her glossy catalogue could sell for upwards of $100,000. The handover loomed large in her mind, not least because of the Chinese government's ambivalent attitude towards the export of antiques. On one hand, some officials tacitly endorsed – and, in the case of the Cultural Relics Bureau, openly supported – international auctions in Beijing, Shanghai and Guangzhou (Canton); on the other, as Grace Wu put it, 'One does hear the constant noise of condemnation of "those who trade in our heritage" et cetera.' The future, therefore, was very uncertain. 'It is guesswork. We don't know.'

In China the trade was governed by the Antiquities Law, which made it illegal for any object over a hundred years old to be exported. However, its enforcement was the responsibility of the Chinese customs, who were well known for turning a blind eye for a small consideration. Grace Wu bought much of her stock from outside China itself, but when importing from the mainland, she was careful to work within the law — at least, insofar as she understood it. Inexplicably, antique furniture itself was exempt from the hundred-year rule, but it was forbidden to export the ancient and precious woods often used to make Ming furniture. The legality of her trade was not in doubt so long as customs officials could be convinced that the wood in her antiques did not fall into the prohibited category. Although she had been scrupulous in demanding an official stamp of approval from the Chinese authorities for every piece which passed through her hands, she was only too aware that she operated in a 'grey area' of the law. Many of her colleagues sidestepped it entirely, thereby — theoretically at least — leaving themselves open to charges which in China carried the death penalty.

The dealers feared that in the 'patriotic' fervour of postcolonial Hong Kong, they would be treated like scavengers. They expected their trade to be sharply curtailed and their possessions to be impounded. Consequently no antiques-dealer or collector of substance had failed to make contingency plans against a crackdown by the post-1997 authorities. Many works of art had already been shipped abroad to second homes or loaned to foreign museums. Of those that were left, every glazed vase had its packing case, each carved goddess its precisely contoured crate, complete with well-oiled casters, ready for a smooth, if unscheduled, departure by air. It was said that the contents of the T.T. Tsui Museum, a breathtaking collection of immeasurable value, had been similarly protected against the prospective vagaries of the Antiquities Law.

Grace Wu wanted to stay in Hong Kong. However, her decision would not be based merely on the prospects for the antiques business but on whether the 'one country, two systems' concept could survive the handover. She lived in a precise but elegant apartment, sparsely furnished in a mixture of modernist and Ming. Sitting there with three friends, all in the antiques trade, she said: 'I think we all feel the same way. We have overwhelming feelings for Hong Kong. I joke that I'm going to be out on the last helicopter, but this is my home. I would leave only if I thought that my personal freedoms were under threat.'

Her friends, for a variety of reasons, were less committed. One, a woman who had been born in Malaysia, educated in the United States, trained at Sotheby's, and now lived in Hong Kong because it was still a 'charmed world' for the collector, was planning to move to England before the handover. Another, a refugee from Shanghai who was a dealer in ceramics, was determined to stay on. 'My concern is to make money,' he explained. He was optimistic that the Chinese would not stand in his way after 1997. Politics did not interest him; as for freedom, he thought that it would still be possible 'to sit at dinner and criticise the government as long as we are not voicing our opinions publicly', and that was fine by him. The third friend, a painter, concurred.

> What is there to complain about if you can have a comfortable living, if you can have your friends around you? You can still enjoy good food in the restaurants and good clothes in the stores. Nothing has changed. There is just a different government . . . You know, artistic freedom is not something that has been important in the past. It's not something we ever had. So I don't think many people understand democracy, or care whether or not we have it. Most people want stability.

Grace Wu disagreed, but seemed uncomfortable doing so openly, as if unwilling to cast aspersions on the narrowly mercantile values flaunted by her friends, and which she, in part, shared. 'In our long history it has always been true that if you did not agree with the ruling dynasty, then you could not voice your opinion. You'd be caught and thrown in jail.' But was it important to her, for example, that newspapers should be free to tell the truth and free to express divergent opinions? 'It is important.' How important? 'Important enough to make me leave, but, having said that, because of our long tradition, I understand why people can feel that it is possible to say, "If I keep out of politics I can be happy." I can understand that.'

Patten's early performance as governor seemed to achieve its primary purpose. A poll conducted by one television station showed over 70 per cent support for his LegCo speech; another suggested that almost 50 per cent of the colony thought he should press ahead even if China were to object. Sixty per cent of the respondents to a poll by Radio and Television Hong Kong (RTHK), the government-owned public-service station, said they believed that the proposed reforms were of the right kind and were being advanced at the right pace.

The pro-Chinese press in Hong Kong was predictably hostile, but in the absence of an unequivocal line from Beijing to guide them, they confined their criticism to vague generalities. Two days after the speech, a Chinese Foreign Ministry spokesman was quoted as saying that Beijing would not be held responsible for maintaining the Patten proposals after 1997, while the Hong Kong and Macau Affairs Office said that the SAR government would reverse any changes that were not in line with the Joint Declaration. Five days later, the deputy director of the NCNA accused the governor, without identifying him by name, of 'masquerading as the saviour of Hong Kong' by offering democratic reform and by appearing to commit the Hong Kong government to proceeding with the new airport regardless of Chinese approval. A columnist in the pro-China *Wen Wei Po* argued that Patten's reforms did indeed violate both the Joint Declaration and the Basic Law, which gave China 'the right to discuss matters relating to the smooth transfer of government in 1997 and the right to be involved in the procedures to be adopted for that transition, both of which Patten has ostentatiously overlooked'. The author was a reliable indicator of Beijing's latent paranoia about what he described as the determination of the British government 'to violate the Joint Declaration and to ignore the need for convergence . . . [and] to impose its representative government system on Hong Kong so that after 1997 it could exert the maximum influence and preserve its interests here'.

The attitude of the British press could hardly have been more different, or more reassuring to a governor who always had one eye on reactions at home. *The Times*, in a leading article entitled 'TYPHOON PATTEN', acclaimed the governor for taking 'a calculated political gamble, on the success of which rests Hong Kong's hopes for giving lasting meaning to the "one country, two systems" formula . . . Mr Patten has set out to recapture the policy initiative from Peking, after a decade of defensive British manoeuvring – and to do so, significantly, from Hong Kong. In this pace setting, he has succeeded.' Peppered with words like 'audacious' and 'challenging', it conceded that Patten would have made himself enemies, and that he had yet to demonstrate 'how effective his bulwarks can be made against post-1997 misrule', but its eulogistic conclusion was that the new governor had made 'a brilliant, eloquent debut'. In similar vein, the *Daily Telegraph* prefaced its accolade with a side thrust at the 'succession of Foreign Office mandarins' who had 'bent before every slightest breeze out of Peking, on the grounds that to attempt to answer back would amount to confronting Peking over the Basic Law on the introduction of democracy and might expose the people of Hong Kong to Chinese retribution'. In taking a calculated gamble, Patten had 'dealt brusquely with this attitude. Someone like Mr Patten should have been made governor decades ago.' In the British media no dissenting voice was to be heard.

The foreign secretary rang to offer his congratulations and the prime minister wrote a warm note of appreciation. Moreover, Patten was advised by Number 10 that Major was due to say what the governor judged to be 'some excessively flattering things' about him in his annual speech to the Conservative party conference. Although Patten was duly grateful, he feared that one phrase in the leader's eulogy would be 'misunderstood' in the febrile atmosphere of Hong Kong:

> He's going to say that he looks forward to me returning to British politics in due course, which I would have deleted from the speech if I'd had any choice in the matter. One of the Peking attacks on me is that I'm not doing this for the people of Hong Kong and that I'm just interested in becoming prime minister or foreign secretary or something. But I couldn't conceivably go back to the prime minister and say that . . . even though the likelihood of my returning to British politics is remote.

Fortified by these public and private endorsements from Britain, Patten kept up a whirlwind round of public appearances, media interviews and private meetings with Hong Kong politicians, diplomats and civil servants, maintaining the momentum in the run-up to his official visit to Beijing, which he had announced in his speech. He was due to leave on 19 October, twelve days after his LegCo address. The Chinese, he judged, were 'confused and angry. They don't quite know what I'm up to . . . It is changing the rules of the game to decline to spend the next five years with one hand tied behind your back.' Although he had the impression that at the most sophisticated level they were anxious about the governability of Hong Kong after 1997, and 'paranoid' about Martin Lee, and despite the fact that the pro-Chinese media in Hong Kong had started to be 'pretty vitriolic', he felt confident enough to dismiss this as an orchestrated onslaught by Chinese officials of only passing significance. He was likewise resigned to facing 'one or two little humiliations along the road . . . Remember, the old emperors, if they had a provincial governor who hadn't entirely behaved, used to send a simple peremptory command: "Tremble and obey." And they will want to try to get me to tremble.'

Patten was anxious to try to establish a personal relationship with his opposite number, the director of the Hong Kong and Macau Office, Lu Ping. 'I've got to have one or two people there who at least start to listen to what I say and take me seriously.' He was concerned, too, about Hong Kong's financial and commercial elite. So far their public reaction had been muted, but he was well aware that, 'on the whole, the business community has never been at the forefront of those who believe in democracy'. At this stage, however, he hoped to win over the sceptics.

> The best way of maintaining political stability is by accommodating, in a modest way, people's demands for greater democracy rather than standing up to them for the next five years. The biggest threat to our wellbeing is an outbreak of trade war between China and the US. I will be incomparably more convincing in Washington in arguing the case for a continuation of most-favoured-nation [MFN] status for China if I'm thought by American public opinion and American politicians to be somebody who battles for Hong Kong.

Although Patten had already tried to persuade some leading business-men of this argument, he was under no illusion that it had carried much weight. Emissaries from the business community had reported their anxieties to him with some precision. The MFN status conferred by the USA on other countries to set quotas and tariffs at favourable levels defined their standard trading relationship with those nations. Around half the world enjoyed MFN status – only pariahs such as North Korea and Cuba were exempt. If the USA were to withdraw MFN status and place higher tariff barriers in the way of Chinese exports, trade between the two states (and others locked into the same system of preferences) would be certain to decline. As the main conduit for the transfer of goods and services between China and the rest of the world, Hong Kong would suffer at once. The prospect that senators and congressmen in the United States, either from a deep-rooted hostility towards communism or from a concern for human rights, might per-suade the US administration to remove China's MFN status was the stuff of nightmares for Hong Kong's business leaders. However, their greater fear was that, in the name of democracy, Patten would – from their perspective – goad China into an overreaction that would frighten the markets and lead to a downward economic spiral which might easily run out of control.

Up to a point Patten shared their concern that Chinese officials 'might be able to roar and shout sufficiently loudly to unsettle the market', and he was uncomfortably aware that there were 'certainly a lot of businessmen around with cold feet. But they haven't broken cover yet.'

Vincent Lo was one of those to keep his counsel, despite his mis-givings. As chairman of the Hong Kong General Chamber of Commerce and president of the Business and Professionals Federation of Hong Kong (BPF), he confided that most of his members were 'expressing grave concern about [Patten's] proposals and what they would do to Hong Kong'. Although they did not wish to voice their concerns in public, their antagonism towards Patten was deeper than he supposed. 'We hoped that democratisation in Hong Kong would go step by step, not trying to create everything in one go. So I think in that sense we do see eye to eye with China.' At this stage Lo was already certain that Beijing would reject the reforms.

> We know that China will react very strongly because we've been dealing with them for years . . . we know that head-on confrontation will not serve our purpose, and we know exactly how China is going to react . . . It's really a myth to think that they will not kill the goose that lays the golden egg. Today, I would say, we need China more than they need us . . . I think we are very close to a breakdown.

Baroness Lydia Dunn, the most senior of Patten's advisers on LegCo, maintained a loyally aloof silence. Although she had none of Lo's ambitious devotion to the Chinese leadership, she shared some of his pessimism. She thought that Beijing must have felt outmanoeuvred by Patten, that they had 'lost face', that they were genuinely angry, and that their sense of paranoia about a 'British conspiracy' would intensify. Although she endorsed Patten's planned reforms, her fear was that China would say 'categorically and publicly, "If you do this we will dis-mantle whatever you have put in place in 1997." Now, that would be a very serious statement, and it would present us with a major dilemma. It would derail the programme; it would, in fact, destroy everything we're trying to achieve.'

Unlike Vincent Lo, who hoped to see the Patten project derailed, Baroness Dunn was cautiously optimistic that the governor could retain public support. Though sustained by the polls, Patten was permanently anxious about the fragility of the backing he appeared to enjoy. Acutely aware that without popular support his plans would collapse, he knew that he was just as likely to become a 'lame duck' governor for 'con-fronting' as for 'kowtowing' to China.

> The Chinese have a tactic, which has worked again and again, which is to scare people, scare public opinion – and it's pretty volatile . . .
> I've got to know Hong Kong as well as you could get to know any

place in four months, but I still have no real comprehension of what makes people tick when they are under pressure or what they really want, or how they'll trade off a bit of short-term security for longer-term security.

Moreover, Patten had not given himself much negotiating leeway in Beijing. 'I'm pretty close to my bottom line,' he admitted.

I finessed on two cards they put on the table: no Martin Lee on ExCo – I wouldn't have put him on anyway, but they were terrified about that for some preposterous reason – and no increase in directly elected seats . . . We are still keeping the question of directly elected seats in play, but by and large they've got those cards . . . You could come up with a different form of Election Committee, but for me it would have to be a democratically elected Election Committee. You could talk a bit about functional constituencies . . . but I haven't got much room for manoeuvre.

He had also set himself a very tight timescale: any agreement with Beijing, he thought, would have to be reached quite early in the New Year – less than three months away. And would he delay beyond that? 'No, because otherwise I'll get into endless discussions.' His reluctance to find himself embroiled in such 'endless discussions' sprang from his fear that the longer the talks continued, the more Beijing would gain the upper hand by frightening the men and women on the 'Wanchai omnibus'.

Patten believed that the prospects for reaching an accommodation with China would be greatly enhanced by a change at the top of the communist hierarchy. 'What I find astonishing is to see people behaving in what is so self-evidently not their best interest. There are things one can't say, but does anybody expect that it will be quite the same establishment in 1997 actually running things in Peking?' To hope that key members of the Beijing gerontocracy might meet their maker or fall from grace in the intervening years was perhaps to place undue faith in the fates. Nevertheless, it was widely assumed that the 'paramount leader', Deng Xiaoping, was close to death, and that, after his demise, China would be sufficiently liberated from its political sclerosis to see the light about Hong Kong. In the meantime, Patten had to consider Britain's interests as well as those of Hong Kong. 'What is the sense in me making accommodations – dishonourable accommodations – now on the assumption that the establishment in Peking is going to remain exactly the same until 1997? What would I look like then? I'd be an ornament – and not a very attractive ornament – for most of my time here. And it would all look like a very dishonourable way for Britain to end an important story.'

As he set off for what he was confident would be the first of many visits to the Chinese capital, Patten expected to be on the receiving end of 'a half beating-up', but he was not in a mood to be cowed. 'I think there is a certain awe about dealing with China, which surprises me,' he commented, 'I think they are bullies in that they've got used, over the years, to other countries applying different criteria in their relations with China [from those] they use in their relations with others. I mean, why should one play the game by their rules?' His hope was that, at the end of the encounter, he would be able to invite Lu Ping and others to his country house at Fanling, near the border, for a follow-up meeting. What he was unable to judge, despite the intelligence available to him from Beijing, was whether the Chinese would want to talk seriously, or 'whether they will want to have a breakdown and say, "That's it. No point in talking about this any more. Good afternoon."'

Despite his reserves of optimism, it was hardly the most auspicious beginning to what he presumed would be the first of many discussions he would have with China over the next five years.

8

'RESTRAINT IN DIFFICULT CIRCUMSTANCES'

Britain and China at Odds

The governor's visit to Beijing for two days of official talks began with a snub. Lu Ping was not at the airport to greet him and sent a junior official instead. Every Chinese with a smattering of Confucian values knew that the message was unambiguous, and accordingly the incident was widely reported in these terms. The governor was resilient and affected indifference the following day.

> The press are frightfully silly about this business of snubs . . . Lu Ping had his first meeting of the Central Committee at the time. He apologised profusely when we met – actually while we were walking past the press – but nobody took a blind bit of notice. But even if there were calculated and deliberate snubs, the idea that anyone who has been through the British political system and lost his seat could actually feel frightfully snubbed by not meeting someone or other is preposterous.

This was not quite the point. Beijing's carefully calibrated attitude towards the Patten visit was calculated not so much to affect him personally as to define the significance the leadership placed on a visit by a wayward emissary of the outgoing colonial power. Patten was cushioned from the impact partly by his failure to appreciate the peculiar obsession that the Chinese have with 'face', and partly by his determination to negotiate on his terms and in his style, regardless of the niceties on which, in his view, the sinologists in the Foreign Office had focused for far too long.

The meeting with Lu Ping took place in a guest house at the

government's Diao Yu Tai complex for foreign VIPs. Patten arrived to face a battery of jostling cameras and journalists. He was greeted by a smiling Lu Ping, and the two men proceeded into an elegant chamber, preserving as much dignity as they could amid the almost uncontrollable media excitement. Patten sat opposite Lu Ping at the centre of an oval table, and their respective teams assembled beside them. They delivered themselves of a few pleasantries for the benefit of the cameras and then began a long session of talks punctuated by a brief luncheon. It was, Patten acknowledged the following day, 'six hours of pretty tough grind'.

Although to begin with the meeting with this 'highly intelligent man' was, according to Patten, 'infinitely courteous', their exchanges were rigorous. The governor reiterated his firm belief that his proposals converged with the Basic Law and were within the framework of the Joint Declaration ('I mean, their arguments that we're in breach of the Basic Law are pretty pathetic'), and that they were designed to secure the stability of Hong Kong. It was soon brought home to him that the Chinese disagreed, and that Lu Ping and his colleagues were even more obsessed with Martin Lee, with Hong Kong becoming a focus for unrest in China, and with the consequent threat to their control over Hong Kong, than he had been aware. He reacted by pointing out that 'if they really wanted to ensure that Martin Lee wins every election there is, they'll go on treating him as a demon'. It was also clear to Patten that the Chinese 'thought we'd pulled a fast one on them by finding ways of extending democracy indirectly'.

Lu Ping adopted what Patten called 'fairly familiar language' to charge the British with breaches of the Joint Declaration, the memorandum of understanding on the airport, the Basic Law and 'past understandings', about the last of which he was, at first, imprecise. Patten noticed that his counterpart had a written text before him which he was waiting to introduce into the argument. Lu Ping delayed reading from this until the late afternoon, and when he did so, Patten gained the impression that he 'toned it down as he went along'. At the end, however, the Chinese negotiator became rather emotional, and as the governor described it immediately afterwards, 'We had a bit of heat in the argument and the allegation that we'd broken understandings that we'd reached in 1989 and 1990.' This was the first and only charge which Patten felt unable to deny with confidence.

The 'past understandings' to which Lu Ping referred were the outcome of the secret visits made by Sir Percy Cradock to Beijing after Tiananmen Square, the subsequent negotiations and an 'exchange of letters' between the foreign secretary and the Chinese foreign minister in January and February 1990. The specific thrust of Lu Ping's case was that Patten's proposals for the Election Committee, which he'd announced in his speech to LegCo, breached these 'understandings', which Douglas Hurd, as foreign secretary, had reached with the Chinese government. It was clear to Patten that what he thought to be a 'rather false point' was one about which Lu Ping felt strongly. The governor's initial instinct was to ascribe this 'flare-up' to pressure from Lu Ping's colleagues demanding, 'How's this guy managing to exploit the Basic Law and the Joint Declaration? You were responsible for the Basic Law. Why has it got these holes in it?'

The meeting broke up in bad humour. Lu Ping stalked out of the chamber, pausing only to inform his guest that if the British could not stick to agreements they had reached in apparent good faith, then there was precious little point in any dialogue between the two sides. He declined to set a date for any future meeting. The British ambassador, Sir Robin McLaren, telegraphed London afterwards to impart the bad news: the session had been grim, the atmosphere appalling. Patten, who underestimated the significance of these 'past understandings' to the Chinese, was less pessimistic. Looking back on the talks at the end of the day, he allowed himself a modicum of satisfaction.

> When you know you are going to get a rough ride, it's quite encouraging to discover that even if you have no saddle and you are going over rather rocky ground, you know what you are doing. And the most encouraging thing of all is to find your arguments are pretty good . . . I've been to European Council meetings, having to put dreadful arguments on things like greenhouse-gas emissions – one against eleven. Now that's a rough ride, because you are arguing from a bloody awful brief. You know you are wrong and you feel cornered. If you feel quite intellectually well defended, even a rough ride isn't too bad. And I think – I hope this isn't vainglory – that I've deployed the arguments pretty well.

Whether or not Lu Ping's 'flare-up' was sincere, the issue which lay behind it was far more explosive than Patten had either imagined or was in an adequate position to appreciate. In all his briefings before he left London, no one had referred to any 'past understandings' or to a correspondence which the Chinese evidently felt to be of genuine significance: not one Foreign Office official; not the prime minister's adviser, Sir Percy Cradock; not Sir Robin McLaren, who had drafted the British documents; nor, indeed, the foreign secretary himself, whose political adviser in Hong Kong, Alan Galsworthy – on second-ment from the Foreign Office and the author of the FO 'bible' on Hong Kong – was similarly silent. As a result, Patten had devised his reforms in ignorance of the exchange of letters between Hurd and Qian Qichen that had in fact formed the most recent round of a pro-tracted negotiation about an important component of the most controversial issue facing Hong Kong.

It was only by chance that, a mere two days before the Government House team set off for Beijing, one of Patten's advisers, Edward Llewellyn, making a final trawl through the papers relating to earlier negotiations with China, came across a brief reference to a set of telegrams of which he and his colleagues had not previously been aware. Thus alerted, Llewellyn contacted the Foreign Office, where an official in the Hong Kong Department drew his attention to the exis-tence of this buried and apparently forgotten correspondence. It was at this point that Patten learned of the predicament in which he had been placed. It was, to put it mildly, a most remarkable gap in his knowledge, and one that he could not possibly acknowledge, at least in public. If the truth were to emerge, his colleagues in the Foreign Office, includ-ing those sinologists seconded to Hong Kong, would be open to the charge of negligence and the Chinese would be handed a devastating propaganda coup. In the process, his own credibility, through no fault of his own, would be severely dented, while the validity of his reforms would assuredly be called even more sharply into question, even by those inclined to endorse them.

For this reason Patten's only public reference to this embarrassing dis-covery was made fifteen months later, in testimony before the Foreign Affairs Select Committee. On 20 January 1994, he volunteered that his reforms had been the product of 'extensive' discussions with a wide range of people and 'some months of advice' from his advisers in Hong Kong and officials in London. He was asked by the committee's chair-man, David Howell: 'You had seen at that stage all the exchanges between Mr Hurd and the Chinese foreign minister, and these were known to you and your advisers fully?' Patten replied:

They were completely known to my advisers, because some of my advisers had taken part, not least in drafting the exchanges. I read in detail all the exchanges before I went to Peking for the discussions that I had with Director Lu Ping shortly after my LegCo speech. My officials, I repeat, were well aware of the exchanges and therefore they were taken into account in framing my proposals in the October speech.

This was not strictly true: neither Leo Goodstadt nor Mike Hanson, who between them had drafted most of the speech, had any knowledge of these contentious documents.

Patten's response was carefully crafted to protect his officials. To his relief, the committee did not take the matter further. Nobody thought to draw attention to Patten's tacit admission that he had not himself been aware of these exchanges in drafting his proposals, or to ask how, in that case, he could be so certain that they had been taken into account when he was preparing his blueprint. Nor was he questioned about when he had seen the documents, or how detailed his study of the material might have been in the few hours available to him before his meeting with Lu Ping.

In fact Patten had had almost no time to assess the importance of the secret negotiations which had led to the 1990 exchange of letters – and certainly not enough to prepare an informed or detailed rebuttal. As a result he went into the meeting prepared to counter any thrust from his Chinese counterpart, but knowing that he had little choice other than to treat the documents as if they were of peripheral importance. He could not possibly concede that his proposals might have been framed in different terms had he been in a position, three months earlier, to form a clear judgement about the status and role which each side had attached to them. Afterwards, Patten reflected, 'It would, I suppose – particularly when I was under a lot of pressure on all of this – have been easier to dump on officials and say, "If I'd known about this it could all have been different."' Although he was furious about this oversight, and it led him to doubt the competence of the relevant officials at the Foreign Office, he also castigated himself for failing to ask whether there were any agreements with the Chinese beyond those limiting the number of directly elected seats to LegCo, on which he had been fully briefed. Although his distrust of the Foreign Office was to grow, Patten was somewhat mollified when the head of the Hong Kong Department, Peter Ricketts – one of the few officials whom he both liked and respected – apologised profusely for his department's failure.

The importance of the correspondence was soon to become a matter of very public and acrimonious debate. Later in the year, the Foreign Office took the unprecedented step of releasing the full text of the disputed, and hitherto secret, papers. This decision was not taken, as the Foreign Office claimed, in the cause of open government, but to pre-empt a leak from the Chinese side. As it was, the British beat them by a mere four hours. It was enough time, however, for Mike Hanson to 'spin' the significance of the documents – momentarily, at least – to Patten's advantage. The British hoped, somewhat desperately, that by giving the appearance of openness they would avoid being put on the defensive by Beijing. In the short term the tactic was partially successful. Few people bothered to read the papers in detail, so, while the conflicting gloss put on their contents by the rival camps carried weight with their own respective supporters, most chose to interpret the row as yet another illustration of the propensity of diplomats to squabble over fine print.

The correspondence consisted of eight letters in all, comprising, for the most part, an attempt by both sides to find a compromise over the rate at which directly elected seats to the Legislative Council should be introduced. In the second of these letters, Douglas Hurd wrote, 'We are not far apart on directly elected seats,' which, it had been agreed by both sides, would reach thirty, or 50 per cent of the total, by 2003. Two letters later, in the same context, the foreign secretary stated: 'I am now able to confirm an understanding with the Chinese government.' Subject only to the proviso that the Chinese included their commitment to this understanding in the Basic Law, which they were already disposed to do, the two sides evidently had a deal. To this extent, the 'exchange of letters' clearly had the status of at least a heads of agreement.

The correspondence dealt similarly with the role and composition of the Election Committee. In his third, and most technically detailed, letter, the foreign secretary suggested five principles which he thought 'could best form the framework for creating an Election Committee system for the legislature'. These included the principles that the Election Committee should be as representative as possible, and that the procedure for the nomination by the Election Committee should be simple, open and prescribed in the electoral law. Nowhere, however, did the five principles prescribe that the 'representative' character of the Election Committee should be secured by a process of democratic elections. This was presumably why the Chinese foreign minister felt free to respond that, 'with regard to the Electoral Committee, the Chinese side agrees with the five principles proposed by the British side'. It must be assumed that for the Chinese, the 'representative' nature of the Election Committee could be achieved as effectively – and certainly more desirably – by a process of selection rather than election.

The British also argued that no member of the Chinese National People's Congress should be allowed to sit on the Election Committee. On this point, the Chinese foreign minister was adamant: the composition of the Election Committee 'should not be subject to change', because it had already been endorsed by the Basic Law Drafting Committee. In response, the foreign secretary noted: 'I agree in

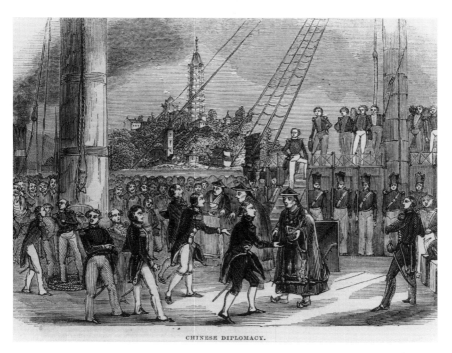

CHINESE DIPLOMACY.

The relationship between Britain and China has been characterised for more than two centuries by misunderstandings, disputes and skirmishes, encompassing the Opium Wars and an enduring sense of shame and grievance in China at Britain's seizure of Hong Kong. Illustrated London News

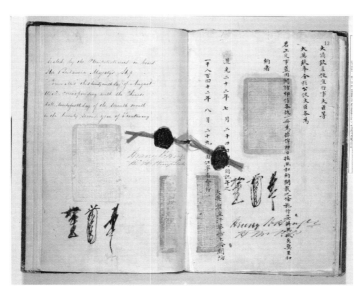

The Treaty of Nanking, signed in 1842, the first of the 'unequal treaties' under which the island of Hong Kong was ceded in perpetuity to Britain. Public Record Office Image Library

Hong Kong justice, circa 1900. Lawlessness was rife, but in their own way the expatriate community behaved no less deplorably than those over whom they held sway. Foreign Office

By the end of the eighteenth century, opium had become the most valuable commodity traded by Britain with China, where its use was commonplace. This contemporary cartoon offers a succinct comment on the relationship between the two nations. Bibliothèque Nationale de France

Aberdeen Street, 1846. Hong Kong remained a colonial backwater until the second half of the twentieth century. Expatriates protected themselves from its disagreeable aspects with a veneer of gentility. HSBC Holdings plc

Demonstrators plaster the gateway of Government House with posters during the riots of 1967. Day after day, thousands took to the streets in the name of the Cultural Revolution, and the authorities were close to despair. Hong Kong Government

The 'policy of co-operation' in action. Governor Sir Edward Youde (second right) and British ambassador Sir Percy Cradock at talks with the Chinese in 1983 about Hong Kong's future. Associated Press

Lord Murray MacLehose, governor of Hong Kong from 1971 to 1982. Hong Kong Government

Chris Patten's predecessor, Sir David Wilson, governor from 1987 to 1992. Hong Kong Government

Prime minister Margaret Thatcher meets Deng Xiaoping in the Great Hall of the People in Beijing in 1984. Associated Press

On 4 June 1989 hundreds of people were killed or injured when the People's Liberation Army forced an end to a student demonstration in Tiananmen Square in Beijing. The atrocity was to have a lasting impact on Sino–British relations and on the negotiations over Hong Kong. Associated Press

Prime minister John Major was obliged to become the first Western leader to publicly shake hands with Chinese premier Li Peng after the Tiananmen Square massacre when the two leaders signed a 'memorandum of understanding' on the new Hong Kong airport in 1991. It was rumoured that Major later came to regret the visit. Associated Press

John Major with his choice as Hong Kong's last governor in April 1992. Patten was the first politician to be given the governorship – 'If you are talking to him, you are talking to me,' Major is said to have told Li Peng. Hong Kong Government

The new governor arrives in Hong Kong with his wife, Lavender, and daughters Laura (far left) and Alice. Hong Kong Government

Chris Patten sets about his momentous task, flanked by the trusted personal advisers he brought with him to Hong Kong, political adviser Edward Llewellyn (left) and private secretary Martin Dinham. Robin Allison Smith

Patten's walkabouts, a novelty in Hong Kong, reflected the importance to him of public opinion. His 'charm offensive' did not please his critics, but it certainly enhanced his reputation among the people of the colony. Hong Kong Government

Open day at Government House. The cultivation of local and international media was another crucial plank in Patten's efforts to secure popular goodwill. Robin Allison Smith

principle with the arrangements you propose for an Electoral Committee which could be established in 1995. The precise details of how this should be done can be discussed between our two sides in due course. Meanwhile, I hope that the five principles to which you have agreed can be reflected in the Basic Law.' It was this 'agreement in principle' which formed the basis of – or the excuse for – China's charge that the Patten proposals had violated a clear understanding between the two sovereign powers.

While the foreign secretary could not be held to have made any secret deal, his 'agreement in principle' and his commitment to discuss the 'precise details' of how the Election Committee might be established for the 1995 elections, is clearly far from the non-committal exchange of views that the British side now tried to claim their correspondence to have been. Certainly, while there were important questions which had yet to be resolved, it was disingenuous of the Foreign Office to claim that 'at the end of these exchanges, the question of electoral arrangements in Hong Kong up to 1997 remained open'. Not closed perhaps, but hardly open. As Mike Hanson noted cryptically soon afterwards, the words 'agreement in principle' had caused the governor 'particular difficulty'. Hanson and his embarrassed colleagues now recognised that parts of the Basic Law had been drafted as if there had been an agreement between the two sides: a 'specific performance' to which contract lawyers, in other circumstances, would attach great importance.

The schism between Britain and China over this exchange of letters was echoed, discreetly but at the highest level, within the British foreign policy establishment as well. Six years later, Douglas Hurd was to maintain:

> [I was] amazed later to hear it suggested that that exchange of letters was thought to govern the framework for the second round [1995] of legislative elections. They never did in my mind. Obviously, we were going to need to consult the Chinese about the second round, but that was common sense . . . But I never supposed that my hands or my successor's hands were tied by what had happened in 1990 as to what would happen in the second round.

However, Sir Percy Cradock has insisted that at the time his interpretation of the letters was that:

> Both sides regarded them as of great significance. The Chinese finalised their Basic Law on the strength of them. And in conjunction

with the Joint Declaration of 1984, the 1990 exchange of letters constituted, you might say, a constitutional and political settlement for Hong Kong . . . and I venture to think this was the view of other figures on the British side at that time . . . There is no doubt at all that the thing was regarded by China as being a settlement on which they could build. And they were taken aback and felt they had been sandbagged when we said this wasn't a settlement, and we were going to do something else.

Significantly, Cradock's interpretation was to be endorsed by Hurd's predecessor, Sir Geoffrey (now Lord) Howe, who helped finalise the terms of the Joint Declaration. Choosing his words with the caution for which he has long been renowned, he said in 1996 of Patten's proposals:

I must say I was startled when I heard of the proposal to reshape and redefine the flightpath towards democracy which had been agreed in correspondence, which had been embodied, as I understand it, in the Basic Law as a fulfilment of the Joint Declaration . . . I think the attempt to change that by redefining some of the components – turning oranges into apples – could certainly be regarded as a departure from the spirit of the Joint Declaration.

Douglas Hurd is dismissive of that view, arguing instead that what really angered the Chinese about Patten's proposals was not so much their content but that their author had failed to conduct negotiations with them on the same terms as before. It is this issue, according to Hurd, which goes to the heart of the whole disagreement he and Patten had with Cradock. In Hurd's opinion it would not have been either right or possible to discuss these matters 'week after week, month after month, in secret', and to inform the people of Hong Kong of the outcome only at the end of a negotiating process from whose terms they had been entirely excluded. 'Certainly the Chinese had rights. They had the right to express a view. But they didn't have a right to insist that that view must be expressed in secret.' To which argument Cradock, supported by Howe in very similar language, has retorted, 'I'm afraid it doesn't lie with us to shuffle off responsibility for Hong Kong on to Hong Kong public opinion which we have helped to create. In the end, we are responsible for Hong Kong up to the last minute of the handover, and it's for us to negotiate with the Chinese. They will only talk to us. They will take no account of Hong Kong, LegCo or the like.'

Underlying this conflict was another, which was sharper and of greater significance. While Cradock genuinely believed that the virtue of secret negotiation was that it allowed the British diplomats to clothe their retreat to China's 'bottom line' with some dignity, Patten, supported by Major and Hurd, was equally convinced that open diplomacy was a precondition for securing public support in Hong Kong for whatever might be agreed in Beijing.

Whatever the case, there can be no doubt that the belated discovery of the 1990 correspondence caused severe embarrassment to the governor. Already committed to proposals for the Election Committee which had been explicitly rejected by the Chinese, he was now exposed to the charge that he had consciously ridden roughshod over the delicate understandings reached between the foreign secretary and the Chinese foreign minister. Moreover, he had been obliged to defend his corner against a sustained and angry barrage from the Chinese, who had at their disposal chapter and verse from the foreign secretary's own pen, which appeared to commit the British to continuing the dialogue between the two sides in a similarly confidential form. It was clearly open to the Chinese to argue that the same 'principle' applied, implicitly, to all the outstanding questions relating to the 1995 elections, not least the most controversial of them: the functional constituencies.

Quite why Patten was not informed of the existence of a formal exchange of correspondence dealing with matters of substance and sensitivity remains unclear. Douglas Hurd believes that there must have been an oversight by Foreign Office officials. 'Chris was not told of them, and I was not reminded of them,' he later recalled. 'It never occurred to officials that there was a read-across from one negotiation to the other. But they should have told him. I mean, he was a newcomer to it. They should have told him of that background, and they should have reminded me of that background.' Sir Percy Cradock, who had two meetings with Patten before the governor took up his appointment, has also acknowledged that he failed to raise the exchange of letters, but he claimed that 'everybody' knew about them, and that 'it was inconceivable that a governor going out to Hong Kong would not have had all of these documents in front of him, and have read them several times. And indeed, many of my comments related to them.'

Patten was not persuaded by Cradock's apologia. 'I think if they were significant to the democratic development of Hong Kong, it's amazing that Sir Percy didn't mention them to me, because he has an all-embracing knowledge of these matters,' he commented later, adding icily: 'Except, of course, that since he doesn't believe there's any commitment to the democratic development of Hong Kong, perhaps he put it to one side.'

It is common ground between Patten and Cradock – almost the only common ground – that Cradock warned the new governor against any attempt to increase the number of directly elected seats, but that he failed to explore with him the implications of tampering unilaterally with the Election Committee. Patten's only public reference to this failure was made, again, in front of the Select Committee. He said then, with strained jocularity: 'When we discussed the difficulties we might have in putting in place electoral arrangements . . . Sir Percy never said to me: "You can forget about any other ideas on political development, old boy. We have agreed all that with the Chinese side. That is all cut and dried. We have had these exchanges with the Chinese side. Everybody has agreed the way forward." '

In a letter to the Foreign Affairs Committee written soon after that testimony, Cradock stated that the main subject of his comments in their conversation had been the 'very limited room we had for manoeuvre, given the existing agreements, which we both understood as meaning in particular the Joint Declaration and the agreement on elected seats of 1990'. He went on: 'My remarks concentrated on directly elected seats because at that time [May 1992] they seemed the problem area. There was no inkling at that time of the plan to circumvent existing agreements.' Patten has since insisted to friends that he made it clear in the meeting with Cradock that he intended to 'look at' ways of reforming the Election Committee, but that Cradock – otherwise so free with his advice – dispensed none at all on this matter.

Although the issue refused to go away, Patten was never to take the view that his ignorance of the exchange of letters had any lasting effect on the crisis in Sino–British relations which followed his visit to Beijing. And in Hong Kong, opinion polls showed that the governor had not been damaged in this skirmish. Convinced from early on that any attempt on his part to establish a fair and open electoral system within the framework of the Joint Declaration and the Basic Law was bound to lead to a row with China in any case, he was unrepentant. Even if he had been in a position to take account of the correspondence in drafting his reforms, it is inconceivable that he would have been willing to modify them either in character or on a scale that would have had any serious impact on the conflict. But there can be no doubt that he would have accommodated the weight given to the exchange of letters by both sides: at the very least, as he has acknowledged to the author, he would have couched his reforms in language which made it clear that he was aware that there had been a set of significant, if indeterminate, negotiations, and that he was not insensitive to them.

On the second day of his official visit to Beijing, the governor met the vice-foreign minister, Jiang Enzhu, who was later to become Chinese ambassador in London. This meeting went no better than the one with Lu Ping, though it was much shorter. According to Patten, the Chinese made it clear that their opposition to his proposals was pretty much root and branch. At one point during a tough exchange, the governor could not resist reminding his interlocutor that, 'Hong Kong, unlike other places, is a place where there hasn't been any social turmoil or political instability for twenty-five years . . . And you worry about instability in Hong Kong in the future? My proposals are likely to produce even more stability.' The message was plain: the Cultural Revolution and Tiananmen Square had not occurred in Hong Kong.

That evening, at the end of an even frostier meeting with the foreign minister, Qian Qichen, Patten was told, 'After our prime minister, Li Peng, saw your prime minister in Rio, we had great hopes of you. But it is clear we have to discuss these matters at foreign secretary or prime-ministerial level in order to resolve these problems.' Undeterred by this put-down, which he chose to ignore, Patten commented afterwards:

> I just thought it was a sign of weakness. There isn't going to be any difference between what John Major says and what I say. And that's one of the things that bothers them, I guess . . . I've made it plain that co-operate means co-operate and consult means consult. Co-operate doesn't mean we'll do anything they want, and consult doesn't mean they've got a veto on anything. It's come as a shock.

Patten suspected that some members of the Chinese team may have wanted a 'complete breach' and to have walked away, which, he acknowledged, would have been unsettling. He was relieved, therefore, by the foreign minister's suggestion that the dialogue should continue, albeit in a forum which would exclude his own participation. Conceding that 'they won't give up, and, in that sense, I don't know where it will end', he had at least averted a total breakdown in communications. Or so he thought.

That evening Patten returned to the embassy to discover that the foreign minister's personal rebuff had already been reported to 10 Downing Street, where the prime minister had become so incensed on his friend's behalf that he had instructed the Foreign Office to withdraw the invitation to the Chinese vice-premier, Zhu Rongji, who was due to arrive in London for an official ministerial visit within the next fortnight. Appalled by the collapse of diplomatic relations which this would herald, a senior official in the Foreign Office at once rang the British embassy in Beijing in the hope of persuading Patten to try to talk the prime minister out of a decision which, he stressed, would 'send a deteriorating relationship into nosedive'.

Patten did not need to be persuaded. He was soon at the switch-board, surrounded by his own team and the British ambassador, who, summoned from his shower, was swathed in a dressing gown, his hair standing on end. Patten was unable to speak to John Major personally as he was chairing Thursday's regular Cabinet meeting. Instead he talked to Jonathan Hill, one of the prime minister's political secretaries. Expressing his gratitude for the prime minister's concern but his horror at what was proposed, Patten urged Hill to ask Major on his behalf to rescind his decision. 'What has happened today,' he told Hill, 'is that they have agreed to further discussions. They've been very tough, but they haven't broken everything off. We've actually come out of it pretty well . . . and not looking too battered and bruised.' He spoke slowly and deliberately but with urgency. If the Chinese were to be rebuffed in the way proposed by the prime minister, he said, 'I think it would bring matters to a head in such a way that it would be more difficult for me to hold public opinion in Hong Kong. It would be regarded with incredulity by the people of Hong Kong, as gratuitously offensive. It would actually lose me support rather than gain it. That is my very strong advice.'

The problem was, as Patten knew only too well, that once a prime-ministerial instruction has been issued it acquires the authority of an edict. The governor told Hill that if necessary he would take the first plane to London to explain his case more fully. 'I'd be very grateful if you would say to him that you hope nothing final would be done until I've managed to make my position clear. I think that would be fatal. All right?'

Within thirty minutes, Patten was in the embassy drawing room exchanging pleasantries with the ambassador's guest of honour for that evening's banquet, Lu Ping. Meanwhile his political adviser, Edward Llewellyn, was on the phone to Stephen Wall, the prime minister's foreign-affairs adviser, who had left the Cabinet room to take the call. Wall reminded Llewellyn that the prime minister's instruction could not easily be countermanded, explaining: 'The PM said that he knew the governor would object or protest that the PM had no need to go to such extremes on his behalf, but that we should go ahead regardless.' However, Wall, appreciating Patten's predicament, agreed to raise the issue again. Slipping back into the Cabinet meeting, he gave Major a note summarising the governor's views. When the prime minister was told that Patten was ready to bring his case to London, he relented, scribbling 'OK' on Wall's message. The immediate crisis was over.

Yet the signs were far from promising. From his vantage point in Beijing, Robin McLaren had been pessimistic from the moment Patten had decided to ignore the Chinese demand that he discuss his proposals with them in secret before announcing them to the world. Nor did he refrain from advising the new governor accordingly.

> I certainly made clear that they wouldn't like it. The Chinese were warned beforehand of exactly what he was going to say. Their reaction was, 'Don't do it.' It was inevitable that they would react badly once we ignored that advice . . . Now the governor was faced with a very difficult dilemma . . . but he was pretty well aware that the Chinese reaction would be extremely hostile. I think he probably thought he could wear that, but that in due course, after time and with difficulty, the Chinese might be persuaded to enter into discussions.

McLaren did not share Patten's optimism, but he did not attempt to dissuade him from the course of action he had proposed. 'You can give advice, but I think that the ambassador's role should not be, "You should not do this." That is, if at all, for ministers in London to do. The ambassador's role is to say, "If you do this, these are likely to be the consequences."' And that, repeatedly, is exactly what McLaren had done. It did not endear him to Patten's team at Government House, one or two of whom had taken to calling him, rather unfairly, the 'White Rabbit'.

Nevertheless, Patten's advisers were impressed by the performance of McLaren and his aides throughout the talks. 'We suspect that they don't like the governor's package very much, and that most of them are very uncomfortable with what's going on,' Mike Hanson confided after the first day of talks. 'They would never have recommended it, but they have been incredibly professional about it. Patten has had superb support from the embassy this week . . . One could have expected a lot of I-told-you-so noises from them, particularly after the meeting with Lu Ping. And we didn't have any of that.' And Patten himself was swift to acknowledge that McLaren had been extremely supportive.

The events of the previous forty-eight hours had confirmed all McLaren's instincts. As he waited to receive his guest, Lu Ping, the ambassador stood unhappily in the foyer of the embassy and forecast for the future record the next move from the Chinese side:

They will say, I think, 'If the governor won't listen to reason, then we will do our own thing in 1997. We will form the legislature in accordance with the provisions of the Basic Law . . .' In other words, you can do what you like in 1995, but there will be no through train. It won't continue . . . And then they will try, through their propaganda, to frighten LegCo off so that it doesn't pass the necessary legislation, and to frighten public opinion. In the meantime, they won't reach agreement over the airport, either. So there will be a feeling that there is no progress on any front. So it will be pretty hard for the governor to maintain leadership . . . The question is, will the Hong Kong people follow when the Chinese turn the heat on?

The ambassador's customary telegram to London reporting on the visit included these points, and was, according to its author, 'a description from me of the extent of Chinese anger that was exhibited during the governor's visit . . . saying that this is something we have to take account of in planning where we go from here'. This was not how his missive was interpreted by the governor, who, according to members of his entourage, regarded it privately as 'McLaren's surrender document', adding with heavy sarcasm that the part which he had most enjoyed was the advice that the British should pay reparations to the Chinese to make amends for their governor's egregious behaviour. According to his officials, Patten's irritation with the telegram lay less with McLaren's account of what had occurred than with his implicit prescription that, 'in the light of these grim circumstances, the only course of action I can see is to find out whether the proposals can be changed without surrendering their central character'.

The governor was dismayed by the British diplomat's eagerness to make concessions so quickly. He was also perplexed by McLaren's assumption that such concessions might secure an agreement with the Chinese, even if the proposals could be amended 'without destroying their central character', which he thought extremely unlikely. McLaren's view, which was widely shared by his senior colleagues in the Foreign Office, was that the governor's stance had been ill judged and that now, before it was too late, he should step back from the democratic brink to arrest the inevitable sharp deterioration in Sino–British relations. To Patten's team, the McLaren telegram embodied all that they most despised about the traditional Foreign Office approach to China.

Patten was furious when the broad thrust of this 'surrender document' somehow found its way from the Foreign Office into the British press. 'I don't honestly think it was Robin McLaren, but I think there are those in the embassy in Peking who've been muttering in that way,' he said. He was more irritated by the fact that more than one foreign diplomat in Hong Kong had told him, 'Some of our officials in Peking are critical of the approach we've been taking on Hong Kong.' He did not approve of such loose talk, especially as no British diplomat had offered such a view to his face. Was there no suggestion from any of them that he had got it wrong? 'No,' Patten replied.

He thought it imperative to conceal any friction in the British camp. Patten had left the Chinese capital secure in the belief that the embassy and his own Government House team had managed to put a constructive gloss on what everyone who had been closely involved recognised to be a damaging stand-off between Britain and China. Before going off to brief the media, Patten told Mike Hanson, 'You want them to say that we've done rather well to avoid a breakdown.'

Hanson suggested dryly, 'Restraint in difficult circumstances?' The governor laughed, and repeated the phrase approvingly in mock-Churchillian tones. 'We want to get the message out that . . . we've had a very severe exchange of views but the relationship is intact,' Hanson explained. 'We can talk to each other. We haven't taken the phone off the hook . . . that's what we want to get out, because all the instincts of the press in Hong Kong are to declare a breakdown.'

The only light relief in a dismal forty-eight hours came at the dinner for Lu Ping, when the governor accidentally tipped his pudding into his guest's lap. As the staff rushed to make amends, the governor rescued the moment by recalling a similar incident at Chequers in which Sir Geoffrey Howe was the victim. Margaret Thatcher had been swift to offer her commiserations – to the waitress.

As the governor's party departed for Hong Kong, Lu Ping held a press conference in which, for the first time, he publicly made clear the extent of the Chinese government's anger. In his 'post-visit blast', as the US secretary of state George Schultz had once described this Chinese ritual to Patten, the director of the Hong Kong and Macau Affairs office said:

We do not want to make public the differences between our sides. Before Mr Patten made public his policy address, the Chinese government said he should not make public his proposals. He should not engage in microphone diplomacy and he should not stir up a public debate between the two sides . . . Regrettably, however, Mr Patten simply did not take into account the views of the Chinese side. He believed he should make public our difference. Since he did that we have to do the same. In my letters to him I told him that if he starts to stir up an open debate then we have to participate in this debate . . . The essence of our differences is not whether the pace of democracy should be accelerated but whether there will still be co-operation or confrontation. If the other side insists on confrontation we have no other choice.

It was the declaration of diplomatic war which McLaren had foreseen, and to which Patten now had to find a response.

9

'THE CRIMINAL OF ALL TIME'

Beijing Campaigns Against the Governor

On 28 October 1992, a week after the governor's return from Beijing, a senior executive from one of Hong Kong's most important companies was invited to breakfast at the NCNA, Beijing's headquarters in Hong Kong. Afterwards he wrote a confidential note to his colleagues about what he billed dryly as a 'discussion among old friends', which was in truth used by his hosts to launch a sustained diatribe against the governor:

> They said that Sino–British relations were at the lowest point since the signing of the Joint Declaration. The main focus was on CP himself: 'He totally lacks sincerity. Had no understanding of China. No understanding of the background of a 150-year relationship and did not understand the character of the Chinese people.' They had warned several times through various channels against letting this situation arise and were very sorry about it as the losers would be the people of Hong Kong . . . It was a great pity that with relations recovering from the events of 1989, there now had to be this setback. The top leaders in Beijing were very upset. It was surprising to them that British business groups in Hong Kong had been appearing to support CP as his proposals would be to their long-term detriment.'

The threat this predictable view contained was characteristically blatant. It also signalled the beginning of a sustained assault against the governor with the clear purpose of undermining his credibility and forcing his departure from Hong Kong. In the closing weeks of 1992, the Chinese escalated their campaign, using ever more strident and vituperative language. Patten fought to maintain his public support while worrying his way through the narrow range of options available to him.

This public excoriation of Patten, which he chose to describe without great conviction as 'background noise', was peculiarly crude and, to a Western mind honed on the invective of Swift or Voltaire, faintly ridiculous as well. How was it possible to take seriously a regime whose mouthpieces chose to denounce the governor of Hong Kong variously as a 'sly lawyer', a 'dirty trickster' a 'clown', a 'tango dancer', a 'strutting prostitute', a 'serpent', an 'assassin', and – Patten's own favourite – the 'Triple Violator'. Lu Ping himself was quoted as saying that 'in the history of Hong Kong the governor should be regarded as the criminal of all time'. These insults seemed more suited to the bar or the playground, yet to patronise Beijing's rhetoric was to miss the point.

As a measurement of China's mood and its determination to unnerve the Hong Kong public, the shrillness of this diatribe, echoed day after day by mainland spokesmen or by unnamed sources in Hong Kong's Beijing-controlled Chinese press, at least demonstrated that the communist leadership was in earnest. Although Patten's personal ratings withstood the onslaught, support for his proposals slipped sharply. By the late autumn, as Sir Robin McLaren had warned, it was not at all clear that the community would stand by him. In a poll taken in mid-November for the *South China Morning Post*, 48 per cent of respondents, compared with 19 per cent a month earlier, said that Patten should abandon his package rather than proceed and thereby derail the through train. Likewise, offered the choice between the governor's blueprint and an agreement on the new airport, a choice which Patten had explicitly rejected, 46 per cent opted for the airport. At the same time the Hang Seng Index, which was monitored with all the care physicians bestow on a severe case of cardiac infarction, began to falter as investors either took fright or realised that it was time to play the market. Hamish McLeod, the financial secretary, was obliged to call a press conference on 19 November. 'I will just say that we must keep things in perspective,' he said. 'Investors should be calm.' But analysts took a different view, prompting the *South China Morning Post* to warn, 'MARKET BRACED FOR NERVOUS SWINGS'. For the first time, China had the upper hand in the propaganda war against Patten.

The chairman of Wheelock, Peter Woo, one of the most influential members of the business elite, had been consulted by the governor on several occasions, and his wife Bessie had become Lavender Patten's golfing companion. They were frequent visitors to Government House and the Pattens liked to think of them as friends. But Woo was also an ambitious man with a highly developed sense of his own worth, who, even by the rapacious standards of Hong Kong, enjoyed a reputation for ruthlessness which had endeared him to very few of his peers. Whatever his personal regard for Patten might have been, he did not allow it to cloud his judgement or perspective. Discreet to the point of opacity in public, he was more forthcoming for the historical record. The essential character of the relationship between Hong Kong and China, he insisted, was economic and financial. All the rest – democracy and human rights, though of course they were not without value – was of secondary importance. Any threat to Hong Kong's role as a 'conveyor-belt' for international trade was, by definition, bad for Hong Kong. The governor's proposals would, he feared, place Hong Kong 'in a very difficult position'.

Justifying the mounting, but still discreet, criticism of Patten by the business community, the Wheelock chairman explained that the effect of the stand-off with China was 'negative'.

> Hong Kong has its own economic agenda and this agenda is being disrupted. We hope that it is not severe. We hope that it is short. But that's hoping. And businessmen don't plan their businesses on hope . . . And that is why the stock market went down . . . It also affects banks. When banks feel uncomfortable they may go back to a borrower and say, 'Look, the margin has shrunk. We may need some more margin.' And this is a sort of momentum; a downward spiral.

At the same time, through the good offices of the NCNA, Beijing started to seed the thought in briefings for business leaders, newspaper editors and sympathetic commentators that Patten's departure was a prerequisite for the restoration of normal relations. As a result, the refrain 'Patten must go' was soon being whispered around the corridors of financial and commercial power. Vincent Lo, the president of the Business and Professionals Federation of Hong Kong, was swift to pass the whisper along. Although the BPF, which listed 130 of Hong Kong's most important companies among its membership, claimed to be non-aligned, it never strayed far from the Beijing stance. While very few of them would speak their minds openly, the luminaries on the BPF's Executive Committee were among Patten's most formidable critics. On 4 November, they had agreed a draft 'position paper' repudiating the proposed reforms and urging the governor to return to the status quo ante. When the paper was released a few days later, it was front-page news. Its publication confirmed the general impression that Patten had 'lost' Hong Kong's business elite. At a press conference on 9 November, Vincent Lo became the first business leader to voice the majority view: 'Democracy is important, but it is not the only goal. A smooth transition is more important.' In private, Lo claimed: 'Even people in the street are asking, "Is he really doing this for us? What is he after? . . . Why should we gamble our future when he says it is just a slight and modest increase in democracy? Why do we have to face all this?"'

As if that were not enough, the rumblings of opposition in the Foreign Office began to find a public outlet in Britain. Among others, the former governor Lord MacLehose emerged from obscurity in the same month to inform his colleagues in the Upper House at Westminster: 'I greatly admire the way in which Mr Patten has endeared himself to people in Hong Kong in such a very short time.' But, he added, they should know that the reforms he had proposed would be 'quite valueless' to them unless they could be carried through 1997. 'Having so much in common with the Chinese government over Hong Kong, is it not a great pity that this dispute has developed into what amounts to a major confrontation?' he asked witheringly. Patten's critics in the Lords were joined by a motley group of back-benchers in the Commons, members of his own party who had identified themselves as 'friends of China' and whose egos were heav-ily massaged by the hospitality bestowed on them whenever they visited Beijing. The most prominent of these was the former prime minister Sir Edward Heath, who was regarded by the intelligentsia in Hong Kong with some contempt. He was known to fall asleep at dinners given in his honour and had a reputation for delivering himself of the most portentous inanities, of which the most notable was his judgement of the Tiananmen Square massacre: 'Probably the students ought to have been told to go home before Mr Gorbachev arrived.' Heath was churlish and rude to those who ventured to prick his certainties with an alternative view of the gerontocracy in Beijing of which he was so inef-fably enamoured.

In this febrile atmosphere, Patten flew to London towards the end of November for a highly publicised set of meetings with the foreign sec-retary and the prime minister – both of whom, like the governor, had underestimated the Chinese reaction to the proposed reforms. Patten reflected ruefully, 'It's certainly at the noisier end of what we were anticipating. And that is, I think, because Deng Xiaoping is himself said to have taken an interest. There is some evidence that he's muttered a few words into his daughter's tape-recorder and that he has said there must be no compromise with the British.' On the other hand, Patten found it hard to believe that Beijing would manage to 'keep up the decibel count indefinitely . . . It's a problem to keep up the same level of hysteria for two, three, four years.'

The ferocity of Beijing's assault was disconcerting, but he was determined not to be swayed by it. 'I don't think one ever cares much for a storm raging around one's head,' he confessed, 'but on this occasion, since I think we're doing the right thing, I don't find it unendurable.' He was far more concerned about the brittle frailty of public opinion in Hong Kong. On the basis of the intelligence available to him from Beijing, Patten maintained that he knew 'for an eighteen-carat fact' that China was overtly blackmailing the business community with 'old-fashioned threats and intimidation'. The Chinese, he said, were warning them: 'Unless you denounce Patten and all his works, you'll have great difficulty in getting this or that franchise after 1997. You'll have great difficulty doing business in Guangdong.'

The governor was in no doubt that the business elite could be 'very dangerous'. It had the potential to undermine public confidence to the point where the wider community might conclude that 'the game's just not worth the candle. I am worried by the danger of them driving a wedge not between me and the UK government, but between me and the people of Hong Kong . . . I've also got to stop the sniping getting completely out of hand. I mean, there is a lot of "get the governor" in it all; the illusion that somehow it's my policy, and that if ever they get rid of me everything will return to normality.' The trip to London was, in large measure, designed to counteract that threat. 'It is essential to set in concrete the government's support for what we are doing and to prevent any backsliding,' he confided. 'I think the prime minister and the foreign secretary intend to manifest their support for me in a pretty straightforward way. I think the foreign secretary will want to make it clear to one or two people who are starting to suggest, if not that we offer reparations, at least that we should start throwing away bits of policy . . . that this is not on.' Patten himself was in no mood to back off.

I don't think that there is a great mystique about foreign policy, and about representing what you believe to be in your own interests. I think that diplomacy is sometimes identified as having a comfortable ride and avoiding rows and avoiding fuss, which isn't very sensible if you are dealing with people who don't care about having a fuss or a bumpy ride. If that's diplomacy, you always lose out . . . I think the

Chinese are bullies. I think there's a certain amount of awe in dealing with China, which surprises me. Why should one play the game
entirely by their rules? Why should one accept their definition of
what a 'principled position' is or what 'consultation' is? We wouldn't
do it with others, so why should we do it with China? If being a
sinologist is taking that view, then I'm quite glad I'm not a sinologist.

Although Patten's immediate predecessor, Sir David (now Lord)
Wilson, had been more circumspect than Lord MacLehose, he was
known to share similar reservations. Likewise, Sir Alan Donald, who
had preceded Sir Robin McLaren as ambassador to China – although
an altogether less substantial player than the others involved – made no
secret of his aversion to Patten. Sir Percy Cradock's bitter hostility was
also well known in Whitehall. One or two officials in the Foreign
Office had been so indiscreet that even the foreign minister of Canada
had got wind of the conflict within the British camp, a fact which,
Patten pointed out grimly, was 'pretty remarkable'. He had little
patience with any of these critics.

Presumably they think they left a policy which was in perfect shape,
which helped to produce this jewel in Hong Kong, and that what
I'm doing may wreck that inheritance. It's also possible, I suppose,
that some of them think that if the policy we're pursuing succeeds, it
may raise question-marks about the approach that's been taken in the
past . . . In the past the assumption has been that really China has all
the cards and that the bottom line has to be getting on with China
and accepting finally whatever China's world view is . . . I think it is
not self-evidently the case that whatever China wants, China must
get.

Indeed, oddly, if not perversely, Patten began to derive added strength
from his Foreign Office detractors. It was almost as if to be attacked by
sinologists was a mark of honour. As for dealing with 'old warhorses'
like MacLehose, Patten liked to borrow Stanley Baldwin's adage:
'When you've left the bridge, you shouldn't spit on the deck.' He
added: 'I think one or two of the most distinguished governors would
have been outraged if their predecessors had criticised what they were
up to. It just doesn't seem to me that that's an acceptable way of behaving in public life.'

Nonetheless, the effect of this muffled cacophony of offstage mutterings against him threatened to exacerbate Patten's difficulties. 'I shall
have a word with senior officials in the Foreign Office and the secretary

of state. To be fair, I don't think there are many people within the diplomatic service who are doing this. I think it's done by senior officials in London.' *The Times* noted with dismay the number of 'old friends' of Beijing who had clustered around the Chinese vice-premier, Zhu Rongji, whose trip to London, saved from cancellation by Patten's intervention, had been timed to overlap with that of the governor. On 20 November, the paper's leading article commented with acerbity:

> Many of them echo Peking's complaints that Mr Patten should have asked China's permission before lifting a finger . . . the real fear of these former architects of China policy is that the pusillanimous character of the advice they have been giving ministers for years will be exposed if he succeeds . . . Where Hong Kong is concerned, the old China hands have not exactly covered Britain in glory. They could usefully refrain from carping in the wings.

Patten was delighted by this thunderous support; the sinologists were furious. For Sir Percy Cradock, in particular, it was an intolerable slur on his reputation. He resolved to hit back openly, but in his own way and in his own time.

Behind the scepticism about his stance, Patten detected a cynicism towards the political future in Hong Kong. This mood was especially prevalent in the 'square mile' of the city, a significant proportion of which, in his words, appeared to believe the Joint Declaration to be 'just a frill, a curtain behind which Britain can withdraw, feeling modestly virtuous', and which did not for a moment imagine that the values it exemplified had any chance of surviving beyond 1997. Patten's tenacious belief that those values could endure was buttressed by two assumptions, neither of which could be said to be grounded in more than an imprecise optimism about China's potential to recast its political values in tune with a rapidly changing economic environment. The first was his confidence that the new leadership cadre emerging in Beijing could be less obsessively concerned about a vestigial form of democracy in Hong Kong. Secondly, while 'I don't think that we're about to see an outbreak of liberal democracy in China,' he found it impossible to imagine that economic reform would not have some effect on politics. 'I don't think you can open up the Chinese economy and keep an absolutely tight grip on political structures . . . It hasn't been possible anywhere else, so why should it be possible in China?'

Patten's adherence to the Western view that authoritarian and repressive regimes invariably succumb to the political imperatives of a market economy, and thus yield to one or another form of representative democracy, was to become one of his recurrent themes. However, he was to win few converts in a region where the 'Asian values' of the kind asserted by Lee Kuan Yew in Singapore seemed no less appropriate. Whether or not one day he would be proved right, it was, in 1992, a fragile base for optimism about China's intentions for Hong Kong. In public, he appeared to have committed himself to the expression of two contrary views about the Chinese. On one hand, he argued that they were to be trusted when they asserted that they would abide by the terms of the Joint Declaration; on the other, that they should not be believed when they threatened, quite unequivocally, to dismantle his reforms in 1997. Patten readily conceded that it was very difficult to have it both ways in the broad light of day.

> It's an argument which is best put on a dark night with a following wind. It is easier to develop in private, because you can say things like, 'Power structures will change in Peking.' If you say that in public, you are challenging them to deny it. You're also making it more difficult for those who will be, one hopes, a more liberal generation of leaders. At the moment they are under intense pressure to demonstrate that they are just as hard-line as the old men in the compound.

As it was, Patten was surprised that only one journalist thought to tax him publicly on such a blatant self-contradiction. Brian Walden, a renowned British television interrogator, identified the inconsistency in late 1992, yet, in the words of Patten's press secretary, 'He set the trap but failed to spring it.' The governor was greatly relieved.

As a pragmatic Westminster politician, Patten had an inbuilt horror of finding himself exposed by his own policies in unfavourable terrain from which there was no discernible means of escape. As a result he spent much time, with his colleagues, with friends and alone, exploring alternative routes, peering ahead into the unknown to reassure himself that whatever he did or said, there was always a way out, even from the worst alley. Despite his contempt for the siren voices urging him to withdraw his proposals, he had already started to prepare his ground for a partial retreat by the time of his London visit, hoping to discover ways in which a compromise could be created in the Legislative Council. The most likely area to do it would be in that of the new proposed functional constituencies, he thought, conceding, 'It would only be a way of shoring up a position. It won't satisfy China, because China's got herself into the position in which nothing except going straight back to the drawing board is satisfactory.' Yet he was hopeful that some such compromise might spike the guns of the business community in Hong Kong and London, and reassure the public that their governor was not bent on confrontation for its own sake. He kept these thoughts to himself, mentioning them to neither Douglas Hurd nor even his most trusted advisers in Government House. 'As soon as anybody thinks I've blinked, I'll be in big trouble,' he explained to the author at the time.

Despite the misgivings in Whitehall, Patten was encouraged to find that the foreign secretary remained robustly supportive. Douglas Hurd, dryly contemptuous of the mindset of the governor's detractors, admonished them as Patten had predicted. He was similarly dismissive of those British businessmen who now started to call in growing numbers for a rapprochement with China. 'There are people who stay in the Mandarin Hotel and listen to a few people and think they know Hong Kong,' he commented. 'They don't see that what is actually happening inside that amazing society is change. And when it is put under their noses they don't like it, because, of course, life would be much easier, more comfortable, if everything went on as before and there were no politics in Hong Kong. There *are* politics in Hong Kong, and ministers have to take account of that the way that *taipans* don't have to.'

The prime minister backed Patten unequivocally, but he had too many other troubles to concentrate for long on those of Hong Kong. John Major's government had just lost the battle to keep sterling in the exchange-rate mechanism of the European Union. Under pressure from currency speculators and despite the frantic efforts of the Bank of England, the pound had plunged through the floor, provoking a financial and political crisis of such a scale that the future of the government and the survival of Major himself had become a matter of intense public debate. On 16 September, the very day that sterling 'fell out' of the system, Patten had a private lunch with the prime minister at the Admiralty. Not surprisingly, Major was somewhat distracted; inevitably, from his perspective, the governor's difficulties were something of a sideshow. Although Patten correctly defined his proposals as being those of the British government, it was only his relentless advocacy that prevented the sinologists in the Foreign Office from devising a retreat from them. The bonds of mutual respect and loyalty which bound Major, Hurd and Patten together were virtually inviolable, but Patten was walking on his own high wire. Had he wished to descend, neither of his colleagues would have instructed him to stay put; by the same token, for as long as he was able to maintain his balance, they would be there as his safety net against those seeking to topple him. Patten returned to Hong Kong confident of this, and hopeful that a measure

of calm would be restored to the debate. Those hopes did not even survive the month.

On 30 November 1992, China suddenly announced that 'contracts,
leases and agreements, signed and ratified by the Hong Kong government, which are not approved by the Chinese side, will be invalid after
30 June 1997'. The £14.8 billion airport project was now joined in
financial limbo by an £800 million scheme to extend the cargo-
handling facilities in the rapidly expanding port known as CT9. A host
of other projects in the pipeline were also under threat. As all infrastructure projects and public utilities in Hong Kong are operated by
private companies under government licence, Beijing's edict sent a
chill through all the businesses involved in communications, transport,
gas and electricity supply, as well as the colony's radio and television
networks, which, with the exception of the government-owned
RTHK, were under franchise. The investment programmes of some of
the colony's most powerful companies, including Hong Kong Telecom
(Cable and Wireless's most profitable subsidiary), China Light and Fuel,
Hutchison Whampoa and Wharf, were in doubt. Theoretically, at least,
even the future of some hospitals and public housing projects was
uncertain.

The pessimism provoked by this announcement was exacerbated by
a report that the Chinese premier had written to the governor upbraiding him for provoking an 'open confrontation', and warning that if
Hong Kong followed his blueprint, there was bound to be chaos in
1997. Earlier, the politburo's mouthpiece, the *People's Daily*, had cautioned foreign investors: '[Those] who support Patten's proposals are
helping to wreak chaos and disaster on the people of Hong Kong . . .
Creating chaos will not only bring calamity to the people of Hong
Kong but will harm the interests of investors of every nationality.'

The icy wind blowing from Beijing dismayed investors. In the space
of five days, the Hang Seng Index fell suddenly by 1,000 points (almost
20 per cent), a crash which seemed to confirm Sir Percy Cradock's view
that the Chinese 'patriots' in Beijing would be quite prepared to inherit
a wasteland rather than permit experiments with democracy of which
they disapproved. Since China was a major investor in Hong Kong, and
especially in some of the companies likely to be worst affected, the
immediate consequence – as Beijing doubtless intended – was to
tighten the screw on the hostility of the business community towards
the Patten plans.

Early in December, Vincent Lo and some of his BPF colleagues
went to Government House to plead their cause. The BPF leader was

reticent about what was said, but later he confided: 'There was no meeting of minds at all.'

Immediately afterwards, apparently more in sorrow than in anger, he volunteered privately:

> Maybe it would be better for him to go . . . I think that unless he's prepared to withdraw his whole proposal and start from scratch, they will not be prepared to come back to the negotiating table . . . There is no way I can see the Chinese government trusting him or working with him in the next four and a half years . . . I think they really believe strongly that there is a grand conspiracy going on in the Western democracies to gang up on China. And I think that is a very frightening thought to them.

However, Lo felt that it was impossible for Patten to go back to the drawing board. 'His own credibility and his own reputation will be ruined. That is why I say that his interests and the interests of Hong Kong may not be the same.'

This was another emerging theme that found a ready echo, and not only in the Beijing lobby: that Patten had accepted the governorship only to prove that he was not a 'broken reed', to 'rehabilitate' himself before a Westminster comeback, to make a mark on the world stage or to 'salvage' Britain's honour. The common thread of these naively disparaging attitudes was that the governor had no intention of serving his full term, and that once his immediate task had been accomplished, he would beat a retreat to some well-paid bolthole in the West. Very little of this conjecture was uttered in public, but conversations about Patten's purpose and his future were the small change of the political gossip which flew from lip to lip in the conspiratorial atmosphere created by the impasse with China. Senior members of the pro-Chinese establishment began to speculate with incontinent enthusiasm about who might replace him. It was suggested by one or two members of the Hong Kong old guard that Sir Robin McLaren coveted the job, and there was even a rumour to the effect that Sir Edward Heath, whose adulation of his fellow gerontocrats in Beijing was much appreciated by the business community, would be summoned from Westminster to act as an 'honest broker' between the two sides.

Of the major companies in Hong Kong, Jardine Matheson, the colony's longest-established firm and still one of its most powerful, was virtually alone in distancing itself from this speculation. The Keswick family, which still dominated the Jardine boardroom, had themselves fallen foul of Beijing but had survived. In 1984 the chairman, Henry

Keswick, had authorised a decision to move the company's base from Hong Kong to the apparently more secure haven of Bermuda, which was widely and correctly interpreted as a vote of no confidence in Beijing. In 1989, after Tiananmen Square, Henry Keswick had used an invitation to address the Foreign Affairs Select Committee to denounce the Chinese government as a 'Marxist–Leninist, thuggish, oppressive regime'. It was no surprise, therefore, that the self-same 'oppressive regime' chose this moment to single out Jardine, the erstwhile opium-dealers, for denunciation. Although no one took the attacks seriously, Jardine's shares fell sharply amid a sudden fear that, after 1997, the company might find it impossible to operate effectively in the new SAR of Hong Kong.

The continuing Chinese assaults on Patten did cause genuine alarm, however. 'They really gave us hell last week,' confided Mike Hanson in December. 'They put immense pressure on the business community, from brutal threats to gentle persuasion . . . They panicked the business community, they panicked the Stock Exchange, they panicked a good proportion of the public and a fair proportion of the civil service.'

On 1 December Sir Percy Cradock broke cover to take revenge on his critics. In a letter to *The Times* defending the policies he and his colleagues had adopted before Patten's arrival, he argued that his policy towards China had been one of 'quiet but tenacious' negotiation,

> pressing hard, but avoiding open breaches and trials of strength for which Hong Kong will have to pay . . . Hong Kong's welfare depends on Sino–British co-operation. If that is a pusillanimous policy, I must plead guilty; and so must the ministers of two governments who endorsed it . . . The logic or fairness of the Chinese response is neither here nor there. What matters is whether they will carry out their threats. If we are sure they are bluffing, all well and good. If we believe, as I do, that they are serious, that is a different matter.

In an interview on BBC's *Newsnight* he went further. Without naming Patten directly, he warned that while 'it might allow us to strike a heroic pose', failure to co-operate with China would do grave damage to Hong Kong. To dismiss warnings that China would overturn the Patten reforms in 1997 would, he said, 'be a serious, indeed a fatal, misjudgement . . . I'm sure they would be ready to dismantle them and impose what they think is a safer system, which by definition means a more repressive system.' He added: 'To find anything like the same state of tension, I think I'd have to go back to the Cultural Revolution in the sixties.' In Hong Kong, it was universally assumed that Cradock was not speaking only for himself but for the Foreign Office community of sinologists of which, until very recently, he had been the most influential member. Echoing Beijing's complaint, the former adviser to Thatcher and Major insisted that British policy had been through a 'one hundred and eighty-degree change' from co-operation to confrontation and, he averred privately: 'If I'd still been at Number Ten when the change happened, I would, of course, have resigned.' The governor had, he asserted later, 'to use a neutral word', been 'incompetent'.

The foreign secretary, who was well aware of Cradock's views, was not impressed by either his timing or his judgement. Hurd held that the former official quite failed to appreciate how, in the wake of Tiananmen Square, Hong Kong had, without British prompting, become 'a political city as well as a money-making city'. He confided that the question in the back of everybody's minds was always:

Are we really going to try to make the Joint Declaration work? Are we really going to try to hold the Chinese to something which we know is very uncomfortable for them; which is gradually turning Hong Kong into a democratic society? Or is that rather a façade, something to get round an awkward corner? Sir Percy would have preferred us simply to find out privately, in secret, without any reference to people in Hong Kong, what the Chinese will accept on a particular issue . . . and then go along with that, present it as best we could.

This dispute between Hurd and Cradock, which predated Patten's appointment, went to the very core of the conflict within the government which had been simmering well before the new governor set foot in Hong Kong. Although Patten had been given a free hand by the prime minister, the foreign secretary's unequivocal endorsement of his approach sprang from a deepening conviction that Cradock was profoundly wrong.

I think if we'd followed Sir Percy Cradock's view, we'd have had a very minimal degree of democracy in Hong Kong – no guarantees, no likelihood of an independent judiciary or a free press, because his argument would have applied at all those points . . . If we had simply accepted that on every occasion we had, at the end of the day, to agree to whatever the Chinese were willing to do, it wouldn't be very long before Hong Kong would be indistinguishable from Shanghai, or perhaps even from Tibet.

In Hong Kong, lesser figures than Cradock took their cue from his public outburst against the government. Among them, Sir David Akers-Jones, a former chief secretary and still on the government's payroll as chairman of the Housing Authority, chose this moment to side openly with China against the governor. As one of those expatriates who had decided to live out his days in Hong Kong, Akers-Jones was not ashamed either to accept an invitation from Beijing to become a formal Chinese adviser, or to join Vincent Lo in publicly endorsing the BPF's criticism of Patten. Though past retiring age, Akers-Jones was by no means a spent force in Hong Kong where, in sharp contrast to Cradock, it was perceived that he genuinely cared about the colony. Fearing that the breakdown was serious enough to prompt the Chinese to move swiftly to set up an 'alternative government' for Hong Kong well before 1997, he let it be known that he thought Beijing's claim that Patten had gone back on an understanding with China was valid. While he conceded that the 1990 correspondence did not constitute a legally binding document, he claimed privately, 'Everyone I've spoken to in Hong Kong believes there was an agreement.' This judgement, delivered as it was by a leading figure in the British community nominally still in Her Majesty's service, had a corrosive effect; moreover, Akers-Jones was known to speak for many more who preferred to stay silent but not loyal. One of his fellow expatriates, a senior civil servant, commented, 'He evidently hasn't taken sufficient notice of the impact of what he is doing on the morale of the civil service. And how he squares what he is doing with the old-fashioned concept of patriotism, I do not know.'

Amid the mood of darkening gloom which in some quarters seemed close to panic, Government House appeared eerily calm. The impression was superficial: for the first time since Patten's arrival there was an atmosphere of real crisis. A mere six months into his five-year tenure, the governor looked exhausted, the ever-present bags under his eyes etched deeper and greyer than before. Though he stayed outwardly calm, in private he seemed sometimes on the verge of succumbing to the view that his venture was in deep peril. In early December Mike Hanson described how the 'boss' would sink into a sombre silence which cast a pall over the office. Patten, who was not given to self-pity, acknowledged that he had a tendency to 'talk myself down' as he surrendered to what he called the 'black dog' of despair. Hanson sensed that his reaction to intense pressure was not coldly to analyse the predicament, but to 'live out' its potential ramifications by saying to himself, 'This could go wrong next. How would we respond? How could we cope? What would it feel like to have to cope?' The self-mortification invariably worked: 'He comes out of the other end. He knows what might go wrong; he knows where the downside is, and he knows how he will cope.'

It was clear now that, in addition to the business community, the traditional elites from both the expatriate and the Chinese population were for the most part antagonistic. To make matters worse, the chief secretary, Sir David Ford, felt bound to report that the civil service, unnerved by the Chinese onslaught, were also 'no longer behind the governor'. As Mike Hanson, himself a senior civil servant, put it, 'There isn't a great deal of stomach for a fight with the PRC in the civil service. There is no doubt about that . . . They ask us, "Why on earth are you leading us into a battle we can't possibly win? You're prepared to make yourself heroes and save your own consciences. But it is we that are going to be here after 1997."'

Privately, Sir David Ford had been sceptical about the rationale behind Patten's appointment. As chief secretary under his predecessor, Sir David Wilson, Ford had been intimately involved in the events leading up to and following the diplomatic watershed of Tiananmen Square. 'Until that moment there was a developing relationship, a relationship even on personal terms,' he recalled. 'If one had a banquet with Chinese officials, one could expect to make good progress on the margins of that banquet . . . they'd talk about the Cultural Revolution and what had happened to their families.' After 4 June 1989 that atmosphere 'absolutely and totally changed', and these genial encounters ceased altogether, despite the most elaborate attempts to restore them. In Ford's view, the Chinese officials were both terrified of making 'mistakes' with the outside world and, by 1992, intensely suspicious of the political process in Hong Kong. In this context Ford did not believe that either Major or Hurd had given sufficient thought to the impact of a 'political' governor on the relationship with China.

Ford and Patten had met in London soon after the announcement of Patten's appointment, and the chief secretary had at once formed the impression that the new governor was 'a man with a real political reputation . . . a man who would find it extremely difficult to abandon his principles in a negotiation with China and simply give up his bottom line to find an agreement'. For this reason, he judged Patten to be the wrong choice for the job, and believed that Sir David Wilson should have been retained to ride the hostility of the democrats and continue the policy of accommodation with China.

Yet Ford conceded that the political environment in Hong Kong was rapidly changing. Nor was he immune to the argument that 'to engage in another secret negotiation would have made it very difficult to maintain confidence in the government'. Patten's appointment had represented a dramatic shift in the authority vested in the governor. 'You don't put a political heavyweight in, such as Chris Patten, and then start to second-guess whether he's right or not . . . It was a sea change in the whole channel of communication and the way in which policy was made.' Hitherto, however strong the individual, and however forceful his advocacy, a 'diplomatic' governor was in the end no more than 'another voice in Whitehall'.

Despite his misgivings, Ford was swift to appreciate Patten's virtues and soon became a loyal lieutenant on whose calm and measured judgement Patten, subjected as he was to a torrent of conflicting advice, came to place great reliance. Ford explained:

> This wasn't a headstrong governor who was overruling his offi-
> cials . . . He was extremely open to argument; he liked to have
> things discussed fully. He had no amour propre at all. He was a real
> person who accepted criticism and voices of dissent. And he was
> refreshing and easy to work with. One never felt inhibited from
> speaking one's mind . . . I think what shone through was his princi-
> ple and integrity . . . and he translated that into the Hong Kong
> situation in a way which was immensely commendable. I never
> thought for one moment that his interest was anything other than
> doing his best for Hong Kong.

For Patten, the situation was made worse by the fact that, with the exception of his wife Lavender, he felt unable to confide fully in anyone, or to share with them the weight of his responsibility. Far away from the Westminster club, he relied heavily on the occasional phone call or brief visit from friends in Britain. Only then could he to some extent unburden himself without risk of undermining the morale of his team. 'You can't help having the odd self-doubt, waking up in the middle of the night and not getting back to sleep again, night after night,' he confided. 'I wouldn't discount the unnerving nature of what's been happening, and I wouldn't underestimate the extent to which one does sometimes wonder, was it worth it? Should I have settled for improving my tennis and having a quiet life and giving in gracefully? But the way the Chinese are behaving actually makes me feel even more strongly that what we're trying to do is right.'

Convinced that he had to win, or at least, not lose a 'very important argument', he drew strength from the fact that, even if the elites might crumble under the threats and inducements from Beijing about their future prosperity, the people on the 'Wanchai omnibus' were still with him. Moreover, his support in the polls had recovered. 'It's amazing and cheering,' he said, as if to comfort himself, 'how much public support has held up. I wouldn't have been at all surprised to see the community simply upping sticks and heading for the hills as soon as the serious noise started.' He cited a degree ceremony at the Chinese University, where he had been guest of honour. 'There were twelve hundred kids and their dads and mums at the back,' and as he walked through their ranks, he reported gleefully, there was a 'sort of rippling of applause down this huge esplanade'.

The Pattens managed to maintain enough of a genuinely private life to keep self-importance at bay and Hong Kong in perspective. On the rare evenings when they were alone or with the intimate circle of trusted friends which they built around them, they dispensed with ceremony, if not with the service of their cooks and orderlies. As a family, they wore their hearts on their sleeves: opinionated, argumentative, affectionate and emotional, they were never constrained by any sense of internal hierarchy. Each voiced what he or she thought and felt, and did so with unabashed vehemence and persistence. If either parent was tempted to presume that gubernatorial status invested an opinion with particular authority or merit, one or more of their daughters would soon puncture that assumption, with affection but emphatically.

At weekends, whenever possible, they usually retreated to their 'country house' at Fanling. It was spacious without being stately: the drawing room was ideal for the family to sprawl in; a verandah overlooked the sloping lawn and there they sipped wine before lunch and sat in the evening. The Pattens used this semi-rural retreat as many other middle-class English families might: they played music, they swam in the pool, they lay in the sun, and in the evening they played tennis. After dinner, they would watch a film on video, usually chosen by Alice. Patten, who worked at his official boxes late into the night during the week, often spent his weekend evenings writing speeches or broadcasts and updating his diary, in which he recorded the confidential details of his governorship.

The whine and whirr of a helicopter fluttering down between violently swaying trees towards their front door signalled the end of their Fanling reprieve. Within minutes they were airborne, leapfrogging the traffic which snaked slowly towards the city. They flew back across the mountains, deeply shadowed in the evening light, over the tenements of Kowloon, skirted around the jets landing at Kai Tak and scudded across the harbour towards the helicopter pad on Hong Kong island itself, where a limousine waited to return them in stately fashion back to Government House in time for dinner.

The governor's advisers were still not sure quite how serious his predicament had become. 'It's difficult to know whether they will go on firing blanks – noisy blanks – or whether they'll try firing live rounds,' Patten noted. He was inclined to discount the plunge in the Hang Seng Index as the product of 'rhetoric, veiled threats and action by mainland firms and banks: you buy forward or sell forward on the futures market, and you drive the price down . . . We know that is what they have been doing.' Meanwhile the 'real' economy, which in Hong Kong meant the property market, had not been affected. Indeed, in the first week of December, one of the most respected credit-rating agencies had put Hong Kong at the top of the international league table. However, he feared that this might tempt the Chinese to 'rattle their sabres louder . . . by taking steps which would really hurt people's wellbeing – even, perhaps, undertaking "big military manoeuvres" on Hong Kong's borders'.

By this time the governor had been driven reluctantly to conclude that Deng Xiaoping did indeed regard his reform proposals as 'part of a global conspiracy to destroy the last communist power'. This disposition on the part of the ailing 'paramount leader' could only have been reinforced by the US decision to sell advanced F16 warplanes to Taiwan, reports that the Germans, French and Dutch were preparing to sell other armaments to the same customer, a visit by the US trade representative to Taipei and doubts about whether the new Clinton administration would renew China's MFN status.

His advisers now presented him with three options, none of them free of danger. The boldest, urged by both his constitutional affairs secretary, Michael Sze, and his private secretary, Martin Dinham, was to present his reforms to LegCo in their entirety. Another alternative, advocated by Sir David Ford, was to divide his proposals into sections and submit them to LegCo one by one. The third choice, favoured by some of the 'old guard' and by the British embassy in Beijing, was to go back to the drawing board in the hope of tempting the Chinese into reopening some form of constructive dialogue. Patten discarded the drawing-board option at once.

Look what I am being asked to do. Would they have connived at keeping Martin Lee out of the 1995 Legislative Council? Because that was China's endgame. I think some of them would have done. Lord MacLehose, who was here the other day, was criticising Martin

Lee – by any definition the most popular democratic politician in Hong Kong. Well, we've got experience of that in our imperial history . . . we went round the world locking up the Martin Lees. Would that have been a good way of finishing our great imperial story? . . . At what point do you draw the line and say, we can't possibly go beyond that?

It was far less easy to choose between the remaining options. Two schools of thought emerged among his senior advisers. One, according to Mike Hanson, argued: 'You must give something to China to head off this awful barrage.' The other urged the governor not to lose his nerve. If he were to start 'backing off', they said, the PRC would draw the conclusion that they could rattle him. The Hong Kong liberals would see this as the sign of betrayal they were anticipating and he might find himself with nothing but enemies on the Legislative Council. 'Get the reforms into the Legislative Council as they stand,' they insisted. The argument went back and forth, with 'all these things racing round in one's head', as Patten put it, until the issue came to a head at the end of that first week in December. Fearful that their boss was about to come down in favour of accommodation, Michael Sze, supported by Hanson and Llewellyn, submitted a paper arguing that Patten would be 'finished' if he were to adopt the option preferred by the chief secretary. If he put the proposals into LegCo piecemeal, 'China would pick off each element of his reforms, one by one'. Sze, a forceful advocate, was, in Patten's view, one of the most brilliant and courageous civil servants he had encountered. Nevertheless the governor was racked with doubt.

Far more cautious than his image suggested, he was tempted by the thought that the Ford alternative might reduce the intensity of the row with China. He was also tempted to propose a conciliatory modification to his blueprint for the functional constituencies. 'It's very difficult,' he confided.

If the parameters were different – if there wasn't this background of liberals feeling betrayed – I'd be, by nature, inclined to suggest a bit of flexibility in areas where I think our proposals will be changed in any case by the Legislative Council. But I feel very constrained about doing that. I don't want to fall down a hole in the middle. I don't want liberals to feel they've been led up the garden path and not to have any support on the other side, either.

It was only after a further protracted round of discussions at

Government House that Patten finally decided in favour of the 'high-ground' option: his reforms would be put before LegCo as one package. And it would be done as quickly as possible, on the pragmatic grounds that 'by definition, you are cutting down the time for trouble'. With the decision made, the tension at Government House visibly eased. Of course, the inevitable confrontation with China would be debilitating, but at least the issues would be fought openly and the choice would be made by the Legislative Council, whose members had recently shown themselves to be reassuringly unflappable in the face of Chinese disapproval. A fortnight earlier, they had debated a motion, sponsored by one of Patten's own appointees to LegCo, Christine Loh, which offered 'general support' for the governor's blueprint; after extended discussion, the motion had been carried by 32 to 19. The angry reaction from the Chinese leadership, which asserted through the NCNA that as an 'advisory body', LegCo had no right to approve a resolution which overthrew Sino–British agreements, left most legislators unmoved. Even if a majority of their number were likely to favour amendments to the Patten proposals, the resultant compromise would at least be seen to have been the product of a quasi-democratic process. And, as Government House totted up the figures, it looked as though the governor could expect to secure a small majority in favour of his reforms.

Patten was given another small boost when, only a few days after its collapse, the Hang Seng Index confounded the specialists by contriving to rise by 6 per cent in one trading session. However, he did not for a moment share the optimism of those financial analysts who attributed this unexpected recovery to the view taken by European investors that the Sino–British conflict would soon blow over.

The excitable Allen Lee expressed his own pessimism in apocalyptic terms – although, for the time being, he shared it only with his fellow members of the CRC. In no doubt that Hong Kong now faced a 'disaster' that could only be resolved by a Sino–British summit, he warned confidentially that the Chinese would set up a shadow government in Hong Kong, which would undermine the current government.

> Chris Patten's power will be gradually diminishing. In other words, the people of Hong Kong will not listen to him any more . . . I am told that they are drafting such a proposal already in Beijing . . . And they will implement it – I'm a hundred per cent certain of that – because they can't work with the British any more . . . It's a disastrous situation for Hong Kong, for Britain and for China. And for what? For a few seats in the legislative assembly.

Lee was so agitated by this prospective calamity that he wrote to John Major seeking an urgent meeting. A few days later he said heatedly:

> The prime minister has got to answer me. And don't tell me he hasn't got time for us over this great impasse between the two countries. If he doesn't want to see us, that leads me to the conclusion that they don't give a damn about Hong Kong and the Hong Kong people; that they don't want to handle it, and they will let Chris Patten do his thing . . . The British rule over Hong Kong will be completely finished and the Chinese hand will be over Hong Kong. If Chris Patten goes on in this way – I put it very grossly – he is digging his own grave.

In his barely suppressed panic, Allen Lee not only spoke for a significant constituency in Hong Kong but also had access to senior members of the Chinese government. Chris Patten, who was well aware of this, recommended to Downing Street that the leader of the CRC should be granted his prime-ministerial audience. Lee could not easily be dismissed as a mere hysteric. The dry-eyed chairman of the Hong Kong Bank, Sir William Purves, was no less critical of British policy, although, as one of the advisers appointed by Patten to his Executive Council, he refrained from saying so for the time being. In private he was scathing about Patten. According to Allen Lee, Purves had recently approached him saying, 'Come on, you've got to provide him with a ladder to climb down.' Lee replied, 'Look, the governor doesn't want a ladder. You must know that.'

Patten had resigned himself to the prospect that Allen Lee would 'go public' after his meeting with Major, which had been arranged for the New Year, but he was taken by surprise when a figure of far greater stature and influence in Asia chose to abuse the conventions of international diplomacy by joining the onslaught against him. On 12 December 1992, the governor was at the Hong Kong University to welcome the senior minister of Singapore, Lee Kuan Yew, who had been invited there to address a gathering of the colony's leading figures. Patten had met Singapore's 'strong man', as he was usually described in the international press, on his way to Hong Kong nine months before. Somewhat in awe of Asia's eminence gris, the new governor had allowed himself to overlook Singapore's abysmal human-rights record, which had earned Lee Kuan Yew a long-established place in Amnesty International's pantheon of states which routinely violated the guiding precepts upon which Hong Kong's unique 'way of life' had been so painstakingly constructed.

Patten's illusions about Lee Kuan Yew were rapidly demolished. The cold venom with which Asia's elder statesman consigned the governor's proposals to the ashcan of history left his host visibly taken aback. 'I have never believed that democracy brings progress,' Lee Kuan Yew informed his admiring audience. 'I know it to have brought regression. I watch it year by year, and it need not have been thus.' In a reference to the recent attacks on Patten by Cradock and others, he commented with arch sarcasm:

> I have been intrigued in the last few days by some very unusual developments, to me unthinkable. Three British professional diplomats, all retired, have come out to state their position on Hong Kong against their political masters. I am truly amazed . . . I think they are signalling something desperately to their political masters – that they have misjudged the situation . . . I therefore expect a real scrap in Hong Kong.

Patten endured this and more in the same vein in silent fury. When the Singaporean leader had finished, he commented, with an irony which most of the audience seemed to miss, 'I hope that some time, perhaps after 1997, I shall have the right of reply . . .' He paused. 'Maybe in Singapore.'

By the end of 1992, it could not be said that the governor relished the prospect of his remaining four and a half years in Hong Kong. 'Deo volente,' he noted wearily, 'I strongly suspect that I'll be here until the thirtieth of June 1997. I try to brace myself up in the morning. It's something I'm not greatly looking forward to, but it's got to be done.'

10

'PEBBLES IN A BLACK HOLE'

Talks About Talks

On 2 February 1993, Chris Patten entered Queen Mary's Hospital in Hong Kong for heart surgery. For several weeks he had complained of extreme tiredness, which he attributed to stress and overwork. However, his family had a history of heart disease (both his parents had died of heart attacks) and the prospect that he too might be affected by it often hovered in the back of his mind. Although he took regular exercise – strenuously on the tennis court – he was significantly overweight. By his own admission, he ate too much of the kind of food of which health enthusiasts disapprove and enjoyed liberal quantities of good wine.

One Sunday in January, he and Lavender were invited for lunch and tennis at a friend's house. Halfway through the match, he was forced to stop playing and lie down beside the court, suffering from what he at first presumed to be acute indigestion brought on by an indulgent lunch of boeuf bourguignon and claret. When the pain became more severe, he decided to return to Government House, where a team of doctors was summoned. They immediately gave him an ECG, which revealed nothing, and a blood test, which showed that he had had an 'episode', though whether it was a full heart attack remained unclear. They told him that he should go into hospital at once for further tests. Anxious to fulfil a dinner engagement the following night with Sir Charles Powell, the former foreign-affairs adviser to Margaret Thatcher, and now a director of Jardine Matheson, he refused. The specialists debated whether to insist, or whether to allow him to remain at his post, a deliberation that was interrupted by a Patten family holiday in Bali over the Chinese New Year.

On his return to Hong Kong, still feeling listless and weary, Patten told the doctors that he had suffered from sunburn but had enjoyed several vigorous walks. Evidently aghast at his folly, they prevailed on him to go into hospital at once, a prospect which filled him with foreboding. They asked him to take a treadmill test, which confirmed within seconds that, in his words, 'something was seriously wrong'. With reluctance, he agreed to undergo a full examination, which revealed that his arteries had 'furred up' and the blood supply to his heart was severely constricted. He had feared that the doctors would recommend a coronary bypass, but the medical team at Queen Mary's decided that they could restore his arteries to full function using the far less taxing procedure of angioplasty. The operation was routine, if disconcerting, but Patten was aggrieved at having to be out of action for even a few days.

The announcement that the governor was to have angioplasty, the medical details of which were explored in colourful detail by the media, provoked a rash of speculation about both the physical causes of his condition and the strain he had been under during the previous few months. The director of the Hong Kong branch of the NCNA, Zhou Nan, whose diplomatic skills had been honed as an interrogator of British prisoners in the Korean War, and whom Patten regarded as a 'nasty piece of work', momentarily suspended his vendetta against the governor to send him best wishes for a quick recovery. Not all of his adversaries were so cordial. In a characteristically vinegarish commentary, T.S. Lo, one of Beijing's official 'advisers', and the owner and editor of *Windows*, a virulently anti-British weekly magazine, suggested to his readers that the angioplasty was Patten's way out of the diplomatic dead end into which he had led himself. Others, who were unnamed, speculated that Patten's condition had provided the British government with a heaven-sent excuse to replace its troublesome plenipotentiary with a figure more amenable to China.

On his admission to Queen Mary's, Patten pledged publicly to stay on as governor until 1997, and his spokesman was repeatedly quoted accordingly. Yet the possibility of his demise had enough resonance in the financial world to produce a rush of buyers for Hong Kong stock in London, with the result that the local closing prices were driven upwards. The going rate for a photograph of Patten on a stretcher was also rising. In pursuit of a fee said to be in the region of HK$400,000, Hong Kong's paparazzi embarked on a form of guerrilla warfare with the hospital security guards. They hid in corners, they climbed scaffolding, they tried bribery, but they failed to hunt down their quarry. After only two days he was out of hospital, and within a fortnight he was back at his desk.

After a lull in hostilities over the Chinese New Year, the conflict was soon resumed in earnest. Deng Xiaoping himself issued a warning (contained in a report from the Central Military Commission, published on 17 February 1993) that China might break its pledges on Hong Kong if Patten refused to withdraw his reforms. The Chinese leader was further quoted as saying that the proposals were part of a Western 'plot' to wage a 'new cold war' against China. He had ordered a harsh policy towards Britain because he believed London's aim was to 'internationalise' Hong Kong and to turn it into a political entity that could not be controlled by China. The conventional wisdom in Hong Kong was that Patten would find it excessively difficult to extricate himself from this impasse.

Just before Christmas, Patten had committed himself to introducing his proposals into the Legislative Council early in February in the belief that, suitably amended to reduce the ferocity of Beijing's objections, they would be on the statute book before the end of the 1993 session in June. Accordingly, the proposals were drafted into legislative form by the end of January. Early in February, the governor's appointed advisers on ExCo endorsed the bill, despite the private opposition of at least three members and the doubts of others. At this point, the British ambassador, Robin McLaren, was instructed to take a copy of the bill into the Foreign Ministry and the Hong Kong and Macau Affairs Office in Beijing with separate accompanying letters from the foreign secretary and the governor which explained the proposed legislative procedure and reaffirmed the readiness of the British side to hold talks. They informed the Chinese that the bill would be 'gazetted' (published, but not tabled for debate in LegCo) a few days later, on 12 February.

A few hours before this deadline, the Chinese Foreign Ministry delivered their response to Douglas Hurd's letter. Beijing was willing to talk 'on the basis of the Joint Declaration, the Basic Law and the understandings between us'. Suspicious of the ministry's motives but cautiously encouraged, Patten decided that he had no alternative but to postpone publication of the bill. On 16 February, the British contacted the Chinese Foreign Ministry to express their pleasure at this development and to inform Beijing that the British team would be led by Robin McLaren and would include a number of named officials of the Hong Kong government. The British proposed that the first round of talks should begin on 24 February, in order to ensure that the Hong Kong authorities could meet the legislative timetable required to establish a new constitutional framework in time for the 1995 elections.

At this point the diplomatic lines to Beijing suddenly went dead.

According to Patten, 'It was like throwing a pebble into a black hole. There was obviously a debate going on in Peking, and I think there were some efforts by Zhou Nan to kibosh the whole process.' The governor now postponed publication of the bill for the second time. Against a background of public anxiety about this delay, he decided, on 26 February, on yet another postponement because, as he explained, 'I felt we had to be falling over backwards to appear to be giving every opportunity for the Chinese to talk.' Patten's suspicion that the hold-up in Beijing was caused by divisions in the Chinese hierarchy was confirmed unofficially (though not to him) by Tsang Yok Sing, the influential leader of the pro-Beijing Democratic Alliance for the Betterment of Hong Kong (DAB). In his role as an official adviser, the DAB leader had attended a 'summit meeting' in Guangzhou, where it became clear that the 'doves', led by Lu Ping, were keen to develop the dialogue with the British, while the 'hawks', led by Zhou Nan, the most ardently anti-British of any Chinese official, wanted to end it. The businessman Vincent Lo, who was also at the meeting, confirmed Tsang Yok Sing's analysis.

It was another two weeks before the Chinese broke what the governor dryly referred to as their 'radio silence' to reiterate their willingness to negotiate. They insisted, however, on a number of preconditions – 'trivial debating points', they seemed to Patten – which included the demand that the proposed talks should not merely be confidential, but that their very existence should remain a carefully guarded secret. The British responded to this with some impatience, telling the Chinese Foreign Ministry, as Patten put it: 'You must be joking. You can't make the existence of these talks secret, because everyone will know they are going on. If senior officials are seen at Kai Tak Airport clutching tickets for Peking, nobody's going to think they are going up there to see their mothers-in-law. It's inconceivable that you can have talks in secret.' Beijing also disputed the right of the British side to include Hong Kong officials in its negotiating team, insisting that, since formal talks could only take place between the two sovereign powers, no servant of the Hong Kong government was entitled to a place at the table. 'It was a rather elaborate, theological point,' Patten commented at the time, 'and you certainly couldn't explain it to a Martian. You couldn't actually explain it to any rational human being.'

So far these manoeuvres had been conducted without any public explanation of what was afoot. Always aware of the need to maintain public support, and acutely sensitive to the suspicions of the liberals that he was going to back away from his commitment to democracy, Patten now felt he could no longer hold the line against a growing public feeling that a deal was indeed being concocted in secret. Unable to stall members of LegCo any longer, he decided that he would have to give them a 'bowdlerised version' of what was going on. On 3 March, in a local television interview, he reiterated, albeit guardedly, his own readiness to talk to Beijing on a basis which would not exclude the alleged 'understandings' contained in the 1990 exchange of letters. This prompted an immediate response from the United Democrats. Though he was very much more discreet in public, Martin Lee was alarmed.

It's really a repeat performance of the Percy Cradock era . . . The only conclusion I can draw is that he is backing down . . . They have deferred gazetting the bill for three weeks now – and we don't even know when the bill will reach us, because the moment they sit down and talk, and if they should arrive at some sort of agreement, then the actual bill will be presented to us according to the agreement, and no longer according to the Patten proposals. I think they are giving in to the Chinese side too much, even before they sit down.

Even so, Martin Lee was somewhat more disposed than his colleagues to give Patten the benefit of the doubt: 'Hopefully he will have the courage in the crucial moment to tell the Chinese, "If you insist on such a bad deal I will not continue with these negotiations but simply present the bill to LegCo and let LegCo decide." But that takes a lot of courage. Once you sit down, you get sucked into the process. Experience tells us that it is very difficult to break off.'

Patten was concerned that Martin Lee would soon broadcast his party's fears, a prospect which put additional pressure on him to maintain a momentum that the Chinese seemed determined to frustrate. 'We've got to deal first of all with the incessant suspicion of the liberals that the British always lose when they negotiate with China, that Hong Kong will be cut out of the debate, and that you can't trust perfidious Albion,' he complained as he and his team prepared three alternative statements for his LegCo appearance the following day. He had to choose between saying, 'There will be no talks, and the bill will be gazetted forthwith,' or, 'Yes, we are going to talk and the date is this,' or, 'I think we will talk – there are just minor points of detail to be worked out, and the sooner we can get a response on these minor points from China, the better.'

In the absence of any word from Beijing, he decided to plump for discretion rather than valour by choosing the third option, on the grounds, yet again, that he had to be able to demonstrate to the community that he could not have tried more; that he had gone the extra mile. As well as informing LegCo that the publication of the bill would be postponed again (an announcement which inevitably provoked headlines the following day of the 'PATTEN'S CREDIBILITY AT STAKE' variety), he used his statement to signal to the Chinese that he would accept Beijing's precise formulation of the terms on which any talks should take place, which included the pertinence of the 1990 exchange of letters.

At this stage Patten was optimistic that his concession would allow the two sides to 'wind up everything in another couple of meetings', and confident that the opening of negotiations would be announced the following week. Once again, though, he was foiled when Sir Robin McLaren (described by Martin Lee as 'a good civil servant, but every cell in his body is Percy Cradock') and Jiang Enzhu (described by Patten as China's 'extremely plodding, bureaucratic vice-foreign minister') became bogged down in an arcane and lengthy debate. It concerned the two unresolved – and what an exasperated governor now called 'ridiculous' – issues: the 'secrecy' of the prospective talks, and the composition of the British team at them.

In themselves the details of these exchanges are of such inconsequence that they are worth exploring only because they reveal something of what was involved in attempting to open serious negotiations on the future of Hong Kong. On 11 March, after five further days of 'talks about talks', the British minister of state, Alastair Goodlad, was finally driven to summon the Chinese ambassador to the Foreign Office to inform him that unless Beijing could agree these outstanding questions by the following day, the governor would go ahead and publish his bill. According to Patten, Goodlad also told Ma Yuzhen that 'the question of membership of the British team wasn't negotiable. We weren't going to change the basis on which previous talks had taken place.' The following morning in Beijing, McLaren and Jiang Enzhu had another marathon session at which, McLaren reported, the Chinese agreed that they would not insist on differentiating between the London and Hong Kong members of the British team. On that basis, Patten decided to extend his deadline by one more day. That same afternoon, however, the 'hard men' in Beijing, as Patten called them, evidently regained the upper hand: Jiang Enzhu contacted the British embassy to inform McLaren that the Chinese side had, on reflection, decided to withdraw their 'concession'. His government was not now willing to permit the Hong Kong members of the British team to be treated on an equal footing in the negotiations.

To break this deadlock, the governor suggested a compromise: the British would not make any public statement about the role allotted to individual members of the negotiating team, and only if pressed would he or his colleagues feel obliged to say, in effect, that there was no apartheid on their side. If the Chinese wished to describe McLaren's team as advisers and experts, the British would refrain from contradicting them. This attempt to fudge the issue failed absolutely. 'We got nowhere,' revealed Patten with a mixture of incredulity and relief.

These fruitless exchanges over status and nomenclature had now lasted a full fortnight, forcing Patten into yet another postponement and prompting the *Hong Kong Standard*, among others, to assert that if the governor dared to announce another such deferral, 'his credibility and the leadership of the government would fall through the floor'. Patten had in any case already decided that he could delay no longer: the more or less secret 'talks about talks' had now lasted for more than six weeks. 'If the talks about talks were going to be like that, I hate to think what the talks themselves would have been like,' he commented.

The Patten bill was duly published on 15 March to a predictable display of outrage from the Chinese. The first blast was delivered by a spokesman from the NCNA in Hong Kong, who declared that there was now no basis for talks between the two sides. The following day, far more seriously, the Chinese premier, Li Peng, in the strongest language yet publicly deployed by the Beijing leadership, denounced Patten for 'perfidiously and unilaterally' crafting proposals designed to alter Hong Kong's political system. Deng Rong, a daughter of Deng Xiaoping, added weight to this peculiarly personal onslaught by saying that the Sino–British row had been entirely the governor's fault. According to Zhou Nan, Britain now had no way out of the controversy. By common consent the intensity of the Chinese response reflected a genuine rage, at least among the Beijing 'hawks', at Patten's temerity. The Hang Seng Index, which had partially recovered from its December fall, reacted by plummeting 201 points (a drop of almost 4 per cent) in thirty minutes.

Patten's public response to the attack by Li Peng was to remonstrate mildly that the interests of Hong Kong were not served by 'excessive language'. Inside Government House, he and his team assessed the situation. Of one thing they were certain: further delay would have been impossible. 'Each week we had to send my press spokesman or even me to the gate to say, "Er . . . um . . . sorry, it's not this week."' The decision to publish the bill had been made only after close consultation with Douglas Hurd: 'If the foreign secretary had thought we were up the pole, he or the prime minister would have said so,' the governor commented. 'In the last twenty-four hours, when London was asleep, we had absolute carte blanche to play the hand.' Although it had been a finely balanced decision, he insisted, 'I don't think there was anybody among my advisers – anybody at all – who thought that another deferral was an option . . . I'm absolutely sure that we'd have been finished, or at least badly wounded.'

Although he was reluctant to admit it, the governor had already compromised his December position. At that time he had been determined to have the bill debated in February. Six weeks later, he reflected ruefully:

> If we had put the bill into the Legislative Council back in February, we'd now be in the middle of a huge ding-dong, but at least things would be happening, and people would have to accommodate themselves to reality rather than rhetoric. But we really, I think, never had a choice, because we're endlessly having to manoeuvre to keep in touch with the middle ground of the community, and that keeps changing . . .

Indeed, the volatility of the community was a major preoccupation at Government House; of greater importance than the condition of the Hang Seng Index, and of no less concern than the diatribes from Beijing. At the end of March, Patten was dismayed by polling evidence which seemed to show that the people of Hong Kong were in 'a pretty odd mood'. While they still supported his reforms, they were divided about whether he had been right to call off the 'talks about talks' merely on the question of the status of Hong Kong's representatives at the negotiating table. For the first time since his arrival in Hong Kong, the governor felt that he had misjudged the community's resolve, and that he was now 'on the back foot'. However, he was certain that he would have been 'shredded' if he had accepted the Chinese terms. He was resigned to the conclusion that, in their confusion and ambivalence, people were bound to 'criticise us for not having a bottom line until we stand on one, at which point they will say, "Perhaps we didn't mean that."'

As evidence of this frustrating mood, Patten cited a member of his Executive Council who had insisted that the question of who should represent Hong Kong at the talks should be non-negotiable. Following the breakdown of the 'talks about talks', the same stalwart suddenly changed his ground, suggesting, 'Maybe we've made too much fuss about representation. Maybe we can look at it again.' Patten remonstrated with him, reminding him of what he had said with such conviction seven days before. 'Ah,' his adviser said, quite unembarrassed. 'That was last week.'

Even more blatant was the volte face made by Allen Lee, who, before the breakdown, had urged Patten to gazette his bill on the basis that 'he could not wait for ever'. Now Lee condemned him for following that very advice: the governor, he complained, had not given himself enough time 'to find out if the Chinese were sincere – which, in my view, they are'. Lee's gyrations provoked some derision in the media, and led one cartoonist to portray the senior legislator as a toad (adding insult by offering apologies to the toad, which, the cartoonist explained helpfully, at least had a backbone). Allen Lee was indignant, not, he claimed, at the imagery, but at the implication: 'I'd rather be accused of being pro-China than pro-British, because I am Chinese. I was furious because I think I am working in Hong Kong's interests.'

The legislator's oscillating judgements were by no means unique in Hong Kong: others, in large numbers, shared his rudderless anxieties but lacked his willingness to unburden themselves so openly. Their volatility, though, was the litmus test by which Patten had to assess the potential of every move he now made. The problem was that the long march to the high ground was bound to take the governor and his team through dangerously exposed terrain. Moreover, their room for manoeuvre was circumscribed by the imbalance of power between the two adversaries and a timetable which was against them. The immediate question facing them was not whether to table the bill, but when. Patten's instinct was to move quickly, but a number of legislators, including some of Martin Lee's supporters, were privately urging him to delay, suggesting that a cooling-off period was needed, and that the proposals should be considered after the Easter recess. A number of sympathetic editorials adopted the same line. Patten was aware that he was now approaching the decisive point of his governorship: 'It's going to be a difficult, cathartic, political moment,' he confided. 'We'll be told it's the end not just of the Hang Seng Index, but of humanity as we know it – or at least, as China knows it.'

At this point, to complicate matters, a number of contradictory signals began to emerge from Beijing. Despite the wrath he had heaped on Patten only a few days earlier, Lu Ping was, according to Patten's sources of intelligence in the Chinese capital, along with Li Peng, 'still trying to flag up their interest in talks'. Making a distinction between publishing and tabling the bill, the Chinese leaders had indicated informally that they had not yet entirely abjured talk of 'co-operation'. Patten was, somewhat reluctantly, drawn to the conclusion that it was just possible that something would start moving. 'I rather doubt it. It's equally possible that something sufficiently provocative will happen to push us into introducing the bill earlier.'

Far from believing that the Chinese were honourably at odds with the British over matters of principle and procedure, Patten was by now more than ever convinced that they were acting in bad faith. In this respect, his indicator was China's attitude to Martin Lee and his colleague, Szeto Wah. Would these Democratic party leaders be allowed to remain as members of the legislature after the handover, or would they be expelled as subversives? For Patten, this was a simple matter of principle. 'I think it goes right to the heart of the argument, and it's what we are fighting about before 1997 . . . If I look at it now, I don't think that they have any conception of a credible Legislative Council after 1997, any more than they have a real conception of the rule of law.'

As he considered how best to nudge his way ahead, Patten parried all public attempts to pin him down to any particular course of action. Meanwhile, he and his advisers identified two alternative ways forward. The first option was, as they put it, to 'buy' peace by contriving arrangements for the 1995 Legislative Council that would guarantee China an acquiescent majority, and from which recalcitrant members could be swiftly removed. As one or two of his advisers were quick to remind him, this would probably secure an agreement on contracts for the new airport, for the container port, CT9, and would be very likely to produce a more secure economic environment in the process. The other option was to risk an economic rough ride, but 'at least to fight for some sort of decency surviving 1997' with a chance, Patten thought, that China would find it difficult to overthrow a 'reasonable set of arrangements' after the handover. By adopting the latter course, Patten argued, 'we'll have established at least some sense of political propriety in that period, and, at the very least, we won't have been behaving in a thoroughly shaming way'.

The question was, what would be judged to be a 'reasonable set of arrangements', and by whom? Many of his admirers in Hong Kong were reluctant to see him rush prematurely into legislation. They believed that the governor's repeated invocation of a deadline which was constantly allowed to slip both exposed the weakness of his hand and was unnecessarily provocative. Patten conceded that: 'Our weakest ground has always been the determination to get things through quickly,' but he was still driven by the conviction that, sooner or later, the community would have to decide whether or not it had a bottom line. 'Let's get it over and done with: if the community decides that we haven't really given it any alternative but to cave in, there is not much I'd be able to do about it, but let's know that soon.' Nonetheless he remained fearful that the public might lack the stomach for such a robust approach.

Judging by the opinion polls, the public was still bewildered. In a telephone poll conducted at the beginning of April for the *Hong Kong Standard*, 78 per cent of respondents said they favoured efforts to achieve more democracy before 1997, even if the territory's economic prosperity were affected as a result. However, 57 per cent also declared that they wanted the governor either to amend or to withdraw his plans in the face of Chinese hostility. A similar poll in the *South China Morning Post* showed that while only 25 per cent of the sample supported the British position, a mere 19 per cent supported the Chinese. No less than 56 per cent of the population was undecided.

With this ambiguity in the forefront of his mind, Patten flew to London at Easter for another round of meetings at the Foreign Office and with the prime minister. The informal evidence from private sources – and in the form of a surprisingly conciliatory statement from the director of the NCNA – appeared to suggest that, despite the governor's obduracy to date, the door was still open for further negotiations if he could be persuaded to desist from further 'criminal' action: in other words, from tabling his bill. To this extent, if to this extent only, the Chinese appeared to have ceded ground. At the same time, Patten began to realise that Beijing had tumbled the fact that the legislative constraints on him – as opposed to the political attractions of an early decision by LegCo – were in fact somewhat less pressing than he had repeatedly insisted. They could therefore pursue their delaying tactics by hinting at the prospect of further Sino–British negotiations without in reality risking the constitutional crisis in Hong Kong that his own statements seemed to suggest would occur. Patten was angry but not surprised to discover, through British intelligence in Beijing, that at least one former diplomat, apparently thoroughly briefed by ex-colleagues in the Foreign Office, had taken it upon himself to inform his contacts in the Chinese government that the timing constraints on which Government House had laid such stress were fictitious, and that the pressure from that source could safely be discounted. Even so, he was astonished by such brazen treachery.

On 13 April, Patten was scheduled to have a lunchtime working session with the prime minister. To his irritation, this meeting was prefigured by yet another Whitehall 'source', who commented for the benefit of several attentive journalists: 'I'm afraid that unless Patten is reined in, China will withdraw all co-operation as Hong Kong heads for the 1997 handover of power, and that would be disastrous for the people living in the territory. Talks between Britain and China could restart tomorrow but for Patten's insistence on having members of Hong

Kong's government on his negotiating team.' Even in the new age of 'leaking' civil servants, specific briefing of this kind was rare. Patten knew that the source could only inhabit the Foreign Office or the Department of Trade and Industry, which was now led by Michael Heseltine, who had recently reinvented himself as the 'president of the Board of Trade'. Heseltine was known to have a rapacious eye on the potential of China's booming economy, and it was no secret that he shared the view prevailing in both departments that Sino–British relations should not be allowed to founder over the intricacies of the electoral arrangements for a territory that would soon be consigned to the margins of Britain's colonial history. Though he did not suspect Heseltine of being in any way implicated personally, Patten was uncomfortably aware that his former Cabinet colleague was likely to share the broad thrust of this anonymous and potentially devastating remark.

In Hong Kong, this 'revelation' served to confirm the impression that Patten was now isolated from mainstream opinion in the government and that he was a 'problem', an obstacle to progress and harmony. It was a perception that was reinforced in Britain by commentators like the former Irish government minister Conor Cruise O'Brien, who called for his resignation, and the ineffable Lord Jenkins of Hillhead, the leader of the Liberal Democrats in the House of Lords, who used a discussion with the governor on BBC Radio's *Any Questions* to express a fastidious disdain for Britain's efforts to introduce greater democracy into Hong Kong at so late a date. The conventional wisdom in the colony, voiced by the ubiquitous Allen Lee, was that the tête-à-tête between Major and Patten would be 'a waste of time'. The legislator was further quoted as saying, 'I do not think Britain has ever given anything to Hong Kong, nor do I either think China will be bad for Hong Kong. If they are going to talk, that is fine. If not, China will have to do what it thinks it needs to do. That is also fine.'

Before the governor and the prime minister had the opportunity to 'waste their time' over lunch the conventional wisdom had been confounded. On the morning of 13 April, Robin McLaren's patience finally bore fruit in the form of a simultaneous announcement from London and Beijing that Sino–British negotiations would after all take place, and that they would begin in the middle of the following week. They would be conducted on precisely the terms which Patten had been demonstrably willing to accept some six weeks earlier, and which involved no discernible retreat by the British on the question of either the 'secrecy' of the talks or of the composition of the British negotiating team. The British side was to be led by Robin McLaren, the British ambassador, supported by Peter Ricketts, the head of the Hong Kong

Department at the Foreign Office; Michael Sze, the secretary for constitutional affairs in the Hong Kong government; his deputy, Peter Lai; and William Ehrman, seconded from the Foreign Office to the Hong Kong government as one of Patten's political advisers. The governor contented himself with saying that the breakthrough had been 'a victory for common sense'. Allen Lee was greatly cheered by 'this excellent news' and the Hang Seng Index responded with Pavlovian predictability by leaping 371 points to 6,789.7 – a record one-day rise to a record high.

Patten was not carried away by this euphoria, estimating that chances of a successful outcome to the negotiations were no better than 'three to one against'. Though he confided that he was ready to dilute his original proposals, he was not prepared to give ground unless the Chinese offered something in exchange, which, he noted, 'may come as a rude shock' to them. Moreover, he was unwilling to let the talks drag on indefinitely, predicting that they would not last more than a couple of months at most. He was right about the odds, but wrong about the timetable.

As agreed by both sides, the talks began within a few days. Three weeks later, and after two rounds of negotiation, neither side had advanced one millimetre. Using the traditional tactic that had proved so effective in the past, the Chinese began by attempting to bind the British side into agreeing a set of broad 'principles' about constitutional structure before moving on to the precise details of the electoral scaffolding. Patten's team was wary, suspecting that to give any such commitment on the functional constituencies or the Election Committee, which were the two most contentious issues, would leave the British with no room for genuine negotiation on either. To make matters worse, Patten also had to accept that it would now be impossible to meet his self-imposed deadline of late July for the passage of his reform bill through the Legislative Council. Instead he began to consider the idea of 'decoupling' those parts of his reform package which applied to the 1994 'local' District Board elections from those which affected the 1995 Legislative Council elections, in which case he would have to table two bills rather than one.

In an effort to make some progress with the Chinese, Patten prevailed upon the foreign secretary to send a message to his counterpart, Qian Qichen, saying, in effect, 'Come on, we can't go on like this: we've got to get down to serious negotiation.' In the absence of a positive response from Beijing, he and his team proposed to bring into play what he liked to describe, with a touch of vainglory, as 'Patten's Maggie Factor': the unstated threat that the governor might suddenly do something wild and unpredictable, such as introducing the legislation without any warning. Whether he could in reality risk putting any such threat into practice at this stage was questionable. Were the British to walk away from the negotiations on the grounds that they were heading nowhere, he feared that a majority of LegCo members would say, 'We're not having any of this. Go back to the Chinese and negotiate something.' And he detected a similar mood among his advisers in ExCo.

Patten now felt himself to be not merely on the defensive but on the retreat. 'I'm in a weaker position because we started negotiating as late as this,' he confided in early May. 'The truth of the matter is that negotiation is inevitable, and a bit of a slippery slope, because people want a successful outcome . . . the further along a road you go like this, there are always a declining number of options.' In the hope of making genuine progress, he had identified two areas for compromise as soon as the Chinese betrayed a willingness to talk in earnest. He was prepared to give ground to Beijing on both the composition of the Election Committee and the size of the electorate for the functional constituencies. The latter, he calculated, could be reduced from some 2.5 million to as little as half a million without undermining their pluralistic flavour. He was insistent that in return he would need guarantees that every member of the legislature elected in 1995 would retain a place on the 'through train'. 'There's not much point in agreeing institutional arrangements that will go through 1997 if people can't as well,' he noted.

During these weeks, Patten's own resolve was put to the test persistently, not only by his own team, which he encouraged to debate every discernible option, but, far less agreeably, by the continuing sniping from the unnamed 'sources' in the Foreign Office, who he had hoped would have been silenced by the foreign secretary's admonition some months earlier.

While Patten professed himself to have been 'overwhelmingly well served' by most of the Foreign Office officials who had worked for him, this handful of dissidents irked him more than he liked to admit. Some, such as John Coles, the permanent secretary, and David Wright, his deputy (whom Patten thought had been overpromoted), frequently adopted an air of courteous but faintly disapproving scepticism. Although Patten dismissed others as 'some old sinologists on the fringes', he detected a disinclination generally in the Foreign Office to stand up to the bitter prejudice of Sir Percy Cradock, even after the latter's retirement. Although he did not put it in precisely such terms, Patten thought of Cradock as the Foreign Office's deus ex machina. It was also plain to him that the former diplomat had 'moved from being a critic on the sidelines to actively working to screw up what we are doing'. Patten harboured the thought that any success on his part would be too painful for Cradock to bear: he remarked acerbically, 'It's curious to take a view of public service that everything you do has to be vindicated, accepted by the outside world as the virtuous activities of a wise senator. Barmy.'

Patten raged against Cradock and his acolytes less for their opinions than for the influence that Beijing might assume they exercised in Whitehall. This concern came vividly into focus just before he made a visit to the States in May 1993, at the invitation (inspired by the prime minister at a meeting with the new president, Bill Clinton) of the White House. As he prepared for his own trip, Patten discovered that Cradock was about to embark on a visit to China. Given that Cradock could oil the hinges of almost any door in Beijing, it came as no shock that, on his retirement from the civil service, he had been able to sell his services to the merchant bankers Kleinwort Benson, who were anxious for a foothold in the People's Republic. However, Patten was surprised to discover that a diplomat so recently retired had considered it appropriate to travel to Beijing, 'purportedly' on his new employer's behalf. He was even more surprised to learn that Cradock's former colleagues in the Foreign Office not only knew about the proposed trip but were busily briefing him for it.

The governor only discovered what was afoot as a result of a casual conversation between Jiang Enzhu and William Ehrman at the customary banquet following the second round of Sino–British talks. The Chinese official told Ehrman that he and his colleagues were greatly looking forward to Sir Percy's visit to Beijing. Ehrman, a loyal if sceptical lieutenant, at once told the governor, who was not amused. He was even less amused when he discovered that the Foreign Office had known for two months that a group of British officials in Hong Kong were proposing to entertain Sir Percy to dinner, but that 'it slipped everybody's mind to tell me. They hadn't thought it was important. I was, as they say in Noël Coward plays, "crawss".'

Patten contacted the Foreign Office at once. 'I insisted they asked Sir Percy Cradock not to go, and I also insisted that they stopped briefing him.' Aware that there was little he could do to snuff out the spirit of freemasonry in London, Patten was sufficiently frustrated to summon his 'local' Foreign Office advisers to Government House where, according to one of those present, he gave them a full-scale dressing down, stating, among other things, that Cradock was now officially 'beyond the pale', and reminding them that 'when we are retreating

under fire, it does help us if we keep good order'. Some of those summoned, who were not implicated except by association, were upset to
have been treated as if they were dissidents; however, one official –
Tony Galsworthy, the Foreign Office's unofficial historian of the
Sino–British negotiations – was overhead to say with relish: 'So he does
realise that it's a retreat. It's the first time he has acknowledged that.'
Cradock's visit to China went ahead, and so did the dinner party.

Patten departed for Washington encouraged by the rough ride given to
Lu Ping by the outgoing Reagan administration the previous year.
Although he was well aware that the Chinese were super-sensitive
about the United States, and that to invoke American support would
open him to the charge of 'internationalising' the Sino–British dispute,
Patten was hopeful that President Clinton and sympathetic members of
the US Senate could be persuaded to use the bait of most-favoured-
nation status to tempt Beijing to be more accommodating about
democracy in Hong Kong. It would be a delicate manoeuvre on his
part. In public, no governor of Hong Kong could be seen to argue
against the renewal of MFN for the People's Republic because the
British colony's own prosperity was so intimately bound to China's
MFN status. However, he thought that it might be possible to exert
pressure on Beijing discreetly by persuading the Americans to hint
obliquely that there was a link, however slight, between the renewal of
MFN and the enhancement of democracy in Hong Kong. To this end
Patten proposed to encourage Washington to confirm, implicitly but
publicly, that by 'standing up' for Hong Kong's way of life, Britain was
in a much stronger position to argue in favour of MFN renewal.

Patten was in his element in the politics of Washington, which had
entranced him as a student when he briefly worked as part of Mayor
Lindsay's campaign team. He was not too blasé to experience a frisson
of pleasure as his limousine swept him through the White House gates
on Pennsylvania Avenue for his audience with the president. The two
men found an easy rapport and the meeting overran by fifteen minutes.
To Patten's delight, Clinton went further than he could have wished in
supporting his stance. Sitting in the Oval Office with the governor
beside him, the president informed the world's media:

I think that the democracy initiative in Hong Kong is a good thing,
and I'm encouraged the parties have agreed to talk about it. You
know, it is one of the world's most vibrant, thriving, important cities.
It is an incredible centre of commerce, and a haven of opportunity
for millions of people. Many of them had not a thing but the clothes

on their backs when they came there. And I think the idea of trying to keep it an open and free society after 1997 is in the best interests of the Chinese. So I think this is an issue which is well founded, and I support it. And I hope it doesn't offend anybody, but how can the United States be against democracy? It's our job to go out there and promote it.

Afterwards, Patten could hardly contain his enthusiasm: 'If you are a politician, being in Washington is like a cricket fan being at Lord's, or a Jesuit being in Rome. It's the centre of all that is most interesting and exciting between politics and the way the world works.' The governor had been far more impressed with Clinton than he had expected; by his physique ('He's so big!'), and by the speed and flexibility of his political intelligence. In addition to his audience at the White House, Patten had been given what seemed to him 'astonishing' access – to the Treasury, the State Department, leading senators and the vice-president, Al Gore. He was confident that this 'red-carpet treatment' would send a clear message to Beijing. 'I hope they will take the point that the US and the rest of the world will be looking at the way Peking treats Hong Kong as a touchstone for how much China can be encouraged to join polite international society,' he said. 'I think it's quite important that China recognises that behaving badly in Hong Kong isn't a cost-free option for them.' In public, however, he took care to ensure that the 'internationalisation card' did not appear to be being played.

The USA visit was judged a success. However, given China's propensity to ignore world opinion, it was perhaps optimistic of Patten to suppose that even the subtlest efforts to 'internationalise' Hong Kong would have a beneficial impact in Beijing. He anticipated the 'usual crude and silly attacks' from China on him for having the temerity to visit the United States at all, but he was not at all prepared to find, on opening *The Times* on the day after his meeting with Clinton, that one of the Foreign Office's freelance communicators had been at work again. The newspaper quoted an unnamed Foreign Office official as saying – in Patten's gloss – 'what a pity it was that President Clinton had expressed support for my proposals on Hong Kong's democratic institutions because that might cock things up. He should have just had his picture taken with me. It was a great pity that he was so effusive.' Patten chose to attribute this war of attrition being waged against him to 'mutterings in the bar at the Travellers Club', but he was angry that a minority of Douglas Hurd's officials should feel free to ignore the foreign secretary's recent strictures, given in his presence, 'about how everyone must be loyal and supportive'.

The pressure sometimes seemed unremitting. With the exception of Lady Thatcher, the procession of grandees from Britain who filed through Government House as his guests frequently exacerbated his sense of isolation. When the former Labour prime minister Lord Callaghan arrived in Hong Kong en route to a gathering of elder statesmen in Beijing, he did not spare his host's feelings. Callaghan argued his case with impressive clarity and courtesy. Patten observed afterwards that this was preferable to the blandishments of those who came to stay at Government House and 'tell me what a wonderful job I'm doing and then go round town sounding gloomy'. Callaghan's view, as reported by Patten, was essentially that Britain should not be overly concerned about 'doing the right thing by Hong Kong'. British interests in China and relations with Beijing were of far greater moment. It was important to protect Britain's commercial interests, to promote British trade with China, and to secure a greater share of China's expanding market. Callaghan's conclusion – 'We can't make very much difference to what Hong Kong is like after 1997, and therefore basically we shouldn't have any arguments with China' – was thoroughly disheartening.

Pessimistically predicting that the conclave of former statesmen gathered in Beijing was likely to share Callaghan's opinion, Patten confessed:

> I do get depressed by the amount of time I inevitably have to spend explaining to people why I'm not a grand poseur. Why what we are doing matters. Why we've taken the decisions we have taken . . . I've got to keep showing them that I'm not just grandstanding; that what we are doing has rational grounds for it and is important for the prosperity of Hong Kong.

As he approached the end of his first twelve months in office, the governor seemed to have lost much of his early bounce. Though he worked tirelessly and sounded no less confident in public, he seemed burdened and careworn in private, his usually bullish stance often yielding to doubt and anxiety. In confidential conversation about his tactics with China, he contrived to be both defiant and defensive. Insisting that his adversaries in Beijing had to believe that the British were serious, he added, in the same breath, 'I mean, we do want to do business. Having got on to this inevitable and slippery slope, we have to complete the journey.'

'THE MAD GOVERNOR FACTOR'

Negotiating in Earnest but in Vain

In the summer of 1993, after two months of negotiation (which had taken them well past the governor's self-imposed deadline), the British team saw a glimmer of hope. Even Chris Patten found himself grasping at the straws which seemed to blow in with the wind from Beijing. Despite China's insistence that the two sides should agree on a list of principles before dealing with matters of substance, the British had not given way. 'If we compromised first, we would have found that the bargain was between our "compromise" position and whatever their position was,' explained Patten. 'So it was imperative that they set out their stall first . . . if there is going to be a compromise, it'll be somewhere between where we started and where they've dug their trenches.' On his instructions, the British side had continued to press the Chinese on the need to establish objective criteria for allowing Hong Kong's elected representatives to travel on the 'through train' across the 1997 barrier. By the end of round three, there had been stalemate.

At this point, however, the Chinese began to shift ground. Although there was no tangible movement in rounds four and five, the British side noticed that the Chinese negotiators had quietly dropped their insistence on establishing 'principles' as a precondition for progress and agreed to proceed to the matters of substance. In the sixth round, the Chinese even laid out their position on the composition of the functional constituencies. Reiterating that the British should drop Patten's proposals for extending the franchise to embrace some 2.7 million people, they demanded that the nine new constituencies should be based on corporate, not popular, votes. It was hardly a leap forward, but it was a step in the right direction, however crabbed. Patten noted dryly, 'Hey presto. They moved. So we did make progress.' Indeed, he even allowed himself to be reassured by the fact that some 'experienced old sinologists' thought the progress made 'spectacular'. For the first time, it seemed to him that the Chinese were serious about negotiating a compromise.

His advisers in Government House were less optimistic. 'The PRC would not ever do a deal, except on their terms,' said one of them. Patten presumed that Beijing's apparent amenability was attributable at least in part to economic factors: 'When the insults were first raining down on the Triple Violator last autumn, if there was economic pressure, it was thought to be on us: British businessmen and Hong Kong businessmen concerned about losing markets in China; concerned that, by standing up to China, we'd ruin the Hong Kong economy.' At that time there had been euphoria about the Chinese economy; nine months later, the Hang Seng Index had risen by almost 30 per cent, while the Chinese economy seemed to be dangerously overheating. 'The Chinese, I think, are feeling they don't want to wreck the Hong Kong economy if they are going to have economic troubles themselves.' To support this theory, Patten cited the fact that the Chinese were about to float ten of their largest companies on the Hong Kong stock market.

> Do they want to carry out these privatisations on a falling, plummeting Hong Kong stock market or one that is stable and rising? The question answers itself . . . The more they worry about their own currency, the more they are stuffing money into Hong Kong . . . So all the signs are that, with Hong Kong representing a fifth – and the healthiest fifth – of China's economy, they aren't going to wreck it.

He was sufficiently confident that China wished to avoid a breakdown to revise his pessimistic assessment of the chances of a deal from three to one against to fifty-fifty. From his vantage point, it now seemed that British resolution was reaping its just reward.

> They wouldn't talk unless the Triple Violator dropped his proposals. They wouldn't talk unless members of the Hong Kong administration were travelling third class. They wouldn't talk if anybody knew talks were taking place. They wouldn't make any progress in the talks unless we compromised first. They wouldn't tell us what they wanted to do until we compromised. At every stage you sit there quietly for a time and they shout and rave and then it happens.

Patten thought that the Chinese, accustomed to a very different style of Sino–British negotiations before his arrival as governor, were now 'recognising that there is slightly less disposition on our side to try to get round substantial issues by clever words . . . We haven't backed off anything. It doesn't mean that we are not going to try to find a compromise, but that it will be a compromise we come to rationally.'

If he was right, then, for the first time, the Chinese were preparing to yield on matters which they had claimed publicly to be issues of overriding 'principle'. For them to cede ground, perhaps to the extent of compromising in favour of Britain's commitment to the 'through train', would be a diplomatic triumph for which Patten would properly be given much, if not all, the credit. Such an outcome would also turn on its head the conventional sinological wisdom about the gerontocracy in Beijing, and call into question the past conduct of relations with China over Hong Kong. Patten was not so incontinent as to speculate in this fashion, but he was, by now, more than ever convinced that Britain had underestimated its position and its strength in the past.

In his new positive mood, the governor was careful to avoid any further public commitment to a timetable for the completion of the talks, a tacit acknowledgement that his previous attempts to do so had been ineffectual, if not counterproductive. Nonetheless he and his team had decided that it would be quite impossible to delay tabling his bill (probably revised as a result of the negotiations with China) beyond the end of the year, which was already five months later than the date he had originally announced.

Patten now flew to London for a well-publicised meeting of the Cabinet subcommittee on 1 July, which was chaired by the prime minister and attended by the foreign secretary and the home secretary, Michael Howard. Its purpose, Patten confided, was to demonstrate 'the harmony between London and Hong Kong and the complete commitment to the approach we've taken, our mild but growing impatience and our shared objectives in the talks – and to give a little burnishing to the threat of the mad governor breaking loose again'. It was duly conveyed to the media afterwards that while the governor had set no deadline for the talks, time was running out, and that, in the absence of a deal, he would press ahead unilaterally by tabling his package in LegCo. The Hong Kong newspapers responded predictably. Pro-democracy commentators noted that the Cabinet endorsement of his approach was a 'victory' for Patten, although they fretted that the British were about to cede too much ground to the Chinese. Conversely, the pro-Beijing press declared that the line adopted by Britain was bound to make the negotiations 'more difficult'. If the

British side persisted with Patten's 'three-violation' package, the talks would fail. While China had always been 'sincere', the 'petty tricks' and unspecified 'unreasonable demands' of the British undermined the prospect of a settlement.

It was soon obvious that this response reflected a renewed obduracy in Beijing, and that Patten and his advisers had misread the signals emerging from the Chinese capital. Within days, the governor's optimism began to evaporate. A meeting between the foreign secretary and the Chinese foreign minister on 9 July – at which, according to Patten, Douglas Hurd intended to 'make it pretty clear that we need to get a move on, that we are serious about trying to negotiate a settlement but we are also serious about walking away from the table if they are just mucking about' – yielded nothing of substance. Hurd was reduced to flannelling in public, effectively saying that the proof of whether or not the visit was worthwhile would be seen in what actually happened later.

During rounds eight and nine of the talks Britain offered further concessions on the composition of the functional constituencies and the Election Committee, but, reverting to their earlier stance, the Chinese refused to shift ground. As for the 'through train', which was for Patten a core issue, they simply refused to discuss it. By the end of round nine the governor was reluctantly forced to reverse his judgement that the Chinese were serious about securing a compromise. Two insurmountable obstacles blocked the way: Beijing's obsession with China's sovereign rights over Hong Kong, which Patten was persuaded would endure until the 'immortals' had finally departed, and the bureaucratic shambles and infighting by which the Chinese administration was so obviously afflicted. As if that were not enough, he was, in blacker moods, also frustrated by what he saw as the innate cowardice of too many members of the Hong Kong community and the greed of the business elite, both of which played into Beijing's hands.

In August the Pattens flew to Italy for a month in the sun. They stayed with friends in an Umbrian villa, where they relaxed in the traditional English way. Patten sat in the full glare of the sun, covered himself with lotion and read Jonathan Spence's *The Search for Modern China*. He played tennis, went for extended walks, swam and almost every day explored the surrounding towns and villages in search of paintings and churches. His friends noted that despite his genial demeanour, he often seemed distracted, his bonhomie uncharacteristically forced. He consumed spaghetti and red wine with his usual enthusiasm, but he often drifted away from the conversation as if wrapped in private worries. On more than one occasion his reveries were punctured by telephone calls from a troubled John Major in London – for the prime minister (though Patten would never have said so) continued to treat his absent mentor as a fount of rare wisdom and understanding – complaining about his treatment at the hands of a hostile Eurosceptical media. Patten did his best to reassure Major and to offer advice, but these interruptions at this time did little to restore his spirits.

It was during these weeks that he began to think his way into the collapse of negotiations which he now considered to be all but inevitable. Although he felt that he had only a little more ground to give, he was still willing to make further modifications to his reforms which would bring them more closely into line with what he would have proposed originally had he been told about the 1990 'understandings', the principal source of his troubles in Beijing nine months earlier. He envisaged a further revision of the composition and size of the functional constituencies, which, he was ready to concede, might be scaled down to 840,000 electors. In the case of the Election Committee, he allowed that it should be formed 'precisely' on the model prescribed in the Basic Law, except that the places on it reserved for those Hong Kong residents who were also members of the Chinese legislature should be filled by election rather than, as the Chinese wanted, by appointment. This prospective retreat, which would have horrified the Democrats had they known of it, was as far as Patten felt he could go without reneging on his own commitment to an electoral process that was palpably 'fair, open, and acceptable to the people of Hong Kong'. It was precisely because he believed that his modified proposals still met these criteria that he was now so dubious about the prospect of agreement with Beijing. As one of Beijing's favoured 'advisers', Sir David Akers-Jones, was to explain, with no sense of irony, to the Foreign Affairs Committee at Westminster a few weeks later: 'The Chinese style is not to rig elections, but they do like to know the results before they are held.'

In the space of a month, Patten's analysis of the Chinese stance had been through a 180-degree about-turn, a fact which he readily acknowledged. As the summer waned he resigned himself to the prospect that any further talks were destined for the quicksands. The one hope was that the Chinese were preparing to make a last-minute concession which might be wrung out of them in New York in a further meeting between Douglas Hurd and Qian Qichen scheduled for early October. It was a remote possibility, but one to which the sinologists in the Foreign Office clung. Meanwhile, Patten began to plan for the anticipated breakdown. He thought it would strengthen his hand as far as public opinion was concerned if the British were to publish a

White Paper explaining how and why the two sides had failed to reach a compromise. He nurtured the hope that this might demonstrate to both Hong Kong and the international community that he had gone as far as it was reasonable to go in a genuine attempt to accommodate Beijing's doubts and suspicions. His immediate inclination was to table his original, unmodified bill in the hope of thus avoiding a confrontation with Martin Lee and the Democrats, but at the same time leaving room for LegCo to amend his reforms if that was the will of the majority. Although he would be denounced by China, he soon convinced himself that this was the only credible way ahead.

With some weariness he predicted a renewed outbreak of panic in Hong Kong at the prospect of a head-on confrontation with China, which might, he feared, provoke one or two of his less stalwart advisers on the Executive Council to resign in protest. However, he thought that his approach would at least be seen as morally defensible and – in political terms – more 'saleable' at Westminster and on Capitol Hill. A collapse of the talks on the grounds he foresaw would at least allow him to argue that the issue between Britain and China was not essentially the previous 'understandings', or whether his proposals constituted a helter-skelter dash for democracy, but whether Hong Kong's electoral system should be conspicuously fair or self-evidently rigged. He was still inclined to believe that if the 1995 Hong Kong elections were conducted on the terms proposed in his original bill, the Chinese would preserve the structure after the handover – regardless of the rhetorical thunderbolts which would be hurled from Beijing in the meantime. If the outcome of the 1995 elections should prove 'so terrifying' that the old men in Beijing felt obliged to dismantle an electoral system approved by LegCo, he thought they would find it exceptionally difficult to justify such vandalism in the eyes of the world. In these circumstances, Britain would emerge somewhat bowed but not entirely dishonoured – a concern which was never far from the mind of a Westminster politician who cared for the national interest, and who wished to retain at least the option of a role in public life after 1997.

Some of his former colleagues in the Conservative party did not want him to wait that long. In the summer of 1993, Douglas Hurd rang Patten to suggest that he might like to return within the next twelve months and re-enter the cabinet as leader of the House of Lords. From that vantage point, Hurd reasoned, he could help shepherd the government, and a beleaguered prime minister, towards the next election. Major's standing had plummeted following the débâcle of Black Wednesday the previous autumn. A catastrophic performance in the 1993 local elections, followed by a humiliating rebuff in the European elections, had led to a mood of panic and rebellion in the parliamentary party. Some senior colleagues who were ideologically at odds with Major's imprecise and vacillating commitment to be 'at the heart of Europe', were in more or less open revolt. Such was the disarray that he was being privately vilified, and none too discreetly, even by members of his own Cabinet – a disloyalty which drove him soon afterwards to refer to the 'bastards' therein. The view that the prime minister was indecisive, weak and incompetent had begun to stalk his leadership to the extent that only a very determined politician was likely to survive the onslaught from his own party and the government's erstwhile supporters in the media, notably the *Daily Mail*, the *Daily Telegraph* and the *Sunday Telegraph*. In vain Major's friends advised him to ignore a media campaign which he believed, with some justification, was being orchestrated to bring him down in favour of a successor committed to leading Britain from the 'heart' to the periphery of the European Union – a prospect from which the prime minister himself recoiled.

As the implications of the Maastricht Treaty began to take effect, the debate over the single currency degenerated into a verbal brawl between senior colleagues, while what had once been an anti-European rump in the Conservative party began to affect the public mood with a potent combination of anti-Brussels rhetoric and jingoism. 'Some pretty nasty people', as Patten described these backbench rebels, had done their best to undermine the prime minister by voting against the treaty, which, Patten said, 'viewed from Hong Kong, is a bit of a fight up a cul-de-sac'. They very nearly succeeded in forcing a vote of no confidence in the administration. The Hong Kong governor shared the view which soon became fashionable in and around Westminster that, with a majority in single figures, the prime minister was in such a perilous position that he might well be driven out of the leadership. Although Major had not yet hinted at this himself, Patten was in little doubt that Hurd's informal overture reflected the prime minister's own sense of impending crisis and his faith that the return of his most trusted colleague could somehow turn the tide.

But it was not a prospect that tempted the governor even for a moment. He was honest enough to confess in private that he was reluctant to mortgage his political future to a permanent seat but a transitory role in the House of Lords. And, while he knew that the prime minister would appreciate his strategic perspective, he was not at all sure that he would be able to help Major steer a more persuasive course through the shoals which beset the government. Nonetheless, if the prime minister had asked him unequivocally, his ties of personal loyalty and political conviction would have obliged him to return. One of

Patten's team recalled later that he had come out of a breakfast meeting with Major, sunk into the back of the car and 'heaved a sigh of relief' that the prime minister had not broached the issue directly on that occasion. Patten informed the foreign secretary that unless the prime minister were expressly to summon him back, he intended to remain at his post until the handover.

The negotiations with China dragged on through the summer and into the autumn. Twelve rounds of talks brought half-promises of a modest harvest while, week by week, delivering only fruit that withered on the branch. Throughout Patten remained in direct command of the negotiations. At the end of each session, he and his team in Government House gathered in his study to read through the telegrams from the Beijing embassy. The governor listened to the advice of his specialists and responded by sending McLaren his 'riding instructions' for the next day. It became an increasingly exhausting process.

On 1 October, three days before his meeting with Qian Qichen in New York, Douglas Hurd reminded an audience in Singapore that Hong Kong had become a 'political city', contradicting a statement by the Chinese foreign minister three months earlier. A day before their meeting, Qian Qichen retaliated by quoting the words of Deng Xiaoping in his meeting with Margaret Thatcher eleven years before: an 'early takeover' of Hong Kong might be necessary, he said, if there were 'major disturbances' in the colony before 1997. This theme was echoed on the same day, the forty-fourth anniversary of the establishment of the People's Republic, by Li Peng in an address to the party faithful in the Great Hall of the People. Patten shrugged off the warning, declaring that if there was any political instability in the region, it was not to be found in Hong Kong. However, the inflammatory tone of the Chinese statement reinforced his doubts.

To no one's surprise, the discussions between the two foreign ministers on 4 October failed to break the deadlock. To the dismay of the British, Qian Qichen made it clear that China intended to reserve the 'right' to exclude from LegCo after 1997 any elected politician of whom he and his colleagues did not approve. After two hours of discussion, Douglas Hurd emerged to comment bleakly, 'There is a considerable gap, and I can't say we have narrowed it today.' It was particularly dispiriting because the British were prone to regard Qian Qichen as a reasonable figure, whom Patten contrasted favourably with 'the hard men who, at the drop of a hat, start to sound like cultural revolutionary nutters'.

In his second annual policy address to LegCo, in October 1993,

Patten confirmed: 'We now have only weeks rather than months to conclude these talks . . . We are not prepared to give away our principles in order to sign a piece of paper. What would that be worth?' Preparing what his team felt to be a 'very shaky LegCo' for the prospect of a vengeful response from China, he urged its members to meet the challenge of Hong Kong's predicament, declaring emotionally: 'We cannot be bolder than you, because liberty stands in the heart. When it shrivels there, nothing can save it.' At a press conference afterwards, he was challenged by pro-Beijing reporters who accused him of delivering an ultimatum to China. Concealing his true feelings in the hope of retaining the diplomatic high ground, he responded breezily. He still had boundless optimism, he said, that a few more rounds of talks could deliver a solution, although he added: 'As the weeks and months tick by, hope becomes a little shadowed by reality.' In his speech, he had been circumspect about the lack of progress in the talks and made no reference to China's failure to make concessions. Afterwards he was asked if the Chinese had moved at all. 'You had better ask them. I don't know how long the answer might take.' Away from the reporters, his answer to the question was that it would take 'about four and a half seconds . . . The Chinese haven't, in practice, budged an inch. Indeed, the more you get ideas out of them, the more alarming they become.' In LegCo he refrained from sharing with his audience his conviction that the Chinese were obsessed with the need to control the legislature after 1997.

Although it was inconceivable that he would even hint at such a bleak appraisal in public while ostensibly the talks had not yet run their course, he was by now quite clear that 'unless something astonishing' were to occur within the next few weeks, he would fly to London for a Cabinet committee meeting in late October at which he would recommend that 'we pull the plug' in November. With this in their minds, Patten's advisers began to shift the emphasis away from the diminishing prospect of a deal towards the 'endgame': making sure that the British side emerged from the breakdown 'looking as good as possible'.

Three more rounds of negotiations had been planned for October, and the revisions that Patten's team had conceived in the summer were duly presented to the Chinese side in the middle of the month. To the governor's astonishment, Beijing once again appeared to shift ground by suddenly proposing, in round fifteen, that the two sides record an 'interim understanding' on five points which had not hitherto been agreed. Once more driven to revise his expectations, Patten concluded that this move was 'substantial enough to be real', and could not be dismissed merely as an attempt to wrong-foot the forthcoming Cabinet committee meeting. The proposed 'interim understanding' related to the reduction of the voting age in Hong Kong to eighteen (the age qualification already in force for 'elections' in China); the right of Hong Kong citizens who were also members of the National People's Congress to stand in local and LegCo elections; a single-vote, single-member system for local elections (but not for LegCo elections); the nature and function of District Board and Municipal Councils (the local authorities); and the composition of these two local assemblies. In the last case, the Chinese appeared to concede the right of the British to replace the appointed members of District Boards and Municipal Councils by elected representatives, but reserved the right of the future SAR government to revert to a system of appointees. These were far from the most contentious issues that divided the two sides, but Patten was encouraged to believe that further concessions would be forthcoming and that, even as it stood, the Chinese proposal held the prospect of a genuine deal.

In the governor's view this eleventh-hour response conceded 'three quarters, maybe half, of the Triple Violator's original package', even though it still left the really awkward issues to be resolved. It was a measure of his eagerness to emerge from these negotiations with an agreement that he allowed himself to be so enthused by what, especially in retrospect, would seem such a nugatory shift by the Chinese. But it was enough to persuade him to change tack. In London at the end of October, he persuaded the Cabinet committee, not to 'pull the plug', but to endorse the notion of splitting his bill in two, 'decoupling' the non-controversial matters referred to in the 'interim understanding' from the less tractable issues in the hope that they could be finessed into an agreed form of words during the sixteenth round of talks and then introduced into LegCo before Christmas. This, he hoped, would at least introduce some momentum into the process. The really divisive issues – the Election Committee, the functional constituencies and the 'through train' – could then be negotiated separately and without quite the same pressure to reach an early agreement.

This way ahead would only be possible if the Chinese were willing to concede that the single-seat, single-vote principle should apply not only to the local elections but to the LegCo elections as well. Otherwise, Patten judged, the deal would not be politically acceptable to opinion in Hong Kong. The Cabinet was sympathetic. After the president of the Board of Trade, Michael Heseltine, had asked 'some perfectly reasonable, legitimate questions' about the impact on Britain's economic interests if China were to start 'trying to take it out on us', Patten was given unquestioning support, both for his handling of the crisis so far and for the strategy he now proposed to adopt. At the conclusion of what was to prove a decisive meeting, the prime minister sent a message to the Chinese premier welcoming the progress made, but indicating that, for practical reasons, it would be necessary to reach agreement very soon. In broad terms, he suggested that he thought agreement should be made forthwith on the 'immediate issues', while the less easily solved questions could be handled in an intensive final phase of negotiations.

Patten's cautious optimism was tempered by his belief that on the more divisive matters, 'the gap between their bottom line and our bottom line is so huge that it's going to be difficult to bridge'. In the case of the 'through train', for example, the Chinese had set out in round fifteen a range of criteria which prospective travellers would have to satisfy, which included a reference to 'sedition'. It was not clear either what they had in mind, or whether their anxiety was about past or future conduct. There was, as Patten observed, 'a world of difference between people promising they won't commit seditious acts in the future and people being pinned for what the Chinese may regard as seditious in the past, like protesting against Tiananmen Square'.

The governor's ambivalence about the negotiating process in which he was ensnared was almost palpable. On one hand, he was inclined to believe that the group in Peking which wanted a settlement was in the ascendant; on the other, he conceded: 'Our assessments of what is going on in Peking are always subject to the caveat that I'm not sure any of us knows what happens in that secret society . . . Who is running China? Is China being run by the president of the All-China Bridge Federation [Deng Xiaoping]? Is China being run by the daughter of the president of the All-China Bridge Federation?'

Patten's private sentiments about the 'Alice in Wonderland' world of Sino–British diplomacy were barely printable.

It's mad. Utterly crazy. Take one issue – the 'through train'. It's inconceivable that with any other country or government you'd actually be arguing about these matters with part of the world standing by and nodding away as though it were a rational thing to be arguing about. And with large numbers of the business community, many of them educated in liberal, plural societies, actually thinking, 'China's got a point. Perhaps we should throw people out of the Legislative Council if they protested against Tiananmen Square.' I mean, it's cloud-cuckoo land.

We are devising the most complicated elections, I should think, in the history of civilisation, with the Chinese trying to devise them in a way that rigs them . . . At the moment there are five functional constituencies where there has never been an election. It's always been a shoe in. In the Chinese commercial functional constituency, which is, by and large, the Chinese Chamber of Commerce – a completely open-and-shut job for Peking – there was a legislator called Mr Ho . . . who, in the run-up to the last LegCo elections, expressed some views about the airport which China didn't like. It was made clear to him that his business interests would suffer. So he stands down and is replaced by a man who's just been chucked out of the stock exchange for his practices . . .

Then there was the regional council functional constituency. The chap representing that is now in Stanley Prison, having been found to have bribed several of the electors. And so you go on. We can't conceivably allow that sort of rot to continue, and we must ensure that the nine new functional constituencies are set up on rather cleaner lines. If not, it will make absolutely certain that it is a rotten legislature in the palm of Peking.

The governor's angry indictment of the prevailing structure contained an implicit criticism, not only of those who had devised it, but also of his own predecessors in Government House, the Foreign Office and the British Cabinet. It was, after all, British officials, endorsed by British ministers, who had invented these rotten boroughs and who had concocted an electoral system – essentially at the behest of Hong Kong's merchant elite – which appeared to accommodate the concepts of freedom and justice, but in reality flouted them. It was not a glorious record, and Hong Kong's last governor was very far from proud of it.

In early November the British returned to the negotiating table for round sixteen with a revised 'memorandum of understanding' based on the Chinese document submitted in the previous round. In an effort to move towards an agreement on objective criteria for the 'through train', the British side submitted a draft oath of allegiance to the special administrative region. But now the British suddenly found themselves in what Patten called 'serious Lewis Carroll country' as the Chinese retreated from what the British believed to be their stated position on the appointment of members to the District Boards and Municipal Councils. Although the leader of the British negotiating team, Robin McLaren, thought he had elucidated the Chinese view (and 'replayed' it back to them twice to make sure), they insisted during rounds sixteen and seventeen that there had been a misunderstanding. According to Patten, the Chinese were only prepared to explain what they had really meant if the British were willing to give up a point of substance in return. In effect they were arguing that their explanation would itself be a concession. They also rejected the British proposal that a first-stage agreement should incorporate a commitment to the single-seat, single-vote formula for LegCo elections as well as the local elections, without which Patten was sure any agreement would be rejected by a majority of Hong Kong's legislators. Acknowledging that Beijing appeared to have 'caught us for another couple of months' of negotiations – which would take them past the December deadline which he had argued only recently would be impossible to postpone – the governor steeled himself for the inevitable complaints from Martin Lee and his democratic cohorts that he was allowing himself to be 'strung along' by China.

At the end of round sixteen – during which, according to Patten, the Chinese made their case with 'pretty ill grace' – Christopher Hum, a Foreign Office official deputising for Robin McLaren, who was ill, was instructed to inform his Chinese counterparts that if they reneged on the agreement the British thought they had made in round fifteen, then it would not be possible to go on discussing these so-called first-stage issues in round seventeen. At the traditional banquet that night, the Chinese were in angry mood. 'There was,' said Patten, 'a huge fuss, and the leader of the Chinese negotiating team behaved in a very ill-mannered and uncouth way.' The atmosphere was the ugliest British negotiators could recall. For the governor's colleagues in Government House, there was a delicious irony in this moment. Christopher Hum, who bore the brunt of the hostility, was one of the governor's most persistent critics in the Foreign Office. Rightly or wrongly, Patten's team believed that Hum was the principal agent of the anonymous leaks from those 'sources in Whitehall' which had so irritated the governor. On this occasion, however, Hum obeyed his instructions to the letter.

At the end of another fruitless round, Hum said simply: 'I have no more authority to go on talking about "first-stage" issues.' After 200 hours of negotiation, the two sides had managed to agree that, whatever form elections might take, the voting age should be reduced from twenty-one to eighteen. And that was it.

Patten now wanted to publish his 'first-stage' bill as soon as the lawyers completed the final draft, and to introduce it into LegCo for debate before Christmas. However, Anson Chan, his choice to succeed Sir David Ford as chief secretary, felt that it should not appear to have been rushed. She advised that what the governor described as a 'more deliberate, orderly' introduction would look better to the community, and so he decided to delay the bill just a little longer. Anson Chan was a formidable character whom Patten had identified within six months of his arrival in Hong Kong as the most suitable 'local' civil servant to inherit a role which had hitherto been the preserve of British officials. She had taken up the post in September, and already her influence was pervasive. Patten readily admitted that he would only take a decision against her advice in extremis. 'I think,' he commented, 'that the most difficult aspect of decision-making and political leadership isn't making up your own mind, but trying to square others.'

Indeed, the question of timing was discussed by ExCo with great passion. Four members, led by Denis Chang, a respected liberal lawyer, felt strongly that Patten should move rapidly. 'If you think something is right,' declared Chang, 'put it in place and – hopefully – it will survive . . .' However, the prevailing view among his colleagues was that the governor should 'be realistic', and Patten was determined to ensure that the majority in ExCo was willing, however reluctantly, to endorse his decision. Denis Chang watched his style with detached admiration: 'He has a very brilliant mind in summing things up, but you can almost hear between the lines what he wants!' he observed. In this case, as Patten explained, 'I summed up against the minority despite the fact that the more I heard of the argument [advanced by Denis Chang], the more convinced I was by it. But . . . I didn't want to make those who were anyway pretty lukewarm or iffy about the course of action we were pursuing to feel they'd had two bloody noses in one day.' It was his constitutional obligation to consult his advisers on ExCo, but it was also good politics to carry them with him: to face resignations from those members of the community whom he had been seen to select as those most able to give him sound and detached advice would have been very much more than an embarrassment.

Patten was more sensitive to the awkward task of dealing with ExCo than some of its members presumed. 'It would be much easier if one just listened to one's own voices and followed one's own instinct,' he ruminated. 'It is quite difficult and a curious exercise, because the Executive Council doesn't have much clout in the community. They are all distinguished people and they very often give good advice very bravely, but . . . I have to think about managing them, and that probably slows me down a bit sometimes.' As it was, several members of ExCo, of fainter heart than he realised, lobbied Patten's team furiously, urging them to intervene with the governor in a last-ditch attempt to persuade him to back away from a showdown with China. They refused.

China's obstinacy was hard for Patten to bear. He found a release for his pent-up frustrations in meetings with his senior staff, who had by now grown accustomed to his expletive-undeleted remarks on the subject. Before his regular question-and-answer sessions in LegCo, a ritual he had instituted soon after his arrival, he prepared himself in dry runs with his advisers so that together they could establish the line to take and he could tailor his responses accordingly. In one such session, on the day before Patten was due to announce that the talks had broken down, Martin Dinham asked him mildly, 'So why was it that in the end you could not reach agreement?'

The governor twirled his glasses, looked at the ceiling as if in search of inspiration, and replied thoughtfully: 'Because they are wankers.'

The decision to delay the first-stage bill would, Patten feared, create more time for 'Chinese intimidation and pressure to work on individual members of the Legislative Council'. Indeed, that pressure had already begun: several LegCo members who had been 'very solid and supportive' the previous week were, Patten detected, already 'peeling off' and, he reported, saying, 'Maybe we could agree all this in a couple of days, and postpone putting in the legislation for another month or six weeks . . .' The reason for this prevarication was, in Patten's mind, self-evident: 'They've had a telephone call from the NCNA.'

There were other reasons for delay. First, even at this late stage, the foreign secretary still harboured a residual hope that the Chinese would return to the negotiating table. Secondly, since Douglas Hurd was to be away from London at a NATO meeting, it would be some days before he could deliver an appropriate parliamentary statement. He therefore advised Patten that it would be wise to proceed with caution. 'London has been extremely supportive,' explained the governor, '[but] I think Douglas's judgement was that London wasn't quite prepared for a breakdown in the way that the community here was.'

Patten continued to insist publicly that the door was wide open for further discussion, and to reiterate his confidence in the willingness of the Chinese to abide by the terms of the Joint Declaration and the Basic Law. Away from the spotlight he noted: 'I hope I'm wrong – and things may change between now and 1997; things may change in Peking – but they give every indication of simply not believing in Hong Kong people running Hong Kong under "one country, two systems". It's all there in the text, but everything they do tells a different story.' It was a dismal thought when he was committed to spending the next three and a half years pretending to the outside world that the reality might be otherwise.

On 6 December 1993 Hurd formally announced that the talks had collapsed. The leader of the Liberal Democrats, Paddy Ashdown, gave the government his support. The Labour party, in the person of the shadow foreign secretary, Jack Cunningham, failed to rise to the moment. In a carping speech in which party points-scoring took precedence over shadow statesmanship, he smirked, 'The central question in response to the right honourable gentleman's speech is what on earth has gone wrong? . . . It seems, Madam Speaker, as though the "through train" of democratic reform has just come off the rails.' In the Lords, the former Labour prime minister James Callaghan was similarly unhelpful. 'The government,' he observed, 'have got themselves into a cul-de-sac. And the cul-de-sac is that they cannot now satisfy the people of Hong Kong and we are endangering our long-term relations with China. This is a terrible example of ineptitude.'

Patten voiced his feelings of isolation.

I suspect one reason why it feels more uncomfortable than most political dramas in which I've been embroiled is precisely that feeling that nobody back home quite knows what it's like. London is in every sense a long way off. Look at the coverage of Hong Kong at the moment in the British media. It's negligible apart from some pretty third-rate sort of Angela Brazil reporting on the BBC . . . There is a bit in *The Times* and in one or two other newspapers . . . but not really the sort of coverage which people here would expect the subject to deserve.

Eighteen months into his governorship, Patten knew that he had reached the point of no return; that the future was all the more daunting for being quite unpredictable.

'WITHOUT FEAR OR FAVOUR'

Defending Free Speech

The ambivalence and uncertainty about the future under China which preoccupied many Hong Kong citizens was typified by the conflicting feelings of one member of the younger generation. In 1992, when Chris Patten arrived in Hong Kong, Norris Lam was a fourteen-year-old schoolgirl living with her parents and her brother in a cramped flat on one of the ubiquitous estates in the New Territories. She had been born in Fujian province in China, where her father was a doctor. In 1980 the family, ostensibly on their way to the Philippines, stopped off in Hong Kong and stayed put. After three months her father, Lam Koon Ying, found a job as an editor at a local news agency.

Norris Lam was already driven by the imperative to succeed that distinguishes Hong Kong teenagers from their Western counterparts. She attended the neighbourhood school, where she was marked out as a star pupil and a natural leader. In addition to her knapsack of books, she invariably carried a mobile phone, which she used to organise a variety of school and community activities with her fellow students. She was studying mathematics, physics, economics and English for A-Level and expected to go on to the Chinese University.

Norris had won a school award for her academic and social record. A member of the school debating team (in both English and Cantonese), she was also chair of the school Community Youth Club, editor of the school magazine, house captain, leader of the Civic Education Group, and, proudly, a member of the Hong Kong Outstanding Students' Association. Cheerful and direct in manner, she talked without priggishness about her urge to make money but also to serve the community. 'We have to show that we can contribute to our society. I am a volunteer at a home for the aged. And we also organised a "workathon" to raise money for World Vision. We like organising camping vacations, and we are hoping to have three days in China.'

Her intention was to use her return to the 'motherland' to discuss the future of Hong Kong with her Chinese counterparts. Although she had not been to the mainland since arriving in Hong Kong as an infant, she thought that it was important to share experiences and to tell her peers about Hong Kong.

> I will tell them about the pace of life here, which is so fast, and about our way of life, which is the trend all over the world. We care about the environment, and about technology, which makes us very efficient. I will tell them that in a democratic country we have the right to speak freely and to have religious freedom. Also voting is important. These are our rights, our human rights. And I think they should know of them, too.

Although Norris had not followed the course of Chris Patten's conflict with Beijing, she was worried that he was moving Hong Kong too far, too fast. 'We are very conservative. I am not even sure that the voting age should be brought down to eighteen. We are not mature enough, I think, for that. But Mr Patten is a real star. Very strong-willed and very hard-working. I think he wants Hong Kong to be a democratic society.'

In July 1993, Norris was able to make her longed-for trip to China. As her bus approached the Lo Wu Bridge, she could see the border. 'I became more and more excited. I kept saying to myself, "I'm nearly there." We all had the same feeling in our group, that we had finally reached Chinese soil and we were back in the motherland at last. Maybe it is because we are Chinese that we have this patriotic feeling.'

This guileless enthusiasm was soon tempered by experience. In the city of Guangzhou, which was growing even faster than Hong Kong, she was struck by the dirt and the drabness. The endless march of new skyscrapers from the impersonal heart of the business centre to the far horizon could not disguise the drudgery, and despite an abundance of Mercedes swirling between new banks and new hotels or from grand apartments to garish nightclubs, the people on the streets seemed down at heel. When the Hong Kong visitors sat down to talk to their Chinese hosts, also students, she voiced her feelings to one of them. 'The things I saw made me a bit depressed. I saw these people in the train station, and they gave me the impression that they were lost and confused.' She was told that they were probably the 'blind flow', migrants from the north travelling south in search of work. The Chinese student explained:

> Economically, Guangdong is quite advanced, but the rest of China is poorer. You can imagine the situation in the north, where fields have been taken out of agricultural production to meet the needs of urban expansion. There are fewer jobs on the land as a result. There are better prospects in the south. If one person from the north finds work in Guangdong this year, he'll go back and bring ten friends down for work next year. Then that ten might bring down a further hundred the following year. Of course, this makes employment more difficult. And when they can't find work, they often commit suicide.

Others in the party from Hong Kong mentioned their own observations. One had seen groups of peasants in a shanty town which looked as if it had been burned down. The government had tried to help these people by resettling them in a better place, but they moved around in search of work, the students were told. The city of Guangzhou had become more unstable and chaotic, and the crime rate had risen. 'These people have no money and no jobs. They are too ashamed to go back home, so they steal and rob from others. As the "blind flow" is always increasing, the government has been unable to cope. Even though some of them will be locked up as vagrants, they will return to the same situation as soon as they are released.'

The candour of the Chinese teenager's response encouraged Norris Lam to ask: 'You witness this depressing fact about this society, and yet you still love your country? What motivates this?' His reply was equally frank: 'I believe,' he said, 'it is the education. The government's emphasis on moral and civil education is very pronounced, especially at primary level. The young are taught about the ideology of the government to make them become more patriotic.'

'And what is the most important aspect of political education?' Norris wanted to know.

'First, you have to be patriotic and passionate towards your motherland, able to understand the basics of the law. Also we have to understand the basic changes of development of the country by the time we reach Form Three. From Forms Four to Six we learn about the basics of business and management. In the beginning, the core thinking is mainly political.' The Chinese student asked Norris about Hong Kong. Was there the same emphasis on political education?

'In Hong Kong they teach you about the basic structure of the government, and they illustrate the rights and responsibilities of the citizen,' she explained. 'We don't usually learn any specific "thinking", as you do. You have lots of activities organised by the government. Students receive their thinking from the government, and pursue these activities. Why are you so obedient to the government?'

Her host's response was simple. 'It's largely because of the political education. The government wishes the young to understand the importance of obedience, loyalty towards your superiors and to the country.'

'We don't have to be obedient towards our parents. We always feel that parents and children will get on better if they are more like friends,' Norris said.

Another Chinese student suggested: 'Maybe we are still inclined to the old traditions. Obeying your superiors is still very important.'

'Tradition may not be as bad as it seems,' offered a third. 'At least it has preserved our society from collapse.'

Norris Lam was a serious teenager, divided from her peers in mainland China by history, not by ethnicity. She wanted to understand, and not to judge, yet she could not begin to comprehend the culture from which she herself sprang, but on which had been superimposed an ideology – communism – which she found alien, and, in her innocence, quite bizarre. Yet she sensed that, if she were to make a place for herself in Hong Kong, which was her home, she would have to adjust to the values her hosts appeared to accept so willingly. Lacking any clear ideological perspective herself, she was troubled by the encounter. Initially she thought it would be a simple, patriotic exploration. Instead it left her feeling that the gulf between her and her counterparts in China was far wider than she had supposed.

In February 1993, nearly four years after Tiananmen Square, the National People's Congress in China had adopted the State Security Law, which criminalised acts 'harmful to state security', either committed by or financed by groups outside the state or carried out 'in collusion with them'. Proscribed activities included 'plotting to subvert the government', 'secretly gathering . . . and illegally providing state secrets for an enemy' and 'other activities against state security'. These 'other activities' related directly to freedom of speech, publication, association and religion. The catch-all nature of these 'offences' was not accidental. Although the law has not been widely deployed, except in respect of 'state secrets', it created, as it must have been intended to do, a climate in which any 'dissident' activity was fraught with even greater uncertainty and danger than before. Potentially, almost any act of defiance against the authorities became subject to severe criminal penalties, not excluding execution.

The same year a well-known journalist, Gao Yu, was arrested and charged with leaking important state secrets. Amnesty International has highlighted her case as an illustration of a judicial system in which the verdict is invariably decided in advance of a trial. This inversion of justice reflected the explicit subservience of the judiciary to the diktat of the Communist party. As the procurator general, Zhang Siqing, later stated in his report to the National People's Congress: 'We should closely rely on the leadership of the party committees and voluntarily accept supervision by the people's congresses. Procuratorial bodies should regularly report to party committees and the people's congresses, seek their advice and consciously carry out their instructions and opinions.'

The implications for Hong Kong of China's attitude towards human rights was brought into sharp focus by the arrest, on 7 October 1993, of Xi Yang, a reporter working in Beijing for one of Hong Kong's leading Chinese-language newspapers, *Ming Pao*. He was held in detention for eleven days before allegedly 'confessing' that he had been 'spying on national financial secrets', the character of which was not disclosed. It appeared, however, that the offence related to a report in *Ming Pao* on 28 July 1993 revealing that the Chinese People's Bank had decided to sell part of its gold reserves to build up its foreign-exchange holdings and that, as interest rates had already been increased twice that year, a third increase was unlikely. The alleged source for Xi Yang's article, an employee of the People's Bank, also 'confessed' to the same 'crime'. The Hong Kong Journalists' Association, a doughty, if isolated, defender of press freedom, pointed out that it was not readily apparent how China's national security might have been endangered by this report.

Margaret Ng, a high-profile columnist and barrister, writing in the *South China Morning Post* a few days after Xi Yang's arrest, offered a disconcerting analysis of the danger facing Hong Kong. Noting that the Chinese law on national security was drawn so widely that what was viewed as perfectly normal journalistic investigation in Hong Kong could be regarded as an unlawful activity in China, she argued that the very existence of a free press in Hong Kong posed a threat to the authorities in Beijing. As China's political, financial, economic and social policies and struggles had an increasingly powerful influence on Hong Kong affairs, so more and more of the colony's journalists would be sent north to cover these developments. Their discoveries would be published in Hong Kong's newspapers, and these in turn would become ever more easily available on the mainland – unless the authorities in Beijing could rupture the cycle of information. 'Not only is China likely to deal harshly with Hong Kong reporters once they are in China,' wrote Ng, 'but [it] is more likely to do everything it can to curtail the freedom of the press in Hong Kong after 1997, probably by getting a similar national security law enacted in Hong Kong if it can.'

One of the troubling features of this case was the way the owners of *Ming Pao* responded to their employee's arrest. They were told by Beijing that they should use the good offices of the British embassy in Beijing to secure Xi Yang's release, and informed that introducing 'self-censorship' in *Ming Pao* would be more likely to bring this about. In these circumstances, the paper understandably refrained from reporting the news of its journalist's detention. However, when the Chinese authorities then pressed charges against Xi Yang, *Ming Pao* abandoned that approach and gave full coverage to this alarming incident. Yet two days later, the chairman of the Ming Pao Group, Yu Pun Hoi, not only took it upon himself to apologise to the Chinese authorities, but declared he had reason to believe that his reporter was indeed guilty as charged – a statement he made without even attempting to consult Xi Yang himself. As Margaret Ng reminded her readers, 'The implication for future freedom of the press is grim.'

The case of Xi Yang not only highlighted the fragility of Hong Kong's freedom; it also threw into sharp relief the shifting attitudes towards that freedom adopted by those of its elite who wished to keep a place in the sun for themselves after July 1997.

By the early 1990s, seventy-six daily newspapers and 663 periodicals were published in Hong Kong, a higher proportion per capita than anywhere else in the world. In this highly competitive marketplace the pressure to cut costs was intense. The culture of investigative journalism was not nearly as developed as it was in the West, and the finance for it was even more limited. While the level of technology was as high as anywhere in the world, the use to which it was put did little to promote adventurous or challenging journalism – to the relief of both the business community and the upper echelons of the civil service, where press freedom was generally regarded as an irritant rather than a virtue. By 1993, the deferential attitude with which Hong Kong's media had long been infected was perceptibly beginning to shift towards self-censorship as more and more journalists, either voluntarily or at the behest of their proprietors, began to heed the pressure from Beijing. Depressingly, it was also clear that the majority in Hong Kong believed this process to be inevitable and irreversible.

In a poll conducted in September 1993, 70 per cent of respondents indicated that they believed the freedom of the press would be eroded after 1997. In the same month, it was reported that the chairman of the Newspaper Society of Hong Kong, Shum Choi Sang, had told the Information Policy Panel of the Legislative Council that many journalists exercised self-censorship because they feared retaliation after 1997. He also estimated that almost three quarters of the profession were worried that they would no longer be able to work in a free environment after the handover.

On 28 March 1994, this pessimism deepened when Xi Yang, who had been held incommunicado for eight months (except for one brief visit from his father), was convicted of 'probing into and stealing state financial secrets'. He was sentenced to twelve years' imprisonment, and his 'accomplice' in the People's Bank received fifteen years. The punishment horrified Hong Kong, and hundreds of local journalists took to the streets to march on the local headquarters of the NCNA in protest. A further 1,300 signed a petition deploring the conviction and the absence of a fair and open trial. The Legislative Council took an unprecedented decision to debate the issue. Nonetheless the message from Beijing was clearly understood: in a poll commissioned by the *South China Morning Post*, 56 per cent of the sample concluded that the sentence was a warning to Hong Kong journalists to be careful and not to do anything with which the Chinese government might disagree.

Almost by definition, it was hard to gauge the full extent of such a closet and insidious practice as self-censorship. However, enough individuals were ready to acknowledge off the record that they exercised it to illustrate the degree to which the independence of the media – one of the defining characteristics of Hong Kong's 'way of life' which was supposed to have been consecrated in both the Joint Declaration and the Basic Law – was under assault. Although all journalists who discover, digest and select facts for publication frequently censor themselves to honour a confidence or to protect a source, it was not this normal filtering process which worried those in Hong Kong who cared about press freedom. In its 1994 annual report, the Hong Kong Journalists' Association explored a phenomenon which it held would 'increasingly play a key role in undermining freedom of expression in the territory', and which, it believed, was infecting the entire industry.

Among other instances, the 1994 report cited the case of Chan Ya, a columnist on the *Express Daily News*, a Chinese-language newspaper which had generally adopted a neutral position on the most controversial issues facing Hong Kong's future. In 1993, shortly after Xi Yang's arrest, Chan Ya's employers told her that they had decided to veto any comment on the case to 'avoid sensitivity'. She agreed to abide by the ruling until Xi Yang's boss made his notorious apology to the Chinese authorities. Incensed, she wrote two articles on the subject, both of which were 'spiked'. In January 1994 she submitted a piece which was critical of David Chu Yiu Lin, a member of the Preliminary Working Committee, a group of pro-Beijing activists appointed by China to help 'prepare' the ground for the transfer of sovereignty. The article was dropped because, according to her editor, it contained an 'indecent metaphor' which he did not choose to identify. Then the paper's chief editor told her that the report was not merely obscene but 'misleading'. Chan Ya's contract was terminated two months later.

A later poll conducted by the Social Sciences Research Centre revealed that over 60 per cent of Hong Kong's journalists felt that their colleagues were apprehensive about criticising the Chinese government, while almost one in three (28.5 per cent) acknowledged that they themselves felt such apprehension.

The term 'self-discipline' was often substituted by editors and reporters, without any obvious sense of irony, for 'self-censorship'. From its own research, the Hong Kong Journalists' Association identified the principal motives for 'self-discipline' from the responses to two related questions: 'Will work which is perceived to be unfavourable to or critical of the Chinese authorities draw repercussions after 1997?' and 'What might the degree of these repercussions be – greater pressures to conform, the loss of one's job, harassment by the authorities, or threats of prosecution for subversion or theft of state secrets?' According to the association, many publishers found it impossible to distinguish their editorial responsibilities from their entrepreneurial priorities. Their attitudes were increasingly dominated by commercial and financial imperatives, which made them unwilling to offend China. Several newspaper proprietors already had extensive investments in China and, whereas Hong Kong's media market was reaching saturation point, the commercial opportunities in China appeared limitless.

The direct but insidious pressure exerted by Beijing on the Hong Kong media played a crucial role in this process. In October 1993, Kam Yiu Yu, the former chief editor of the daily newspaper *Wen Wei Po*, China's unofficial voice in Hong Kong, gave an interview in which he explained, with the authority of an insider, the methods used by Beijing to secure greater compliance from Hong Kong's sometimes wayward media. Some of them were uniquely despotic. Selecting correspondents from supportive papers for favoured attention by giving them 'inside' stories or even headline news is a technique frequently deployed by democratic governments. The Chinese went further. Targeting what

Kam Yiu Yu called the 'economic bases' of Hong Kong's media, they set about acquiring a controlling stake in individual newspapers or media groups by encouraging pro-Beijing investors to purchase the requisite number of shares on their behalf. The purpose of this infiltration, according to this former chief editor, was to gain control of editorial policy and the newspaper's direction of public opinion.

An even more direct pressure was exerted through advertising. Guided by Beijing, Chinese-owned companies had started to offer lucrative but conditional advertising contracts to targeted newspapers, magazines and broadcasting companies. Beijing's trade-off was crude but effective: a boost to company revenue in return for a supportive editorial line. Evidence of this tactic surfaced on 4 June 1993, when *Ming Pao*, one of the few independent Chinese-language papers, published the contents of two internal notices issued by the Bank of China's Hong Kong and Macau office. These instructed all organisations under the bank's extensive control not to place advertisements in eight newspapers and eleven magazines, including *Ming Pao* itself. These diverse periodicals shared one feature: none of them had been willing to toe the Beijing line.

The task of securing the undivided loyalty of Hong Kong's media was reinforced by what Kam Yiu Yu referred to as 'undercover agents': loyal party members sent to work as reporters and editors for Hong Kong papers, usually on the 'China beat'. Many of these mainland correspondents were veterans of the official China News Agency or the semi-official New China News Agency. They were readily hired by Hong Kong editors because their links with the communist hierarchy in Beijing were held to be valuable in themselves; moreover, they held the promise of a major 'scoop'. After the failure of Hong Kong's media, including otherwise loyal newspapers, to endorse the 1989 massacre in Tiananmen Square, Beijing had apparently redoubled its use of these 'agents', first to recover the loyalty of the errant communist press, and secondly to work on the rest.

According to what the 1995 report of the Hong Kong Journalists' Association referred to as 'informed sources', the second of these two objectives was tackled with some sophistication. In addition to direct infiltration, some agents were instructed to offer freelance articles to a variety of newspapers and magazines – an important way, apparently, of 'occupying more bases of public opinion'. Others were to befriend journalists with the purpose of influencing their judgement. As with the other forms of pressure, it was impossible to quantify how widespread or effective these efforts were, but in the tense atmosphere of Hong Kong, they were enough to perturb those who wished to remain journalists after 1997.

In addition the Chinese used the NCNA to bully and threaten recalcitrant journalists, to castigate 'hostile' publications and to instruct editors to undertake their 'patriotic' task with greater dedication. In July 1993, *Next* magazine, a Chinese-language weekly similar to *Time* or *Newsweek*, drew attention to allegations of self-censorship within the Sing Tao Group of newspapers, owned by Sally Aw, who had a reputation in Hong Kong as a tough proprietor with strongly pro-Beijing sympathies. After the sudden resignation of *Sing Tao's* editor in chief, *Next* reported that Aw had berated her editorial team, complaining that the Chinese had expressed unhappiness about a *Sing Tao* editorial on human rights, which they adjudged to be 'biased', a view with which she concurred. She issued instructions that future editorials should be 'fair, neutral, and objective', but did not specify how these standards were to be measured. Sources at *Sing Tao* interpreted the ruling to mean that any news about the pro-democracy movement in China, or about hostility towards Deng Xiaoping, should be regarded as 'unhelpful'. Soon afterwards, reports that a group of students on a Beijing university campus had dared to demonstrate against the authorities, which received extensive coverage elsewhere, were ignored by every paper in the Sing Tao chain. Was it a coincidence that the Sing Tao Group had decided to co-operate with a subsidiary of the *People's Daily* in Beijing to produce a monthly magazine called *Starlight*? Or that, at the same time, *Sing Tao's* office in Guangzhou had set up a TV magazine called *Screen Friends* in collaboration with an official Cantonese television station? Independent observers drew the obvious conclusion.

Yet the trade-offs were not quite as simple as such a bald analysis might imply. At least in comparison with the mainland, the consumer in Hong Kong was highly sophisticated and would certainly be alienated by any overt sign of subservience to Beijing. Few editors were willing to curry favour with the politburo at the risk of decimating their circulation, and therefore only a handful of Hong Kong's newspapers openly campaigned against the principles of democracy. Although it was still easy to distinguish between pro-British and pro-Chinese coverage of the Sino–British conflict, every newspaper of note liked to claim that its editorial stance was merely 'pro-Hong Kong'. Of the mainstream Chinese-language papers, only the *Hong Kong Economic Journal* was stalwart in support of democratic reform; most of the rest sheltered behind the demand for 'consensus' and 'compromise' without specifying how these admirable objectives might be achieved in the circumstances.

In 1994, the chairman of the Hong Kong Journalists' Association,

Daisy Lee, contributed an article for a programme compiled by the Hong Kong News Association for the Three Coast Forums, an annual seminar on journalism attended by delegates from Hong Kong, Taiwan and China. 'The Hong Kong media is in a state of growth and crisis; an era of hope and challenge,' she wrote. 'As long as we don't rush to censor ourselves and compromise our principles, the present freedom of the press can be maintained after 1997.' The piece was removed from the programme. Denying that this decision was a precise illustration of Daisy Lee's warning, the Hong Kong News Association told Radio and Television Hong Kong that the issue of press freedom was both 'too minor' and 'too sensitive' for discussion at the forum.

Broadcasters, too, came under pressure. RTHK was financed directly by the Hong Kong government but prided itself on exercising a similar independence to that enshrined in the charter of the BBC. RTHK's director was Cheung Man Yee, a former civil servant who had emerged as a tenacious advocate of broadcasting freedom. Under her leadership, RTHK maintained its reputation for fair and impartial journalism and as a station that did not shrink from contentious public debate. To protect RTHK from interference after 1997, Cheung Man Yee had pressed for the state broadcasting system to be incorporated as an independent public institution. However, China at once made it clear that this would be regarded as a hostile move by the colonial authorities, and the Hong Kong government decided that it would be a bridge too far, a decision reluctantly endorsed by Chris Patten. Morale at RTHK was severely affected, and it took all Cheung Man Yee's formidable powers of leadership to prevent her colleagues from succumbing to fatalism about 1997 – especially when it became ever more obvious that Beijing was unable to distinguish public-service broadcasting from state propaganda.

The colony's other two terrestrial broadcasters, the commercial stations TVB and ATV, were less stalwart. They competed for audiences with the mix of game shows, comedy and serials which form the staple diet of 'tabloid' television all over the world. Their most popular current-affairs programmes were frothy in content and sensationalist in tone, and shared a penchant for voyeuristic reporting of 'human-interest' dramas and crime. 'Is A.A. Ying's sex drive really strong?' inquired one TVB programme, reporting the alleged rape by a taxi-driver of a sexually promiscuous woman. The manager of TVB's 'Enrichment' Department justified their prurient coverage: 'There were reports in the press about this amazing woman. We had to support our story with in-depth reporting . . . If you stop reporting things you consider bad taste, then I think you are adopting an undesirable attitude as far as disseminating information and communicating are concerned.'

This intrepid approach did not extend to what might more usually be regarded as 'current affairs'. In 1993, TVB bought the rights to a BBC documentary called *Mao Zedong: The Last Emperor*, which took a distinctly less reverent view of the 'great helmsman' than the two portraits already transmitted by local commercial channels. Although it was the programme's revelations about Mao's sexual proclivities which attracted headlines in the West, its contention that he was indeed an emperor of the old school, remote from his people and ruthless in his means, was far more likely to inflame opinion in Beijing. Indeed, the Chinese had already unsuccessfully attempted to pressurise the Foreign Office into asking the BBC to drop the programme, and the Foreign Correspondents' Club in Hong Kong to cancel a private screening. When TVB failed to transmit *The Last Emperor*, it was widely presumed that either the station had yielded to pressure from Beijing, or, at China's behest, had bought the rights precisely to prevent its transmission in Hong Kong. TVB also acquired the rights to another BBC documentary, about China's labour camps, which contained secretly shot footage of prisoners toiling in the fields and on their way to work in prison factories. The film included interviews which revealed the appalling conditions under which 're-education through labour' took place. As in the case of *The Last Emperor*, the documentary was not shown, a decision which angered some legislators. TVB explained: 'It is just one of the documentaries we've bought in and we do not have a schedule for it yet.'

Whether or not TVB was exercising 'self-discipline' in these two cases, it was notable that both TVB and ATV refrained from featuring news likely to provoke Beijing's wrath. When Jung Chang, the author of *Wild Swans*, arrived in Hong Kong, both stations declined to interview her, even though her book was a world bestseller and she herself was generally fêted wherever she went. *Wild Swans* was not only a history of modern China, but a searing indictment of the Cultural Revolution, written from the author's first-hand perspective with an eye for coruscating detail. Similarly, in November 1993, both TVB and ATV decided to ban further interviews with the veteran dissident Wei Jingsheng, who was at the time nominally, though temporarily, a free man. He had served fourteen years in jail in China for trying to protect rights granted by the law but systematically violated in practice before being released that September – nine days before China's thwarted bid to host the Olympics in 2000. The two broadcasters vehemently denied the ban, but when an enterprising journalist rang Wei

Jingsheng in Beijing, he confirmed that TVB, at least, had recently cancelled an appointment to interview him.

Other examples abounded, among them the decision by ATV to drop *News Tease*, which, with an audience of over half a million, was one of the most highly rated and discussed programmes on Hong Kong television, compared locally with CNN's *Larry King Live*. ATV's management explained the cancellation as an editorial decision, claiming that the programme had lost its flair. Yet it was widely recognised that – certainly by Chinese standards – the programme was remarkably sharp-edged and tenacious. It was also noted that one of its interviewers, Wong Yuk Man, had made no secret of his antipathy to communism. Without naming him, a number of pro-Beijing papers, led by *Sing Tao*, had mounted a campaign against the programme, accusing Wong Yuk Man of abusing the freedom of the media, of being 'anti-China', and of 'talking too loudly and being too hostile'.

ATV was embarrassed when, in the spring of 1994, six senior members of the News Department resigned in protest against the decision by its chief executive to cancel the planned broadcast of a documentary made by a Spanish television company to commemorate the fifth anniversary of Tiananmen Square. As edited by ATV, the documentary included a brief segment filmed in the square in the early hours of 4 June 1989. In later evidence before the Legislative Council, the senior managers who had taken the decision to withdraw the programme explained that the film failed to show the 'overall' situation in Tiananmen Square, and that, in any case, they thought it would be 'unhelpful' to pore over the details of that unfortunate episode yet again.

After a protracted debate in the media about this decision, ATV shifted their ground, insisting that there had not been a ban but a misunderstanding: it had always been their intention to transmit the documentary, but in a different slot from that proposed by the News Department. In the event, the programme was transmitted on the anniversary as originally scheduled, but none of the six journalists accepted ATV's offer of reinstatement, preferring instead to use the incident to campaign against the growing threat of self-censorship. 'I don't think there is any room for compromise,' one of them commented. 'One alternative is to give up. But if you carry on, you have to take a journalistic stance. The most important thing is that we journalists are able to maintain our journalistic ethics. Of course, journalists are only one part of the media. The companies themselves, and the public, should also act as watchdogs if they want to maintain press freedom.'

An even more craven example of 'self-discipline' was provided by the world's most powerful media proprietor, Rupert Murdoch. In 1994, as part of his restless search for global supremacy, the owner of News International bought Star TV, a rapidly growing satellite station owned by one of Hong Kong's most powerful entrepreneurs, K.S. Li. K.S., as he was known locally, had sold space on Star's northern beam to the BBC, which used this access to transmit its new World Television Service into Hong Kong and China. In the past Murdoch had made much of the virtues of satellite broadcasting, declaring that global communications of the kind he owned would be the 'biggest catalyst for peaceful co-existence'. The freedom of the airwaves, he intimated, transcended national borders and would liberate countless millions of people trapped in ignorance by the propaganda of oppressive regimes. Soon after his takeover of Star TV, he made a speech in London during which he reiterated that 'the march of telecommunications technology has been the key factor in the enormous spread of freedom that is the distinguishing characteristic of recent years'. Within weeks of that speech, however, Murdoch informed the BBC that Star TV satellite system would no longer be available for its World Television Service.

Had this decision merely been the product of the tycoon's insatiable urge to crush his rivals, it might have been understandable; indeed, Star TV insisted at first that it had been taken for entirely commercial reasons. It was left to Murdoch himself to reveal the precise character of those 'commercial reasons' for denying viewers in China access to the freedom of the airwaves about which he had recently waxed so eloquent. In an interview with his biographer, William Shawcross, for *Esquire*, he acknowledged that his decision would appear cowardly and that he was 'well aware the freedom fighters of the world would abuse me for it', but, he explained, the Chinese authorities 'hate the BBC'. As a result, 'We said that in order to get in there . . . we'd cut the BBC out.' Shamelessly, Murdoch also volunteered that the reason why he had sold most of his shares in the *South China Morning Post* before his acquisition of Star TV was another move to minimise the risk of conflict with China. 'We certainly don't want Star to be shut down because of the opinions of some of our newspaper editors,' he said. Perhaps the only virtue of Murdoch's confession was that he gave expression in public to attitudes shared in private by the overwhelming majority of his peers in the international business community.

It was in this context that Chris Patten decided to give vent to his own fears about the freedom of the press in Hong Kong. Worried about the growing extent to which the Chinese, through the NCNA locally, were 'leaning' on the broadcasting companies and individual newspapers, he used an invitation to address the World Press Freedom

Conference in Hong Kong in the autumn of 1994 to urge journalists and proprietors to stand firm. 'This governor will defend the freedom of the press up hill and down dale . . . All of us in Hong Kong need our free press now, more than ever.' Entreating the media to give the news 'true and straight, without fear or favour', to 'investigate, analyse and explain', and to 'ask the difficult questions and insist on the answers', he spoke with a conviction that clearly touched his audience. 'For our system in Hong Kong to survive and prosper,' he declared, 'proprietors, editors and journalists will have to demonstrate that they too believe passionately in the values of an open society. I am sure they will not betray that trust.' In truth he had no such confidence. He knew that in the scramble for trade with China, proprietors were suggestible and biddable, and, with a handful of exceptions, indifferent to the principles on behalf of which he was so agitated. He knew, too, that many of their employees lacked the stomach for a prolonged struggle on behalf of cultural values which were still novel, if not alien. Even if some of them had the courage of his convictions, they would not easily withstand such political and mercantile pressures.

As the tide in favour of an accommodation with China became more and more difficult to resist, it became evident that fewer and fewer media outlets in Hong Kong could be trusted persistently to champion the values of an open society in the way that the colony's last governor had hoped. The peculiarly personal character of China's onslaught against Patten, combined with the deep-seated if anonymous resentment against him in the business community, found a ready welcome in an increasingly ambivalent media.

By the end of 1993, it was almost impossible to find a British investor in China with a good word to say about Patten's policies for Hong Kong. The governor was the principal subject of dinner-party gossip as bankers and investors gave free rein to their resentment and disdain. Those of his friends who monitored the shifting attitudes of this elite detected from the dismissive hubbub that Patten's standing in this sector of the community was at its lowest since his arrival. Late in 1993, a private dinner party given by Peter Woo and his wife, Bessie, for the chairman of the Hong Kong and Shanghai Bank, Sir William Purves, who was relocating to London, exemplified the mood. Peter Woo made a speech heaping praise on Purves. Purves spoke about his sadness at leaving Hong Kong. He uttered not a word about freedom or democracy or human rights, but made a promise that, back in London, he would 'raise the flag' for Hong Kong as much as he possibly could. Reminding his approving audience that Hong Kong had to 'get on' with China, he expressed the hope that relations would soon be restored and that the 'cack-handed' manner in which these had been handled in recent months would soon be rectified.

When he heard about this, the governor was not so much surprised as disappointed at the disloyalty of a senior adviser who, as a member of ExCo, had not only been privy to his strategy but had failed to speak against it at the time. Word of what Purves had said at his valedictory dinner soon swept through Hong Kong's establishment, as he must have known it would. Indeed, when he returned to his table he had commented in a gleeful aside, 'Well, I expect I have lost some of my more liberal friends now.' A few nights later, at a dinner for Purves at Government House, Patten made a glancing reference to the banker's assessment of his conduct of Hong Kong affairs. According to one guest, 'It was gently done, but Purves was flattened. He had very great trouble making a coherent response.'

Patten's contempt for Purves originated in an incident which had taken place some months earlier. The chairman of the Hong Kong Bank had come to Government House to threaten Patten that if he did not change course, he would face dire consequences. In so many words he told the governor, 'The prime minister is in very considerable political difficulty, a very weak position. I'm thinking of taking along a lot of businessmen to see him to tell him he has to change his policy on Hong Kong and China. You'd better understand that.' On another occasion, the chairman of Shell came to see him and made similar threats. He behaved, as Patten put it, 'with the sort of crudeness which I don't think the Mafia would show'. Patten was not used to such raw conduct and it genuinely shocked him.

One of the more painful episodes for Patten in this period was a visit from a former Cabinet minister, Lord Prior, who had re-emerged into prominence as the chairman of GEC. In government, where he had served as minister of agriculture and secretary of state for Northern Ireland, Prior had earned a reputation for affability and decency, if not for strength of purpose or intellect. Patten, who had served under him in Northern Ireland, had grown to like and respect him. As a prominent 'wet', Prior had had an uncomfortable relationship with Margaret Thatcher, who made no secret of her disdain for his 'one-nation' Toryism. As chairman of GEC, however, he was a surrogate for Lord Weinstock, and in this role he appeared to shed these values – at least in relation to Hong Kong. Those close to the governor revealed that Prior used his visit to Government House to berate his former colleague, showing a disconcerting lack of perspective and an embarrassing ignorance of the colony. The governor was by now familiar with Prior's message, which had already been delivered to him by other panjandrums of British industry for whom the rights and aspirations of the people of Hong Kong were apparently of little moment. Nonetheless it distressed him that Prior could so easily discard the principles which he had once seemed to hold dear.

He was less surprised by the animosity of another former colleague, Lord Young, the chairman of Cable and Wireless. Unlike Prior, Young had been one of Thatcher's favourites, an abrasive businessman who had never claimed a serious interest in political ideas. He was an entrepreneur by instinct and talent, a man of energy and enthusiasm whose 'can-do' attitude to apparently intractable problems prompted the prime minister to bring him into the Cabinet for a brief but inconsequential spell in the eighties. His contempt for the niceties of diplomacy was well known. In the case of China he believed simply, as he explained in 1996, 'It is trade that strengthens relationships, not treaties.' In 1984, following the signing of the Joint Declaration, he had led a British trade mission to Beijing during which he laid the foundations of a productive relationship with the Chinese leadership. As a former secretary of state for trade and industry, he liked to regard himself as an 'old friend' of China. Moreover, as the chairman of a company hungry for business in China, he conveniently found himself in sympathy with many of the attitudes of the country's leaders. By the early nineties he had come to the view that 'if you allowed too much openness in China . . . it would go back to warlordism'. The danger, he thought, lay in disparities in living standards between the north and, for instance, Shanghai, where, in 1995, 'Ferrari opened a car showroom and sold four cars in the first weekend to local Chinese. Well, they don't do that in London.'

It was from this standpoint that Lord Young assessed Patten's programme for Hong Kong. 'I think a number of us saw that there were opportunities in China on a heroic scale. That we could go back and reclaim markets that were ours in the last century. And that, I thought, would be a great prize: to retreat with honour and actually have a relationship.' Tiananmen Square, he conceded, was 'of course, appalling; it was a terrible miscalculation', but he was encouraged when one or two of his friends in Beijing acknowledged that this 'miscalculation' was the product of inexperience. Indeed, he had some sympathy when they told him, 'This was the first demonstration we'd had since 1949 which we had not organised ourselves. We were clumsy.' The problem, as it was explained to him, was that they had 'put in people who had no idea about crowd control'. Young was also persuaded by his Chinese hosts that the demonstrators were not entirely blameless, either. Although he did not know how many had died, he suspected that 'a lot of these people' had been 'stoked up'.

> They had been talked into democracy and they got talked into doing a number of things which an ageing leadership felt, I suspect, struck at the very heart of what they were trying to do . . . They were humiliated. The worst thing you can ever do is to make people lose face in that part of the world . . . And then I suppose they reacted – and that's not to apologise for them; what they did was wrong in every way – but you could begin to understand.

This 'understanding' had allowed Lord Young, among others, to nurture his relationship with China – even when, as a member of the Cabinet, he was subject to the bar on ministerial meetings with the Chinese imposed by the European Community after the Tiananmen Square 'miscalculation'. Young thought that it was 'extraordinarily important to keep the relationship going', regardless of the sanctions. To this end he even managed to arrange a meeting to discuss the expansion of the Anglo–French nuclear plant at Daya Bay by inviting the relevant Chinese general to meet him in a box at Ascot Races. 'I passed a very pleasant five minutes with him and off I went,' Young said. The general was able to report back that he had 'met' the trade secretary, while Young could claim that their 'chance encounter' did not breach the sanctions. As Young put it, 'Everything was plain sailing from then on.'

Soon after his appointment as governor, Patten had been invited to lunch at Cable and Wireless, where Young and his colleagues had put their case for accommodating China in the interests of British industry. According to Young, they went out of their way to tell Patten how things should be done in private rather than in public, and how 'face' was very important. Patten did not seem overly impressed, and made it clear, Young says, that he was going to 'look at this with different eyes'. Afterwards Young recalls turning to a colleague and saying of Patten's appointment: 'I'm very worried. I am not sure this is going to be such a good idea.'

Young's doubts turned to dismay when he heard that Patten had decided to forgo the governor's plumed hat and official dress.

> You see, the governor is not an elected individual. The governor should be an aloof person who represents authority . . . Chris behaved as if he was canvassing for votes . . . you know, going round and kissing babies . . . I thought it demeaned the position of governor. I was concerned at his whole style . . . it is not the way to deal

with the Beijing leadership where, in my book, you should say everything to them privately and agree what you're going to say publicly. It's not kowtowing to Beijing; it's simply the best way of getting agreement out of them.

At that time Cable and Wireless was the only foreign telecommunications company – through its subsidiary, Hong Kong Telecom – permitted to operate inside China. Young had worked hard to secure a closer relationship with the Chinese leadership. 'I had invested an enormous amount of time and effort seeing everybody – the president, Jiang Zemin, the premier, Li Peng – in order to find a way in which we could play a role . . . in what would be by far the largest market in the world,' he explained. 'It was incredibly important.' As he saw it, Patten's desire for democracy in Hong Kong not only threatened his own company's interests, but, more generally, promised to cause unnecessary damage to Britain's trading prospects with China. 'I do not believe that it was his job to sell out the people of Hong Kong for the benefit of the United Kingdom,' he said later. 'But I do believe there was a balance . . . and I think that balance went too far.'

Patten's refusal to be swayed rankled with Young. During a trip to Hong Kong, Young visited Government House on three occasions to press his case, all to no avail. If Patten managed to conceal his contempt for what he felt to be Young's crude approach and narrow focus, he gave the chairman of Cable and Wireless no comfort. 'We'd started on a confrontational approach, and I was trying my very best to plead the course of agreement with him,' Young recalled. 'We didn't have a row – my personal relationship [with Patten] was very good, and I think he's a very honourable, decent human being – but it was obvious I was not being listened to. And if you think you are not being listened to, you think to yourself, why bother?' After the third visit he did not seek any further meetings. Nor, he reflected, was he invited.

After his departure from Cable and Wireless following a long and highly publicised boardroom struggle, Young was unrepentant. Insisting that his overriding concern was the 'people of Hong Kong', the 'vast majority' of whom were 'entirely unpolitical', he declared Patten's term to have been a 'disaster'. 'The business community in Britain is totally against the governor,' he volunteered, 'and the business community in Hong Kong is totally against the governor.' He added: 'When you find this unanimity of opinion, you have to ask yourself why.' For Young the answer to the question was as honourable as it was self-evident.

Patten found it very difficult to take Young seriously. 'He never put those arguments to my face, though I used to hear what he said behind my back. That happened regularly over the years,' the governor commented dismissively. 'I think that is perhaps characteristic of Lord Young's style. But I can never remember him coming and having a serious discussion with me about our obligations to the people of Hong Kong.'

Young's response to the charge of cowardice was to say, somewhat limply, 'I did not risk having an argument with him because I didn't want to bring any animus into the relationship we had, because that would react on my company.'

Patten's contempt for individuals like Purves and Young extended to many of their Chinese counterparts in Hong Kong. 'Some of the business leaders in the community appear to have been prepared to accept a sort of Faustian deal,' he noted with disdain. 'In effect they say to the Chinese leadership, "Well, nobody gives a button about a free press or all this other stuff the Brits went on about and stuck into the Joint Declaration. So long as we can go on making money, everything is all right."'

Patten's critics in the business community were now becoming more outspoken. Even the silkily oblique Peter Woo allowed something of his resistance to the Patten reforms to emerge, if only for the future record. While he and his wife, Bessie, continued to cultivate the Pattens socially, he spoke insinuatingly of the damage caused by the proposals 'the governor is supposed to have put on the table'. In so doing Patten had provoked the raising of a voice which had hitherto been silent: 'The business voice, saying, "We don't like it." Look, we don't try to control Hong Kong – it is not the business people's desire to control Hong Kong. But they don't want to see that they have no say in the future.'

Vincent Lo expressed his hostility with less guile. 'To be blunt,' he said towards the end of 1993, 'I think he has done what he has done. So if there is a good assignment for him in London or elsewhere, maybe he can go and we can have a new governor who can really understand the reality of Hong Kong and work with Beijing so that we can get a better deal.'

Patten had only one unequivocal champion in Hong Kong: the flamboyant and outspoken Simon Murray, former managing director of Hutchison Whampoa. Murray's endorsement of Patten had irritated the company's chairman, K.S. Li, who was avowedly pro-Beijing. Though neither of them would concede the point publicly, their conflict over this issue was instrumental in Murray's decision, late in 1993, to resign. As he moved easily between the expatriate and the local elite, Murray was in a unique position to assess the motives of his fellow businessmen.

Visitors always asked him similar questions: 'Why doesn't Patten keep quiet?' 'Why doesn't he shut up?' 'Why doesn't Britain co-operate?' Some of them, assuming that Murray shared their views, would complain about 'this bloody Patten'. Murray gave them no quarter.

> You simply do not understand. Who the hell are you, coming from France, or London, or wherever, to start telling me that Patten is wrong? You haven't even understood one fraction of the issue, and yet you are coming out here telling us what the score is . . . You say, 'Patten seems to be the problem.' Well, he may be the problem for your particular business. But there are five or six million people here for whom Patten is not the problem. Patten is their life-saver. OK? Have you thought about their position? The ordinary Hong Kong citizen has run away from China. He's a refugee. We are handing over Hong Kong to a third party which happens to be the last bastion of hard-nosed communism in the world. Examine the human-rights record. Every so often they release a guy who's been in jail for twenty-seven years and never actually been on trial, and they'll say 'It's all getting better.' Yes, it is getting better, but China's record is still pretty bad, and this leaves a lot of people in this place who are absolutely terrified of what comes next.

Murray was resigned to the fact that his would remain a lone voice, even though his listeners sometimes appeared to be impressed that one of their own should speak with such conviction. He was by no means self-righteous. It was simply as a matter of fact that he noted: 'Businessmen are interested in their money, and that is all they are interested in.'

Murray pressed Patten's cause with his counterparts in terms which Patten could not himself deploy, even in informal gatherings. Insisting that only a more broadly based, and thus more democratic, Legislative Council could protect Hong Kong from the corruption that was endemic on the mainland, he argued that if LegCo were to be elected on Beijing's terms, it would be a very small body and dangerously open to bribery and coercion. 'Anybody in his right mind would say that we've got to have a wider electoral body to ensure that we do not have a corrupt Legislative Council, and that we can throw them out if they turn bad on us.' Murray believed that many of his peers privately shared this opinion but were afraid to speak out. He persevered.

> The only way we can have any hope of continued success is by being different. Who needs Hong Kong? The weather's OK, and it

is quite a nice place to live, but it would be irrelevant for our business. We'll all go and open our offices in Shanghai. Outsiders will not invest in Hong Kong if the business is exactly the same as in China. Hong Kong's GDP will begin to fall, and Hong Kong will begin to fade. It will cease to be important. It is important today because of the freedoms and because of the law.

Murray often found that he could 'swing a dinner table round', but his success was invariably short-lived. 'The following day they are back under their tables. They are fearful and they want to keep their mouths shut and hope it will all go away. In many ways it's pathetic.'

Patten only occasionally gave vent to his own frustration. Rarely raising his voice, even in private, he invariably encased his feelings with a carapace of heavy irony. At a particularly exasperating moment in December 1993, when his responsibilities seemed 'fairly nerve-racking', he noted that he had 'learned to worry less about the ammunition which is going to be fired at you from the other side than the ammunition which comes zinging at you from behind your back'. A few months later he was less oblique. The most depressing thing about the first two years of his governorship was the extent to which the business community had been prepared to 'sell out completely without really bothering whether or not China lives up to the bargain it undertook in the Joint Declaration, and without bothering whether China actually lives up to all its commitments on preserving the values of Hong Kong. I think that is pretty treacherous.'

I3

'A BRACING AND
BRUISING EXPERIENCE'

Charges and Counter-Charges

The collapse of negotiations with China at the end of 1993 provoked a protracted bout of political soul-searching in Government House. Although he could hardly admit it publicly, Chris Patten felt a sharp sense of liberation and relief that the Chinese negotiators had at the last moment reneged on their apparent readiness to do a deal. In particular he had not enjoyed having to concede ground on the electoral franchise; nor could he rid himself of the sense that to negotiate with Beijing involved a through-the-looking-glass journey in which the awareness of delusion was always mockingly at hand. The future was daunting, but at least he was once again in control of events – insofar as it was possible to dictate a process so fraught with uncertainty.

The governor knew that he had to regain the initiative and to reinvigorate Hong Kong with the confidence and enthusiasm for his reforms which had noticeably dissipated in the long months of haggling. On 3 December 1993, he announced that ExCo had sanctioned his plan to introduce the first (and least controversial) part of his reform package into the Legislative Council on 15 December. The Chinese responded with a predictable outcry and, taking its cue from Beijing and the business community, Allen Lee's Liberal party (the Co-operative Resources Centre had reinvented itself in March) voiced severe misgivings about Patten's decision to press ahead in the absence of China's blessing.

Patten was far more concerned about the Democrats. Martin Lee had expressed his dismay that the governor had ever allowed himself to be drawn into the charade of negotiations with China. By now the two men knew each other well, and Martin Lee had privately left Patten in no doubt about his party's 'bottom line'. Patten's decision to table his original bill, albeit in two parts, was not only a matter of political instinct. It was also governed by the knowledge that he would lose the support of the Democrats if he were to table the 1993 version of his proposals watered down in an attempt to reach agreement with China. Martin Lee's Democrats might well join Allen Lee's Liberals in an unholy alliance to wreck any bill thus amended. In these circumstances, public confidence, already fragile, would be shattered, as would his own credibility. The demands for his departure would reach a crescendo and, as he privately acknowledged, it would be very difficult for him to remain in office.

As it was the path on which he now had little choice but to embark was hazardous. Even if he could muster the votes for the relatively innocuous first stage of the bill, he knew that LegCo would be split down the middle over the second stage. He was not at all confident that he would emerge triumphant from such a fracas. Whatever the final outcome, he was all too conscious that the months ahead would put his political acumen severely to the test. He had a foretaste of this when Martin Lee, ostensibly one of his few allies in Hong Kong, attacked his approach while on a trip to Washington to drum up congressional support. Warning that the governor's decision to table the bill in two parts would give the Chinese even more time to derail the reforms, Martin Lee declared that he no longer trusted Patten to fight for democracy in Hong Kong. In characteristically exaggerated language, he claimed that the governor had 'talked a great deal but delivered nothing'.

The days leading up to Christmas were consumed by a dreary routine of charge and countercharge which aggravated the deteriorating relationship between Britain and China. Beijing accused the British of being responsible for the breakdown; London retorted that it was the other way round. Each side claimed that it was willing to recommence negotiations and blamed the other for failing to respond. On 17 December a Chinese Foreign Ministry spokesman reiterated that any legislation passed by LegCo in the absence of a Sino–British accord would not straddle 1997. He added that trade relations between the two sovereign powers would be adversely affected, although he did not specify in what way or to what extent. Patten reacted swiftly by pointing out that China enjoyed a trade surplus with Britain, and that he could not imagine that Beijing would wish to damage that advantageous imbalance. On 27 December, in their most unequivocal statement so far, the Chinese issued a formal warning that there would be no 'through train' for the legislative assembly, or for the two tiers of local government, the District Boards and the Municipal Councils. On 1 July 1997, they announced, all individuals elected to these three bodies would cease to hold office, and a new three-tier structure of government would be 're-established in accordance with the relevant Basic Law stipulations'. This was the most unnerving declaration of intent yet to issue from Beijing.

To add to the mood of pessimism in Hong Kong, a leading NCNA official served notice that senior government officials would not automatically be allowed to remain in office following the handover. This threat to derail the administrative 'through train' along with its political counterpart was calculated to alarm not only civil servants but also the business community, for whom the survival of an experienced and independent civil service was critical to ensure stability. The Basic Law stipulated that all civil servants would have the right to remain in service after 1997. However, the NCNA spokesman said, the mechanism by which this process was to have been achieved had been severely damaged by Patten's insistence on pressing ahead with his constitutional reforms in defiance of China's will. As a result, the first chief executive of the SAR would (as stipulated elsewhere in the Basic Law) nominate senior officials who would be appointed by the central government of the People's Republic. The implied threat was self-evident: senior civil servants who had the temerity to honour their obligations as loyal servants of the British crown might have to look elsewhere for employment after 1997.

Anson Chan, the chief secretary, responded mildly but firmly that it was 'important to maintain the continuity of the civil service'. Her words disguised the anxiety felt by all her colleagues in the upper echelons of the government, many of whom had already privately made it clear that they had no faith in Patten's 'confrontational' approach. The governor's press secretary, Mike Hanson, one of his most loyal officials and himself a civil servant, was frustrated by the erosion of morale among his colleagues. Many of them complained that the governor had been too distracted by the conflict with China to address other important issues; that they had been isolated from the policy-making process; that they no longer trusted Patten to act wisely in Hong Kong's interests. Hanson noticed that on a number of domestic issues they were becoming increasingly recalcitrant – even to the extent of failing to co-operate in the preparation of the governor's 1993 address to LegCo. Instead of identifying and exploring a range of alternative policy options, some chose, in Hanson's words, to 'cut off the options in advance'.

Simon Vickers, another expatriate who had joined the Hong Kong civil service in 1979, was equally disturbed. He had served in various departments, including the chief secretary's office, before joining the Security Department in 1992, with responsibility for immigration and nationality policy. The impact of Tiananmen Square had forced him, like so many others, radically to adjust his views about the future of Hong Kong. The optimism of the mid-eighties, when he had been sure that he and his family would be able to stay on after 1997, swiftly gave way to uncertainty and then to pessimism. After Patten's arrival and the outbreak of diplomatic hostilities between Britain and China, he had noticed a shift of attitude among 'local' civil servants. Though ostensibly loyal to their present sovereign, he sensed that a lot of them had 'fallen away' from Patten because 'he was causing too many problems for them in their daily lives'. According to Vickers, they were frustrated that many of their otherwise non-contentious policy proposals for the development of Hong Kong were being blocked by Beijing in the Joint Liaison Group (JLG), the forum through which the Chinese exercised their right to be consulted on all matters relating to the handover. Rather than blame their future masters for this impasse, they tended instead to blame Patten, lamenting, 'It wasn't like this in the old days.' The warnings from China that their jobs would not be secure after 1997 served only to sharpen this alienation which, Vickers detected, was accompanied by a surge in 'patriotic' sentiment. He saw this as a threat to the colony's post-1997 prospects. 'It doesn't leave room for Hong Kong to say, "Well, we are part of China, but we do things in a different way."'

One incident was to lodge in Vickers' mind to illustrate this anxiety. A year or so on, in 1995, as a reliable expatriate, he was transferred to the Judiciary Department, where he was charged with the sensitive task of separating those personnel files that would be made available to the Chinese in 1997 from those to be retained or shredded. On one occasion, when he was deputising for the department's senior administrator, he came across a note from one of the colony's most senior Chinese judges, which was clearly not intended for his eyes. Attached to a clipping from a newspaper article about the alleged superiority of the Chinese IQ over that of other ethnic groups, the judge had written: 'How much longer must we carry on this charade of subordination?' The latent hostility towards the British from such an important member of Hong Kong's judicial establishment intensified Vickers' own growing sense of isolation and reinforced his intention to take his family back to Britain before the handover of sovereignty. Vickers shared Hanson's view that the governor would have great difficulty retaining the loyalty of the most senior civil servants in the final stages of the handover. Hanson was reluctant to add to Patten's troubles by voicing such fears. 'I don't think the governor realises how isolated he is,' he said.

As Christmas approached, in his rare moments of respite from the increasing pressures of his governorship, Patten tried to make the most of the personal comforts his surroundings offered. If Hong Kong is light on culture, it is a cornucopia for those in need of retail therapy, and the governor was an avid shopper. In Bath, he had been a familiar sight in supermarkets, delicatessens and wine stores, not propositioning constituents but buying the weekend groceries. On holiday in France (where the Pattens were to buy a house in 1994), his daily routine was constructed around his mission to attend every local market of significance. As these occurred at least three times a week, he was kept very busy. Despite Lavender's attempts to curtail his enthusiasm, he invariably returned from such expeditions heavily laden with cheeses, wines, meats, fruit and pastries, concerned only about whether he had purchased enough to meet their needs before his next foray.

In Hong Kong, where he did not need to buy his own food, he browsed in the antique shops which line Hollywood Road, a mere ten minutes from Government House. He also enjoyed buying clothes for himself and for his family, choosing dresses for his wife and daughters – even for Laura, who now worked in London for *Harpers & Queen*. On one occasion he selected for her a scarlet slip of a dress designed by Jean-Paul Gaultier: it fitted perfectly. He was also taken with Shanghai Tang, owned by one of Hong Kong's most imaginative entrepreneurs, David Tang. Here he bought a long green *cheong sam* as a surprise for Lavender and a velvet Chinese jacket lined with vivid cartoon prints for himself. When friends came to stay he took them to Shanghai Tang and urged them to follow his example.

In Hollywood Road, calling in on the way to buy his favourite sweetmeats from a corner store which proudly displayed a photograph of him with the owner, he would happily spend a couple of hours wandering from shop to shop, admiring the ceramics, bronzes, ivory and jade on display. Patten soon acquired enough antiques to adorn both the private quarters at Government House and the main rooms at Fanling. The housekeeper at Fanling, evidently unaware of the importance attached by collectors to the original pigment on 2,000-year-old ceramics, noticed one day that the rough pieces of ancient pottery seemed grubby. She decided to attack them with hot water and cloth. Soon they were free of all dirt – and almost all colour. The Pattens sighed, but did not complain.

In January 1994, Patten flew to London to give evidence before the Foreign Affairs Committee of the House of Commons. In his opening statement to the assembled MPs, he intimated something of the pressure to which he had been subjected. Offering an otherwise robust account of his stewardship, he volunteered that the attempt to negotiate the transfer of sovereignty was 'occasionally a more bracing and bruising experience than any of us would like'. Answering the charge that he had been responsible for violating the Joint Declaration, the Basic Law and other agreements between Britain and China, he asserted that no Chinese official had yet 'been able to identify precisely where these perfidious crimes have taken place'. As for Sir Percy Cradock's accusation, made before the same committee a month earlier, that Patten had 'refused consultations with the Chinese', it was, he insisted, 'completely untrue – whether the result of misunderstanding or whether the result of other motivations is for Sir Percy to explain in due course'.

In an indirect riposte to Cradock, who had gone on to accuse him of a 'reckless' disregard for the interests of the people of Hong Kong, Patten poured scorn on those unnamed officials who liked to approach negotiations in the belief that 'if you find a suitably opaque form of words, full of strong nouns and weak verbs, it can provide a curtain behind which you can retreat on matters of substance'. A little later in his evidence, he challenged Cradock directly to 'say openly that basically his point of view is that we should settle for whatever China will provide'. Remarkably, this swingeing assault – his only public reprimand until that point for the prime minister's former adviser – was barely noticed by the media, whose attention was otherwise engaged. Privately, Patten expressed his contempt for the 'appeasement' policy advanced by Cradock, his loyalists in and around Whitehall and a significant proportion of the international business community. 'You know, I dare say there are some who, if China was saying, "Well, our price is slaughter of the first-born," who would say, "Well, maybe it is not unreasonable in the circumstances. You know, you have to allow for different cultural traditions." I mean, do we ever have a bottom line?'

The animosity between the governor and the former diplomat not only reflected their mutual contempt but their mutual incomprehension. The non-debate between them exposed contradictory certainties about Britain's responsibilities towards Hong Kong and, consequently, about what strategy to adopt with China. These divisions, long suppressed by the diplomatic evasions and self-delusions of the Foreign Office, had allowed both Britain and China to pretend to themselves that fundamental questions about freedom and justice could be avoided or postponed. By insisting that these issues could not honourably be ignored, and that, diplomatically, Britain should not be intimidated by China, Patten had not only brought them to the surface but had obliged Hong Kong, China and Britain to confront the perilous realities which faced them.

But Patten had now advanced too far down his chosen path to be diverted for long by a thwarted ex-official who refused to keep his own counsel. Bombarding the committee with carefully marshalled arguments, he reiterated his belief that his proposals were not only modest but well within the terms of the Joint Declaration and the Basic Law. He concluded – carried away more by his own rhetoric than by a genuine conviction – with the assertion: 'I am optimistic about Hong Kong's future. I am optimistic about the likelihood of our values and our way of life surviving, because I think that what Hong Kong represents is the future, not the past.'

Meanwhile, there was the present. Asked about the deadline by which the two parts of his bill would have to complete their passage through the Legislative Council, he answered, 'We need to have the main legislation in place by July . . . these are fantastically complicated elections. They involve, as honourable members can, I am sure, imagine, about forty different pieces of subordinate legislation or administrative guidelines . . . All these things are hugely complicated and July is cutting things very fine indeed.' This was the first deadline he had set which genuinely could not be extended without severely disrupting Hong Kong's electoral timetable.

On 24 January, the Cabinet once again endorsed the governor's approach and strategy. In what by now had become a routine procedure, the foreign secretary stood beside Patten at a press conference after the Cabinet meeting to make it clear that the governor had the 'unanimous support' of his colleagues in government. This statement of the predictable was ignored by the British media, for which, in any case, it was not principally intended. It played well in Hong Kong, however, where a distinctly more credulous school of journalism prevailed, and where every inconsequential phrase from a figure of authority was likely to be treated as a tablet from the mount. It also served to remind Beijing that the 'Triple Violator' and the British prime minister were not easily to be unyoked, however rough the terrain might become. Both men genuflected towards a resumption of talks, but the press conference did elicit two points of substance: that the governor had not yet decided when to table the second part of his reform package, and that the decision was to be his alone, subject only to consultation with the foreign secretary.

Meanwhile, the possibility of Patten returning to London to help restore the fortunes of an ailing government was given an airing in the British press. The *Daily Telegraph* reported that a number of senior officials had privately urged that the governor should be summoned back from Hong Kong in the hope of restoring Sino–British relations. His skills, they noted dryly, could perhaps be put to better use in a less sensitive role. More flatteringly, an editorial in the same paper observed: 'Minister after minister has lamented privately that Mr Patten, among the ablest of Tory strategists, is absent from the bridge in the government's hour of need.' This was certainly true: the Conservatives were still stricken by divisions over Europe and the failure of the 'feel-good' factor to emerge at the end of Britain's longest postwar recession. The party had also exposed itself to contempt and ridicule with a succession of financial and sexual scandals, and the term 'sleaze' had attached itself, limpet-like, to the reputation of an unpopular government. Whether or not Patten could have made a significant difference was, however, open to question. Although he sometimes allowed himself the thought that he might have been able to steer Major around some of the pitfalls into which he had fallen, the government's problems were as much matters of substance as of presentation, and Patten had been far too preoccupied with his own drama in Hong Kong to do more than commiserate with his friends and colleagues at Westminster. In any case, he was as robustly determined to stay as he had been six months earlier when Douglas Hurd had first mooted the possibility of a premature return to the government. In an attempt to deter further wishful thinking by his former colleagues, Patten used an interview with Max Hastings to scotch rumours that he had his sights on an early departure from Hong Kong. He was only too aware that if they were to gather force, his credibility would be further endangered. Hastings clearly got the message: although he ruminated on the prospect of the governor's return, the burden of the *Telegraph*'s editorial on the subject was summed up in the headline, 'PATTEN SHOULD STAY'.

In Hong Kong, it was widely presumed that the first part of Patten's bill would emerge unscathed from LegCo. Regardless of the mutterings from Beijing, it seemed unlikely that the anti-Patten coalition within LegCo could mount a significant threat to a set of proposals whose most controversial point was lowering the voting age to eighteen. All attention was therefore now focused on the fate of the second part of the package. The question lobbed back and forth in the media and between the competing political parties was whether Patten should table his original 1992 proposals or the 1993 version watered down in the vain attempt to secure a deal with China. Patten, of course, had

The throbbing megalopolis of Hong Kong, until 1997 the last significant jewel in Britain's colonial crown, has been variously described by Western writers as 'pure joy to the senses' and a 'permanent parasite' upon the skin of China. Robin Allison Smith

The leader of the Liberal party, Allen Lee, a toughened but compliant advocate of the business community and their allies in China. Robin Allison Smith

Margaret Ng (below), the fearless political columnist elected to the Legislative Council in 1995. Robin Allison Smith

Martin Lee, the leader of the Democrats, who recorded a landslide victory in 1991, when, for the first time, a proportion of the seats on the Legislative Council were directly elected. Robin Allison Smith

The Legislative Council chamber (below), the setting of many scenes in the remarkable political drama which unfolded during Patten's governorship. Robin Allison Smith

The redoubtable Emily Lau. 'Emily is a sort of yardstick against which the rest of us have to measure ourselves,' remarked Patten. Robin Allison Smith

Christine Loh, originally the governor's own appointee to the Legislative Council, emerged as a politician in her own right in the countdown to the handover. Robin Allison Smith

The author in conversation with Tsang Yok Sing, the leader of the Democratic Alliance for the Betterment of Hong Kong. Robin Allison Smith

Property developer Vincent Lo, an influential voice in both Hong Kong and Beijing. Robin Allison Smith

The trials and the triumphs of Patten's term of office were monitored assiduously by the local press. FormAsia Books Ltd

British ambassador to China Sir Robin McLaren faces the press after the fourth round of talks in 1993. Associated Press

Sir David Ford, chief secretary in Hong Kong from 1986 to 1993. Hong Kong Government

Sir Len Appleyard, McLaren's successor as British ambassador in Beijing during the final years of British rule in Hong Kong. London Pictures Service

The prime minister's adviser Sir Percy Cradock arrives at Kai Tak Airport in 1993 en route for Beijing, a visit undertaken against the governor's wishes. David Wong, South China Morning Post

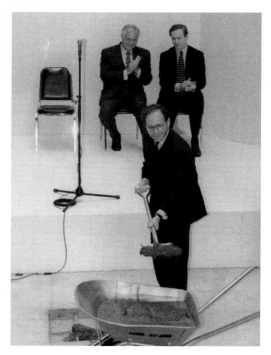

Foreign secretary Malcolm Rifkind, watched by the governor, performs the topping-out ceremony at the British consulate building in Hong Kong on his first official visit to the territory in January 1996. Hong Kong Government

The country retreat at Fanling provided some respite from the pressures of Government House, but there were always official boxes to attend to. Robin Allison Smith

already made up his mind in favour of the 1992 proposals the previous summer, but had not disclosed this to his colleagues until his return from holiday. Although the Cabinet meeting on 24 January 1994 had formally endorsed his decision, he refrained from committing himself in public. Indeed, as a precautionary measure, the lawyers in the Constitutional Affairs Department had been instructed to draft a parallel bill based on the 1993 concessions. The governor and his team resolutely denied the existence of such a draft, knowing that it would be used by his adversaries to undermine the case for the original bill.

In early February, Patten made an official visit to Australia, where the foreign minister, Gareth Evans, paid fulsome tribute to his 'modest' reforms. In contrast, the premier, Paul Keating, whose anti-British chippiness was well known, was notably reticent about the need for greater democracy in the British colony, an omission which was gloatingly picked up by the NCNA. At the same time, Beijing reacted to news that, on Patten's advice, the Foreign Office was about to release a White Paper detailing the background to the breakdown of the Sino–British talks with a tit-for-tat promise to produce their own version. Irreverent observers noted wryly that only a serious breakdown in relations could prompt either Britain or China into such an uncharacteristic display of open government.

In fact Government House had been involved in a fierce argument with both the Foreign Office (where Christopher Hum, one of Cradock's acolytes, was particularly influential) and the embassy in Beijing about whether it was necessary or advisable to give the Chinese formal notice of the decision to publish the White Paper and of the proposed timetable for the LegCo debate. In the end, as one of Patten's disgruntled aides put it, 'the diplomats won'. It was agreed that the British ambassador, Sir Robin McLaren, would deliver a letter to Lu Ping on 17 February. But the day before a member of ExCo leaked the proposed LegCo timetable to the *Economic Journal*, which duly published the details. When the British embassy pressed for a meeting with Lu Ping, there was no response. As a result McLaren had to leave the letter at the Hong Kong and Macau Affairs Office without even seeing its director. A measure of the relationship between Government House and the embassy may be gauged from the report of one of Patten's aides that the governor had chortled mirthlessly: 'The cowardly sods gave it to the receptionist and ran.' A few hours later, Lu Ping's office rang wanting to know why the British ambassador had not had the courtesy to await a response. When this was finally delivered, down the phone line, it was, said Mike Hanson, 'terrible'.

The Foreign Office released their White Paper on 24 February, timing it to coincide with the passage of the first stage of Patten's reform bill through LegCo in the early hours of the same day. The Electoral Provisions (Miscellaneous Amendments) (No. 2) Bill, as it was officially known, confirmed that in the 'geographical' constituencies at all three levels of government elections would be on the basis of a single-seat, single-vote system; that appointments to Municipal Councils and District Boards would be abolished; that the voting age would be reduced to eighteen; and that restrictions on the rights of Hong Kong residents who were simultaneously members of the Chinese People's Congress to stand for election in the territory would be lifted. The bill was passed on second reading by a majority of 48 to 2 after a motion proposing its postponement had been rejected by 36 votes to 23.

Anson Chan welcomed the outcome, and despite Beijing's fury at Britain's unilateral decision to forge ahead with the unamended second-stage bill, made emollient noises about future co-operation with China. Moving forward with the second stage was complicated by the fact that several senior civil servants, increasingly fearful of Beijing's wrath, had hoped to appease China by running with the 1993 version. The secretary for constitutional affairs, Nicholas Ng, who had replaced Michael Sze, was particularly negative about the decision to press on with Patten's original proposals. His attempts to defend it in public were notably lacklustre and, at times, incompetent.

Patten formally announced his decision to proceed with his 1992 proposals a few hours after the publication of the White Paper, at one of his regular question-and-answer sessions in LegCo. The bill, he informed the legislators, would be tabled on 9 March. The response from China and the pro-Beijing lobby in Hong Kong was immediate and predictable. Patten was denounced for 'sabotaging' the Sino–British negotiations and, yet again, for violating the Joint Declaration and the Basic Law. Beijing fulminated that the decision to publish the White Paper was both a breach of confidentiality and a 'bid to deceive the public and mislead public opinion'. Anson Chan countered that the White Paper was 'the truth', and a Foreign Office spokesman reiterated that the decision to table the second stage of Patten's reform bill had been made after close consultation between the governor and the British Cabinet. Beijing responded by restating that as the bill had no status in Chinese law, the three tiers of councils 'unilaterally established by the British side' would be abolished at the handover.

Bracing themselves for further Chinese reprisals, the independent *Ming Pao* and an official Beijing newspaper, *Overseas China Daily*, warned that Beijing might also exact an economic price for Britain's political démarche by retaliating against British firms trading with the mainland. The *Overseas China Daily* warned that the Chinese might form their own 'shadow' tiers of government before 1997, or even make moves to take Hong Kong back earlier. It was unavoidable, the paper declared, that China would strike back. The *South China Morning Post* summed up the general view of relations between Britain and China with the headline 'NOW IT'S ROCK BOTTOM'.

Patten now found the ranks of his detractors swelled by the Democrats, apparently fearful that the governor was only half-hearted in his commitment to electoral reform. Martin Lee, in particular, was agitated by Patten's persistent public reminders that the Legislative Council had the authority to amend or annul any legislation proposed by the government. As the governor had tried to intimate to Martin Lee, this did not mean that he would refrain from advocating the virtues of his proposals or, indeed, from lobbying for them. Lee was not impressed. His anxiety that the reforms would be shredded by hostile amendments was exacerbated by the suspicion that Patten had done a secret deal with China. He confided his concerns soon after the bill had been tabled.

> I am afraid Patten may be doing a very clever thing and a very dangerous thing. He knows that he could not possibly have introduced the '93 version of his reforms, so he introduced the '92 version, which is more democratic. But as for telling members, 'Well, if you want to amend it, I will accept it,' I have never heard of a government which says to its Parliament, 'Look, we are presenting this bill to you because we think it is good, but please, if you don't like it amend it in any way you like and we will accept it.' He calls this 'an executive-led government'. I think this is very dishonest.

Martin Lee's suspicions had been fuelled some weeks earlier, before the publication of the White Paper, at a lunch with Tsang Yok Sing, the leader of Hong Kong's most significant pro-Beijing party, the DAB. Asked by others at the table if, despite the breakdown of negotiations, agreement between Britain and China was still possible, Martin Lee responded with an unequivocal no. 'I don't agree,' countered Tsang Yok Sing, explaining, according to Martin Lee, that there would be an agreement because Patten had already made enough concessions (in the 1993 negotiations) to satisfy the Chinese. As Tsang Yok Sing was known to have the ear of Beijing, Martin Lee leaped to the conclusion that, in the course of those negotiations, the British had retreated far enough to ensure that Beijing could control the legislature. Knowing

that amendments tabled by pro-Beijing legislators to the 9 March proposals would be designed to dilute them to satisfy China, Martin Lee
was moved to complain privately that Patten's stance was a 'devious and
dishonourable and dishonest way' of appeasing Beijing. Despite Patten's
original insistence that he had no hidden agenda for Hong Kong, the
colony was rife with rumours of plots and conspiracies and, not for the
first time, Martin Lee allowed himself to fall foul of the prevailing
atmosphere.

Although Patten had, in fact, engaged in no such legerdemain,
Martin Lee's interpretation of his motives was closer to the mark than
he would have liked to acknowledge.

> I suspect he is trying to make life easier for himself in two ways. He
> wants to make sure that when he leaves Hong Kong no one can say,
> 'How could you, the British government, sell Hong Kong down the
> river to a very repressive communist regime without leaving some
> democratic institution to protect human rights and the rule of
> law? . . . And he can do that by presenting a bill which, if passed in
> its present form, would give us those safeguards. But he then leaves
> it to the Legislative Council – which is highly undemocratic – to
> water it down so that the legislature which China inherits in 1997 is
> one that it controls . . . He can then say, 'Look, it's not my fault. I
> tried to give Hong Kong democracy but they were too nervous to
> accept.' In other words, he's trying to put the blame on the people of
> Hong Kong.

Martin Lee's assumption was unjust, but it reflected a genuine fear that
by standing aloof from the legislative fray the governor would, by
default, aid and abet Beijing's purpose. For the first time, but not for the
last, Patten was irritated by Lee's lack of faith. 'The refusal to rule out
any amendment at all produces, yet again, charges of conspiracy,' he
protested wearily. 'But I went through the eight, nine, ten previous
occasions on which Martin and his friends had said we were about to
rat on them, and pointed out to them that after eighteen months there
was still no rat. So maybe they should just be a bit more patient.'

Patten's analysis of China's attitude to the events now unfolding in
Hong Kong was based as much on intuition as evidence. He was puz-
zled, confiding that he was unable to predict China's next move. 'I now
have sufficient confidence in my knowledge of China to say we haven't
got the faintest idea what they'll do next,' he said dryly. Yet he remained
optimistic. 'I think there is a very good chance – though I don't intend
saying it very much in public because it just pushes them into saying,

"Ya boo, you're wrong" – of the electoral arrangements we put in place this year surviving through 1997.' Allen Lee reacted scathingly to this tentative prognosis, commenting with an air of finality, 'No way. That's a myth. That's Chris Patten's line. It will never have a future.' Patten had a delicate path to tread: to intervene strenuously in the debate about his reforms would lay him open to the charge of misusing his executive authority; to stand aside would allow Martin Lee and others to allege that, for all his rhetoric, he was indifferent to Hong Kong's fate. In an attempt to weave a path through this political minefield, he decided to increase his public appearances, carefully orchestrating them to ensure that he could react swiftly to criticism and, where possible, get his retaliation in first: 'I have to be, as they say, out and about pretty well every day, being seen in public.' Taking care to avoid proselytising for his reforms, he took every opportunity to reassure people that his proposals were good for Hong Kong; that they fell within the Basic Law; but that, of course, in the end, it was for the people of Hong Kong, through their representatives on LegCo, to decide.

As the July deadline drew close, the battle for votes in LegCo intensified. A visit to Hong Kong by Lu Ping at the beginning of May exemplified the contrasting behaviour of Patten and his Chinese counterpart. As soon as the visit was announced, Patten issued Lu Ping with an invitation to Government House, which he duly refused: Lu Ping, the governor was told, would be too busy to meet him. Government House expressed its regrets but assured the director of the Hong Kong and Macau Affairs Office that Patten would interrupt his own hectic schedule at any time to facilitate a meeting. Patten was in fact concerned that he would be marginalised by the visit but, in a generally successful attempt to turn it to his advantage, he repeated his invitation at every opportunity, even suggesting that Lu Ping might like to return to the territory to join the guests at his forthcoming fiftieth birthday party. For the next few days the two men circled each other in Hong Kong, vying for public attention as they respectively hurried from one pressing engagement to another. Farcical though this stand-off appeared, the media was swift to side with Patten. The week before, Government House had nudged the *Oriental Daily* into conducting an opinion poll which demonstrated overwhelming support for a meeting between the two leaders (though the sample of 206, as Patten's press aide gleefully admitted, was 'sentiment, not science'). The findings were widely reported and seemed genuinely to confirm the mood of the public.

Under pressure from the media Lu Ping issued a statement explaining that he would not be in a position to meet the governor until the differences between the two governments had been resolved. The contrast between the governor's openness at press conferences and during walkabouts and Lu Ping's stiff and formal style was widely noted, again to the former's advantage. Tsang Yok Sing confided, 'I believe Lu Ping should and could have done a lot better . . . we can't see what China or Lu Ping himself can lose by meeting the governor.' Except, he might have added, 'face'. Even Vincent Lo, China's most loyal advocate, admitted: 'I would like to see the two of them sit down and really thrash things out.' But he judged that China was making an explicit and fundamental point.

On the third day of his visit, Lu Ping and his entourage were stricken by food poisoning. Government House (which monitored the NCNA offices just as carefully as the Chinese were presumed to bug the British embassy in Beijing) discovered that Lu Ping himself had had to be given glucose intravenously. Muttering, 'It wouldn't have happened here,' Patten took malicious delight in sending Lu Ping his best wishes for a speedy recovery. By the time of the director's departure, it was quite clear that he had signally failed to dent Patten's image.

The concern within Government House about public opinion sometimes bordered on the neurotic, and the relief when Patten's ratings survived the visit intact was palpable. Yet his need to demonstrate that he remained at the centre of events, still confidently guiding Hong Kong's destiny, was not narrowly egotistical; his desire to secure the passage of his reforms through LegCo, notwithstanding Martin Lee's scepticism, governed his every move. Perhaps for this reason, Patten still allowed himself to believe that Lu Ping would have to meet him before long: nothing would do more to enhance his local standing and to undermine his critics. Patten's problem, which he sometimes seemed to forget, was that the Chinese were as aware of this as he was.

An illustration of the governor's sensitivity at this time was his response to the news that Sir Percy Cradock had once again chosen to intervene in Hong Kong's affairs. On a visit to the colony immediately before Lu Ping's arrival, Cradock had gone straight from the airport to meet the director of the NCNA, Zhou Nan, where, according to Tsang Yok Sing, who leaked the story to journalists, he advised Zhou Nan that Lu Ping should refuse the governor's invitation. He was reported to have warned that such a meeting would send the wrong message from China to the British government and would demonstrate that Beijing could be bullied into submission; that it would have overtones of the Opium Wars. As soon as this alleged act of treachery was reported to Government House, one of Patten's aides was on the line to the Foreign Office, demanding that Cradock issue a statement to clarify his comments. Instead, after an interval, the former diplomat simply denied that such a conversation had occurred. Some days later, one of Patten's friends confided that the governor was still 'spitting' at this latest 'betrayal'.

Patten's resolve was also being tested from another quarter. Despite his brisk rejection of Douglas Hurd's suggestion the previous summer that he was needed back home, the issue had not gone away, and Westminster gossip continued to float his candidature for a senior position in the government. At the end of May 1994, these rumours reached Hong Kong, where newspapers reported that John Major had asked him to return as Conservative party chairman, an offer which he had refused. With the fate of Patten's reforms teetering in the balance, the suggestion that the prime minister wanted to withdraw him from Hong Kong was very far from helpful. Government House at once issued a statement dismissing the reports as nonsense and reiterating that the governor would stay until 1 July 1997. As it stood the statement was true – the prime minister had not asked Patten to return as party chairman – but it was also misleading. For while Patten was not seeking to leave Hong Kong prematurely, he knew that the prime minister was anxious to secure his services. Indeed, early in the summer, Major approached Patten directly 'as a friend', to ask whether, once he had steered his electoral reforms on to the statute book, he would consider returning to the Cabinet as his most senior colleague.

The prime minister offered his trusted political ally an astonishing brief: he could become leader of the Lords and foreign secretary, as well as taking over the vacant role of deputy prime minister. Apart from Major himself, Patten would become the most powerful man in the Cabinet. Patten was flattered, but once again he declined, observing gently that the prime minister really needed someone like Lord Whitelaw, who had served as Margaret Thatcher's shrewd and unflappable deputy prime minister in the eighties. Major replied that this was precisely why he wanted him back in London. But Patten insisted that, unless instructed otherwise, he could not honourably renege on his duty to Hong Kong.

Although he sympathised with Major's plight, Patten thought that the prime minister's approach reflected a failure to recognise the significance of the responsibility he was attempting to discharge on Britain's behalf as the colony's last governor. It was a feeling he had had when Douglas Hurd had approached him the year before. On that occasion it had seemed to him somewhat perverse that a British foreign secretary, of all people, should appear to place the difficulties of the Tory party above the reputation of a nation. Although he had by no means 'gone

native', Patten retained an acute sense that his was a momentous assignment, and he was disappointed that Major, like Hurd, appeared unable
to share that sense of history. Instead, yet again, and in an exceptionally
demanding period, the prime minister had unwittingly left Patten with
the impression that Britain's mission in Hong Kong somehow mattered
less in 10 Downing Street than the future of his troubled administration
at Westminster. For a while Patten brooded on this: it did nothing to
cheer him.

There were other irritations as well. Henry Keswick, the chairman
of Jardine Matheson, one of the most powerful 'Hongs', had been one
of the very few international business leaders not to have deserted the
governor early on in his battle with Beijing. Now he, too, abandoned
him – and in circumstances which infuriated Patten. After transferring
the company's place of incorporation from Hong Kong to the apparently safer financial haven of Bermuda in 1984, the Jardine board had
refrained from criticising the British stance as the company continued
to weather China's outbursts of hostility. Although Patten was not so
naive as to suppose that Keswick's tacit support sprang from altruism, he
was dismayed when the magnate began to behave in a way which
clearly suggested that he expected a return on his investment. It was
Keswick's habit to fly into Hong Kong three times a year, usually
accompanied by senior members of his 'absentee' board, for an intensive round of meetings with key executives in Hong Kong. Invariably
on these occasions, they would expect, and duly received, an invitation
to Government House. In March 1994, in his capacity as a member of
Jardine's main board, Sir Charles Powell, Margaret Thatcher's former
adviser at Number 10, made use of this access to press Patten to exercise his authority on Keswick's behalf.

In 1991, Henry Keswick had decided to move Jardine Matheson's
primary stock-exchange listing to London, leaving only a secondary
listing in Hong Kong. By 1993, Jardine was operational in thirty countries and employed a workforce of more than 200,000. Keswick was
impatient to liberate the company from the constraints of the Hong
Kong takeover code, and his lawyers embarked on discussions with the
Securities and Futures Commission (SFC). Arguing that the company
was soon to become subject to Bermuda's takeover code, they tried to
convince the SFC that its shareholders would lose none of the protection afforded them by the Hong Kong code. The SFC was not
impressed. Keswick was enraged by what he regarded as pettifogging
and vindictive decisions by second-rate bureaucrats.

Powell was dispatched to Government House to demand that Patten
exercise his gubernatorial powers to overturn the SFC's decision. Patten

refused. The governor's aides, reflecting his own strong feelings, emerged from this meeting filled with indignation at what they saw as a blatant attempt to 'call in the favours' that the Keswicks had hitherto bestowed on the governor. At a subsequent meeting a few days later, at which Powell was joined by Henry Keswick's brother Simon, the two men made the case again. Once more they were rebuffed by Patten, who insisted that it would be quite improper for him to intervene. 'We won't be bullied,' he said afterwards.

Keswick ran Jardine as if it were his own fiefdom, although by now his family owned only some 15 per cent of the shares. In March 1994, thwarted by the SFC, the company took the drastic step of withdrawing its listing from the Hong Kong Stock Exchange. Keswick declared that his decision did not signal any lack of confidence in the future of Hong Kong itself. 'We are as confident as ever in Hong Kong's future . . . we wish to continue to expand our investment in and business links with Hong Kong, China and the whole Asia Pacific region,' he said. This did not find favour among his employees in Hong Kong, who regarded the decision to delist as an act of pique and a betrayal of their loyalty by an arrogant and distant board as indifferent to their individual fates as it was to that of Hong Kong. The governor had similar feelings. He was not surprised when the Keswicks ceased to press for invitations to Government House, although Sir Charles Powell remained one of his confidants. The discovery that Keswick now referred to him as 'that bloody little socialist' merely confirmed Patten's impression that the tycoon was faintly ridiculous.

At the end of May Patten found himself under assault from his democratic allies on another front. It emerged that he had authorised a decision to bar two Chinese dissidents now resident in the United States from coming to Hong Kong to take part in the annual 4 June rally in Victoria Park to commemorate Tiananmen Square. Under pressure from the local media, Government House insisted, without much conviction, that Hong Kong could not be used as a base for dissidents. The governor's apparent failure to live up to his own rhetoric about human rights provoked the censure of democratic activists, which embarrassed and irritated him. As one of his aides commented privately, 'I'm afraid we have handled this very badly. It has been looked on by some as another example of the government kowtowing to China.'

Patten earned even more opprobrium from the same quarter when he made it clear that he opposed the establishment of a Human Rights Commission for Hong Kong. Arguing that the Bill of Rights, which was already on the statute book, was protection enough, he claimed that his forthcoming Equal Opportunities Bill would take care of all outstanding issues, and faced down the human-rights activists in LegCo – even to the extent of barring Anna Wu, a respected independent member, from tabling a motion in favour of a commission. For good measure he made it clear that he would also reject an Access to Information Bill proposed by Christine Loh. Both these decisions were presented as if they had emanated from ExCo, but no one was in any doubt that they originated with the governor. His reason for refusing to countenance the 'all-singing, all-dancing legislative effort', as he described Anna Wu's motion, was that, as he confided later, he had come to the conclusion that the community would not stomach another huge fight with China. He argued that the same ends could be achieved by other means which might involve 'running skirmishes with the Chinese rather than another nuclear confrontation'.

Christine Loh was one of the governor's own appointees to LegCo. Brought up to enjoy the middle-class comforts of a prosperous merchant's family, as a teenager in the late 1960s she had been more interested in sport than politics. Her father was a refugee from Shanghai but unusually, her mother, who had been born in Hong Kong, could trace her family back through four generations as colonial subjects. Like that of most of her peers, Loh's knowledge of China was culled from newspapers and television; the vicissitudes of life in the People's Republic did not impinge significantly on her early life. At the end of that decade she was sent to school in England and did not return to Hong Kong until 1979. At the age of twenty-three, armed with a law degree and a belated zest for public affairs, she took lessons in Chinese and soon became involved in 'fringe' politics as a member of a group called the Hong Kong Observers, which lobbied for the extension of human rights and democracy in the colony. Although Loh had reservations about the Joint Declaration, it was not until the Tiananmen Square outrage that she became convinced that the 1997 transition would be fraught with danger. Encouraged by the appointment of Chris Patten as governor, she was astonished, in October 1992, to be invited up to Government House, where the chief secretary, Sir David Ford, asked if she would accept the governor's appointment to a seat on the Legislative Council. She thought, 'My God, I can't believe this!' Over the next few hours, she discussed the offer with other activists, all of whom advised her to accept. 'This is a vital opportunity to promote the liberal cause,' they told her. She took their advice. Six months later, she said, as if still off balance, 'Chris Patten has completely changed my life.'

But now some of the governor's liberal critics began to wonder whether his genial demeanour concealed an authoritarian streak. Six months earlier, in November 1993, Patten had made a speech at the Foreign Correspondents' Club in which he had attacked those moral relativists who liked to believe that the issue of human rights was essentially a Western obsession amounting to a 'neo-colonial incursion into Asian affairs'. Put the other way round, if it were argued that human rights weren't really appropriate for Asia, Latin America or Africa, the proposition would, he avowed, rightly be regarded as sanctimonious, if not racist.

> If you are a journalist locked up for months for telling the truth; if you are a trades-unionist incarcerated for championing workers' rights; if you're thrown out of your country and deprived of your rights; if you're beaten over the head, or worse, by a policeman, the brutal result is the same, whether it happens in Europe, or Asia, or America, or Africa. Human rights are indivisible and interdependent.

It was a stirring dissertation no previous governor would have essayed. That China was the principal object of his scorn was in no doubt, yet – or so it seemed to the activists in Hong Kong – the self-appointed champion of human rights seemed overly willing to retreat from these heady values when it came to the crunch. They were disappointed and angry.

To make matters even more tiresome, two of his senior officials disagreed in public about the scope of the government's Equal Opportunities Bill. Patten wanted Anson Chan to handle the presentation of the policy, but she insisted that it was the responsibility of the home affairs secretary, Michael Suen. Evidently ill briefed, he mishandled the press conference. On the most sensitive issue of all, he stated that the government's bill would not include proposals to outlaw sexual discrimination in the workplace. Mark Fisher, a British Labour politician who was in Hong Kong to support Christine Loh's unsuccessful attempt to introduce her Freedom of Information Bill, watched bemused as the hapless official stumbled through his brief. It was, Fisher judged, a 'pitiful performance'.

The following day, members of LegCo, led by Anna Wu and Christine Loh, expressed their fury at the government's apparent indifference to the issues at stake. To limit the damage, Patten's press secretary, Michael Hanson, rushed out a statement insisting that, despite what Michael Suen had appeared to say, the government's Equal Opportunities Bill would after all include measures relating to sexual harassment. The home affairs secretary doggedly stuck to his guns. He was not aware that the scope of the bill was to be extended in this way, he said, adding: 'Mr Hanson does not represent the government.' Patten was furious. Although he eventually prevailed, the incident could not have occurred at a worse moment. As one of his aides admitted, 'It was a huge cock-up.' It certainly confirmed the impression, seized on by his adversaries, that, as an administrator, Patten was not infallible.

The governor was under too much pressure to dwell on adversity. In early June he was censured by the Legislative Council in the unprecedented form of a vote of no confidence. The issue, which involved property rates, was of little significance constitutionally and the effect of the censure was merely symbolic. But in such a feverish atmosphere, symbolic gestures mattered. The episode served to remind the governor that the independence of Hong Kong's legislators, for which he had so ardently proselytised, could backfire on him personally. With the vote on his reform package only three weeks away, anything that could undermine his authority was a potential threat to its passage. In this case he was quick to turn the setback to his advantage, using his question time at LegCo to declare, 'I will always defend the right of this council to criticise the government and the governor. I hope we can take this for granted after 1997.'

In the days leading up to the anniversary of Tiananmen Square, Beijing's 'friends', led shamelessly by the former prime minister Sir Edward Heath, urged Hong Kong to forget the massacre or at least to reinterpret it less harshly. In his weekly column in the *South China Morning Post*, Tsang Yok Sing, the most politically sensitive of Beijing's allies in the colony, advised his readers not to 'reopen the wound'. It was all the more telling, therefore, when, in an interview for CNN on the eve of the vigil, he broke down in tears as he remembered how the entire school where he was headmaster had wept that day in 1989. The trauma of Tiananmen Square still echoed through all discourse about democracy in Hong Kong, and it was not only the democrats who were offended by the crass intervention of Heath and others.

Tsang Yok Sing, the leader of the DAB, was born in Hong Kong in 1947 and educated at the colony's leading Roman Catholic school, St Paul's College. He went on to study at the University of Hong Kong, where he became caught up in the high drama of the Cultural Revolution. With his brother, Tsang Tak Sing, he helped to organise the student demonstrations against the British which erupted in the riots of 1967 and nearly brought colonial rule to a premature end. The authorities had been obliged to fall back on the draconian powers embodied in the Emergency Regulations, yet even these measures would not have prevailed had it not been for a simultaneous instruction from the Beijing Maoists to their Hong Kong cadres calling a halt to the uprising. The repressive methods adopted by the British, which led to Tsang Tak Sing being jailed for two years, confirmed his brother's antipathy towards colonial rule and his intellectual commitment to Marxism. Although Tsang Yok Sing was always to insist that he never joined the Communist party (which was, and remained, outlawed in Hong Kong), he soon established himself as one of the most loyal supporters of Beijing in the colony. In 1969 he became a mathematics teacher at the Pui Kiu Middle School, one of more than a dozen 'patriotic' schools. He took over as principal in 1986, by which time he had already been appointed by the politburo in Beijing as a delegate to the People's Congress in Guangdong.

The Tiananmen Square vigil, on 4 June in Victoria Park, took place only three weeks before the LegCo vote on Patten's reforms, which gave it a particular poignancy. It was a wet night, and a crowd of over 30,000 sat on plastic sheets or newspapers holding lighted candles protected by rice-paper shades. At a crescendo in the music the candles were held aloft and glittered through the rain across the park. The quiet resolution of the people affected even the most hardened observers, and it was impossible to conclude that the hunger for freedom and democracy in Hong Kong was a popular spasm exploited by irresponsible elements among the colony's chattering classes. Edward Llewellyn, the governor's political adviser, was spotted watching from the sidelines by a reporter from *Ming Pao*. The pro-Beijing *Wen Wei Po* picked this up and inevitably saw in the aide's presence a British plot. The following day the NCNA made two official complaints to the governor.

In the run-up to the decisive vote on Patten's reform package, Government House began to lobby intensively to secure its passage. To win, Patten needed at least half the votes in the sixty-seat council; to win convincingly he needed a big enough majority to offset the effect of the votes of three 'ex-officio' LegCo members (the chief secretary, the financial secretary and the attorney general) who, as government employees, were obliged to support the bill. With LegCo almost evenly split, the outcome hinged on a handful of wavering votes. These included those of the so-called 'Breakfast Group', an alliance of disparate interests featuring, among others, a senior executive of Jardine Matheson, Martin Barrow, who had a reputation for listening with very great care to his paymasters' voice; Hui Yin Fat, of the social workers' functional constituency; and Simon Ip, an amiable but lacklustre barrister who represented the legal profession on LegCo. Patten homed in on this group, joining them for breakfast on several occasions to make his case. The task of corralling other floating votes was entrusted to Nicholas Ng, the constitutional affairs secretary, and his deputy, C.M. Leung, who spent long hours in the council ante-chambers openly lobbying against his adversaries in the Chinese camp.

Their job was made more difficult by the positions taken by Martin Lee and Emily Lau, the governor's two most impressive but unpredictable allies on LegCo. Lau, the most forceful and eloquent politician in Hong Kong, had argued vigorously that the three government officials appointed to LegCo should be released from their obligation to support Patten to join her in voting against his package in favour of her own bill, which called for direct elections to all sixty LegCo seats. Her proposal was regarded by Patten, in the words of one of his staff, as 'not only crazy, but certain to send China berserk'. Nonetheless it had the potential, as a grand but futile gesture, to scupper his reforms by luring away one or more of the Democrats' crucial votes. Even more seriously, opponents of the Patten reforms, notably the pro-Beijing Liberals, might decide to vote for Emily Lau's 'impossibilist' bill to embarrass him. From the perspective of Government House, Emily Lau's perversity was matched by Martin Lee's failure to rally support for the governor. Although he had been surprised and delighted by the Patten proposals, he had yet to endorse them in public; formally, the Democrats were still committed to an increase in the number of directly elected seats for the 1995 elections from twenty to thirty. To Government House this seemed pointless, as Lee had made it quite clear privately that his party would in the end endorse Patten's reforms. 'Martin seems to be doing nothing,' one of the governor's aides complained in exasperation a few days before the crucial debate.

To complicate the process, there were fourteen amendments to Patten's bill, the most dangerous of which had been tabled by the Liberals. At first the governor's team took comfort from the fact that this attempt to redraft his package was so clumsy that even some in the pro-China camp were embarrassed by it. In seeking to scale down the functional constituencies, for example, Allen Lee had found himself proposing restriction of the franchise in one functional constituency to a maximum of 153 senior executives. Patten's allies were optimistic that none of the 'floaters' would be attracted by such blatant efforts to subvert the democratic process. Nonetheless, they knew that the pro-Beijing bloc in LegCo would throw its weight behind the Liberal amendment. If so, Patten would need to secure every last possible vote for his bill to survive more or less intact.

14

'INSIDE I'M CROWING
LIKE MAD'

LegCo Votes on Patten's Reforms

On the eve of the vote on the Legislative Council (Electoral Provisions) (Amendment) Bill 1994, the outcome still hung in the balance. In Government House the mood was gloomy. Though even his closest colleagues did not know it, Patten believed that it would be impossible for his governorship to survive a defeat at the hands of the Liberals. Lavender, whose public performance as the governor's wife had earned her plaudits throughout Hong Kong and across the political spectrum, knew this, but kept her nerve. Although she did not volunteer strong opinions in public, she understood his predicament with clarity, and did not hesitate to express her thoughts within Government House. In this case, she shared her husband's view: he had invested too much of his reputation in his reforms for his credibility to withstand their defeat.

Behind the scenes Martin Lee was almost in despair at what he regarded as the governor's failure to secure enough support for his bill, and complained that he had only himself to blame. 'I told him he had to lobby hard, but I think he thought all would be fine. Now they appear to have only twenty-eight votes, and that is not enough. I am very unhappy, and very annoyed. He is supposed to have a good reputation for twisting arms. I just cannot believe he could not have done better.' If Patten were to lose the vote, he fretted, 'It would be the cruellest thing that could happen to Hong Kong. It would have been better if Wilson had remained, toeing his line of appeasement. We will have been betrayed.'

Within twenty-four hours of the decisive vote, it began to look as though the bill would fall. Not only had LegCo's pro-Beijing bloc confirmed publicly that it would almost certainly support the Liberal amendment, but, despite Patten's breakfast appearances, the independents seemed likely to follow suit. The remaining waverers were wobbling so violently that it was impossible to tell which way they would eventually vote. One by one they were summoned to Government House to hear the governor make his case yet again. One or two of them indicated that he would have their vote; others listened intently but refused to declare themselves one way or the other. 'I've been Clintonising since the end of last week,' remarked Patten. 'I don't much like it. I'm not one of nature's whips. But there it is, it had to be done. I don't want to go through this again.'

At the eleventh hour, Martin Lee finally came to the governor's aid by agreeing to make a speech, at the request of Government House, in which he not only called on all instinctive democrats of whatever party to support the Patten proposals, but also named the remaining undecided voters who could tip the scales either way. In an intriguing development, he also undertook to lobby Lau Wong Fat, the deeply conservative leader of Heung Yee Kuk, a residents' association bloc from the New Territories, with whom he was deeply at odds on almost every issue. Indeed, his own amendment to the Patten bill proposed the abolition of Heung Yee Kuk's three seats in LegCo. Now, after much prompting from Patten, Lee promised that he would try to cut a deal with Lau Wong Fat by undertaking to withdraw this part of his amendment in return for a commitment from the Heung Yee Kuk leader that he and at least one of his colleagues would either vote against, or abstain on, the Liberal amendment.

On the night before the most crucial day in his political career, Chris Patten went to bed, well supplied with sleeping tablets, not knowing whether the next day would bring glorious victory or ignominious defeat.

The morning of 29 June 1994 began as usual for the governor with a workout on the tennis court. In his private office, his team vainly scoured the newspapers for developments. The only new story was in the *Eastern Express*, which reported that John Major had intervened to secure a crucial vote 'as the fate of Chris Patten's reform proposals hung in the balance'.

According to the *Post*, the prime minister had, in some unspecified way, persuaded Henry Keswick to secure the support of Martin Barrow, the Jardine Matheson executive on LegCo. The previous day, Barrow, whose own hostility to the Patten reforms was no secret, had suddenly upset all calculations by announcing that he would not after all be supporting the Liberal amendment of which he himself was a principal architect. When Patten arrived in the office, he dismissed the report. He had, he said, himself momentarily considered ringing the Jardine chairman, but had managed to resist the temptation. 'Hand on heart, I did not call Henry. I just thought it would put me in the position of a supplicant.' Barrow, too, insisted that it was his 'personal' decision. 'It was going to be such a dead-heat situation. I didn't think that I should be the one with the casting vote.' Yet it was widely presumed that Barrow would not have switched his loyalties so suddenly without instructions from his chairman. Despite Keswick's falling-out with Patten, Jardine Matheson was a significant contributor to Conservative party funds, and the family was believed to maintain close links with the government, not least through Keswick's wife, Tessa, who was the political adviser to the chancellor of the exchequer, Kenneth Clarke.

Whatever the truth, Allen Lee, who had been relying on Barrow's support for his Liberal amendment, was furious, though less with Barrow than with the governor. Before announcing his decision, the Jardine executive had rung the Liberal party leader to break the news of his defection. According to Lee, Barrow was reticent about his change of heart.

> He told me he had changed his mind for personal reasons, and that it had nothing to do with the governor, but I couldn't get any explanation. We've been working on this for two weeks. He was instrumental in designing our package. He had devised a lobbying plan; he told us how to lobby Chinese support and how to lobby local support; he told us who we had to discuss our plan with in Beijing, and that this was the way to secure the support of pro-China legislators here . . . He was working with us day and night. Now, at the last moment, he drops out. There must be a reason . . . Somebody must have got to him. I told him, 'Martin, your heart must be bleeding.'

Allen Lee, never known to understate a case, claimed that Patten's lobbying tactics had been excessively brutal. 'Their limbs have been taken off by the governor. He is twisting their arms and legs . . . Is this fair? Is this British politics? Is this letting the Hong Kong people decide? We had thirty votes; now the fate of Hong Kong is being changed by one man. I've never seen anybody operating like that.'

Edward Llewellyn acknowledged that Government House had been like a whip's office on the previous day, and that Patten and his advisers had managed to 'square' Martin Barrow. While the governor admitted that he had lobbied 'vigorously', if with some distaste for the process, he was adamant that the proprieties had been scrupulously observed.

> I can say hand on heart that we didn't promise anybody anything and we didn't threaten anybody. What we said was that we thought that a defeat would be extremely bad for the authority of the government; that it wouldn't end the political argument; that . . . it would make sure the argument rumbled on for the next two or three years with the pro-democracy politicians becoming increasingly difficult to handle. Why? Because they would feel, understandably, that they'd been robbed.

After breakfast, Patten's team huddled in the private office to project the impact of Barrow's about-turn. At first, on the basis of the latest reports from LegCo, it looked as though they were likely to scrape home with a 28–25 majority. Mike Hanson announced, to no one in particular, 'We've got it in the bag.' It was soon clear that his optimism was premature.

The debate began at 9am but it was expected to be at least ten hours before the crucial vote on the Liberal amendment was taken. With television and radio coverage of the proceedings droning in the background, Martin Dinham and Edward Llewellyn orchestrated the last-minute effort to keep the wavering legislators on side. But despite the assiduous lobbying of Nicholas Ng and C.M. Leung, at least three of them were still under intense pressure to abstain or vote against the Patten proposals, not only from their colleagues but, as it soon transpired, directly from Beijing. Patten's support was starting to crumble.

China's original tactic had been to remain aloof from the proceedings. But in the days leading up to 29 June, in the wake of the Barrow-inspired efforts of the Liberals, the Chinese had shifted their ground. Not only had Lu Ping issued his allies on LegCo with instructions to support Allen Lee's amendment, but now, on the day itself, he was secretly lobbying himself. In perhaps the most breathtaking attempt to destroy Patten's reforms, the now London-based chairman of the Hong Kong and Shanghai Bank, Sir William Purves, also chose this moment to turn against the governor. The previous day, a respected member of LegCo, Vincent Cheng, who was on the board of the bank, told Government House that he had decided to abstain on the Liberal amendment. Now, twelve hours later, with the debate underway, he rang both Dinham and Nicholas Ng in some distress to tell them that he had come under great pressure from Purves to switch his vote in favour of the amendment and felt obliged to do so. Purves had, Cheng reported, made it clear to him that 'his job was on the line'. Purves's call had been followed up by another from Lu Ping. Patten knew that Purves had seen Lu Ping the previous day and half suspected that the two men were even now in the same office. He was aghast. 'That's Willie Purves, true to the last,' he said contemptuously. Later, still angry, he was more explicit:

> The Hong Kong Bank owes something to Hong Kong . . . the chairman of the Hong Kong Bank was a member of my Executive Council when we were first pushing these proposals and knew about them before they were announced . . . but the most disgraceful aspect of this is that someone can phone up an employee on an open line from Peking and tell that employee how to vote. What's the employee supposed to say, knowing perfectly well that the phone call is probably being listened to? It is mind-boggling.

When Lavender Patten walked into the private office and heard the news, she spat, 'Bloody traitor,' before recovering her poise. An aide spluttered: 'If we win, we'll get him for this.'

Vincent Cheng's defection was likely to influence other undecided legislators to follow, and by mid-morning, Hanson was obliged to adjust his optimistic forecast. 'Down in the hothouse of LegCo, four or five votes are dodging around quite a bit. They keep changing their minds. At the moment we don't know which way it's going to go. It's very, very close.' In Government House, the atmosphere became more and more oppressive: faces were drawn and anxious; fingers drummed on desks against the background babble of the televised debate.

A little later, news came through of another intervention from Beijing. Lu Ping had been on the phone again, this time to Hui Yin Fat, the elected representative of the functional constituency representing the social workers. This time, however, Dinham was able to confirm: 'Hui has told Lu Ping to get lost, I'm glad to say.' According to Dinham, Lu Ping had urged Hui Yin Fat to abstain. 'All I ask of you,' the Beijing official had said, 'is that you leave the chamber when they vote.' Hui Yin Fat apparently had the courage to retort, 'I am not prepared to do that.' Another of Patten's aides reported that the legislator felt under such pressure that he had hidden himself away in his office, refusing to take calls from anyone.

Lu Ping tried the same tactic with one of Hui Yin Fat's colleagues, Pan Chung Hoi, urging him: 'I don't care what you do. Just go to the toilet if necessary when the vote is cast.' Pan Chung Hoi, too, stood firm.

Patten mused: 'What's it going to be like after 1997? They won't have to make phone calls from Peking to get them to vote the right way then. Just a local call.' 'And they are free,' quipped Dinham.

Lavender Patten sat in the private sitting room upstairs. The last week or two, she reflected, had been testing.

> I try to give Chris a little bit of reassurance if I can, but it is very hard. I can't reassure him that the votes are there if they aren't. So I suppose all I can really do is say to him, 'There is still time to capture the votes, and we'll deal with what happens if we don't win afterwards.' There's no need to anticipate disaster, because that can paralyse you. But it's easy to say that, and impossible for him not to think about the effects if it goes the wrong way . . . I've got to support him and not panic. I wouldn't be much good to him if I was screaming . . . Who knows, perhaps by this time next week we will have retired.

By lunchtime, the figures were looking bad. All hope of a three-vote majority had now evaporated, and defeat seemed to beckon. Edward Llewellyn, who was keeping a running tally, estimated that the race was neck and neck at 27–27. Patten's survival now appeared to depend on Martin Lee's ability to deliver his deal with Lau Wong Fat of Heung Yee Kuk. If this were to collapse, one horrified aide whispered, 'It's awful, we fall.' Llewellyn hurried to warn Patten, who had temporarily retired to his study.

Unhappily, Martin Lee's flair as an advocate was not matched by his skill as a broker. It rapidly became clear that his efforts were foundering. In the early hours of the morning, the leader of the Democrats had finally persuaded his own colleagues to accept the proposed trade-off with Lau Wong Fat. As the morning wore on, however, Allen Lee had discovered what was afoot and had threatened that unless the Heung Yee Kuk leader and his colleagues voted for the Liberal amendment, the Liberals would themselves vote to abolish his functional constituency, and thereby his seat on LegCo.

Incomprehensibly, Martin Lee, apparently believing that he could afford to increase the pressure on Lau Wong Fat, chose this moment to jettison the deal which he had persuaded his colleagues to endorse only a few hours earlier. Not content with an abstention, he now demanded that Lau Wong Fat and his colleagues vote against Allen Lee's amendment. This was a miscalculation. In high indignation, Lau Wong Fat broke off negotiations. When news of this reached Government House, Patten was almost speechless with frustration. 'Martin is mad,' he expostulated. 'It really is like trying to deal with the entire Society of Jesus.' He could not understand how the leader of the Democrats could be so incompetent and self-regarding as to jeopardise the prospect of extending the franchise to 2.5 million new voters. 'Martin has really fucked this up,' he finally exploded, and retreated upstairs to the family sitting room.

Meanwhile, in a meeting room in the precincts of the Legislative Council, Nicholas Ng tried desperately to persuade Martin Lee to see sense. Llewellyn went upstairs to warn Patten that defeat was not only possible but probable. The governor said: 'I'll do anything Nicholas wants me to do. It'll be so annoying if Martin cocks up this deal. You know, actually arguing about whether somebody should vote against the amendment or abstain, I mean . . .' His voice trailed away as he returned to the strained hubbub of the private office. An unidentified voice in the LegCo chamber rose and could be heard to say, 'There are people who appear to be gripped by horror and frightened to death.' The governor paced abstractedly back and forth, then slumped into an armchair, head in hands. He roused himself once to remark, in self-mockery, 'I think what is called for is a prayer. What time do we meet at the cathedral for early mass tomorrow if it goes right?'

In the afternoon, there were public duties to briefly take Patten's mind off the battle for votes. He departed by helicopter for an official visit to Tsing Yi – 'being gubernatorial', as he described it – where he inspected an environmental scheme and planted a tree, cautioning the local officials, 'Don't let it die.' Llewellyn, who accompanied him, monitored the LegCo debate on a transistor radio. Patten reflected on the fragility of Hong Kong's political courage. 'What I can't imagine is telling someone I would do something and then not doing it,' he said, bemused by the way votes were even now shifting from one side to the other. He prepared himself for the recriminations which would follow a defeat, especially from the Democrats. 'What will irritate me most,' he sighed, 'will be the allegation that we didn't try; that we meant to lose all along.'

At a press conference he was asked about the LegCo proceedings. He replied smoothly, 'I think the issue is being resolved in the right way by the representatives of the people of Hong Kong: in the open, not in secret behind closed doors, and that is a very important step forward.'

Back in the helicopter, a call came through from 10 Downing Street: the prime minister wanted a progress report. Llewellyn replied that while he remained optimistic, the outcome was still uncertain.

Patten returned to his private office to resume his original position, slouched in an armchair alternately sucking his spectacles and whirling them round distractedly. At one point he exclaimed restlessly, to no one in particular, 'I'm no good to you in here like a jaded lemon,' and walked out, only to return to his post a few minutes later. As he waited, he crossed his fingers in unconscious supplication. On another occasion, he interrupted his silent ruminations to bewail the absence of Baroness Lydia Dunn, his most senior adviser on ExCo, who had left for Britain in the crucial run-up to the vote. 'She's not really in London arguing for passports, you know. She's been on holiday for the last three weeks.' He raised his eyes towards the ceiling as if to say, 'Why wasn't she here helping to get the bill through?'

There were only two hours to go before the first vote was due to be taken. The government's officials on LegCo redoubled their efforts to shore up their support. C.M. Leung lobbied two legislators who had confided separately to him that they were frightened about being out on a limb if they abstained on the Liberal amendment. Edward Llewellyn suggested, only half jokingly, that each should be told that if they were to abstain together, neither of them would be alone. Patten fretted about Simon Ip, the representative of the legal functional constituency, who was easily driven by the shifting winds. The night before, Ip had been frog-marched into a hastily arranged meeting of the Bar Council by Margaret Ng, the diminutive but forceful barrister-cum-columnist, where he had been lobbied furiously to vote for Patten and against the Liberal amendment. But the larger part of his constituency was made up of solicitors who were less enthusiastic about the Patten proposals, and twelve hours later, he was still adrift.

Margaret Ng, born in Hong Kong in 1946, had graduated from the University of Hong Kong with a degree in philosophy and comparative literature. She then studied in the United States at Boston University and in England at Cambridge, where she acquired respectively a PhD in philosophy and a BA in law. In the eighties she had worked variously as a university researcher and administrator, and, for a time, at the local headquarters of the Chase Manhattan Bank. In this period she wrote and broadcast prolifically for the Hong Kong media, earning herself a reputation for clinical analysis and fearless commentary. By the time of Patten's arrival, she combined a twice-weekly column in the *South China Morning Post* with a growing practice at the bar. She had at once warmed to Patten's style but, as she said at the time, she gave herself 'no room for pessimism or optimism' about the prospects of the 'one country, two systems' concept surviving the handover. Britain's impending departure made her 'very, very depressed' – not because she wished British rule to continue, but because 'we are to be returned to a communist regime over which we have almost no influence and over which I have no influence whatsoever. We are now going to be taken over by a government which will have no qualms about riding roughshod over our opinion, whatever we want.'

Like many other people, Ng had only realised the significance of the Liberal amendment to the governor's bill in the hours leading up to the debate. Until then she had merely been pleased that the decision was to be taken by Hong Kong's legislators and not 'rammed down our throats' as the result of a secret deal between Britain and China. However, on the eve of the debate, Denis Chang, a fellow lawyer and a Patten loyalist, whom the governor had appointed to ExCo soon after his arrival, had told her that China was working very hard to secure the Liberal amendment.

Mortified that Simon Ip, the representative of her own constituency, might have the decisive vote, she had deployed her formidable powers of argument to win him over. At first she had been optimistic, but later she discovered that he was backsliding under pressure from the solicitors. Now, only three hours before the vote, she rang Chang and told him, 'Frankly, my feeling is that it is very dodgy. It depends on who gets to him last.' With the moment of decision rapidly approaching, Denis Chang at once rang Government House to pass on this news. Martin Dinham tried to engineer a meeting between Simon Ip and C.M. Leung, in the hope that the latter might be able to stiffen the lawyer's resolve. 'I've got C.M. to lay a trap,' Dinham said. He had arranged for Denis Chang to waylay Ip and lead him casually into the LegCo meeting room, where C.M. Leung had taken up temporary residence on Patten's behalf.

In the meantime Margaret Ng called Government House to tell Llewellyn that she and Denis Chang were determined to see Simon Ip once more, 'just to make sure that he is on track'. She had some sympathy for Ip. 'It was a moment of crisis,' she recalled afterwards. 'I felt I was much involved in a moment of history . . . I was very tense, looking down at Simon to see which way he would vote. He looked pale and totally unhappy. I felt very sad for him, because he had obviously been subjected to a great deal of pressure.'

By six o' clock in the evening, Patten's team was assembled in the private office, watching the debate on television. The vote was still too close to call, but it was too late to do anything about it now.

'If anyone presses the wrong button, we're done,' the governor commented gloomily.

'You *are* a morale-booster,' retorted Llewellyn.

Dinham joined them to discuss the wording of two alternative telegrams, one of which would have to be sent to London. Martin Barrow, belatedly loyal, rang to say that he thought he had managed to

secure Simon Ip's vote. Patten was nonplussed and unimpressed. 'The
trouble is Simon is so weak. Anyway,' he went on disbelievingly, 'why
is Martin now lobbying for us?' A few moments later, they heard that
Ip had undertaken to abstain. Patten could barely control his relief.
'Fucking hell, fucking hell!' he muttered loudly, smashing his right fist
into the palm of his left hand. 'Let's hope the vote comes before Simon
changes his mind again.'

A few minutes later, Patten was given another break. Nicholas Ng
phoned in to report that one, if not two, of the wavering Breakfast
Group, infuriated by the tone of a speech in support of the Liberal
amendment, were likely to vote for Patten after all. Sustained by this
crumb of comfort, the governor retreated to his study to wait with
Lavender.

By 7.30pm, thirty minutes before the vote, the phones in
Government House had ceased to ring. At 7.45, the vote on the Liberal
amendment was finally called. The legislators pushed their buttons,
and the result flashed up on the television screens instantaneously: 28 in
favour, 29 against. The governor's package had survived by one vote.
His team erupted in triumph. All decorum vanished as they waved their
arms in the air, clapped and embraced one another. 'Fucking hell!'
yelled Llewellyn; Dinham, discarding his usual reserve to punch the air,
repeated over and over again, 'Yes! Yes! Yes!' There were other amendments to follow, but this was the one that mattered. An elated Patten
hurried to the office, flushed with relief, and called for champagne all
round. Llewellyn rang the Foreign Office to report the good news.

It was not the margin of victory for which they had hoped. Without
the three ex-officio votes, Patten's bill would have fallen to the Liberal
amendment. Patten saw a way of pre-empting the mischief an embit-
tered Allen Lee might try to cause by alleging that Government House
had fixed the result. If a majority of those legislators who had been
directly elected in 1991 had voted against the Liberal amendment, he
could at least blunt any such attack by pointing out that a one-vote victory it may have been, but it had been sustained by a substantial
majority of those who had been democratically elected. Sitting at
Dinham's desk, he pored exultantly over a list of legislators, shouting
out their names one by one: were they elected or appointed? As his
team yelled back the answers, he was overjoyed to discover that only
one of the eighteen directly elected members had voted against him,
while Allen Lee's support came overwhelmingly from legislators
appointed by his predecessor. The governor's relief was palpable: 'That's
the answer we've got to keep on using if people talk about the "official"
votes.'

In public Allen Lee contained his rancour, and refrained from identifying Martin Barrow as the defector who had helped to destroy his amendment. In private, however, he fulminated against Patten.

> He didn't win. He bulldozed it through. He won by one vote. He didn't let the Hong Kong people decide. He's been lying to the Hong Kong people. And finally he uses the three official votes to get it through. He now has a system for 1995 which has no future after 1997. His package has no chance, absolutely no chance . . . For Christ's sake, we're not morons. We're not kindergarten kids. I think he is bad for Hong Kong, really bad for Hong Kong. A failed politician coming here and playing politics. This feeling will never wash off me. I'm going to be here in 1997. He is not.

Meanwhile, Martin Lee, who had failed to deliver his deal, was blithely unaware of the frustration he had provoked at Government House. Instead he rejoiced in Allen Lee's defeat as though he had masterminded it himself. The Liberal leader's credibility, he chortled, had been severely damaged.

> You have to remember that the majority of the Liberals were appointed by Patten's predecessor, Sir David Wilson. The only way for them to preserve their position was to make sure that the future electoral arrangements would not be fair or open or democratic. With undemocratic elections, as proposed by their amendment, they would have stood a good chance of getting themselves, in effect, appointed to the Legislative Council – to serve China, no doubt. So they've had their own interests to serve.

Patten's bill was still not quite safe. The Democratic party now tabled an amendment designed to extend the number of directly elected seats for 1995 from twenty to thirty in accordance with their publicly stated objective. This was a clear violation of the Basic Law. The government team feared that Allen Lee might now urge his party members to vote for Martin Lee's amendment in the hope of wrecking the Patten reforms, which would, Llewellyn warned, leave them 'in deep shit'. This time, however, the leader of the Democrats saw the light. After a brief but genial conversation, Patten put down the phone to announce with relief, tinged by self-satisfaction, 'Martin is withdrawing his amendment.'

Now, at last, the governor knew that his bill was through, and that he and the British government had been spared a humiliation which would have had lasting personal and political consequences. In the end, his margin of victory on the substantive motion was larger than he had expected. Once every hostile amendment had been defeated, a number of jittery legislators finally screwed up enough courage to bow to the sentiment of LegCo's elected majority. As a result, after more than seventeen hours of debate, the Patten bill was endorsed by a comfortable majority of eight votes (32–24). Of the eighteen directly elected members of LegCo, only Emily Lau voted against it, and that was because it failed to satisfy her own rigid aspirations. Her decision combined principle and pragmatism, but it had caused a jolt of last-minute anxiety at Government House. Patten admired Lau, but not unequivocally. 'Emily is a sort of yardstick by which the rest of us have to measure ourselves. Every community needs a sea-green incorruptible,' he observed. Then he added: 'It does make her from time to time absolutely infuriating.' Immediately before the third reading of his bill, Patten had telephoned Lau to ask for her backing.

'Look, you may actually endanger the vote if you don't vote for it,' he said.

'You've got enough votes,' Emily Lau replied.

'We can't be sure of that. And at the end of the day, you're going to be voting with the Liberal party and all those pro-Peking legislators. Is that really the sort of company you want to be in?'

But Emily Lau did not yield. Her own bill, which demanded universal adult suffrage on the Westminster model, was due to be debated immediately after the vote on the Patten reforms, and it would clearly have weakened her cause to have supported the governor so soon before seeking LegCo's support for her far more radical proposal. Patten remarked, less than graciously, 'She voted against us just so that she could stay greener than green.'

If that was Emily Lau's inspiration, she was not alone. In the early hours of the following morning, the minority of legislators who had stayed up through the night to debate her bill did reject her passionately argued case, but only by the wafer-thin margin of one vote. Patten had not expected the result to be quite so close, and he was more relieved than he liked to admit to have escaped what would have been a severe embarrassment. Although he conceded that there was a moral case for complete democracy in Hong Kong, he would not have hesitated to veto her bill for the same reason that he would have felt obliged to reject Martin Lee's amendment: neither was compatible with the Basic Law. Acknowledging that if Emily Lau's amendment had been carried, 'it would have given her another stick to beat us with', he added, with greater generosity, that in the months ahead she would have 'plenty to shout about, and she will shout with great eloquence. The fact that she'll still be there shouting in 1997 is good for an awful lot of people in Hong Kong, who may think she is a pain in the backside. But you actually need people like that to be able to go on living in a free society.'

The next day, the liberal media expressed a widespread cautious relief. However, commentators were scathing about both Martin Barrow and Simon Ip. Regardless of the fact that their abstentions had helped to save the Patten bill, their reputations were destroyed. The *Eastern Express* declared that they had both 'shirked their duty' in failing to come out in favour of democracy. 'When for whatever pathetic reason, they are unable to take a stand on the most important political issue facing Hong Kong,' the paper thundered, 'they should vacate their seats to allow in someone who has more stomach for the job.' The two men stayed put.

Buoyed by his victory, Patten declared that the result was 'historic', but he was careful not to elaborate. He confided: 'I've got to avoid triumphalism, and I've got to build as many bridges as possible, not just with China, but with those people who feel bruised by what has happened.' He was reminded of something the former Conservative Cabinet minister William Whitelaw had once said: 'Everybody tells me I mustn't crow. I'm certainly not going to crow. But inside I'm crowing like mad.'

Patten's internal triumphalism was reinforced by the response of the community to LegCo's decision. 'The conventional wisdom was that we couldn't have a political argument about Hong Kong without the roof falling in here,' he said. 'Well, the Hang Seng Index went up by over a hundred points this morning . . . I think some of the conventional wisdom got heavily bombed over the last twenty-four hours.' Another piece of conventional wisdom to be called into question was, as Patten noted dryly, that 'you couldn't have an argument with China and at least in the short term – we don't know about the long term – do any other business with them'. The LegCo vote did not deter China from concluding – after seven years of frustrated negotiation – an agreement the following day in the Joint Liaison Group on the future of the colony's defence lands, which were due to be handed over to the People's Liberation Army in 1997. This deal, the first of several which would have to be struck for a smooth transition through 1997 to be secured, gave Patten reason to hope that the Chinese were indeed prepared, as some of their spokesmen had hinted, to separate economics from politics.

He even allowed himself to believe that he might restore his personal relationship with the Chinese leadership. Although Lu Ping had snubbed Patten a few weeks earlier on his official visit to Hong Kong, the governor was now sure that a meeting would, after all, take place. To this end, he resolved to be 'as positive as possible, and to avoid being unnecessarily provocative'. An embrace of this kind from China would not constitute the seal of approval from Beijing, but it would go a long way to restoring Patten's credibility with his critics. Did he really think that he would be given another chance to visit Beijing? 'Oh yes,' he replied airily. 'Sooner or later.' In this respect, as in others, he woefully overestimated his own hand, and greatly underestimated the unforgiving nature of Hong Kong's future overlord.

Immediately after the vote, Edward Llewellyn dictated a statement on behalf of the governor over the phone to the *Times* correspondent in Hong Kong, Jonathan Mirsky: '"This has been an important day and night for Hong Kong. I welcome the council's decision. This has been a vigorous debate which ends a significant chapter in Hong Kong's history. We must now turn the page." That's it.' As Mirsky, among others, prophesied, it wasn't.

The intoxication of victory was short-lived. Although the local elections in September, conducted on the basis of Patten's reforms, attracted a record turn-out of over 30 per cent, Beijing's attitude towards the governor did not soften. By the late autumn, various official spokesmen had made it clear that no Chinese official would conduct negotiations directly with the governor of Hong Kong. He was openly castigated by local critics, while further afield, politicians and businessmen kept asking him for assurances about the future which he felt unable to give against what he called a 'backdrop of growing anxiety, suspicion and concern about China'. Clear evidence that the mainland's economy was overheating combined with some glaring examples of endemic corruption to dent what Patten referred to as the 'global euphoria' about China's economic miracle. Any disruption to the country's economy was bound to blow back into Hong Kong and, given the breakdown of political relations with Beijing, Patten was well aware that he would certainly take some of the blame, however unjust this might be. He was particularly worried about the property market in Hong Kong. If anxiety about the future were to translate into fears about property values, then prices could tumble sharply as people hurried to cash in their assets.

His worries were reinforced by evidence that morale in the civil service had plummeted. In an internal survey of opinion among the staff of the MRTC (Mass Transit Railway Corporation), 20 per cent of senior managers declared that they would leave Hong Kong before 1997. How many others in similar roles in the private and public sec-tors had made the same decision, or would do so if fears about their prospects after 1997 became widespread?

At the end of 1994 the columnist Margaret Ng spoke privately of her conviction that Hong Kong would face a 'very tough takeover'. It was, by now, quite clear to her that 'Peking is going to take control of this place before it will allow local people to have any say . . . there may be a period when there will be a lot of persecution with people like me being a target.' She was depressed by the superficial appraisal of Hong Kong's prospects so often parroted by outsiders.

> Every visitor will tell you, 'Hong Kong is a vibrant place. The econ-
> omy is growing,' but you can feel that a lot of your fellow workers are
> on the edge of breakdown. You know, sometimes you feel that on a
> bad day all you have to do is to light a match and the whole house
> would blow up because everyone is under tremendous pressure. No
> one likes to acknowledge it, because that is not our style . . . but
> there are lots of inexplicable cases of people suddenly breaking down
> and weeping. If you look at the broader picture, there is this tension.
> We are going berserk. There is no doubt about it.

Margaret Ng was not an excitable woman and she spoke reflectively, more in the manner of a psychiatrist than a polemical writer.

The governor was far from sanguine. 'My worry six months to a year ago was that we might find ourselves in the last couple of years facing a downturn in the Chinese economic cycle and a shift of mood from euphoria to pessimism, which is more abrupt in relation to China than anywhere else in the world,' he confided in late 1994. 'Well, it seems to me that it is happening, all too much on cue.' In such circumstances Patten's isolation would place him in a most precarious position, and he knew it.

> We'll be pressed with increasing stridency by some sections of the
> community to do more to safeguard human rights . . . whereas ever
> more limited efforts to do that will draw down on our heads huge
> denunciations from the Chinese leadership . . . This will provoke
> even more rows each time . . . I think this job is going to be trickier
> in the coming year than it was last year.

Patten managed to mask his anxieties to enter into the spirit of his social duties as governor. The Pattens' desire to make extensive use of the ballroom at Government House was enthusiastically welcomed by the organisers of local charities, who knew that the cachet of a Government House event attended by the governor and his wife was a sure-fire fund-raiser in this competitively generous community. One evening in March 1995, organised by two local children's charities of which Lavender was patron, was typical. A visiting company from Britain, the European Chamber Opera, gave a performance of Mozart's *Così Fan Tutte*. The occasion, sponsored by two of Hong Kong's most formidable institutions in the Hang Seng Bank and Jardine Pacific, attracted a swathe of the colony's grandees.

Quite what the Chinese guests made of Mozart's most absurdly complicated plot was unclear, especially as the opera was sung uncompromisingly, if with verve, in Italian, and without the benefit of scenery. It was perhaps not surprising that at least some of the guests soon allowed their imagination and attention to wander. The Europeans present, if only to confirm their familiarity with the work or the Italian language, laughed noisily at appropriate moments. For the detached observer, no cultural occasion could more vividly have pinpointed the cultural divide between the races: the intense concentration of the Europeans set against the bemused indifference of the Chinese. Afterwards, Patten joined the performers for a late-night drink. His day of meetings and visits had begun at 8am and had been interrupted only by a luncheon for the Mayor of Westminster. Yet one of his guests remarked that he seemed more animated than he had been in the morning. He chatted to the young singers and musicians, praising their performance, listening to what they had to say about England and telling them about Hong Kong, until well after midnight. As his friend observed, 'Somehow, it seemed to make him feel at home again. These were his people, and his country.'

This was also the weekend of the Hong Kong Sevens rugby tournament, the highlight of the colony's sporting year, for which the world's leading teams arrive to compete in the fiercest seven-a-side competition on earth. As guests of honour, the Pattens were escorted to their blue-canopied box along with their house guests, who included the governor of Macau and his wife. Patten was in his element. Sweeping his binoculars around the crowd of 40,000, mainly Europeans, who danced and yelled their way through the afternoon, he grinned delightedly. 'Look at that! Isn't it a marvellous sight?' At school he had been fanatical about rugby; now he showed the restraint befitting the guest of honour as each match was battled out in front of him. Nevertheless he obeyed the entreaties of the abandoned crowd and rose self-consciously when a Mexican wave swept round the stadium engulfing the stand in which he and other VIPs were sitting. Afterwards he walked behind the stands, where young British expatriates were draining jugs of beer in convivial satisfaction. 'All right, then, Chris?' they asked, raising their glasses to him. He smiled easily, the politician at home among his own.

15

'A MATTER OF DECENCY'

A Row Over the
Court of Final Appeal

In the prevailing atmosphere of renewed anxiety, the governor now had to confront a raft of unfinished but highly contentious business which had been delayed by the protracted conflict with China over his political reforms. Detailed negotiations covering a wide range of crucial issues – including the airport project, the CT9 container port, the sale of defence lands, immigration and passports – had come to a virtual standstill. And then there was the matter of human rights. Patten's refusal to countenance a Human Rights Commission earlier in the year did not mean that the question had fallen off Hong Kong's agenda. To bring the legislation into line with the 1991 Bill of Rights, he had been advised by the government's lawyers that he should abolish a range of longstanding repressive laws which had been a source of embarrassment to the Hong Kong government for years. Britain had done little or nothing about the issue before Patten's appointment, and the desultory approach of his predecessors had left the governor doubly exposed: he now had to act not only under the critical scrutiny of human-rights activists in Hong Kong and the hard-line regime in Beijing, but against a very tight deadline. Patten thought that the readiness of officials in London and in the colony to see the protection of human rights in Hong Kong in terms of diplomatic settlements with China was another example of how Britain continually viewed Hong Kong 'through the prism of our relationship with Peking'. It had made his task far more difficult than it would otherwise have been.

A case in point were the laws grouped together under the colony's Emergency Regulations, last used in the riots of 1967, when the authorities feared that the survival of Hong Kong hung in the balance. To deploy the Emergency Powers Ordinance would be tantamount to a declaration of martial law, and Patten had no choice but to abolish it, not least because Hong Kong's law officers were in no doubt that these residual powers contravened the Bill of Rights. Although China had undertaken in Article 13 of the Basic Law to protect 'freedom of the person, of speech, of assembly, of association . . . of strike, of demonstration' in Hong Kong after the handover, Patten predicted that he would face a hostile reaction from Beijing once he announced his decision to follow his own official advice.

> When we first go along to them, clearing our throat and saying, 'Well, you know, we've got to do something about these emergency powers, because they are not in line with the Bill of Rights,' they will say, 'But they've been all right for governors to have in their back pockets in case they needed them. Why are you now changing them? . . . You just want to create chaos. What you want is to go round unloosening all the screws.'

Although the Legislative Council had passed the appropriate measure to abolish some of the harsher elements of the Public Order Act, the governor was inclined to get rid of the Emergency Regulations using a swifter and more surgical method: exercising his executive powers, authorised, or rubber-stamped, by his advisers on the Executive Council. Even though Beijing was likely to 'blow a gasket', he had persuaded the Cabinet in London to recognise that this was his best available option. However, he confided, 'I still have to carry London on the timing.'

He was well aware that the Chinese would be bound to interpret his decision as a deliberate indication to the outside world that his successors could not be trusted to exercise the same degree of restraint as his predecessors. As it turned out, when Patten did eventually abolish the Emergency Powers by executive fiat, to his relief and astonishment, Beijing seemed not to notice.

There was no chance of finessing past Beijing an even more controversial issue which had the potential to explode into a terminal conflict with China, and which was therefore almost certain to become yet another cause of friction between Government House and the Foreign Office. Once again the crisis he now foresaw had been inherited from a chain of events which predated his appointment, and once again, the focus was on human rights. In this case, the context was the judicial system, and notably the status and composition of the Court of Final

Appeal, which was to replace the Privy Council as Hong Kong's court of last resort.

In 1991, the terms of the secret agreement between Britain and China on the Court of Final Appeal had been unveiled before a sceptical Hong Kong public, whose suspicions were duly confirmed. As Patten later commented, the deal reflected a 'particular style of diplomacy of which I am not wholly enamoured'. Britain, he complained, had been willing to reach 'pretty fundamental agreements with the Chinese without taking much notice of what people in Hong Kong thought'. The main area of contention concerned the Basic Law's imprecise definition of 'acts of state', over which, under Article 18, Hong Kong courts would have no jurisdiction. The issue of exactly what activities – if any – in addition to foreign affairs and defence, might fall into this category had been skirted by Britain and China and was still unresolved. Several legislators and a number of prominent lawyers, led by Martin Lee and Margaret Ng, also expressed their dismay that the British had apparently colluded in an interpretation of an ambiguity in Article 82 of the Basic Law which would, they argued, severely damage the credibility of the Court of Final Appeal.

This article stated that judges 'from other common-law jurisdictions' could be invited by the chief justice 'as required' to sit on the court. But the British negotiators had yielded to China's insistence that Article 82 should be taken to mean that only one 'foreign' judge could sit on the court at any one time. From the critics' perspective, the presence of expatriate judges sitting with their local counterparts at the highest level of the Hong Kong judiciary would both enhance the standing of the court internationally and act as a counterweight to any interference, however discreet, from Beijing. But limiting the court to one 'foreign' judge would invariably leave the verdict – by a potential majority of four to one – in 'domestic' hands, a prospect which threatened to undermine these twin objectives.

Patten had been warned before his arrival in Hong Kong that the Court of Final Appeal would cause him trouble. He was aware that the 1991 agreement had, as he put it, 'left one or two bits of shirt-tail flapping', but he thought, somewhat casually, that it still left Hong Kong with 'quite a reasonable' deal. The colony's legislators, kept in the dark during the course of the 1991 negotiations, had responded with predictable hostility once the terms of the agreement became public. 'As soon as it saw the light of day,' Patten reflected, 'the agreement was howled down by the legal profession in Hong Kong and voted down by the Legislative Council'. Nonetheless, the British felt that they had no option but to draw up a bill based on the agreement. It was this bill which was Patten's inheritance.

According to the terms of the Joint Declaration, the forum for discussing all these issues was the Joint Liaison Group between the British and the Chinese. In the wake of the collapse of relations between their respective sovereign masters, communication between the two sides in the JLG had reached a nadir. Before Patten's arrival, for example, it had been the tradition for the leaders of each delegation to entertain one another – at the theatre, the ballet, and even at home for dinner – during their regular sessions in Beijing or London, regardless of how fraught matters at the negotiating table had been. This display of social amity had been suspended during the seventeen rounds of intergovernmental negotiations about Patten's electoral reforms, and although the custom was re-established in the summer of 1994, it had done nothing to accelerate progress.

In May 1994, the head of the British delegation at the JLG, Hugh Davies, had presented the Chinese with Hong Kong's proposed bill establishing the Court of Final Appeal, but amid this dialogue of the deaf the Chinese refrained from making any response until almost four months later. Eventually, they deigned to raise what the British side considered some 'rather puerile questions' about the bill. According to one long-serving and long-suffering participant, the discussions now became impatient to the point of acrimony. 'Their tempers rise and so do ours. But we don't shout at each other . . . The only way out is to break and try to reassemble in smaller groups.' It was not until the early spring of 1995 that the Chinese returned to the table again, armed this time with a set of more serious questions which nevertheless served only to convince the British that they had 'decided they would prefer not to reach an agreement'.

In the face of such obduracy, the governor had to consider his options in earnest. Exasperated by the unwillingness or inability of the Chinese to reach any decision on any significant issue, he characterised their attitude as one of 'mendacity, fabrication, incompetence and wishful thinking'. They had raised three issues relating to the Court of Final Appeal Bill, all of which suggested that they had it in mind to curtail sharply, if not terminally, the independence of the Hong Kong judiciary. First, they argued that the court should not be permitted to pronounce on the 'constitutionality of laws' – for example, on cases arising out of the Bill of Rights. Secondly, they sought to include a mechanism for what they described as a 'post-remedial verdict', which would allow the National People's Congress to overturn any judgement reached by the Court of Appeal. Thirdly, they intimated that the definition of 'acts of state' would have to embrace 'other things' in addition to foreign affairs and defence. They also demanded that the bill should contain a clause specifically drawing attention to the fact that any 'acts of state' thus defined would not fall within the jurisdiction of the Court of Final Appeal, a requirement which the British had hitherto resisted. For Patten, the implication of these demands was as crude as its purpose was self-evident: 'If we – the Chinese – don't like the result, we've got to find some way to overturn it.'

Given the character of the objections of the Chinese and their refusal to negotiate, Patten came to the conclusion that it was going to be impossible to reach an agreement with their officials 'in their present mood'. Yet the Joint Declaration had specified that the court was to be established in advance of the 1997 handover. The governor was running out of time. Although this did not emerge publicly, he now faced his most daunting quandary since his appointment. For the first time, he found himself facing the prospect of conflict not only with officials in the Foreign Office, but potentially with senior members of the Cabinet as well – even those who trusted him most – and certainly with the president of the Board of Trade, Michael Heseltine. In March 1995 he explained his predicament:

> London accepts the argument for trying to set up a Court of Final Appeal before 1997. After all, we negotiated the agreement. But London also wants to minimise the number of rows that we have with China. There is still the view – more among diplomats than politicians – that if only we could somehow get on better with China, everything would be easier and Sino–British relations would produce an aura of sunlight in which problems could be solved and trade would be better.
>
> Here in Hong Kong, we feel very strongly that we've at least got to have a go at setting up the court, but we are still dealing with a Legislative Council which we don't think will vote in very large numbers for the court. So do we press ahead on our own without Chinese agreement? If we do, and there is a row, can we get the bill through the Legislative Council? What sort of situation is this in which to persuade London that we should go ahead? We have a row with China, and we fall flat on our face in the Legislative Council.
>
> The position I am in is one in which my political judgement is going to be taken rather less seriously by my former colleagues from now on. Over the electoral provisions we won. We had a row, but we won. But to go into the Legislative Council [on this issue] wondering whether we can win or not poses a real dilemma.

Indeed, the pro-China legislators would have been bound to oppose any measure not approved by Beijing, while the Democrats had made it plain that they would also vote against the bill unless it was modified in ways which Patten believed would violate the 1991 agreement with China. It was quite possible that the Democrats might amend the bill in an effort to alter the composition of the court to ensure that more than one foreign judge could sit on it at the same time – the point on which the British had given way in 1991. Were this to happen, Patten would be constrained by what he regarded disdainfully as a 'sacred text between Britain and China'. For the governor to give his assent to a bill thus amended by the Legislative Council would, he believed, be tantamount to advocating a breach of the agreement between the two sovereign powers. 'I don't think I could have done that. I don't think the foreign secretary or the prime minister could have accepted it,' he concluded.

Meanwhile, the British ambassador in Beijing, Sir Len Appleyard, was sending anxious messages to London warning that it would be 'ill advised' to press ahead with the CFA bill. He argued in what Patten's team regarded as an 'unhelpful memo' that to confront China over this issue would damage British interests in China and provoke Beijing to be even less conciliatory on all matters in the run-up to 1997. Appleyard was known by bolder spirits in the Foreign Office as 'Applecart'; at Government House, he was roundly distrusted for what Patten's advisers regarded as his readiness to appease his Beijing hosts. As on other occasions, they believed he had succumbed to the temptation to load the evidence and exaggerate the prospective damage to win his case. 'Sir Len will do almost anything for an easy life,' remarked one of them bitterly.

Although both the foreign secretary and the prime minister had made it clear to Patten that if he thought it was right to go ahead and try to legislate, they would back him, the Foreign Office sinologists had other ideas. On this occasion they had a powerful ally in Michael Heseltine. Officials in the Department of Trade and Industry had spent several months putting together a team of prominent British industrialists for a trade mission to China, scheduled for mid-May 1995, to be led by the president of the Board of Trade. The visit was being promoted as the first major trip of its kind since the eighties, when Lord Young had been tour leader on the DTI's behalf, and Heseltine was expected to meet the most senior members of the politburo. It was soon clear that Heseltine's team was determined that his thunder should not be stolen by what they saw as an avoidable quarrel with China. Patten, they argued, should be restrained from pursuing his arcane obsession with the Court of Final Appeal with such undue haste.

The governor was intuitively sceptical about the value of the travelling circus of industrialists Heseltine was intending to parade around China. Although he refrained from expressing direct criticism of his former Cabinet colleague, his team in Government House was well aware that he had long been suspicious of the 'grandstanding' instincts of the Cabinet's most colourful character. Although there were those, Patten mused, who 'think that having receptions for ministers and businessmen, signing letters of intent and memoranda of understanding, is the same as getting contracts and winning exports', he also recalled, with a touch of savage satisfaction, that Lord Young's endeavours in this respect during the eighties had failed to stem a decline in either British exports to or Britain's share of trade with China. And he pointed out that, despite the political breakdown with Beijing in 1992, British trade with the People's Republic had grown rapidly ever since: there was no evidence that 'kowtowing' made any difference to the prospects for trade or investment.

Patten's overriding worry about the Heseltine mission was the potential it had to undermine the British government's stance over Hong Kong. He feared that it would be bound to signal to China that, from London's point of view, trade with the People's Republic mattered more than human rights or the rule of law in the future SAR. His concern was increased by the fact that China had already intimated to the British embassy in Beijing that a 'warming in the economic relationship' might be in the offing if only the political environment could be improved. Officials in the Department of Trade and Industry and the Foreign Office, supported by Sir Len Appleyard, pressed this argument vigorously. The disagreement continued back and forth between London and Government House without resolution throughout the spring of 1995. In the end, Patten decided against adopting what he described as the 'Rorke's Drift approach to politics'. He reluctantly agreed to postpone tabling the CFA bill, at least until Heseltine had returned from China.

During this period, the foreign secretary, Douglas Hurd, came under intense pressure from both Heseltine and Patten. 'I really did have very considerable difficulty with these two colleagues,' he commented later.

Michael's preoccupation was entirely justified. He is different from Percy Cradock because Cradock's concern is mainly political. But Michael sees this immense market growing at a huge rate. He sees the Germans and the French powering in there with huge delegations, and he wants to do the same. And Hong Kong is an impediment to that process . . . Michael and I are friends. We've not had a real row in our lives, and we certainly didn't then. We circled round each other to a certain extent, and you assess the size of each other's arguments and who is likely to support them . . . I was always asking Chris, 'Can you not postpone it for a little [longer] while I handle Michael?' But for Chris, the Court of Final Appeal was an absolutely crucial point.

With the prime minister watching from the sidelines, Hurd advised Patten that he should stand by to return to London after Heseltine's visit to argue his case against the president of the Board of Trade face to face in the Cabinet. Patten was not at all certain that he would win, not least because he knew that he would have to share his fear that LegCo was likely to reject his proposals for the Court of Final Appeal, an admission of weakness which would make it even harder for him to prevail in Cabinet. Yet, although he was reluctant to make the CFA a resigning issue, he was by no means sure that he could return to Hong Kong as governor if he failed to get his way in London.

Patten was tempted to think that Heseltine had allowed himself to be flattered into seeing his visit to Beijing as a possible turning point in Sino–British relations. Certainly this was the line taken by the Foreign Office, and by Heseltine's prospective Chinese hosts – egged on (it was presumed at Government House) by the ubiquitous Sir Percy Cradock, who had himself recently returned from Beijing. To the governor's team it was clear that the forceful head of the Hong Kong Department in the Foreign Office, Sherard Cowper-Coles, was using Appleyard's reports from Beijing to promote the view that trade with China should take priority over Hong Kong's post-1997 legal system – urging, in effect, as one of them put it, that 'we should wash our hands of Hong Kong and rebuild our relationship with China'.

Patten was contemptuous of the view that there was a 'cornucopia in China waiting to flow over our slippered feet if only we would recognise the importance of "restoring good relations" . . . I think the Chinese have managed to turn otherwise rational and sensible people inside out by dangling these great, fat carrots.' By the time of Heseltine's visit in May 1995, a year after the draft CFA bill had originally been submitted to the Chinese in the JLG, the governor's impatience with the Foreign Office sinologists and their allies in the DTI had reached a new intensity. The interminable conflict over how to deal with China over this issue, he confided, had become

more debilitating than the rows about anything else, and certainly more debilitating than having an argument with the Chinese about democracy . . . Looking over your shoulder while you are trying to take on an important issue is always rather tiresome. I've always thought that we were in a somewhat difficult position . . . trying to implement it in the teeth of opposition from China, and from parts of the local community. What I guess I hadn't entirely expected was that there would be opposition on one's own side, too.

Claiming that the ins and outs of bureaucratic politics did not usually engage him, he volunteered that in the case of the Court of Final Appeal he had been 'surprised and mildly shocked by some of the tricks and devices' which had been used against him by the sinologists. Though he was unwilling to go into detail, the precise cause of his deepening anger was easily apparent. His closest advisers, who shared his opinion, were furious at the way in which, as it seemed to them, both Appleyard and Cowper-Coles had usurped their proper roles as subordinate officials to undermine the governor's position. In particular Patten's aides resented the eagerness of one or two people in the Foreign Office to put it about that their 'boss' was not only intellectually arrogant, but refused to listen to counter-arguments or superior wisdom.

The Chinese treated the arrival of the British president of the Board of Trade as an event of great moment. According to most observers in Beijing, Heseltine was magnificently presidential in bearing and made an excellent impression on his hosts. He saw all the top leaders, with the exception of Deng Xiaoping, and, amid all the flummery and fanfare that such formalities invariably engender, the two sides duly signed letters of intent worth hundreds of millions of pounds. In Hong Kong, the governor's enthusiasm for Heseltine's coup de théâtre was muted.

> I think trade missions are important to any country, and I think it is absolutely fair to say that the president of the Board of Trade has been terrifically supportive of British business all around the world . . . I very much hope that Michael's visit will lead to big business coups for Britain. He carries these things off with more chutzpah than anybody else could manage. But at the end of the day the Chinese do business on business terms.

Reiterating that while Britain, the European Union's biggest investor in China, had enjoyed 'huge increases' in its exports to the People's Republic over the previous two years, he was also at pains to point out that British trade with Hong Kong was of even greater significance. 'I want to see the best possible trading relationship between Britain and

China,' he maintained. 'But what I don't agree with is that in order to do business with China you should ignore your obligations to Hong Kong, not only because it is a matter of decency, honour, Britain's word and Britain's place in the world, but because I think that a huge commercial interest of Britain's is that Hong Kong should continue to succeed.'

Appleyard's valedictory telegram to London after Heseltine's trip confirmed all Patten's fears. Both oleaginous and, from the standpoint of Government House, defeatist in tone, it lavished praise on the president of the Board of Trade for what Appleyard described as an 'outstandingly successful visit'. As a direct result, he reported, British companies were now chasing business worth more than £5 billion, while deals to the tune of £1 billion had already been concluded. The showpiece of the event, a meeting between Heseltine and Li Peng, had, according to Appleyard, sent a message throughout China to the effect that Britain was greatly valued as a trading partner. Even more importantly, the visit had apparently been viewed by both sides as an important landmark in the process of the 'gradual restoration of good relations' between the two nations. In his tête-à-tête with Heseltine, Appleyard reported, Li Peng had made it clear that the two countries could have even closer ties if only the stumbling block of Hong Kong could be removed. While Beijing was anxious to co-operate and to reach agreement on the outstanding issues between them, the ambassador concluded, failure to achieve this desirable outcome would be bound to have an adverse effect on trade relations between the two nations. He and other British officials were careful to avoid using phrases such as 'turning point', but Appleyard nonetheless declared that the time was ripe to capitalise on the achievements of the mission.

This was precisely what Patten had expected from the outset. Although he took pains to avoid blaming Heseltine – who he knew had not once strayed from the Cabinet's agreed stance over Hong Kong while he was in Beijing – he was disconcerted to be told that, on one occasion, the president of the Board of Trade and the British ambassador, closeted in a Guangdong hotel owned by the People's Liberation Army, had discussed the best way of handling the 'Patten problem'. He was far more dismayed by the zeal with which, on his return to London, Heseltine set about attempting to shift the government's priorities towards Hong Kong. Arguing that British trade with China should take precedence, he claimed that, if it was not to be severely damaged in the months ahead, Patten had to be prevented from causing yet another showdown with the People's Republic over the Court of Final Appeal.

In Beijing Heseltine had formed the view that the Chinese were willing to compromise over the CFA. Indeed, according to a member of Patten's team, one of Li Peng's aides had even told the British Cabinet minister that the Chinese were willing to look again at the quota of foreign judges allowed to sit on the supreme court. Encouraged by this apparent flexibility, Heseltine urged that Patten should be instructed by the Cabinet to delay tabling his bill for a further six weeks to allow more time for the exploration of the potential for a negotiated settlement. On the face of it, as Patten ruefully acknowledged, the president of the Board of Trade had a powerful case.

In Hong Kong, where the Court of Final Appeal had now emerged publicly to become a subject of acrimonious debate, Patten's imperatives were of a quite different order. To delay tabling the CFA bill would, he was convinced, be interpreted as a sign of weakness on his part at the worst possible moment. Reiterating the governor's stance, his chief secretary, Anson Chan, had only recently voiced the opinion that failure to set up the court before 1997 would leave Hong Kong's legal system with a 'vacuum at the apex'. Any delay, she declared, would lead the Hong Kong government to be 'rightly criticised for not meeting our obligations under the 1991 agreement'. Rumours that Beijing was seeking to impose restrictions on the powers of the court had started to leak into the local press, and though Patten had managed to sidestep anxious questions from legislators, he knew he would have to act swiftly to avert a crisis of confidence. It was essential, he believed, to head off Heseltine. To this end he sent an impassioned telegram to London insisting that it was vital that the bill was tabled without further delay. If he were to acquiesce to Heseltine's plan, he wrote, his own authority in Hong Kong would be fatally undermined; it would be seen as a 'betrayal of the principles that we have constantly said we stand for'. Moreover, to postpone the decision would send precisely the wrong signals to both Beijing and the community in Hong Kong, and would almost certainly result in the establishment of a court 'even less to our liking'. He informed London that his approach had the support of the legal profession, the civil service and − for once − the business community as well; the media, apart from the irredeemably pro-Beijing press, were also urging him to forge ahead. It was extremely important, he maintained, that the Cabinet should not be 'seduced' by 'reassurances' from Li Peng about Hong Kong; in the past these had amounted to very little.

Patten knew that Michael Heseltine had been urging the prime minister to send a conciliatory message to Li Peng stating, in effect, that he was sure they could reach agreement on all sorts of matters that concerned Britain, including the outstanding issues in relation to Hong Kong, and that if it would help, Britain would certainly be willing to come to terms on the question of the appointment of judges to the Court of Final Appeal. The governor repeated that Heseltine's approach was, if well-meaning, misguided. Adamant that the government should put as much space as possible between Heseltine's visit and any action over the CFA, he advised that, if the Cabinet insisted on endorsing the approach suggested by the president of the Board of Trade, he would feel bound to fly back immediately to fight his corner. He warned that the mood in Hong Kong was now so volatile that this in itself would be enough to shatter the territory's confidence as it was bound to be interpreted as evidence of a serious rift with China.

The implicit, if unstated, message of Patten's telegram was 'back me or sack me'. The warning was not lightly given. Although he was sure that he still enjoyed the confidence of the prime minister, he also knew that, following a disastrous showing by the Conservatives in the 1995 local elections, John Major would find it hard to confront Heseltine directly on the issue. Heseltine had become the lynchpin of the administration, and the merest hint that he was unhappy with the prime minister's handling of affairs would give credence to the growing murmur that Major would face a leadership challenge in the autumn of the kind which had dealt Margaret Thatcher's premiership its fatal blow five years before. The Conservative backbenchers were dangerously demoralised and restless, and calls for Major's resignation had started to reverberate around Westminster. The continued support of Heseltine, his most powerful Cabinet colleague, was indispensable to Major's survival as leader of the party. In these circumstances Patten was less sanguine about his own position in Hong Kong than at any time since his arrival.

For several days, Major stood aloof as the battle over the CFA was fought out between the president of the Board of Trade and the foreign secretary, who remained entirely loyal to Patten despite pressure from his own civil servants. According to the reports which reached Government House, there was a 'real stand-off' between the two Cabinet heavyweights. Finally, prompted by Patten's telegram, the prime minister consulted the chancellor of the exchequer, who endorsed the governor's stance. Soon afterwards he summoned Douglas Hurd, Kenneth Clarke and Michael Heseltine to a meeting at Number 10. They had three papers before them – one from the embassy in Beijing, one from the Cabinet Office and one from the governor of Hong Kong – all offering conflicting opinions. As the story was relayed to Government House, Heseltine argued, in effect, 'For God's sake, I've made this trip. Don't screw up the prospects. I've had good conversations with the Chinese. They are saying we can make progress if we don't throw the CFA at them.' The same points were made by some of his officials in what Patten described as a distinctly less sophisticated way.

After a vigorous debate, Patten was informed by the Foreign Office that he had won the day and that Heseltine had yielded with characteristic grace. In the absence of agreement with China within the next few days, he was, free, as he interpreted it, to 'go ahead and legislate'. Government House had planned to gazette the CFA bill on the third Friday in June, which, it was calculated, would leave just enough time for the Legislative Council to vote on it before the summer recess. Heseltine was apparently mollified by the prime minister's decision to take his advice and send a message to the Chinese premier indicating, in Patten's gloss, that he 'very much hoped we would be able to reach an agreement, and that he welcomed the success of Michael Heseltine's visit to Peking'. This communication may or may not have had an impact on what happened next.

Events now moved with unexpected speed and in an unpredictable manner. The Cabinet had given Patten full authority to oversee a last-ditch attempt to secure a deal with China, and this decisive meeting of the Joint Liaison Group was held on 30 May 1995. Towards the end of the session, the leader of the Chinese side, Chen Zuo'er, made a number of suggestions and indicated for the first time that Beijing's principal anxiety was the timing of the establishment of the Court of Final Appeal. Even though the 1991 agreement committed both sides to establishing the court before the handover, he made it clear that, for reasons the British could not fathom, Beijing would prefer the court not to 'open for business' until 1 July 1997.

That evening, after a rapid round of consultations, Chris Patten authorised Richard Hoare, the acting head of the British negotiating team in the JLG, to inform his Chinese counterpart that, while the British would like the court to be set up before 1997, it was not as fundamental to them as the nature of the court that was actually to be established. Patten was to argue that this compromise (or climbdown, as his critics described it) was a sensible trade-off, a relatively modest price to pay for the possibility of an agreement with China on the structure and function of the court. On the plausible assumption that the Legislative Council would approve a bill endorsed by China, he asserted privately that his concession on timing would ensure that there would not be a rupture in the rule of law after the handover.

A week earlier, the Hong Kong government had redrafted parts of the bill to bring it in line with six of eight demands made by the Preliminary Working Committee, the body set up in Hong Kong in 1993 by Beijing as an alternative centre of influence to Government House, allegedly to assist the smooth transfer of power following the collapse of negotiations between the two sovereign states. Hitherto Patten had loftily ignored the ruminations of the PWC. Now, although the body's recommendations for the Court of Final Appeal dealt essentially with technical issues, the governor's willingness to redraft his bill basically on their terms was a significant shift towards the Chinese position which could not have gone unnoticed in Beijing.

Beijing responded by dropping its original demands that the bill should contain a 'post-remedial verdict mechanism' and that the court should be debarred from adjudicating on the 'constitutionality of laws'. China also backed away from its earlier intimation that the bill should define 'acts of state' more precisely than they were defined in the Basic Law. In return, the British side was authorised by Patten to concede that the bill would, as Beijing had insisted, contain a clause confirming that all 'acts of state', howsoever defined in the Basic Law, would be excluded from the jurisdiction of the Court of Final Appeal.

The British negotiators presented Patten's revised bill to their counterparts in the JLG at the beginning of June. The Chinese moved with surprising dispatch, and on 7 June, the two sides signed an agreement to set up the Court of Final Appeal on 1 July 1997. At first Patten was jubilant. Although he acknowledged that it would have been 'incomparably better if we'd been able to establish the court now', he explained that he had been boxed into a corner, not so much by pressure from London as by the prospect of certain defeat in the legislative assembly had he pressed ahead with the CFA bill without China's consent. 'The position we were in was very different from the argument over electoral reform,' he explained. 'On this occasion it looked more and more as if legislating on our own was going to be charging the guns. It would have been magnificent, but ultimately not wildly successful.' In this case it was, as he saw it, a straightforward choice between having a say in the nature of the court and not having the court set up until 1997, or not having a say in the court and still not having the court set up until 1997.

Quite why the Chinese had suddenly decided to compromise was the subject of much speculation at Government House. Patten had not yielded to Heseltine's argument for delay, nor had Britain ceded the right to table the bill in the absence of China's approval. Patten himself thought that Beijing must have reached the conclusion that they were 'running out of time to screw us up, just as we are running out of time as the sovereign power in Hong Kong'. He also felt that they had started to worry about the low morale among civil servants, for whom British standards of justice and law were a sine qua non of civil order, and about the possible exodus of capital from Hong Kong that could so easily be precipitated by a failure to resolve such a crucial issue. Indeed, if they agreed with Patten on few other matters, the colony's business leaders were united with him in the conviction that the survival of the 'rule of law' was vital to their prosperity after the handover. However, not one significant voice in the business community expressed anxiety about whether Beijing would interpret the controversial clause about 'acts of state' in a repressive fashion. Their worry was that Hong Kong's post-1997 judicial system might lack international credibility: it was essential that foreign banks and corporations should regard the Court of Final Appeal as a truly independent body with the power of ultimate adjudication, especially in relation to the law of contract. Otherwise, as they warned Beijing with growing urgency, the world's major investors would inevitably shy away from negotiating deals under Hong Kong law.

Patten was convinced that the Chinese had also been impressed by the 'mad governor' factor; by the evidence that, following the Cabinet decision in his favour, the British would not, in the end, be deterred from establishing a Court of Final Appeal even in the absence of an agreement with China. According to Patten, Douglas Hurd shared this assessment. 'I think the foreign secretary was as surprised at the outcome as we were. But I think, like us, he believed that the real reason we got a deal was because the Chinese believed we had a bottom line, and that we were going to go ahead if we reached the deadline.' Whatever the explanation, Patten was relieved that the deal 'enabled us to dig ourselves out of a hole', and freely conceded that, when the prospect of an agreement appeared, he 'grabbed at it with both hands'.

Throughout the process Patten had been scrupulous in closely consulting Martin Lee. He not only shared with the leader of the Democrats some of his frustrations and dilemmas, but even indicated in broad terms some of the pressures he had been under from London. The governor was indignant, therefore, when the CFA bill was published, that Martin Lee not only failed to applaud the breakthrough but chose to denounce the terms of the deal with China in the most strident and contemptuous fashion. The two erstwhile allies at once found themselves locked in an unusually vituperative public battle. For the first time, Government House experienced the full strength of the Democrats on the offensive. Patten's team reflected ruefully on how dangerously abrasive their relationship would have become if the governor had failed to introduce his political reforms.

Their bitter row went to the heart of an issue which deeply troubled both men: Britain's inability to impose limits on the action the Chinese government would be able to take in Hong Kong after 1997. The first round was fought in the pages of the *South China Morning Post* on 15 June, when Martin Lee accused Britain of allowing the sun 'to set in shame' over its colonial history and Patten of doing 'Beijing's dirty work'. The fundamental cause for the legislator's outburst was what he described as Britain's 'explicit acceptance of China's faulty definition of "acts of state"'. The following day, Patten responded in the same newspaper with a ferocity Hong Kong had not previously witnessed, and which betrayed the governor's acute sensitivity on the issue. Charging Martin Lee with resorting to 'pejorative clichés' and 'inventing quotes and ascribing them to me', he argued that, far from accepting China's definition of the 'acts of state', Britain had merely agreed to 'incorporate the precise wording of the Basic Law into the CFA bill'. He continued, in a tone of exasperation, 'The plain fact is that the Basic Law will be the law of Hong Kong after 1997, and whatever we do now, the CFA would have to be compatible with the Basic Law after 1997 anyway.' Urging Martin Lee to abandon his 'knee-jerk stuff', he criticised the leader of Hong Kong's only directly elected party for doing a 'disservice to Hong Kong people and to the rule of law which both he and I cherish so much'.

To illustrate the nub of his argument, Martin Lee cited a hypothetical but by no means far-fetched scenario.

> Supposing the People's Liberation Army, who will be stationed in Hong Kong, were to arrest somebody and just keep that person in prison without a trial. And suppose his family were to go to court and ask for habeas corpus, according to the common law which will apply in Hong Kong after 1997. And the court says, 'Quite right. You cannot imprison someone in this way without charge. What do you think you are doing?' But the PLA says, 'This is an act of state; we are acting to protect the security of the government in Beijing. This man is a dissident, a counter-revolutionary.' That could be the end of that man's freedom . . . In other words, Beijing will decide, effectively, the cases which our courts can try and those they cannot try.

Patten could not contradict the point directly, and he knew it. Instead he claimed, wrongly and limply, that hitherto the issue of 'acts of state' had not been raised by Martin Lee and his civil-libertarian allies. As they were quick to counter, the issue had been central to their concern during the drafting of the Basic Law and one of the reasons why the Legislative Council had been so suspicious of the 1991 agreement between Britain and China. In any case, Patten's critics wondered, was the governor suggesting that the British would have been more stalwart if the Democrats had been more vociferous? Or was he merely seeking to blame them for delivering such an unpalatable message through the letterbox of Government House?

The slanging match lasted for almost a month as each side cast around in vain for the linguistic stiletto that might inflict the fatal wound to the other's case. The rawness of their exchanges, laced with sharp debating points and a genuine sense of grievance, owed a great deal to the fact that they shared very similar anxieties and a genuine dismay that they should find themselves at each other's throats. Lee agonised privately, 'I feel betrayed. I think he's betrayed the Hong Kong people's trust in him. When he came it was like a breath of fresh air. He effectively took over from us our banner for democracy . . . I feel terrible . . . I mean, what difference is it from the good old Percy Cradock days?'

Almost symmetrically, Patten confided, 'I think Martin Lee is the most important elected politician in Hong Kong, and that is why I think his attitude to this is so profoundly worrying.' Acknowledging that he was indeed in a 'terrific state' about Lee, Patten complained bitterly about the self-righteousness of the legislator's onslaught. 'It's as if Martin's got a monopoly on concern about – he'd almost go as far as to say knowledge of – the rule of law in Hong Kong.' However, the governor's dismay went deeper than this. It was, though he did not explicitly admit it, as much a manifestation of his own fears as it was a reflection on Martin Lee. 'The frustration is to have the argument turned to issues on which one can't give reassurance,' he said. 'Instead of being about the composition of the court, the argument has become about something which he knows we can't give a one hundred per cent answer on . . . The argument is now about China's understanding and comprehension of the law after 1997.' He appreciated the skill with which Lee had marshalled his case, but he protested that it was nonetheless neither particularly decent nor honourable. 'If Martin spends the next two years saying, "It is all going to be hopeless. Hong Kong is finished. It's a disaster," I can give my opinion, which is maybe matched against his, but I can't stop people in this community and elsewhere becoming either excessively fatalistic or excessively pessimistic about Hong Kong.'

As the two men traded blows they each attracted impressive support. Some of Britain's most important allies – the Americans, the Australians, the Japanese, the Hong Kong Chamber of Commerce and the chief justice – lined up behind the governor. Martin Lee was able to call on the Bar Council, every international human-rights organisation of any note and some of the most eloquent columnists in the colony. Privately, he also had the support of one or two of Patten's most trusted lieutenants who had not broken ranks before. One of them complained:

> The governor is just wrong. I've seen the Executive Council papers on this, and it was agreed that we must not yield on 'acts of state'. It was very clear that this should not be included in the bill as this would be to surrender on an important principle. Now this has been turned upside down overnight. Even if Chris can justify this on the grounds of force majeure – that he had no option on broader diplomatic or political grounds – he should not now turn round and blame Martin for defending a position which he himself once defended as being very important . . . He should have come clean and said, 'It is the best we could get.'

The aide was reminded uncomfortably of Sir David Wilson's governorship, and in this he was not alone. 'In those days they would identify a set of points on which they agreed they should not compromise. Then, after years of futile negotiation with the Chinese, they would meet again and redefine their definitions and then go and present abject defeat as astonishing triumph,' the official explained. 'That is exactly what the governor is trying to do now. It may be inevitable, but it leaves a bad taste.' Later Patten came to regret his decision to allow the Chinese to incorporate the 'acts of state' clause into the CFA bill – a lapse of judgement which perhaps should be attributed more to the intense and sustained pressure imposed on him by London and Beijing than to any indifference to the potential consequences of his retreat from what had once been an important point of principle.

On the eve of the debate on the bill in the Legislative Council, the principal combatants once more drew their swords in public. Patten accused Martin Lee and his supporters of talking in 'irresponsible and exaggerated terms about the destruction of the rule of law in Hong Kong', an approach, he warned, that created the real danger of doing before 1997 the damage they claimed the Chinese would do afterwards. Far from fighting for the rule of law, he said, Lee and his colleagues were virtually 'raising the white flag'. Lee countered that

Patten and his officials had 'graduated from distortions to comical hyperbole'. He noted that his fellow barristers on the Bar Council had condemned the CFA bill in ten specific areas for undermining the rule of law and the independence of the judiciary. To rub salt into the wound, he also quoted Sir Percy Cradock, who, as one of the architects of the 1991 agreement, had made the most egregious intervention of all, taking it upon himself to warn that Patten's bill incorporated a 'dangerously broad definition of "acts of state"'. As Martin Lee observed caustically, 'When Sir Percy describes something as dangerous, it must be very dangerous indeed.' He concluded, with all the hyperbole of which he had accused the governor, 'By being craven and giving in to Beijing's demands, Mr Patten is not doing Hong Kong a favour. He is doing all Chinese people the gravest disservice in the long term, and dashing our hopes of Hong Kong helping to set an example for China in the future . . . He has abandoned ship.'

The outcome of the vote in LegCo was never in doubt, and on 26 July, after formal negotiations with China lasting seven years, the Legislative Council voted overwhelmingly, by a majority of 38–17, in favour of the CFA bill. The governor expressed his satisfaction. 'I am sure it will be welcomed by the whole community and by international investors as a vote of confidence in Hong Kong's future,' he said. The media were distinctly less euphoric. The *Eastern Express* commented that 'despondency carried the day', and elsewhere that it was a 'dark day' for the human rights of the Hong Kong people. While the *South China Morning Post* condemned Martin Lee for 'whipping up fears', it noted that many legislators were unhappy with the lack of a clear definition of acts of state. 'Every possible effort must now be made to find out how much broader the scope will be, so that real concerns – as well as scaremongering – can be laid to rest.' The paper's cartoonist depicted the governor at the wheel of a giant steamroller flattening Martin Lee into the ground.

The leader of the Democrats was defiant, informing his colleagues after the vote was cast, 'I'm down, but I'm not out.' The truth, on this issue at least, was that the juggernaut had already moved on.

16

'A GOOD MOMENT'

The First Fully Elected LegCo

Surrounded as he was by adversaries on so many fronts, Chris Patten rejoiced in the discovery of a new ally. Jimmy Lai was an immigrant from the mainland for whom the Hong Kong version of the American dream had come true. An enthusiast for Western notions of freedom and democracy, he was alone among his peers in the business sector in using his fortune to advocate these twin causes and to make money in the process. As a small boy in the 1950s, he had hustled in the streets of Shanghai, 'trying to sell this and that to make some money'. He noticed that visitors from Hong Kong were sleek and well dressed, and he was envious. One day one of them gave him a bar of chocolate. 'I tasted it and said, "What's this? Where's it from? Hong Kong?" I thought Hong Kong must be heaven.' Later he stowed away in the bottom of a boat, arriving in Hong Kong as an illegal immigrant. By 1981, he had accumulated enough capital to set up in business on his own. He opened a clothes shop which he called Giordano, selling cheap but fashionable designs for the young 'me' generation of the early eighties. The company grew at the rate of 30 per cent a year, and within little more than a decade, the Giordano empire owned 300 shops throughout Asia and was valued at around $US400 million.

Jimmy Lai did not belong to Hong Kong's elite and he did not share their reticence. A bulky man, restless and energetic, he dressed flamboyantly in casual suits and coloured shirts and sported loud braces. Nor was he ashamed to express his opinions or feelings. 'I'm always a troublemaker. I love trouble. I love the intensity of trouble,' he proclaims with the air of a naughty child who knows that no one, nowadays, is likely to gainsay him. It was in the spirit of entrepreneurial flair and personal iconoclasm that he decided to divert some of his fortune into publishing. His first venture was a weekly magazine called *Next*, which, under his idiosyncratic tutelage, swiftly emerged to challenge and then conquer the existing market in Hong Kong. Often scurrilous, sometimes investigative and frequently prurient, *Next* managed to combine the virtues of *Newsweek, Hello!* and *Private Eye*. It irritated, offended, entertained – and it made money. Never afraid to use *Next* to expose and lampoon the powerful, Lai soon acquired more enemies than friends, especially among the cadres in Beijing whose financial dealings in Hong Kong came under damaging scrutiny in the pages of his magazine.

Lai grew increasingly politicised as a result of his foray into journalism, and his criticism of the People's Republic was often vehement. After the 4 June massacre in 1989 he cast off restraint entirely, using what had now become a bestselling periodical to publish a coruscating 'open letter' of condemnation to the Chinese premier, Li Peng. 'I was so mad,' he explained later. 'It was a very nasty, rude letter. I called him . . .' – he paused at the reminder of the enormity of what he had written, and lowered his voice – 'I called him the son of the turtle egg, which is very rude. I don't want to translate it.' He had indeed caused grievous offence to the Chinese leadership, and Beijing's retribution was not long delayed. Within days of the appearance of the offending article, the authorities closed his Giordano shop in the Chinese capital and warned the company that it would not be permitted to trade there again as long as Jimmy Lai remained in control. And that was not all: 'I got bombs thrown into my house here in Hong Kong. I got people coming to my office, ransacking my computer.' Undaunted, Lai removed himself from the board of Giordano, divested himself of his shares and used some of the proceeds to expand into newspapers. In the spring of 1995, his *Apple Daily* hit the news-stands amid an avalanche of publicity. Cleverly targeted at the mass market, *Apple Daily* established itself within days as one of the colony's most popular daily newspapers. Scantily dressed girls vied for the reader's attention with reports on the criminal underworld and a political message which was unequivocally in favour of human rights and democracy.

Not everyone appreciated the new addition to Hong Kong's crowded and cut-throat media market. Jimmy Lai's journalists were threatened, news-vendors were warned not to stock the offending journal and, the proprietor reported, 'We got papers thrown in the harbour and our Giordano shop in Macau was set on fire. Maybe it was because some of the things we wrote offended the triads and they wanted us to know that they didn't like it.' Whatever the motive, these tactics had no effect other than to make Jimmy Lai rue his decision to spend so much on the launch of *Apple Daily*. 'Had I known they would do that, I would have spent much less on promotion. We had all the publicity we needed from these people trying to stop us.'

As the 1995 election approached, Lai's editorial message to his fast-growing readership was simple: 'Don't have fear.' Explaining his enthusiasm for Patten's reforms, he spoke with defiance and intensity. 'Hong Kong is our home. Hong Kong is where we want to protect our freedom. I don't give a shit what happens in China – this is my home.' And if, after 1997, the authorities were to suppress *Next* or *Apple Daily*? 'I will just lie low and wait for the right time to come back again. I am young. Unless my life is threatened I will stay here. This is my home.' As he reiterated the last four words, his face creased and his eyes filled with tears.

A few days before the voters of Hong Kong went to the polls to choose the first fully elected Legislative Council in the history of Hong Kong, David Chu Yiu Lin boarded his motor yacht for the outlying island of Ping Chau. His mission was to solicit one vote from the leader of the local council, which he was confident would be enough to secure his place in the legislature. The twenty seats on the Legislative Council which were to be directly elected would be decided on the first-past-the-post system in geographical constituencies covering the entire territory; another thirty were to be elected in the functional constituencies. The remaining ten would fall to candidates elected by the Election Committee, which consisted of 266 people representing the District Boards, who had themselves been elected in the 1994 local elections. It was one of these latter seats that David Chu coveted.

Hong Kong's most ebullient apologist for Beijing had not run for an election of any kind before, and, by his own account, it was an exciting if daunting experience. Born in Shanghai in 1944, David Chu had fled with his family to Hong Kong to escape the rigours of early Maoism. When he was fourteen, they emigrated to the United States, where he acquired an American accent, some influential friends and an MBA from the Harvard Business School. In 1977, now a senior financial executive, he returned to Hong Kong, soon to be headhunted by Jardine Matheson. In 1984 he launched his own company specialising in property development. Before long he was a multimillionaire.

His business acumen notwithstanding, he was better known in Hong Kong for a penchant for fast motorbikes ('I go fast to scare myself') and dangerous sports. In August 1995, at the age of fifty-one, he was able to boast that his most recent escapade – paragliding from Hong Kong to Beijing – had not only broken three world records but raised US$130,000 for charity. His image as a middle-aged playboy was complicated by his passion for political debate and an irrepressible and apparently guileless optimism about Hong Kong's future under Chinese rule. In 1992 his loyalty had been rewarded by Beijing with a role as an 'adviser' on Hong Kong affairs, and the following year he was appointed to the Preliminary Working Committee. In this capacity he wrote articles for a variety of newspapers and magazines denouncing the alleged perfidies of Chris Patten and his democratic allies in the Legislative Council. His breezy disdain for the political freedoms he had enjoyed as a naturalised citizen of the United States was offset by a personal charm. As a result he was readily forgiven – if not taken very seriously – by those he chastised in print.

Chu's sincerity was not in doubt. Unlike many of his colleagues in the business community who protested their allegiance to China but, in the governor's phrase, had 'British passports tucked in their back pockets', he had recently taken the rare step of surrendering his Western (in this case, American) passport to demonstrate his commitment to the mainland. In this campaign his message was to be simple, if not simplistic: 'You may say I am extremely optimistic. I fully expect things to be better after 1997. I expect Chinese people will be able to rule Hong Kong even better when the British have left . . . When Hong Kong is ruled by Hong Kong people, we'll be so proud.' As for the danger that China might intervene to repress personal liberties, he placed his trust in the Basic Law. 'You know, China is not allowed to close down democracy. It is not permitted by the Basic Law. I have faith in the Basic Law, and in my ability to make China behave according to the Basic Law. The Basic Law is not only a constitution for Hong Kong, it is also a contract between Hong Kong and China, and neither side can break that contract for fifty years.' He conceded that some Chinese officials were bemused that such a colourful individual as himself could be so dedicated to Beijing's cause. 'My personal lifestyle is vastly different from that of a Chinese official, so they look upon me as a really strange animal, but I am quietly friendly to them, and genuinely patriotic.'

For many liberals in Hong Kong, David Chu was the almost acceptable face of a regime which they not only loathed but feared. In the summer of 1995, however, only the most courageous individuals were still prepared to speak their minds regardless of the consequences. With the business community and its acolytes in the media ranged against them, they faced isolation and ridicule from those who damned them with the faintest of praise as idealists or romantics or self-righteous publicists. Along with Emily Lau, Martin Lee and his colleague Szeto Wah, Christine Loh had emerged as one of the few public figures to speak out publicly in favour of human rights and in defiance of Beijing's animosity, and she shared none of David Chu's optimism about their future sovereign. Although she had not yet decided whether to give up a successful career in business for the vagaries of full-time politics, her scepticism about China's readiness to allow Hong Kong a 'high degree of autonomy' after 1997 had by now turned to pessimism. By the end of 1993, she had made up her mind to run as an independent candidate in the 1995 elections, commenting wryly, 'I never thought I would be in this predicament, but I have to be positive, to say that there is a way forward, because if we can't believe that, then the future is pretty bleak.'

As the 1995 election campaign approached, Christine Loh maintained this façade, but in private she was warding off despair. The repeated warnings from Beijing that after the handover the entire political structure of Hong Kong would, as she saw it, be 'liquidated' was 'really, really bad news'. Yet instead of taking to the streets to demonstrate their disapproval, as she had hoped and half expected, the people seemed to have 'numbed themselves' to the prospect. 'I am pessimistic,' she told her friends, 'but I can't do the job I do if I can't get up in the morning and believe that there are still some things we can do. I'm not going to rule out the Hong Kong people . . . Why should they take this lying down?'

Christine Loh was to stand against a veteran legislator called Peggy Lam, a vigorous ally of Beijing. Lam had nurtured her constituency in Central, and enjoyed a reputation as a doughty political infighter. It would not be an easy contest. Loh's overriding reason for running against such a stalwart opponent was, she declared, 'to fight for our own identity'. She believed that there were many who shared her inability to express any patriotic fervour for the motherland. 'I do not know whether I can ever stand up and say, "I'm a citizen of the People's Republic of China,"' she confessed privately. 'Maybe people like me will have to be phased out.' She had been angered by a conversation she had recently had with a senior Chinese official, Jiang Enzhu. He had told her, 'If you really feel this way about us, why don't you just leave?' She had replied, 'Hong Kong is my home. You can't say that to me.' She went into the campaign in this mood of defiance, reflecting, 'Of course, if we are talking about tanks rolling over the border, then I concede right away. But we have to continue to argue that that's not going to happen . . . It's a last stand, in a way.'

Margaret Ng shared Christine Loh's pessimism, but felt it even more keenly. After playing a decisive part in preventing the lawyer's representative, Simon Ip, from voting against Patten's reforms in 1994, she had found herself more directly involved in the political process, but with dwindling expectations. By the summer of 1995, she was not only despondent about China but also bitter about what she regarded as the governor's acquiescence in a fatally flawed compromise with Beijing over the Court of Final Appeal. 'Relying on logic,' she commented, 'there is every reason to be pessimistic, to believe that the rule of law will be non-existent after 1997. But, of course, hope defies logic.' It was in this spirit that, at the last moment, she decided to run for a place in the legislative assembly, aspiring to represent the legal profession in a functional constituency whose size had been significantly increased by the Patten reforms to embrace almost 2,000 registered voters. Superficially, at least, her decision to enter the political fray was paradoxical. 'There is nothing to stay here for. People don't want people like me. I won't be able to find a job. No one will hire me as a lawyer, no one will print my articles,' she had said to herself. Like many others who would never admit it publicly, her growing despair had led her to start flat-hunting in London, for a bolt-hole to which she could retreat in a hurry, if necessary. She was well aware that it would be difficult to earn a living in Britain, but she was ready to work, 'as a charlady' if she had to. 'I think it is a perfectly respectable way to live. You offer a service which is needed, and you get paid for it. I would still be able to amuse myself by reading books, even by writing books. I think what is important is the inner life.'

But by September 1995 these plans had been put in abeyance as Margaret Ng prepared to enter a political campaign which, if she were successful, would almost certainly oblige her to stay in Hong Kong until after the handover. A few weeks earlier, a group of like-minded lawyers had approached her to ask her to stand in the elections. She was neither flattered nor excited. She had never contemplated a political life, and she knew enough about LegCo to conclude that it was 'very boring' for most of the time and that it would interfere with her personal freedom. She also sensed that the focus of attention between 1995 and 1997 would shift from the legislative assembly to the Preparatory Committee which, under the terms of the Joint Declaration, was due to be set up in 1996 to replace the Preliminary Working Committee, ostensibly to ensure a smooth handover. She was well aware that she would therefore have limited influence, and, if successful, she expected to have to fight hard for very little. She was not even looking forward to the campaign itself. 'It involves thinking about problems you have found very boring to think about before. It involves listening to the views of a lot of people. It involves cheering the troops. It involves canvassing for votes. It involves election meetings and giving people tea . . . It's all terribly tedious.'

Nonetheless she felt obliged to submit herself to an ordeal to which, with no false modesty, she thought herself to be particularly ill suited. Before acceding to her colleagues' request, she asked herself whether there was something, despite all that, which made it worth doing. Her answer was positive, and her certainties lacked any hint of bravado or vainglory, but seemed to be driven by a fierce moral imperative.

> There might come a moment when something needs to be said. You might be able to change the political culture. You may be able to bring into question a taboo that no one has realised before. You may be able to offer your time, your knowledge and your skill to ensure that certain bills are constructed to protect the rule of law . . . It is very much a matter of 'maybe', but I do not see that it is impossible.
>
> What do I stand for? An uncompromising attitude towards all things which are fundamental to the liberty of the individual. For the quality of professional service. For integrity. Not being afraid to speak the truth. Not putting your own interests first. Being able to face whatever it takes to say the honest thing. I don't know if they are of use to anyone, but such as they are, I offer them.

These attitudes were not calculated to endear her to the post-1997 sovereign, as Margaret Ng knew only too well.

Of the established politicians, Martin Lee was the most prominent figure in the campaign. The two most notable candidates standing against his Democratic party were his old rival Allen Lee, an appointed member of the Legislative Council and the leader of the pro-Beijing Liberals, and Tsang Yok Sing of the Democratic Alliance for the Betterment of Hong Kong, the pro-Beijing coalition he had helped to found in 1992. Neither man had stood for election before, and they formed an unlikely alliance: Allen Lee, the muddled voice of vacillating compromise, and Tsang Yok Sing, the Marxist intellectual, publicly loyal but privately troubled by the predatory instincts of the repressive regime in China.

In the 1980s Lee had been an assiduous champion of open government and democracy; by the time of Patten's arrival he had fallen under the influence of Sir S.Y. Chung and, along with his mentor, had switched allegiance from the colonial authorities to the future sovereign. 'I have thought many times,' he confided in the run-up to the

1995 elections, 'do we really need democracy in Hong Kong while we enjoy all the freedoms under British rule, where our businesses flourish and Hong Kong has become a great international centre?' His born-again reluctance to make any link between freedom under the law and democratic accountability was an attitude endemic in Hong Kong among civil servants, the business community and those like himself who had been plucked from obscurity and given some power and much prestige under Britain's relatively benign patronage.

After 1989, the language people chose to use about the killings in Tiananmen Square was a revealing indicator of feelings towards China. For some it was an 'atrocity'; for others, 'unfortunate'. Allen Lee saw it as a 'tragic' episode, a 'very sad' period that could have been resolved peacefully, not least if the student leaders had been less 'distasteful and impolite' to the Chinese premier, Li Peng. The sharpening divisions between Martin Lee's Democrats and Allen Lee's Liberals dated from this period, the Liberals taking the view that Beijing should not be shunned but 'engaged in discussion', a standpoint which coincided precisely with that of Allen Lee's political partner of convenience, Tsang Yok Sing.

Notwithstanding their assiduous attempts the previous year to torpedo the Patten reforms, both Tsang Yok Sing and Allen Lee decided that in order to retain any vestige of political credibility in Hong Kong, they would have to undergo the novel experience of running for direct election. Tsang Yok Sing's advisers selected what they thought to be the safest seat, Taipo in the New Territories. Embarrassingly, and for the same reason, Allen Lee made the same choice. Protracted negotiations ensued in an attempt to avoid certain defeat for one of them and con-ceivably, through splitting the pro-Beijing vote, for both. At first Tsang Yok Sing tried to persuade Allen Lee to bypass the test of a direct election and instead, as Hong Kong's 'most experienced legislator', to ensure himself a place in the chamber by running for a safe seat via the reformed Election Committee system. His suggestion fell on deaf ears. Beijing, in the person of Lu Ping, intervened directly to break the deadlock by instructing Tsang Yok Sing to withdraw his candidature for the Taipo seat. The DAB leader reluctantly obeyed this edict, only to come under intense pressure from his party colleagues, who urged him to take himself the indirect route on to LegCo which he had vainly pressed on Allen Lee. 'If there is any chance of winning in one of the geographical constituencies I should go for it,' Tsang Yok Sing argued. 'If I am to lead the election campaign, I want to do it as a participant, as someone standing for election, seeking a popular mandate.'

It was intriguing to witness how far both Tsang Yok Sing and Allen

Lee had already been swayed by the process put in train by the Patten reforms. Although each deplored the governor's measures, neither could ignore the political lesson generated by the subsequent public debate about democracy. The prospect of two of Patten's principal adversaries seeking a popular mandate for their platform of public opposition to the very electoral system in which they were about to be such prominent participants did not go unnoticed at Government House, where it caused a degree of complacent mirth.

Tsang Yok Sing had to fight a fierce internal battle with his DAB colleagues to win their consent to stand in what some of them thought to be 'futile' elections. He maintained that it was vital 'to show people both in the pro-China camp and in society at large that we can win support from the voters'. However, this was not an end in itself. On the eve of the elections, in a confession which would have astonished the Hong Kong public and horrified those in China for whom he was an important apologist, he volunteered his hope that, if his party performed well in the elections, Beijing might be persuaded to withdraw its threat to dismantle the legislature in 1997. 'If most people were to agree that the results of the elections reflected the intentions of the voters it would be easier for us – for people who believe in the present system – to convince the Chinese officials that it won't be disastrous for the establishment of the SAR to keep the electoral system more or less the same.' Patten could hardly have wished for a more full-hearted endorsement of his reform package; unhappily, he did not even know of it, because Tsang Yok Sing, not through cowardice but in order to retain his moderating influence in Beijing, had at no stage felt able to rally support for the governor in public. The DAB leader eventually persuaded his colleagues that he should contest a seat in Kowloon, where he would be competing with a popular local member of Martin Lee's Democratic party. His opponent would be sustained by a far more sophisticated electoral machine than the DAB possessed. The DAB had ample funds, but lacked any experience of electioneering.

By British standards, the election campaign was a muted affair. Although hoardings were littered with the portraits of the candidates, some of whom took to the streets with aplomb, complete with megaphones and video displays, the contest was remarkably free of vulgarity or venom. Contenders for the twenty seats to be directly elected set up their stalls outside underground stations or bus terminals or near busy markets. Supporters, carrying bright banners and wearing identical T-shirts, lined the pavements to exhort the public to back their candidate. Often two or three candidates arrived to occupy the same pitch at the same time. Once or twice there were scuffles but for the most part they contented themselves with out-shouting the opposition. Very few voters seemed to take much notice.

The media reflected this apparent lethargy. The newspapers carried summaries of the competing platforms and interviewed the most prominent candidates in the most closely contested seats, but election news rarely made the front pages. The tabloids preferred to focus on an unpublished government report suggesting that pornographic videos were a principal cause of rape in the colony's jails. And Typhoon Kent, which hit Hong Kong at the beginning of September, was a far bigger story: traffic was brought to a standstill for eight hours, railways and bus routes were closed and the Tuen Mun road, part of a main artery between Hong Kong and the New Territories, had to be shut for emergency repairs to prevent a landslide. By 6 September, the papers were calling on the governor to apologise for the disruption caused by the road closure. Patten refused to oblige, and *Sing Tao* editorialised: 'Patten's mentality is typical of a "sunset governor" who cannot be bothered even to go through the motions of expressing his concern for the inconvenience caused to the public.' Typhoon Kent eventually gave way to the arrest of three police officers on corruption charges and the trial of Albert Yeung, the chairman of a large corporation, who had close links with Beijing, also on a corruption charge. On 12 September, five days before the election, the media devoted front-page coverage to a confrontation between Han Dongfang, a Chinese dissident expelled from China and now living in Hong Kong, and officials of the local branch of the NCNA. On 13 September, the lead story in most newspapers was a road accident in which eleven pregnant women, all illegal immigrants from the mainland, were injured. They had been smuggled across the border to give birth in the territory, thereby giving their children the right of abode in Hong Kong. This drama all but smothered Patten's comments expressing his hope for a large turnout and urging that this 'milestone' election should not be seen as the last which would be conducted freely in Hong Kong. It was with only three days to go that the 'milestone' election finally came to dominate the news.

On Sunday 17 September, the voters went to the polls, filing into schools and other public buildings in a quiet and orderly fashion, confirming the view that the citizens of Hong Kong were quite mature enough to participate in the democratic process so belatedly bequeathed to them. It was, however, far more complicated than the British elections which in other respects it so closely resembled. Many voters had also registered for their respective functional constituencies and therefore not only had to select their chosen candidate for the geographical constituency in which they lived but had to vote a second time for a candidate on that slate as well. An overall turnout of 35 per cent was lower than the governor might have hoped for, but, given the complexity of the new system, it bore favourable comparison with the presidential elections in the United States and with local elections in Britain. In the case of the twenty directly elected seats, the turnout was 3.5 per cent down on the 1991 elections, but the total number of voters had risen by 170,000 to a record 920,000. Although fewer than half a million of the 2.7 million people eligible had cast a vote in the functional constituencies, it was widely recognised that this was due less to apathy than to a failure by many voters to identify which of the nine new functional constituencies was 'theirs'.

When the polls closed, the ballot boxes were conveyed in sealed boxes under police escort to the International Trade Mart to be counted. Here, at last, it was possible to experience the 'election fever' hitherto so markedly absent from the campaign. The trade mart had been turned into a vast electronic theatre with a giant video wall relaying the images of frantic activity on the floor caught by endlessly roving cameras. Anxious candidates and their supporters watched as the votes piled up for and against them on long tables. Tellers and runners, dressed according to their role and status in uniform reds, yellows and greens, dashed back and forth across the hall with well-drilled urgency. Newspaper journalists from all over the world, there to record Hong Kong's first – and possibly last – genuinely free election, sat in a tier of reserved seats waiting for the results in an atmosphere of real excitement. Television and radio reporters from more than a dozen countries stood ready to deliver a well-turned phrase to their audiences. In an outer arena, four local television channels provided live coverage of the count, their star presenters, proficient and cool under the arc lights, talking endlessly despite the absence of news. Rumours abounded: the Democrats had won by a landslide; Allen Lee had lost; the DAB had been trounced. By midnight only a handful of votes had been counted. By two o'clock, the result was still uncertain. Famous local figures, a beaming governor to the fore, strode purposefully across the set. Anxious candidates wandered from table to table, going nowhere. The fast-food counters around the main hall were soon littered with empty bottles and screwed-up napkins and the residue of innumerable Cokes, Pepsis and pizzas. In the end it took fifteen hours to count all 1.4 million votes cast.

To those with feelings of foreboding about 1997, the good-natured enthusiasm of a new political class – men and women at last liberated to exercise rights which should, and could, have been theirs for a generation – was both impressive and touching. Before each result was announced, the candidates were summoned to a long dais to await the verdict of the voters. The winners stood for photographs and sometimes uttered a few words for the cameras before being swept away into the enfolding arms of friends and supporters. Christine Loh, who won Hong Kong Central with almost twice as many votes as Peggy Lam, was visibly moved at her startling share of the vote. Margaret Ng was even more astonished to emerge comfortably ahead of her two rivals for the legal functional constituency, but she declined to make a victory speech and could barely face the cameras. David Chu, who in the end failed to secure the support of the local councillor on Ping Chau Island, still garnered enough votes to win one of the ten seats chosen by the 283-member Election Committee. He could hardly contain his delight, but no one asked him to make a speech. Martin Lee won easily in Hong Kong Island East; and, despite his own pessimism, Allen Lee was victorious in a three-way contest in the New Territories North-East after what was widely regarded as one of the most effective campaigns in the entire contest. Emily Lau, the territory's most charismatic politician, who had poured scorn on China and Britain in equal measure while still demanding direct elections for every seat in the legislature, secured the largest personal vote (39,265) of the twenty geographical constituencies – almost 2,000 more than Martin Lee. However, they were both outdone by Elizabeth Wong, a much-admired civil servant who had taken early retirement to contest the community and social services functional constituency as an independent. She secured more than 40,000 votes from workers in that field, a turnout of over 40 per cent.

Aside from the defeats of Peggy Lam and her fellow pro-China veteran Elsie Tu, the most significant casualty was Tsang Yok Sing, who was comfortably beaten by a relatively unknown candidate from the Association for Democracy and People's Livelihood (ADPL), which had close links with Martin Lee's Democratic party. Tsang Yok Sing's personal credibility had been damaged by a revelation about his family which had first surfaced six months earlier. Soon after Tiananmen Square, his wife and daughter had secured Canadian passports and retreated to Vancouver. Though Tsang Yok Sing himself had remained in Hong Kong, his opponent in the campaign had insinuated that the DAB leader could easily 'jump a plane' out of Hong Kong if he wished to escape Chinese sovereignty. Tsang Yok Sing indignantly denied that he possessed a foreign passport of any kind, but the mud stuck. The only smear of note in the campaign, it was, as Tsang Yok Sing himself conceded, remarkably effective.

Yet it was not in itself the reason for his downfall. It was clear that the voters had not been convinced by Tsang Yok Sing's assiduous efforts to distance himself from Beijing. His failure to persuade the electorate that he was not merely China's mouthpiece had not been helped by repeated warnings from Beijing – one on the very eve of the vote – that the entire electoral edifice would in any case be dismantled on 1 July 1997. Frustrated by China's clumsy belligerence, Tsang Yok Sing had gone out of his way to insist during the campaign that the 1995 election should be regarded as a valid test of opinion, and, immediately after his defeat, he reiterated publicly that there was 'no evidence to show that the elections were unfair'. Privately he went further: 'I will advise the Chinese government and the officials in charge of Hong Kong affairs to say nothing more against these elections. It will not help in any way . . . I do not think it is wise, although there are obviously some people in the Chinese government who think it necessary to remind people in Hong Kong that there will be no "through train".'

The DAB leader drew comfort from the fact that seven other members of his party had won seats in the Legislative Council. These, combined with the ten seats won by Allen Lee's Liberal party and a small bloc of pro-China independents, meant that the Democratic party, the largest single bloc with nineteen seats, would have to depend on the support of independents (among whom only Emily Lau, Christine Loh and Margaret Ng could be relied on) to form even a small majority in the legislature. Tsang Yok Sing saw this as precisely the 'balanced' outcome which should hold no fears for Beijing. 'If anybody in Beijing or Hong Kong believes that by scrapping the present system we could replace it with another that was acceptable to the people of Hong Kong yet composed of very different people from what we now have, then he is certainly wrong,' he confided. It was a judgement which revealed the depth of foreboding felt even by this honourable communist about Hong Kong's future.

If the DAB leader was dismayed by the behaviour of Beijing, he was appalled that so many of his 'friends' in the community, assuming his to be a sympathetic ear, went out of their way to stress to him that they shared China's concerns. The Legislative Council would have to be reconstituted in 1997, they said, both to maintain social stability and to create a 'conciliatory' relationship between the legislature and the government. Though he was not altogether surprised that such sentiments should emerge from the business community, it shocked him to discover that 'there are people within the Hong Kong government who believe it will be really difficult to work with a legislature dominated by members of populist political parties', and that there was still a 'proportion of our population who don't believe that democracy as we see it in some Western countries is really good for Hong Kong'.

Tsang Yok Sing was tempted to voice these concerns, but he concluded that to speak his mind openly would be counterproductive. 'If I am not mistaken, the Chinese government does not accept this form of lobbying. Doesn't like it.' Such honesty in the aftermath of his own defeat was remarkable, not least because he was determined to press this case behind the scenes with Beijing while being quite willing for his real views to be made public after the handover. If the old guard in Beijing were to live up to their well-earned reputation for vengefulness, Tsang Yok Sing's prospects after 1997 were likely to be dramatically diminished.

As if to confirm his anxieties, China reacted to the election result in precisely the way he had predicted. The NCNA in Hong Kong declared that the outcome had been 'unfair and unreasonable'. In Beijing, Li Peng announced that China would not recognise any political structure that violated the Joint Declaration and the Basic Law. A Foreign Ministry spokesman said that the election result 'did not reflect public opinion', and the Hong Kong and Macau Affairs Office confirmed that 'China's decision to terminate LegCo on 30 June 1997 is strong and firm: it will not be changed by the election results'. Unnamed 'sources close to China' advised that Beijing's attitude would become 'harsher' as the leadership was bound to conclude that 'Hong Kong people now support those who confront China'.

Martin Lee, whose party's nineteen seats included twelve of the twenty directly elected seats, was undeterred by China's response. 'The principal reason for our victory is that the voters trust us to stand up for Hong Kong . . . Hong Kong people cannot be intimidated into submission. They love democracy and they want their human rights to be preserved.' Chris Patten was almost as exuberant. Congratulating the Democrats on maintaining the momentum in the four years since their previous triumph, he declared that their 1991 victory had clearly not been a flash in the pan. 'Four years nearer to the transition, we have people standing up and saying the same things, and saying them with a great deal of conviction.' He countered China's threat to 'terminate' LegCo by warning of serious international repercussions if they were to contravene the Joint Declaration and the Basic Law. However, he was careful not to specify what would constitute contravention, or what action would be taken and by whom.

On the day after the vote, in the relative tranquillity of Government House, Patten struggled to express his mixed feelings. The election which he had devised, and for which he had fought for three years, was

'Being gubernatorial'. Patten with the Prince of Wales, on an official visit to Hong Kong (top), and inspecting a guard of honour (below). His decision to dispense with the ceremonial uniform traditionally associated with the post was a disappointment to some.
FormAsia Books Ltd

The people of Hong Kong look forward to the future with mixed feelings. The Ngs and their children (top left); Hari Harilela and his extended family (below left); George and Rowena Chen (top right); and Norris Lam. Robin Allison Smith

Will the freedoms enshrined in the Joint Declaration survive the handover? Dick Lee of the Hong Kong Police (top) is optimistic about China's intentions, but street demonstrations by Hong Kong citizens, such as this one photographed in 1997 (below), are under threat. Robin Allison Smith

Two of Hong Kong's most prominent characters: David Chu (top), posing with his beloved motorbike, and the irrepressible Jimmy Lai (left), proprietor of the hugely popular newspaper Apple Daily. Robin Allison Smith

Chris Patten with Baroness Thatcher in 1997 (top) and in conversation with a supportive President Clinton during his successful visit to the USA in 1993. FormAsia Books

The governor with chief secretary Anson Chan. Patten considered her a vital link in ensuring a smooth transition between the outgoing and incoming administrations. 'If she goes, it will be a very bad blow,' he noted. FormAsia Books Ltd

Chris Patten pictured with the author shortly before the handover. Robin Allison Smith

The last governor with his family in front of Government House – from left to right: Laura, Lavender, Alice and Kate – not forgetting local stars Whisky and Soda. Government House

over. It had self-evidently been free and fair: it was not only a personal triumph, however transitory, but a huge relief. He said that he was 'sort of cheerful', but that he had a sense of 'slightly alarmed astonishment' because 'the people of Hong Kong couldn't have more decisively demonstrated that we haven't been entirely out of tune with them for the last three years'. This made him feel 'slightly emotional'. An American friend of his, a professor of politics, who had been staying at Government House and who had gone out touring the polling stations, had been captivated by the experience. He returned to tell Patten, 'You know, what was wonderful was seeing all these people who are proud of their freedom practising it.' As he related his friend's thought, the governor found himself unable to continue. Tears came to his eyes, and there was a long pause before he said, with unintended bathos, 'So it was a good moment.'

His sang-froid restored, he went on: 'I don't see any way in which the Chinese can simply ignore this result. I imagine the New China News Agency will have a bit of trouble explaining it away, and that there will be those who'll say, "We've just got to look more positive if we are going to win a few hearts and minds before 1997." Because, as sure as hell, they haven't done that yet.' He was by no means confident that the gap could be bridged.

His own difficulties were compounded by the attitude of his civil servants. In the face of Chinese attrition, their morale had continued slowly to erode. The intention of Michael Sze – who was widely admired for the tenacity he had displayed, as secretary for constitutional affairs, in the face-to-face negotiations with China – to depart from government for a job in the private sector (though in the end he decided against this) deepened the gloom in Hong Kong's corridors of power. Patten was frustrated by the fact that 'a lot of my administration, a lot of my civil servants, will not want to be doing things which undermine "executive-led government"'. His words echoed Tsang Yok Sing's concerns. It would not be easy, he said, to bolster the standing of the legislature, but it was part of the democratisation of the community. He feared formidable opposition: indeed, earlier in the month, his own appointee as chief secretary, Anson Chan, had led a powerful delegation of civil servants to Government House to urge Patten to redraft the constitution to reinforce the concept of an 'executive-led government' by forbidding the introduction of any private member's bill without the prior approval of the governor.

Patten had been horrified by this proposal. It demonstrated an alarming failure on behalf of the colony's future administrators to appreciate an important channel for the expression of democratic opinion, and furthermore he knew that such a regressive change would fundamentally undermine his own position in the community. Patten respected Anson Chan for her judgement, intellect and integrity, and if he was aware of this authoritarian streak in her character, it was counterbalanced for him by her evident ability to 'stand up for Hong Kong'. He shared the widespread view that she would be the lynchpin of the post-1997 administration, and that if she was removed from office by the Chinese, the civil service would rapidly crumble. He was therefore dismayed by her advocacy of what he regarded as a 'rotten case' for constitutional 'reform'.

Like many of her colleagues in the government, Anson Chan was ambivalent about the growth of the democratic spirit in Hong Kong. Ill at ease with the freedoms enjoyed by the media, whose practitioners she was prone to regard with disdain, she had rarely displayed great sympathy for the efforts of Hong Kong's elected politicians to flex their fledgling muscles. Whether this merely betrayed an efficient administrator's frustration at the messiness of democracy, or whether, as some of her critics feared, it revealed the narrow vision of a thwarted autocrat, her distrust of Hong Kong's democratic momentum troubled her admirers no less than her detractors.

Patten had listened to the case made by his most senior bureaucrats, but ended the meeting by making it clear that he would not contemplate acceding to his chief secretary's proposal. He pointed out to her and her colleagues that, as governor, he already had far-reaching constitutional powers, and that if he were to 'pick a constitutional row' with Hong Kong's legislators on the issue of private members' bills, they might refuse to co-operate with the executive by, for instance, refusing to approve the budget. If the civil servants were not convinced by his stance, they soon realised that the governor was not to be swayed.

Patten derived little consolation from this victory. He was well aware that he could not afford to alienate his senior colleagues. After the election he noted, 'I have a civil service which I want to keep loyal, which I don't want to see starting to look towards a less democratic future as the answer to their prayers.' At the same time, in the form of the Legislative Council, he had another constituency which he had to handle with care. Together, the members of a newly credible legislature and the traditionalist civil service represented, as it seemed to Patten, the 'political schizophrenia of Hong Kong . . . I want to persuade the administration to look for ways of co-operating more with the Legislative Council. At the same time, I want to try to persuade the Legislative Council to do things which are sensible on the economic and social front rather than to go in for knee-jerk populism.'

Patten knew that much would depend on whether Martin Lee and his colleagues used their new power with discretion. If they did, he argued, it would be far harder for senior civil servants and the business community to point an accusing finger at Government House, complaining, 'You see? As soon as you have a more democratic legislature, they cock up the economy.' Moreover, it would be very much more difficult for China to remove Martin Lee and other 'subversives' from the 'through train', or to deny them a role in Hong Kong's political future. Patten believed that in this respect the future stability of the territory was at stake.

> What will be the consequence of the Chinese continuing to try to anathemise Martin Lee and the other Democrats? The consequence, if they do that beyond 1997, is, inevitably, political turbulence. You can't, in a community like Hong Kong, simply shut out the opinions, the views, the aspirations, the ambitions, the fears, without there being socio-political consequences.

Patten's faith in the colony's democratic potential was undimmed; indeed, in the wake of the elections, it burned even more powerfully. In his certainty, he had been a combative but measured campaigner, tenacious, eloquent and inspiring: now, his judgement about the people of Hong Kong vividly confirmed, he longed for a legislature that would display the kind of political maturity which would make it even harder for Beijing to snuff out the light of freedom after the handover.

For this reason he worried about the Democrats. 'The easy thing for Martin Lee to do now,' he confided, 'would be to spend the last two years of British sovereignty demonstrating that the last British governor wasn't elected, didn't have a democratic mandate and was the representative of an external colonial power a long way away.' Although Patten suspected that this would 'doubtless satisfy some of his American entourage' – the latest in a line of Martin Lee's political advisers, Minky Worden, had a born-again attitude towards democracy which so irritated Patten's team that, in schoolboy fashion, they had nicknamed their cheerful adversary Stinky – he hoped that the leader of the Democratic party might be both 'more open and more generous' and 'more responsible in the sense of less populist' than he feared would be the case.

As it was, Martin Lee had started to reflect on the fruits of victory in terms that would have delighted the governor and indeed even surprised himself. It was not until several hours after the final declaration of the results that the leader of the Democrats began to realise that he and his allies would be able to form a clear majority in the legislature on almost all issues of any substance. On the basis of his party's analysis of the Patten reforms, Martin Lee had long ago concluded that the Democrats would remain in opposition as a minority party after the election. 'We never thought that we could form a majority. It was a very very pleasant surprise.' He also felt somewhat chastened.

> People kept on saying, 'Look, the Tiananmen effect has gone. The people of Hong Kong have learned to be more pragmatic. They want to work with China . . . That means, if necessary, working on China's terms.' The British bought that line. And I almost bought it. I and my party assumed that the Hong Kong people didn't want trouble with China. So the results of the poll shook me. They were a very strong vindication of what we had been doing, although in our hearts we thought we had lost their support.

The following morning, his exhilaration rapidly ebbed away to be replaced by a political hangover. His electoral mandate, combined with the enhanced status devolved to the Legislative Council by the Patten reforms, was bound to alter the contours of political debate. With characteristic candour, he confessed that his party was uneasy with the unexpected authority bestowed on it by the voters.

> I was extremely worried, thinking to myself that with this majority there comes responsibility. We have to be more careful in everything we say from now on . . . Every time we take a stance on anything, we really have to be very careful. If we get it wrong, maybe the government will actually do what we want them to do . . . We will have to be much more reasonable and sensible in all our statements, because it could make a difference. If we get it wrong, the community will suffer and we will have to take the blame.

In opposition, the only role he and his colleagues had effectively previously experienced, his task had been simple. As the colonial government had been able to ignore LegCo, individual legislators had been free to indulge in 'gesture' politics – a memory which already seemed to be provoking a glow of nostalgia in Martin Lee. 'Even if the government did something that was quite generous to our people – and which some of our members may have privately applauded – in public we could complain that it was not enough . . . No party had any obligation or responsibility, really. Whatever the government did, you could simply say that it was not enough.' To Martin Lee's frustration, his senior lieutenant, Szeto Wah, led a faction that was reluctant to adapt to the new situation. 'He wants to be in the minority all the time, and he thought we would be,' he said dismissively. However, the party leader reminded Szeto Wah and his colleagues:

> It has happened: we are the majority, and if we don't take what I consider the sensible approach, and we merely criticise the government strongly for another two years, then at the end of that time we might not have done anything for our people. We will have criticised a lot, but what will we have done? With compromise the chances are that, with the co-operation of the government, we could actually do something.

Chris Patten was keen to restore the goodwill between himself and Martin Lee which had been ruptured by their public slanging match over the Court of Final Appeal. Although Lee was still fiercely critical of the governor's actions in that matter, he was by now ready to concede that Patten might have been under pressure from the Foreign Office and the British government. Personally, he still considered Patten a 'genuine and interesting person, a nice guy', and, as a fellow Catholic, he was enthusiastic about the prospect of future 'co-operation'. But he warned: 'Of course, we will never concede on principle on issues like the rule of law and individual liberty.'

The governor, not yet aware of Martin Lee's intentions, did not in any event have time to dwell on the happy outcome of the elections. Within a week the triumph of democracy was driven out of the headlines by an issue which had long been lurking in the political undergrowth, tinder waiting for a match: in this case, however, the governor's principal adversaries were not to be found in Hong Kong or China, but in Whitehall.

17

'NOT REMOTELY ACRIMONIOUS'

Tackling the Home Secretary

On Friday 22 September 1995, Chris Patten appeared in an edition of the BBC Radio 4 programme *Any Questions*, which was broadcast live from Government House. In response to a question from the former BBC correspondent Anthony Lawrence, the governor declared that more than 3 million subjects of the British crown in Hong Kong should be given right of abode in Britain. In elaboration he said:

> I don't think that a British passport should just be a more convenient way of getting on and off an aeroplane. I think that a British passport should be about more than helping you to travel comfortably around the world, and I think that those who qualify for a BDTC [British Dependent Territories Citizen] passport – a British passport – should qualify for something that, if necessary, gives them right of abode. I don't think that more than three million Hong Kong citizens are suddenly going to arrive at Heathrow. Nobody seriously supposes that. And, to be blunt, if they did that, they certainly wouldn't be living on the welfare state.

Patten had chosen his words with care. Knowing that the issue was likely to be raised in the programme, he had debated with his advisers how best to respond. He concluded that he would have to give a direct answer. Anything less, he explained afterwards, would have caused a 'huge fuss in Hong Kong'. As it was, his words caused a huge fuss in London. Traditionally xenophobic newspapers like the *Sunday Express* led the way. Patten had 'lost touch with reality', its leader-writer spluttered, 'for the reality is that the "full up" sign should have been hung up on these islands years ago. And Governor Patten doesn't seem to know it. Maybe he has spent too much time in his colonial mansion, decorated in exotic taste, surrounded by flunkies. Maybe the £150,000-a-year salary and the chauffeur-driven car have gone to his head.' With the notable, and surprising, exception of the *Daily Mail*, the other tabloids were scarcely more restrained. The broadsheets, led by *The Times* and the *Daily Telegraph*, reflecting longstanding editorial policies, were, however, supportive. Nonetheless, under the headline 'TORY FURY AT PATTEN CALL FOR 3M PASSPORTS', the *Observer* reported that many right-wingers on the government's backbenches were incensed that the former party chairman should seek to reopen an issue which they thought had been closed more than five years earlier when the House of Commons passed the 1990 British Nationalities (Hong Kong) Act in response to the killings in Tiananmen Square, and thereby marginally 'liberalised' Britain's strict immigration regulations for the first time in almost thirty years by offering the right of abode in the UK to 50,000 selected British subjects.

Since then, the formal policy of the Hong Kong government had remained that all existing BDTC passport-holders should be offered right of abode in the United Kingdom, and Patten's comments on *Any Questions* were, as he was ingeniously swift to remind the Home Office, merely a repetition of this. He was, however, under no illusion that the government (of which, incidentally, he had been a loyal member when the 1990 act came into force) would fail to respond to his challenge, and he was not at all surprised when, two days after the broadcast, the home secretary, Michael Howard, hurried to the microphone to reassure the public in Britain that there was no question of a change in policy and that the matter had been settled once and for all by Parliament in 1990. On immigration, at least, New Labour, like Old Labour, was not to be outflanked from the right: the shadow home secretary, Jack Straw, was similarly quick to criticise Patten. He could not resist a cheap political shot at the governor's expense, asserting that his plea for more passports 'must raise questions about his own confidence in the stability of the arrangements he has put in place for after 1997'. Despite this rebuff from Westminster, the Government House spokesman, Kerry McGlynn, who had succeeded Mike Hanson earlier in the year, confirmed that the governor would continue to raise the issue 'when appropriate'.

In reality, Patten had no such intention, because he knew perfectly well that it would be a waste of his time. In any case, he had to face what was, to his mind, a far more important battle with the Home

Office, and one he was determined to win against an obdurate home secretary. For some months his team had been sounding out their counterparts in Whitehall on two crucial issues which, Patten confided in September 1995, 'could cause us very, very considerable difficulty and embarrassment the closer we get to 1997'.

The first of these was the question of Hong Kong's non-Chinese 'ethnic minorities', which, as Patten said that autumn, 'still sits there waiting, I think, to hit us in the solar plexus as we're leaving'. To date Home Office officials had been adamant that none of Britain's 5,000 or so non-Chinese colonial subjects born in Hong Kong, who were mainly of Indian origin, would be eligible for full British passports unless they had been selected under the 1990 act for one of the 50,000 BNS passports. Similarly, although the imprecision of Beijing's concept of nationality as defined in Article 24 of the Basic Law made it difficult to be sure, it appeared to exclude Hong Kong's 'ethnic minorities' from the right to acquire Chinese citizenship either. If so, in the absence of a British passport, Hong Kong's Indian community would in effect become 'stateless', even if they were permitted to remain in Hong Kong as residents.

Privately, the governor sympathised strongly with their predicament, and he believed that the British government had a moral obligation to provide them, as British citizens, with full UK passports. A failure to do so had the potential, he felt, to inflict severe damage on Britain's international reputation. However, the public position of the government, as outlined in a carefully crafted 'information note' from the chief secretary's office, was that 'effectively no one will really be *stateless* in Hong Kong in 1997'. To those who might have been perturbed by the weasel words 'effectively' and 'really', the note made much of the fact that 'the small minority of Hong Kong people . . . who have no right of abode elsewhere than Hong Kong will automatically become British Overseas Citizens (BOC) with right of abode here [in Hong Kong] too'. However, the chief secretary's civil servants were careful to avoid mentioning the fact that the BOC passport was a travel document of extremely limited use, providing visa-free access to very few countries outside the United Kingdom and no right of abode in Britain itself. Indeed, in Hong Kong, as elsewhere, a BOC passport was held to do little more than identify with cruel precision the 'effective' and 'real' statelessness of its holder. The Hong Kong government was prone to reiterating the 'assurance' of the British government given to 'those with solely British nationality' that if they had to leave and had nowhere else to go, they would be 'considered sympathetically for entrance into Britain'. If anything, this attempt at reassurance served only to increase the level of anxiety among the Indian community.

The second of Patten's preoccupations had even greater potential to wreak havoc – indeed, he was afraid that it might make governing Hong Kong very difficult in the following eighteen months. This issue was whether the 3 million people who would automatically acquire HKSAR (Hong Kong Special Administrative Region) passports in 1997 should be offered visa-free access to the United Kingdom. The SAR passport was to replace the identity cards held by the ethnic Chinese and would also be available to all Hong Kong citizens who failed to qualify for BNO passports but were likely to satisfy Beijing's as yet ill-defined criteria concerning nationality.

Patten believed that it would be an act of great folly for Britain to withhold visa-free access from SAR passport-holders. Failure to grant SAR and BNO passports similar status would, he thought, have calamitous consequences, not only for Hong Kong but for British interests throughout the region. Yet, as in the case of the ethnic minorities, he suspected that the weight of opinion in the Cabinet would be against him. And he knew for certain that the secretary of state responsible for immigration, Michael Howard, was, as he put it, 'implacably opposed to making any change'.

In the autumn of 1995, the governor, Edward Llewellyn and Martin Dinham began what they knew would be a war of attrition with the Home Office. Their aim was to create a consensus in and around the Cabinet strong enough to force the home secretary to abandon his rigid stance. 'We have to persuade the Home Office in general, and the home secretary in particular, that, though his argument may be intellectually logical, it's politically, and, I think, morally, wrong,' Patten explained. 'What I have to do is mobilise support in London.' Failure would be intolerable, but the chances of success were not good. Not only had Howard staked out his opposition unambiguously, but any retreat would dent his carefully honed image as a populist hard-liner on immigration.

There were glimmers of hope. 'There isn't an MP who's come here in the last months who hasn't gone away convinced of the strength of our case,' said Patten, and he was confident that the media – 'at least the quality end' – would be supportive. But the issue of visa-free access for SAR passport-holders had yet to become a matter of public debate in Hong Kong, and, given the political minefield ahead of him, Patten was at this stage anxious that it shouldn't 'surface prematurely'. He wanted to start lobbying in London before any hint of the emerging conflict between the governor of Hong Kong and the British home secretary leaked out. If necessary, however, he was quite ready to turn a private negotiation into a public battle.

It was not simply a matter of two men's credibility. On the surface, at least, the home secretary had a formidable case. In political terms, he could argue that it would be hugely damaging for a Conservative administration, pledged to maintain strict limits on immigration, to approach the next election committed to giving millions of ethnic Chinese from Hong Kong the right to enter Britain at will, albeit without any right of abode. He could argue, as many of his most reactionary colleagues on the Conservative backbenches were sure to do, that the electorate, egged on by a xenophobic tabloid media, would not easily distinguish between the right to enter Britain and the right to stay there. Not only would the Conservative party's already enfeebled electoral prospects be further weakened, but, as Patten recognised, a Cabinet decision to 'open the floodgates' would also be subject to merciless exploitation by a Labour party which, on such issues, was equally opportunistic. Perhaps more persuasively, Howard would be sure to point out that to grant visa-free access to SAR passport-holders would set an unwarranted precedent. As Patten summed it up: 'The home secretary could reasonably ask why we should be obliged to give people with Chinese passports in Hong Kong after 1997 – when we will not be sovereign – rights which they didn't have before 1997, when we were.' It was, he conceded, a good question.

The governor's counter-case centred on the likely repercussions of the denial of such access. First, there would be alarming consequences for BNO passport-holders. China would be infuriated by Britain's stance, and might well retaliate by lobbying every other member of the United Nations to treat BNO and SAR passports on the same footing. As most countries were already dubious about offering visa-free access to holders of BNO passports, there was a real risk that they would respond to Chinese pressure by barring that right to both categories. If this occurred, Patten had little doubt that prospective holders of BNO passports would become extremely nervous about whether their new travel documents would be worth anything after 1997. One of his team summed it up more bluntly: 'If we don't give free access to SAR passport-holders, we'll kill the BNO passport.'

Secondly, another, more direct, form of Chinese retaliation was likely. After the handover they could require all UK citizens to obtain visas before entering Hong Kong. In 1995, some 14,000 Hong Kong Chinese carrying Certificates of Identity (all of whom would become SAR passport-holders) travelled to Britain annually, whereas more than 400,000 British citizens travelled from London to Hong Kong. 'Given the extent to which Hong Kong is our jumping-off point for China and Asia,' Patten reasoned, 'it really would be a case of shooting oneself in the foot.'

More generally, and perhaps even more damagingly, another of the 'extremely disagreeable consequences' would be that the Chinese would portray Britain as having no real interest in the future wellbeing of Hong Kong. To refuse visa-free access to SAR passport-holders would, Patten believed, 'trigger a good deal of criticism of Britain, tinged with a certain view that we are behaving in a racist way'. The prospect exasperated him. 'I mean,' he said, clenching his fists in frustration, 'everybody now talks about us having a more assertive role in relation to Asia, and making the most of our opportunities in China through Hong Kong. If one's serious about that, how could one seriously lash oneself to a policy as misguided as the one we've been talking about?'

The Government House tactic against the Home Office was to lobby key members of the British government and their civil servants, reiterating and elaborating Patten's case, hoping to pick them off one by one. By mid-September 1995, the governor's 'campaign', as he called it, was already underway. By the end of the month he had rallied some key figures to his cause, including the Conservative chairman of the Hong Kong Parliamentary Group. He was also confident that the Labour party and the Liberal Democrats would not be 'difficult about it'. The affable minister of state at the Foreign Office, Jeremy Hanley (one of Patten's devotees), and the permanent secretary, John Coles, both of whom had just been in Hong Kong, were also supportive. However, he was less certain about three more important players: the foreign secretary, Malcolm Rifkind, who had replaced Douglas Hurd in a government reshuffle in July; the deputy prime minister, Michael Heseltine, promoted to that role following his part in securing John Major's self-imposed re-election as party leader in June; and the chancellor, Kenneth Clarke. Patten's team decided to direct their fire at Hanley and Coles in the hope that, according to one of those directly involved, they would 'go back and push the argument with Rifkind'.

In June, just before his departure from the government, Hurd, who strongly supported Patten on the issue, had called together a small group of senior Cabinet ministers for an initial discussion, prompted by an alarming proposal from immigration officials in Brussels that Hong Kong should be placed on a list of countries whose citizens would require mandatory visas to enter the European Union. At that meeting, Howard had shown his colours, not only making his case against

visa-free access for SAR passport-holders, but also seeking to pre-empt
further debate by announcing the decision publicly. Moreover, he had
made it clear that he was in favour of extending the visa requirement to
BNO passports as well – a stance, according to Government House,
that was supported by Clarke. Rifkind, as defence secretary, had been
at best equivocal. Hurd was appalled by Howard's lack of perspective
and, by his own account, told the home secretary: 'Hold your horses –
don't let's stir up an unnecessary row in Hong Kong until we've all
looked at it seriously.'

The governor knew he had no hope of victory without winning
over the new foreign secretary; nor did he underestimate the magnitude
of his task. 'I'm not saying he's hostile, it's just that he needs to be persuaded that this is an issue which demands a fight.' He suspected that
Rifkind, for whose forensic cast of mind he had great respect, would
not be won over until he had seen Hong Kong for himself. His first
visit to the colony as foreign secretary was scheduled for November
1995, when, as one of Patten's team put it, 'we will really expose him
to the arguments'. As the governor left for London in early October, he
knew that, sooner or later, there would be a fight. The Home Office
was still intransigent, or, as he put it, 'being a bit silly' about the possibility of Hong Kong citizens overstaying their official welcome: if there
were to be a problem of 'visa abuse' after 1997, he complained, 'then
they can deal with it as they've dealt with other examples . . . by slap-
ping in a regime, a restrictive set of controls'.

Patten's arrival in London almost coincided with the departure of the
Chinese vice-premier and foreign minister, Qian Qichen, making his
first visit to Britain since the row over Patten's reforms. Qian Qichen
had prefaced his trip with a sideswipe clearly directed at the governor
for advocating that Britain should grant right of abode to the 3.3
million holders of BDTC passports. This intervention was, he said, one
example of 'troublemaking' by the Hong Kong authorities which stood
in the way of further improvements in the relationship between Britain
and China. Although he did not mention it himself, several pro-China
newspapers in Hong Kong, citing sources in Beijing, reported that the
Chinese foreign minister intended to use his London visit to demand
visa-free access to Britain for SAR passport-holders. There was now a
danger that Patten's own rift with the Home Office would leak into the
British media, making his task even more difficult. The governor was
in a most curious situation: singled out for condemnation by Beijing for
promoting democracy in Hong Kong, he was about to become the
most insistent – if not the only – significant advocate of China's case for
SAR passports. If Beijing's renewed campaign to have him removed as

governor were to succeed, the prospect of securing such access for those passport-holders would almost certainly vanish with him.

As it turned out, the passports issue was to be temporarily over-shadowed by an unexpected, if superficial, thaw in Sino–British relations. On his first day in London, 2 October, Qian Qichen met the deputy prime minister, Michael Heseltine, after which it was reported that both men had agreed that closer co-operation between the two sovereign powers was required to secure a smooth transition and that, with this in mind, Qian Qichen had invited Heseltine to pay a return visit to Beijing in 1996. The following day, the Chinese vice-premier attended a three-hour session with Malcolm Rifkind at the Foreign Office, where they were joined briefly by the prime minister. Their dis-cussions produced a number of 'understandings', or what was described as a 'consensus', designed to improve official contacts between Britain and China at all levels in the run-up to 1997 and beyond. They also agreed that the handover ceremony itself should be 'solemn and digni-fied'. Afterwards, the foreign secretary emerged with Qian Qichen at his side to inform the assembled media that they had had an 'extremely important and satisfactory session'. The Chinese foreign minister described it as 'positive, useful and productive'. Although the 'consen-sus' lacked any single measure of substance, the Hong Kong media promptly deduced that Sino–British relations were back to normal. One correspondent, writing in the *South China Morning Post*, was so carried away by the warm words emanating from each side that he informed his readers that the two governments had managed to 'draw up a new road map for a smooth transfer of the territory'.

The Foreign Office did nothing to dispel this illusion. Indeed, offi-cials were on hand to point out for the benefit of attentive journalists that no representative of the Hong Kong government had been present at the talks. Just in case the significance of that should fail to seep into the collective consciousness of the media, at least one of them went on to confide, anonymously: 'We don't always have to see Hong Kong through the prism of Chris Patten's eyes.' It was a lethal remark, which, since it came from an apparently unimpeachable source, drew both the British and Hong Kong press to the obvious conclusion: Patten had been sidelined and isolated in an effort to put Sino–British relations back on course.

With the lines between London and Hong Kong humming, Patten was at once caught in a new crossfire. Detecting a Foreign Office 'sell-out', Martin Lee noted that Malcolm Rifkind had failed to confront Qian Qichen over the latter's public reminder that LegCo would be abolished on 1 July 1997. In their joint press conference, the Chinese foreign minister had responded to a question about the 'through train' with the words, 'We did not discuss this question. The issue has already been resolved.' However, the new British foreign secretary had failed to reiterate the official British position, that there was no justification for preventing the members of LegCo from serving a full term, i.e., until 1998. 'It is obvious,' Martin Lee reasoned, 'that economic interests have become the primary concern of the British side in dealing with China.'

The governor now had the delicate task of endorsing Rifkind's bullish remarks about his meeting with Qian Qichen while denying that he himself had been sidelined or that the talks had been a 'sell-out'. Officially he confined himself to saying that the proposals for improving co-operation between Britain and China had emanated from Government House; that the position of the British government remained that there was no reason why the Legislative Council should be demolished; and that, as for his own role, 'I continue to be in regular touch with the prime minister and the foreign secretary.' Martin Lee was not mollified. 'As Britain and China tango cheek to cheek,' he said on RTHK's *Letter to Hong Kong* a few days later, 'they are trampling Hong Kong.' Any sense that the rapprochement between China and Britain would benefit Hong Kong was swept aside in a renewed bout of doubt and suspicion about the real purpose of the British government and the future role of the governor.

Patten seethed with frustration at the impact in Hong Kong of the words attributed by the media to 'senior officials' from the Foreign Office. 'It was irritating,' he confided, 'not really because it bruised my ego – though it would be dishonest in the extreme to pretend that occasionally that sort of thing doesn't piss one off in a fairly substantial way – but because there really was a good story for Hong Kong to tell, and quite an important story, which got completely screwed up.' The important story was that he and his colleagues had 'stood firm on a number of matters of principle – particularly on decent elections – and we've still managed to do serious business with China within a couple of weeks of those elections'. From his point of view, the significance of this was – or should have been – 'what we've argued all along: that they are obliged to do business on some issues as we get closer to 1997, and one shouldn't think one has to throw in all one's cards to do business with them at all'. All this had been put in jeopardy by the Foreign Office.

'So what happens? Instead of that being the story, the story which spins out – as though the New China News Agency were running the Foreign Affairs News Department – is, "Ah! We've managed to do all these deals with China because we've bypassed Hong Kong . . . and the clever old Foreign Office in London has done it all."' Patten was far from pacified by what he referred to as the 'Foreign Office line' relayed to Government House 'rather nervously', to the effect that the unnamed officials had been misquoted. Patten had no doubt that the newspaper reports were accurate: two of the three journalists involved were people, he said, who 'I know are straight, and on whom I would completely rely'.

Yet the governor was inclined to believe that the Foreign Office had been inept rather than treacherous. 'There was,' he complained, a 'complete lack of comprehension of the sensitivities in Hong Kong, of the extent to which people simply don't trust Britain and have, actually, in some respects, quite a good pedigree for that particular opinion or prejudice.' He was also sure that real damage had been done to Britain's negotiating stance with Beijing. 'I have no doubt that Qian Qichen would have left London thinking that there was a difference between the governor of Hong Kong and the British government. No doubt at all.'

This impression of disharmony could only have been exacerbated, to Patten's dismay, by the fact that, at the grand dinner given for Qian Qichen, one of the guests had been Sir Percy Cradock. Soon afterwards, Cradock was heard describing Patten as the 'incredible shrinking governor' in a radio interview, designed, in the latter's view, 'to do maximum damage and to create the impression that the only role I had in the future was to stamp on the Democrats when they got out of line'.

Patten was swift to exonerate the foreign secretary from any blame for the débâcle. It was clear to him that Rifkind had been mortified by his failure to rebut Qian Qichen at once over the 'through train'. As soon as the story broke, he had been on the phone to Hong Kong to say how unfortunate it was, and how he would immediately put his position on the record. Patten offered an explanation for Rifkind's uncharacteristic lapse. 'When you are a new foreign secretary coming to a brief which is as complicated as Hong Kong, it's a miracle if you get the main tune right. If you manage one or two grace notes as well, it is astonishing.' Moreover, the oversight was partly attributable to Patten himself. Before Rifkind's meeting with his Chinese counterpart, Government House had prepared a brief for the foreign secretary listing the main points Patten wanted him to raise with China. Assuming that he was bound to reiterate the British position on the 'through train', Patten's team failed to draw attention to the need to remind him of it. The governor conceded:

Maybe we should have banged our fists on the table more vigorously before the meeting, and said, 'It's imperative that before you start talking about anything else, you just remind the Chinese what our position is on the Legislative Council'. . . But we are always sensitive to the charge that we are party-poopers, that we are not sufficiently concerned about – what's the phrase? – 'warming up the relationship with China'.

Patten's scorn for the in-house language of the Foreign Office and the 'exceptionally unhelpful' behaviour of some of its officials was fuelled by personal resentment, but it was driven by a genuine and deepening anxiety. The perception of disunity in the British camp was likely to encourage the Chinese to be even more intractable. In particular, he feared that they were likely to be much more assertive in their threats to dismantle Hong Kong's protection of human rights contained in the Bill of Rights.

To forestall this, Patten now resolved to challenge Beijing openly on both the Bill of Rights and the legislative assembly. If he was prone to overestimating the strength of his hand – in late 1995 he still allowed himself to believe that it would be 'extremely difficult' for the Chinese to dismantle his reforms – it was because he found it hard to credit that the gerontocracy in Beijing would, in the end, act so blatantly against China's own interests. To this extent he suffered from a form of intellectual schizophrenia, apparently convincing himself that a regime which he judged to be generally vindictive, irrational and incompetent would nonetheless act in this respect with goodwill, common sense and at least a modicum of competence. If officials at the Foreign Office continued in their efforts to baulk him, he intended to make an unequivocal response. 'I'll do what I've always done, which is to take the first opportunity in front of a television camera to set out my views.' He recognised that pressure of this kind was likely to increase up to the handover, and that it would be far more problematic to resist afterwards. In theory Britain had the right and duty to monitor, through the Joint Liaison Group, the execution of the Joint Declaration for a further decade. Given the attitude of the Foreign Office, he feared that, in practice, it would be 'even more difficult to win the argument that Britain has to demonstrate a commitment to Hong Kong. You can imagine the sighs of relief in some parts of the bureaucracy on 1 July. You know, "Now we can get back to trying to get the sort of relationship with China that Germany has . . ."'

The foreign secretary had not only intimated that he wished to make political amends for his failure to tackle Qian Qichen on the 'through train' issue: according to Patten, he wanted to be 'rather more supportive than we thought entirely sensible'. Rifkind was evidently appalled by the way in which Beijing saw fit to treat a British governor. His instinct was to respond by suggesting that Patten should, in future, accompany him whenever he met the Chinese leadership, either in London or in Beijing, to make it clear not only that Patten remained the driving force behind British policy towards China over Hong Kong, but that the territory remained the government's first priority. Patten was encouraged by Rifkind's robust attitude, but he resisted the proposition, explaining, 'In practice, it doesn't make very much difference, and I wouldn't like to become part of the problem.'

He was encouraged, too, by the response of a growing number of his former colleagues to the passport issue. Still intent on keeping the latent tensions within the Cabinet from surfacing too soon, he focused on his main concern now: restraining some members of Parliament, including those on the Conservative benches, from 'leaping in and starting to lobby too early'. None of his ministerial colleagues were yet prepared to commit themselves in favour of visa-free access, but the prime minister, the foreign secretary, the deputy prime minister and the new president of the Board of Trade, Ian Lang, had at least listened carefully to his case without argument – although Lang had seemed less than impressed.

With the home secretary, however, it was different. While their conversation, according to Patten, was 'not remotely acrimonious', the governor was frustrated by Michael Howard's 'slightly annoying barrister's habit of merely repeating his best point, while arguments you advance yourself are allowed to whizz overhead'. In any event, Howard remained firm. As Patten had predicted, the home secretary warned, as the governor phrased it, 'I'm not proposing to change anything. At the moment, if you are a Certificate of Identity holder – a future SAR passport-holder – and you want to go to London, you require a visa. And you will require a visa after 1997 as an SAR passport-holder. So what is the difference?' When Patten reminded Howard that visa policy had changed dramatically since 1990, when visa-free access to Britain was granted to Czechs, Hungarians, Poles, Latvians, Lithuanians and Estonians, bringing the total number of foreigners who now enjoyed such access to over 2 billion, the home secretary was dismissive. According to sources close to Howard, he thought Patten's argument 'simply didn't wash' and that the fact that 'hundreds of millions of people already have visa-free access does not seem to be remotely a reason for deciding whether a particular group of people should have visa-free access in the future'. Patten disclosed that, as far as Howard was concerned, the only question at stake was not whether to introduce visa-free access but when the government should announce publicly that SAR passport-holders would require a visa to enter Britain after 1 July 1997. As Government House had forecast, Howard seemed to take the view – mistakenly, in Patten's opinion – that the British public would not be able to distinguish between immigration policy and ease of travel.

Patten returned to Hong Kong with the issue still unresolved. The schedule for the foreign secretary's first visit to Hong Kong happened to dovetail with the timetable for a set of related negotiations in the Joint Liaison Group, where, according to one of Patten's aides: 'Our line with the Chinese is, "Of course we're happy to give visa-free access for SAR passports, but we can't do that until we know the form of the passport – who is eligible for it, and how it will be issued; will it be properly secure?"' When the foreign secretary's visit was put back from November to January, Patten's team found itself in danger of reaching an agreement on the technicalities of the SAR passports without being at all sure that London would be willing to deliver on the governor's implicit, if provisional, undertaking to secure visa-free access for them.

In December the British continued to press the Chinese through the JLG on the 'integrity' of the SAR passport. In London Qian Qichen had shown off what Patten described as a 'technologically gee-whizz' document which would be hard to forge. However, there was still some doubt as to whether Hong Kong would be the only authority permitted to issue SAR passports. In the absence of such a guarantee, few states would be willing to grant visa-free access, and some would be reluctant even to accept the new passport as a valid travel document. In Patten's blunt assessment: 'There are going to be immigration authorities all round the world who will see that it is a more useful document than the Chinese passport and will therefore – I am sure incorrectly – leap to the conclusion that there won't be a cadre's son or daughter in Peking who won't have a copy of it.'

It was important therefore for the Chinese to confirm unequivocally that the SAR passport would only be issued in Hong Kong by the appropriate authority, and would be available only to those citizens entitled to hold it. Although the Chinese had been characteristically oblique until now, Patten's hope was that they would satisfy these requirements before the foreign secretary's rescheduled visit to Hong Kong. If so, Patten was confident that Rifkind would endorse his case and go back to London ready to confront Howard directly. Patten suspected that the foreign secretary would fare no better than he had done himself. In this event Rifkind would almost certainly lay out his views in letters to his Cabinet colleagues. This would be followed by what Patten hoped would be a decisive meeting of the Cabinet Committee in the spring, at which, with luck, the home secretary would find himself outnumbered. In the meantime, the governor was determined to keep up the momentum with discreet but sustained lobbying in Whitehall and Westminster.

Back in Hong Kong, banquets and grand balls followed one another relentlessly. The Pattens were invariably invited as guests of honour and were duty-bound to attend the most important events of the social calendar. The highlight of the 1995 Christmas season was the party given by the banker and former attorney general, Michael Thomas, at the end of December in honour of his wife, Baroness Dunn. Invitations to this function were prized above all others. Lydia Dunn, the political doyenne of Hong Kong, was the most elevated public figure in the Chinese community. Invariably dressed in white, perfectly coiffed, exquisitely poised, she looked deceptively like an alabaster doll, unlined and ageless, but she was a canny, tough and perceptive insider who knew most, if not all, Hong Kong's secrets. Patten had been impressed by her knowledge and judgement, and, in the early months of his governorship, he had had regular tête-à-têtes with her which had proved invaluable.

The banquet, held in the Grand Hyatt, was to be Baroness Dunn's formal farewell to Hong Kong as she and her husband had decided to move to London, where he was due to take up a new appointment. To mark the significance of the occasion, the banqueting room of the hotel had been remodelled for the evening, fitted with false walls and hung with paintings to provide a more intimate atmosphere for the 220 guests. That night Hong Kong's elite was on display. In one of several delicious ironies, Lavender Patten was seated next to William Purves, the man she had metaphorically denounced as a traitor for his covert efforts to destroy her husband's reforms during the marathon LegCo session the previous year. Purves's wife sat beside the governor. Paul Cheng, the chairman of the Chamber of Commerce, one of Patten's smoothest but bitterest foes, was also there, as were critics such as the tycoons Sir S.Y. Chung, Robert Kuok and K.S. Li, who had long ago made their peace with China on Beijing's terms. They smiled politely and engaged in small talk with the governor whose efforts for Hong Kong they abhorred. Peter Woo and Bessie, his wife, were present. Bessie and Lavender Patten had forged a genuine regard for one another; Peter, who had not yet judged it impolitic to be regarded as a confidant of the governor, was, as ever, charming. Another guest was Peter Sutch, the *taipan* of Swires. The most powerful of the colony's expatriate entrepreneurs, Sutch had lived in Hong Kong for twenty years. He was a 'company' man who had risen through the ranks to become its unassuming chief executive. Respected for his business acumen and his far-sighted approach to management, he had made no secret of his reservations about Patten's reforms, but, unusually, he had at least expressed his views with courtesy and to the governor's face. As a result, the two men had remained on cordial and mutually respectful terms.

In this gathering of Hong Kong power-brokers it was not easy for the governor to count many allies. At a neighbouring table were Tung Chee Hwa and his wife, Betty. C.H., as Tung was known by everyone locally, was a shipping tycoon who had close links with the Beijing leadership. C.H. had a reputation for being incorruptible, his own man. Patten, seeking the authentic voice of traditional Chinese conservatism, had persuaded him to join the Executive Council in October 1992, where he had proved to be cautious, sincere and worldly-wise. One or two insiders had started to champion him as a possible successor to Patten as Hong Kong's first chief executive.

The chief executive would be the most important figure in post-handover Hong Kong. Appointed by Beijing, he would have full authority over the SAR as specified in the Joint Declaration – in theory, only foreign affairs and defence would remain with the government in Beijing. It was widely thought that C.H. possessed the attributes such a demanding role would require. However, in his deceptively avuncular manner, he had been quick to disown any such ambition. At dinner, insofar as conversation was possible above the cacophony from the dance floor, he intimated that, if the truth were known, he was really a man of very little importance. He spoke with affection of Liverpool, where he had attended university, and with adoration of his grandchildren whom, he said, he made a point of visiting every day. His wife, meanwhile, engaged in a discussion about democracy. Like C.H., Betty Tung was held in high regard. She worked for charity, she was generous, shrewd and kindly. But democracy – which she identified principally as a source of communal friction and potential disharmony – clearly remained an alien notion to her. She very much liked the governor, she said, but added, as if speaking for her husband as well, 'We do not really understand this idea of democracy. We believe in freedom, but democracy is complicated.' Another guest suggested that democracy and freedom were intertwined, arguing, 'Freedom cannot survive without accountability. In the West we believe that accountability is best secured by democracy in the form of universal adult suffrage.' Betty Tung shrugged, and the conversation moved on. 'What we would really like to do when C.H. retires is to live in San Francisco,' she confided. 'The weather is beautiful, the atmosphere is friendly. The only problem is that it is more expensive to hire staff in America, and it takes much longer to get a washing-machine mended. Sometimes it takes days. Here you make the call and someone is round immediately.'

By the late autumn, public attention in Hong Kong had begun to focus once again on human rights. Three weeks after Qian Qichen's 'successful' visit to London, Beijing had confirmed Patten's fear that the politburo would be ready to exploit any perceived divisions in the British camp. It was announced, in the guise of a 'recommendation' of the Preliminary Working Committee, that the Bill of Rights was in need of fundamental revision. Following the enactment of the Bill of Rights in 1992, scores of anachronistic ordinances had been amended or were in the process of revision. The most important of these concerned individual rights to free assembly, free speech and the free expression of opinion. The PWC's proposal, which was immediately endorsed by Chinese officials in Hong Kong and on the mainland, was that a number of vital safeguards should be removed from the Bill of Rights. In particular, the PWC recommended that three crucial articles – 2 (3), 3 and 4, which stated that no Hong Kong law enacted either before or after the Bill of Rights should contravene any of its provisions – should be deleted. They also argued that six ordinances which had already been amended should be restored to their original form. The Chinese claimed that the amended versions of these ordinances 'seriously weakened the government's authority and are not conducive to a smooth transition'. Citing three broadcasting ordinances, and three relating to public order and the use of emergency powers – all of which, before being amended, had not only contravened the relevant international covenants but had also been allowed to gather dust for almost two decades – the NCNA declared that the decision to introduce a Bill of Rights had been motivated by Britain's determination to 'undermine the authority of the post-1997 administration'. The British were, the Chinese asserted, gambling with the stability and prosperity of Hong Kong. For good measure, Beijing, in the person of a Foreign Ministry spokesman, offered a ritual denunciation of the Bill of Rights as a 'serious violation' of the Joint Declaration and the Basic Law.

So preposterous was this latest Chinese onslaught that even some of Beijing's most dutiful supporters were embarrassed. The business community, as usual, refrained from expressing any opinion that might have been taken as evidence of a collective conscience or moral backbone, but a number of 'anti-British' legislators like the Liberal party's Selina Chow condemned the PWC's proposal. Similarly, Tsang Yok Sing, speaking for the DAB, and effectively for a much wider constituency in the colony, was careful to distance himself from the recommendations, noting publicly that they were 'worrying' and set a 'bad precedent'. Answering questions from journalists, Patten said that the PWC's proposals called into question their commitment to the rule of law, and indeed, their understanding of it. 'It does immeasurable damage to confidence, and therefore immeasurable damage to Hong Kong's prospects . . . I very much hope that wise counsel will prevail.'

His hopes were vain. Even before the 'Triple Violator' had arrived in Hong Kong, the Chinese had made clear that in devising the Bill of Rights, Britain had 'disregarded' what they chose to describe as a matter of principle, and that, accordingly, Beijing reserved the right to 'review' that document and all other legislation. Throughout the late autumn of 1995, competing lawyers examined the fine print of the Basic Law to establish to their own satisfaction that the Bill of Rights most certainly did, or did not, depending on which side they were representing, constitute a violation of the Basic Law. In reality, however, the controversy was far less a dispute about constitutional niceties than a bitter political conflict clothed in legal jargon which reflected the deep-seated insecurities of the totalitarian regime in Beijing. As with the Legislative Council, China's attitude, expressed through the PWC, provided unsettling evidence that, as 1997 approached, the politburo was finding it increasingly difficult to tolerate the vision of a genuinely autonomous Hong Kong.

Even the leader of the Liberal party, Allen Lee, was uneasy. The Chinese would have to find ways to back off, he said unofficially, or the public would become extremely demoralised. 'If you ask a common person in the streets about the content of the Bill of Rights, they don't know. But they feel . . . that it will protect them from abuses by the government . . . I think Hong Kong people don't want them to screw around with the Bill of Rights . . . The Chinese are walking on a very thin line.'

Then a single indiscretion by Hong Kong's chief justice, Sir Ti Liang Yang, detonated a furious public row. Towards the end of October, the colony's senior law officer had been invited to dinner by the deputy director of the NCNA, Zhang Junsheng. In the course of what he apparently considered a private conversation, the chief justice confided to his host that he shared Beijing's view that the Bill of Rights threat-ened to undermine Hong Kong's legal system. His comments were inevitably leaked to the media by the mischief-making official. At first, the hapless chief justice responded to the consequent uproar by claim-ing that he could not remember what he had said at dinner. Then, to make matters even worse, he shifted his ground, intimating that what-ever he had said, it should not be regarded as the product of careful thought on his part as he had not yet studied the matter in any detail; for this reason, whatever he had said could not be taken to represent his final opinion. Zhang Junsheng immediately countered by observing that the chief justice's comments had been 'well thought out and deliv-ered prudently'.

In other circumstances, this Ruritanian dialogue might have been entertaining; as it was, the prospective dismemberment of the Bill of Rights was the most sensitive legal question facing Hong Kong. The breathtaking incompetence displayed by the individual charged with interpreting and defending the law from political interference hardly inspired confidence in the attitude of the judiciary after 1997. Although the chief justice was ridiculed by liberal politicians and commentators, the incident left the impression that, if he remained in his post after the handover, Sir Ti Liang Yang was likely to prove as biddable as Beijing hoped and Hong Kong feared.

In the middle of November, the Legislative Council debated the PWC's recommendations for the Bill of Rights, and, by 40 votes to 15, passed a motion deploring them. The motion also urged the governor to review all existing laws to ensure that they were in line with the bill. A fortnight later, maintaining the pressure, Martin Lee led a delegation of Democrats to Government House to urge Patten to press ahead with the repeal of all the 'colonial' legislation still on the statute book, including the Official Secrets Act and the Crimes Ordinance (which in any case required amendment to reflect the Basic Law prohibitions against subversion, secession, sedition and treason). Although Patten was not yet ready to show his hand, he gave the Democrats a sympathetic hearing.

As only his private office knew, his desire to face down the Chinese over the Bill of Rights and its associated legislation had not merely remained undiminished but had been actively fuelled by Beijing's animosity. 'It is exceptionally important . . . and it goes right to the heart of the central issue: whether the Chinese really are committed to upholding Hong Kong's way of life, and whether they are prepared to show that restraint in dealing with Hong Kong which is implied by the concept of "one country, two systems",' he remarked in December.

The fact that the PWC had been 'ventriloquised' by Beijing into advocating the dilution of the bill so soon after Qian Qichen's visit to London was, for Patten, a 'nice reminder to those who subscribe to the notion that you have a nice meeting with the Chinese, and everything proceeds as it would with anybody else' of how little there was to be gained from that course of action. Phrases like 'warm afterglow', 'gradual restoration of relations' and 'preserving the channel to Qian' had become the small change of Foreign Office memoranda. They were held in such contempt at Government House that as soon as a new one entered the mandarinate's lexicon, Patten's advisers would pin it up on a pillar in his private office which he christened Democracy Wall. It was astonishing, Patten fumed, that within days of the Chinese foreign minister's return from London, Chinese officials had no qualms about threatening to dismantle the main protection for Hong Kong's civil liberties or making proposals which would involve absolute direct contraventions of the Basic Law.

It was inevitable that the clash between Government House and the Foreign Office which had long been simmering beneath the surface should now be exposed. In Government House, the obligation to protect Hong Kong's 'way of life' within the framework of the Joint Declaration was not merely a slogan but a commitment which coursed through the veins of those who now surrounded Chris Patten. His private secretary, Martin Dinham, his personal political adviser, Edward Llewellyn, the government's political adviser, Bob Peirce, and several others, including his press secretary Kerry McGlynn, were unswerving in their belief that Britain had a moral duty to protect and enhance freedom and democracy in Hong Kong, even at the risk of alienating China. Nor did their attitude spring only from the feeling that the British should depart from their last significant colony with pride and honour. Many of them found it bizarre that Whitehall should set so much greater store by the bilateral relationship with China than by the indirect but organic growth in trade and influence which Britain enjoyed throughout the region as a result of its presence in the enterprise capital of Asia. Britain's trade with Hong Kong was three times more valuable than the direct flow of exports to the People's Republic. In any case, trade between Britain and China had grown sharply despite the presence of the 'Triple Violator' in Hong Kong. Between 1990 and 1995, Britain's exports to China had risen by 75 per cent. The share of this trade which flowed into the People's Republic through Hong Kong had risen from 24 to 36 per cent, and it was to rise dramatically again, to 46 per cent, in 1996.

Although he remained grateful for what he continued to regard as the generally excellent service provided to Government House by the Foreign Office, Patten viewed with mounting incredulity the gap between style and substance which often seemed to permeate the departments with which, through his advisers, he had most contact. 'There is a difference between real diplomacy and shaking hands and smiling,' he said. In some parts of the Foreign Office, the failure to make that distinction had become 'part of the wallpaper', a weakness which, he suspected, 'sometimes affects our dealings with, and attitudes to, other parts of the world as well'.

In respect of Hong Kong at least, this criticism was damning, but the implications of Whitehall's shortcomings were far less damaging than they might have been had anyone other than Patten been governor. None of his predecessors, diplomats rather than politicians, would have had either the authority or the willpower to withstand the persistent pressure from the Foreign Office to compromise again and again to placate Beijing. Even if they had been blessed with an appetite for bureaucratic infighting, they lacked the institutional and political clout to prevail against a Whitehall consensus which implicitly, if not always consciously, favoured 'co-operation'. To the frustration of some mandarins, Patten's unique advantage, from the point of view of Government House, was that he could, and, whenever necessary, did, bypass the Whitehall machine to press his case directly with his former colleagues in the Cabinet. They did not easily forget that his predecessors had, in matters of policy, been answerable to them.

As he looked towards his final full year in office, Patten was in no mood to be diverted from his course. The public indignation in Hong Kong over China's brutish attitude towards the Bill of Rights could, he thought, increasingly give way to apprehension, and he was worried that people would begin to 'vote with their feet'. The demand for foreign passports was growing steadily; any surge in that demand would not only undermine confidence in the colony's future but had the potential to trigger the mass exodus which was the great unspoken fear of every senior official. Patten still retained a residual hope that the Chinese position was perhaps given a harder edge than they intended by the individuals they had chosen as spokesmen or advisers in Hong Kong. In his opinion, most of these representatives 'couldn't persuade their way out of a paper bag . . . They display all the finesse of a bacon-slicer when dealing with some of these issues.' In any case, his self-appointed and overriding task now was to promote Hong Kong's liberties in every possible forum in the colony itself, in London and in every other significant capital city.

It touches on something I'm beginning to feel more and more. That is that what happens here is at the heart of the debate about what happens in China, both economically and politically. And for Chinese spokesmen to be so nervous about what sort of slogans people should be allowed, under the law, to shout in the streets in Hong Kong, suggests a lack of self-confidence which doesn't bode particularly well.

Yet for many citizens, it was the economy rather than politics which remained the most significant factor in their personal lives. George Chen was born in Hong Kong in the 1950s. His father was one of the thousands of Chinese who had fled Shanghai when the Communists took over in 1949. George had a conventional upbringing until he was a teenager, when he met Rowena, the girl who was to become his wife, at their piano-teacher's house. They fell in love almost at once, and although they were both only seventeen, they were determined to marry as soon as possible. Their parents thought that they were too young, and said so. They decided to elope, and emigrated to Canada. When they arrived in Vancouver they had two suitcases and 500 Canadian dollars between them. Financing their way through college by working part-time as shop assistants, they graduated, and six years later went back to Hong Kong as Canadian citizens to register their marriage. Two years after their return they set up a trading company, buying and selling cheap clothes. Rowena, who had always wanted to be a fashion designer, taught herself how to sketch and to cut fabrics and began to experiment with her own designs. Within a few years the company had expanded enough to finance the purchase of a garment factory in China, and Rowena was marketing her designs under her own label.

In the boom of the late 1980s, their principal market was in Japan. 'We positioned ourselves to serve the better end of the market . . . the only thing we worried about was how much could we produce. Did we have enough capacity to meet the demand?' George explained. Then the Far Eastern bubble burst and suddenly their company was on the point of collapse. The Chens decided to take advantage of the new opportunities opening up in China's rush towards capitalism. In corporate terms, they were minnows, but they knew that to survive they had to move faster than everyone else. In the fiercely competitive world they had chosen to inhabit this meant ensuring that the Chinese factories in which they had invested produced clothes of a range, quality and price which would attract their customers – wholesalers and retailers in other parts of Asia and Europe. By 1993 their high-turnover, high-risk business had seemed secure and the Chens had laid plans to expand further in China, producing clothes to meet the burgeoning consumer demand in the north, which was starting to benefit from an economy growing at upwards of 15 per cent a year.

George Chen's world was bounded by horizons which seemed limitless. He dreamed of creating an 'information highway' for the clothes trade.

> The customer comes to see me. We sit down. I ask him, 'What do you want? Tell me your total concept.' After I've listened to him, I say: 'These are the fabrics you want. This is the factory you should go to. This is the design . . .' My customer is not buying a product, but a collection, so that he can create a market. My vision is to mastermind the whole process, from the production of the material right through to what the customer buys. We have a project in China for a million-square-foot shopping mall. We are going to put different retailers into the mall and we will manage them collectively, doing all their merchandise. Different labels for a specific market. That is two hundred shops with two hundred different needs all coming back to me along my information highway. So I am very excited.

George Chen was not only infatuated by his 'concepts', but with the jargon of hi-tech commerce. He explained that he and his wife could not realise their vision without their base in Hong Kong, because Hong Kong was at the 'interface' of China and his potential markets in the rest of the world. Likewise, in terms of fashion, it was the 'interface' between Western designs and the Chinese consumer. 'Without Hong Kong, I very much doubt that I could be in business. Singapore? I doubt it. Shanghai? Maybe in ten years' time.'

Except ethnically, both George and Rowena Chen seemed to be children of the West, embracing 'global-village' assumptions in style and manners. And yet their notion of freedom did not readily embrace the concept of democracy. For the Chens, freedom was defined vaguely in terms of 'lifestyle', not of political representation or the accountability of the executive, nor even of the right to free speech and assembly. When he spoke of such matters, George Chen's techno-fluency faltered.

> What is politics? This is a new language for us. I'm patriotic, but patriotic to what? Let's forget about it. Let's hold on to our normal life. Hong Kong is so busy, we have never had spare time to think

about politics . . . You talk about freedom . . . The question is, does it affect me? I'm a very selfish guy . . . the monetary thing is very important to me. I have a young family. If the political situation changes so that I cannot make my living here, or I cannot maintain my lifestyle, then I would move on . . . If Hong Kong cannot give that to me, then in order to maintain our dreams and continue our life, maybe somewhere else could satisfy our needs.

The recurrence of the word 'lifestyle' spoke partly of glossy magazines and holiday brochures but, for the Chens, it clearly defined somewhat more than this, however imprecisely. Their work was all-consuming. They wanted the 'good things', but they seemed to have them already: they ate in good restaurants, they had a bright, fast car, and their apartment was expensively furnished. They did not seek leisure; on the contrary, leisure was for them a form of idleness, an indulgence they could not afford and did not crave. Their 'lifestyle' encompassed the right and the ability to travel freely and to set up their stall in the global marketplace. For them, freedom of speech and freedom of assembly lacked intrinsic merit but were accidental and agreeable, if inexplicable, byproducts of the capitalist system. They were clearly bewildered by the notion of representative democracy. From their perspective, Chris Patten's row with the Chinese was 'unnecessary', a conflict about 'face' between the two sovereign powers which threatened to damage their interests. Nevertheless it left them 'uneasy' and on the alert. If the outcome was good for business they would stay; if not, using their Canadian passports, they would quietly slip away. They had a choice, but they did not yet have to decide.

As if to confirm the governor's somewhat broader anxieties, on 13 December 1995 China sentenced its most prominent dissident, Wei Jingsheng, to another fourteen years' imprisonment for allegedly attempting to overthrow the government. Wei Jingsheng was familiar with Chinese prisons: he had served almost fifteen years in jail before being paroled in 1993 during China's unsuccessful bid to host the 2000 Olympic Games. He was rearrested the following year after meeting a senior human-rights official from the United States and held incommunicado until the subversion charges which led to his sentence were finally laid against him. Although the Chinese authorities had said that he would have an 'open' trial, all journalists and foreign diplomats were barred from the proceedings, which were conducted in secret and lasted five hours. According to the evidence presented against him, Wei Jingsheng's capital offence included alleged plans to purchase newspapers and to establish a Hong Kong-registered company to organise non-governmental cultural and artistic activities, and thereby to set up a 'propaganda and liaison base [in an attempt] to raise a storm powerful enough to shake up the present government'. The three judges took thirty-five minutes to reach their verdict.

The United States and major European Union governments at once condemned the sentence, and in Hong Kong, even pro-Beijing legislators expressed their abhorrence of the harshness shown by the regime. As several commentators observed, Article 45 of the Chinese constitution, on which Wei Jingsheng had based his unsuccessful defence, was replicated almost word for word in Article 27 of the Basic Law, which reads: 'Hong Kong residents shall have freedom of speech, of the press and of publication; freedom of association, of assembly, of processions and of demonstration; and the right and freedom to form trades unions, and to strike.' Wei Jingsheng was convicted of subversion against the state, an offence which would be a crime under Article 23 of the Basic Law after the handover. It was hardly surprising that those in Hong Kong who treasured their legitimate freedom were consumed by trepidation.

For Chris Patten personally, it was discouraging to receive at precisely this moment an emissary from Lambeth Palace, who told him that the archbishop of Canterbury, George Carey, would not be accepting an open invitation to stay at Government House on his forthcoming visit to the colony. Carey had evidently been advised by the Anglican bishop of Hong Kong that it would be 'unhelpful' and an 'unnecessary provocation to China' to be seen to consort with the governor. Recalling ruefully the enthusiasm for democracy and human rights displayed by both Lambeth Palace and the Synod before his departure from England in 1992, Patten did not remonstrate with Lambeth Palace, but away from the spotlight he was scornful of what he regarded as a feeble-minded and cowardly decision.

Not to be outdone, Carey's predecessor as archbishop of Canterbury, Robert Runcie, also chose to ally himself with what Patten's closest friends regarded as Lambeth Palace's 'trahison des clercs' by writing to say that he, too, would be declining the hospitality offered by Government House when he came to Hong Kong. In explanation, he informed the governor that he had consulted two specialists, Sir Percy Cradock and Sir Edward Heath, both of whom had counselled him against accepting the hospitality of Her Majesty's representative in Hong Kong. Patten assumed that the clerics had been advised that the prospect of ending religious persecution in China would be enhanced if they took care to avoid causing the regime in Beijing unnecessary offence. For him it was further dispiriting evidence that the 'warm-afterglow' school of diplomacy was not confined to the Foreign Office or to the business community.

Patten shrugged off these discourtesies, although he was not able to disguise the hurt they momentarily caused. More to the point, the accumulation of petty slights reinforced his prediction that the last year of his governorship would be no less testing than the first four. He presumed that the Chinese would continue to be difficult and obstructive in 1996 and he was resigned to the likelihood of even more debilitating arguments with the Foreign Office. He knew that the mandarins' case was, superficially, persuasive – even to the point where some members of the Cabinet might begin to recycle it. 'Look, we've gone a long way with Chris, it is now time to face up to reality,' he could hear them saying to each other. 'What happens after 1997 will happen. We have to deal with China, so let's not put unnecessary obstacles in the path of that relationship.'

There were rare moments to be relished. In the middle of December, the leadership of the People's Republic used a meeting of the Joint Liaison Group to express its dismay at Patten's proposal to increase Hong Kong's nugatory welfare budget to take better care of the elderly. The leader of the Chinese side, Chen Zuo'er, evidently encouraged by Lu Ping, denounced Patten in a sustained burst of petulance, culminating in the charge that the governor was a 'big dictator'. Entertained by the idea that China could regard him simultaneously as a big dictator and a lame duck, Patten nonetheless asked the Foreign Office to make an official complaint about this unwarranted interference in Hong Kong's internal affairs. In the absence of an ambassador (Ma Yuzhen had returned to Beijing, and his successor had not yet been appointed), the hapless Chinese chargé d'affaires, Wang Qilang, was summoned to the Foreign Office to receive a dressing-down from the deputy under-secretary, Andrew Burns, during which he was told that the Chinese outburst could be interpreted as jeopardising the level of autonomy for Hong Kong promised by China after 1997. The Chinese official appeared chastened and, evidently caught off guard, even acknowledged that welfare spending was important.

Such priceless incidents aside, Patten's pessimism was aggravated by a flurry of anecdotal evidence that a growing number of people in Hong Kong were losing their residual confidence in China's good faith. He had his own example, the case of a prominent doctor who told him that he was about to take early retirement. Patten asked him why. 'Well,' the doctor explained, 'if I retire now I can be sure of receiving my pension. But if I wait another five years, who knows?' The governor reminded him that he had rights under the law of contract; that there was an agreement with the Chinese government and that his pension entitlement would have to be honoured. The doctor replied, 'Yes, my wife said you'd say that.'

'What more could you say?' Patten reflected. It was a small but bleak reminder of Hong Kong's fragility.

18

'THANK YOU FOR THE VISAS,
PRIME MINISTER'

John Major Brings Good News

L ate in the evening of Saturday 6 January 1996, the British foreign secretary, Malcolm Rifkind, arrived in Hong Kong. The follow-ing day he joined the governor and his predecessor Douglas Hurd, who was in Hong Kong on private business as a director of the NatWest Bank, for a day-long walk on Lantau Island. It was, according to one of those involved, a 'very good bonding session'. At a three-hour working dinner that night at Government House, Chris Patten's ad hoc team of advisers (Martin Dinham, Bob Peirce and Edward Llewellyn were joined, significantly, on this occasion by the chief secretary, Anson Chan, and the financial secretary, Donald Tsang) briefed Rifkind in detail on the most pressing questions facing them. 'He'd read about all the issues in his briefing papers, but the case is much more persuasive when you're hearing about them from the individuals directly affected,' one of Patten's team noted. They lobbied him 'pretty hard' on visa-free access for SAR passport-holders. Rifkind also came under pressure from legislators, from the Executive Council and from businessmen, which 'helped finally to convince him that visa-free access was extremely important'.

At an open session in the Legislative Council, he parried questions about visa-free access, but he was given a rough ride when he informed his audience that the government's decision not to grant UK passports to Britain's soon-to-be former subjects was irreversible. Afterwards, in private, he said that Patten, as governor, was bound to act as Hong Kong's champion; as foreign secretary, he thought it would not be 'reasonable or appropriate' to give British citizenship to 'millions of people who have an identity that is essentially Chinese'. This was virtually the only point of disagreement between himself and Patten. However, on the eve of his departure, Rifkind reassured Patten that, in relation to visa-free access, he had finally been persuaded by the evidence to remove himself from the political fence on which he had perched for so long. For the future record, he confirmed this, albeit inexplicitly: 'I shall be making it very clear where I stand to my colleagues in the near future. I will be making a recommendation, because it needs collective discussion. I shall be making a clear and unequivocal recommendation.' His caution was understandable: like Patten, he knew very well that Michael Howard was not only a dogged opponent but that he might easily be joined by his predecessor as home secretary, Ken Clarke, who was an even more formidable member of the government.

Rifkind left Hong Kong on Tuesday 9 January for Beijing, where he was given a warm welcome by the Chinese leadership. Despite the fact that the visit coincided with the transmission in Britain of *The Dying Rooms*, a horrifying television documentary about the ill-treatment and neglect of Chinese orphans, Qian Qichen was evidently in 'warm-up' mood. He even invited the foreign secretary to look round the orphanage at the centre of the scandal to see it for himself, an invitation which Rifkind neatly sidestepped. After a three-hour formal meeting, the foreign secretary emerged to announce that the two sides had reached an understanding on a range of matters. As it happened, the Joint Liaison Group negotiations on the details of the SAR passport had progressed more slowly than had been anticipated, and so, fortuitously, Rifkind's delayed visit now coincided with an interim agreement on the main technical points. This meant that the two sides were able to sign a formal minute covering these issues, which had, in fact, been finalised only the previous day in the JLG. According to one of the individuals closely involved, the agreement, which was not published, stipulated that the SAR passport would be available only in Hong Kong, to people who had permanent Hong Kong identity cards, and that it could be issued only by the Hong Kong immigration authorities. Nor, he added dryly, could the passport easily be faked: 'We are to have a computer system which will digitise details of the passport . . . this is a facility which can't be replicated in Guangdong or the Chinese embassy in Bratislava.' As a result, Britain would now be willing to endorse the SAR passport as a bona-fide travel document, a commitment which would be crucial in persuading other states of its validity.

Rifkind also briefed the media that the Cabinet would decide within two to three months whether or not to grant visa-free access to people holding SAR passports. The one issue which was not yet resolved, and which the British side had originally asserted would be a sine qua non of granting visa-free access, was the 'eligibility' criterion: who would or would not be granted these passports? This question begged another: who would be granted right of abode in Hong Kong after 1997? Beijing's utterances on this matter had been so impenetrable as to confuse every constitutional specialist, each of whom was driven to the conclusion that China did not yet itself know the answer. Six weeks later, Beijing had still not responded to this question. Scores of thousands of Hong Kong Chinese living in Canada, the United States, Australia and elsewhere still had no idea whether, or on what terms, they would be granted right of abode in the future SAR, and therefore, whether they would be eligible for an SAR passport. In December, China had sent a diplomatic note to most UN states asking them to enter negotiations with Beijing about 'reciprocal' visa agreements, implying obliquely that in the absence of such an agreement, the SAR might require visas for visiting foreigners. As one of Patten's team put it, 'Some of these countries, I think, are likely to reply to the Chinese note that they'd love to be able to take a decision about visa arrangements, but that they will need a clarification on the right-of-abode issue before they do that.'

In London, despite the efforts of the foreign secretary, Michael Howard remained intransigent. Britain, he thought, had been unwise to grant UK citizenship to three million BNO passport-holders, and he was not going to compound that error by extending visa-free access to a further 3 million Hong Kong citizens. However, a decision could not be postponed indefinitely. The prime minister was due to make his last visit to Hong Kong at the beginning of March, by now only a matter of weeks away. If he failed to confirm the visa-free status of the SAR passport, the reputation of the British government would plummet. Patten's advisers made it clear to London that if Major were to arrive empty-handed, his visit would be a diplomatic disaster. According to Patten himself, Major's visit was to prove the decisive factor. 'It was the fact that he became personally interested in, and committed to the issues. At every stage of nuancing on all the issues we resolved, the prime minister's instincts and decency took him into a position nearer to Hong Kong rather than further away from Hong Kong,' he explained. With the prime minister on side, Rifkind had a one-to-one meeting with Howard ten days before Major's departure, at which, related a Patten aide, the foreign secretary 'set out all the arguments we've been using – in particular, of course, that this decision was one that could be reviewed, like all other visa arrangements: if there was abuse or trouble, a visa regime could be imposed'.

Howard, who was still obsessed by the prospect of a flood of Hong Kong Chinese pouring into Britain, now knew that he was not only outnumbered, but likely to be a lone voice in the Cabinet. He surrendered. His friends would later maintain that he was eventually persuaded by Rifkind's presentation of the case, and especially by the point that if a catastrophe in Hong Kong should lead to a stampede of refugees, Britain and all other countries would be obliged to impose a visa 'regime' on both BNO and SAR passport-holders to control the potential deluge of immigrants. Patten's colleagues, however, insist that Howard was well aware of these arguments from the start, and that his climbdown was calculated to avoid a debate in the Cabinet which he knew he would lose. As one of them put it, 'He wasn't overruled by the PM or by the Cabinet, because he was ultimately prepared to sign a recommendation to the Cabinet that visa-free access should be allowed.'

At the beginning of March 1996, John Major arrived in Hong Kong from London via Bangkok after a trying domestic week for his government. After the Commons debate on the Scott Report into the 'Arms to Iraq' scandal, a testy Anglo–Irish summit and many late-night phone conversations with the taoiseach, John Bruton, Major had flown to Thailand for the first heads-of-government meeting between European and Asian leaders, where he met the Chinese premier (to discuss Hong Kong) and the Vietnamese premier (to discuss the Boat People still languishing in camps in the British colony). After two days in Bangkok, he flew into Hong Kong and went immediately to the governor's country residence in the New Territories. There, in the relative balm of Fanling, he worked with Patten to put the finishing touches to a speech he was to make to the Chamber of Commerce, which was to be widely regarded as the most important statement of British attitudes towards Hong Kong and China since the Joint Declaration in 1984. It was certain to be the last such speech made by a British prime minister.

After their return from Fanling to Government House for a formal dinner in the banqueting hall on the eve of his speech, Major and Patten retreated upstairs to the governor's private sitting room for a final meeting with their closest aides. Very late on that Sunday night, Major made clear his view that it would not be enough merely to say that Britain would watch closely what happened in Hong Kong after 1997; it was vital to demonstrate that no future prime ministers, within the limits of their power and influence, would merely look on. The speech was once more adapted to reflect that very personal commitment.

On Monday 4 March, Major delivered the speech, which had been drafted by Patten himself with the help of the government's political adviser, Bob Peirce, whose influence had grown rapidly since his recent appointment, and Edward Llewellyn. It began with a lucid exposition of Hong Kong's remarkable economic development, highlighting the 'energy, dynamism, the sheer guts in business enterprise' and the vital contribution made to the territory's pre-eminent role in Asia that flowed from the commitment to the rule of law, individual freedom and the free movement of information. Reminding his audience at the British Chamber of Commerce that these values had been underpinned by the Joint Declaration, Major reported bluntly that at his meeting with Li Peng the two leaders had reached no agreement on the future of the Legislative Council, or on the issues relating to the Bill of Rights. 'We did not agree to disagree, we just disagreed,' he added. 'We are not going to leave it there . . . We will say only what we do believe. We do not, and will not, simply lie down and accept what we are told.' He went on to warn China and to reassure Hong Kong. 'If there were any suggestion of a breach of the Joint Declaration, we would have a duty to pursue every legal and other avenue available to us . . . Britain's commitment to Hong Kong will not end next summer. Far from it.' Then, to Chris Patten's delight, in the passage he had rewritten the night before to toughen up the Government House draft, the prime minister announced:

> We in Britain will have continuing responsibilities to the people of Hong Kong, not just a moral responsibility as the former colonial power, and as staunch friends of Hong Kong, but a specific responsibility as a signatory to the Joint Declaration. We shall watch, vigilant, over the implementation of the treaty to which Britain and China have solemnly committed themselves . . . Every member of the international community, all Hong Kong's friends and partners around the world, in both hemispheres and five continents, will be watching to see that the letter and spirit of the Joint Declaration are honoured, now, next year and for fifty years beyond. And we will be making sure that they do.

These were not the words of a sinologist anxious to retreat to China's 'bottom line', nor the product of the collective wisdom of those officials in the Foreign Office and the DTI whose priority was to 'warm up' the relationship with Beijing. As the democratic majority in Hong Kong recognised at once, the prime minister's declaration of intent was an act of statesmanship, an express commitment from which no future British government would find it easy to resile. Major's decision to throw down the gauntlet in these terms had not been taken lightly. The foreign secretary, who was consulted, shared the view that the time was right to be unequivocal about Britain's readiness to mobilise international public opinion.

The prime minister had another piece of news, which he had revealed an hour earlier at a closed session of the Legislative Council, and repeated publicly in his speech. 'I have reflected carefully on this with my Cabinet colleagues in London, in the light of the powerful arguments made by the governor, the Legislative Council, by business people and by the wider community in Hong Kong in recent months,' he told his audience. 'The answer is, yes, we shall extend visa-free access [to SAR passport-holders].' Under the terms of Major's announcement, SAR passport-holders would be free to enter Britain for up to six months but, as in all other such cases, they would be forbidden to work, study or draw social security.

News of Major's announcement, though it had not been unexpected, spread fast. Within two hours of his address, the prime minister went on a walkabout in the New Territories town of Shatin, where, in places, the crowd was twenty feet deep. Many shouted out, 'Thank you for the visas, Prime Minister.' At a primary school he shook hands with six-year-old Yip Kwan Ho. 'He is the King of England,' she beamed proudly. It was not the kind of welcome to which the beleaguered leader of an unpopular government was accustomed.

The media in Hong Kong were surprised and thrilled by this prime ministerial pledge. 'YOU'LL NEVER WALK ALONE' was the banner headline the following morning in the *Eastern Express*, and, in its leading article, the *South China Morning Post* commented,

> Just for once, a visiting minister did not fail to live up to expectations. Indeed he exceeded them . . . Mr Major struck an impressive note. After the trade-obsessed approach of deputy prime minister Michael Heseltine, whose evasiveness so angered legislators during their recent visit to London, it was refreshing to hear yesterday's pledge . . . such a pledge provides that, in the unlikely event things did go wrong after the handover, Britain would not wash its hands of the problem.

There was an unexpected bouquet from a newspaper which was not renowned for its enthusiasm for the colonial administration. 'MAJOR MOVE SAVES BRITAIN'S HONOUR', the *Hong Kong Standard* declared, praising his decision, after 'all the years of weasel words and humming and hawing that Hong Kong people have had to endure', to grant every holder of an SAR passport visa-free access to Britain after all.

Major's speech was somewhat less well received by some of his own backbenchers and their acolytes in the tabloid media who shared Michael Howard's prejudice. 'OPEN INVITE TO 2 MILLION' was the banner headline in the *Daily Express*. John Wardle, a former immigration minister, warned that the change would lead to further abuses of the system, and that anyone, like the foreign secretary, who thought otherwise was 'talking through his head'. Teresa Gorman, a 'rent-a-quote' right-winger, demanded 'urgent reassurance' from the government and warned shrilly, 'We had better be prepared for the worst.' Norman Tebbit, who had been bitterly opposed to the 1990 Nationality Scheme, commented caustically, 'I wonder how much money John Major has collected for the party in Hong Kong.' Yet this backlash lacked teeth: Major's enemies in his own party were far too preoccupied with plotting against him over Europe to waste more than a spasm of energy on the distant 'threat' from Hong Kong.

In the colony there was a further cause for rejoicing. At 8am, on the morning of Major's speech, Jack Edwards, a seventy-seven-year-old British expatriate who had for ten years led a one-person crusade on behalf of a dwindling band of Hong Kong war widows denied full UK citizenship, had arrived outside Government House with his Union Jack and a petition for the prime minister. Edwards, himself a former prisoner of war, was far from optimistic that the British government could be persuaded at this late stage to legislate in favour of the remaining twenty-nine wives and widows of ethnic Chinese subjects who had fought for king and country in the Second World War. Edwards did not know that the governor shared his view that the British stance was both shameful and unsustainable, and that in fact Patten had been lobbying London accordingly for at least nine months, albeit to no apparent effect. He was surprised, therefore, when one of the governor's aides came down to the front gates and asked him to return at midday.

Once again, it was the home secretary who had been the stumbling block. His particular fear in this matter was that a host of other 'special cases' would be tacked on to any primary legislation designed to appease the war widows, thus, as he saw it, reopening the floodgates for a Chinese invasion from Hong Kong which he hoped had been dammed permanently in 1990. However, neither Howard nor indeed the British government had bargained for the wave of disgust the callousness of this attitude would create. In 1994, under pressure from Government House and the House of Lords, the home secretary had grudgingly agreed to send a letter to the twenty-nine widows reassuring each of them that, in return for their 'late husband's services to Hong Kong', they would, after all, be free to enter Britain at any time and to settle there if they so wished. However, he explained, they would not have a right to a British passport. This concession served only to inflame the moral outrage of Jack Edwards and the international body of opinion which he had helped to mobilise. The force of their case – that Britain owed these elderly women British citizenship in view of the sacrifice made by their husbands' service to the crown – continued to reverberate. Their cries left a powerful and potentially indelible impression that, on this issue, the British government had demonstrated at best an impoverished sense of honour. It was a failure of political imagination which left Patten quite incredulous.

The issue remained unresolved until the weekend before Major's departure for Hong Kong, when he was given his brief for the visit together with the draft of his speech to the British Chamber of Commerce. At this point he decided to act with the decency ascribed to him by the governor. According to a member of Patten's team, there began at once a 'great flurry of activity' which continued until after the prime minister's arrival in Bangkok. The Private Office at Number 10 was instructed to ask the Home Office for some new options for progress. Initially, Michael Howard was reluctant to respond and, according to his friends, capitulated only when it became quite clear to him that the prime minister was determined to 'bear good tidings' with him to Hong Kong. In the volte-face necessary to accommodate this political imperative, Howard 'discovered' that, after all, it would be possible to introduce into Parliament a 'carefully circumscribed' private member's bill which would not have the damaging implications for immigration that he had until that moment foreseen.

When Jack Edwards returned to Government House at midday as instructed, he was unaware that at the time of his earlier visit the prime minister had been about to inform LegCo that the British government had relented. Now he was ushered in to see John Major, who walked up to him, placed a hand on his arm and said, 'I've got some good news for you.' Edwards left, visibly affected, for a round of radio and television interviews. In one of these, he said of Major, pointing to his now redundant petition, 'I have called him a hypocrite before and I have called him all sorts of names. But today he is a gentleman.'

The last-minute decision to provide passports for war widows and visa-free access for SAR passport-holders still left one group of British subjects without the protection of a full British passport or the right to carry an SAR passport – the 'ethnic minorities', most of whose families had emigrated to Hong Kong from the Indian subcontinent, where they had become subjects of the British crown. Although Beijing did propose to grant this group right of abode in Hong Kong, albeit as officially stateless persons, they would be unable to travel as Chinese citizens. Only those fortunate enough to have acquired one of the 50,000 British passports available under the 1990 British Nationality Act had the security, protection and identity of citizenship. The endemic anomalies and apparent arbitrary nature of this selection process had served only to exacerbate the anxiety and dismay of the leaders of the Indian community. The situation was particularly painful for a group which was not only closely knit and self-contained but also bound together by ties of blood in a network of extended families. Only a minority of the 5,000 or so citizens of Indian origin had been granted British passports, and the relief of these 'winners' was tempered by the knowledge that their friends, brothers, sisters, sons and daughters had emerged as losers.

One of the most prominent Indian families in Hong Kong was led by Hari Harilela, who emigrated to the colony as a young man in the mid-1930s. Working first as a newspaper-vendor and then as a salesman, he went on to create a chain of hotels which, by the time of Patten's arrival in Hong Kong, had given him a substantial entrepreneurial toe-hold throughout the region as well as in Britain, Canada and the United States. In the manner of a minor maharaja, he had built a palatial Indian compound in Kowloon containing separate apartments which were allocated to upwards of forty relations spanning three generations. His contribution as a pillar of the Indian community – he was a longstanding justice of the peace – had been recognised, in 1979, with the award of an OBE. Harilela was more perplexed than angry to discover that he and his wife would be granted British citizenship while his son, who was nineteen and had a shareholding in the family empire worth HK$100 million, had been rejected. Too proud, and perhaps too embarrassed, to suggest openly that the British government's attitude was tinged with racism, he could not fathom why his hard-working, law-abiding and prosperous family should be thought unfit to enjoy right of abode in Britain – which, as it happened, none of them wished to exercise, except in extremis. On their behalf, he felt humiliated.

We are a British-orientated people. I was shocked when we realised that we would be refused British passports – in my immediate family, out of six members, four get it and two don't. After all, we have been here for sixty years. My son's accent is just like yours, just like a British accent. In the case of my elder brother, his elder son has a passport, his second son is denied. It is so piecemeal, so arbitrary. Can you tell me why we have been rejected? We took the oath of allegiance to Her Majesty the Queen. Now we will be a broken family.

Hari Harilela's younger sister, Leila, said: 'My husband and I got rejected last week. My husband's younger brother will be sworn in next month. I was very upset, hurt. I was in tears. It is like a betrayal. All of a sudden we are nowhere.'

Despite the entreaties of the Indian community the British government's position on the issue had not changed. Following a report of the Foreign Affairs Select Committee in March 1994, the Home Office had stated explicitly that discrimination against them would be a factor in determining whether members of the ethnic minorities in Hong Kong had come 'under pressure' and therefore whether 'sympathetic consideration' should be given to an application to settle in Britain. Michael Howard had regarded even this 'concession' as one too many, and he was not now willing to go further. Yet again – as in the case of the SAR passport-holders and the war widows – the governor believed Howard's stance to be untenable. He was sharply aware that it lacked moral credibility, and he knew that in the run-up to 1997 Britain would come under increasing pressure to relent.

At Patten's instigation, Government House had started to lobby discreetly on behalf of the ethnic minorities in mid-1995, urging the Home Office to provide them with at least the same degree of protection that Howard had originally been prepared to offer the war widows – namely the right to settle in Britain if they chose to do so, albeit without the right to a British passport. Howard refused on familiar grounds; indeed, in the case of the ethnic minorities he had been even more stubborn. However, he had reckoned without the prime minister's 'decency' and his tacit alliance with Patten. At the instigation of Number 10, Malcolm Rifkind had lobbied Howard with what Patten described as 'considerable verve and tenacity' both before and after the prime minister's departure for Bangkok. Memoranda and draft statements flew between London, Hong Kong and Bangkok, but still Howard did not relent. Finally, a few hours before Major's flight from Bangkok to Hong Kong, Michael Heseltine, as his deputy, was drafted in on the prime minister's behalf. In the course of a long three-way telephone conference between Heseltine, Howard and Rifkind, the home secretary was finally persuaded to accept a new formula, which was put to Patten a few hours before the prime minister's arrival. Although the governor thought the proposed offer was still inadequate, he decided not to press for more at that stage, hoping that Howard had been driven to shift just far enough to deal with what he described as the 'real anxiety' among the ethnic minorities. Two days later, in Hong Kong, the prime minister duly announced the revised British position in his speech to the Chamber of Commerce: 'Let me make it clear to this group that we are prepared to guarantee – repeat, guarantee – admission and settlement if, at any time after 1 July, they were to come under pressure to leave Hong Kong.' As if to reassure the home secretary and his right-wing backers in the media, Major added: 'It is the position, of course, that this group do not wish to leave Hong Kong; they are settled here; their businesses are here; their family ties are here. But they want to be sure that if they come under pressure to leave they will have a country to go to. From today, they have that assurance.'

Major's visit was a rare success for the British government. Martin Lee was moved to comment that the prime minister's speech was the 'strongest statement of support for Hong Kong yet from any British minister. At a time when we believe that the British interest in Hong Kong is only in terms of dollars, I think this is a very pleasant surprise.' Even Emily Lau, who had awarded Major 'ten out of a hundred' for passport commitments, was teased by him into conceding, 'Oh, all right, eleven, then.' The prime minister set off for London garlanded with accolades from the local media and reinvigorated by Patten's company. On the flight he was relaxed enough to share his feelings about the governor's virtues with the Westminster lobby correspondents travelling with him. His praise for Patten, particularly in an interview with the BBC's political editor, Robin Oakley, prompted that questing posse to draw the unanimous conclusion that the prime minister had deliberately chosen this moment to anoint the Hong Kong governor as his chosen successor as leader of the Conservative party.

Only thirty-six hours earlier the governor had himself said enough to persuade the Westminster media that he was intent on making a political comeback in Britain. Pressed by the assembled political editors, who betrayed distinctly more curiosity about his own future than they did about that of Hong Kong, he said, 'I am a political animal. I could not fail to be interested in the issues, and I follow what goes on at Westminster pretty closely.' Volunteering that he missed the atmosphere of the Commons, 'though not the clubbiness', he added, 'I am not ruling anything in, and I am not ruling anything out.' His remarks produced headlines in the British press the next day of the 'Patten signals his return to Commons' variety. Recalling that the governor had recently made a speech extolling the virtues of the so-called tiger economies of Asia, all of which maintained low levels of public spending, the journalists also reported that he had recently 'told friends' that he was becoming increasingly sceptical about the merits of a single currency. On this basis, they speculated that he was eager to shed his image as a Tory 'wet' in order to place himself in a stronger position from which to claim the Conservative crown.

In Britain, the apparent endorsement of the prime minister for Patten's supposed hunger for high office after the handover not only produced headlines, but led to a number of leading articles which fully exposed the raw wounds of a Conservative party racked by ideological conflict and personal animosity. When Patten saw these, he was shocked by the vituperation heaped on him by some commentators for daring to presume that the Conservative party would ever accept him as leader. Despite his tough political hide, he was hurt and bewildered. Attempting to make light of this hostility, he joked that at least he had managed to 'bring into an unholy union the *People's Daily* and some of the populist tabloids'. But a few days later he admitted, 'It didn't make me any more enthusiastic about the prospect of going back into British politics.' He knew that Major's remarks had been injudicious, if well meant, but, somewhat disingenuously, he observed, 'The prime minister did no more than say that he thought I was a decent bloke. I guess it would have been more of a story if he'd said what a terrible tosser I was. But he was kind and friendly and amiable about me. I should think he was surprised at the subsequent fuss.'

The truth was that Patten faced an insoluble dilemma. He knew that it would be exceptionally difficult to parachute back into British politics, even if a seat could be found for him. In any case, he was not yet at all sure that he wanted to re-enter that insular and incestuous world, which, viewed from Hong Kong, sometimes seemed to be dominated by the vanities of a preposterous cast of also-rans. He had already been approached directly by the local leaders of two safe Tory constituencies, who asked him if he would become their prospective parliamentary candidate in the forthcoming general election. One offered a new constituency in East Anglia, close to Major's Huntingdon stronghold; the other was – yet again – from Kensington and Chelsea, where, he was told, Nick Scott would either stand down voluntarily or be deselected to make way for him. Patten declined both invitations, repeating that since he still intended to remain in Hong Kong until the handover, it would be impossible for him to consider either of them: the election, as they all knew, would have to be held before the middle of May 1997 at the latest.

In April 1996, Patten confided that he thought the option remained 'live, but difficult', adding, oddly, 'not least because I don't have any roots in British politics'. He reiterated that, although there would be 'all sorts of hurdles to clear', if he did decide to re-enter the fray, he did not intend turning his back on political issues. 'I hope I can find another job in public service, but whether I want to go back into the House of Commons, or whether a constituency would have me, are both issues to resolve in the future.' Even though he had little appetite for the prospect of leading of a broken opposition party at war with itself over Europe, he did sometimes indulge in prime-ministerial reflections. With characteristic but not entirely convincing self-deprecation, he adopted a sporting metaphor to explain:

> If you are a club cricketer, I guess there are times in a hot bath after a game when you imagine yourself walking down the steps at Lord's. So when I go back to see John at Number Ten, I do think about what it would be like to live there myself. But if you ask me as a sentient, rational human being whether I think I will ever be prime minister of Great Britain and Northern Ireland, the answer is, no, I don't.

Two years earlier he had described the prospect of a return to British politics as remote. Now, a year away from the handover? 'Distant.' It gave him a moment of amused satisfaction to receive a letter from All Souls, Oxford at the height of this dramatic sideshow inviting him to become the next master. In truth, he did not spend a great deal of time thinking about what he would do in the future: there were too many imponderables and there was too much uncertainty. Moreover, there was still much to be done in Hong Kong.

Immediately after the prime minister's departure, the Chinese government reiterated that it would dismantle the Legislative Council and replace it with a provisional body that would be 'elected' later in the year, confounding Patten's earlier confidence that, in the end, Beijing would hold back from such drastic action. Soon afterwards, the members of the Beijing-appointed Preparatory Committee voted by 148 to 1 to endorse the Chinese threat. The only member to vote against the establishment of the provisional legislature, Frederick Fung, was not only reprimanded by the director of the Hong Kong and Macau Affairs Office but removed from the committee and told that he would not be permitted to play any further part in Hong Kong's future governance unless he was ready to recant. In private Patten responded to what he

described as a 'nasty, bullying bit of old-fashioned Leninism' with suppressed anger, noting that Beijing's 'decapitation' of Fung would send
'some pretty nasty messages around the world'.

Paradoxically, this latest example of intimidation, which happened to
coincide with another crackdown on 'dissidents' in China, offered
Patten some respite from the charge that his approach had been overly
confrontational. His persistent refusal to acknowledge the validity of
what was now widely regarded as a puppet body began to seem far less
obstinate than his critics had sought to establish. In public, he was seen
to occupy the high ground; in private he rejoiced that the heat was now
on China.

> Nobody can now seriously believe that the argument has been about
> whether or not we somehow broke the Joint Declaration or the
> Basic Law or the understandings or agreements between the two
> sides . . . The Joint Declaration is about establishing democracy in
> Hong Kong, the sort of democracy they have in Taiwan, Korea,
> Japan and – it has to be said – the same sort of democracy that we
> have in the United Kingdom. That's what China signed up to – the
> development of representative government. So don't let's have any
> more pretence that somehow the argument has been about the 'triple
> violations'. The only violations there may be will be from the
> Chinese side . . . They're in the throes of defining words in the Joint
> Declaration in their own terms.

In support of this contention he quoted China's foreign minister, Qian
Qichen, who had recently declared in a disconcerting blend of neo-
populist and sub-Marxist jargon: 'To mechanically ape the Western
democratic model does not accord with Hong Kong's actual
conditions.'

In his contempt for Beijing, Patten sometimes allowed himself to
invest the Joint Declaration with a far less equivocal commitment to
'Westminster' democracy than the wording of the treaty itself, with its
opaque references to elections, could sustain. Nonetheless, his essential
point was valid: China had wrenched the treaty's ambiguities out of
context in order to justify the suppression of democracy in Hong Kong.
Patten foresaw a long battle ahead after the handover. He noted
privately in April:

> I dare say we'll spend the next five or ten years arguing with China,
> and with some apologists for China, about whether democracy really
> means choosing your representative institution, or having it chosen

by the people of Hong Kong; about whether protecting human rights really means closing down newspapers and locking up editors, or whether it means allowing freedom of speech.

Patten could not speak in public about his fear of China's repressive intentions without risk of precipitating an onrush of panic in the population, but in private he was more scathing than ever about his critics, and in particular the sinologists in London. Unmoved by their case, he commented for the future record:

> Stripped of its sinuous charms, the argument amounts to this. You should have ratted, in practice if not in rhetoric, on the undertakings given to people in the Joint Declaration. You should have risked Britain leaving Hong Kong with maximum obloquy after years of fighting Martin Lee and the Democrats, after years of fighting internal opinion. And you should have accepted the undertaking to do China's dirty work for it, and to try to chloroform Hong Kong and international opinion as Hong Kong was frog-marched into the future. I think that would have been appalling.

It was the fiercest defence of his own approach he had yet essayed, and it was underpinned by the confidence that the roots of democracy in Hong Kong had grown much deeper since his arrival. Every significant poll showed that at least 60 per cent of the public continued to support the Democrats, despite the 'subversive' tag Beijing had placed so ostentatiously around the neck of Martin Lee:

> Nobody now doesn't know that there is a Hong Kong, and what is happening in Hong Kong, and I think that there is in Hong Kong enough momentum behind the development of representative government and civil society to make those things in the long term unstoppable. You can wind up the Legislative Council, but you can't actually wind up the sixty to seventy per cent of the population which still supports the Democratic party.

But you could, surely, crush that expression of support? 'Maybe for a bit . . . I don't believe that 30 June represents the end of democracy and pluralism in Hong Kong. I think those things may have been turned into papier mâché if one had followed some of the sinologists' advice.'

If he was right, the prospects for a confrontation between China and Hong Kong were greater, and more alarming, than he seemed able to recognise. Nevertheless, he took heart from his belief that, in the cliché so often deployed by optimists, China would not wittingly destroy the goose that laid the golden egg.

> What the Chinese are trying to do at the moment is to bludgeon public opinion into submission . . . What I think it all tells one is that they are very anxious about political control; that they are very sensitive about the extent to which civil society and democracy have developed in Hong Kong. And I fear that nervousness means they are handling these matters with a very shaky hand. It was very ham-fisted, very maladroit.

Patten's view that, on the one hand, China was not willing to tolerate dissent from a community which had become irreversibly pluralistic, while on the other, Beijing would contrive to avoid open confrontation with the people of Hong Kong after the handover, was contradictory. It was a flaw in his reasoning that he skirted for the time being by boasting that China's belligerence did not make it any more difficult for him to govern Hong Kong because 'it is such a clumsy piece of authoritarian artifice'.

Three days after Major's departure from Hong Kong, China started a nine-day missile test off the coast of Taiwan to 'preserve the territorial integrity' of the People's Republic. US naval forces were diverted into the area. Deng Xiaoping was reported to be 'very concerned' about this show of strength, and a Chinese source held that Beijing's policy had shifted from 'peaceful reunification' to 'defending reunification by force'. An official from the Foreign Ministry in Beijing said that the people of Hong Kong should not be worried but 'pleased with the strengthening of the power of defence of their own country'. Partly as a result of the tension over Taiwan, and partly because of a sharp fall in the US stock markets, the Hang Seng Index plunged by 820.34 points, or 7.3 per cent, to 10,397.45, the largest reverse recorded in the Asia–Pacific region. The financial secretary, Donald Tsang, claimed that there was no cause for alarm. In a telephone survey conducted by the *Apple Daily*, 50 per cent of respondents agreed that the live-ammunition exercise in Taiwan had undermined their confidence in China's commitment to the idea of 'one country, two systems', which had originally been applied by Deng to Taiwan and only later to Hong Kong.

At the end of March, the Royal Hong Kong Police had to move in with batons to quell a scuffle that almost became a riot after tens of thousands of people arrived en masse at the Wanchai Sports Stadium to register their applications for BNO passports twenty-four hours before the closing deadline. Although hundreds of extra staff had been drafted in to cope with the last-minute rush of applicants, emotions were running high. This stampede for BNO passports, coming as it did only three weeks after the British prime minister had assured the Hong Kong citizenry that SAR passports, for which all of those in the stadium would be eligible, would enjoy visa-free access to Britain, was an eloquent illustration of the tensions which ran only just below the placid surface of the colony. As one correspondent to the *South China Morning Post* wrote:

> I am ethnic Chinese and was born and bred in Hong Kong . . . the silent majority feel helpless. But they do not bother to take their discontent to the street, or make their voices heard through any channel. Their feelings will only be expressed in incidents like a scuffle in a crowd . . . I am glad I obtained my BNO passport long before the deadline for applications and did not need to join the queue the other day, otherwise I could have been involved in a scuffle too . . . I would rather be a third-class national of Britain than a 'loyal' and 'patriotic' Chinese puppet.

In one of Beijing's crasser attempts to secure the allegiance of Hong Kong, the civil service came under increasing pressure to demonstrate its 'patriotism'. Soon after the 'decision' by the Preparatory Committee to set up a 'provisional' legco, officials in Beijing issued a statement in which they tried to coerce Hong Kong's civil servants into showing their loyalty to the future sovereign power. Civil servants should offer to co-operate with the provisional legco, even at the expense of violating their obligations to the present sovereign, a spokesman cautioned; otherwise, they would not be able to 'transit' into senior posts after the handover. This caused such a spasm of alarm that Beijing half withdrew the threat, though not before its significance had hit home. Such pressure on the civil service had become a source of growing anxiety at Government House. Nine months earlier, one of Patten's most senior advisers had identified the threat to Hong Kong's civil servants as coming from a disparate combination of Chinese officials (both within Hong Kong and on the mainland), the Bank of China and the People's Liberation Army, 'each thinking that 1997 would tip the balance in their favour', albeit against one another. The aide argued then:

> There will be no institutional defence against Peking if they decide, damn it, we're going to crush Hong Kong. That is a possibility. But if Peking sobers up, then it is a matter of the Hong Kong system being strong enough to resist encroachments from the Public Security Bureau telephoning the police and saying, 'That bloke you

arrested the other day is actually a friend of mine. Could you please just deliver him to the border and not put him on trial?' Or a Chinese company leaning on someone in the Legislative Council, or someone on the Central Tendering Board saying, 'If you know what is good for you, deal us into this consortium.' It is that we have to guard against, and that all depends on the individuals in the system.

At that time, Patten's advisers believed that Hong Kong's protection in this sense hung, by a thread, on a handful of the colony's most senior public servants, including the chief secretary, Anson Chan; the financial secretary Donald Tsang; Michael Sze, now head of the Hong Kong Trade and Development Corporation; and the constitutional secretary, Nicholas Ng. The pivotal figure was Anson Chan: were she to resign or to retire before the handover, Hong Kong's self-confidence would be irreparably damaged. 'I don't think there is anyone who matters as much as she does,' Patten noted. 'If she stays, if she is part of the system, then a lot of other decent people will stay as well . . . If she goes, it will be a very bad blow. For other, very good, civil servants, I think, she is the determining factor in whether they stay in public service.' Although the civil service was blessed with a wealth of talent at first-secretary level (individuals who might expect to inherit the top jobs within a decade or so), they did not yet have the experience or authority to take over. If Anson Chan and her most senior colleagues were unable to sustain the pressure from China, Hong Kong, in the view of a Patten adviser, would soon be left with a 'flabby, Third World bureaucracy' which would rapidly succumb to the predators from the mainland. Patten and his aides were keenly aware that an exodus from the civil service could easily be triggered by Beijing's bullying ineptitude. In the words of one senior official:

You can't underestimate the extent to which these people have options . . . They've all enjoyed tremendous asset inflation over the last few years . . . Anyone who took out a loan immediately after Tiananmen is sitting on several million dollars of profit. So you can sell your three-bedroomed apartment here, buy a six-bedroomed ranch in Vancouver and still have several million in the bank. It is pretty tempting when you compare that with the prospect of having to deal with Lu Ping's emotional outbursts, and the creeps from the NCNA trotting around poking their noses in your files.

Now, in the spring of 1996, the focus of media attention began to switch from Patten to Anson Chan. In the two and a half years since her appointment as chief secretary she had become a very public figure. Her dress sense was closely observed while her penchant for ballroom dancing had rejuvenated the foxtrot and the quickstep at every fashionable party she attended. The public was by now familiar with her potted life story: how she had been born in Shanghai in 1940, the daughter of a famous painter and the granddaughter of a Chinese general who fought with great gallantry in three separate wars, only to be assassinated in the year after her birth; how her parents had fled to Hong Kong, and how the star pupil had joined the civil service in 1962 and risen steadily through the ranks to become Hong Kong's first high-flying female public official; how her uncle, Harry Fang, a distinguished doctor, maintained a close relationship with the family of Deng Xiaoping because he had attended the Chinese leader's disabled son; and how, over the years, she had demonstrated great administrative flair but developed an ill-concealed animosity towards the media. It was well known that this hostility originated from an incident in 1986, when, as director of the Social Welfare Department, Chan had presided over an over-enthusiastic posse of social workers who had taken it upon themselves to storm the apartment of a mentally ill client to rescue her child. Her defence of the individuals involved had been high-handed and self-righteous; murmurs in the media that she was unsuited for so sensitive a post grew to a noisy crescendo before fading soon afterwards from almost every memory – except hers. Years later, Anson Chan still bridled at the memory of the 'persecution' she had had to endure from the media. 'I have no hang-ups about the press,' she insisted, while demonstrating quite the reverse, 'but some seem to think that if you're in public office, you're supposed to take all that flak. I can take plenty, but there is a limit to what one can bear.' Some feared that this antipathy, combined with a well-honed streak of arrogance, would make her a less enthusiastic defender of Hong Kong's rights and freedoms than Patten had allowed himself to believe.

Yet as chief secretary Chan had rapidly developed an astute sense of public relations. The dour, unsmiling persona with which she had been invested by her critics before she came to prominence was replaced by a stylish image in which an air of easy authority blended with an apparently warm smile. In July 1995, she had accomplished a secret mission to Beijing to meet Qian Qichen and Lu Ping and had demonstrated a flair for diplomacy. At the same time she had been able to reassure the Legislative Council that her trip had been a 'get-to-know-you' exercise and that there had been no secret deals. Although the governor and his entourage had been dismayed by her ill-judged attempt in September 1995 to nobble the right of Hong Kong's newly elected politicians to introduce private members' bills, and by an earlier incident in which she had ordered a government bill to be withdrawn after it had been amended by LegCo (when she confided none too discreetly that her dubious decision had been taken to 'teach the Democrats a lesson'), she had otherwise demonstrated a refreshing fervour for the Patten project. In March 1996, she won herself plaudits from a suspicious media for expressing her regret at China's decision to establish the provisional legislature. 'I hope that the Chinese side would explain clearly to the Hong Kong people the reason behind that,' she said. 'In any case, we will not undermine the authority and credibility of the existing legislature.'

In the face of Beijing's threat to disown civil servants who failed to support the provisional legislature, she remained defiant – China's decision was 'bound to cause confusion and uncertainty', she declared. The mood of the moment was well caught in a leading article in the *Eastern Express*, which praised her bravery and dignity under the headline 'COURAGE IN THE ABYSS OF DESPAIR'. On 30 March 1996, on the advice of Patten's political advisers, she took the diplomatic initiative, inviting Lu Ping to meet her on his next visit to Hong Kong so that they could discuss the issue of 'loyalty' and 'other transitional issues'. A week later, the director of the NCNA, Zhou Nan, announced that he would be hosting a dinner for Lu Ping and the chief secretary on 18 April, when – conveniently – the governor would be away in London. Sixty per cent of the respondents to an opinion poll criticised the director of the Hong Kong and Macau Affairs Office for refusing, yet again, to meet Patten.

Lu Ping arrived in Hong Kong on 12 April to be confronted by a small but angry group of demonstrators protesting against the continued imprisonment in China of Xi Yang, the *Ming Pao* journalist. In the governor's absence, Anson Chan showed herself to be a doughty defender of Hong Kong's rights and freedoms, and a fortnight later, in response to an invitation from Lu Ping, she flew to Beijing to discuss the transition. Patten not only welcomed her growing assurance but encouraged her to step into his limelight, recognising that, for Hong Kong's sake, she had to walk a tightrope between loyalty and independence.

He was perturbed, therefore, to discover, in May 1996, that his trusted lieutenant was planning to deliver a series of speeches in the United States in which she would appear to be signalling her readiness to soften her opposition to the provisional legco. Any suggestion that he and Anson Chan were at odds on this matter would severely damage both his own credibility and public confidence. Halfway through her visit, Patten sent an urgent message to New York asking her to amend her speeches to bring them back into line with government policy. At first she was reluctant to comply with his request. It was only when he spoke to her directly, insisting that her remarks were open to damaging misinterpretation, that she agreed to redraft the speeches to take account of his anxieties. It was an uncomfortable moment in an otherwise increasingly harmonious relationship, and it demonstrated the extreme delicacy of their joint predicament in the countdown to the handover.

Patten had himself just returned from a fourteen-day trip to the United States and Canada, where he had made eleven speeches, given thirteen press briefings and held several dozen meetings with government officials and politicians, including President Clinton. By this time, the media had started to run 'Patten's last year' articles summarising his achievements and his troubles. One of these, a cover piece in the American magazine *Newsweek* of 13 May, headlined 'THE BETRAYAL OF HONG KONG', greeted him on his return. Above a picture of a symbolic Chinese 'prisoner' with the number 97 stamped on his forehead, the magazine asked, 'With a year to go, who speaks for his future?' In combative style, the writer, Dorinda Elliott, noted how easily China had 'recruited so many of Hong Kong's tycoons' and speculated that 'this tiny elite may go down in history as the class that betrayed Hong Kong'. With the exception of T.T. Tsui, a tycoon with close links to the Beijing leadership, who told his interviewer that Hong Kong was like a 'family company; you don't have your arguments in the open', the objects of Elliott's scorn preferred, as usual, to conceal their animosity towards the governor.

Alongside its main article, *Newsweek* carried an interview with Patten. In answer to the query, 'What motivates the rich people to do Beijing's bidding?' he posed his own question: 'Why is it that privileged people sign up to arrangements whose sole intention is to choke off the voice of those who by every measure represent the majority of public opinion? Well, I'll say this: they wouldn't be doing it if most of them didn't have foreign passports in their back pockets.' Patten's long-concealed contempt for the spinelessness and hypocrisy of the business community had, at last, broken through the surface. His remarks ricocheted around Hong Kong, finally exposing the wound between the governor and the business elite which had festered for so long. Interpreting his incautious comments as an endorsement of the 'betrayal' headline, the leaders of Hong Kong's commercial sector were swift to indulge a spasm of self-righteous indignation.

At the instigation of Beijing, a Hong Kong executive called Nellie Fong (nicknamed Snow White at Government House), who was known to be exceptionally close to one or two members of the

Chinese leadership, orchestrated the response of an apparently apoplectic business elite. She drafted a letter denouncing Patten for the leaders of seven Chambers of Commerce (whom the governor called the Seven Dwarfs) to send to the prime minister in London. Her protest was couched in language of such incontinent ferocity that even China's most fervent apologists felt obliged to modify its tone before dispatching it to London on 18 May. The letter stopped short of demanding Patten's recall, but expressed 'profound disappointment' at the remarks quoted in *Newsweek*, which, tycoons complained, showed that the governor had failed to recognise the scale and quality of their contribution to the wellbeing of Hong Kong. 'Mr Patten,' they declared, 'has, through his unjustified attacks on the business community, ended up doing Hong Kong a great disservice.' On 21 May 1996, they wrote to Patten expressing:

> the concern of the business community on the Hong Kong government's position on the future provisional legislature, and, in particular, about the adverse effect which non-co-operation will have on the smooth transfer of sovereignty. We wish you to know of our sincere belief that the interests of Hong Kong will be better served by accepting the reality that a provisional legislature will be established.

Patten's response was to the point: 'Come off it.' The Chambers of Commerce received an equally dusty answer from the prime minister. Describing Patten's visit to America as a 'formidable success', during which he had 'vigorously defended and promoted Hong Kong's interests – not least the interests of the business community which you represent,' Major commented on their failure to give any public support to the judiciary, the civil service or the elected Legislative Council, adding tartly:

> It would be helpful . . . if the leadership of your chambers could make its voice heard on these issues too – just as you have to me about remarks inaccurately attributed to the governor. The governor has always been an admirer and energetic advocate of the great contribution which the business community has made to Hong Kong's spectacular economic success. I suggest you rather owe him gratitude for working so hard to make your case.

In America Patten had been on the receiving end of what he described to the press on his return as a 'massive and growing scepticism about Hong Kong's prospects'. Many of those he had met in the States, he reported, had told him that they had been briefed by Hong Kong business visitors who had struck them as defenders of Chinese policies rather than advocates of Hong Kong. This in itself had raised questions in people's minds about 'one country, two systems'. 'Does it matter that our American and Canadian friends are sceptical about the future for Hong Kong? I think it matters a great deal . . . We cannot afford to lose their confidence. But we must recognise that their confidence has been damaged by recent actions and decisions by China.'

Off the record, Patten was even less repentant. Some of his detractors, he noted, had simply been driven into saying things publicly which they were saying privately anyway – 'I think, more for Peking's benefit . . . to demonstrate their credentials.' Those who had lined up against him in the Chambers of Commerce, who included the chairman, James Tien, had now taken the 'dangerous' step of joining the united front 'in the trenches against anybody who believes in democracy or protecting civil liberties in Hong Kong'. They had allowed themselves to become, collectively, a 'megaphone for Peking . . . I think they've let Hong Kong down'.

Exhausted by the American trip and somewhat deflated by the row with the business community – especially given that, in the States, he had managed to sound 'wearily bullish' about Hong Kong's future and the remarkable achievements of the colony's entrepreneurs – Patten was consoled by a comment by the *Asian Wall Street Journal*. Quoting from memory, he recalled that the newspaper had observed: 'This is a controversy about something which the governor didn't say, which, if he had said it, would have been regarded by the man in the street as being completely uncontroversial.' He believed that the 'international card' was a very important element in the 'survival of decency' in this very international city.

> If I belted up it would be so much more difficult for anyone else to speak up about those things which are important and of lasting value in Hong Kong. I've got to go on making sure that not only is Hong Kong not chloroformed into the future, but that the rest of the world notices what is happening.

However heavy-going the effort now seemed, Patten remained convinced that he had no choice but to carry the fight for democracy and freedom to his adversaries.

19

'THE HEADBANGER
IN HONG KONG'

China Maintains the Pressure

In the midst of the governor's conflict with the 'Seven Dwarfs',
Michael Heseltine swept into Government House for a twenty-
four-hour stopover on his way back to London from another
triumphant mission to China. To his evident satisfaction, he had once
again been fêted by the leadership in Beijing; as on his trip a year earlier, he had been accorded the privilege of a tête-à-tête with the
premier, Li Peng, and the president, Jiang Zemin, which, he reported,
had been most productive. 'The truth is,' the British deputy prime
minister said at a press conference in the Chinese capital, 'that our
interest and the Chinese interest in Hong Kong are identical, and that
we have got to bring about the transfer of Hong Kong in the condition
of prosperity and stability. That is what we are totally committed to, and
I believe that this is what will happen.' Echoing Heseltine's tone, a
spokesman for the Chinese Foreign Ministry added that, during the
deputy prime minister's visit, 'both the Chinese and British side have
expressed their full confidence with regard to China's re-exercise of
sovereignty over Hong Kong in 1997'.

At Government House there was no such confidence. Heseltine's failure to caution China publicly, and his evident eagerness to trust Beijing's
good faith, stood in stark contrast to the stance taken by the governor.
Patten admired Heseltine, but disagreed deeply with his judgement. He
observed that on this occasion the deputy prime minister had been the
only Western politician of note who had managed to complete a visit to
China in recent years without making one mention of human rights,
even in private conversation with the Beijing leadership.

At a private dinner at Government House, Heseltine caused

resentment by informing the guests – who included leading members of the civil service, the judiciary and LegCo, as well as a number of Patten's senior advisers – that they had 'nothing to fear' from China. On the basis of his meetings in Beijing, he declared, he could assure them that China would honour the Joint Declaration and the Basic Law and that, 'from the president downwards', the leadership was committed to the future stability and prosperity of Hong Kong. For such an accomplished states-man, it was – even in the eyes of his admirers – a lamentable homily: complacent, jejune and ill informed. His failure to rise to the moment was symbolised, for his critics, by an unaccountable lapse of either knowledge or memory: he rephrased Deng Xiaoping's famous dictum as 'one nation, two states'. If he could not even be bothered to find the term that was supposed to define his rosy vision of the future, they won-dered aloud, how could anything he said about China or Hong Kong be taken seriously – except as an apologia for Beijing on behalf of the Foreign Office and the Department of Trade and Industry?

The following day, Heseltine's performance at a press conference con-firmed the widespread impression in Hong Kong that the deputy prime minister cared less for freedom and democracy in the future SAR than he did about British trade with the People's Republic. With the governor beside him, looking glumly embarrassed, he delivered himself of some vague generalisations about China and the injunction that, in effect, the media had a responsibility to look positively towards the day when Hong Kong would once again be part of China according to the guiding prin-ciple of what he referred to this time as 'one nation, two regimes'. He made no significant mention of the mood in Hong Kong and his appar-ent ignorance of the fundamental issues at stake incensed many of his listeners, who went away convinced that his insouciance reflected the British establishment's indifference to their fate.

It was an uncharacteristically inept display. Using one of the gover-nor's favoured words, Patten's press secretary, Kerry McGlynn, professed himself 'gobsmacked'. The media, he said, were bound to conclude that 'there is not just a cigarette paper between the governor and Mr Heseltine, but a whole packet of cigarettes'. Patten's aides did their best to explain away Heseltine's performance, and, as it happened, McGlynn managed to 'spin' a way out of the situation the deputy prime minister had created. But neither McGlynn nor Patten was in any doubt that Beijing would have been delighted by this indication, however unwit-tingly made, that the support from London enjoyed by the governor was not as wholehearted as he liked to claim.

The governor was worried that Heseltine's high-handedness might undo some of the good done by the prime minister's visit in convincing the public that Britain was committed in the long term to Hong Kong. Stressing that the deputy prime minister had 'never done anything, or acted in a way, which was remotely disloyal', Patten explained that Heseltine was, and always had been, 'sceptical about the idea that we really can do anything in Hong Kong which the Chinese don't care for to safeguard its liberties . . . And he's very trusting of the economic opening up of China – safeguarding Hong Kong without having to bother about "all that stuff in the Joint Declaration".' Patten felt that, in his keenness to open up trade with China, Heseltine was overly susceptible to Beijing's blandishments. 'I think he takes the assurances that he is given and the welcome he gets at sort of face value – I think sometimes to the surprise even of those who are themselves enthusiasts for, or apologists for, China. I mean, he can go over the top on this.' Patten's sensitivity here was acute. After Heseltine's previous trip to Beijing, the British ambassador, Sir Len Appleyard, had claimed that the agreement on the Court of Final Appeal, which came soon afterwards, 'was all because of the "warm afterglow" from Michael's visit'. Patten did not believe this, although he conceded that it was important that 'it looks as though Sino–British relations are better – it is no help to us if people think they are still in the refrigerator'. Nonetheless, he worried perpetually that the 'warm afterglow' argument would acquire enough momentum to suffocate his reform programme, which was not yet complete. 'The Chinese, of course, use these things to try to isolate me from the British government,' he complained.

You know, 'We'd have this wonderful relationship with you if only it wasn't for the headbanger in Hong Kong.' The danger is that they think these things are just sort of pro formas; that I, for some eccentric British reason, have been given Hong Kong to play with, but the broader strategic question of Sino–British relations is in good and more experienced hands.

If Patten's amour propre was pricked a little by Heseltine's failure publicly to endorse his stance, the issue between them nevertheless went to the heart of British policy. Aware that it was important for him 'not to turn into the all-time party-pooper', the governor believed with a passion that, for the foreseeable future, Anglo–Chinese relations were bound to be focused principally on how China behaved over Hong Kong. 'I suppose that really is the disagreement – the extremely civilised disagreement – between Michael and myself,' he said. 'I think Michael is hugely right about some things – inner-city deprivation and Europe – and wrong about one or two others. And I think China is an example.' The deputy prime minister had not made his role in Hong Kong any easier. 'I find myself living between those who think that Hong Kong *is* being sold out for British trade, and those who think Hong Kong *should* be sold out for British trade.'

Soon after Heseltine's departure, Patten sent him a genial note enclosing a pile of press cuttings, notably from the *Wall Street Journal*, about 'what I call showbusiness – that is, the extent to which these trips by trade ministers and politicians are mostly show rather than real business'. The grandee of the Tory party did not feel this gesture of lese-majesty required a response.

Despite the proclaimed success of Heseltine's second visit to China, its tangible fruits were not easy to discern. In particular, it soon became clear that his rapport with the Chinese leadership had failed to unblock the negotiations between the two sides in the Joint Liaison Group over the arrangements for the handover ceremony, which was now only a year away, and to which both states attached great importance. The discussions had spluttered on to the JLG agenda in the previous autumn, when the Chinese foreign minister and Malcolm Rifkind had agreed in principle during Qian Qichen's visit to London that the ceremony marking the transfer of sovereignty should be, in Patten's translation of the Mandarin, 'grand, solemn and decent'. Some months before this, early in 1995, the British had unilaterally decided to resist the temptation to leave the colony with any overt display of triumphalism. For this reason, although a British task force was due in the area in 1997, Patten advised that it would send the wrong message to have an aircraft-carrier on show. It seemed important to exploit what was bound to be a great media occasion to best advantage; 'to show', as Patten foresaw the historic moment, 'that China and the United Kingdom, members of the Security Council, had resolved their problems relatively peacefully . . . and that they had created together a government which was going to continue to give one of the greatest cities in the world the prospect of even greater prosperity in the future'.

On this basis, Britain proposed a day of celebration on 30 June, followed by a formal handover ceremony in full gaze of the people of Hong Kong which might also be etched on the televisual retina of the international community. The Chinese response was frosty. As characterised by Patten:

> They wanted to have a ceremony in the City Hall, which will take about a thousand people and is a pretty grotty little building, at which we would, as it were, sign a piece of paper saying, 'Here's Hong Kong – we're sorry we've been here.' There'd be a glass of

warm Asti Spumante and that would be that. There would then be a separate military ceremony behind the closed walls of the Tamar Barracks, at which a flag would go up and a flag would go down. I mean, the whole thing is preposterous. Here we are being told that there are likely to be six thousand journalists from all over the world; that there are likely to be up to a hundred television companies wanting to broadcast live – and we are told this is the way the SAR intends to start life.

By the spring of 1996, Patten thought the situation had become 'absolutely crazy'. He appreciated that the Chinese were inevitably worried about security, and in particular about the risk of hostile demonstrations – 'We'd proposed a ceremony at which members of the public would be present, and I suppose they might wear T-shirts or hold up banners' – but he and his advisers sensed that the underlying reason for China's reluctance to discuss the handover was Beijing's refusal ('which one understands in historical terms') to accept that there was any question of a change of sovereignty. The stand-off over what Government House had hoped would be a relatively simple negotiation became increasingly bizarre and fraught. At one point the Chinese side in the JLG informed their British counterparts, according to Patten, that 'they didn't understand why any foreign visitors were being invited. This was merely something that had to be resolved between Britain and China.' At the same meeting they proposed 'joint vetting' of all journalists who applied to cover the ceremony. 'What,' Patten wondered, 'is "joint vetting" a euphemism for?' Memories of the heavy-handed treatment of the media at the International Women's Conference in Beijing the previous summer were not a source of encouragement that 'joint vetting' would serve the interests of either Hong Kong or a free press.

By May, Patten had resolved to avoid spending the next six months arguing with the Chinese about the nature of the ceremony. 'If, at the end of the day, we have to have a departure ceremony rather than a handover ceremony, so be it . . . But I'm not going to connive at us leaving Hong Kong with our tail between our legs in a sort of hole-in-the-corner way.' As it had already been agreed that the Prince of Wales would be on hand, and that both he and the Pattens would depart Britain's last significant colony aboard the royal yacht, making her final voyage, it seemed unlikely, in this respect at least, that the last governor would have any difficulty in accomplishing this modest purpose.

On 2 October 1996, the governor delivered his fifth and final policy address to LegCo. It was a long speech, lasting ninety minutes, carefully crafted and rehearsed to set the seal on his own accomplishments and to lay down no fewer than sixteen 'clear benchmarks' by which, he proposed, the world should judge Hong Kong after 1 July 1997. It was both an unsurprising and an uncompromising speech, delivered, by convention, to a silent and impassive chamber. He began by promising that he would speak in more personal terms than was customary on such occasions, although he invited his audience to accept that this did not mean that 'the government is closing down or going into hibernation for nine months . . . We still have plenty to do'.

Patten was addressing his audience in his role as the quasi-mayor of Hong Kong, the head of a mini-state in which he had over-arching responsibility for every area of public life. Reminding the legislators that when he arrived he had promised a more open and accountable government, he recited the list of performance pledges by which this objective was being achieved. 'I doubt whether there are many, if any, governments anywhere which try to be as frank about their failures as their successes,' he boasted. Yet, because of the diplomatic crisis with China, his achievements had received less attention than he, and his admirers in Hong Kong, felt they merited. As one of those politicians who enjoyed the practice of administration, he had, as it happened, derived greater satisfaction from his role as a social reformer in Hong Kong than from his reputation as a 'head-banging' adversary of the People's Republic.

With the assistance of a dedicated civil service, he had delivered virtually all the policy commitments he had made on his arrival: schoolchildren, students, the disabled, the disadvantaged, the sick and those in need of homes had all benefited. A surge in public spending had brought more teachers per pupil, more nurses and doctors, more hospital beds and a cut in waiting times for outpatients from one hour to thirty minutes. There were thirteen new clinics, a new Comprehensive Social Security Assistance Scheme (the first in Hong Kong's history), more than 5,000 'care and attention' beds for the elderly (another first), a Disability Discrimination Ordinance and greatly improved access to buses and trains for the disabled – a project which the governor had overseen personally. More than 100 new flats were being built every day and the numbers living in slum-like 'temporary housing' had been reduced from more than 65,000 people to fewer than 18,000, despite the influx of new arrivals from China at the rate of 150 a day. Since the start of Patten's governorship in 1992, the deployment of 1,500 more police officers on the 'front line' had helped to cut the overall crime rate by 9 per cent and violent crime by 23 per cent. The crime rate in Hong Kong was now on a par with that of

Singapore, and, as Patten observed, much, much lower than those in London, New York, Tokyo and Toronto. Even the environment had been improved: pollution in rivers and streams in the New Territories was down by 70 per cent; most cars now used catalytic converters and ran on unleaded petrol; the government at last had put in place, though not yet implemented, a proper strategy to dispose of Hong Kong's ever-growing mountain of waste, the cause of appalling marine pollution.

Patten's record of social reform and welfare expenditure still left Hong Kong languishing behind any advanced Western country: unemployment benefits and a universal pension scheme, for example, were still conspicuous by their absence. Nonetheless, he had overseen a leap forward in public spending targeted at needy individuals and the community which obliged even his bitterest adversaries to concede the seriousness of his intent and the competence of his administration. Nor could the business community complain unduly: despite Britain's row with China, Beijing had, under pressure from Hong Kong's tycoons, eventually allowed the major construction projects to proceed. The first phase of the new airport would be finished, complete with roads, bridges and metro system linking it to the city centre, in 1998 – only nine months behind the original schedule. Work was about to start on Container Port 9, and plans for a further two container ports were already underway. Hong Kong had also embarked on what Patten described as 'one of the most advanced and competitive telecommunications systems in the world', complete with four alternative fixed-telecommunications network services operators, four cellular-phone operators, six personal-communications service operators and thirty-one paging operators.

The government had abolished or reduced a range of charges and taxes, notably cutting the corporate profit tax to 16.5 per cent from an 'already low' 17.5 per cent. Even so, the administration had begun work on a multibillion-dollar extension to the Convention Centre to ensure that Hong Kong remained the 'best conference venue of southeast Asia', a HK$50 million new technology training scheme, a HK$300 million investment in the Employees Retraining Board and numerous other grants designed to keep the territory at the forefront of Asia's tiger economies. Despite the cost of this programme of public expenditure, since 1992 the government had also contrived to increase the basic tax allowance, the married person's allowance and the single-parent allowance by 44 per cent, the first-child allowance by 16 per cent and the second-child allowance by 56 per cent. As a result, 60 per cent of the working population now paid no tax at all and only 2 per cent

paid the top rate of 15 per cent. The virtuous circle which allowed the
governor to reap the political benefit of tax cuts while increasing public
spending was a reflection not only of Hong Kong's work ethic and
entrepreneurial verve, but also of the territory's geographical location at
the gateway to China. 'We all recognise that our economic success is
part of a region-wide story,' Patten said. 'When the tide comes in, all
the boats rise . . . China's success is Hong Kong's opportunity. That is
the case today. It will be even more so as Hong Kong takes its place as
the richest, most outward-looking and most modern city in China.'

In his recital of the colony's achievements under his guiding hand he
was able to record that, on a per-capita basis, Hong Kong, with an average income of US$23,200, enjoyed a higher standard of living than
Australia, Canada, 'and – I whisper it quietly – the United Kingdom'.
As the eighth-largest trading community in the world, Hong Kong
already had the world's busiest container port and would soon have the
second-busiest airport. Since Patten's arrival – although, as he was
quick to point out, not because he arrived – Hong Kong's gross domestic product had grown by almost a quarter, exports by almost two
thirds and investment by over 40 per cent. 'We have been through
some stormy seas during that time; stormier than any of us would have
liked,' he declared, 'but we stayed true to our course, true to ourselves.
Hong Kong has weathered the storms.'

A later passage of his speech was a stinging riposte to those who had
sniped at his welfare programme.

> It seems to me to be preposterous to claim, as some do, that to
> respond to the community's desire for a little more compassion is to
> strike at the heart of the Hong Kong success story; that to channel a
> little of our new wealth to help the elderly, the sick, the disabled and
> the disadvantaged is to undermine our public finances and our system
> of government. This is propaganda dressed up as prudence, cant dis-
> guised as conviction.

Then, less like a retiring governor than a party leader seeking a second
term of office, he highlighted five areas in which his administration had
made no fewer than twenty-seven new 'policy commitments', almost
all of which were designed to improve the territory's infrastructure, services, openness and accountability, or to make Hong Kong a better
place in which to live and work. 'Our economic and social accomplishments here will give the new government of the special
administrative region the best possible start in life,' he said in a sideswipe
at those Beijing officials who had suspected that the last governor

would take Hong Kong's family silver with him on the royal yacht. He pointed to fiscal reserves in the region of HK$320 billion, equivalent to seven times the government's annual capital spending programme, which, he said, constituted a 'serious downpayment on the future'.

Next he turned to the political relationship between Britain, China and Hong Kong, echoing the prime minister's pledge: 'Britain's moral and political commitment to Hong Kong will remain, inscribed in a binding international treaty spanning the next fifty years.' Reflecting on the ties of history and family which bound Britain and Hong Kong together in a mutually supportive embrace, he expressed the hope that these bonds would continue to flourish. In 1992, before his departure for Hong Kong, he had spoken of a smooth handover to China as an imperative. Now he declared: 'A community is a living thing which grows and changes . . . A "smooth transition" is certainly not an end in itself. What we want is a successful transition, which we would also like to be as smooth as possible. But reaching the right destination is more important than the occasional bump on the way.'

He was also at pains to point out, in language which scarcely disguised his personal resentment, that those who liked to divide the period after the Joint Declaration neatly into two phases – a period of 'fruitful and harmonious co-operation' up to 1992, followed by 'relentless and largely profitless hard pounding since' – were guilty of a 'travesty of history, in which some of the participants appear to have rewritten their own parts'. In support of this personal apologia he claimed, with some justification, that it had been 'tough going' from the start, and even more difficult since 1989. The prolonged argument with China over the Bill of Rights and the airport, for example, had long preceded his arrival. 'We have also sometimes suffered from the pretence that things are other than they are, and that words mean other than what the dictionary has always told us they mean,' he continued in a criticism aimed at sinologists in London and business leaders in London and Hong Kong as well as at his adversaries in Beijing. 'Freedom of speech, the obligations under international covenants, the political neutrality of the civil service, elections, co-operation. All those things should be clear, but they have provoked storms of debate.'

Then, in a trenchant defence of his democratic reforms, Patten warned against those who would 'snuff out legitimate aspirations and shut out those politicians who can most authoritatively claim to hold a popular mandate'. But he reserved his full firepower for an onslaught on the provisional legislature which China was proposing to establish as a rival parliamentary forum to the Legislative Council elected in 1995. The governor had been under great pressure from Martin Lee and the

Democrats to charge China with a violation of the Joint Declaration. Privately, he believed that such a challenge would be profitless; that if pressed as a legal challenge, it would take many years to prosecute and be difficult to prove. He regarded China's repudiation of the terms and spirit of the treaty as a matter of urgent political significance, the character of which could easily be distorted or lost if the matter were taken either to the United Nations or to the International Court of Justice in the Hague. For this reason he chose to focus the attention of his audience on some of the threats that sprang from China's decision.

> The role of this institution, its credibility and legitimacy, lies at the heart of wider doubts about the future of pluralism and freedom in Hong Kong. How can you have complete faith in the future of the rule of law if you worry about the integrity of the institution which makes the laws? How can you have complete faith in the future of free speech if this assembly only allows it for some? How can you have complete faith in the future probity of government if openness and accountability are to be limited by what is deemed to be politically convenient?

In response to those who thought that he should accommodate China's prospective fait accompli by allowing the civil service to co-operate with the provisional legco, he was unequivocal: 'It is unnecessary as well as provocative, and we will have nothing to do with it. We will not assist a provisional legislature's establishment, its operation or its ability to withstand legal challenge.' And defying Beijing's threat to reverse his decision to bring Hong Kong's laws into line with the Bill of Rights, he said, 'We have done about eighty per cent of the work and we will invite this council to help us finish the job.'

In the final part of his speech Patten identified his sixteen 'benchmarks', the criteria by which he believed the international community would judge Hong Kong in the future. They merit restating.

> Is Hong Kong's civil service still professional and meritocratic? Are its key positions filled by individuals who command the confidence of their colleagues and the community and owe their appointments only to their own ability?
>
> Is the SAR government writing its own budget on the basis of its own policies, or is it under pressure to respond to directives dictated by Beijing?
>
> Is the Hong Kong Monetary Authority managing Hong Kong's exchange fund without outside interference?

Is Hong Kong behaving in a truly autonomous way in international economic organisations?

Is the Hong Kong legislature passing laws in response to the aspirations of the Hong Kong community and the policies of the SAR government, or is it legislating under pressure from Beijing?

Are Hong Kong's courts continuing to operate without interference?

Is the Independent Commission Against Corruption continuing to act vigorously against all forms of corruption, including cases in which China's interests may be involved?

Is Hong Kong continuing to maintain its own network of international law-enforcement liaison relationships?

Is the integrity of the Hong Kong–Guangdong border being maintained, including the separate border controls operated by the Hong Kong Immigration Department?

Is the Hong Kong press still free, with uninhibited coverage of China and of issues on which China has strong views?

Are new constraints being imposed on freedom of assembly? Are the annual commemorations and vigils of recent years still being allowed?

Are foreign journalists and media organisations in Hong Kong still free to operate without controls?

Is anybody being prosecuted or harassed for the peaceful expression of political, social or religious views?

Are Hong Kong's legislators, at successive stages of transition, fairly and openly elected, and truly representative of the community?

Are democratic politicians continuing to play an active role in Hong Kong's politics, or are they being excluded or marginalised by external pressure?

Is the chief executive exercising genuine autonomy in the areas provided for in the Joint Declaration and Basic Law?

It was a blunt set of questions which identified with clarity precisely those concerns agitating the chanceries of the West, not to mention the incumbent leader of Hong Kong. Patten concluded his speech by offering the cold comfort that Hong Kong's autonomy need not be destroyed by China. Instead, those who had most power and influence in the territory – businessmen, politicians, journalists, academics and other community leaders – should resist the temptation to sell Hong Kong short to further their own interests as some of their number had already done. As if shaking himself free of such a morbid prospect, he ended the last policy address of the last British governor with the statement: 'I hope that Hong Kong will take tomorrow by storm. And when it does, history will stand and cheer.' It was made with more faith than certainty.

The audience remained silent in their seats: there was not a murmur of approbation or dissent, no applause, no smiles, no frowns. The legislators who had in so many ways imbibed the virtues of the democratic process on this occasion obeyed the dictates of convention: their governor had descended among them, he had delivered himself of his final formal testimony, and he would depart as he had arrived, without fanfare or gratitude.

As soon as Patten left the chamber, the legislators rose from their places and made for the exits to be met by probing cameras in search of soundbites. Apologists for Beijing used the freedom they still enjoyed – and which the governor had so assiduously promoted on their behalf – to demonstrate their unswerving loyalty to their political masters. From the right, Allen Lee complained that the governor had failed to make good his promise to increase co-operation with China; from the left, the DAB representative on LegCo, Ip Kwok Him, accused him of 'dividing Hong Kong's people and spreading pessimism in their midst'. Emily Lau, who rarely allowed her hatred of Beijing to diminish her hostility towards British colonialism, dismissed the governor's attempts to 'get Britain off the hook' of history and thundered that the Hong Kong authorities were doing 'sweet nothing' to ensure that China implemented the Joint Declaration.

More surprisingly, Margaret Ng, the most thoughtful of commentators, was infuriated by a passage of Patten's speech in which he had reminded his audience that, at the end of the Second World War, when the population of Hong Kong was no more than 600,000, the colony had been 'devastated by conflict, occupation and pillage', and yet over the next three decades, 'wave after wave of refugees swam, walked, ran and climbed over barbed wire to find a new life in this city. Why did they come and what did they find? The peace and safety guaranteed by the rule of law. Not rules, not laws, but the rule of law, that vital protection against arbitrary government.' As Ng explained later, it was not so much the values implicit in Patten's words which provoked her wrath, but the assumption of colonial virtue by which they were underpinned. Interpreting his litany of Hong Kong's qualities under colonial rule as a self-regarding apologia on Britain's behalf, she protested: 'We are the people who climbed the barbed wire.'

Ng's complaint went to the heart of a disconcerting ambiguity in the relationship between a colonial administration, however enlightened, and its subject people, however liberated. 'I was very upset. I felt very alienated. I had to exercise a good deal of self-control not to walk out of that chamber.' The governor had been 'condescending'; he had talked of Hong Kong as a 'British possession', and of 'how much Britain had done for Hong Kong. We were back to a hundred and fifty years ago. I don't think it is even a matter of colonialism. It's a matter of cultural superiority, which, let's face it, plagues the British as much as it plagues the Chinese.' Although the governor was taken aback by this reaction, it struck a chord with him. Margaret Ng, he reflected, saw Britain's colonial record 'through the prism of a thousand little humiliations and acts of discrimination' and the failure to begin the process of democratisation and protection of civil liberties early enough. As far as she was concerned, he concluded, there would never be a positive case to be put for Britain's administration. 'I respect her because I know that much of what she is saying about past discrimination is correct.' However, he maintained that in all fairness she should have conceded that it was indeed a British creation which attracted those waves of refugees, and that the institution of liberal values in Hong Kong had been a product of British administration. Yet at the same time the ferocity with which Margaret Ng launched her criticism encouraged him: she represented, he judged, the 'best and most constructive sort of intellectual awkward squad', the kind of person Hong Kong could ill afford to lose. He was also relieved that, even though so many legislators felt obliged to find fault with his final address, some of the Democrats, at least, had gone out of their way to tell him privately how pleased they were with the focus of his speech. The international response, too, was favourable, and the local polls showed him to be as popular as ever with the ordinary people of Hong Kong. His personal-approval rating rose in the days after his address from 65 to almost 69 per cent.

The pressure on Hong Kong from China was relentless. On 16 October, the *Wall Street Journal* carried an interview with Qian Qichen, in which, as if delivering a direct rebuke to Patten, he gave an ominous warning against the overt manifestation of dissent in Hong Kong after the handover. 'In the future,' he told his interviewer, 'Hong Kong should not hold political activities which directly interfere in the affairs of the mainland.' For good measure he added that, after 1997, the Hong Kong media would be free to 'put forward criticism, but not lies; nor can they put forward personal attacks on Chinese leaders, for that would not live up to the morality of their occupation . . . and is not compatible with personal moral ethics.' This prerequisite, coming from such a senior figure in Beijing's ruling elite, provoked a roar of dismay from those at whom it was aimed: the organisers of the annual vigil to commemorate Tiananmen Square retorted that they would go ahead regardless after 1997. Newspaper editors joined forces with lawyers to insist that the Chinese authorities had no legal right to threaten the free expression of opinion – a fact which, no less ominously, Qian Qichen had himself acknowledged in his interview. 'I don't believe that [future] laws will make such stipulations,' he had said, as if to indicate that, under pressure from China, the future executive of the SAR would intervene to enforce 'personal moral ethics' regardless of the law, in much the way as the Chinese authorities did on the mainland. So much for at least half a dozen of Patten's 'benchmarks'. Although a spokesman for the Chinese Ministry of Foreign Affairs later back-tracked, claiming that Qian Qichen's comments had been misinterpreted, the Chinese leader of the JLG was quoted as saying that 'spreading rumours and lies is a different matter from press freedom'.

In London, the foreign secretary issued a statement expressing the British government's concern. 'The Chinese should make clear that they have no intention to depart from "two systems, one country" and from the provisions of the Joint Declaration.' Chris Patten, who was in London to see the prime minister and other members of the Cabinet, remarked privately: 'My biggest worry was that it showed a complete lack of understanding by senior Chinese leaders about how Hong Kong works . . . Plainly Mr Qian doesn't understand the difference between the rule of law and the rule of man. But maybe the fact that he's a senior Chinese cadre makes that inevitable.' Nor was he optimistic that the Chinese could be brought to a more sensible view. Qian Qichen's words, according to Patten, reflected the 'implacable political will of the Communist party in Peking. And what is always a worry is that there will be people in Hong Kong who will say, "Oh, this is terrible, but I suppose we've got to be understanding and go along with it."' Although he had a residual faith in the local media, the rule of law, the democratically elected legislators and the source of their support, the citizenry itself, he was painfully aware that Hong Kong's ability to resist Beijing's 'implacable will' lay principally with whoever was selected to replace him as the SAR's first chief executive. 'We've got to hope,' he confided in the middle of October, 'that a chief executive of Hong Kong will encourage Chinese officials to keep their fingers off.' The auguries were not encouraging.

The main contenders for the post of chief executive had recently emerged from relative obscurity, blinking in the glare of local and international publicity. There were to be four candidates of note: a retired justice of appeal, Simon Li; the former chief justice Ti Liang Yang; the business tycoon Peter Woo and, in spite of his previously professed reluctance, the shipping magnate C.H. Tung. There was much speculation about the likely victor, although it was generally presumed that C.H. was China's preferred choice. In January 1996, the president of the People's Republic, Jiang Zemin, had been steered across a gathering of Hong Kong 'patriots' to shake him warmly by the hand, a mark of distinction which did not go unnoticed in Hong Kong.

All four candidates had remained conspicuously silent about the threats made so lately by the Chinese foreign minister. Patten was depressed by this reticence, but not surprised.

> They ran for cover, and, I think, were very reluctant to say anything which suggested that they were prepared to stand up for the things which are guaranteed in the Joint Declaration and which Qian Qichen was specifically attacking. I don't think they will want to do anything at this stage which might annoy China, because we all know that the main ingredient in the selection is who gets China's blessing . . . I hope it will be different after a chief executive has finally emerged.

Under the terms of the Basic Law, the chief executive was to be chosen by a selection committee of 400 people, ostensibly elected by the Preparatory Committee, but in practice appointed by China. Nevertheless, for six weeks from the end of October 1996, the four candidates engaged in a semblance of an election campaign, producing personal manifestos, staging press conferences and walkabouts, giving interviews on radio and television and canvassing support among those who might have some influence with the Selection Committee. As the outcome had been preordained, this exercise in democratic accountability was a charade. Nonetheless it was not entirely unimpressive: all four candidates set about their self-imposed task with sub-Pattenite prowess, deploying some of the populist techniques the last governor had introduced to Hong Kong: they kissed babies, travelled on the MTR underground rail network and beamed delightedly amid a populace from which their power, influence or wealth had hitherto protected them. For democrats, this shadow contest was a bittersweet illustration of Hong Kong's thwarted potential. It offered a glimpse of what might have been – a genuine campaign for popular support from which one or other of the candidates would have surfaced legitimately triumphant – but the skill and sincerity with which the ritual was enacted mocked the very purpose it appeared to serve.

Pundits wondered what had prompted the other three contenders to enter a race that C.H. Tung had already won. Was it vanity, self-delusion or a bid for a place at the top table after the campaign? Certainly, the two lawyers, whatever their other virtues, were regarded as political lightweights without significant administrative experience. Peter Woo, though an able entrepreneur, had persistently denied any aspiration to lead Hong Kong, and most observers had thought that his apparent reluctance to succeed Patten showed sound self-judgement on his part. He lacked any significant base of support in China, and was intensely disliked by many of his peers in Hong Kong, some of whom were only too ready to recall the occasions on which they had been worsted, slighted or cold-shouldered by an arrogant competitor. As a result, he had too many enemies in and around the Selection Committee to be confident of more than a derisory vote, even in a rigged election where the votes would be carefully distributed to preserve the illusion of a genuine contest. His peers believed either that he was too thick-skinned to appreciate their disaffection for him, or that he was driven, forlornly, by a longstanding and bitter rivalry with the far more influential Tung, the preferred candidate even of those who did not vote for him.

Patten, who had long expected C.H. Tung to win, privately believed that the combination of the shipping tycoon as chief executive and Anson Chan as chief secretary was as near to a 'dream ticket' as Hong Kong could expect. C.H.'s contribution to ExCo's deliberations had left Patten with few doubts about his lack of enthusiasm for democracy or freedom; moreover, the governor felt that, as a deeply conservative and traditional figure, C.H. would find it very difficult to stand up for such issues. Nevertheless he had half hoped that C.H. would be prevailed upon by Beijing to stand for the leadership. As a decent and honest individual, he was more likely than any of his rivals to secure the confidence of the international community without betraying his loyalty to China.

Born in Shanghai in 1937, C.H. was the son of a prosperous merchant. In 1949 the family fled to Hong Kong, where his father built up one of the world's largest shipping fleets, Orient Overseas. C.H. was educated locally and then in Britain at Liverpool University. Later, he worked for General Electric in the United States before returning to Hong Kong to join the family business, which, by 1980, owned a fleet of 150 container ships. Yet by the time of his father's death in 1982, Orient Overseas was facing an acute financial crisis. Despite a deep recession in shipping, exacerbated by the war of attrition between Iran and Iraq, C.H.'s father had ignored all advice to the contrary and continued to expand his fleet. C.H.'s inheritance, therefore, was a growing mountain of debt which, by 1985, had reached US$2.6 billion. On the brink of bankruptcy, he had to placate some 200 bankers, a handful of whom could easily have co-operated to destroy his late father's empire overnight. At a meeting in Tokyo he faced his creditors, taking personal responsibility for his father's errors and promising to repay all his debts if they would stand by him. According to impartial observers, his sincerity and dignity won them over within fifteen minutes.

A consortium of American banks undertook to take on some of his debts, but the decisive factor was a loan of US$120 million from China, a rescue operation co-ordinated by a Hong Kong tycoon and Beijing apologist called Henry Fok. Thanks to China's munificence, Orient Overseas' fortunes were gradually restored until, a decade later, in 1995, the company was able to report a profit of US$60 million. C.H. Tung had much for which to be grateful, and, although no one suggested any malfeasance on his part, it was widely presumed that, as an honourable man, he would not regard his debt to the People's Republic to have been discharged merely by the repayment of the outstanding loan.

As soon as he had received President Jiang Zemin's 'blessing', C.H.'s aptitude for the post of chief executive came under close scrutiny. His tenacity in adversity was noted with approval; likewise his links with the international community and his close acquaintance with luminaries in Washington and New York. No one doubted that he had the capacity to represent Hong Kong with decorum and dignity. The question was whether he would be able or willing to stand up for Hong Kong's 'autonomy'; indeed, whether he even valued the crucial distinctions embodied in the concept of 'one country, two systems'. After much speculation, amid which C.H. let it be known that he felt he was too old for the post, and that, in any case, he preferred a quiet family life to the vicissitudes of public responsibility, he had finally announced his candidature in September 1996. To the governor's private consternation, he soon made it clear where his instincts and his loyalties lay.

On 28 October, using terminology that could have been dictated from Beijing, he warned the people of Hong Kong to be alert to the threat of 'international forces' seeking to use the territory in a campaign to isolate China. He volunteered that it would not be easy to balance the need to guard against such external threats with protecting freedom of expression in the future SAR. Although he promised that the 4 June commemorative activities would still be permitted as long as they were 'peaceful' and 'lawful', he used a series of subsequent public statements to distance himself from Patten's reforms and criticised the governor obliquely for initiating them without Beijing's prior approval.

Moreover, far from condemning China's decision to establish a provisional legislature, he made it clear that he thought the administration should co-operate with the new body, and that it should be given quasi-legislative responsibilities even before the handover. In particular he argued that the provisional legislature should draw up a law on 'subversion' in line with Article 23 of the Basic Law, which stipulated: 'The HKSAR shall enact laws on its own to prohibit any act of treason, secession, sedition, subversion against the central People's Government.' He did not say – he did not need to – that, after the handover, this self-same law might be used to determine whether the Tiananmen Square commemorations which so offended China would be 'lawful' or not. Criticising Martin Lee's Democrats for their 'confrontational' stance towards China, he called on them to be more 'constructive' by agreeing to stand for the provisional legislature rather than attempting to mount a legal challenge to its creation.

No one doubted that he spoke sincerely, an assumption that made his remarks even more disconcerting. One or two of Patten's advisers were perplexed. In private, C.H. had often spoken with admiration of what one of Government House's most assiduous China-watchers described as the 'lobotomocracy' of Singapore and expressed his fear that Hong Kong was losing 'its Chinese values' – 'Whatever they might be,' added one of Patten's aides cynically. From his public pronouncements, it was not clear to Government House whether C.H. hoped to preserve Hong Kong's status quo; whether he would encourage the police to behave differently under Chinese sovereignty, regardless of the law; or, even more alarmingly, whether he would listen obediently to what Beijing might whisper in his ear and order the Hong Kong Police to behave accordingly.

Fears about what Beijing might require of them, and about their own security after the handover, had been rife among members of the police force itself. When Patten had first arrived in Hong Kong, the chief superintendent commanding Wanchai, a commercial district by day and the centre of the colony's nightlife in the small hours, was Dick Lee. Born in 1950, he was one of six children brought up and educated in Hong Kong. After graduating in history from the Chinese University, he joined the Royal Hong Kong Police Force in 1972. Identified as a 'local' with high-flying potential, he rose steadily towards the top via the Metropolitan Police Training School at Hendon on the outskirts of London, a public-administration course at Oxford University and secondment as an instructor to the Police Staff College at Bramshill in Hampshire.

In 1992 Dick Lee had been responsible for two divisions and 700 officers policing a citizenry of just over a million people. His officers confronted the usual catalogue of burglaries and street crime, though on a far smaller scale than in any European city. Apart from routine raids on brothels masquerading as nightclubs, and attempts to penetrate and combat the protection rackets run by the triads, Lee's team concentrated their operational efforts on the surge of firearms, including AK47s and grenades, smuggled across the border with China for armed robberies, and to an even greater extent on the crime syndicates who controlled the booming trade in cars stolen from Hong Kong and ferried in specially modified speedboats to secret destinations on the mainland at a rate, on average, of more than one a day. This illegal trade had reached such a level of sophistication that the triad bosses in southern China had begun to specify precisely the make, model and colour of vehicle required by their clients, many of whom held senior positions in the Communist party. The gangs operated with such speed and precision that it was almost impossible to apprehend them. Once afloat, the Chinese speedboats, travelling at upwards of 40 knots, could easily elude all but the fastest patrol boats.

Dick Lee was an impeccable public servant with the traditional virtues of his profession. In the early days of the governor's conflict with China, he had for the first time begun to focus on the post-handover uncertainties. He had been privately dismayed by the deteriorating morale of the men under his command. A tall man, erect in a neatly pressed uniform, he spoke slowly and with dignity, but without pomposity. The question which was uppermost in every mind, he said, was what would happen to them after 1997.

Before Chris Patten's proposals, before the argument, we believed that the Chinese side was genuinely supporting the police service in Hong Kong, and that we would continue to receive the same conditions of service, the same salary, the same standard of living that we are getting from the current government. But what we now see is a different side of the Chinese government: they do not want to accept any proposals from the Hong Kong government. They say that if the attitude of the governor remains unchanged they will do things their own way after 1997. So there is uncertainty: what will the Chinese do with the police after 1997?

Some of the officers trained in the traditions of the British police were even more anxious about what the Chinese might expect of them. 'If you look at the policing methods and the legal system in

China, it is very, very different from what we have here,' Dick Lee had explained.

Our fear is that after 1997 we police officers will be directed to per-form in the same way as Chinese police officers do. Say, in a crowd-control situation. What we are doing now is maintaining law and order, but perhaps after 1997 we'll be asked to exercise force on the crowds when that is unnecessary. Put simply, we are afraid that we will be ordered to do things that we don't want to do.

And how would he respond to such an order? In late 1992, Lee had been unequivocal. 'As a professional officer trained in Hong Kong, I have to stand up and say no.' He would refuse to obey orders? 'I would, if I am asked to do things that, in my opinion, are immoral and incor-rect.' His answer was given deliberately and without bravado; a line drawn in the sand.

Dick Lee's abilities had led to swift promotion. By 1996, he was a deputy commissioner responsible for security affairs. His viewpoint had changed as well. A study visit to China had reassured him about Beijing's intentions, and now he saw his task as 'enforcing the laws of Hong Kong. Whatever the law says, we carry it out.' Even if the law is unjust? 'If the new government changes the law, then the police have to enforce it.' It was a small shift in attitude, perhaps, but coming from such an eminently reasonable and honourable police officer it was a worrying augury, not least because Dick Lee himself seemed quite unconscious of the implications of his words.

'WE ARE NOT SIMPLY LIMP VICTIMS'

The Governor's Authority Begins to Crumble

The dismay caused by Qian Qichen's threats and C.H. Tung's authoritarian utterances was compounded by renewed evidence of China's indifference to international opinion about human rights. The most spectacular example of Beijing's insouciance was the case of Wang Dan, who was charged on 17 October 1996 with 'instigating turmoil' and 'creating public opinions' with the intention of 'overthrowing the state power and socialism'. The main indictment against him – conspiracy to overthrow the government – related to thirty articles the twenty-seven-year-old dissident had written for newspapers in Hong Kong and Taiwan since his release on bail, pending subversion charges, almost four years earlier. If found guilty he would face a minimum sentence of ten years' imprisonment. Thirteen days later, on 30 October, after a hearing lasting three hours, Wang Dan was sentenced to eleven years in jail. The governor was swift to state that Wang Dan's activities would be regarded as quite legal in Hong Kong. Martin Lee warned: 'What happened to Wang Dan may happen to us after 1997.' His colleague Szeto Wah added: 'Wang Dan's case shows there is no judicial independence in China. The function of China's judiciary is to attack citizens and to prosecute opponents.' Even Allen Lee, on behalf of the Liberal party, said, 'It's a severe sentence for a young person like Wang Dan,' but he continued, reassuringly, 'We should not be so disappointed, as there is an appeal system in China.' Of the four candidates for the leadership of Hong Kong, the two lawyers declined to comment; Peter Woo advised: 'We should keep a mutual respect and attitude towards China's system, and not intervene,' and C.H. Tung said: 'China has China's law, and Hong Kong has Hong

Kong's law; the two laws are different, and I think we should understand this point.' Two weeks later, the Beijing Higher People's Court
took ten minutes to uphold the sentence. Wang Dan was refused leave
to address the judges. His mother told reporters, 'The verdict was all
prepared in advance. It was very unfair.'

In London at the end of October, Patten met both the prime
minister and the foreign secretary to discuss the implications of the
threats made by the Chinese foreign minister and the arrest of Wang
Dan. He argued that these incidents made it an urgent imperative to
put the revised Crimes Ordinance (covering sedition, treason, subversion and secession) before the Legislative Council. The governor was
well aware that to introduce legislation covering these so-called Basic
Law Article 23 offences, which China had already insisted would be for
the future government of the SAR to determine, would be likely to
cause yet another conflict with Beijing, but he advised the foreign
secretary that if he failed to act, 'people would think we'd piked out of
trying to complete our work on civil liberties and human rights'.

Not for the first time, Patten found himself up against senior officials
in the Foreign Office, who had carefully briefed Malcolm Rifkind
against him. The foreign secretary, whom Patten described as a formidable analyst, was in his most forensic mood. 'You do feel as though
you've been gone over by George Carman [Britain's most famous libel
lawyer] in the witness box . . . a two-hour meeting with a very well-
informed Malcolm Rifkind, who's very anxious to find out exactly
what one's objectives are, is itself pretty punishing.' But the governor
stood his ground, asserting that 'we have to finish the job we have
started'. According to Patten, one or two of Rifkind's officials were
'anxious to egg him on to come down against the governor', which
made the process even more exhausting. His most difficult moment
came when the foreign secretary asked if he could guarantee that the
appropriate legislation would be passed by LegCo. Patten's answer had
to be no. He explained that he found himself 'in the usual Hong Kong
position, in which some of those who criticise us if we go ahead with
the legislation would criticise us on the other flank if we didn't; some
of those who press us to go ahead won't actually vote for us if we put
it forward'.

Rifkind's officials, led by the head of the Hong Kong Department,
Sherard Cowper-Coles, intervened at this point to provide the foreign
secretary with a list of names designed to show that Patten was bound
to lose the vote in LegCo. The team from Government House speed-
ily demolished Cowper-Coles' argument by demonstrating that his
statistics were fundamentally flawed. One of them commented, 'You

could see the foreign secretary shift ground at once.' Patten himself confided: 'It has to be said that the foreign secretary – after quite properly quizzing me on every option, on every angle – was prepared to accept my political judgement.' In return, the governor agreed to postpone publication of the bill for a fortnight so that it would not coincide with the visit to London of a group of senior diplomats from Beijing. With that, Patten left the foreign secretary's office, convinced that, as far as Rifkind was concerned, the issue had been settled in his favour.

However, immediately afterwards, Cowper-Coles continued the argument with Patten's advisers, telling them that the matter should not be finally resolved until the next meeting of the Cabinet subcommittee. According to one of those present, the departing Patten overheard this, turned on the official and informed him that the matter was closed. Cowper-Coles, who had a reputation for stubbornness and who, one of Patten's aides reported, was 'pathological' on this issue, evidently detected the menace in the governor's voice and made no further comment.

It was not the end of the matter. Within days Government House received the first in a deluge of telegrams from the Foreign Office, in which, according to Patten, 'Those officials who weren't hugely delighted by the decision which the foreign secretary had come to . . . spent two or three weeks trying to unpick the agreement.' This campaign achieved the desired effect: according to one of the governor's advisers, Rifkind was eventually 'ventriloquised' by Cowper-Coles into reopening the issue as if nothing had been agreed. Patten confirmed that, three weeks after his meeting with Rifkind, 'we fetched up with it looking as though the foreign secretary was going to reverse the decision and to propose that we should spend more time trying to reach an agreement with the Chinese'.

It was quite apparent to the British negotiators in the JLG that no such agreement was in the offing. The Chinese had made it clear in early October that they would oppose any attempt by the British to adapt the relevant Hong Kong legislation, and in early November they indicated that they would not discuss the matter any further. Patten maintained that it was vital to publish the revised bill before the selection of C.H. Tung as chief executive designate – if only to diminish the risk of an open breach with his appointed successor over whether or not he should press ahead with legislation to which Beijing was so resolutely hostile. After a strenuous effort, Patten finally prevailed, and the Crimes (Amendment)(No. 2) Bill 1996 was duly published in the last week of November.

The Chinese had already indicated in 1995 that they would reinstate the six laws relating to the right of assembly and free speech which had been amended to bring them into line with the 1991 Bill of Rights. It was no surprise, therefore, when Beijing reacted adversely to the publication of the new Crimes Bill, which so amended the concept of 'subversion' to ensure that no individual could be convicted of subversive behaviour unless that person's 'intention of overthrowing the government' involved the use of force. It would thus be virtually impossible to use the Crimes Ordinance to prosecute individuals in Hong Kong for the kind of 'dissident' activities for which Wang Dan and many others had been jailed in China. To Patten's surprise, Beijing's response to what the Chinese described as 'further provocation' was unexpectedly imprecise and muted. This did not prevent the hapless British ambassador in Beijing, Sir Len Appleyard, from dispatching an alarmist telegram to London which claimed, yet again, that the Crimes Bill would 'affect co-operation across the board'. One of Patten's advisers dismissed Appleyard's warnings that the 'roof would fall in' and that the bill would be the 'end of civilisation as we know it' as 'cobblers, and demonstrably cobblers'.

The gulf of perspective between the Foreign Office and Government House was growing ever more difficult to bridge. Patten's closest aides admitted that the 'realists' in the Foreign Office, represented by Cowper-Coles, were even more intransigent than the 'sinologists', the most significant of whom had, by now, either retired or been promoted into other departments. Patten himself thought that over the previous few months the 'realists' had 'persuaded themselves that this great big beautiful thing – the Sino–British relationship – is starting to show signs of life again and that it needs more pampering and more encouragement, and that we should avoid argument at all costs . . . That is complete nonsense, but there it is.' He was becoming increasingly concerned about the impact the conflict was likely to have on his senior civil servants in Hong Kong – and especially on Anson Chan. It was all very well for him, he argued, to insist that Britain had a moral responsibility for Hong Kong, 'enshrined in an international treaty' that would last for fifty years after the handover, but what store would Chan and her colleagues set by such rhetoric against the evidence from the Foreign Office? 'I think they must ask themselves the obvious question,' Patten noted. 'If British officials – or some British officials – are like this now, what are they going to be like afterwards?'

On Wednesday 11 December, C.H. Tung was duly anointed as the first chief executive of the Hong Kong special administrative region. The 400 members of the Selection Committee were required to cast their votes in public in an elaborate ritual conducted at the Convention

Centre. Mimicking the formalities of Western democracy, Qian Qichen presided over the proceedings as if to give them his seal of approval. In an earlier round, the four leading candidates had been reduced to three: C.H. Tung, Peter Woo and Ti Liang Yang. While they waited for the verdict, a large ballot box was placed in the centre of the floor in front of the Selection Committee and a battery of camera crews and photographers. For the benefit of the press, an official inspected the ballot box, turning it this way and that to show that it was quite empty with all the showmanship of a children's conjurer. Evidently satisfied that the ballot could not be rigged, the organisers gave the instruction for the votes to be cast. One by one Beijing's appointees filed to the dais, smiled for the cameras and deposited their voting slips in the box. At Government House, Patten's officials failed to suppress their mirth at these televised proceedings. Patten himself declined to watch, claiming the pressure of other work.

In an attempt to inject further drama into the occasion, the organisers had rigged up an electronic scoreboard on which the 'results' could be displayed as each vote was counted. The votes were called individually and, digit by digit, the board duly illuminated the scores of the candidates. It was an excruciating process, aggravated by the knowledge that all involved were participating in a humiliating legerdemain. When the verdict was announced – C.H. Tung: 320; Ti Liang Yang: 42; Peter Woo: 36 – there was a polite murmur of applause before the Selection Committee hurried away to go about their normal business. In a chamber now deserted except by the media, the chief executive (designate) read from a prepared statement, expressing his gratitude for the 'highest honour of my life', and his undertaking 'to do my very best to create a better future for Hong Kong'. He also declared: 'Our society has become too politicised in recent years,' and, reiterating a theme of his campaign, urged the people of Hong Kong to 'try their very best to strike a balance between rights and obligations' now that 'we are finally masters in our own house'.

Although Chris Patten was by now far less confident than he had been even a month earlier that C.H. Tung would exercise his authority to protect Hong Kong's freedoms against China, he joined the foreign secretary and other international leaders in offering his congratulations. He made no comment about the 'election' itself, but was careful to remind C.H.:

The community will be looking to the chief executive to provide strong leadership with vision, integrity and determination; to defend Hong Kong's interests . . . and to preserve the cornerstone of Hong

Kong's success – the rule of law, a level playing field for business, the
protection of individual rights and freedoms in an open and accountable society.

Privately he observed, 'I think it would have been as surprising to the
politburo in Peking if C.H. hadn't been elected as it would have been
for the Cabinet to discover in June 1992 that I wasn't going to be the
next governor of Hong Kong.'

Simultaneously, an equally bizarre 'election' process for the provisional legislature was now reaching its final stage. On 13 December, the
presidium of the National People's Congress in Beijing had approved a
shortlist of 130 approved candidates from which the sixty-seat 'shadow'
legco would be chosen by the Selection Committee. The ubiquitous
Qian Qichen announced that he would like to see as many incumbent
or former legislators as possible taking their places in the new body. As
Martin Lee's Democrats and a number of independents had long since
decided to boycott what they regarded as an illegitimate exercise, only
thirty-four official LegCo members, including Allen Lee, had put their
names forward. Patten was optimistic that at least some of these 'pusillanimous and pathetic' politicians would end up losing all credibility. 'It
is not quite so easy for mainland officials to control the way four hundred people vote for sixty candidates as it was to stage-manage the way
four hundred behaved over three,' he surmised. But not for the first
time, he had allowed himself to underestimate Beijing's corrosive will.
On Saturday 21 December, the results of the 'election' were
announced. Of the thirty-four 'pathetic' aspirants for 'shadow' power,
thirty-three were duly chosen. The remaining twenty-seven seats were
taken by a small army of obedient 'patriots', notable among whom
were a handful of former legislators like Peggy Lam, Elsie Tu and
Tsang Yok Sing – all of whom had been rejected by the voters in
1995. So much for democracy.

Any remnants of optimism Patten still harboured about C.H. Tung
quickly evaporated. A week after his appointment, the new chief executive (whose office lost no time in dropping the 'designate' appendage
from his official title) hastened to Beijing to be sworn in. Before leaving Hong Kong, he used a press conference to attack the governor,
declaring that it was wrong to 'ignore the reality' of the provisional
assembly, which, he claimed, would have a useful role to fulfil now that
the 'through train' had been derailed by Britain's failure to abide by the
Basic Law. Some of Patten's advisers had hoped that C.H. would use his
newly acquired authority to demonstrate his independence from
Beijing; instead, he was sounding ever more like his masters' voice. At

a reception in the Great Hall of the People in Beijing, the president, Jiang Zemin, echoing the words of Deng Xiaoping almost seventeen years earlier, reassured his guest that he should put his 'mind at ease', because, 'from now on, we shall strictly abide by the Basic Law when handling the issues of Hong Kong. We will definitely not interfere with matters that are within the high degree of autonomy promised for the SAR.' It was a statement which, of course, begged every important question now facing the British colony. C.H. Tung responded by promising his host that he would do his best to contribute to the well-being of both the SAR and China.

Precisely what this might mean for Hong Kong after 1997 was unlikely to emerge for some months, but it became increasingly clear that there was small chance of the new chief executive deviating from China's own sense of Hong Kong's priorities. During an eighty-five-minute meeting with the governor on 23 December, he restated his support for the provisional legislature: it was, he said, 'the wish of Hong Kong's entire six million people that we have a smooth transition', and it was therefore very important that there should be 'co-operation' between the Hong Kong government and the 'SAR government'. Patten's press secretary Kerry McGlynn reported bluntly that the pair had 'agreed to disagree'.

On 31 December, the new chief executive had an informal lunch with forty-eight members of the provisional legislature. Congratulating them on their success, he told them that although they would not be called upon to pass any legislation before the handover, they would have an important role in the months ahead. They would sit across the border in Shenzhen and prepare laws that would be enacted as soon as power had been ceded formally by the British, and his office would give them as much administrative support as possible. Soon afterwards he announced the appointment of his Executive Council: as Government House had feared, its balance was tipped heavily in favour of Beijing. Only one of its fifteen members had been heard to speak openly in support of freedom or democracy. The rest, led by the seventy-nine-year-old Sir S.Y. Chung (once staunchly pro-British) had shown themselves to be conspicuously hostile to Patten's reforms. Responding to criticisms that the post-1997 ExCo would be dominated by the anti-Patten business community, Sir S.Y. commented: 'We can only talk about social welfare and civil rights after we have made money.' It was the authentic voice of Hong Kong's elite.

There was worse to come. After a meeting on 17 January 1997, the so-called legal subgroup of the Preparatory Committee published proposals for abolishing or amending the civil-liberties legislation which, under Patten's instructions, had been revised to eliminate from the statute book those colonial measures which infringed the 1991 Bill of Rights. This threat to reimpose controls that would inhibit rights to assembly, free speech and free association sent a shiver of horror down the spine of Hong Kong. Patten described the proposals as 'legal nonsense', and, a few days later, used his monthly question-and-answer session to express his scorn for those present and former members of LegCo and ExCo who had once endorsed the very Bill of Rights which, at China's behest, they now seemed eager to repudiate. Several hundred members of the Democratic party and Emily Lau's new Frontier party picketed the NCNA's office in protest. Even the usually discreet financial secretary, Donald Tsang, felt moved to warn that international investment might flow out of Hong Kong if the rights of free speech and free assembly were withdrawn from its citizens.

Initially, C.H. Tung refused to comment, but on 23 January, at a dinner where he was honoured as 'leader of the year' by one of the territory's most fervently pro-Beijing newspapers, he asserted that the legislation proposed by the Preparatory Committee was indeed 'consistent with the Basic Law'. Later he was besieged by reporters outside the hotel where the dinner was held. In response to their questions, he snapped, 'We will find a way forward.' He paused before adding angrily, 'But it may not be the way you like.' Hong Kong had not heard such harsh words from this apparently mild elder statesman before, and, in the current febrile atmosphere, they set alarm bells ringing. According to a poll conducted by the Hong Kong University, his popularity plummeted overnight by 15 points.

No one was more disconcerted by C.H. Tung's apparent submission to Beijing than Anson Chan. At a breakfast meeting on 28 December, C.H. had asked her to remain in her post after the handover and, after careful thought, she had agreed. Patten knew that she would find it hard to serve two masters, and he was prepared for her to drift away from him in the months ahead, but he had not expected her to be caught quite so early in what she now described publicly as a 'very delicate situation'. Acknowledging her disquiet, she tried to skirt around the clash of loyalties she now faced by refusing to echo Patten's condemnation of the provisional legco. Instead she expressed the hope that the provisional body would not try to legislate in parallel or in competition with the existing, elected legislature. Within days observers had begun to speculate about how long she would manage to straddle the divide. At Government House, where her colleagues viewed her situation with sympathy, one or two people started to wonder whether she would be able to survive as chief secretary after the handover.

The governor's own troubles had been compounded by a visit to
Hong Kong by the former foreign secretary Lord Howe at the beginning of January. In a speech at a joint gathering of the British and
Australian Chambers of Commerce, he took it upon himself to caution
the democrats that 'Hong Kong is not entitled to regard itself – would
be very unwise to regard itself – as a bridgehead for revolution within
the People's Republic.' Howe's appreciation of Beijing's concerns had
recently been enhanced by his appointment to the board of GEC,
which was increasingly active in China. He told his audience: 'Hong
Kong cannot and should not expect to transform China. Trying to do
so could risk destroying Hong Kong itself.' As one or two of Patten's
aides observed, this warning could easily have issued from a spokesman
for the Chinese politburo. Warming to his theme, the former foreign
secretary urged the local media to exercise caution and restraint in its
coverage of China, reassuring them that developments in the SAR and
China would be under the careful scrutiny of their colleagues around
the world. One or two of Howe's friends believed that the former
foreign secretary had himself coveted the governorship of Hong Kong.
Certainly he did little to dispel the suspicion that he considered his own
ultra-emollient approach to be more suited to the conduct of relations
with China than Patten's less equivocal stance.

Martin Lee denounced Howe's comments as 'shameless', adding that
the former foreign secretary was simply trying to prove that the
'kowtow' policy of which he had been a principal agent had been correct. Patten himself was frustrated, although he did not realise the depth
of Howe's aversion to his stewardship, or that, for the future record,
Howe would volunteer the opinion: 'It would have been so much
better if Hong Kong had got in place a governor who would have
played that crucial part of managing the process of transition right up
till the last minute.' Had Patten known of Howe's disdain, it is conceivable that he might have taken the opportunity to repudiate his
views; as it was he grumbled in private but kept his counsel.

On 23 January the provisional legislature held its first meeting, electing one of Beijing's most unremitting apologists, Rita Fan, as its
president. In his regular *Letter to Hong Kong*, broadcast by RTHK the
following day, Patten declared, 'We are not simply limp victims of
other people's decisions . . . Those who have agreed to help close
down Hong Kong's elected legislature' – the 'honourable members'
who had decamped to Shenzhen the previous day – 'can at least prevent
the trashing of Hong Kong's civil liberties. Many of them actually
voted for our Bill of Rights.' He signed off with a question: 'Is Hong
Kong going to have the same freedoms after 1997? Yes or no?' His

words were intended as a challenge, but they betrayed his growing despair.

On 29 January the re-elected president of the United States warned China to honour the commitment to 'one country, two systems'. Bill Clinton said that he was not sure Hong Kong could 'exist, with all its potential to help China modernise its own economy and open opportunities for its own people, if the civil liberties of the people are crushed'. C.H. Tung, who was in Beijing for a plenary session of the Preparatory Committee, responded that certain sectors of people around the world were being misled. 'They should spend more time to understand what is going on in Hong Kong.' He was immediately contradicted by the governor, who said that Clinton was concerned because these issues were not 'marginal issues . . . he is not misinformed about what is going on in Hong Kong'.

On 1 February, the Chinese foreign secretary opened the two-day plenum of the Preparatory Committee with the formal announcement that Government House had long feared and Chris Patten had once thought would never be heard. Qian Qichen told his audience that members of the provisional legislature would be free to scrutinise and approve legislation before 30 June, although it would not be enacted until after 1 July. The timing and scope of their work would be based on rulings by the Preparatory Committee and the National People's Congress.

As the 134 members of the Preparatory Committee readied themselves to cast their votes in favour of the 'recommendation' to repeal the civil-rights legislation put in place under Patten's administration, a storm of debate erupted in Hong Kong. Scholars, lawyers and politicians united to denounce the proposal to abolish or amend these crucial safeguards. Even Allen Lee was perturbed. 'I have read the Basic Law again, but I cannot see how it is infringed,' he told the *South China Morning Post*. 'I and my colleagues believe the ordinances have not damaged public order.' Declaring, 'There is no way I will change my view on this subject,' he vowed to oppose any attempt to repeal the Public Order Amendment and Societies Ordinances. On 2 February, 124 members of the Preparatory Committee voted in favour of dismantling the legislation after the handover. Ten members abstained. Only the indomitable Frederick Fung registered his dismay with a 'no' vote. The provisional legislature was thus authorised to act as China's Trojan horse for Hong Kong. Empowered by the National People's Congress to draw up a set of laws to inhibit human rights and civil liberties, they would also be given the task of drafting new legislation on subversion, secession, treason and sedition to replace the Crimes

Ordinance which had by now been negotiated through a second reading in LegCo.

Now, somewhat later than he had originally anticipated, the governor's authority began to crumble. Although he remained astonishingly popular in the community, winning just under 60 per cent support in the most recent polls, his power was ebbing away, and everyone knew it. He had slipped from the centre of attention; increasingly, he became a spectator, if not a spectre, at an unpalatable feast. His hopes for Hong Kong, expressed with undiminished energy and eloquence in speeches and interviews on radio and television, were more frequently at odds with the presumed certainties of his listeners. His words therefore hung in the air, forlorn echoes of what might have been, no longer carrying conviction.

By the beginning of 1997, Hong Kong's psyche seemed to have been gripped by a combination of resignation and suppressed panic. This contradictory mix was expressed most emblematically in popular ambivalence towards Britain. On one hand, it was becoming de rigueur to display a patriotic conviction that Hong Kong's return to the 'motherland' was a matter for unbridled celebration; on the other, any suggestion that the British might not honour their post-handover obligations under the Joint Declaration prompted intense indignation. This latent schizophrenia reached into the upper echelons of Hong Kong and was most evident in relation to the passports issue. Those who had been selected for one of the 50,000 United Kingdom passports granted under the 1990 British Nationality Scheme guarded their secret acquisitions jealously. Hong Kong's sensitivity on this subject was dramatically, if inadvertently, exposed by Britain's senior trade commissioner in Hong Kong, Francis Cornish, who was due to become Britain's first consul general after the handover. Showing reporters around the new British post-1997 consulate – a confident if fortress-like edifice designed by the British architect Terry Farrell – Cornish mentioned that holders of British passports granted under the Nationality Scheme could not be guaranteed consular protection after 1997 as the Chinese had refused to recognise the validity of the passports. As a result, he said, 'you end up with the situation of dual citizenship, dual nationality'.

Cornish's remarks caused an immediate outcry. Every news bulletin in Hong Kong and almost every front-page headline carried his chill warning: 'NO CONSULAR SHIELD FOR UK SCHEME PASSPORTS'; 'BRITAIN BLASTED FOR DENYING PROTECTION'. Politicians and civil servants, many of whom had placed their faith in the future in the protection apparently offered by these passports, rounded on the British authorities, accusing them of bad faith and treachery. 'The British passport,' a senior civil servant complained, 'will become a blank paper with no purpose at all . . . I am supposed to be a real British citizen, so how can Britain treat us differently?' Furious at what he regarded as Cornish's clumsy comments and alarmed by the sudden panic they had triggered, Patten summoned him for an explanation. Cornish was unrepentant. He reminded the governor about the limits of Britain's authority. Regardless of the fact that passports granted under the British Nationality Scheme were full UK passports, there was nothing to stop the Chinese asserting that any individual who held a Hong Kong identity card or an SAR passport would be treated as a Chinese citizen even if he or she were suddenly to produce a BNS passport to prove UK citizenship. As Cornish put it later, 'This group of people, to the Chinese, are Chinese nationals. China doesn't recognise dual nationality. To the British, they are British, and there is a full British passport to prove it.' In these circumstances, Cornish believed it would be virtually impossible for the British consul in Hong Kong (or, indeed, China) to guarantee this group of British citizens the usual degree of protection. In spite of the furore he had caused, he thought he had been right to explain the facts as he saw them.

> This is an excitable place and this is a neuralgic issue . . . but I think it is very important not to give any impression that you can do more than, in the real world, you can – which is not quite the same thing as saying you won't try. What it boils down to is that we are the absolute authority on who is British, but we cannot set ourselves up as any kind of absolute authority on who the Chinese regard as Chinese.

Patten was well aware that what Cornish had said was true, but he blamed the British official for expressing himself in terms which were bound to excite rather than to allay Hong Kong's anxieties. After a flurry of telephone conversations between Government House and London, he persuaded the foreign secretary to issue a statement in the hope of limiting the damage. Rifkind duly announced: 'We would not regard any claim by the local authorities that a British passport obtained under the local British Nationality Scheme was acceptable evidence of dual nationality.' This attempt at reassurance made little impact. Patten was anxious about the gulf afflicting the colony 'between what people say, the confidence they claim, and the boiling emotions there are under the surface, particularly the nervousness about what life is really going to be like after 1997, whether the communist cadres have really changed their spots or not'. He also feared that the headlines would lead the public to believe that 'this was just the British ratting again: that we'd given these passports, that they were really worthless, that we weren't going to make even modest sacrifices for anybody in Hong Kong'. He was no less concerned that, if Hong Kong's civil servants started to believe that Britain 'would not lift a finger for people after 1997', they would start to wonder what point there was in remaining loyal to Britain and British political values.

In an effort to dispel these fears, Patten took the unusual step of inviting himself to LegCo, where, in what even his critics conceded to be a bravura performance, he insisted that Britain would not discriminate between a UK passport obtained under the BNS scheme or by any other legitimate means. Nor would a British government accept that 'the way in which a British citizen obtained his or her passport would be of itself evidence of dual nationality'. And he promised that even in cases of dual nationality, 'Britain will not stand idly by if British nationals are in trouble'.

He was brought up short, however, by Margaret Ng. She did not question his good faith, but asked for reassurance that the Chinese authorities would have no way of establishing how or where a British passport had been obtained. He answered with care. 'I do not believe that there is any way in which Chinese authorities will know how somebody acquired a British passport.' He then drew attention to what he described as a 'chilling' statement by an NCNA official, who was reported to have to have told the *Hong Kong Standard* that identified BNS passport-holders would be regarded as Chinese nationals even if they had lived in Britain and returned to Hong Kong as British citizens, and that China would be able to trace such people even though their files were kept by Britain. Patten then asked with barely suppressed fury, 'What is it, what state of mind is it, that brings people to make statements like that when all we are attempting to do is to give people in Hong Kong reassurances about their future, about their future stability and their future freedoms?'

Margaret Ng persisted, asking what had happened to the files containing the details of those who had applied for British passports under the British Nationality Scheme. Patten replied that, as far as he knew, the information was held by the Immigration Department and would be sent back to London through the consulate general before the handover. He added, 'I want to assure everybody in Hong Kong that we do everything humanly possible, technologically possible, to keep the material secure and to keep that material confidential.'

Emily Lau returned to the issue a little later, raising the suspicion that the Chinese government might already have access to the list of people who had been granted BNS passports. Patten retorted sharply:

> I don't know how, if one's veracity is suspected, one can put the point more strongly than I am going to do: I know of no evidence, have no evidence, that Chinese officials have lists of those people who are beneficiaries under the British Nationality Scheme. I have no evidence whatsoever of that. I am not surprised, when things like this are said, that people worry. I can understand it – I would worry myself . . . I would not, I hope, even if I was a liar, put the point as explicitly, as comprehensively, as I have just done.

Emily Lau had perhaps touched on the most sensitive aspect of this tortuous and delicate issue. Six months earlier, the director of the Immigration Department, Laurence Leung, had suddenly resigned, on 'personal' grounds. Rumours soon began to spread that he had been forced to hand in his notice, and that the Hong Kong government, led by Patten, was engaged in a cover-up of Watergate-type proportions of Laurence Leung's activities. One of these whispers had it that the Hong Kong official had managed to acquire the list of BNS passport-holders and had handed it over to Beijing. This story, among others, soon became a subject of open conjecture and rapidly acquired the status of a revealed truth. Patten's attempt to quash the rumours in LegCo was soon to be undermined by Laurence Leung himself.

On 10 January, the former director of immigration had been summoned to LegCo, where a committee had been set up to inquire into the circumstances surrounding his sudden departure. He told the legislators that, far from offering his resignation, he had been forced to resign on the instructions of the governor and the chief secretary. He went on to relate that in 1995 he had been the subject of an official investigation by the Independent Commission Against Corruption (ICAC), which had been unable to establish that he had acquired his wealth by improper means. The government was forced to concede that Laurence Leung had been under sustained investigation, but that the facts which had been uncovered about his activities were not adequate to justify his dismissal. Despite the agitation of a feverish media, the authorities had little more to say, except that, in the circumstances, it had been agreed that Laurence Leung would be allowed to depart from office with his honour, officially, intact.

The integrity of the Immigration Department was also crucial to Britain's efforts to establish the SAR passport as a valid international document which could not be faked. Worried officials from more than one country who were considering whether or not to grant visa-free access to SAR passport-holders now hurried to seek reassurance from the Hong Kong authorities. What if, as a result of lax security or internal corruption, the Chinese had acquired enough information to issue SAR passports illicitly either on the mainland or in any of their embassies around the world? The foreign consulates were particularly concerned about triad gangs or Chinese agents infiltrating their borders. On this question at least they were offered an unequivocal response. Even if any official had in the past enjoyed improper links with the mainland – and there was no evidence of this – the security features of the SAR passport, which had only recently been finalised, were intact: they had no cause for alarm.

The senior British officials most closely connected with immigration were convinced that Patten's uncompromising statement about the integrity of the British passports issued under the BNS scheme was justified. According to one of them, only one person had access to the list of people who had been given BNS passports, and none of this individual's colleagues had ever asked to see the list – which, as it happened, was due to be taken back to London before 1 July by the same official. So the list was safe. In any case, it was common knowledge at Government House that the fears which had led to the aborted investigation into Laurence Leung did not relate to the integrity of the Immigration Department, but to other matters, which – for good reason in an open society replete with libel laws – it was not possible to air publicly.

Patten himself was intensely irritated by what he regarded as the contemptible efforts of over-excited conspiracy theorists in the media who refused to accept his word on the subject. Privately he dismissed them as a 'relatively small group of expatriate journalists', and 'one or two people with axes to grind in the Legislative Council' – individuals who, he complained, 'think that Anson Chan and I are not only telling lies but are political innocents out of the kindergarten'. The issue soon faded from the headlines but the anxieties which it had brought to the surface were not erased.

In all these matters the honour and reputation of Britain was at stake. Patten had given as much reassurance as he could to British passport-holders. After a long battle, he had finally persuaded the home secretary to grant British passports to the war widows and to grant the same rights to those with SAR passports as those enjoyed by holders of BNO passports. As a result, almost every citizen of Hong Kong would have the right to enter the United Kingdom without a visa after 1997. Only the ethnic minorities were still without that security. On his visit to London the previous October he had tried unsuccessfully to persuade the home secretary to relent. In December, he returned to the issue again, reminding Michael Howard that the Labour party had committed itself to offering these soon-to-be stateless British subjects right of abode in Britain with the opportunity to acquire full British citizenship after five years of continuous settlement in the United Kingdom. He pointed out that as a result the government 'would not be in any political difficulties if it took what would be regarded as a generous-minded approach'. As he had expected, Howard was unwilling to give any more ground. Enough had been done already, the home secretary told him, and nothing had changed to warrant a shift by the government. Even though this was a special case, it was not special enough to justify offering British citizenship to up to 7,000 people from the Indian subcontinent who would not lose the right to stay in Hong Kong after 1997. 'I got nowhere,' said Patten after their meeting.

He was not willing to leave it there. 'I think it is inconceivable that we can be in that position come 30 June 1997,' he said flatly just before his last Christmas in Hong Kong. 'I think the story of Britain's departure from Hong Kong will be told at least partly through the experience of four or five thousand South Asians who think they're being abandoned. I think it would be regarded by a lot of people around the world as pretty shameful.' Acknowledging that he personally would also feel ashamed, he admitted, 'I think it will be something of a failure on my part if I don't get a better deal for them.'

'WE ALL KNOW THE END OF THE PLOT'

Wrangling About the Handover

The leaders of the Indian community in Hong Kong now saw that time was rapidly running out for them. The sense of despair in Hari Harilela's household was pervasive and overt. What would happen, one of his family asked, if they were in trouble with the authorities after 1997? 'I don't have a passport. I am in jail. How can the British get me out? What is this "guarantee"? We have no protection. If we have a British passport then we have protection. All China can do then is to say, "OK, we will deport you." As it stands, they can still deport us but we have nowhere to go.' Hari Harilela estimated that a third of his relatives had been granted passports under the BNS scheme; the rest would be stateless. His son was still without a passport. 'He has his PhD from England. He has lived there for thirteen years of his life,' Harilela entreated. 'They have promised me. In September, October, November, December, I call them. They say, "Yes, yes, yes," but so far, nothing. Strange. I don't understand.' As a last resort he went to see the chief secretary, Anson Chan, who was clearly embarrassed. It was not her responsibility, she explained; it was British law, and not in the hands of the governor. Hari Harilela concluded: 'I think the Home Office is behind it. But I don't know why. I just don't understand.'

At the Harilela family's weekly get-together one of his sisters said, 'I am very uncomfortable about what might happen in the next two years. Maybe it will be smooth to start with, but after that . . .' She spoke softly and her voice trailed away. Then she added, 'We've been abandoned.' Another explained, 'My father was a British subject. I am second generation. I was born and bred in Hong Kong. You ask what

I think? The initial emotion is anger; then the anger subsides, and it becomes sorrow.' A cousin had an even more complicated problem. 'My situation is OK – I have a British passport; my wife has a passport. My daughter has a passport, but my two sons do not. I mean, how are we to stay together if we have to move out of this place?'

'Of course, I understand the "floodgates" argument, that the British can't let everyone in,' said Hari's stateless son in a voice tinged with sarcasm. 'But in the face of statelessness it feels different.' He outlined a depressing potential post-1997 scenario.

In the case of my parents and myself, we will walk up to Immigration as a family, but they will look at our passports and see that they are different, and then they will question us. 'Are you really a family? Explain, how come you have different passports?' I get a lot of hassle at Heathrow. I have an identity card, I have a student visa, but I don't have a British passport. Or maybe it is because I am not British by race or origin. My parents go straight through . . . We fear being separated in the future. In our culture we live as a family, together, until we are married. We are one family, but the British government does not acknowledge that.

His father interrupted. 'You know, we feel proud because we've grown up in this colony and we have lived with the British. And then all of a sudden, they deny us. That is what hurts.'

His youngest sister added, in a hesitant whisper as if ashamed to utter the thought, 'When the Falklands were invaded, Britain ran down there immediately. And there were just a handful of people stranded. It makes me feel that probably it is because we are not white. That is why we are stranded.'

When Chris Patten heard about these remarks, he said bleakly, 'She is trapped between the explicitly racist nature of Chinese nationality policy and the British Home Office. And precisely how you describe the British Home Office's attitude on these matters, and precisely how you compare it with Chinese nationality law, I leave to you.' And where did that leave Michael Howard? According to the governor, weighing his words with care, 'The home secretary has a political agenda which is different from mine. I think the home secretary believes that he should be seen as a tough home secretary, not just tough on crime, but also tough on the number of immigrants coming into the country.'

Howard's tenacity, however, was matched by Patten's. And the governor had an advantage: he knew that the foreign secretary shared his view, and he was confident that Michael Heseltine could be brought on side. The prime minister had always been sympathetic – he had already told one of his private secretaries that the present position was 'morally untenable' – and although he was not willing to confront Howard at this stage, Patten felt confident that, if it came to a Cabinet show-down, the home secretary would be overruled. Howard clearly thought otherwise; he made it clear to his friends that he would fight until the bitter end to maintain the status quo. According to his critics he even persuaded the chief whip, Sir Alastair Goodlad, one of Patten's close friends, to tell the prime minister that the Tory backbenchers 'wouldn't wear' any further concessions.

On 19 December 1996, Malcolm Rifkind, who believed that this was the last piece of important unfinished business to be resolved, had had a meeting with Howard at the Home Office. He suggested that the home secretary should at least shift to the position already adopted by the Labour party. At first Howard resisted, but under sustained pressure from the foreign secretary he eventually agreed to look at the situation again to see whether there was a case for strengthening the prime minister's March 'guarantee'. He insisted, however, that he would not agree to make any change at all unless it was discussed and agreed by the full Cabinet. Rifkind's officials were pessimistic about the prospects of winning Howard over, but the foreign secretary interpreted his reference to a Cabinet meeting as a concession in itself.

In January, the Foreign Office and Government House joined forces for a further assault on the Home Office, making it clear that it would not be good enough 'merely to tinker with the wording' of the com-mitment to the ethnic minorities. With the full backing of the foreign secretary, Patten had another meeting with Michael Howard at which he challenged the home secretary directly, asserting that it was specious to claim that the issue had been resolved by the 1990 Nationalities Bill. At that point, the exceptional predicament of the ethnic minorities had not even been identified, let alone debated by Parliament. The ethnic minorities had been sidelined in 1990, and it was most unfair to suggest otherwise. At the end of their session, Howard, courteous as ever, said, 'You've set out the arguments more eloquently than ever before,' but he made it obvious that he had not changed his mind. This time, however, the Government House team came away with the impression – if only from his body language – that the home secretary was not quite as unmovable as he might have wished them to believe. They also detected that Howard's officials, who had come under persistent pressure from the Foreign Office and from Government House, had begun to distance themselves from their political master. Even his political advisers now intimated that they thought Howard would be unable to stand fast.

At this point the home secretary's fortress began rapidly to crumble. On 30 January, a House of Lords bill to grant full British passports to Hong Kong's ethnic minorities reached its third reading stage. The bill's author, Lord Willoughby de Broke, who had campaigned tirelessly for many months, secured the support of many Conservative peers, two previous governors, Lords MacLehose and Wilson, and Lord Bramall, a former commander of the Hong Kong garrison, who accused the government of a 'cruel and heartless' approach. Baroness Blatch, for the Home Office, tried in vain to defend Howard's position. She emerged from her drubbing with the words, 'This is an untenable policy' – a judgement Chris Patten was careful to pass on to the prime minister at a private lunch a few days later.

Approved by the Lords, the Willoughby de Broke bill went straight to the Commons, to be introduced there by an elder statesman of the Tory backbenches, Sir Patrick Cormick. He told the house: 'This small group of people should be granted the security their loyalty to the crown merits.' It was by now doubtful that the government would be able to hold the line. Four days later, on 3 February, the home secretary, finally recognising how isolated he had become, asked to see the prime minister at 10 Downing Street. 'I've changed my mind,' he told John Major. The next day, in the House of Commons, Howard announced his surrender in a written reply.

> I have carefully reviewed the position of the solely British ethnic minorities in Hong Kong, in the light of expressions of concern in both Houses of Parliament here and in Hong Kong . . . It is clear that the assurances which they have been given over a number of years have not allayed this concern. I therefore intend to make provision enabling them to apply for registration as British citizens, giving them right of abode in the United Kingdom.

Jubilant at Howard's volte-face, Patten said: 'The case has been put with dignity and vigour, and today the right decision has been made.' Privately he added dryly, 'It shows how open-minded the home secretary is.' It was the first piece of good news he had received for many months. It was likely to be the last.

With six months to go before the handover, the Pattens were counting the days. 'Since we all know the end of the plot, the sooner we get to the last page, the better,' the governor commented cryptically. 'I'd now like to get on with the packing and get things over and done with.' In truth there was little left for him to do except to fulfil his official duties, to preside over the mundane task of finalising the details of the hand-over ceremony and to continue to stand up for the principles which had animated his governorship. The pleasures of Hong Kong had begun to pall many months before, and he looked forward to returning home. In January he and Lavender began to search in earnest for a house in London. Their friends speculated about his future. Would he return by some means to British politics after the general election, which it was presumed the Conservatives would lose? Would he succeed Sir Leon Brittan as European commissioner – a role it was widely thought would be available to him if Tony Blair were to form the next government? Would he be offered a senior posting at the United Nations? Would he accept an invitation to run an Oxford or Cambridge college? Would he take to the lucrative international lecture circuit? Or would he simply bide his time?

Patten had already made up his mind to stay away from Britain for at least six months. His intention was to live at the house he and Lavender had bought in France, at least until the spring of 1998, and to write the first of three planned books about his experiences of Hong Kong and the Far East. In this first book he would lay out his ideas about the success of the Asian economies and its implication for Britain and Europe. In the process he would almost certainly define his reformulated attitudes towards the European Union and Britain's part in it, his scepticism towards the European currency, his enthusiasm for otherwise widening and deepening the union and his conviction that the 'democratic deficit' should be made good through a strengthened European Parliament. By keeping away from Westminster, he hoped to escape the insistent speculation over his political future, about which he was himself entirely uncertain in any case. He had not completely written off a Westminster comeback, although he was not sure either how this might be achieved, or even that he really wanted to return to what seemed to him – in some moods – a tawdry and parochial stage. He certainly had little appetite for conscripting himself into the trenches for what he feared would be a vicious civil war in his party over Europe; nor was he tempted to pick up the clutch of company directorships that would doubtless be available to him on his return. However, at the age of fifty-three, he needed to earn a living and wanted to have a purpose worthy of his talents.

Some observers wondered if the Pattens would find it difficult to wean themselves off the grandeur of their Hong Kong status: the secretaries, chauffeurs, footmen, butlers, cooks, cleaners, gardeners and bodyguards. Would they miss the Rolls–Royce, the yacht, the official mansion and the grace-and-favour country house, and the deference with which, in public at least, they were treated? Would the governor find it hard to adjust to a world in which he did not have automatic access to presidents and premiers? The truth, as their friends knew, was that they would find it a relief to be free of the formalities by which their lives had been bounded for the previous four and a half years. Although Lavender Patten had developed the poise and style of a first lady, she had never allowed herself the indulgence of presuming that this elevation was anything other than accidental and short-lived. She had enjoyed the tennis and the golf and the walks which characterised the days of so many fellow expatriates. She had made friends in the Chinese community, although she was perplexed, if not resentful, when the wives of prominent local figures began to distance themselves from her as the relationship with China deteriorated. As the patron of more than a score of charities, she had attended luncheons, made speeches, and, with evident conviction, visited the sick and the needy. She had emerged from this experience confident but without vainglory.

The governor kept up the momentum of work without the illusion of power. By January his diary was crammed for the following months with routine business and official farewells. During his governorship he had made sixteen overseas trips (excluding his eighteen visits to London on Hong Kong business) and had been granted audiences with one emperor, three presidents and eight prime ministers. There had been innumerable formal speeches, ceremonial functions, district visits, political events; meetings with business and community leaders; charitable, academic, professional and sporting receptions. He had opened exhibitions and other cultural events, and together the Pattens had hosted 320 official dinners, 243 official lunches, and 175 official receptions at Government House, wining and dining for Britain with a dutiful vengeance. More than 500 visiting guests had stayed at Government House, some of them on several occasions – among their number four members of the royal family, Cabinet ministers, politicians, ambassadors, Lady Thatcher, Sir Edward Heath and the archbishop of Canterbury. It had been demanding, stimulating and frequently enjoyable. But neither the governor nor his wife regretted for a moment that it would soon be all over.

The removal men had already been booked. The Chinese chests, sideboards, chairs and tables, antique pots, vases, boxes and sculptures Patten had accumulated in his frequent forays to the shops in Hollywood Road were to be packed and shipped in the spring along with their books and the other modest possessions they had brought with them to Hong Kong. All that would remain on the day of their departure aboard the royal yacht would be a suitcase or two. The future of Government House itself was still uncertain. It seemed unlikely that C.H. Tung would consider it appropriate to take up residence in what, psychologically, would have become be a colonial relic. Some thought the house should become a museum, with its grounds open to the public and available for concerts; others that it could be used as a government guest house in the Chinese tradition. Some suggested pulling it down to make way for a commercial redevelopment. When the governor discussed the options with his successor, C.H. indicated that he was worried about the 'bad *feng shui*' of Government House. Although some years earlier a tree had been planted strategically in the garden to offset the adverse effects of the Bank of China's sharp-edged profile, which pierced the very heart of Government House, the incoming chief executive was evidently concerned about the Japanese tower at the eastern end of the building: the *feng-shui* man had told him that it would need to be redesigned in the shape of a dome and painted gold to create the good *feng shui* without which, C.H. was warned, he would be ill advised to take up residence therein. Patten, a devout Catholic who understood the pull of mysticism, nevertheless found it quite impossible to fathom such superstition. Although Betty Tung, Hong Kong's future first lady, had indicated to Lavender that she relished the prospect of inheriting Government House, she had intimated that her husband was strongly against the proposal. At the end of May, C.H. Tung confirmed that they would not be moving in when the Pattens left.

Whatever became of Government House, there was no question that Britain's colonial footprints would soon disappear from this most unsentimental of societies. Symbolically, the Royal Hong Kong Golf Club, the Royal Hong Kong Jockey Club and the Royal Society for the Prevention of Cruelty for Animals (HK) had already discarded their emblematic relationship with the crown. In May 1996 the Royal Hong Kong Yacht Club voted narrowly to retain their link. Nevertheless, in early 1997 members decided to ask the Chinese president, Jiang Zemin, to replace the Queen as their patron and C.H. Tung to take over from the governor as vice-patron. It was doubtful, however, whether either would accept while the colonial stain remained on the crested note-paper. The 'Royal' was also due to be removed from the Royal Observatory, and, inevitably, from the Royal Hong Kong Police Force. In common with fourteen other public services, the police were to replace the crown on their insignia with a representation of the five-petalled bauhinia flower after 1997. But the stylised view of the Hong Kong waterfront which was to succeed the nineteenth-century trading schooners at the centre of the police badge had been carefully designed to exclude the headquarters of Jardine Matheson, Jardine House, one of the colony's most prominent waterside landmarks. The head of public relations for the Royal Hong Kong Police said, 'It's our badge, so we can do what we want with it.' He did not mention that the final design had required the approval of the new chief executive and the Chinese authorities. On Jardine's behalf, an emollient Martin Barrow retorted, 'Neither I nor anybody else is overreacting. We are here to stay. If anybody chooses to do anything of this sort, then fine, but I don't think one can read too much into it.' Traditionalists, sentimentalists and historians were relieved that there were no plans to erase British links with scores of streets, roads and drives, or Victoria Park and the Prince of Wales building on the waterfront in Central.

In February, a firm in the Chinese city of Guangzhou completed the first batch of 1,200 Chinese national and Hong Kong SAR flags ordered by the colony's pro-Beijing Federation of Education Workers. All were snapped up at once by schools throughout the colony, who were uncertain which of the two flags they would be required to fly after 1 July. The handover logo (featured on a selection of forty souvenirs), a smiling pink dolphin designed to highlight the threat to this endangered species, found itself in the troubled waters of cultural misunderstanding. The deal between an American company, CYRK, and the 'Association for the Celebration of Reunification of Hong Kong and China' gave CYRK a monopoly of official memorabilia. However, one of the colony's leading fashion designers, Mickey Li Honming, criticised the graphic and the colours selected by the Americans.

The pink dolphin could usefully have served as a symbol of the way in which the future of Hong Kong continued to thwart efforts by Foreign Office officials to 'warm up' the relationship with China. Politicians and diplomats on both sides continued to smile and shake hands for the cameras, but still they could find no common ground on democracy or human rights. As the handover approached, the language of diplomacy grew sterner. In Singapore for a joint meeting of ASEAN and European Union foreign ministers, Malcolm Rifkind had yet another fruitless conversation with Qian Qichen, the last scheduled under the current regime. Afterwards, the British foreign minister conceded that it would be naive and unrealistic to expect the Chinese to reverse their policy towards the provisional legislative council or human rights in Hong Kong. Some days earlier, in a characteristically quixotic gesture, Beijing announced that the Hong Kong journalist Xi Yang, sentenced to twelve years in prison in 1993 for 'stealing state secrets', was to be released. The crass cynicism of this arbitrary show of lenience did little to soothe the ever-deepening anxiety about the future of human rights in Hong Kong. Likewise, the promulgation of a directive instructing China's journalists how to report the world about them – which explicitly reminded them of their duty to 'promote patriotism, collectivism and socialism' and enjoined them to 'uphold the truth in news' – sent another chill wind through those parts of the media which had not yet succumbed to the inevitable. A few days later, a spokesman for the Hong Kong and Macau Affairs Office in Beijing gave a briefing for Hong Kong reporters to remind them that there was 'no such thing as absolute rights and freedoms'.

The feeling that Britain was on the back foot in Hong Kong was compounded when the *South China Morning Post* gave prominence to Singapore's senior minister Lee Kuan Yew's optimistic assessment of the territory's future. Echoing the thoughts expressed earlier by Lord Howe, the architect of Asia's model state (who was greatly admired by Hong Kong's future chief executive), Lee Kuan Yew wrote:

> Hong Kong looks set to prosper for many more years, provided its people mind Hong Kong's business, and do not meddle in China's politics. Hong Kong's people have to make up their minds whether they want to prosper under 'one country, two systems', or to engage China on human rights and democracy as the Hong Kong 'democrats' have been doing, encouraged by American human-rights groups, the US media and by Governor Chris Patten and his policies. No human-rights and democracy hero can reverse the inevitable – that over time Hong Kong will become more of a Chinese city, if nothing else than by osmosis.

Such sentiments could as easily have been expressed by C.H. Tung or by a host of other luminaries, including the chairman of the Hong Kong and Shanghai Bank, Sir William Purves; almost any member of the Chinese or British Chambers of Commerce in Hong Kong; a significant proportion of the British Foreign Office; the British ambassador to Beijing, Sir Len Appleyard; two former governors, Lords MacLehose and Wilson; Sir Percy Cradock and a sprinkling of super-annuated Cabinet ministers, led by Lords Howe, Prior and Young. This knowledge aggrieved and offended Britain's last governor almost more than anything else.

In Europe on a month-long tour, Martin Lee continued to pursue his case for genuine autonomy, warning Beijing not to 'meddle' in Hong Kong's affairs. C.H. Tung retaliated by castigating Martin Lee for 'bad-mouthing' Hong Kong overseas, declaring angrily that he had 'blackened the reputation of Hong Kong . . . giving the impression that Hong Kong is collapsing'. One of Martin Lee's colleagues, Dr Yeung Sum, responded sarcastically, accusing the future chief executive of being a 'megaphone for China' and adding, 'I want to ask Mr Tung whether, from now on, people who intend to make visits abroad have to seek his permission. I think Mr Tung is more interested in policing what people say both inside and outside Hong Kong . . . than [in] trying to reflect people's anxieties.'

The gulf between the chief executive and the leader of the most widely supported political party in Hong Kong was proving ominously difficult to bridge. By the day it became clearer that C.H. Tung was fiercely committed to the authoritarian assumptions of Beijing. 'We should sit down and talk about our family matters in our home . . . Do we have to ask foreigners to tell us what to do? Why can't we decide our own fate and future?' he said in the course of an attack on Martin Lee for an article denouncing China in the *Asian Wall Street Journal*. The question on the minds of commentators was whether Martin Lee would be allowed to play any public role in Hong Kong after the hand-over, given that his 'patriotism' was already under such hostile scrutiny. The pro-Beijing *Wen Wei Po* remarked approvingly that C.H. Tung wanted to make the point that 'Hong Kong people should respect their own race and respect the dignity of the SAR government when he says that people should love the country and love Hong Kong'.

It seemed increasingly likely that the Democratic party would be obstructed after the handover. Not content with reintroducing the most repressive clauses of the Societies Ordinance and the Public Order Ordinance, Beijing now indicated through the Preparatory Committee that the provisional legislature would be invited to reinstate the system of appointments to the Municipal Councils and District Boards which, under Patten's reforms, had been replaced by elections. The prospect that Beijing was bound to vet such appointments exacerbated fears that the authorities in China would leave no aspect of Hong Kong's political life alone. There were even deeper anxieties. Margaret Ng was not alone in suggesting that C.H. Tung would use his executive author-ity to exclude the Democrats from any future electoral process that China might put in place for Hong Kong. Her reasoning was precise and chilling: to allow the Democratic party to compete in elections once China's proposed restrictions on political freedom and dissent had been put in place would be to hand Martin Lee a landslide victory on a silver platter – an outcome which both C.H. Tung and Beijing would find unacceptable.

The most effective way of achieving the exclusion of Lee and his cohorts, Ng argued, would be to reinstitute the kind of 'loyalty test' that China had apparently been willing to discard seven years earlier. The future chief executive had already asserted on more than one occasion that public figures should be seen to 'love Hong Kong, love China and uphold the Basic Law'. It would not be difficult, Ng predicted, to revive the subjective concept of love as a test of any candidate's willingness to 'uphold' the Basic Law and his or her 'allegiance' to the Hong Kong SAR, as required by the 1990 decision of the National People's Congress. Writing in the *South China Morning Post*, she commented:

> Once 'love' is revived, vetting by some kind of nomination committee is the next easy step, and it would not matter how many people have the vote, or how many voters want to vote for democrats – democrats will never even be allowed to stand as candidates. However, once this path is chosen, there will be nothing left of the credibility of Mr Tung's government at home or abroad.

Perhaps Margaret Ng was overly pessimistic, but no one was confident enough to mock her grim scenario.

In an interview with the *Australian* on 6 March, Chris Patten forecast that even if Martin Lee was not outlawed by any 'loyalty' test, the Democrats would be sidelined in any future election by the introduction of proportional representation for LegCo's twenty directly elected seats, in which they had almost swept the board in 1995. 'I'll tell you what will happen,' he prophesied gloomily. 'The Chinese officials will propose, for example, that instead of having twenty single-member constituencies, we should have ten two-member constituencies – thus, at a stroke, halving the number of Democrats who can get elected . . . That is what will happen, I can tell you now. Watch this space.' If so, instead of winning at least seventeen of these seats, the Democrats would be confined to ten at most. Patten was proved right. By restoring the gerrymandered character of the other forty seats in LegCo, Beijing, acting through the provisional legco, could easily ensure that Martin Lee and his allies would become an impotent rump in any future official LegCo.

As the provisional legislature began to flex its muscles in Shenzhen, across the increasingly nominal border with Hong Kong, doubts about the future independence of the judiciary began to surface once again. Under the Basic Law, the Legislative Council was required to endorse the appointment to and removal of judges from the Court of Final

Appeal. So, on 11 February, Rita Fan, the president of the provisional legislature, suggested that she and her colleagues should be given responsibility for vetting candidates for these senior posts. A fellow member of the provisional legislature, Ambrose Lau Hon Chuen, the influential leader of the Hong Kong Progressive Alliance, was enthusiastic. Using as yardsticks 'personal integrity' and 'professional standing', his colleagues should, he said, be free to 'nosy around' to familiarise themselves with the judges under consideration for the Court of Final Appeal. Members should, if they so wished, have 'some direct access to the individual, but not in the form of a hearing – I would prefer a private meeting', he told the *South China Morning Post*. The DAB leader, Tsang Yok Sing, was more cautious. His party did not yet have a policy, he said, but he would not wish the provisional legco merely to rubber-stamp appointments to the Court of Final Appeal.

Once again Margaret Ng was the first of her colleagues to denounce this prospect as unacceptable, while Raymond Wacks, professor of law at Hong Kong University, warned that any such proposal would 'strike at the core of our system'. The vice-chairman of the Bar Council, Lawrence Lok Ying Kam, argued that the role of the provisional legislature should be severely circumscribed. 'Why should a body that is not fully recognised as lawful be given the power to veto judges?' he asked. His question went unanswered as the conviction grew that the provisional legislature would not only curtail the community's human rights but impose on it, at the highest level, a biddable, if not suborned, judiciary. Even the *South China Morning Post*, which had recently demonstrated a growing commitment to 'patriotism', was moved to comment anxiously: 'Of all the issues surrounding the handover, few are more crucial than the independence of the judiciary.' Pointing out that the judiciary was facing far-reaching change, not least in the matter of finding fifteen lawyers of equal talent and inclination to fill the places left by those retiring or leaving before 1 July, an editorial warned of the danger of nominated judges being cross-examined about their views on the Bill of Rights or the legitimacy of the legislature. 'If the independence of the judiciary is compromised, the common law system will face serious damage . . . In these times when everything is coming under the microscope, Hong Kong needs to have the fullest assurance that the rule of law is being maintained by a free and unfettered judiciary.' No such assurance was forthcoming.

Britain's foreign secretary arrived in Hong Kong from Singapore on 15 February 1997 on his second, and last, visit to the colony. Asked whether he thought that C.H. Tung was a puppet of Beijing, he responded ambivalently. The future chief executive, Malcolm Rifkind noted, had been very emphatic that he was not under the direction of the Chinese government. Nonetheless the foreign secretary appreciated the unease in Hong Kong generated by the fact that C.H. Tung's 'opinions on some very controversial matters have been very similar to the views of the Chinese government'. While he praised the governor for showing 'huge courage and conviction' in standing up for Hong Kong at times and in places where others had been reluctant to do so, Rifkind was unable to conceal the fact that Britain had lost the argument with Beijing over the provisional legco and human rights. When pressed about the impotence of the British government he became tetchy. A headline in the *South China Morning Post* on 17 February, 'RIFKIND CONCEDES DEFEAT', which prefaced a report on an uncomfortable session with the handful of LegCo members who bothered to turn up for a meeting with him at Government House, provoked him to an uncharacteristic display of public discourtesy. The newspaper 'should be ashamed of itself', Rifkind said dismissively on the *Hong Kong Today* programme, going on to tell his mild-mannered interviewer to stop asking such 'stupid questions' about the future: of course Her Majesty's government would not walk away from its responsibilities to Hong Kong after the handover. The foreign secretary's ruffled demeanour left a poor impression on a jittery colony, which was aggravated by his sudden departure for London to vote in a Commons debate about Britain's BSE crisis in which the government's majority of one was under threat. 'Britain may be anxious to leave Hong Kong "with honour",' the *South China Sunday Post* commented sourly, 'but its words now sound so hollow that one understands why some politicians here accuse London of simply playing games in the last months of its rule.' The headline over this editorial reflected a widespread resentment: 'WHEN MAD COWS MATTER MORE THAN HONG KONG'.

2 2

'HONG KONG CAN'T BE LOBOTOMISED'

Patten Runs Out of Time

In the last few months of British rule a note of self-justifying cynicism could be heard in Hong Kong. It was as if Britain's failure to secure the eternal verities of Western liberalism in perpetuity for its last significant colony might serve as a convenient excuse for those in the civil service, the media, the law and business who had already resolved to adapt to future diktats from Beijing without a murmur. It had become unfashionable to express any nostalgia for the departing power, or to allow any sense of regret to seep into public discourse. Yet not everyone was indifferent or hostile to the recent history of the colonial authorities. On 14 December 1996, Captain Albert Lam, one of the last 'local' officers in the British Army to be demobilised, was on duty at the disbandment parade of the Hong Kong Military Service Corps on Stonecutter's Island, where the Royal Navy still maintained three patrol craft to fly the flag and to combat smuggling.

Captain Lam's father had been a soldier, and although he had himself originally trained as a tailor, a better-paid trade, he had soon followed his father into the ranks. He had now been a soldier for twenty-four years. 'Today,' he said quietly, 'I am very, very sad.' He watched as the column of men filed on to the parade ground – mechanics, carpenters, dog-handlers, chefs and chauffeurs, for whom square-bashing was not a regular routine – marching with precision under the proud gaze of families with clicking cameras. The Band of the Royal Hong Kong Police strutted back and forth playing those military airs which bring a lump to patriotic throats. The Union Jack hung limply from a flagpole, stirred occasionally by an idle breeze. Sergeant-majors bellowed. In charge was a brigadier, dressed in tropical kit, his sword vertical in his right hand. The parade fell silent. After a few moments the governor arrived with his wife in the back of the colonial Rolls–Royce. A retired colonel in the VIPs' stand muttered tetchily, 'He could at least have worn his uniform and his hat. It's not right.' Women and children waved as Patten approached the dais, took the last salute and then inspected each detachment, stopping frequently to show that he cared. An army chaplain said prayers in English and a Buddhist monk chanted from the holy writ. The regimental flag was carried solemnly to a table in front of the troops, furled carefully for the last time and then blessed. There was a dragon dance, the band played 'The Last Post' and the Hong Kong Military Service Corps passed from existence into memory.

Afterwards, there was a buffet lunch in the outdoor shooting range which was soon to be handed over to the People's Liberation Army. Hamburgers sizzled on a charcoal griddle, wafting smoke through the assembled multitude of retired comrades, heavily laden with medals, who reminisced over pints of beer. The wives stood in clusters together as home-counties officers and squaddies from Newcastle, separated by rank but not by emotion, exchanged awkward condolences. Captain Lam spoke of his pride and sorrow. 'The parade was really impressive, but now we go our own ways. And, sadly, we may not see one another again. I have been British for a long time.' Each local regiment had been allocated British passports by quota. 'We have done quite well – one in six.' Which meant than five out of six did not receive British passports? 'That's right.' And did that matter? Captain Lam was hesitant, apologetic. 'If you ask me – because we really served the British army, we served the Queen, we gave everything to the Queen when we joined the service – I think everybody should have a passport.' It was not a subject on which he wished to dwell.

This was Captain Lam's second disbandment parade. In September 1995, he had also been on duty at the closing ceremony for the Royal Hong Regiment, the volunteers, founded in 1854. In the battle for Hong Kong against the Japanese in 1941, 10 per cent of the regiment had been killed or reported missing in action. 'I actually saw people in tears at the last parade. When the men marched by for the last time, one of our honorary colonels, who is now in his seventies, could not stop crying. And loudly. And I absolutely understand his feelings. I think, today as well, everyone has the same feeling.' Captain Lam paused as his own tears welled up. 'I have had a long service in the army, and I have never regretted joining the British army,' he continued after a moment. 'But unfortunately I can't serve any longer. I have a terrible pain inside.' He pointed to his heart and the tears flowed freely.

The commander, British Forces, Major-General Bryan Dutton, preferred to look on the bright side. However, like Albert Lam, he was
troubled by Britain's failure to pay its debt of honour to those members
of the Hong Kong Military Service Corps who had been denied British
citizenship.

> They are loyal, hard-working and amazingly gentle and courteous.
> They will need to find another job, another life, in a situation which
> will be very different for them. We have set them up as well as we
> could. There is generous financial provision; we are generous with
> retraining. We are setting up an ex-servicemen's association with the
> British Legion, I hope with a clubhouse. Yet, at the end, we've been
> rather mean-spirited in not giving them unequivocally a passport in
> recognition of their service. I think that is a great shame.

The general was responsible for the final stage of the run-down of
British forces in Hong Kong. Appointed commander in July 1994,
when the British garrison numbered almost 10,000 personnel, he had
'drawn down' 5,000 military personnel by the end of 1995. Two years
later, the garrison had a symbolic complement of fewer than 2,500 men
and women from the three services, all of whom would have to depart
before midnight on 30 June. At the twenty-ninth meeting of the Joint
Liaison Group in June 1994, immediately after Chris Patten had secured
a one-vote victory in LegCo for his electoral reform package, the two
sides had agreed the terms under which fourteen military sites – the
'defence lands' – would be handed over to the Chinese authorities in
1997. Since then the British had evacuated most of these bases, and
by early 1997, aside from the garrison headquarters in the Prince of
Wales Barracks in Central, they maintained a skeletal presence on
Stonecutter's Island, in Kowloon and at Kai Tak Airport only.

The prospect of their replacement by 10,000 men of the People's
Liberation Army was not calculated to enthuse the citizens of Hong
Kong. General Dutton, a bluff soldier with an eye for public relations
and a uniform which had started to bulge at the seams, had had the task
of introducing his successor, Major-General Liu Zhenwu, to his forthcoming command. The Chinese general made two visits to the British
colony in 1996 to visit all the 'defence lands' he was about to inherit.
He was briefed on all aspects of the garrison's responsibilities; everything, according to General Dutton, 'from how we live, how we feed
the troops, how we train, how we liaise with the police, how we interface with the law – the list is endless. We covered every facet of life for
a garrison of 10,000 men.'

It had been obvious to Dutton and his colleagues that the Chinese team had no experience of any similar operation, but that they were keen to make it work. At one point one of them asked for clarification about the garrison's padre, whom they evidently equated with a PLA commissar. 'They wanted to know what control he had over me,' Dutton recalled a few days later. The general was anxious for it to be known that while the two armies were 'very different', he did not wish to make any criticism of the PLA. He explained:

> We are a small, regular, highly professional force, volunteers . . . We are used to being deployed to carry out quasi-diplomatic missions as much as straightforward military commissions . . . They are a con-script force of three million. They have been living in Chinese garrison towns in central China, doing things the Chinese way with very heavy Communist party control. Their conscripts are pressed men. They are paid as conscripts. They live in very harsh conditions compared with us. The whole ethos of the two forces is totally different.
>
> It will be a totally new world for General Liu's soldiers. For instance, his privates are paid enough to buy one beer a month in Wanchai – forty yuan . . . They will have a hard life here, only allowed out on controlled visits, for sporting occasions or cultural trips, usually in organised groups. But it is very important that they do establish contact with the community. One of the greatest dangers to the future would be to have a PLA garrison here which was isolated from the community, from the realities of life here.

Dutton reported that General Liu was likeable and responsive. According to the British commander, when he explained that it was of great concern to the people of Hong Kong that the PLA should not be above the law, General Liu and his colleagues responded eagerly. 'We understand that,' they told Dutton. 'We want to use Hong Kong as a window on the world.'

'You've heard of Tiananmen?' General Liu asked the British com-mander. 'We want to leave that image of the PLA behind us. We want to use Hong Kong as a means of rehabilitating the world's image of the PLA and show them that we are now a mature, modern armed force.' For a Chinese general to share such a confidence – when, according to the official version of the events of 4 June 1989, the PLA, insofar as it had been involved at all, had operated with restraint merely to assist in the maintenance of law and order – was a remarkable lapse of military discretion. Dutton was encouraged. However, it would not be easy for the PLA to adapt. 'The law in China is an instrument of government and is not about the rights of individuals,' he said. 'Military personnel are only liable to the military law. They are not liable to civil law at all.' For the benefit of his Chinese counterparts, Dutton had identified a variety of legal predicaments they might face in Hong Kong: 'What would happen when a Chinese military truck with a drunken driver knocks over a Chinese granny in Wanchai at a pedestrian crossing and kills her? Could he be breathalysed? Could he go to jail? Which court would he go to? Could he be arrested? Whom do the family sue for compensation? Which court do they sue in?' General Dutton had more questions than General Liu had answers.

The rapport between the two generals was not reflected in the negotiations between their respective governments on the role of the PLA before the handover. With less than 100 days to go, the two sides were still wrangling in the JLG over the number of PLA troops to be deployed in Hong Kong before the transfer of sovereignty, the date of their arrival, and whether they should enjoy diplomatic immunity or be allowed to carry weapons. The British argued that a small advance guard of unarmed PLA troops would be quite sufficient to meet China's needs; Beijing countered that at least 250 troops should be deployed, and that they should be free to cross the border without inspection. The British side realised that the Chinese team was coming under growing pressure from the PLA, which had originally demanded a presence in Hong Kong from January.

By mid-March 1997 Patten had authorised his negotiators to turn up the heat on the Chinese by linking any agreement on the PLA troops to another issue on which Beijing's JLG negotiators had long been stalling, even though there was no real disagreement between the two sides: the right of abode. Although all Hong Kong Chinese resident in the territory knew that they would continue to enjoy right of abode after the handover, the JLG negotiators had refused to finalise an agreement on the status of either foreigners resident in Hong Kong, or the million or more Hong Kong citizens who had emigrated to America, Canada, Australia and elsewhere. From the British standpoint, these emigrés retained their right of abode in Hong Kong, but the Chinese had refused to confirm this formally. This apparent impasse was the cause of significant public anxiety. Would they all be required to return to the territory before 1 July to qualify? And would the children of Hong Kong residents away at school in Britain and elsewhere also have to come back before the handover? The Chinese had been procrastinating with the evident objective of preventing the administration from putting the agreed legislation before the Legislative Council for approval. The ulterior motive was not hard to fathom: if the legislation had to be in place before 1 July, and if, as the Chinese maintained, it could not be enacted by the British, then as far as they were concerned any agreement between Britain and China should be put before the provisional legislature. As one of Patten's team complained wearily in mid-March, it was 'transparently an attempt to create an argument for the provisional legislature to exist at all'.

In an effort to reach a compromise the British now suggested that the two sides should announce that they had reached an understanding on the key issues, and that appropriate legislation would be enacted formally after 1 July. If they had a written agreement on the substance, issued by the JLG, which could then be sent to the four corners of the earth, that would be fine. The Chinese response to this proposal came from Lu Ping, who told the British ambassador that Beijing would agree, but only if the British were willing to concede that it should at least be endorsed by the provisional legislature, on 1 June, a month before the handover. To the irritation of Government House, Sir Len Appleyard appeared to believe that Lu Ping's suggestion constituted a step forward. From Patten's perspective, it offered nothing of the kind. To concede Lu Ping's case would be tantamount to recognising the provisional legislature, the legality of which, Patten had already suggested, was a matter for determination by the International Court of Justice in the Hague (even though he did not think it worthwhile to seek a judgement there, not least because a settlement of the question would require the co-operation of the People's Republic). One of the governor's team commented: 'I don't want to be unfair to Appleyard and suggest that he is deliberately working against us. He just isn't quite on track.'

Although it was a tactic which they had themselves frequently deployed in the past, Beijing's negotiators affected to be furious at Britain's decision to contrive a link between agreement over the PLA's role and status in Hong Kong before the handover and the resolution of the right-of-abode issue. One of their number castigated the leader of the British side, Alan Paul: 'The man who thought that this was a good idea should know that he is in danger of torpedoing the "dignified" handover.'

Meanwhile, the man in question was locked in yet another bout of internal diplomacy with the Foreign Office, this time over the handover itself. The head of the Hong Kong Department, Sherard Cowper-Coles, had been charged with the task of drawing up the list of those who should be invited to join the Prince of Wales and the foreign secretary in the official British party at the handover ceremony. When the draft list was sent to Government House for approval, Patten was astonished to discover that the name of Sir Percy Cradock had been included. An explanation from Cowper-Coles, to the effect that Sir Percy had not only been the architect of Sino–British relations for more than a decade, but for some of that time Her Majesty's ambassador in Beijing, failed to placate the governor. He was particularly irritated that, clumsily if unwittingly, the Foreign Office official had placed him in the demeaning position of having to either allow Cradock to join the official party or exercise his gubernatorial veto, which was bound to be interpreted by Cradock's acolytes as pique on his part.

He could not understand why Cowper-Coles seemed so insensitive to the message that Cradock's presence at the top table would send to Beijing. Giving the Chinese the opportunity to fête a bitter foe of British policy so blatantly was bound to encourage them in the hope that, once the troublesome governor was out of the way, appeasement would once more be in the offing: that the hegemony of the diplomats would be restored; that the British did not intend to be unduly officious in their role as guardians of the Joint Declaration; and that a transgression by Beijing in Hong Kong would not be permitted to ruffle the restoration of good relations with the leaders of the People's Republic.

As it happened, Patten was spared further embarrassment. One of his aides proposed a neat diplomatic manoeuvre which would exclude Cradock without denying the former diplomat the chance to attend the historic occasion: instead of inviting all former ambassadors to join the Prince of Wales, he suggested, why not rule that only the present incumbent, Sir Len Appleyard, and his immediate predecessor, Sir Robin McLaren, should be among the official party? Cradock, along with a clutch of other diplomats and ministers of state, could be invited instead to join the much larger group 'accompanying' the official party. As guests of the British government at the farewell parade, the banquet and the handover ceremony, this group would be observers, not participants. They would also be required to pay for their own travel and accommodation. In the event, Cradock declined to attend.

Fortuitously for Cowper-Coles, Patten had not yet read Cradock's most recent onslaught on his 'incompetent' handling of the relationship with China. Had he done so, he would have had even greater cause to be aggrieved by the official's proposal. In an article for the April 1997 edition of the influential monthly magazine *Prospect*, Cradock cast aside all restraint. In characteristically precise but waspish prose, he charged Patten with taking 'at best a wild gamble with the future of over six million people' who had been encouraged by him to have 'unreal expectations' about the future and would now be left to 'face the consequences of a confrontation they never wanted'. Noting proudly that until 1992, British policy towards China had been guided by officials, and that recommendations by sinologists in the Foreign Office and Number 10 were usually accepted by ministers, Cradock observed disparagingly that thereafter, 'politics was in command. Officials were told to stand back.' Rehearsing his familiar argument in favour of 'co-operation', he accused the governor of abusing his role for his own selfish political ends. 'As a rising politician, he had his name to make. A tough rearguard action, without glory, was not an attractive option. He made instant democracy his slogan.'

It was the naivety as much as the venom of this allegation that lent credence to the view long held by Patten's allies in Hong Kong and at Westminster that Cradock was obsessed with the urge to wipe the stain of 'appeasement' from his own reputation, and that this had thoroughly distorted, if not unhinged, the judgement of this eminent diplomat.

A side-effect of the diplomatic hostilities for which Cradock blamed Patten was that the Chinese government dragged their heels over agreeing the international guest list for the handover. As late as March, embarrassed British officials were confiding to their counterparts in other capitals why it was not yet possible for London to issue formal invitations to attend the ceremony. The foreign secretary personally contacted his peers to ask them to ring the date in their diaries for what both sides had agreed eighteen months earlier should be a 'solemn and dignified' occasion. A spokesman for Malcolm Rifkind was quoted as saying: 'It's not yet at the stage of an international incident, but we do want to get things moving. No one wants it to be a hasty affair, after all.'

This ludicrous diplomatic impasse was rivalled in Hong Kong itself by a local wrangle over a concert by Elton John planned for the run-up to the handover. A group of urban councillors exercised their powers to stipulate that the singer should be seen but not heard. They declared that the 40,000 fans expected to attend the performance should be required to listen to the music through individual headsets so that local people would not be disturbed by any untoward noise. The concert promoter pronounced the idea 'tragic' and an editorial in the *South China Morning Post* tried to mock the local worthies into reconsidering their proposal, suggesting that to ensure the success of the scheme, fans should also be issued with gags and gloves in case they felt tempted to sing along to the music on their headsets or clap to the rhythm. It was to no avail. When news of the edict reached Elton John, he decided to cancel his appearance. It was both a severe disappointment to the governor personally and a microcosmic illustration of his waning authority. In the hope of

having the councillors' decision reversed, Government House hur-
riedly canvassed members of the Legislative Council, only to discover
that none of them was prepared to rally to the support of either
Patten or the singer. Kerry McGlynn said morosely: 'It didn't look as
though we would get a single vote. It's very surprising and very sad.
We thought an Elton John concert at that particular time would have
been quite an event. It will be difficult to explain to the rest of the
world.' In truth, the rest of the world was indifferent. Britain might
have retained the vestiges of power, the symbols of constitutional
authority, but the focus of attention was now almost exclusively on
the incoming rulers.

Virtually every element of the prospective SAR was now in place.
C.H. Tung had selected his new Executive Council, and the provisional
legislature was already at work debating the 'reform' of Hong Kong's
Bill of Rights and the proposed amendments to the territory's civil-
rights legislation. The budget for 1997–8 had been agreed between the
two sovereign powers, and, despite earlier threats to the contrary, the
heads of the main civil-service departments had been reassured that
they, at least, would be free to travel on the 'through train' from 30 June
to 1 July. On the surface Hong Kong was calm. The exodus, either of
people or capital, which Patten had once feared had not taken place, or
not yet, anyway. The stock exchange was steady and the property boom
was reaching new heights. On the surface the overwhelming majority
of the population appeared to have come to terms with the inevitable.

In March the authors of the Hong Kong Transition Project, the
most reliable statistical analysis of public opinion in the territory, published their most recent findings, based on a detailed study of a
randomly selected 'focus group' of more than 500 respondents. The
project's researchers, who had monitored shifts in public opinion from
soon after Patten's arrival, produced an illuminating explanation for the
apparent insouciance of the community during the intractable stand-off
between Britain and China. On the face of it, optimists about the
future outnumbered pessimists by ten to one, but when the researchers
distinguished between economic and political optimism, the results
differed dramatically.

While 60 per cent of the sample claimed to be optimistic about
Hong Kong's economic future, only 40 per cent had a similar degree of
political optimism. In this context, exactly half the respondents
expressed anxiety about personal freedoms after 1997. The same
number feared for the political stability of Hong Kong, and a higher
proportion of the entire sample were more concerned about these two

issues than any other. Intriguingly, a third of the sample, given the hypothetical choice, said that they would prefer Hong Kong to remain a British colony or to become independent (perhaps as a member of the commonwealth) than to be absorbed into the People's Republic. For the first time since the survey was initiated, however, a clear majority (62 per cent) expressed a preference for Chinese sovereignty over any other alternative. An overwhelming proportion (90 per cent, the highest figure ever recorded) declared that they were content with their lives under British rule, while Patten continued to enjoy the support of over 60 per cent of respondents, as opposed to 52 per cent for his successor, C.H. Tung. The authors concluded:

> As the sun sets on British administration in Hong Kong, many aspects of life under [British] rule seem suffused with a 'golden haze'. The burden remains, rightly or wrongly, on the Chinese government and SAR government to establish their own competence and good faith in maintaining a way of life and opportunity that the vast majority of the Hong Kong people support. On 1 July 1997 the transition does not end; the most difficult aspects of transition actually begin.

At Government House, the unease about that transition was palpable. The principal focus of anxiety was C.H. Tung himself. Patten did not directly criticise his successor in public, but for the post-handover record he conceded that he was dismayed by the chief executive's performance in the three months since his appointment. 'I think the charitable view is that Mr Tung has to deal with bombs rather casually left around by Chinese policy. Others would argue that he seems to share and endorse some of the Chinese views on democratic development and civil liberties. Time will tell whether his view of Hong Kong is right, or whether my view of Hong Kong is right.'

The chief executive's impatience with journalists was evident in the abruptness and ineptitude with which he handled awkward questions at press conferences. The contrast with the performances of the governor, who could be fierce and direct or oblique and obfuscatory as the situation demanded, was starkly apparent. If C.H. Tung was grateful to Patten for elevating this means of communication to the forefront of Hong Kong's public life, he showed little sign of benefiting from it. He rapidly developed an aversion to foreign correspondents. Those seeking interviews with him were required by his office to provide examples of their previous work on China or Hong Kong. They were also required to submit in writing a list of the questions that they wished to ask. More than one correspondent was reminded of the pre-censorship demanded by insecure dictators in third-world countries. It was a retrograde step, and a worrying indication of C.H. Tung's insensitivity to international opinion.

Hong Kong seemed increasingly benumbed. On 10 March, the Chinese foreign minister informed the Chinese People's Congress that a revision of Hong Kong's textbooks would be required after the handover. In the jargon favoured by communist apparatchiks, he advised his audience that the 'contents of some textbooks currently used in Hong Kong do not accord with history or reality, contradict the spirit of "one country, two systems" and the Basic Law, and must be revised.' The governor was quick to confute Qian Qichen. 'The Joint Declaration and the Basic Law are clear that educational policies are to be set by the post-handover government, and not to be vetted for political correctness,' he said. 'In a free society, teachers are not told what facts they can teach and what facts it is politically wrong for them to teach.' At a press conference the following day, C.H. Tung stood firm. 'Obviously textbooks need to be rewritten, especially those relating to the colonial past,' he declared. Asked whether the events of June 1989 would have to be rewritten too, he avoided the question, merely commenting, 'You may be interested to read what is written about the Opium Wars.' When a Hong Kong government official had suggested a year earlier that some textbooks might have to be rewritten, there had been an outcry in the press. It was a measure of the altered times that now the media scarcely bothered to report this exchange, except in the margins.

At the same press conference, a foreign correspondent asked the new chief executive whether he had ever said no to Beijing. Clearly angered, C.H. Tung pointed at his interrogator and said, 'Let me ask you, during the hundred and fifty years of British rule, have you ever seen a British governor talking back to the prime minister so openly?' Patten was outraged. Not only was C.H. Tung apparently content to underwrite China's decision to remove the protection of law promised to Hong Kong under international covenants; not only was he 'setting up a Mickey Mouse legislature'; but now he seemed willing to rewrite Hong Kong's history as a defence against journalists' questions about his attitude to Beijing. 'Nobody has ever suggested for one moment that we don't make our own decisions here in Hong Kong – of course, with the authority of the Foreign Office and the foreign secretary and the prime minister – but nobody thinks of me or my administration as a sort of transmission mechanism for decisions made in London,' he said.

C.H. Tung's appointment of Elsie Leung as secretary of justice (designate) did not reassure the sceptics. Although she was considered a kind-hearted lawyer, and had a reputation for protecting the interests of the elderly and impecunious, her loyalty to Beijing as a representative of Hong Kong in the National People's Congress sent a ripple of anxiety through the legal profession. Within days of her appointment, she delivered her first public statement of significance, volunteering that after the handover it would be illegal to shout slogans like 'Down with Li Peng'. In an evident misunderstanding of the Crimes Ordinance, she justified her stance by claiming, incorrectly, that chants such as 'Down with the Queen' were already prohibited in Hong Kong under the British common law. This bizarre intervention embarrassed some of Beijing's allies in Hong Kong. The editor of *Ta Kung Pao*, Tsang Yok Sing's brother Tsang Tak Sing, attempted to soothe his journalistic colleagues by saying he thought it most unlikely that the prospective secretary for justice would in reality press charges against a newspaper 'just for being critical' of the Chinese authorities or the SAR government. 'I doubt if anyone will be arrested for saying "Down with Li Peng".'

In view of the warnings already given by Qian Qichen, Lu Ping and C.H. Tung – who was careful not to contradict Elsie Leung – Tsang Tak Sing's assurances did not carry great weight. It was not so much the specific threat to freedom that alarmed human-rights activists as the repressive attitudes Elsie Leung's statement appeared to reflect. In private, the governor wondered, 'How can you try to inflict on this incredibly sophisticated city those sort of attitudes through the statute book? What is it going to lead to? Hong Kong can't be lobotomised.'

Once again Margaret Ng was the first commentator to identify with precision this new threat to Hong Kong's legal autonomy. 'If Beijing insists on asserting its own ways of thinking, Ms Leung will soon find herself the wrecker of the law to which she has dedicated all her life,' she declared.

'I think that people tend to underestimate the extent to which Hong Kong people value their freedoms,' one of Patten's advisers disclosed, looking ahead to the possibility of serious confrontation after the handover, and even on the day itself.

> If they have a law on 1 July which requires people to seek permission to demonstrate at forty-eight hours' notice, then people are going to disobey that, because they will definitely want to demonstrate on 1 July, with six thousand press and forty foreign ministers and Li Peng and whoever else is there . . . So they will deliberately test the law. And then the police have to decide whether they arrest people . . . The police will have the task of enforcing it and beginning a

completely new relationship between themselves and the community. It will be a new method of policing, a new situation in which the police commissioner has no discretion as to how far to go or how literally to interpret the law.

The same danger was likely to arise in the case of the ban on flying the Taiwanese flag. Under the existing law the police were free to exercise discretion, and did so by refusing to countenance any attempt to hoist the nationalist symbol on any public building while ignoring those which fluttered all year round in villages where loyalty to the national-ist cause remained strong. Government House wondered whether this flexibility would survive the handover; if not, trouble was inevitable.

The apprehension of Patten and his advisers was sharpened by C.H. Tung's treatment of Anson Chan. Despite their deep divisions on other issues, the community was of one mind about the chief secretary: she was Hong Kong's lynchpin, the guarantor that the civil service would remain genuinely autonomous and incorruptible, that the administra-tion would be efficient and dispassionate, and therefore that the high standards of public life would prevail against any incursion from the mainland. For this reason, C.H. Tung had been widely applauded for persuading the governor's appointee to stay in her post after the hand-over. It may be that a nervous community invested too much faith in the potential of a single individual, but the prospect that Chan would remain at the apex of the SAR administration was a source of undisguised relief.

Government House was therefore perturbed when Chan intimated privately that her relationship with C.H. Tung was in serious difficulty. Her senior colleagues knew her to be resilient and discreet, and con-sequently the fact that she felt obliged even to hint that C.H. appeared unwilling to consult her on any issue of substance immediately alarmed Patten's senior advisers. Anson Chan had known C.H. for many years, and it had been widely supposed that the two partners on the erstwhile 'dream ticket' would easily develop the professional rapport without which a working relationship cannot prosper. The mutual regard between Chris Patten and Anson Chan had been a critical factor during the transition: the two met frequently and informally; they spoke on the phone on a daily basis; and, as Patten had freely acknowledged, he would never have made a significant decision without the support of his chief secretary. Now Chan found herself excluded from Tung's inner counsels, her advice ignored. In the early weeks of 1997, she had taken the view that he was still adjusting to his new role and had not yet discovered the crucial importance of identifying priorities and developing strategies in close consultation with the head of the civil service. She was patient, if frustrated and anxious.

By March the formal meetings between the two of them had become even more cursory, the telephone conversations inconsequential. As one of her friends put it, 'Most of what he says or decides, she reads about in the papers first.' Tung's manner towards her, though courteous, tended increasingly to the Olympian and sometimes bordered on the peremptory. Instead of reading and digesting the papers she put before him, he appeared instead to spend most of his time either glad-handing senior Chinese officials at the NCNA or closeted with his personal advisers. These 'self-appointed misfits', as a member of Patten's team described the clique which now surrounded C.H., seemed to have acquired an extraordinary degree of influence. Of these, Nellie Fong, who was credited by some with the attributes of a latterday Mata Hari, and Paul Yip, a shadowy individual around whose past activities rumour clung with fetid persistence, were the two most prominent acolytes. Both were known to have exceptionally close links with Beijing and to be fervently antipathetic to Britain. It was no secret in the civil service that Anson Chan regarded their talents with distaste. The fact that C.H. Tung had clasped them to his bosom was dispiriting but illuminating.

Drawn ineluctably to the conclusion that she was being sidelined by these parvenus, the fears of the chief secretary – not for own future, about which she had long been quite sanguine, but for that of Hong Kong – began to coalesce. In public there was always a smile on her face; behind the scenes, her friends soon realised that the doughtiest and most able woman in Hong Kong was under intense strain. 'She thought it was going to be a partnership, but she is one item in his weekly diary,' one of her colleagues revealed of her relationship with Tung. 'I think she is beginning to wonder whether she really knows the man, whether she really has known him over all these years. I don't think she can put it right. The question is whether she is prepared to carry on at all – and that still hangs in the balance. She is in a terrible state.'

On 11 March, Anson Chan agreed to be interviewed by the BBC. Probed gently by their correspondent, James Miles, about some of C.H. Tung's inauspicious public comments and the difficulties they might pose for their relationship, she suddenly snapped. Cutting off the interview, she leaped up, saying, 'You are impugning my integrity!' and stalked from the room. The BBC team assumed that this sudden petulance sprang merely from the streak of irritable authoritarianism with which her relationship with the media had long been afflicted.

They did not appreciate quite how painfully they had brushed the exposed nerve-endings of a deeply unhappy chief secretary. Patten was appalled when he heard later what had happened. Knowing that she was bound to face much more of the same in the run-up to the hand-over, and conceivably beyond, he was concerned that a repetition of that outburst would inevitably expose the fragility of the most important professional relationship in Hong Kong. If it became known that Hong Kong's 'dream ticket' was not beating with one heart, it could do untold damage to confidence, both locally and internationally.

It was also rumoured in the Hong Kong establishment that the days of the financial secretary, the widely respected Donald Tsang, were numbered; that – apparently at the behest of Lu Ping, who could not abide Hong Kong's second most senior civil servant – he would be ditched by Tung soon after the handover in favour of a more malleable candidate. This was bad enough. The thought that Anson Chan might also depart prematurely was inconceivable. Her dilemma was neatly summed up by a senior British official. 'It would be a catastrophe if she went now, but it would also be a recognition of a catastrophe to come. If things are so bad that she gives up, then she couldn't actually keep things on track for very long by staying. She'd simply be providing cover.' In any event, the odds that Chan would remain in office for long after the handover had shortened dramatically. 'If you want my bet,' said one of her colleagues, 'I think she'll be living in Pinner by the end of the year.'

Government House strove assiduously to disguise this situation, but it tempted some expatriate analysts towards an extremely gloomy prognosis. They foresaw that C.H. Tung would become the unwitting victim of a Chinese pincer movement in which the concept of 'one country, two systems' would lose all significance, except as a slogan. The NCNA would still be in place as the unofficial representative of the Chinese Communist party, exerting ever greater control. In addition, the headquarters of the new Ministry of Foreign Affairs Liaison Office was already near completion on the hillside looking down over the British Consulate, and would soon be occupied by a staff of perhaps 300 Chinese officials under the direction of the senior diplomat Jiang Enzhu. Both institutions would become alternative, if rival, centres of power, and C.H. Tung's only way of containing their influence would be to preserve his own channels to the very top layer of authority in Beijing. 'If he allows himself to be dragged down into the Chinese bureaucracy,' said one British official, 'if he is docking with China at the same level as Jiang Enzhu and whoever replaces Zhou Nan at the NCNA, then both of them will have him for breakfast, because they know their way around the system.'

At Government House, Patten's feelings were mixed. He was delighted to be close to the end of his mission but increasingly worried about the 'rotten international press' to which Hong Kong had been subjected since the appointment of C.H. Tung.

> I think events in the last couple of months have made people seriously question whether Hong Kong is really going to enjoy its autonomy after 1997. All the rhetoric seems to have been about one country, and there doesn't seem to have been much about two systems. And I think there are worries about the way China and the SAR government will handle the whole range of political issues after 1997, which if mishandled, could go badly wrong . . . At the moment Peking seems to be getting its own way in Hong Kong.

British officials were dispatched to America to attempt to shore up support in the media and in Congress, where a growing number of Republican representatives were agitating for the chance to use the situation in Hong Kong against China. Their message was that reports of Hong Kong's death were premature. As long as Anson Chan and Donald Tsang were still in place, they maintained, the game was still worth playing. They urged the Americans:

> Don't use Hong Kong as a stick with which to bash China. Keep boosting your bilateral relationship with Hong Kong. Keep the focus on Hong Kong. Deal with the people here as international partners. Then you bolster their morale and their determination to keep operating as they do now. In the process you will also raise the political threshold for China. The moment you start to treat Hong Kong as part of China, then China is more likely to treat Hong Kong as part of China.

One of these emissaries, who was far more pessimistic about the future than he had revealed to his American audiences, said, 'I can just about square my conscience with that theme.' Patten tried to spread a similar gospel. 'Frankly, there is not much reassurance I can give about the future. I find myself giving endless interviews in which I'm asked what I think is going to happen in Hong Kong, and I find myself repeating, parrot-like, the same formula. So I shall be pleased when it is the end of June.'

Deng Xiaoping's death at the age of ninety-two had been so long fore-told that the announcement of the event itself, in February 1997, was almost an anticlimax. The eulogies that poured forth from official scribes in the Chinese capital, written months or conceivably years earlier, reminded the Chinese people of the remarkable achievements of the last significant survivor of Mao's Long March. A close confidant of the 'great helmsman', he had been at Mao's side throughout the first tumultuous years of communist rule. He had been purged in the frenzy of the Cultural Revolution, and 'rehabilitated' in time to be purged again by the 'gang of four' in 1976. He had re-emerged to take power as Mao's successor in 1980. Restoring a semblance of order to a chaotic society, he began to lead China away from the orthodoxies of state ownership and collectivism towards the free market. The public was encouraged to regard individual salvation in the form of personal wealth as a desirable objective. Extolling his extraordinary achievements as a great reformer, the official media in Beijing contrived to ignore the events of 4 June 1989. Nor did they make any reference to the repressive structure of political control over which Deng, and those who now jostled to succeed him, had presided with evident equanimity.

In Beijing the official mourning lasted for twelve days. In Hong Kong, the governor felt bound by convention to join the throng who attended the offices of the NCNA to pay their respects. Like them, Patten bowed his head three times before a black-bordered photograph of the man to whom he had once referred sardonically as 'one of the great immortals'. Deng's demise had no immediate impact in either China or Hong Kong. The caretaker administration of Li Peng had been in day-to-day control of the People's Republic for at least three years. Beijing's ritual denunciations of Patten and his works had certainly not been crafted by Deng himself, although it was rumoured that he had occasionally murmured in the ear of his daughter, who had long been the only link between the 'paramount leader' and the mortals who interpreted his will. It was the future that worried Hong Kong. Which faction would emerge from the inevitable struggle for power to succeed him? Would a 'modernist' or a 'traditionalist' triumph? Would the contest be peaceful, or, as in the past, accompanied by bloodletting and repression? And would the consequences, whatever they were, spill over into Hong Kong?

No outsider could penetrate the secret society of oligarchs who ran China. Rumours, based on conjecture for which there was no evidence, held sway: Jiang Zemin had enough backing from the military to consolidate his power base as president; Jiang Zemin, an ineffectual and backward-looking figure, would be removed. The stolid but crafty Li Peng would take the helm; Li Peng would be ousted. While no one, perhaps least of all the candidates themselves, could predict the outcome, it was generally assumed that momentous changes were afoot and that the mists would clear at or around the Party Congress in October 1977. In the meantime, Hong Kong had other worries.

Although it seemed insensitive to make the point, Deng's death had at least lifted one uncertainty about the handover. Until then, it had been widely presumed that a cortege would bear the ailing leader from Beijing to Hong Kong, allowing him to 'reclaim' the stolen territory in person on behalf of the People's Republic. If the citizens of Hong Kong grieved that fate had intervened to prevent this symbolic démarche, they managed to contain their emotion.

Aside from the continuing wrangle over the international guest list, the preparations for the day of departure were now in place. The choreography of Britain's valediction was in the hands of a production company reporting directly to the governor. Patten knew what he wanted: 'We will have a ceremony at dusk with bands and colour and light and spectacle at which we will say farewell, but I hope in a way which indicates that we are not just sugaring off and leaving Hong Kong to its own devices.' There was still a minor wrinkle in the plans for a squadron of Harrier jump jets to hover in final salute over the royal yacht, *HMS Britannia*, which was to be moored alongside the parade ground in front of the Convention Centre. The presence of a British aircraft carrier in Hong Kong's waters might be interpreted by China as a provocation, but without such a vessel, the Harriers could not fly. Eventually, the navy suggested that the ship could be stationed outside but just close enough to China's territorial waters to allow the Harriers to complete the round trip to Hong Kong. The diplomatic question was when to advise Beijing of the plan: to give no warning might easily provoke the Chinese military to scramble their own warplanes to 'intercept' the unknown intruders; to give too much notice might well lead to an inconclusive contretemps with Beijing about whether the presence of the Harriers was conducive to good diplomatic relations. It was, Government House allowed wryly, a delicate matter of judgement which would require careful finessing.

After this ceremony – with or without the Harriers – there was to be a gigantic firework display of the kind at which Asia excels. Then the British party, led by the Prince of Wales and the new prime minister, Tony Blair, was to file into the Convention Centre for a banquet for some 4,000 guests. (Blair had rejected Patten's advice, given even-handedly to John Major and himself before the general election, against attending in person.) Just before midnight, under the eyes of a watching world, the British flag would be lowered for the last time and the SAR flag would be raised in its place. It would be a confusingly emotional moment: tears of nostalgia and regret would mingle with genuine feelings of liberation and hope. A footnote in the history of the world, the ceremony would be a defining moment in the story of the twentieth century. Careful to contain his own mixed feelings, Patten liked to describe his vision of the closing moments of Britain's colonial rule with calculated schadenfreude: 'Bands will play, and the Prince of Wales and the governor and family – minus dogs – will get on *Britannia* and sail off down the harbour.'

EPILOGUE

I n the final weeks before the handover, Hong Kong was shrouded in
fatalism. The absence of any 'end-of-empire' elation about the
future was matched by a lack of sentimentality about the past. By
now every argument had been played out. As if numbed by what had
become a ritualistic conflict over freedom and democracy, the citizens
of what was about to become an SAR of the People's Republic of
China awaited the transfer of power with stoicism: the optimists clung
to their faith that Beijing would tread with care, while the pessimists
prepared for the worst.

The portents were not encouraging. Late in April C.H. Tung published a set of proposals for 'public consultation' which were designed
to curtail precisely those freedoms his apologists in Hong Kong liked to
believe the new chief executive would seek to protect. Under a variety
of proposed amendments to the Societies and Public Order ordinances,
it would be forbidden to form any organisation without first register-
ing it with the police, and permission to proceed could be withheld 'in
the interests of national security'. Political groups would not be able to
accept funding from abroad, and, for the sake of 'public order', no
demonstration of more than thirty people would be permitted in the
absence of a formal 'notice of no objection' from the police at least
seven days in advance.

These proposals provoked an angry reaction from a wide cross-
section of the community, led by Government House. Evidently taken
aback, the chief executive retreated. At the end of a three-week consultation period, on 15 May 1997, C.H. Tung's office released a
statement modifying the proposals: political organisations would, after
all, be able to accept donations from abroad, but only from individuals,

not from 'foreign forces'; and, although the police would retain extensive powers to ban public gatherings, it would not be necessary for protesters to secure a 'notice of no objection' before staging a demonstration. Nevertheless, the chief executive would retain the authority to curtail a wide range of freedoms 'in the interests of national security'.

C.H. Tung invited the community to accept that he had thereby struck a 'proper balance between civil liberties and social order'. He had indeed shown that he was not entirely deaf to public opinion but the emphasis – and the drift – of Beijing's legislative priorities was depressingly obvious. As if a further illustration of this were needed, the provisional legislature chose this moment to publish the text of a bill which would make it a criminal offence to 'defile' the new SAR flag. From 1 July, any individual found guilty of this crime would be subject to a fine of $HK50,000.

C.H. Tung's subservience to Beijing's diktat did not go unnoticed abroad. In the early spring, the chief executive had made plans for a visit to the United States, where he hoped to meet Bill Clinton and leading members of Congress. However, his advisers soon realised that he would be given an extremely critical reception. Nor were they at all sure that he would be able to handle the hostility of the American media. In May, rather than risk a public-relations fiasco, they quietly cancelled the visit on the grounds that the chief executive was too busy in the run-up to the handover.

In a symbolic rebuke to C.H., on 4 June, some 60,000 people attended the vigil on the eighth anniversary of the massacre in Beijing. The new chief executive, who had persistently warned against the threat of subversion against China, had urged Hong Kong to 'put the baggage of Tiananmen behind you'. In the centre of the demonstrators, who carried candles in memory of the dead, was a huge stone statue, the Pillar of Shame. A large sign lit up the sky with the words: 'Fight to the End'. The question in everybody's mind was whether the commemoration of this anniversary would be permitted in 1997.

It was in an atmosphere of uncertainty and foreboding that Hong Kong prepared for the arrival of 4,000 dignitaries and even larger numbers of the world's media to witness Britain's departure from Hong Kong. As the Pattens packed their remaining personal belongings and prepared to leave Government House for the last time, they drew comfort from the genuine friendships each of them had formed and from the goodwill, or perhaps the absence of ill will, of the community.

Certainly the Ng family bore the governor no ill will. Their prospects had changed little. Mr Ng still worked for the refuse company, but he had been promoted to foreman. The family's income had risen a little above the level of inflation, but he and his wife were still concerned about employment and the future stability of Hong Kong. Like so many ordinary citizens of the future SAR, the Ngs did not wish to say more than 'Life will go on.' It was, they believed, wise to speak cautiously.

The schoolgirl Norris Lam who had organised the school trip to China to exchange views about democracy was now twenty-one years old. A graduate of the Chinese University, she had studied for a year in the United States, where she considered her fellow students inclined to idleness. As an 'outstanding student' of her generation, she had not only met the governor (an encounter which confirmed her first impression that he was a 'real star'), but had also become a 'youth representative' on a government task force chaired by the chief secretary, Anson Chan. In the spring of 1997, Norris joined the HongKong and Shanghai Bank at the start of what all who knew her presumed would be a high-flying career. She remained an optimist about China. 'Yes, we have differences. Maybe we want to go faster towards democracy and they want to go slower. But we share the same culture.' If Hong Kong lost its freedoms, then she would leave and start again somewhere else. But that, she was confident, would not happen.

Grace Wu, the antiques-dealer, was less sanguine. Although she did not intend to sell her apartment in Hong Kong, she expected to move most of her business abroad, to Europe or the United States. 'For the moment I have decided that this is my home, but it will depend on whether I can work here or not.' She had already sent many of her possessions abroad, fearful that she would be forbidden to export them after the handover. 'I am not a communist, but this is my country. It is a dilemma for me.' In the past she had worried about her rights to move freely, to talk freely and to read freely. 'They still matter to me, and I believe that is true for many people in Hong Kong. Many people. Yes, many . . .' Her voice tailed away. And if those rights were curtailed? Her dilemma would be resolved at once: 'I will leave.'

Hari Harilela and his family, now secure in the knowledge that they could leave, intended to stay. 'I am really proud of Chris Patten,' Harilela said. 'I knew he would do it. He is just one those people who succeeds.' The 'ethnic minorities' were grateful for their passports and Britain had finally fulfilled a 'legal and moral duty'. In the words of Hari's sister, the family was now 'so happy' that a British government 'had not determined a policy on the basis of racism'. Hari interrupted: 'The credit, if you don't mind my saying so, goes to Chris Patten. He worked very, very hard. Very sincerely.'

Then there was Jimmy Lai, the penniless immigrant who became a multimillionaire publisher.

Chris Patten gave people the sense of choice, the sense of what is right. He has raised their aspirations. And those the Chinese government will have to take into account if they want Hong Kong to be stable. After 1997, Hong Kong will not just be China's window on the world – it will be China's face to the world . . . I want to say one more thing. It is a shame to have your country colonised, but I have never had this sense of shame, because I have been a free man living in this colony. I have been blessed with a wonderful life.

He paused. His eyes filled with tears, and then he added: 'So long, the British. May God bless you.' Occasionally what was said behind the governor's back was worth hearing.

For the previous five years, Allen Lee had been a political weathervane in LegCo for Hong Kong's most powerful tycoons. Since 1995 he had also been an elected representative of the people. Despite his failure ever to offer a significant criticism of China, even he was disconcerted by C.H. Tung's apparent readiness to dismember the Bill of Rights and to curtail the rights of assembly and demonstration on Beijing's behalf. Earlier in the year Lee had raised the issue with the chief executive in person. C.H. had told him that his 'reforms' were not intended to take away the civil liberties currently enjoyed by the people of Hong Kong. Was the chief executive right or wrong? 'I won't use the words right or wrong,' said Lee. 'It is simply that he and I had a difference of opinion. I won't say whether he is right or wrong because on this kind of issue there is no clear-cut right or wrong.'

Such equivocation only a few weeks before the handover testified to the genuflectory mood of the political old guard. Yet Allen Lee, like several of his peers, reacted with genuine dismay to the charge that he would soon be seen as a mere messenger for C.H. Tung. 'He is a very close friend of mine, but I do not agree with everything he does.' So would he resist any attempt by the new chief executive to stifle Hong Kong's freedom of expression? 'The Basic Law states very clearly that we have freedom of the press. It is up to the media people. They must not exercise self-censorship. If they do so in fear of Beijing's interference, then I do not think they should be in that profession.' So would he speak out against legislation banning media attacks on the Chinese leadership, which some of C.H. Tung's appointees seemed keen to accomplish? Allen Lee hesitated. 'Well, it depends on the issue. If we are simply talking about a slogan, then I would certainly not agree. I would say that that would contradict the Basic Law . . . If anybody tries to tinker with the Basic Law as far as these freedoms are concerned, I would not only oppose them, I would raise hell. If our chief executive thinks he has to make laws limiting the freedom of speech . . . he will embark on a very slippery slope, and I think support for him will slip.' But Allen Lee's confidence in C.H. Tung was, in his own words, 'absolute . . . I think he has no intention of making laws limiting the freedom of Hong Kong people . . . I don't think he is that kind of person.'

Like Allen Lee, Tsang Yok Sing had been disconcerted, or, as he put it, 'surprised' by C.H. Tung's eagerness to curtail individual freedoms in the interests of public order. But, he said, he was even more surprised by the fact that 'the media and all those critics who have never been slow to point out the mistakes of the Chinese government or those of us in the "pro-China" camp in Hong Kong, were very, very kind to C.H. Tung'. He also declared himself surprised by C.H.'s accusation that Martin Lee and the Democratic party were hostile to China: 'Before that he didn't appear to be a really tough person, or high-handed.' The leader of the DAB party hoped that the new chief executive's 'tough line' was part of a strategy that would allow him to adopt a 'more moderate and conciliatory' tone after the handover. But if that was not his strategy; if he persisted on the present course? 'Well, we have our position. We have our principles. And if we believe he is doing something wrong, then we will speak up and try to stop it.'

Tsang Yok Sing's political adversary Martin Lee had already lost faith in C.H. Tung. According to the leader of the colony's most popular party, Hong Kong's future after the handover looked bleak. 'Big brother is already here and in control . . . If they press one button they can get one thing done; if they press another, another thing is done,' he noted. Resigned to the fact that C.H. Tung – 'a good man forced to do evil' – would seek to marginalise his influence, Martin Lee assumed that any future electoral system would be rigged to exclude the Democrats from effective power. He believed, too, that a cowed media would take their cue from Beijing and suppress coverage of him and his allies in the hope that they would thereby become 'non-persons'. He did not, however, intend to acquiesce in this plan.

> I cannot believe that, in the long term, the leaders of China can for ever stand in the way of democracy. The whole world is marching towards democracy, human rights and the rule of law – except Hong Kong, which is going in the opposite direction. But we don't have to

worry: as long as we keep on fighting, the tide is in our favour, and one day democracy and human rights will come to China and return to Hong Kong.

In the meantime, he was prepared for trouble. 'I still don't think the chances of my being thrown into prison are high, though I can't rule that out altogether. We are prepared for the worst but hoping for the best,' he said. 'Of course my wife and son are worried. But there are times when people must make a choice between the community and their own families. The Hong Kong people need a voice, and we will be that voice.' He anticipated that the new chief executive would be unable to stifle free expression and protest.

When you see people now demonstrating outside the New China News Agency, they chant slogans to give vent to very strong feelings. Then they go home and watch television or play mah-jong. If you don't allow them to express a very strong grievance, it might explode. So what Mr Tung is proposing to achieve by limiting the right to demonstrate will have the opposite effect. He will find out that you can suppress some people but you can't suppress all the people. And they will burst like a volcano.

The persistent failure of C.H. Tung to resist the blandishments of Beijing left Margaret Ng feeling 'desperate' about the future. At midnight on 30 June, her role as an elected representative of the legal profession in the Legislative Council would be abruptly terminated, and her place would be taken by a member of the provisional LegCo selected by China's appointees. 'What will I do? I imagine I will spend more time on my practice as a barrister,' she mused. 'But I will give some of my time to public issues. If I can still publish a column, I will publish a column. If I can still lobby, I will lobby. If there is a demonstration to join, I will join that.' Only two years earlier she had been ready to leave Hong Kong for London rather than endure life under China, but her unexpected electoral triumph in 1995 had made that option impossible, notwithstanding her impending removal from LegCo. 'My constituents elected me to a term of four years, and my obligation is still to them. I have to stay around. One of my duties to them must be to press for the early return of democratic elections.'

Margaret Ng predicted a collision between China and Hong Kong, but what she could not foresee was the scale of it or the character it would take. Invisible but fundamental, the replacement of one sovereign by another, she thought, could quickly change the political culture and, with that, the public sense of what constituted appropriate behaviour.

> I don't think that C.H. Tung knows at this point how strong the opposition is to him. I think he is a very sheltered man. I think he believes he has very wide support when he says we should have less politics . . . I think when he sees how naked the opposition against him is, he will be very angry. I don't think he will stay his hand. So I see confrontation.
>
> If you ask me what is best for Hong Kong, I would say the only viable future is to fight for autonomy, for democracy and for the rule of law, because otherwise we sink into darkness. But because I was brought up in the kind of society Hong Kong is, it is difficult for me to want that confrontation . . . We may have to pay a very severe price. It may bring on a great deal of very strong suppression from China. It may cost lives. So it is daunting for me to think of that price now.

At the same time Ng was encouraged by the resilience she found in the community. Although people who talked to her 'in the streets or in taxis' usually told her that it was 'unrealistic' to oppose the imposition of the provisional legislature by China, they invariably dissented when she countered, 'Would you then rather I shut up?' 'No, no, no, no,' they would say. 'It is all very well for us to keep quiet, but we want you to speak out.' She had no doubt that the underlying support for democracy and human rights was deeply felt.

> Perhaps a majority would not stand up − particularly if it means confrontation − but I think there may still be quite a lot of people who would be prepared to do that. I understand the fear and hesitation in their hearts. But even those who are not going to join demonstrations and express their views publicly want us to do it for them, and they will support us in spirit. And we − and this is not just those in LegCo who believe in democracy, but other bodies as well, like the legal profession − will not stand by and remain silent when the rule of law is being undermined. And the future administration under C.H. Tung is going to be very intolerant. It will not admit that we may be right and he may be wrong.

Christine Loh, who had also found herself catapulted into public life by her own commitment to human rights and the impact of Patten's

electoral reforms, spoke in less apocalyptic language but she shared
Margaret Ng's foreboding. The outgoing governor, she believed, had
opened up the political process.

> I think politics is no longer for the elite few, and I am very concerned
> that the new administration will want to put it back the way it was.
> But how much of this genie can you put back into the bottle when
> Hong Kong people are now so used to all kinds of political pressure?
> It is now normal to have a demonstration. We have demonstrations
> about all sorts of things every day. That is now taken as very much
> the political culture here, and it is very good and dynamic compared
> to the rest of Asia. We are very, very different.

Although Loh knew that she was about to enter the 'political wilder-
ness' she was not proposing to give up and tried to maintain her
optimism. 'I hope I won't get snuffed out one way or another,' she
said. Like Margaret Ng and Martin Lee, she was optimistic about the
long term. In May 1997, she founded a new political party, the
Citizens Party, to focus on issues like the environment, equal opportunities and a range of other 'domestic' concerns sometimes
overlooked by those democrats, like Martin Lee, for whom the relationship with China had been of pre-eminent if not all-consuming
importance. 'I am going to have times, I am sure, when I will wish I
was not doing this,' she admitted. 'I constantly get asked by members
of my family, "Why are you doing this?" But I also feel a certain
excitement that, in the historical sense, this really is a great step forward for China as a nation.'

Christine Loh, Margaret Ng and Martin Lee had not been uncriti-
cal of Patten's governorship. Ever suspicious of Britain's motives, they
had been inclined to see a prospective sell-out to China in any of his
public statements which failed their ambiguity test: the merest hint of
equivocation had been enough to send them reaching into their extensive armoury of verbal grapeshot. Yet they admired the last governor.
He had, said Martin Lee, 'stood up for Hong Kong whenever threats
were made from Beijing, and he would respond immediately. That is
something his predecessors would never have dared to do.' But more
than this, all three of them agreed, he had transformed Hong Kong's
'political culture'. True, it was too late to make up for the time lost in
the seventies and eighties by his ineffectual predecessors, but, at the very
last moment, he had at least helped the people of Hong Kong to find
their 'political identity' and potential, which, they believed, would be
of lasting benefit. 'We now have open debate,' said Margaret Ng, 'more

straightforward expressions of our differences of opinion. You can now criticise the government and the government can answer back. I think that has been very important for Hong Kong.' 'He has been good for Hong Kong,' Martin Lee concluded.

A few weeks before Patten's departure, Martin Lee and his colleagues gave him a farewell dinner at which Szeto Wah, the most radical of the Democrats, presented the governor with a piece of calligraphy he had painted himself. Punning with the symbols used to depict Beijing's denunciation of Patten as 'a criminal for a thousand years', Szeto Wah had transformed an abusive slogan into an affectionate tribute to a governor whose character and beliefs would 'charm and intoxicate for a thousand years'. Patten was greatly touched.

Tsang Yok Sing, the colony's most prominent ally of Chinese communism, did not entirely dismiss Patten's term of office, either. Inevitably, he condemned the last governor's role in the 'confrontation' with Beijing, judging him to have been a 'divisive' force who had polarised debate in Hong Kong. Discussions had too often been conducted 'in terms of black and white', he explained, a 'Western practice' which had not been good for 'our' community. But, echoing the words of his democratic counterparts, Tsang Yok Sing also volunteered approvingly that Patten had brought a 'new political culture' to Hong Kong. 'Nobody in Hong Kong has ever before seen such an eloquent politician,' he said thoughtfully. 'He has made the government more open and accountable. C.H. has a lot to learn from him.'

Allen Lee was less forgiving. In his valedictory assessment of the man who had removed him from the Executive Council almost five years earlier, Hong Kong's longest-serving politician commented:

> Mr Patten's tenure has been very, very unfortunate. He said when he arrived that he wanted to establish trust with the Chinese, and he failed to understand why, on his terms, that would be impossible. He has succeeded in establishing himself as a China-fighter, but that has certainly not been conducive to a smooth transition. We will long suffer what he has done for Hong Kong. He was a China-fighter, that's all. He has no other achievements.

Those sentiments were almost universally shared by members of the local and expatriate business community, whose leaders – with the exception of the Patten loyalist Simon Murray – had always managed to identify their individual and collective avarice with the presumed needs of the wider community which they affected to represent. In his quiet but insistent way – and, as ever, more in sorrow than in anger – Vincent Lo summed up the view of his fellow tycoons. 'I look forward to a new era for Hong Kong when we can do away with all this politics for a change, really start a new chapter and get on with life again.'

Despite – or perhaps because of – 'all this politics', Patten remained remarkably popular in Hong Kong. Within weeks of his departure, his favourable ratings in the polls, which still hovered around the 60 per cent mark – testified at least to a rare political talent. But on its own, as he would himself concede, public support for his leadership was not a sound basis on which to make even an interim assessment of his governorship. His critics claimed that this very support pointed to a cruel and deplorable lack of judgement on his part. By encouraging the illusion that political freedom and democracy on the Western model was a universal right from which no member of the community should be excluded, he had, they claimed, indulged himself at the expense of the Hong Kong people. China's probable retaliation, springing from an atavistic fear of subversion from the West, was likely to be severe, and certainly harsher than it would have been if the governor had made it his business to reconcile the community to the realities of Chinese sovereignty. Instead of surrendering to the demands of Martin Lee and the Democrats, he should have faced them down, regardless of how unpopular it made him.

This line of argument was based on a dubious premise: that in the post-Tiananmen Square era it would have been possible to govern Hong Kong as if popular opinion could be ignored. From the view-point of Government House, the implicit assumption that Patten could have overridden the electoral mandate secured by Martin Lee and his allies before his arrival was inherently implausible. To assume that the forces of democracy would have submitted to Beijing's 'bottom line' without a sustained struggle appeared preposterous. It seemed more likely by far that the 'debate' would have spilled on to the streets, which would have had an incalculable impact on Hong Kong's political and economic stability.

As we have seen, throughout his governorship, Patten's fiercest antagonist was Sir Percy Cradock. The way this former diplomat chose to deliver his judgement on Patten – through a battery of media interviews and articles – sharply diminished his reputation among those of his peers who felt that the former civil servant should have resisted the temptation to 'go public' so damagingly during such a delicate period. However, his views had a seductive clarity which lent them a carapace of intellectual rigour beneath which others of a more primitive cast of mind were able to shelter. According to Cradock, the governor's 'incompetence' sprang from a deplorable failure to engage in 'co-operative' dialogue with China and the pursuance instead of a self-promoting and destructive path of 'confrontation'. Cradock's corrosive judgement hung on twin assumptions that were rarely questioned by his acolytes: first, that Patten had chosen 'confrontation', and secondly, that 'co-operation' would have secured an acceptable agreement with Beijing.

The evidence for the first assumption was at best tenuous. Certainly the governor failed to 'consult' Beijing before announcing his electoral proposals, and Beijing did react with fury. But had his approach been 'confrontational'? Patten had made it clear in advance that his blueprint for electoral reform was negotiable and that he was anxious to discuss the entire package with China accordingly. Indeed, lengthy – though fruitless – negotiations eventually took place. To the detached observer, if not to Cradock, the word 'consultation' had clearly acquired a quite different meaning in China's diplomatic lexicon from that which usually described this form of dialogue between sovereign states. As understood by Beijing – and apparently by Cradock as well – the process of 'consultation' presupposed an acknowledgement that China had a right of veto. To consult, in this context, meant to secure prior consent, in the absence of which, the supplicant (in this case Britain) would be unable to proceed. In short, though the term 'consultation' had a sinuous charm, the process it described was, a priori, a sham. If refusing to participate in such a charade constituted 'confrontation', then Patten would be obliged to plead guilty.

In any event, the second of Cradock's underlying assumptions, that 'co-operation' – his neatly alliterative alternative to 'confrontation' – would better have protected Hong Kong's 'way of life', is no less fragile than the first. That 'co-operation' on the terms accepted by Cradock would have secured a settlement with China is hardly in doubt. It would have delivered an electoral system to Beijing's liking, a Bill of Rights similarly amended to limit Hong Kong's pre-existing freedoms and an agreement not to dismantle any of the draconian measures that were incompatible with the Bill of Rights. A 'co-operative' governor would have stayed silent in the face of threats to curtail the freedom of expression in Hong Kong; silent about the gerrymandered procedures for the selection of the chief executive and at the hint of an impasse on any other issue. He would have crumbled before the Chinese threat to forbid the major construction projects, and he would have made no allusion at any time to the character of the Chinese regime. But what would he thereby have achieved for Hong Kong that would not have been achieved in any case?

To put the matter the other way round: if, as all the evidence suggests, China was not willing to interpret the concept of 'one country, two systems' in such a way as to allow Hong Kong to preserve and develop its existing rights, freedoms and aspirations, what would 'co-operation' have delivered that 'confrontation' failed to provide? This question acquired an ever sharper edge as the noose of the future tightened around Hong Kong, and Britain's critics there inveighed anew against past 'betrayals' which had left them deprived of their democratic rights and dangerously exposed to the vagaries of the volatile Chinese regime. The case against Britain focused once more, but with growing resentment, on the period (covered in Chapter 6) between the signing of the Joint Declaration in 1984 and the decision by the British government in late 1987 not to introduce direct elections the following year. Allegations made at the time by Martin Lee, and later by an American journalist, Mark Roberti – that Britain had 'betrayed' the colony by colluding with the Chinese government in 1987 to thwart the expressed will of the Hong Kong people – were given renewed currency in a *Dispatches* documentary for Channel 4, 'A Very British Betrayal', broadcast in the spring of 1997.

At this last-ditch point in Britain's colonial history, it is clearly important to establish whether or not this charge is valid. If it is true, then Britain's reputation, not least in Hong Kong, is likely to be permanently tarnished. If it is false, then a festering sore can be healed, those who are innocent will have the cloud of suspicion removed from them and Britain's honour will be redeemed. In the absence of official documents it is impossible to establish, beyond peradventure, what happened and why, or who said what to whom and when, not least because the relevant British diplomats have been remarkably reticent about this crucial period. For example, the self-confessed overlord of Sino–British relations at this time, Sir Percy Cradock (who has written extensively about his 'secret' missions to Beijing in 1990), does not offer any explanation for Britain's postponement of the introduction of direct elections in 1988, after they had been proposed in the 1984 White Paper and enthusiastically endorsed by ministers at that time. In *Experiences of China*, he refers obliquely to the fact that there was a 'further review of the situation in 1987', and to a 'Sino–Soviet understanding' about the British decision to introduce 'ten directly elected legislature seats in 1991'. And that is all.

However, in the closing weeks of British rule, a final attempt to penetrate this protective shell has made it possible – at least in outline – to piece together some of the key elements of what happened before and after the 'consultation' of the Hong Kong people about direct elections which took place in the late summer of 1987. The available facts provide compelling, if not conclusive, evidence that the charge of 'betrayal', though emotive, is by no means ill founded.

The process seems to have begun at the second meeting of the Joint Liaison Group, in November 1985. The Chinese were in suspicious mood. In response to their warning that the People's Republic would not tolerate the establishment of direct elections in 1988, the British side reassured the Chinese that the 1984 White Paper proposal to that effect should not be interpreted as a commitment. On the contrary, the government would decide how to proceed only after soliciting the views of the Hong Kong people and taking into account other relevant factors. No deal was struck at this meeting, but it is clear that the two sides reached an understanding of each other's position which was to have a significant impact on Britain's strategy thereafter.

Fourteen months later, in March 1987, Sir Robin McLaren, the senior negotiator in the JLG, reiterated the 1985 stance and, for good measure, informed his opposite number, Ke Zaishuo, that the British government would, in any case, move towards direct elections only with extreme caution. Thus encouraged, China maintained the pressure. In the following months, they used every formal and informal channel to insist repeatedly that the introduction of direct elections in 1988 – even for a small minority of the LegCo seats – would constitute an unacceptable violation of the principle of 'convergence' to which the British negotiators had keenly assented after the Joint Declaration. In response, McLaren and other Foreign Office officials – including the governor, Sir David Wilson – not only confirmed Britain's commitment to 'convergence' but volunteered that the British side had no preconceived views about the desirability of direct elections in 1988, or indeed at any time before the handover. And they went a stage further, promising that, although the decision would be influenced by the outcome of the public consultation process, it would by no means be bound by it.

As the negotiations continued into the summer, the foreign secretary, Sir Geoffrey Howe, intervened. He suggested to the Chinese foreign minister, Wu Xueqian, that Beijing might care to indicate that the Chinese had no objection in principle to the creation of direct elections at some point after the promulgation of the Basic Law, which was scheduled for 1990. This, Howe intimated, would go a long way towards dampening down Hong Kong's impatient demand for more democracy in 1988. At this stage, there was no specific commitment from either side, but the seeds of a secret deal, nurtured by nods and winks, were starting to sprout.

Before long this Sino–British understanding became explicit. The Chinese implied that they would indeed be willing to make a pronouncement in favour of direct elections at a later date, but only if the British could undertake not to introduce such measures in 1988. As both sides now acknowledged, the only obstacle to this agreeable outcome was the will of the Hong Kong people – who, of course, had no idea that such talks were taking place.

The formal process of public 'consultation' began in July 1987 and was due to end three months later. It soon emerged that there was a groundswell in favour of direct elections in general and, specifically, of the 1988 start date. Informed of this not only by their own sources in Hong Kong but directly by British officials, the Chinese became increasingly agitated. Through the JLG and in private meetings, they began to press the British on how the authorities in Hong Kong would respond if – as now seemed possible – it were to emerge that a majority did indeed favour the establishment of direct elections in 1988. At a JLG meeting in London, Robin McLaren used stronger language than ever to make it clear that, while the British could not guarantee to veto this prospect, they shared China's antipathy to it. And, on Britain's behalf, he made yet another move towards Beijing by reassuring his opposite number in the JLG that, regardless of the result of the survey, the British government would not even consider introducing direct elections in 1988 without first consulting the Chinese.

As the consultation process intensified, the British, too, became increasingly concerned about the strength of opinion in Hong Kong. The foreign secretary had made it clear that the survey had to be genuine and open, but this did not prevent other British officials from encouraging Beijing to urge their allies in Hong Kong to make their own views known on an 'individual' rather than a collective basis. As we have seen (pages 107–8), those 'individual' submissions, in the form of preprinted letters distributed by these self-same allies, were to play a decisive part in the distortion of evidence eventually engineered by the Hong Kong government.

In late September, a few days before the end of the consultation period, Sir David Wilson made an official visit to Beijing, where he met leading members of the Chinese government. In a meeting with Zhou Nan, he discussed the Survey Office report in some detail. Although he indicated that the preliminary results did indeed show a majority in favour of democracy in 1988, albeit not a substantial one, he explored the implications of this in terms which led the Chinese to conclude that the British government would nonetheless not feel obliged to abide by this verdict. Zhou Nan's impression that the two

sides had now reached a private understanding to this effect was doubtless reinforced when Wilson ventured that, in this case, a significant
section of the community – the influential middle classes – would be
gravely disappointed. It was, the governor intimated, a situation which
would have to be handled with extreme delicacy.

Wilson stressed that the terms of his understanding with Zhou Nan
were both preliminary and conditional, but they turned out to be final,
if not entirely unconditional. In November, as the Hong Kong government considered the evidence, McLaren followed Wilson to
Beijing. At a meeting with Ke Zaishuo, he reported that the full survey
report had confirmed the governor's initial assessment in September. A
majority of the 135,000 'individual' submissions expressed opposition to
the direct elections in 1988, but more than 230,000 individuals had
signed petitions advocating them. McLaren did not feel obliged to
point out the self-evident truth that the survey had produced an embarrassingly large majority in favour of the 1984 White Paper proposal.
However, echoing Wilson, he did voice concern that a significant
number of those who endorsed the 1988 option came from the middle
and managerial classes, on whose commitment to stay in the territory
Hong Kong's future was so dependent.

Early in December 1987, Wilson returned to Beijing. Arguing now
that the final statistics had failed to show a clear majority, he nonetheless reminded his Chinese hosts that every independent opinion poll
had done so, and confessed that he had not anticipated that the signature campaign would deliver quite such a huge number of supporters of
the proposal. In an oblique reference to his own administration's decision to turn the statistics upside down, he reported ruefully that some
individuals had accused the Hong Kong government of rigging the figures in order to achieve the result the Chinese wanted.

Wilson then confirmed the secret deal the two sides had struck a few
months earlier. As the British had already half promised, the White
Paper on democratic development which was due to be published in
February 1988 would defer the introduction of direct elections as long
as the Basic Law included such a commitment for after 1997. Wilson
intimated that the Hong Kong government would hope to isolate its
more vociferous critics by promising a limited number of directly
elected seats for the 1991 LegCo elections without violating the principle of 'convergence'. It was very neat, and precisely what Zhou Nan
must have been hoping to hear. He responded sympathetically. It was,
he did not need to say, the final triumph of 'co-operation'.

With the benefit of hindsight, it is hard to exaggerate the implications of this outcome. A 'virtual' historian might judge that if direct

elections had been introduced in 1988, the prospects for the survival of democracy after 1997 would have been immeasurably enhanced. With what would by now have been the experience of three 'direct' elections and almost ten years in which to bed down this novel form of accountability, even the most antagonistic tycoon and the most dubious civil servant might have discovered that democracy was not incompatible with economic prosperity or executive efficiency. Moreover, the establishment of direct elections would have been accomplished before Tiananmen Square, at a point when the Chinese, though suspicious, were far less paranoid about 'subversion' than they subsequently became. In any case, it is almost inconceivable that even the Chinese would have been willing to defy the world by openly dismembering a democratic process which self-evidently enjoyed widespread support in the community.

Almost inconceivable, but not entirely so. Doubtless Lord Howe, Sir Percy Cradock, Lord Wilson and Sir Robin McLaren will in due course provide their own explanation for the 'betrayal' of which they stand accused by liberal opinion in Hong Kong. It may be that they will claim a victory; that the trade-off with China secured Beijing's commitment in the Basic Law to the introduction of direct elections after the restoration of Chinese sovereignty. They might indeed argue that this could not have been achieved in any other way and that the price of their success was having to conceal these realities from the people of Hong Kong.

It is too early to judge whether some such justification – or any other – will find general favour. In the meantime, when pressed for a reaction, officials in Hong Kong were unwilling to discount the plausibility of the above account of what happened in 1987. In the absence of any better explanation, the former foreign secretary and the officials then under his authority will find themselves open to the charge that the consultation exercise over which they presided was indeed the sham their detractors have alleged it to have been. They will be accused variously of arrogance, cynicism and dishonourable conduct. The bitterness in Hong Kong will fester and Britain's reputation there will be indelibly stained by the mark of appeasement.

Against this background, any judgement of the last governor must take into account not only what he set out to achieve, but what it was possible to achieve. In 1992, Patten had hoped to accomplish a delicate manoeuvre: first, to engineer the smooth transfer of sovereignty from Britain to China according to the principles laid out in the Joint Declaration and the Basic Law; secondly, to prepare the people of

Hong Kong for that future; and thirdly, to extricate Britain from its last significant colony in a dignified and honourable fashion. On the first count, he failed. The 'through train' hit the buffers, and on 1 July 1997 the provisional legislature will replace the Legislative Council which was elected in September 1995 under the Patten 'rules'. The provisional legislature lacks credibility in Hong Kong and abroad (to the extent that, when C.H. Tung indicated in May that its formal inauguration would form part of the handover celebrations in the early hours of 1 July, he was notified that the American secretary of state, Madeleine Albright, would in that case not attend the proceedings). Nonetheless the new body will be charged to rubber-stamp proposals for its own replacement with a gerrymandered Legislative Council which will be structured to ensure that its deliberations will not prove 'subversive'. However, in the face of China's obduracy, Patten's failure was effectively preordained. To have been 'co-operative' might have secured a 'smooth transfer' (though even that is open to question); it would most certainly have required Britain to surrender to China's perverted notion of the concept of 'one country, two systems'.

As it was, no one was able to identify any tangible benefits that would have accrued either to Hong Kong or to Britain if Patten had succumbed to the policy of 'co-operation'. In economic terms, the 'golden goose' was as fecund as ever. Growth was steady. The property market was booming. All the construction projects which Beijing had threatened to veto were on course, albeit marginally delayed. Nor was there any evidence that Britain's direct or indirect trade with China had suffered as a consequence of the Triple Violator's sundry impertinences. Patten had certainly underestimated the intensity of Beijing's animus against him, and to this limited extent, he overplayed his hand. Ironically, however, the only economic 'punishment' inflicted on Britain by China bore no relation to Hong Kong at all. In the second week of May 1997, China cancelled a trade mission from the United Kingdom scheduled for the end of the month. Officially described by Beijing officials as a 'postponement to a more opportune moment', the decision was made in retaliation to Britain's endorsement of a UN resolution in April criticising China's record on human rights.

So what of the second criterion by which Patten might expect to be judged? How well prepared were the people of Hong Kong for what they were to face once Chinese sovereignty took effect? Certainly they had been steeled by the conflict between their governor and his adversaries, not only within the colony itself but in London and Beijing. As a result of his commitment to 'open' government, they were sharply aware of the issues which were supposed to underpin the concept of 'one country, two systems'. The transparency with which, for the first time in their history, a governor had conducted diplomacy on their behalf, had both exposed them to the arguments and included them in the dialogue. Again and again they had endorsed his stance, despite the verbal abuse Beijing had rained upon his head. By no stretch of a patronising imagination could they now be thought to be 'sleepwalking' into the unknown. Yet there was no evidence of panic; no rush for the boats. By the same token, romantic delusions were notable by their absence: to depict Patten as a latterday Robespierre urging the mob to self-immolation at the barricades in the name of 'direct elections' would not convince. Late in the day – unforgivably late – Britain, under Patten's 'reign', had encouraged the people of Hong Kong to participate in the political process on similar terms to those enjoyed by their counterparts in civilised societies. Could it possibly be argued – except by anti-democrats or communist cadres or purblind tycoons – that this either ran against the interests of the people or, in some unspecified way, threatened their prospects after the handover?

The third criterion was Britain's credibility in the world. In the United States, the European Union and south-east Asia, the last governor had been under close scrutiny – often closer, indeed, than at Westminster or in the British media. In most eyes Patten had come to be regarded as a belated advocate of important principles and values. In America, in particular, where anti-colonial sentiment and moral certainty formed a potent alliance, Patten's public declaration in support of democracy and human rights, combined with his readiness to 'confront' China on matters of principle, confirmed the impression that Britain was, in the end, mindful of past obligations and future duties. The passports issue was a case in point. As Patten entered the final days of his governorship, he could be confident that the international community would judge his tenure of office with favour and thus with benefit to Britain's reputation and interests, especially in the emerging democracies of south-east Asia.

Patten's critics, notably Sir Percy Cradock, had claimed or implied that his strategy had been driven by arrogance or by the frustrated ambition of an aspiring prime minister. According to this thesis, Patten used his time in Hong Kong to parade his admittedly formidable talents before an admiring audience in Britain which would, as a result, welcome him home as the nation's future saviour. This argument was not only vindictive but jejune, revealing more about the judges than the judged. Patten did not lack ambition, but he was never in its thrall. As a pragmatic politician, he was uncomfortable deploying the language of morality except in relation to personal behaviour; he preferred to talk of decency or, occasionally, of honour. Yet he did believe that politics had a moral dimension, and he felt that strongly in relation to Hong Kong. The evidence makes it preposterous to suggest that he conducted himself as the governor of Hong Kong with an eye on the main chance at Westminster.

In the wake of the humiliating and historic defeat of his party in the general election on 1 May 1997, Patten's allies in politics and many Conservatives throughout the country bemoaned his absence from the contest to succeed John Major as leader. Patten did not allow himself to indulge in the 'what if' school of contemporary history. From the moment of his own defeat in Bath in the 1992 election he had refused to participate in any of the schemes cooked up for him by his supporters for a return to Westminster. Adamant that he would remain in Hong Kong for the duration, he was well aware that the longer he was away from London, the less likely it would be that he could successfully rejoin British politics. In the absence of any self-delusion about his prospects of re-entry, he had been liberated from the constraints and disappointments that such ambition might otherwise have imposed. Although he did not entirely rule out a return to the British political stage, the result of the election served merely to confirm his judgement. Eighteen months earlier, he had confided to friends his intention to stay away from London after the handover and to spend the rest of 1997 writing in the seclusion of his home in France. Two weeks after the election (when he was in London to meet Tony Blair) he confirmed that intention. Despite the entreaties of some former colleagues, who chose to believe that he alone could save the party from itself, he reiterated that for the foreseeable future he would stay well away from Westminster.

Chris Patten had fought a sustained public and private battle to carry through his project for Hong Kong: publicly against the Chinese and a powerful minority in Hong Kong; privately against an influential number of politicians, diplomats and officials in London. It had been a gruelling and often lonely five years. The scale of his purpose and the character of his responsibility had required rare qualities of leadership: a clear vision, an abnormal resolve and a profound sense of public duty. The last governor of Hong Kong had arrived in the colony as a politician, hopeful of success. He would depart as a statesman, knowing failure as well as victory, but in dignity and with honour.

SOURCES AND
FURTHER READING

U nless otherwise attributed, the quotations in *The Last Governor* are taken from conversations with the author. Almost all of these interviews, amounting to several hundred hours and more than a million words, were recorded on tape. A handful of my interviewees wished to protect their anonymity. With this exception, the transcripts of all interviews (which were conducted in parallel for this book and for the BBC series *The Last Governor*) are to be lodged in the William Mong Collection at the University of Hong Kong, where they will be available to researchers.

For background material, I have also drawn on a range of second-hand but authoritative sources, of which the following have been the most instructive. For my account of nineteenth- and early twentieth-century Hong Kong, I am indebted to Frank Welsh's *History of Hong Kong* (HarperCollins, 1993). As a scholarly, perceptive and entertaining guide through the thickets of that period, Welsh has no peer. Robert Cottrell's meticulous and balanced account of what he refers to as the 'secret diplomacy of imperial retreat' in *The End of Hong Kong* (John Murray, 1993) will be invaluable to those who seek to understand the crucial events leading up to the Joint Declaration and its consequences. Percy Cradock's *Experiences of China* (John Murray, 1994) is a vivid and elegant autobiographical portrait of a dramatic period in Sino–British relations, when, as the chief architect of British policy, Cradock was perpetually in the eye of the storm. Steve Tsang's *Democracy Shelved* (OUP, 1988) is a detailed examination of postwar British policy towards Hong Kong. His view of Britain's alleged perfidy is cautiously phrased but leans towards the trenchant certainties of Mark Roberti's *The Fall of Hong Kong*, which is subtitled 'China's Triumph and Britain's Betrayal'

(John Wiley, 1994). Roberti draws on his own experience as an American correspondent in Hong Kong and readers may detect an anti-British as well as an anti-colonial bias in his analysis. However, at least in the case of Britain's failure to advance the cause of democratic reform in the late 1980s, his conclusions bear close examination. In this respect, as I argue in the Epilogue to *The Last Governor*, the evidence appears to be on Roberti's side.

The media summaries produced by the Hong Kong Government Information Service have provided a useful digest of news and views culled from the principal English-language and Chinese-language daily press, and the Hong Kong Yearbooks published by the Hong Kong government supplied exhaustive annual facts and figures.

The reports produced by Amnesty International and AsiaWatch, who monitor human-rights violations in China (and Hong Kong) with diligence, are sources of vital knowledge.

I have also quoted briefly from David Owen's *Time to Declare* (Michael Joseph, 1991), *Excellency, Your Gap is Growing* by John Walden (Hong Kong, 1987), Ian Fleming's *Thrilling Cities* (1963), John le Carré's *The Honourable Schoolboy* (Random House, 1977) and Jan Morris's *Among the Cities* (Penguin Books, 1985).

INDEX